RICHARD VINEN

National Service

Conscription in Britain, 1945–1963

ALLEN LANE
an imprint of
PENGUIN BOOKS

ALLEN LANE

Published by the Penguin Group

Penguin Books Ltd, 80 Strand, London WC2R ORL, England

Penguin Group (USA) Inc., 375 Hudson Street, New York, New York 10014, USA

Penguin Group (Canada), 90 Eglinton Avenue East, Suite 700, Toronto, Ontario, Canada M4P 2Y3
(a division of Pearson Penguin Canada Inc.)

Penguin Ireland, 25 St Stephen's Green, Dublin 2, Ireland (a division of Penguin Books Ltd)

Penguin Group (Australia), 707 Collins Street, Melbourne, Victoria 3008, Australia
(a division of Pearson Australia Group Pty Ltd)

Penguin Books India Pvt Ltd, 11 Community Centre, Panchsheel Park, New Delhi – 110 017, India

Penguin Group (NZ), 67 Apollo Drive, Rosedale, Auckland 0632, New Zealand
(a division of Pearson New Zealand Ltd)

Penguin Books (South Africa) (Pty) Ltd, Block D, Rosebank Office Park,
181 Jan Smuts Avenue, Parktown North, Gauteng 2193, South Africa

Penguin Books Ltd, Registered Offices: 80 Strand, London WC2R ORL, England

www.penguin.com

First published 2014
001

Copyright © Richard Vinen, 2014

The moral right of the author has been asserted

Set in 10.5/14pt Sabon LT Std
Typeset by Jouve (UK), Milton Keynes
Printed in Great Britain by Clays Ltd, St Ives plc

ISBN: 978–1–846–14387–8

For my mother, Susan

Contents

CONTENTS

Appendices:

List of Maps

List of Illustrations

List of Tables

Abbreviations

ACC	Army Catering Corps
CCF	Combined Cadet Force
CSM	Company Sergeant Major
ILP	Independent Labour Party
KAR	King's African Rifles
KRR	King's Royal Rifle Corps
MRLA	Malayan Races Liberation Army
NATO	North Atlantic Treaty Organization
NCO	Non-Commissioned Officer
NS	National Service
OR1	Other Rank 1 (a potential officer)
OR4	Other Rank 4 (a potential NCO)
OTC	Officer Training Corps
RAC	Royal Armoured Corps
RAEC	Royal Army Education Corps
RAOC	Royal Army Ordnance Corps
RASC	Royal Army Service Corps
RAF	Royal Air Force
REME	Royal Electrical and Mechanical Engineers
RPC	Royal Pioneer Corps
RSM	Regimental Sergeant Major
TUC	Trades Union Congress
USB	Unit Selection Board
WOSB	War Office Selection Board

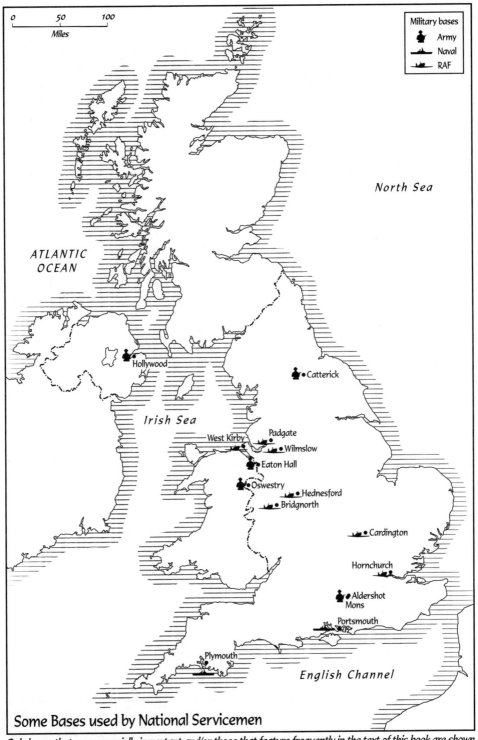

Some Bases used by National Servicemen

Only bases that were especially important and/or those that feature frequently in the text of this book are shown

DISPOSITION OF BRITISH TR
ALL RANKS AND WOMEN INCLUD

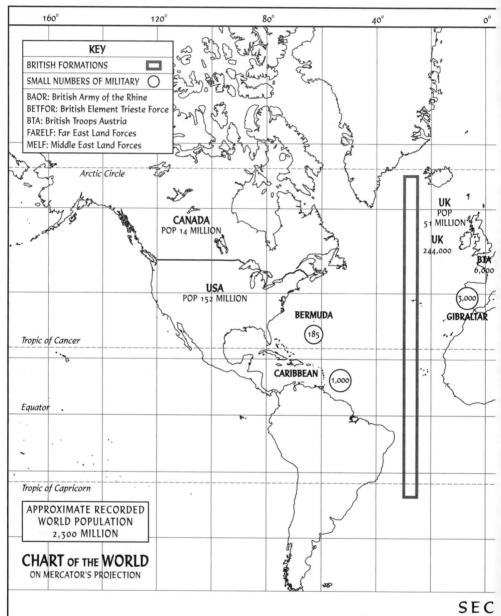

160°   120°   80°   40°   0°

KEY

BRITISH FORMATIONS	▭
SMALL NUMBERS OF MILITARY	○

BAOR: British Army of the Rhine
BETFOR: British Element Trieste Force
BTA: British Troops Austria
FARELF: Far East Land Forces
MELF: Middle East Land Forces

Arctic Circle

CANADA
POP 14 MILLION

USA
POP 152 MILLION

BERMUDA
(185)

CARIBBEAN
(1,000)

UK
POP
51 MILLION
UK
244,000

BTA
6,000

(3,000)

GIBRALTAR

Tropic of Cancer

Equator

Tropic of Capricorn

APPROXIMATE RECORDED
WORLD POPULATION
2,300 MILLION

CHART of the **WORLD**
ON MERCATOR'S PROJECTION

Reproduction of War Offic
The War Office did not show Japan on this map,

OOPS AS AT 31 MARCH 1951
ED (LARGER FIGURES ROUNDED)

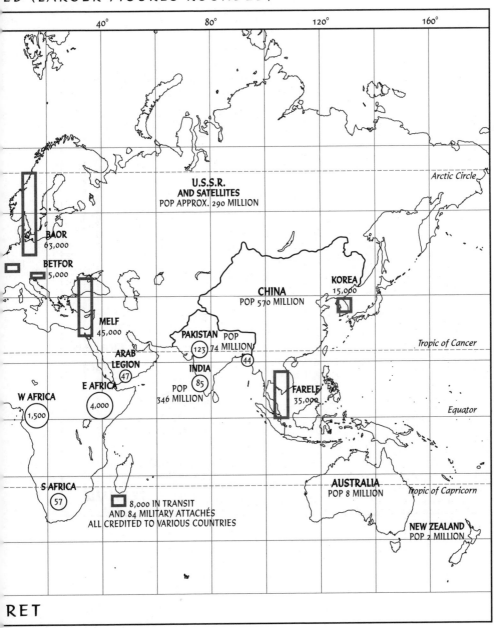

40°   80°   120°   160°

Arctic Circle

U.S.S.R.
AND SATELLITES
POP APPROX. 290 MILLION

BAOR
63,000

BETFOR
5,000

KOREA
15,000

MELF
45,000

CHINA
POP 570 MILLION

PAKISTAN POP
123 74 MILLION

ARAB
LEGION 47
44

INDIA

Tropic of Cancer

E AFRICA
4,000

POP
85
346 MILLION

FARELF
35,000

W AFRICA
1,500

Equator

S AFRICA
57

8,000 IN TRANSIT
AND 84 MILITARY ATTACHÉS
ALL CREDITED TO VARIOUS COUNTRIES

AUSTRALIA
POP 8 MILLION

Tropic of Capricorn

NEW ZEALAND
POP 2 MILLION

e Map from TNA WO 384/1
though there were British troops there in 1951

ETHIOPIA

UGANDA

KENYA

SOMALILAND (now SOMALIA)

Aberdare Mountains

Nakuru • Nyeri * Mt Kenya
Gilgil • • Fort Hall
Naivasha •
Nanyuki

Lake Victoria

Nairobi

Mt Kilimanjaro
Arusha •

Indian Ocean

Mombasa

TANGANYIKA
(now TANZANIA)

Pemba I.

ZANZIBAR

Dar-es-Salaam •

Kenya

Miles
0   100   200

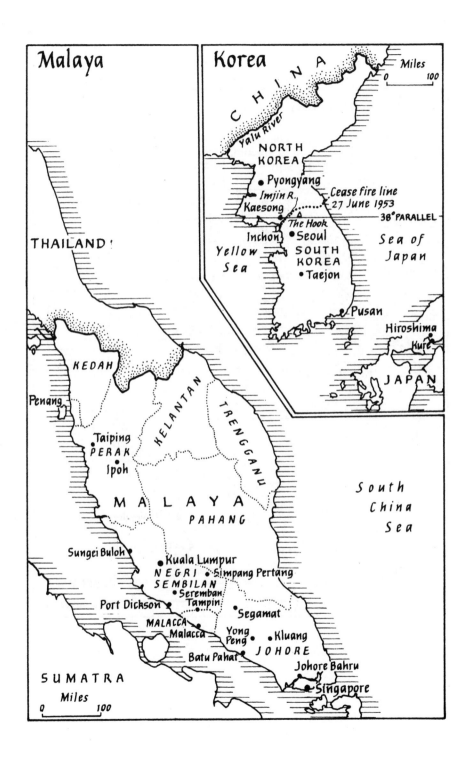

Malaya

Korea

THAILAND

KEDAH

Penang

Taiping
PERAK
Ipoh

KELANTAN

TRENGGANU

MALAYA

PAHANG

Sungei Buloh

Kuala Lumpur
NEGRI
SEMBILAN
Simpang Pertang
Seremban
Tampin

Port Dickson

Segamat

MALACCA
Malacca

Yong
Peng

Kluang

Batu Pahat

JOHORE

Johore Bahru

Singapore

SUMATRA

Miles

0   100

South
China
Sea

CHINA

Miles

0   100

Yalu River

NORTH
KOREA

Pyongyang

Imjin R.

Kaesong

Cease fire line
27 June 1953

The Hook

38° PARALLEL

Inchon

Seoul

Yellow
Sea

SOUTH
KOREA

Taejon

Sea of
Japan

Pusan

Hiroshima
Kure

JAPAN

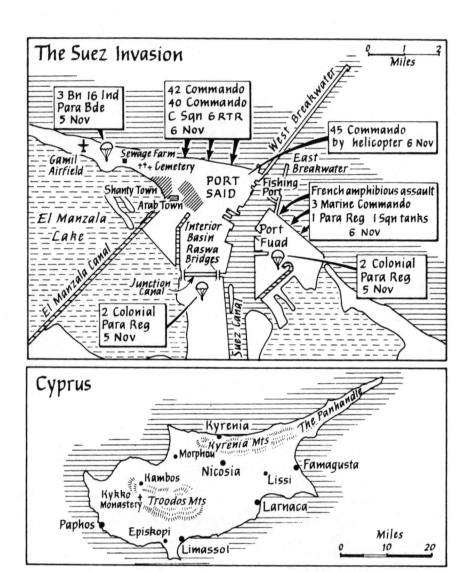

The Suez Invasion

3 Bn 16 Ind
Para Bde
5 Nov

42 Commando
40 Commando
C Sqn 6 RTR
6 Nov

45 Commando
by helicopter 6 Nov

West Breakwater

Gamil
Airfield

Sewage Farm
+++ Cemetery

East
Breakwater

Shanty Town
Arab Town

PORT
SAID

Fishing
Port

French amphibious assault
3 Marine Commando
1 Para Reg 1 Sqn tanks
6 Nov

El Manzala
Lake

Interior
Basin
Raswa
Bridges

Port
Fuad

2 Colonial
Para Reg
5 Nov

El Manzala Canal

Junction
Canal

Suez Canal

2 Colonial
Para Reg
5 Nov

Cyprus

Kyrenia

Kyrenia Mts

The Panhandle

Morphou

Nicosia

Famagusta

Kambos

Lissi

Kykko
Monastery

Troodos Mts

Larnaca

Paphos

Episkopi

Limassol

Miles
0   10   20

A Personal Preface

*The question of conscription would indeed be a tedious topic
to pursue ... to which no doubt in years to come dull history
professors will direct their duller research students.*

Robert Blake (1955)[1]

I was born in March 1963 (two months before the last conscript left
the British army). I grew up in what must be the most unmilitary
square mile of England – the Bournville Estate in Birmingham, which
was founded by the Quaker Cadbury family to provide workers for
their factory. The Cadburys had abandoned their pacifism by the late
1940s, but here was still a sense that Bournville was a Quakerish area.
Conscientious objectors, destined for the Friends' Ambulance Unit,
were gathered in Bournville during the late 1940s and former prefects
from Bootham, the Quaker public school, put them through the 'Con-
chie Commando course' in Manor Park, which is round the corner
from my family's house.[2] I also grew up in an unmilitary age: 1968 was
the first, and last, year in modern times when no British serviceman
was killed in action. Northern Ireland simmered during the 1970s but
Britain was not involved in a real war until the Argentine invasion of
the Falklands in 1982.

Having said all this, military matters impinged on my childhood,
partly because my father served in the air force in 1948 and 1949. He
had hoped to become an educational sergeant but accepted a posting
as a clerk because an officer told him (untruthfully) that all educationalists would be recruited from among clerks. He rose to the rank of

corporal and never left England, though he did, unlike most RAF conscripts, occasionally fly in aircraft.

In fact, many of the adult men I have known for much of my life – i.e. the majority of those born between 1927 and early 1939 – would have been national servicemen. My father-in-law was a second lieutenant in an anti-aircraft regiment of the Royal Artillery – his background was similar to that of my father but he had been educated at a slightly grander grammar school and had officerly qualities because he was a Christian and a rugby player and endowed with the confidence that was so highly valued by the War Office Selection Board.

Sometimes the ubiquity of national service has made it invisible. We tend to take it for granted, like some large, immobile and, at first glance, not very interesting object in the background of a familiar picture. People of my own generation sometimes refer briefly to the military service of their fathers but rarely know much about it and, sometimes, the things that we 'know' turn out to be wrong. Half-remembered and half-understood conversations form the backdrop to my own research on national service. For example, in 1984 I read an article in *The Spectator* by Geoffrey Strickland in which he described having been trained to torture when he was a conscript in the Intelligence Corps in 1949.[3] He remembered, in particular, instruction on the matter from an officer who had served in the Far East during the Second World War. The article provoked a blistering rejoinder from an officer – one who served in the very camp in the Far East that Strickland mentioned – saying that the British army had never tortured. I discussed the matter with my friend Giles Ockenden, who said, in passing, that his father, John, had been trained to torture during his national service in the Intelligence Corps.

John Ockenden died in 2003, but his sons lent me his unpublished memoir – which does indeed refer to training in interrogation but not to torture. I asked Giles, who recalled his father talking about torture, though he thought, on reflection, that he had been taught *about* it rather than *how to do* it. I have, in fact, come across other accounts by men who were in the Intelligence Corps and who seem to have trained in techniques that might be described as torture – though many who served in the Intelligence Corps do not mention the subject. Most revealingly, I discovered that Strickland had been trying to publish accounts of his experience since the 1960s, and that the Ministry of Defence had been keen that his articles should not reach the public.[4]

Talking to national servicemen has raised one particular question in my mind: how far does it matter if my view of their experiences is different from their own? One former national service officer remarked, after hearing me give a paper, that he 'vaguely recognized the universe' I described, but felt that 'the planets were all in the wrong place'. Sometimes, I have been gripped by genuine uncertainty because the picture that emerges from archives is so different from what is remembered by national servicemen themselves.

There is a difference between the interpretation of the historian – usually looking for some overall pattern – and that of the individual – prone to explain his own life in terms of particular choices and chances. I suspect that, in particular, national servicemen will object to two aspects of my account: some will say that I am too negative and fail to allow for the beneficial or enjoyable aspects of national service. There is probably an element of truth in this. It is hard for someone of my generation to recapture the excitement felt by men who might otherwise never have left home about the novelty of life in the forces and, in particular, about the prospect of being sent abroad. One should, however, add that contemporary documents, including those produced by the armed forces, rarely suggest that conscripts were happy. Many former conscripts will also probably feel that I lay an excessive emphasis on the role of class divisions in British society. I would reply that social class is often now an unfashionable topic for academics and an embarrassing subject for ordinary people, but it was a matter of almost obsessive interest in the 1950s.

Conversations with national servicemen are often interesting precisely because they suggest different ways of interpreting the same experience. Sometimes, there are contradictions within the same account. The historian could tell the same story in several different ways but individual national servicemen also seem to tell the same story in different ways or to tell several different stories within a single memoir or interview. Conscripts describe experiences that sound almost unendurable – such as being taken prisoner in Korea – but then say that conscription was a good thing and that they would do it all again.[5]

A working-class man from the East End who was called up into the Black Watch talks about hand-to-hand fighting in Korea. He saw one of his comrades split a Chinese soldier's head open with a trenching tool: 'guys I had had breakfast with . . . they were getting bits of their body blown away'. He struggles to explain what it was like: 'probably now with the distance of time it seems not so bad as it was, but it was bad'. He had a nervous breakdown some years later, as events in Korea caught up with him. He also served in Kenya during the Mau Mau Emergency but is more reticent about what happened there: 'there were things that went on, that wouldn't have happened with the Chinese in Korea, because [in Korea] it was soldier against soldier'. He was offered the chance to come home as part of a detachment that attended the coronation but refused because: 'If I had come, I think I would have trotted [i.e. deserted].' At the end of a conversation that must have lasted several hours, the interviewer asks how he feels about having done national service with an illustrious regiment. He replies simply: 'very proud.'[6]

In 2007, Andreas Whittam Smith, the founding editor of the *Independent*, gave an interview in which he described his two years as a private soldier in the Cheshire Regiment. He was, by this stage, a successful man with a cheerful manner and an attractive propensity for self-mockery. He recalls getting to know men from different backgrounds. He travelled: getting off the ship at the Hook of Holland, he said to himself, 'So this is abroad.' He was posted to Berlin before the Wall went up. He discovered opera and went to nightclubs in the cellars of bombed-out buildings. He watched soldiers, returning from drunken evenings out, throw the German drivers off and drive the trams themselves. It all sounds fun. Suddenly Whittam Smith says that he has mentioned the good times but 'basically it was excruciatingly dull'. He was unhappy and prevented from going absent without leave only by the knowledge that time spent in prison would keep him in the army longer. Prison itself did not worry him, because it would have been much like the army.[7]

I have noticed in my own researches that, after formal taped interviews, men sometimes say things that put their recorded comments in a different light. Peter Duncumb was one of the rare men who learned to fly during his national service in the air force. Interviewing him, I asked whether there had been a distinction between public school boys and grammar school boys during his service. He said not and I sensed that, though he was too polite to say so, he thought this an odd question. After the interview, as we walked to lunch, Peter returned to the subject. Now he thought about it, when they had chosen their rooms in training, all the public school boys shared with other public school boys and the grammar school boys shared with other grammar school boys. He did not think that there had been any animosity or awkwardness between the two groups – indeed, like many airmen, he felt that the rigour of their training had quickly knitted them together. There had, however, on reflection, been some kind of separation.[8]

Similarly, I talked to a former officer who encouraged me to investigate the role of homosexuality in the armed forces during the national service period – while making it politely clear that he was not going to discuss his own experiences of this. Months later, I was having coffee with him near King's Cross in a café, full of labourers from a nearby building site. He disagreed with my view that there was a sharp separation of officers and other ranks in national service but then, he added: 'I felt already that my sexual career would mainly involve the working classes.'

I think that Duncumb and my informant from the King's Cross café were both interested, and even amused, by the differences of interpretation that emerged from our talks. Sometimes exchanges have been more awkward. When I wrote to men asking for permission to quote letters and diaries they had deposited in archives, one rang me up. He was friendly and keen to help but told me that he had not written the words that I quoted and that, in fact, they described an episode that could not have happened. He offered to check the original of his letter. When he returned to the telephone, the tone of our conversation changed. It turned out that he had indeed written what I attributed to him, but he was surprised and perplexed. He did not want me to quote the letter, because it would give an entirely misleading impression. A few days later he wrote me a very gracious note saying that I could quote the letter after all – 'it must have been true at the time'. I decided, in the end, not to do so.

Introduction

Over 2 million men were conscripted into the British armed forces between the end of the Second World War and November 1960; the last of them were demobilized in May 1963. In addition to this, hundreds of thousands jumped before they were pushed and volunteered for regular service. Many such men regarded themselves as conscripts in all but name. Every man born between 1928 and September 1939 was affected – either because he was called up, because he failed the medical (itself sometimes a disturbing experience) or because he sought to avoid service. Evasion became easier in the late 1950s but no one was certain that they had avoided it until they saw the newspaper headlines saying that the last man had been called up.

Conscription bit into the lives of tens of millions of people. On board a troopship – the *Dunera* – in May 1951 Lt Colonel Andrew Man drafted a brief account of how the national servicemen who made up over half of his own battalion, the 1st Middlesex, had acquitted themselves in the Korean War. He began: 'It is probably true to say that no subject receives greater attention in the English home today than the National Service Act and its repercussions upon the growing son, who must one day and for a time become subject to military law.'[1] For some families the intrusion of national service was particularly violent. Thirty-one soldiers from the Middlesex did not come back from Korea – several were recorded as having 'no known grave'.

National service seems, as a former conscript mused in 1996, 'more than a generation ago'.[2] The world in which young men submitted themselves to the, usually, petty humiliation and brutality of peacetime conscription appears, oddly, more remote today than do the two world wars. The British value institutional continuity and their perceptions of the post-war years tend to emphasize things – such as the creation of the National Health Service or the 'permissive' legislation of the 1960s – that seemed to change society in a permanent way. National service, by contrast, belongs to that part of post-war Britain that was improvised and jerry-built. Almost no one thought that peacetime conscription could, or should, be permanent.

Even at the time, national service was 'foreign' in the sense that it formed no part of British tradition. Conscripts were ubiquitous but also, so far as certain sorts of public discussion were concerned, invisible. Books on the 'youth culture' of the 1950s and early 60s depict a world of espresso bars and jazz clubs but servicemen pop up only when there is some, otherwise unexplained, reference to a man who has recently come out of the forces.[3] Furthermore, a significant minority of conscripts served abroad. Many men had never been more than a few miles from their home and regarded travelling on escalators on the tube as they passed through London as an adventure in itself. They might then be packed off to countries they had never heard of. Men served in Aden, Cameroon, Cyprus, Egypt, Germany, Hong Kong, Jamaica, Kenya, Libya, Malaya, Malta, Nigeria and Sierra Leone. They passed through South Africa and Sri Lanka. A few fortunate men went to the Allied Control Commission in Trieste or to NATO headquarters in Fountainebleau. Some were unlucky enough to experience trench warfare in Korea or to endure the heat, dust and bitter local hostility of the zone around the Suez Canal.

Men on troopships would spend four weeks getting to the Far East – in March 1954, there were 13,000 British soldiers 'in transit'. In an age of full employment, this might be the longest period of relative inactivity that a working-class man would have until he retired in the 1990s. Other ranks lived in conditions of appalling squalor on ships but, once they had recovered from seasickness in the Bay of Biscay, the mind-boggling novelty of what they saw sometimes struck them more forcibly than physical hardship. Men remembered flying fish and the lascars on the boats – sometimes the first non-white people they had ever seen in the flesh. A soldier might wake up one morning, look out of a porthole and spot an Arab riding a camel along the banks of the Suez Canal: 'like a picture in an early geography book come to life'.[4] In Malaya, national servicemen fought alongside Gurkhas from Nepal. In Hong Kong, they turned a blind eye as refugees crossed from the Chinese mainland. In Korea, they were treated for their wounds by doctors from an Indian parachute field hospital. In Aden, a pharmacist drafted into the RAF was required to learn a couple of hundred words of Arabic – so that he could treat men from the locally recruited Levies – and spent part of his time administering buckets of Epsom salts to sick camels.[5] In Libya, conscripts met Greek sponge divers who had crossed the Mediterranean in small boats.[6]

The peacetime armed forces were, in some respects, 'foreign' even for men who never left mainland Britain. Conscripts learned to understand alien customs and languages. They picked up an understanding of military dialect – part bureaucratic formulae, part obscenity and part Hindustani slang. They learned that old soldiers called bayonets 'swords' and that second lieutenants had to be addressed as 'Mr'. They learned elaborate drills designed for infantrymen in the eighteenth century and they learned not to ask why such drills were necessary for men who were being trained as clerks in the Royal Army Service Corps. Those who became officers went through rituals in the mess that sometimes seemed odder than those of the headhunters who led some national servicemen through the Malayan jungle.

From 1939 to 1945, the entire population had been mobilized for war. After 1945, by contrast, there was a clear separation between men in the forces and the civilian population. The former were subject to different rules and the sense of living under externally imposed constraint was particularly strong for young conscripts – men who had not chosen a military life and who, usually being at the bottom of the hierarchy, felt the force of discipline especially hard.

After 1945, national service took men into a kind of nether world. They were trained for war but rarely saw any fighting. Most of them were being prepared for a conflict with the Soviet Union that everyone devoutly hoped would never happen. Even those sent to theatres of real fighting might never see an enemy soldier. For most men, national service meant one of the huge camps that once dotted Britain. Tens – or even hundreds – of thousands of men were churned through the RAF bases at Padgate, Cardington and West Kirby. The Royal Artillery kept four training regiments at Oswestry in

Shropshire. Catterick near Richmond in Yorkshire was the largest, and probably the least attractive, camp in the British Isles. It was a training depot for the signal and tank regiments. Conscripts remembered the signs at the station: 'Signals to the Right; Armoured Corps to the Left'. By the mid 1950s, 16,000 soldiers – mainly national servicemen – were stationed there. It was so large and chaotic that it was possible for a soldier to disappear entirely; a signalman charged with desertion turned out, in fact, to have stayed in the camp hiding in the toilets and stealing food. He had lived like this for six months.[7]

Douglas Hurd, returning from reserve service in the artillery, wrote about how army camps disfigured Salisbury Plain and how future archaeologists might suppose that such camps had been built by the Saxons to protect Wessex: 'who in the future will believe that Englishmen of the twentieth century were so foolish as to snatch for the purposes of war thousands of acres of beauty and fertility from the heart of a country which has seen little war since Alfred beat the Danes?'[8] Barracks could seem bizarre places. Sometimes they were huge, old, brick buildings that dated back to Crimea; sometimes they were made up of huts that had been thrown up, usually during the war, on patches of ground that soon turned into seas of mud. Some civilians had no sense of what a military camp might look like. A female member of the Wolfenden Committee, investigating 'vice', enquired – innocently or mischievously – whether sexual acts in barracks might be said to occur 'in private'.[9]

The perimeter fence around each camp was the most ruthlessly enforced frontier that most British people encountered. Until the construction of the Berlin Wall in 1961, it was relatively easy to move from the Communist-ruled countries of central Europe to the West or vice versa. Some conscripts noted with alarm that Warsaw Pact armoured divisions would have to cross nothing but a white line painted on the trees of a forest if they smashed their way into western Europe. A soldier undergoing basic training, on the other hand, might have to get past barbed wire and Alsatian dogs if he wanted to go out for a bag of chips.

The frontiers between military and civilian life could be found in the oddest of places. Waterloo station was a frontier post, patrolled by military policemen and sometimes thronged with young men on their way back to garrisons in Hampshire. On troopships, soldiers – apart from officers – were kept separate from the civilian passengers. On the *Empire Orwell* in 1954, a national service private was posted as a 'children's picket' to prevent his comrades from reaching those parts of the deck reserved for 'first class ladies and children'.[10]

Some former national servicemen, perhaps with a mocking nod to the patois of their grandchildren, describe their national service as 'gap years'.[11] A few men really were called up between school and university. Some drafted applications to grand Oxbridge colleges on NAAFI writing paper,[12] or while recovering from wounds in Korea.[13] Men who undertook national service before university sometimes came to talk as though their experience was universal: 'I don't know anybody who didn't go from school to national service and then to university.'[14] In reality, only a small proportion of national servicemen would have stayed at school until the age of eighteen.[15] Most boys spent several years at work before they joined the forces. Some deferred their service to complete apprenticeships, and might have worked for seven years or more between school and the armed forces. During the 1950s, the word 'gap' was, in fact, used in relation to national service to apply to the awkward years through which working-class boys passed between leaving school and being called up.[16]

National servicemen who went into the forces before university were a minority, even among the already small minority who went to university at all. Most men with university places deferred their service until after they graduated. Those who went into the forces before university were largely those who were going to the universities of Oxford or Cambridge. These men had an importance that bore little relation to their numbers. This was partly because they were so culturally influential. It was also partly because they were socially significant. The military authorities regarded them as the best source of 'officer material', but civil servants and politicians were also keen to ensure that military service should interrupt their educational careers as little as possible. Anyone who imagines that national service involved equal sacrifice should remember that men holding places at university were the one group regularly excused part of their national service.[17]

The tendency to see national service as something that happened between school and university goes with a tendency to downplay it. For most educated men, conscription meant a few weeks of fear, followed by around eighteen months of mild boredom. In the long term, it was often just a backdrop against which the more agreeable aspects of their lives could be highlighted.[18] Those who went on to be successful were particularly prone to present national service as an interlude. Bill Rodgers, a politician of the 1970s and 80s, wrote that his time in the army was 'less a chapter in my life than a short story, complete in itself, with a beginning and an end'.[19]

In one sense, all the years from 1945 to 1963 were gap years. The period is overshadowed, on one side, by the anti-fascist struggles of the 1930s and the Second World War and, on the other, by the cultural revolution of the 1960s. Even the Attlee governments of 1945 to 1951 are often presented as the culmination, or sometimes the betrayal, of wartime projects. National servicemen were frequently conscious that their experience seemed in some way less important than that of both those older and those younger than themselves. Partly this was a matter of demographics. Birth rates in the 1930s were low. In 1952, there were 1,393,000 boys aged between fifteen and nineteen in England and Wales, almost all of whom would have registered for national service at the age of eighteen. By contrast, in the same year there were, even after the casualties of the Second World War, 1,603,000 men aged between thirty and thirty-four. Even more strikingly the national service generation was thrown into relief by the high birth rates of the subsequent period: the number of boys aged from five to nine in 1952 (all of them young enough to escape conscription) was 1,787,000.[20]

Low birth rates were particularly pronounced among the lower middle classes, which tended, in the inter-war period, to favour small families – the air force, recruiting largely from the children of 'black coated' workers, found that 23 per cent of its conscripts were only children; the figure for the army was 6 per cent.[21] The national serviceman hero of David Lodge's *Ginger, You're Barmy* is an only child of elderly, lower-middle-class parents: 'Sometimes I wondered if they had stumbled on the trick of procreation by accident'.[22] The high birth rates of the late 1940s, and the consequent burst of young people who entered early adulthood in the late 1960s, increased the sense that former national servicemen were a marginal group. Lodge's later novels are largely about men born in the 1930s, who reach early middle age in a world that seems dominated by *soixante-huitard* students.

The sense of being an 'in-between generation' was cultural as well as demographic. One defining feature of national servicemen was that they had all lived through the Second World War (no one born after September 1939 was called up) and many of them were acutely conscious that their own military experience seemed petty compared to that of their fathers or older brothers. The most educated national servicemen also reflected on the ideological conflicts of the 1930s. Even pacifism felt more passive in the 1950s than it had twenty years earlier. David Batterham, a conscript in the Canal Zone, wrote to his father, who had been a conscientious objector during the war: 'Generally speaking pacifism is less political now than between the wars, would you say? . . . less idealistic and more personal.'[23]

Those older than national servicemen sometimes regarded them with condescension. Gwylmor Prys Williams was a statistician who wrote on the problems of teenagers in the late 1950s – he was especially interested in the effects of military service. He thought that young men of the 1950s lacked the sense of purpose that had animated his contemporaries in the 30s and then in the war. This was partly because of national decline: 'In my early youth Great Britain was still a first-rate power. We thought we had won the 1914–1918 war and I think that most teenagers had that illusion until 1948 or 1949.' It was also because he saw the foundation of the welfare state as marking the end of a period of a heroic political struggle: 'To live in the aftermath of a Social Revolution is disturbing to youth, whose instinct is to alter the existing order.'[24]

In an influential book, Noel Annan (born in 1916) defined his generation thus:

> If you had asked Maurice Bowra, the most famous Oxford don and wit
> of his day, how old someone was, as like as not he would have replied:
> 'Our Age'. He meant by this anyone who came of age and went to the
> university in the thirty years between 1919, the end of the Great War,
> and 1949 – or, say, 1951, the last year in which those who had served
> in the armed forces during the Second World War returned to study.[25]

The Annan/Bowra definition revolves around the two wars (the second in particular) and around the formative effects of political commitment between those wars. However, post-war conscripts are conspicuous by their absence. Annan writes about John Wolfenden and Douglas Jay but not these men's sons – both prominent members of what Annan himself would call 'the intellectual aristocracy', and both national servicemen. Even those post-war conscripts who were famous, or notorious, members of Annan's Cambridge college – Neal Ascherson and Simon Raven – are not mentioned.

Former national servicemen also use the word 'generation' when talking about their own experience, but they use it less frequently and with less confidence than their elders. In some ways, national service actually undermined men's sense of generational identity. The pattern of peacetime conscription encouraged men to think of their 'contemporaries' in narrow terms. Among themselves, conscripts regarded a man of twenty-two as being old. When one historian assembled the letters written by his friends, he described them as the 'generation of 1949' and regarded the experiences of those who left his Nottingham grammar school and were called up in that particular year as being quite different from those of men who were just one year older or younger.[26]

Though national service lasted for eighteen years, a single conscript was rarely in the forces for more than two years. The conditions in which men served changed enormously. Those who lay under rough blankets and broke the ice on their barrack-room latrines during the bitter winter of 1946 were worse off than those who were called up in, say, 1958 – though civilian conditions improved more quickly than those of the armed forces and it may, therefore, be that the conscripts' sense of relative deprivation actually increased. Early conscripts still lived in a world that was overshadowed by the war and, for that matter, by the threat of another war that seemed to go with the Berlin airlift. Conscription seemed more legitimate and necessary to them than it did to men who came ten years later.

The rhythm of call-up and demobilization encouraged men to think of themselves as belonging to a cohort that changed every two weeks as new recruits arrived or left. 'Get some in' – one of the phrases most associated with the memory of national service – was used by conscripts and applied to those of their comrades who had been called up just a few months later than themselves.

If men born from 1928 to 1939 think of themselves as having something in common, then this sense tends to come from civilian experiences – education and post-war prosperity – rather than military service.[27] If such men refer to military experience, they generally assume that the defining characteristic of their generation was the fact that they escaped from conscription during the war and were thus, in John Osborne's words, 'too young to fight, too old to forget'.[28]

National servicemen were overshadowed by those who were younger than them as well as those who were older. The sharp rise in birth rates that began in the late 1940s went with social changes that produced more confident and vociferous representatives of 'youth'. This was especially true of those who were academically able. Children born around 1948 gained most from the Butler Education Act of 1944, which increased the number of free grammar school places, and the Robbins Report of 1963, which expanded universities.

Britain, or at least London, is often presented as a place in which the 1960s were lived with particular intensity – the French historian Michel Winock describes them as '*les années anglaises*'. One effect of this was to relegate the preceding decade to a kind of long Victorian age. Significantly, this (1963 to be precise) is the moment that conscription ended – though, also significantly, historians rarely allude to this fact: they are more likely to make Larkinesque reference to the *Lady Chatterley* trial or the advent of the Beatles. National servicemen were aware that they did not fit into the culture of the 1960s: 'Our ambitions then were probably more lined up to 1930 values than perhaps to 1960 values, but that was perhaps inevitable because in a sense the country had gone into a sort of hiatus in the early 1940s.'[29]

Though the culture of the 1960s did not have much of a place for national servicemen it did, curiously, have a place for their elders. The 1960s saw increased interest in the two world wars and in the ideological struggles that lay between them. The First World War was presented as important because it epitomized the tragic futility of conflict (the musical *Oh! What a Lovely War* was first produced in 1963).

The Second World War and the anti-fascist crusades of the 1930s were held up as examples of 'good wars'. The result of all this was that the 1950s appeared as a valley of quiescence wedged between mountain ranges of political commitment. More specifically, national service came to seem like a parody of real war that had all of its farce and none of its tragedy. In generational terms, it was as though the radicals who were twenty in 1968 were conducting a conversation with the radicals who had been twenty in, say, 1936, but conducting it over the heads of the generation, made up of men born in the 1930s, that stood between them.

The idea that national service was laughable came to influence national servicemen themselves. In 2007, when David Batterham deposited his national service diary and letters in the Imperial War Museum, he appended a note: 'For many years after I left the army, the question "Where did you do your National Service?" was a common greeting among all young men. I last heard it, after a long gap, from a pompous pub bore in about 1975.'[30]

There are some specifically academic reasons for the neglect of national service. The end of national service overlapped with the beginning of the golden age of British sociology, but sociologists took oddly little interest in the armed forces. A few researchers exploited the information about young men provided by conscription, but these researchers usually thought of themselves as specialists in 'public health' rather than sociology, as it was coming to be understood. Often their studies had started looking at a particular generational cohort before they reached national service age, or even before conscription had been introduced in Britain, and simply followed their subjects as they were called up. Sometimes such work had begun with assumptions that were starting to seem old-fashioned by the late 1950s.[31] The sociologists who were appointed to newly created or expanding university departments in the early 1960s usually showed little interest in national service. This is all the more striking because many of these sociologists had themselves been national servicemen – indeed some seem to have turned to sociology partly as a reaction to their military experience.[32]

Sometimes, national service seems a gaping hole in works of sociology. In her study of Ship Street in Liverpool, Madeline Kerr gives information about the work of every one of the 120 adult males in the area and then adds: 'The boys in between 18 and 20 are of course doing national service. Twelve of the boys below this age are in Borstal or some other approved school.' Kerr later mentions in passing that some men refused to come back home after their national service.[33] These are the only references to national service in the whole book. A later section on 'going away' is about prison.

National service is also conspicuous by its absence in the studies of 'affluent workers' published in the 1960s. The authors were interested in how well-paid workers in engineering factories thought about their social position. A large proportion of these men, all aged between twenty-one and forty-six, would have served in the armed forces, either during or after the Second World War. Interviewers were specifically asked to prompt workers about military service when asking about previous jobs. Their handwritten notes sometimes record extraordinary experiences; one of the workers had fought with the Special Air Service.[34] Notes on interviews reflect a bored familiarity with the military world: 'rather thick ex-military policeman (I know the type well from extensive experience)'.[35] There is, however, almost no reference to military experience in the published study.[36] There is, for example, no enquiry into whether service in the RAF – which recruited many skilled workers and which had been shaken by large-scale 'strikes' in 1945 – might have helped foster a particular kind of working-class culture.

Absence is most striking in *Education and the Working Class*, the beautifully written study by Brian Jackson and Dennis Marsden of ninety-eight children (over half of them boys) educated at grammar schools in Huddersfield. Jackson and Marsden, born in 1932 and 1933, were both national servicemen,[37] and their book contributed to a debate about educational potential that had been ignited, in part, by the Crowther Report of 1959, which drew much of its information from national servicemen. But *Education and the Working Class* says little about the fact that almost all the male subjects of the book would have spent two years in the armed forces. There is just one explicit, and tantalizingly brief, reference to a working-class grammar school boy who found that national service 'offered some kind of respite' from the aimlessness that had afflicted him after school.[38]

Why were the most influential sociologists of the 1950s and 60s so uninterested in national service? Partly, no doubt, the answer lies in a link between an absence of a tradition of conscription and the absence of a tradition of military sociology. The fact that the armed forces had usually been small, and made up of long-service regulars, contributed to the sense that it was a subject for specialists that could have no broader implications for civilian society. Universal military service did not last long enough to change academic assumptions in this area. Furthermore, the most influential sociological works of the period were usually 'community studies'. Most of them involved studying a particular town, suburb or neighbourhood.[39] This intense focus on an area meant that anything that took people away from it tended to disappear from view.

What of historians? The generation born in the late 1940s has been especially influential in the historical profession and its members have sometimes assumed that recent British history overlaps substantially with their own autobiography.[40] This does not mean that they ignore what happened before their birth or during their youth but it does mean that they tend to focus on those things that were to have an obvious impact on their own lives – the welfare state, social mobility, meritocracy. For such people, however, national service exists only as a vague blur on the periphery of their vision.

Tony Judt recognized that not being conscripted had defined his own generation: 'I was born in England in 1948, late enough to avoid conscription ... but in time for the Beatles.'[41] But the absence of conscription also came close to defining his vision of the whole post-war period:

> The 1960s saw the apogee of the European state. The relation of the citizen to the state in Western Europe in the course of the previous century had been a shifting compromise between military needs and political claims: the modern rights of newly enfranchised citizens offset by the older obligations to defend the realm. But since 1945 that relationship had come increasingly to be characterized by a dense tissue of social benefits and economic strategies in which it was the state that served its subjects, rather than the other way around.[42]

Remarks about national service in most studies of British history are cursory.[43] The subject does not fit neatly into any of the categories under which post-war British history is usually studied. Historians of grand strategy and high politics say something about government policy on conscription but not much about the experience of conscripts. Old-fashioned social historians (those on the frontier of labour history) tend to be interested in adult men who voted, worked in industry and belonged to trade unions. New-fashioned social historians (on the frontier of cultural history) tend to be interested in immigrants, women and children. The notion that it might be possible to write a social history of the armed forces themselves has been relatively slow to take hold.[44]

Oral history has widened the gulf between military historians and those who work on more broadly 'social' themes. Anyone who conducts interviews is obliged, in a literal sense, to formulate questions before they begin their research and this makes frontiers between the sub-disciplines of history more rigid. David Lance, himself a former national serviceman, did much to develop oral history when he worked at the Imperial War Museum. However, he recognized that oral history was largely conducted by people with different interests, and he felt uncomfortable among what he described as the 'oral history establishment' in Britain. He regarded it as having a 'very left-wing orientation', and he was disillusioned by the 'dominance' of 'social history' and 'sociology'. For Lance, the Oral History Society (founded in 1973) was dedicated to 'social history meaning the history of the working classes as opposed to other kinds of social history'. He felt that 'I carried this Imperial War Museum label. I felt as if I had been put into a box.'[45]

Lance's conflation of 'sociology', 'social history', 'left-wing approaches' and 'the history of the working classes' is not entirely fair, but it is revealing. The interviews conducted by Lance's own colleagues at the Imperial War Museum and those conducted by those historians who are primarily interested in civilian society differ strikingly. The military interviewers sometimes pass over every aspect of civilian life – which means that they occasionally move men born in the 1930s straight from their last memories of the Second World War (usually of victory celebrations in May 1945) to the moment when they were themselves called up.

By contrast, interviewers who are primarily interested in civilian society ask little about national service.[46] The 'City Lives' interviews, with figures from the London financial establishment are particularly suggestive. The interviewers are drawn in part from Lance's 'oral history establishment', they are all scrupulous, and they cannot in this case be accused of confining their interest to the working class: most of their interviewees are bankers and stockbrokers. All the same, they often approach national service as though they find it a perplexing episode in the lives of their subjects. Sometimes they simply pass over it and then retrace their steps when they realize that there is a two-year gap in someone's biography: 'I'm sorry we missed out your national service. I'd forgotten about that.'[47]

The relative neglect of national service as a topic for research in Britain is highlighted by international comparison. Americans have always taken the social history of the armed forces seriously – perhaps because military service so often provided a route to education and social mobility. Samuel Stouffer's study of the American soldier put the phrase 'relative deprivation' into circulation[48] – though the English sociologist who made most use of this concept, a national serviceman, applied it exclusively to the civilian world.[49] More specifically, conscription was a topic of interest for US scholars because it became so controversial during the Vietnam War.

Even more strikingly, military service was, until its abolition in 1997, important in France. French historians, and historians of France, have always studied compulsory military service. They have examined it as an object in itself and they have studied it, as Eugen Weber famously did, as one of the means by which the state transformed 'peasants into Frenchmen'.[50] The historians of the Annales School used conscription as a source of information that could be subjected to statistical analysis.[51]

This interest has not crossed the Channel. The British, unlike the French, did not use military service to mould national culture. The authorities excluded from conscription anyone whose attachment to the nation seemed problematic – including the entire population of Northern Ireland. The links between military service and national identity were therefore less explicit than in much of continental Europe. As for the attempts by the Annales School to use military service as a source for social history, many of those British historians who did most to diffuse the influence of the Annales School were themselves national servicemen, but they do not seem to have thought that national service itself might be an interesting object of study. Indeed, Peter Burke has suggested that the effect of national service was to make young men who had been posted to Malaya, like himself, or Jamaica, like Keith Thomas, interested in anthropology and hence to turn them away from twentieth-century Britain towards the apparently exotic cultures of early modern Europe.[52]

The French interest in conscription was enhanced by the fact that so many conscripts fought in the Algerian War of 1954 to 1962. This war, and the rebellion by army officers against the decision to withdraw from Algeria, stimulated interest in the sociology and social history of the army.[53] Important historians – such as Robert Bonnaud, Antoine Prost and Alain Corbin[54] – served in Algeria and wrote about their experiences there. Most importantly, the perception that conscripts in Algeria had been involved in torture and other atrocities encouraged a generation of historians born in the early 1970s – notably Raphaëlle Branche and Claire Mauss-Copeaux – to interview former conscripts.[55]

The British colonial wars – in Malaya, Kenya and Cyprus – also involved conscripts but they have not directed British attention to conscription in the same way. The number of conscripts mobilized in British wars of decolonization was relatively small – the recent burst of writing on British repression in Kenya has mainly involved regular soldiers and policemen.[56] The very fact that British conscripts fought in more than one conflict meant that there was no single war that focused discussion in the way Algeria did for the French or Vietnam did for the Americans. Atrocities were less widely discussed in Britain than in France – perhaps because the British authorities did not persecute anti-colonial militants who were of European origin.

The aim of my book is to use national service as a means to study a series of broader questions about modern Britain. I am interested in how national service might have affected society, and preventing change is as much of an effect as precipitating it. I am also interested in how national service reflected society as it was. I have approached the topic in a way that does not begin and end at the gate of the barracks and examined the penumbra of conscription. I have looked at what men did before they were conscripted, and what effect the prospect of conscription had on them before they were called up. I have explored the relationship between women and national service: it is significant that the armed forces often regarded the mothers of conscripts with hostility and that young women were often so indifferent to men of military age. And I have looked at who did not do national service and why the British state did not want to conscript certain categories of men.

I should explain features of my work that may seem strange to some readers. The first relates to national servicemen in the wars of decolonization. I recognize that conscripts were often involved in the administration of violence. I have not, however, entered into the wider debates about how common violence was. Furthermore, I have not touched on what one historian has called the 'juridification of the past'.[57] I mean by this that I have not attempted to determine how far violence might, or might not, have been legally defensible. From the point of view of national servicemen themselves, what mattered was the act of killing – particularly killing in the uncomfortably intimate circumstances that often marked the wars in Kenya and Malaya, where soldiers frequently fired at very close range – not the question of whether any particular kill was legal.

Second, I have not sought to write a faithful account of daily life as experienced by an ordinary conscript. A few literal-minded conscripts wrote letters or diary entries of exactly the same length on every single day of their service. Reading such documents gives the historian an uncomfortable insight into how tedious national service could be, but I have written most about those aspects of service – travel abroad, combat and, most important for most men, basic training – that loomed largest in men's memories. Similarly, I have devoted attention to groups whose experience strikes me as significant. I have written about two conflicts – Korea and Suez – that involved relatively small numbers of conscripts (very small numbers in the case of Suez) because these were conflicts that were, for very different reasons, seen as important by many British people. Similarly, I have written at length about the social extremes. This is partly because we learn about the armed forces, and indeed British society, by looking at those whose success and failure were most marked and, in the context of national service, this means looking at the group of men (5 per cent at most) who were commissioned and the even smaller proportion who were most likely to end up in Colchester Military Detention Centre. I have also tried to take national servicemen at their word. Since so many of their accounts emphasize the social integration of a process that allegedly mixed boys from Borstal and those from grand public schools, it is worth examining these groups. Large numbers of the former were 'direct entrants' into the Pioneer Corps and a significant minority of the latter would have joined Brigade Squad of the Household Division. Both these groups were separated from other soldiers from the first day of their service.

The third characteristic of my work that might require some explanation relates to memory. Recent historians have tended to divide into two camps. Those writing for the general public are increasingly interested in personal recollections; some present their work as a collage of first-hand accounts. Such an approach has been especially influential in histories of national service – because, until recently, few other sources were available. Several writers have either edited collections of autobiographical essays or synthesized the memories of national servicemen.[58] Keith Miller, Trevor Royle and Adrian Walker have generously deposited their sources – sometimes composed of long and striking accounts by individual servicemen – so that they can be consulted by other historians.[59] On the other hand, academic historians have become increasingly prone to see problems in the use of what they call 'ego-documents' as historical sources. Some of them see all autobiographical accounts as a kind of 'fiction' based on a false notion of the unity of the self. Such scholars often believe that the operation of memory itself should be an object of study.

I have attempted to steer a middle course. I have, to quote a critic who is hostile to such an approach, used autobiographies 'for useful facts to pick out, like currants from a cake'.[60] I have treated personal accounts as I would treat any other documents and tried as far as possible to check one kind of source against another. I am aware, as many former national servicemen are themselves, that memory plays tricks and that there is sometimes a fine line between fact and fiction. Some of the best-written and most amusing accounts of national service, ones on which I have myself drawn, contain assertions that cannot be true. Julian Critchley claims to have been offered a commission in a smart regiment because an officer noticed that he was circumcised and thus concluded that he was a public school boy – one could write a whole chapter on why this story is implausible.[61] It would, however, be wrong to assume that unreliable personal memoirs can be juxtaposed with a world of austere fact to be found in official archives. The service ministries compiled 'ego-documents' themselves because they often drew on interviews and questionnaires to examine the experience of conscripts. Furthermore, official bodies, like individuals, have personalities, which express themselves in documentary records. The brisk empiricism of the air force contrasts sharply with the more emotional and Panglossian views of the army. Most of all, Whitehall departments had interests of their own to defend. One collection of documents concludes with a revealing remark by a civil servant: 'I understand that one of the purposes of the survey was to provide ammunition to enable S of S to deal with critics of national service.'[62]

Sometimes the things that men remember and forget can themselves be revealing. Working-class conscripts frequently refer to national service pay – 28s per week with deductions for barrack-room breakages. For boys who had been called up when they had been at work for several years and were sometimes earning as much as £10 per week, this was a matter of bitter resentment. Middle-class men, by contrast, rarely remember what they were paid. For boys who came straight from school, it mattered less. A few wealthy men do not remember what allowance they received from their parents (though some regiments discouraged men without such resources from applying for a commission) or even whether they received an allowance at all.[63] Even the national service number tells us something. Men almost invariably remember it. During basic training they had to shout it out when asked to identify themselves – a private who told a court martial that he would answer to his name but not to his rank or number got fifteen months.[64] Men who were commissioned got new numbers but they rarely remember them: an officer was identified by name rather than by number.

Sometimes the inconsistencies of memory can be dramatic. Consider one of the most notorious episodes of the national service period when a patrol of the Scots Guards killed twenty-four Chinese men in Malaya in December 1948. There was a major division in the way in which men on the patrol recounted the incident. Some, mostly regular soldiers, stuck to the official line that the Chinese had been 'shot while trying to escape'. Others, mostly national servicemen, said that the victims had been murdered. Even among those who said that there had been a massacre, however, there were important discrepancies. Men disagreed about who had given them orders and about whether or not individual soldiers were offered the chance not to participate. Finally, one guardsman recognized that his own memories ebbed and flowed with time:

> it's been bothering me recently [in 1970] more than when it actually happened, or immediately after it happened . . . It hasn't been comfortable. It has drifted at times, I've forgot about it and then television and suchlike and different things suddenly bring it back and then it goes again as quick and then arisen again as quick.[65]

What, then, might the historian gain by looking at national service? First, the answer to this question lies in a shift in perspective that may make recent British history appear less benign. Studying national service means turning away from the experience of the post-war baby boomers to examine the generation of men whose childhoods had been overshadowed by economic depression and war. It also means recognizing that the upwardly mobile grammar school boys, who have provided some of the most famous accounts of national service, were a minority. Many young men did not encounter the benign state of Beveridge and Butler. Their education more or less stopped with elementary school and was, at least for those of them born in the early part of the 1930s, disrupted by the chaos of war. The most important state interventions in their early lives came from evacuation or from the conscription of their own fathers. Their view of the state revolved around coercion as much as welfare.

Secondly, national service is useful for anyone who is interested in social class. Class might seem an intangible category to anyone working on civilian society in modern Britain, and many historians have begun to question whether it is useful at all, but people in the 1950s did think in terms of class. Those who talked most about class tended to do so with reference to the civilian world and they sometimes pointed out that class distinctions were becoming more fluid and permeable, which did not mean that they were disappearing. However, the armed forces had their own class system – which involved distinctions between ranks (especially the all-important distinction between officers and 'men') but also more complicated hierarchies involving the different services and the different units within them.

Thirdly, national service tells us about masculinity. The armed forces had explicit and aggressively enforced notions of what constituted properly 'masculine' behaviour. They also took an intrusive interest in the lives of recruits. Seeing how young men responded to all this tells us much about how they thought about notions such as 'adulthood', 'sexual experience', 'homosexuality' or, indeed, 'normality'.

Fourthly, national service relates to Britain's position in the world. Between 1945 and 1963, Britain changed from being the greatest imperial power that the world had ever seen into a small island that ruled over a few other small islands. It also acquired nuclear weapons and adopted a foreign policy that revolved around the containment of the Soviet Union. Usually this process is seen in terms of high policy and grand strategy, and national servicemen appear only as part of the 'resources' that Britain was able to deploy. Studying them shows something of how the big strategic changes affected ordinary people. Relations with empire are particularly important in this context. It was during the last years of the British empire – from, say, 1943 to 1958 – that ordinary Britons were most likely, as conscript soldiers, to go to many of Britain's imperial possessions. Furthermore, their experiences – in the jungles of Malaya or the hills of Kenya – did not always fit neatly into the hierarchies of race and class that we usually associate with empire.

Finally, national service is worth studying because of what it tells us about the armed forces themselves. Regular airmen, sailors and soldiers (especially those who serve in the ranks) are rarely very articulate or given to recording their impressions. Often they take the codes and customs of the military world for granted and feel no need to explain them to outsiders. National service provides a rare window on to this world.

I

Definitions, Facts and Uncertainties

Along with their kit, national servicemen were issued with instructions on how the armed forces worked. These often reflected an extraordinary set of priorities. Lectures on 'how to survive a nuclear explosion' seemed to be given the same billing as ones on 'the ranks and identification of officers from all the different services'.[1] At the risk of sounding like a drill sergeant, I propose to begin my study of national service with a series of brief factual statements – though I want to stress that, behind the confident assertions that are often associated with any discussion of national service, much remains in doubt. I hope that this chapter will provide the reader with the equipment to understand the rest of the book. Some of the points I discuss in this chapter and, indeed, in later parts of the book may sound arcane to modern readers. However, historians ought always to begin their examination of past societies by looking at those aspects of them that seem initially to be obscure and this is even more true of the relatively recent past than it is of, say, medieval monasticism. For example, the relative social position of 'the Brigade' (which usually means the Brigade of Guards) and the Rifle Brigade (which is actually a regiment) tells us much about the class system in the 1950s.

WHAT WAS NATIONAL SERVICE?

I have used the term to apply to all military conscription after the end of the Second World War. However, the first National Service Act was passed in 1939 and, in its widest sense, national service should apply, and occasionally was applied, to all men called up after this date. The first post-war act defining national service was passed in 1947, revised in 1948 and came into force in January 1949. So, in its narrowest sense, national service should apply only to men called up from January 1949. Men continued to be called up after the end of the Second World War under wartime legislation that required their services 'for the duration of the Emergency'. In May 1946, it was announced that men were to be called up for a fixed period of time – initially, two years – and this rule was applied from January 1947. In April 1950, War Office statistics relating to the army distinguished between 'National Servicemen, 1939–1946' (there were 536 of them); 'National Servicemen, 1947/1948' (there were 24,389 of them) and 'National Servicemen, 1949' (there were 148,886 of them).[2]

Post-war conscripts were often confused about what the term 'national service' might mean and how far it might be applied to them. A working-class man from east London made a shrewd, if technically incorrect, distinction. He believed that the war had seen something called 'people's mobilization' and that 'conscription came in after the war'.[3] Godfrey Raper began a course of officer training at Oxford before the end of the Second World War but became a full-time soldier after its end. He said later that he was not sure 'whether national service as such had been formed yet'.[4] Jeremy Morse joined the army in February 1947 and said many years later:

> In fact, formally speaking, national service began on January 1st 1947. Those who joined up in 1946 were still under wartime conditions. I found that out later because I was actually the first national service officer to be commissioned into the Rifle regiments.[5]

Morse is right to say that the beginning of 1947 marked the end of 'wartime conditions' for conscription, and it is very likely that his brother officers described him as a 'national service officer' when he was finally commissioned, which was not until a year after his initial call-up. However, he was not 'formally speaking' a post-war national serviceman – because he was not called up under the 1948 Act. Morse is described in the *Army List* for 1948 as the holder of an 'Emergency Commission'.[6] The first 'National Service Officer of the Regular

Army', the honourable R. E. L. Johnstone, did not make his appearance in Morse's regiment until the following year.[7]

Even the Secretary of State for War was not sure exactly how the term 'national service' should be used. In September 1948 he said: 'Of the Brigade of Guards sent to Malaya, only 400 men were conscripts. I mean they were National Service men. Although the National Service Act has not come into operation as yet.'[8] Writers whose autobiographical works did much to inform images of national service were not always, in the strictest sense of the words, national servicemen. Tom Stacey, who wrote an influential autobiographical essay in a collection of accounts by 'national servicemen',[9] was described in the *Army List* as an 'Emergency Officer'.[10] The novelist Alan Sillitoe wrote a number of autobiographical essays and stories about national service but he had sought to join up before he was conscripted and, in at least some of his accounts, he continued to describe himself as a 'volunteer'.[11] By the time he was interviewed in 2000, he was uncertain about his own status and that of his contemporaries:

> very complicated to me this nomenclature of what people were. I mean some of them were conscripts. Because they were calling them up during the war and, after the war, it never stopped whether they called them conscripts or national servicemen or people in for the duration of the present Emergency.[12]

There was similar ambiguity about the end of national service. Regular officers, including senior ones, often did not know exactly when national service had ended.[13] Henry Askew was born in 1940, and described his time as an officer in the Grenadier Guards thus:

> well, you see, I was the first age group that didn't have to do national service, but my father volunteered for me. So I did a course called voluntary national service and I signed on for a bit more, so that basically, I did six months training and three years commissioned service.[14]

The phrase 'voluntary national service' has left no trace in official records but one assumes that Askew did not just dream it and that it must have been used in the army in the early 1960s.

WHAT WAS THE DIFFERENCE BETWEEN A NATIONAL SERVICEMAN AND A REGULAR?

A regular is, strictly speaking, a soldier undertaking full-time service rather than one in the part-time Territorial Army. The *Army List* refers to men as being 'national service officers of the Regular Army'. In practice, though, the word 'regular' was widely understood to mean a professional serviceman rather than a conscript. Professionals were volunteers; they served for longer and they received higher pay. Divisions were not clear-cut. Some men became regulars after having been called up. Matters were made particularly complicated because, in 1950, the forces created three-year engagements, which attracted regular pay. It was widely recognized that some of these men were conscripts in all but name, and would not have signed on for three years if they had not known that they would, in any case, be called up for two. Three-year men frequently described themselves as conscripts and official reports conceded that this was fair. Senior officers often recognized three-year engagements as being 'extended national service'.[15] When a soldier appeared as a witness before an official inquiry in 1953, he was described as a 'national serviceman' and the president of the board asked 'two or three years?'[16]

HOW LONG WAS NATIONAL SERVICE?

The authorities planned to call up men in January 1947 for two years and then to reduce the period of service gradually to eighteen months. Briefly, between late 1947 and late 1948, it seemed that the period of service would from January 1949 be set at just one year. However, this decision, taken as a result of a rebellion by Labour MPs, was reversed before the National Service Act came into force, and the period was set at eighteen months. It was extended to two years in late 1950 because of the Korean War. Not all men served for the stipulated term. Some were released early to go to university. Towards the end of national service, some conscripts were also discreetly released before their normal date because the forces simply did not need them.

Some conscripts were retained for longer periods. Many of those serving in 1948 were kept for an extra three months because of the Berlin airlift. It says something about the uncertainties attending post-war conscription that in 1953 a civil servant in the Ministry of Defence, reviewing call-up figures, could not remember why men had been held back for three months: 'I share your recollection that it was connected with the Berlin Air Lift but I have not been able to check this in the time available.'[17]

Some conscripts were again retained during the early 1960s so that the last national servicemen, having been called up in November 1960, were not released until May 1963. A few unfortunate men not only served at a time when most of their contemporaries escaped military service entirely, but were kept in the forces for longer than any other conscripts since 1947.

WHAT PART-TIME OBLIGATIONS ATTACHED TO NATIONAL SERVICE?

All conscripts were obliged to serve for a time in the reserve forces. Traditionally, proponents of conscription in Britain had presented it primarily as a means of building up reserve forces and the first post-war projects were designed to do precisely this. It was, at one time, intended that men should perform just one year of full-time service before spending six years in the reserve. In the end, the legislation of late 1949 required men to spend eighteen months in the forces followed by four years in the reserve. Reserve service was then reduced to three and half years when full-time service was increased to two years in 1950. Soldiers were required to serve in either the Territorial Army or the Army Emergency Reserve. The former required them to undertake three annual two-week camps and a further fortnight of training; the latter generally involved just annual camps. In 1955, however, as national service began to run down, the reserve obligations for most national servicemen were reduced to twenty days in total.[18] Some men escaped from all or part of their reserve service in

5

various ways, and towards the very end reserve commitments were all but abandoned – the last men to be called up simply received rail warrants and instructions that they were to report to particular bases if required but did not, on the whole, ever have to put their uniforms on after their full-term service was finished.

Reserve service had an effect on the way the armed forces treated conscripts – in particular, the need to provide officers for the Territorial Army forced the War Office to concern itself with the geographical, and thus with the social, origins of national service officers. Reserve service also mattered during the Suez crisis of 1956 – though even then the number of men who remembered being frightened that they might be recalled to service was much greater than the number who actually were. Generally, however, few men took reserve service very seriously. Men who returned for a two-week camp usually lost whatever acting rank they had held at the end of full-time service and were often assigned to duties that had little to do with what they had done during full-time service. Military discipline, which had seemed so terrifying and novel when they were first called up, was often now treated as a joke. One airman recalled for reserve service was quietly advised to disappear from his base during working hours – he spent some happy days in Blackpool.[19] A trained paratrooper turned up for reserve training with long hair and a beard.[20] National service memoirs usually devote long passages to the first few weeks of basic training – most of them dismiss the few weeks of reserve obligations with a single flippant sentence.

DID ALL THE SERVICES TAKE CONSCRIPTS?

All three services took some conscripts. The army took most – around two thirds of all those called up between 1949 and 1960. The navy took about one in forty of them; the Admiralty often toyed with the idea of doing away with national service sailors entirely and sometimes stated its intention to limit entrants to 2,000 men per year, though they did not achieve this figure until the last couple of years of the call-up. At the very end, national service became almost

6

exclusively a matter for the army. Of the last conscripts to be called up, in November 1960, 2,000 went to the army, fifty went to the RAF and none to the navy.[21]

Many accounts of national service, particularly those written at the time, simply ignore the navy. I have included all three services – partly because the differences between them are frequently revealing. I have, however, given most space to the army. This is partly because it took most national servicemen. It is also because men from the two social extremes – the lowest part of the working class and the most privileged part of the upper-middle class – went almost exclusively into the army, which is, therefore, of special interest to the social historian.

WHAT RANKS DID NATIONAL SERVICEMEN HOLD?

All three services are divided into 'officers' and 'other ranks'. Officers hold a 'commission' from the Queen. 'Non-Commissioned officers' – corporals, sergeants and warrant officers – have more limited authority and never outrank officers. A 'junior' officer means a second lieutenant or lieutenant. NCOs are promoted, having begun their careers as privates. Towards the end of the Second World War, and for a short time after it, all army officers were required to begin their careers in the ranks. All national servicemen began in the ranks – though from 1948 'potential officers' were identified quite quickly.

National service officers mostly finished their full-time service with the rank of second lieutenant – or the equivalent rank in the other services. A few were made acting lieutenants or acting captains. Graduates commissioned into the Royal Navy held the rank of sub-lieutenant, equivalent to that of full lieutenant in the army. Doctors, who undertook their national service as medical officers at the end of their clinical training, were given the rank of captain. A tiny group of men (presumably doctors who had been called up late) held the rank of major. Rank was one of the topics about which myths of national service flourished. It is, for example, often said that the politician Ian Gow was a major during his national service;[22] according to the *Army List*, he was a lieutenant.

7

Among other ranks, quite large numbers of conscripts rose to lance corporal or corporal during their service. There were also some national service sergeants and a tiny number of men who became staff sergeants or warrant officers. Many national service NCOs and most sergeants held their rank because they exercised some particular function – as a clerk or as a teacher in the Education Corps rather than because they gave orders in a platoon of a fighting unit.

All ranks can be acting or substantive. An acting rank is temporary and may expire when its holder moves to a different role. A substantive rank is retained unless the soldier is demoted for some offence. Some national servicemen believed that there was a formal rule that non-commissioned conscripts could not hold ranks above that of corporal. This is untrue. It was also sometimes believed that national servicemen could be promoted only to an acting rank and that all must therefore have finished with the substantive rank of either private or second lieutenant. The record-keeping department of the War Office appears to have thought, wrongly, that this might be the case.[23]

HOW MANY NATIONAL SERVICEMEN WERE THERE?

Historians, and indeed official figures, often conflate different things when talking about national service. Official figures often refer to men of national service age who were posted to the armed forces – not all of these men, in fact, would have been conscripts. The total number of men of national service age who entered the armed forces from January 1948 to December 1960 was over 2 million. However, only 1,718,884 of these were conscripts. Similarly, some authors mix up the number of men called up under the 1948 Act with the number of all post-war conscripts. Thus historians write that there were 2,301,000 national servicemen in all, that there were 33 soldiers for 12 airmen and 1 sailor or marine, and that the army took 1,132,872 servicemen in all.[24] Anyone with a pocket calculator can see that at least one of these numbers must be wrong, and it seems likely the figure given for the army here refers to the period after January 1949 while that given for all servicemen refers to the period after 1945.

The Ministry of Labour seems to have had the most reliable figures for conscription,[25] and it gave a detailed breakdown for conscripts entering the three services from 1948 to 1960 (see table).[26] These figures more or less match those given by the War Office for the number of conscripts arriving at Army Basic Training Units from 1949 to 1960.[27]

Postings of National Servicemen to the Armed Forces

	Navy	Army	RAF	Total
1948	3,700	100,500	46,700	150,900
1949	8,100	115,400	43,100	166,600
1950	1,300	120,600	52,300	174,200
1951	2,728	118,376	47,547	168,651
1952	3,716	126,720	39,948	170,384
1953	3,544	113,611	36,909	154,064
1954	5,875	108,616	33,484	147,975
1955	6,105	108,656	42,072	156,833
1956	4,350	89,479	36,194	130,023
1957	2,727	77,852	20,586	101,165
1958	1,077	68,090	12,041	81,208
1959	255	49,739	11,234	61,228
1960	106	46,777	8,770	55,653
Total	43,583	1,244,416	430,885	1,718,884

The Ministry of Labour also gave overall numbers for conscripts entering all three services in 1946 and 1947. These were, respectively, 266,000 and 183,000.[28] These figures suggest that a total of 2,167,884 men were conscripted between January 1946 and December 1960. However, this is not, in fact, a perfect guide to the total number conscripted. First, it does not tell us how many were called up between the end of the Second World War and December 1945. Secondly, it is not really possible to distinguish between conscripts and regulars before January 1947. Thirdly, the number of men called up and posted is not the same as the total number of national servicemen. Some men – quite large numbers in the early 1950s – would have switched to regular engagements (especially three-year ones) after arriving in the forces.

WHO WAS LIABLE FOR NATIONAL SERVICE?

The only exemptions from national service were accorded to those who were clergymen (relatively easy to establish with regard to the major Churches) and those who had been certified insane or blind. In practice, some men were never called for medical examination because they suffered from some physical or psychological problem that was too obvious to require further investigation. Large groups of men were granted deferments and it was expected that coal miners, fishermen, merchant seamen and, at first, agricultural workers would defer until they reached an age when they would no longer be liable for service. All men called to register for national service underwent a medical and some failed this. Failure rates changed over time – mainly because the authorities used medical inspections to regulate the number of men called.

Men usually became liable for national service in the year when they were eighteen. However, the government varied the age of call-up from time to time. This was done either by suppressing one of the quarterly registrations in a year, which meant that the age of conscripts would rise by three months, or by adding an extra registration, which meant that it would drop. The age of call-up was never brought below eighteen and overall it drifted upwards. Men who wished to complete their studies or apprenticeships could defer their national service, which meant that they usually entered the forces when they were twenty-one. Men who wanted to discharge their military obligations as soon as possible (usually this meant public school boys with places at university) were allowed to register for national service early.

National service had a blurred end. No one born later than September 1939 was called up. However, deferment, medical rejection and increasing delays in the administration of the call-up meant that the majority of men born in 1938 and 1939 were never posted to the forces.

Not all national servicemen were young. Some men born in 1927 or earlier were called up after 1945 – even though they had reached military age during the Second World War. Some of these had deferred their service. A medical student, for example, might have trained during the war and then been drafted into the armed forces as a qualified doctor in his late twenties. The usual age at which men ceased to be liable for national service was, initially, twenty-six – it was raised to thirty-five in the mid 1950s in order to prevent men from evading their obligations by spending some time abroad. However, special rules applied to doctors, who had rarely completed their training much before the age of twenty-six. They could be called up until they were thirty-one and it was theoretically possible for men who had deferred their service further in order to complete specialized medical qualifications to be called up until they were forty-one.[29] On 30 June 1950, there were ninety-two national service officers in the army who had been born between 1920 and 1922 and a further 531 who had been born between 1923 and 1925. It seems reasonable to assume that most, if not all, of these men were doctors who had been medical students during the war and who had, therefore, deferred their service until after they qualified.[30]

More perplexing were those other ranks who were much older than their comrades. In June 1950, the army contained seventy-one national servicemen who had been born before 1914, including one who had, apparently, been born in '1898 or earlier'.[31] The army statisticians appended a note saying that some of these men had been called up during the war and retained in the forces. Some conscripts were not discharged because they had committed offences and the time they spent in detention did not count towards their service, or because they had deserted. Arrested wartime deserters were still brought back to their units until a general amnesty of 1953.

A study by an army doctor of the physical condition of recruits alluded to one man called up *for the first time* in 1951 who had apparently been born in 1902. The doctor discounted the individual from his study on the grounds that he was 'unrepresentative'. Curiously, neither he nor the army statisticians suggested that the Edwardian conscript might have been a clerical error and that the man in question had been born in 1932.[32]

WHAT WERE THE CASUALTIES AMONG NATIONAL SERVICEMEN?

The total number of all servicemen who died between 1 January 1948 and the end of December 1960 was 19,521. Most of these died in the UK. Korea was the most dangerous place in that 1,135 men died there; it was also the only theatre of war in which most deaths (905 of them) were due to enemy action.

It is usually said that almost 400 conscripts were killed in action.[33] This number seems to have come from an answer given by the Secretary of State for War in parliament on 1 August 1963. He said that, between 1949 and 1962, 395 national service soldiers had been killed or died of wounds while on active service. The minister also said that a total of 2,578 soldiers had died of all causes during their national service.[34] In January 1956, a previous Secretary of State for War had given a slightly more detailed answer. He said that 397 conscripts had been killed in Malaya, Korea, Kenya and Cyprus.[35] Oddly, he also said that he had no separate figures for national servicemen killed in Malaya before November 1949 – though his predecessor had told the House of Commons that five national service officers and eleven other ranks had been killed in Malaya between 1 May 1948 and November 1949.[36] This would bring the total of dead to at least 413. One assumes that even this was not a final figure and that some national servicemen would have been killed in conflicts – Malaya, Cyprus, Suez and Aden – after January 1956.

None of the figures are as clear as they might seem at first glance. Being 'killed on active service' was not the same as 'killed in action' – the former figure would have included, for example, those men who died when their improvised petrol heaters blew up in their dugouts during the Korean winter. The army also sometimes published separate figures for men who were killed by terrorist action (an important category for those serving in the Canal Zone) and for those who died in captivity (important for men in Korea). It is not clear whether these figures were included in the final tally of national service deaths in action. Most men who died during national service did so for reasons that had nothing to do with enemy action – one conscript died from a surfeit of cream cakes.[37] A national serviceman in West Germany thought it possible that his regiment had lost more men in a NATO exercise, in which some soldiers were drowned and run over by tanks, than it did during a tour of duty in Malaya.[38] Flying accidents, the single most common cause of death, killed 3,145 servicemen in the period. Learning to fly a Meteor was almost certainly more dangerous than leading a fighting patrol in Korea.

WHAT ASPECTS OF NATIONAL SERVICE REMAIN UNCERTAIN?

Military facts and figures are subject to all sorts of uncertainty. The British armed forces often arranged servicemen into categories that seem entirely arbitrary. A list of languages spoken by army interpreters, for example, put speakers of Danish and Chinese into a single undifferentiated group.[39]

Sometimes the information that interests national servicemen themselves most is unavailable. One conscript wrote: 'I'd like to see the suicide figures for the national service intakes.'[40] Suicide among conscripts was certainly discussed and it is hard to believe that the forces did not carry out enquiries of some kind. One national serviceman claims that a friend of his, serving with the Intelligence Corps, was sent as a spy to join training units and investigate allegations of brutality.[41] If this was so, however, no records have come to light and the Ministry of Defence say that they have no statistics on suicide for the national service period.

Sometimes, the military authorities were reluctant to record embarrassing facts. Under the Attlee governments of 1945 to 1951, some Labour MPs, believing that the Brigade of Guards incarnated the inherited privilege that they had been elected to sweep away, pressed for information about the background of its officers. Initially, the army responded with a petulant suggestion that collecting such statistics would be impossibly complicated: 'In view of this and the fact that the type of school has no bearing on selection for a commission will you please ask US of S whether he still wants this information.'[42] Eventually, the guards conceded in September 1951 that just one national service officer,* out of ninety commissioned in the Brigade since January 1948, had not been educated at a public school.[43]

Attlee was succeeded as Prime Minister by Churchill (Harrow and the Hussars), Eden (Eton and the Rifle Brigade) and Macmillan (Eton and the Grenadier Guards). Not surprisingly, pressure on smart regiments to reveal their techniques of officer recruitment declined – though Labour MPs continued to squeeze details out of the War Office.

Generally speaking, the armed forces produced information only when they sought to address some specific problem and they usually stopped collecting it if they thought that the problem had been solved. The forces had little interest in the past for its own sake. It is, for example, relatively easy to find out how many British soldiers were in Korea at any one moment, a fact that had military value, but hard to find out how many men passed through Korea during the whole period of hostilities there.

MPs sometimes elicited facts from the service ministries – it may be that the advent of nuclear weapons, with their attendant shroud of secrecy, meant that national service was one of the few areas of defence policy on which Labour MPs could hope to be well briefed in the 1950s. George Wigg, in particular, exasperated the services by repeatedly pressing for information.[44] Sometimes this produced clear statistics; more often it produced revealing vignettes about individual cases, including the story of the national serviceman who wished to return to Europe so that he could compete in the world solo accordion championship.[45]

The forces knew their information about some matters was imperfect. The army, for example, compiled detailed statistics about the

---

* The one officer in question was presumably Simon Coke – who had been educated in Canada. There was also one non-public school boy among the twenty-one short service officers in the Brigade; there were none among the 127 regulars.

incidence of venereal disease among troops in various parts of the world. However, the quality of its information depended on circumstances. VD statistics were probably accurate with regard to foreign postings in the late 1940s, but, at least as far as soldiers in Britain were concerned, they were undermined by the National Health Service and penicillin. Men who could get treated discreetly by civilians were hardly likely to submit themselves to the army's tender attentions.[46]

Sometimes simple incompetence undermined military statistics. On matters as basic as the proportion of national servicemen in the army, different numbers were given within a single document. Records were often kept by nineteen-year-old national servicemen who took their duties lightly: Harold Evans claims that, as a clerk in the RAF, he once issued an instruction that officers should count the number of flies stuck to flypaper at all bases.[47] In 1948, an army inspection team from York commended the records of the Royal Warwickshire Regiment. In fact, just before the inspection, a single national service clerk had spent an entire night in the office, with bottles of different coloured ink, filling in forms. Much of the information that he recorded was fictitious.[48] In the early 1950s, national service 'sergeant testers' were attached to Ministry of Labour Offices to administer intelligence tests to men who were called up. The War Office decided, however, to pass this work to civilians after it noticed discrepancies that suggested that the sergeant testers had invented results to cover up their own mistakes.[49]

National servicemen themselves took the assertions of the armed forces with a pinch of salt. For example, medical statistics detailed the weight and height of conscripts, and even made allowances for the quarter of an inch that would be added to the height of an average airman by his socks.[50] John Inglis, a conscript in the RAF Regiment, recalled being weighed as part of his pre-demob medical in 1953. The doctor remarked that he had gained seven pounds since his entry into the forces; Inglis did not have the heart to point out that he had been naked when weighed at his initial medical and was now wearing the full uniform of a motorcycle dispatch rider, which included boots, helmet and a spare motorcycle chain.[51]

2

National Service Writing

This enormous social upheaval has passed unnoticed into history. Where are the novels, the poetry, the films of National Service?

John Boorman, *Adventures of a Suburban Boy* (2003)

A writer's job is to remember for everybody ... better than they can remember for themselves.

David Baxter, *Two Years to Do* (1959)

John Boorman is right to say that national service has not left the kind of cultural residue that is associated with, say, the Algerian War in France or the Vietnam War in America. It is not, however, true that there are no novels, poems or films about national service. The first national service novel – *The Dead, the Dying and the Damned* – was published by John Hollands in 1956 and the most recent one – *Heroes of the Hook*, also by John Hollands – in 2013. In between there have been autobiographical novels by David Lodge, Alan Sillitoe, Andrew Sinclair, Leslie Thomas, Gordon Williams and Christopher Wood, as well as a novelistic autobiography by David Baxter.[1] There have been at least four plays, three films and two television comedy series about national service. In addition to this, national service is often dealt with in the autobiographies of eminent men and is the subject of numerous memoirs, often privately published, by those who are not well known.

Writing assumed particular importance for national servicemen. Sending letters home provided them with a sense of association to the outside world at a time when they frequently felt lonely and scared – though they often sought to hide their loneliness and fear from their families when they wrote. Writing autobiographical accounts could be a form of therapy for men who were haunted by the memories of their national service experience. John Hollands believed that the catharsis of writing about Korea helped him to keep his sanity when he returned from the battlefield.[2] Even for men who never saw active service, writing was sometimes easier than talking. One national service airman told an interviewer that he found it easier to read aloud his memoir of being in the psychiatric ward of a military hospital than to answer her questions.[3]

In some ways, the problem for the historian is not the absence of writing by national servicemen, but its abundance. So many conscripts have written about their experience in terms that they partly derived from their own reading that, as some national service writers came to admit, they themselves found it hard to dig out the real experience from underneath the layers of literary representation. Alan Sillitoe reckoned that he had reworked the same material about his military service in fourteen different accounts – ranging from articles that he wrote straight after coming out of the air force in 1949, through a novel of 1961 to his autobiography in 1995. In 2000, however, he told an interviewer preparing a radio programme on national service that they would have to go back to sources before 'a certain literary stereotype developed'.[4]

The first way in which the literary conventions of national service writing can deceive us is by suggesting that the armed forces were always inimical to the written word. Educated conscripts often portrayed themselves as having been isolated among the philistine horde of their semi-literate comrades. William Donaldson, a national service naval officer between Winchester and Oxford, wrote of his basic training: 'They had never seen someone read a book before. They were like natives watching a white man shave.'[5] Michael Holroyd, a national service army officer between Eton and becoming a full-time writer, wrote that 'only in Anthony Howard [the journalist] did I find someone for whom books were a part of life'.[6] These judgements were unfair. Holroyd and Howard were not only allowed to read and write but actively encouraged to do so by their commanding officer, Brigadier Bernard Fergusson, who was himself an author of military history.

Furthermore, the soldier-servant whose services Holroyd and Howard shared, a working-class private, read Simenon and Kerouac in his time off from polishing shoes and pressing uniforms.[7] As for Donaldson, national service naval officers were required to read and write and, in particular, to keep a journal. Some long-suffering lieutenant commander would read these journals, correct spelling, suppress redundant words (men who had been trained to prepare signals for transmission by semaphore valued concision)[8] and laugh out loud when a nineteen-year-old who had read too much D. H. Lawrence compared a shoreline to 'the swell of a woman's breasts'.

National servicemen belonged to a bookish generation. They had grown up after Allen Lane's paperbacks democratized reading and at a time, particularly during the war, when there were not many other forms of distraction. Regular soldiers and airmen were less educated than conscripts, but they read slightly more.[9] Even semi-literate soldiers were sometimes enthusiastic about books.[10] Servicemen, especially regulars, read thrillers and, most of all, westerns – one thinks of the sergeant in *The Third Man* who admires *Death at Double X Ranch*. 'Modern novels', by contrast, were read by a small, but significant, proportion of conscripts.[11]

Even during the hellish chaos of basic training, some men managed to snatch a few minutes with a book: 'read us a bi' said P. J. Kavanagh's scouse comrades as he lay on his bed in Catterick with a French translation of Kafka.[12] Once training was over, vistas of unfilled time opened up before many conscripts. A radar operator on night shift in Germany might spend two hours checking his equipment and then, unless the Red Army attacked, have nothing but reading, and writing letters, to distract him until morning. Alan Sillitoe, who had left school at fourteen and whose father was illiterate, had encountered almost no adult books when he joined the RAF. The enforced idleness of thirty-one days on a troopship to Malaya introduced him to reading,[13] and, on his first night in a radio operator's hut, he noticed that his predecessor had left a copy of Balzac's *Droll Stories* lying on the table.[14] By the end of the year, he had read thirty-six books, recording their titles in his radio logbook. Sixteen months in a military hospital – he had caught TB in Malaya – meant yet more reading, and, by the time he finished *Cakes and Ale* on the train home, he had decided to become a writer himself.

Getting books was easy. Battered paperbacks were passed around the barracks. Men who were posted overseas bought cheaply printed editions. A scholarly soldier might pick up 'the new Pelican on Confucianism'[15] from a Tamil bookseller in Singapore. Men passing through Port Said would buy a cheaply printed edition of *Lady Chatterley's Lover*,[16] along with half a dozen dirty postcards and a fake leather handbag for their mother. Many bases had their own libraries,[17] which provided a refuge from the noise and promiscuity of the NAAFI. One conscript reckoned that the library of the training camp at Oswestry contained 7,000 volumes.[18] Men in garrisons around the world found libraries that could get them quite a long way into an undergraduate reading list.[19]

Some always intended to use military service for literary purposes and the number of men who kept diaries or letters with a view to writing books was greater than the number who eventually published anything on the subject. Young men of the 1950s knew how previous writers – Siegfried Sassoon, Robert Graves, George Orwell – had turned encounters with violence and squalor into literature. Some of them regarded military service as a source of 'experience' about which they could write. John Hollands volunteered for service in Korea to provide him with raw material for his first novel.[20] Karl Miller had already written an army short story before he was even called up and looked forward to 'mooning by a Nissen hut with a book in my hand'.[21] Malcolm Barker had been a journalist in Brighton before his national service. He kept a diary 'with the idea of one day writing a book'.[22] Peter Duffell was also a trainee journalist in the late 1950s. He actively sought to get called up at a time when national service was beginning to taper off. He did so for partly literary reasons: 'I simply saw national service as an opportunity for travel and to gain material for these wonderful novels that I was going to write.' Duffell liked the army so much that he joined the Gurkhas (having been attracted to the regiment by reading John Masters' autobiography *Bugles and a Tiger*), stayed on and became a lieutenant general.[23] J. M. Lee was excused military service on medical grounds in 1949 but he kept letters from his friends in the armed forces partly because, as he later put it: 'I had a plan at the time to write on the Oxford/National Service/provincial grammar school boy theme.'[24]

Peter Burke was an extreme example of the bookish national serviceman – his father had been a bookseller and Burke *fils* would, eventually, become professor of cultural history at Cambridge University. He kept a diary during his service as a pay clerk in Singapore. The diary is partly a book about books: 'Usual day: Galileo, Gide';[25] 'Rain, Rimbaud'.[26] Burke also wrote about writing. He reflected on how he might record his experience. He flirted with the idea of writing an autobiographical novel about his service and repeatedly wrote about how he might use his letters – 'predominantly extrovert' – and his diary – 'introvert' and 'a sketch of mental landscape' – to provide material for the novel.[27] References to the 'unwritten novel of Army life'[28] and the 'shadow novel'[29] came to permeate the diary.

Even national servicemen with no literary ambitions wrote. They were posted away from home at a time when letters provided the only means of keeping in touch with their families. Illiterate conscripts would often ask their friends in the barrack room to write something to their parents or girlfriends – a process that sometimes gave the designated scribe an insight into the life of the lumpen proletariat.

Some men wrote home on almost every day of their service and left caches of hundreds of letters. Vocabulary changed in revealing ways. 'Mummy' became 'mum' or 'mother'. Men who were on their way to wars in which they would kill and risk death sometimes wrote home in the same terms that they must have used since prep school: 'the food on board is simply wizard'.[30] Many tried to spare parents from knowing the worst details of what was happening to them. On 23 August 1950, men of the Middlesex Regiment heard that they were to be posted from Hong Kong to Korea. After a chip sandwich and a mug of tea, they made out their will forms and wrote to their parents: 'the composition intended to allay any suspicions at home that we were in any danger'.[31]

Letters from the front line often played down danger. An officer added a brief note to a letter from Korea at Christmas 1951: 'p.s. we had a bit of a battle yesterday.'[32] Trying to recapture his experience of Korea, Robert Gomme recalled: 'Reading my letters home is disappointing. My parents were so sure that I would be killed that I was careful not to worry them with any mention of the war.'[33] An officer in the marines, about to go into action at Suez, wrote his parents a letter that was designed to 'give something to take a line from if I was killed'.[34] Some letters were deliberate works of fiction. Officers, some of them nineteen-year-old national servicemen, had to write to the parents of men who were killed. The letters – with their stock phrases about how the victim 'must have died instantly' – were, as one national service officer recalled, easier to write if you did not know the man concerned well.[35]

Many men drew on their letters to write later accounts of their national service – some of them were already conscious that their letters would, one day, serve as an autobiographical aide-memoire when they first wrote them'.[36] Other men came upon old letters that they had not looked at for years and the uncertainties that sprang from this rediscovery are themselves interesting. At the age of sixty-five, P. J. Houghton-Brown found a collection of undated letters that he had written to his mother when he was a national serviceman from 1955 to 1957. He scoured them for glimpses of his experience as an officer with the Wiltshire Regiment in Cyprus and added some notes from his own memory. However, he wrote: 'Normally if you set out to write something you have some thought before you start as to where it will all end up, but in this I have no idea. Will memory feed memory?' Houghton-Brown did not always recall the incidents recounted in his letters and does not always seem to have felt that he had much in common with his nineteen-year-old self – though, unlike many veterans, he did not censor his letters before depositing them in an archive. Most striking of all is an absence from the letters to his mother:

> There is no record, for some unknown reason, of the worst thing that happened to affect me personally. I wondered why I had not got my usual cup of tea one morning, only to find my Batman had been shot dead while on patrol that night . . . We never found who did it. I remember so well the funerals, the coffins, it was all very poignant. I found it difficult to write the letters [i.e. the letters to the families of the dead men].[37]

Many national servicemen kept diaries, an activity that fitted in well with an obsessive desire to tick off days of service. It is tempting to say that the diary – contemporaneous and apparently written for no one but the author – is the most 'authentic' form of national service writing. Certainly some diaries seem to capture the full tedium of military life. One airman recorded the exact menu for many of his meals.[38] The most banal aspects of a diary can be revealing. F. N. E. Starkey made regular entries through his school days, his training as a solicitor's clerk and then during his national service in the RAF. Starkey's own language changed during his service. Early in basic training he referred to 'bullshit' in inverted commas, then, as the profanity of military life stamped itself into him, he used the word without inverted commas. Finally, when he moved into the comparatively civilized world of a clerical unit, he used the word 'bull'.[39]

Diaries are not, however, as simple as they seem at first glance. Not all of them were written up every day and few of them, at least very few of those that eventually reached the historian, were written without some thought of how a reader might respond to them. Many men – especially those on active service – made entries several weeks after the events described. Some diaries were deposited in archives only after their authors had typed them up and, often, edited them.

National service pushed a few young men into literary composition because those who claimed to have conscientious objection to military service usually produced brief essays setting out their objections for the benefit of the tribunal that adjudicated on such matters. These often drew on published writers – Michael Randle's was a 'rehash of Aldous Huxley'.[40] The playwright Harold Pinter produced a piece that referred to 'Jesus Christ, the great mystics and the Dostoevsky'.[41] Later he also produced a fictionalized account of his confrontation with the military authorities – telling his biographer that he had refused to 'hide under the convenient shelter of pacifist or religious principles' and that he had stood up to 'colonels and major generals' on the tribunal.[42]

So far as published work was concerned, the pattern of national service writing changed over time in revealing ways. The earliest books and articles were written by well-connected men from privileged backgrounds, usually those who had the contacts needed to get published at an early age. Two of the first national service authors, Tom Stacey and Andrew Sinclair, were Etonians.[43] As time went on, national service authors became more plebeian. The characteristic author/hero – Baxter, Lodge, Thomas – was now a pay clerk rather than a guards officer.

Increasingly, such authors were likely to identify themselves as 'angry young men'.[44] David Lodge, discussing his own national service novel, remarked that the 'angry young man' tag was attractive because it could be applied to both 'fictional characters and their authors'. Lodge identified the characteristics of the angry young man's writing as:

> gritty realism, exact observation of class and regional differences in British society, a lower-middle or working-class perspective, anti-establishment attitudes, hostility to all forms of cant and pretentiousness, a fondness for first-person, confessional narrative technique.[45]

The national service writer himself became a literary stereotype. Cecil Blacker, an intelligent man but one who affected the manner of the caricature cavalry officer, commanded a training depot for the Royal Armoured Corps at Catterick, the camp in which Lodge's novel is partly set. Blacker wrote:

> Catterick camp in North Yorkshire in the 1950s was the perfect background for the plays which have appeared on television about the horrors of National Service and iniquities of the army generally. The writers had usually failed as soldiers and become embittered; many had tried for commissions and been found wanting. The icy Nissen huts with their stone floors and coke stoves, the bleak east wind and driving rain which whistled round them, the brown-grey monotony of the landscape and the general ghastliness of the camp in those days must have been manna from heaven to these authors as, many years later, they dipped their pens in bile and began to write.[46]

Professional writers, or men who were on their way to being professional writers, came to dominate accounts of national service. This was true even of collected works that claimed to provide representative samples of national service experience. The collection of memoirs of the 'call-up' edited by Peter Chambers and Amy Landreth contained one account, presumably ghost-written, by an illiterate and eight by men who were 'ordinary' in the sense that they had not attended university and had, in most cases, left school at fourteen. However, there were also two essays by men who had already, in their twenties, published books, one by 'one of the more intelligently vociferous young journalists in Fleet Street today' and one by Peter Wiles, who had been born into a working-class family but edited *Isis* at Oxford and 'hoped eventually to live by his writing'.[47]

The collection also contained at least one essay by someone whose own self-depiction was a kind of fiction. The biographical notes on John S. Bingham said that he was from Yorkshire – 'I have lived in Sheffield all my life . . . and I like it very much' – that he was the product of a 'sturdy northern grammar school' and a 'family of publicans', and that he hoped to pursue a career in commerce.[48] Readers of this account might have been surprised to learn that Bingham had also been a fashionable figure at Oxford (an 'Isis idol') who had written a number of short stories.[49] Another collection, edited by the novelist B. S. Johnson in 1973, consisted of accounts by, or about, twenty-five men of the national service generation, of whom ten might be described as being professional writers – several more were artists or worked in films.[50]

Young men seeking to make a reputation were concerned with the style and form of their work and aware too of the ways in which their writing might fit in with that of writers they admired. The narrator of *Ginger, You're Barmy* – who is, like the author of the book, a graduate in English literature – writes a 'prologue' in which he says that his initial intention had been to write a purely factual account but that he has been influenced by 'the insinuations of form' to produce something more artful and contrived. Lodge himself then wrote an 'afterword' to the 1982 edition of his novel, in which he discussed his literary influences and suggested, in particular, that Graham Greene's *The Quiet American* had affected his novel. David Baxter's *Two Years to Do* was published while Baxter was still an undergraduate, reading English literature and much taken with such matters as the different types of irony in the work of Gibbon.

Most significantly, accounts of national service often blurred the lines between fact and fiction. All writing is partly factual in that no writer can describe anything without drawing on their experience, and almost all writing is partly fictional in that it always involves an element of artifice. Writing about national service, however, presented a particularly striking example of these blurred lines. Other military experiences have evoked 'pure fiction': Sebastian Faulks, born in 1953, has written novels about the First World War and the French Resistance; Alexis Jenni, born in 1963, won the prix Goncourt in 2011 for a novel about the French wars of decolonization (from 1945 to 1962). However, as far as I know, no national service novel has been written by anyone who was not a national serviceman.

If no account of national service was entirely fictional, no account was entirely factual either. Peacetime conscripts often regarded their years in the armed forces as crushingly dull and assumed that their stories could be rendered readable only if they were in some way embroidered. Sometimes the consequences of this embroidery can be found in the oddest places. The entry in the *Dictionary of National Biography* on the publisher John Blackwell contains the following passage:

> The details of Blackwell's military service are clouded in a certain amount of mystery, which he himself encouraged rather than dispelled. It is known that he was trained as a coder, and took a course in Russian at the Joint Services School for Linguists at Crail, Fife. At some point in his naval career he was stationed in Turkey, monitoring Russian radio traffic in the Black Sea region, a clandestine operation from which he had to be hastily airlifted by the American military in circumstances that remain obscure. According to family tradition John did not take his intelligence duties altogether seriously, and claimed to have recorded Russian radio programmes for children at half speed and sent them to the Admiralty for analysis.[51]

One suspects that Blackwell, sociable and fond of a drink, had told this anecdote so many times that he had come to believe it and, perhaps, also that the author of his *DNB* entry, David Lodge, had added an imaginative twist to the tale. Lodge wrote of his own novel: 'the need for a fictional story was self-evident since my own national service experience was almost totally devoid of narrative interest'.[52]

National servicemen were often conscious of the fine line between fact and fiction in what they wrote. Alan Burns wrote a 'memoir' of national service in the first person, though it was in fact about his brother Peter. Alan explained: 'I tell his story rather than my own for two reasons: my novel *Buster* covered the same ground so effectively (for me) that I am now unable to disentangle fact from fiction; and Peter's story is better than mine.'[53] Some subjects were easier to approach if camouflaged as fiction. The Conservative politician John Nott broke out of his conventional autobiographical account of national service to include a short story that he had written about a young officer who begins to feel 'the stirrings of manhood, buried under a Prussian public-school training of eighteen years'.[54]

The frontiers between fact and fiction were particularly porous in the works of those writers – usually men from relatively humble backgrounds – who took longest to get published and who consequently rewrote their material repeatedly. Peter Nichols wrote his play about national service – *Privates on Parade* – in the early 1970s but he had begun to record his own experience when he first set out as a passenger on a converted Liberator bomber on a frosty morning in late 1945:

> I'd decided to send home two parallel accounts of my life abroad; on one hand personal letters with news, gossip and appeals for cash, on the other a properly-written diary, sent piece by piece, a vivid account of my great adventure. Sadly, it is the last that survives. Though jotted down in pen or pencil on whatever paper came to hand, it is clearly meant to be a literary composition, eighty-seven chapters, each with its snappy title – the first 'Tense present', the last 'Prologue.' The tone changes over the two years and four months but only superficially. Reading it now, one longs for more facts, fewer purple passages.[55]

Nichols began his career as a writer while he was serving with the air force. His first fiction was to adopt the pseudonym of Gene Maxwell. It was designed to sound American – like Eugene O'Neill – and might have been an attempt to distance himself from those English writers – Maugham, Coward, Rattigan – who still cast their shadow over his own style. He later noted that one character in his play

Privates on Parade had been based on a real man but one whose 'reality had been blurred by several attempts to write him down'.[56]

Arnold Wesker's play *Chips with Everything* was finally performed in 1962 but drew on an unpublished novel he had written soon after leaving the air force in 1952, which, in turn, drew on his letters. Interviewed in 1970, Wesker described the process thus:

> Certainly the characters are drawn from characters in the novel, who are drawn from characters in the Air Force. I'd decided that I was going to write something about square-bashing and so every day I wrote home a long letter to a friend or relative and asked them to keep it and then I assembled them all at the end in chronological order and from those letters created the novel.[57]

In his autobiography, published in 1994, Wesker described a scene in the play and the incident in his own national service on which the scene was based. He then added: 'I'm using these extracted, highly stylized scenes as autobiographical stand-ins. I'm not even sure if such a scene took place between me and my Scottish hut-mate whose real name was Bill – or whether it was a conversation with myself. Art and experience – the boundaries become blurred.'[58]

Perhaps because national service so often went with a sense of artificiality and performance, theatre was an important element in its recollection. Peacetime conscription coincided with an exciting period in British theatre. During the 1950s, young writers – most notably John Osborne – set themselves up in conscious opposition to the traditionalism of men such as Terence Rattigan, whose plays had often seemed to celebrate military patriotism.

The most privileged and educated national servicemen went to the theatre and understood something about the changes going on it – a candidate for a naval commission in 1956 gave his assessors a mini lecture on 'London theatre' that included references to Jean Anouilh.[59] A larger group went to the cinema: one conscript reckoned that he saw 300 films in the course of his service.[60] Many British films in the 1950s were just plays projected onto a screen, and works by Coward and Rattigan were quickly translated to the cinema. Some men understood their military service in theatrical terms. They realized that much of service life involved, in one way or another, 'putting on a show'. 'Performances' in the forces could be as funny, and as sinister, as the absurdist plays at the Royal Court. One conscript remembered the ceremony with which Colonel Willie Officer (it was his real name) greeted recruits. They marched into the depot cinema to find:

> The band playing the corps march while the curtains slowly drew back to reveal the colonel standing in the middle of the stage on what looked like a large soap box with the Union Jack draped on it. After his rousing address of welcome, the 'finale' consisted of playing the National Anthem while the curtains slowly closed in front of the spot-lit colonel standing at the salute on his box.[61]

Public school boys often remarked smugly on the ways in which team games or the Officer Training Corps had prepared them for life as an officer but a couple of the shrewder ones (including one who later became a general) said that the most useful aspect of their education had, in fact, been the school play.[62] At one point, national service officer cadets were shown an old training film in which David Niven played the 'good officer' and Peter Ustinov was the 'bad private'.[63] A national serviceman remarked that officers assembling to conduct a court martial looked 'like something out of *Carrington VC*' – a film that had used national servicemen as extras.[64]

Theatre sometimes implied a degree of comedy, and writing about national service was often intended to be comic. Indeed, the notion that national service ought to be funny came to dominate many memoirs and perhaps even memories. A former conscript who was asked by an interviewer whether he had any 'funny stories' about national service replied: 'I suppose it was all a funny story.'[65] Jeff Nuttall – who became famous as an artist and organizer of 'happenings' – describes his military service as 'funny, ludicrous, archaic . . . And it was all still funny.' It ceased briefly to be amusing when he saw his first example of real brutality but then it became a 'kind of majestic farce'. He laughed when a squaddie was left out standing to attention in the cold until he almost passed out and he laughed when a naive private was persuaded that he was about to be shot and told to write a last letter to his girlfriend. Lewis – a 'high-grade mongol who should never have got into the army' – was locked in the cellar to keep him out of the way during a parade. 'Lonely and frightened in his dark cellar', Lewis tried to hang himself with a piece of string but the string broke. The sergeant told him: 'Good job for you you're so fuckin' thick.' And 'Everybody, including Lewis, laughed about the incident for days.'[66]

The most important films and television programmes about national service were comedies. *Carry on Sergeant*, which appeared in 1958, was the first and most innocent of the long *Carry On* series of British films. It was filmed at a real army camp. One hard-bitten real-life sergeant, a veteran of the Second World War, shouted at a private to put his beret on properly and received the reply: 'I'm with the film crew duckie.'[67] It also featured some actors who had been national servicemen: Kenneth Williams was both an actor in *Carry on Sergeant* and a model for one of the characters in *Privates on Parade*. *The Army Game*, which described the fate of conscripts, was aired on British television from 1957 until 1961. *Get Some In!*, about conscripts in the RAF, was shown on ITV from 1975 to 1978.

The end of national service coincided with the beginning of the cultural era known as 'the Sixties', which actually lasted from about 1963 until about 1973. This was a period marked by a self-consciously irreverent attitude towards the British establishment, class system, patriotism and history (evident in the satirical reviews of the early 1960s, especially *Beyond the Fringe*, and in *Private Eye* magazine) and by the rise of youth culture and the kind of rock music that began with the Beatles. National servicemen were sometimes part of the culture of the time but they seem to have felt that their military experience would not fit easily into the new world they inhabited – most of them either ignored it or played it for laughs.

Those who had already written about national service turned away from their subject. *Chips with Everything* was Arnold Wesker's least favourite play. David Baxter was aware that there was something archaic about his own book on the subject, *Two Years to Do*, almost as soon as it appeared. He had been prompted to write it by a publisher and it attracted considerable attention from people older than himself – it was reviewed in national newspapers and he was interviewed, along with an irate brigadier, on television. However, student newspapers at Cambridge, where Baxter was still an undergraduate, barely mentioned the book, and Baxter himself moved on to other things.[68] David Lodge occasionally referred to national service in his later novels but the references became brief and dismissive as though Lodge himself was bored with the subject: 'I have described it in detail elsewhere. So have others. It is always the same.'[69]

By the early 1980s, national service was a non-subject for most professional authors. Books about it were published but there was an increasing sense that it was not the kind of topic that serious writers ought to deal with. Stanley Price wrote novels, stories, plays and film scripts, but his television play about his own national service experience and his relationship with his commanding officer, Archibald Wavell, was never performed.[70] He composed a chapter entitled 'The Fucking Army' for his autobiography but it was removed at the request of the publisher so that the published version has just a few pages on national service, squeezed between school and Cambridge.[71]

The disappearance of national service from published books by well-known professional authors does not mean that it has vanished as a subject for all writers. Many national service memoirs have appeared since the 1990s. Retirement, the wish to explain their lives to grandchildren and the rise of desktop publishing encouraged a generation of men to write about their youth.

Some recent national service memoirs revolve around a comparison between the 'present day' and the apparently more innocent era of national service. Occasionally it seems as though the angry young men, who resented everything that happened during national service, have been replaced by angry old men, who resent everything that has happened since they left the forces. Berwick Coates published a book in 2009 that was intended as an explicit riposte to the most promin-ent national service writers of the early 1960s. He presented himself as 'an alternative voice to those "literary forces" that have a propen-sity to focus on the bad parts' and argued:

> Firstly, that those vociferous, intellectual critics might be wrong.
> Secondly, that the abiding impression about national service that has
> reached us has been conditioned, even totally shaped, by the memories
> of those very critics, for the simple reason that they were the ones

who got into print, into the newspapers, on the radio, and on to the box.

He described his own background thus:

> It was the 1950s. A respectable suburban house. No teenage purchasing power. No Top of the Pops. No school counsellors pushing stuff into your head about 'talking things through'. No politicians droning on about a children's charter . . . 'Young people' didn't exist. The world had barely got used to the term 'teenager'.[72]

'Shiner' Wright in his memoir of national service in the navy – *Jack Strop, VD and Scar* – writes:

> I'm gonna tell yer a story of how it was in the Royal Navy of the 'Swinging Sixties'. Days when life was simpler. Days when being gay didn't mean being a 'fairy'. 'The Glory Days', before the roof fell in, when our, *now floundering*, country was known as Great Britain, respected throughout the world . . . Yes, a time before decimalization, inflation, greed, laziness, drugs, AIDS, political correctness, racism and now, **thanks to our leader**, terrorism.[73]

'Political correctness' is often deployed to explain the difference between the 'present day' (i.e. some point since 1990) and the period of national service.[74] A national service medical officer attached to the Black Watch remarked that that 'pernicious corrosion (political correctness)' would now prevent the tying of a well-known 'Cypriot sympathizer' to a jeep.[75] An officer who served in Kenya told an interviewer: 'They were all dead by the time we'd finished with them. You didn't capture too many Mau Mau; a waste of money. Shouldn't say that should I, that's not politically correct.'[76]

Not all memoirs are bitter about the present or regretful for the days of national service. Many are, in fact, marked by an engaging sense of uncertainty and/or self-mockery and this is sometimes true even of writers who start out by presenting themselves as denouncers of political correctness. Authors often recognize that their recollections are uncertain or that they see their youth through a haze of nostalgia. One memoir is entitled *Remembered with Advantage*.[77] Another, unpublished, quotes the conservative opinions recorded in a national service diary: 'At home the basic need is initiative, keenness and enthusiasm for the job of reconstruction as was shown at Dunkirk and after.' The author then writes: 'All this expressed in those highly authoritarian and downright tones to be expected of intolerant youth.'[78]

Two partly related things have had an effect on how national servicemen have 'remembered' their experience in recent years. The first of these is television. Television came to Britain during national service. In 1947, just one person in 500 lived in a house with a television.[79] It was so unusual that a middle-class conscript wrote in his diary 'go to television' – it is unclear whether this meant that he had been in a studio audience or that he had been to some place with a television set.[80] By early 1959 television was so ubiquitous that men in a military prison rioted when they were not allowed to watch their favourite programme.[81]

Most former conscripts watched television, particularly during their old age. This reinforced their sense that their own youthful experience was forgotten or, perhaps, unimportant. Apart from the comedies discussed above, post-war conscription rarely featured on television. For British television, military life meant feature films and documentaries about the Second World War and re-enactments of even more distant conflicts. It also meant reporting from Vietnam, the Falklands and Kuwait. Finally, it meant 'reality TV', in which programmes, beginning with the BBC's *Paras* in 1983, purported to show how servicemen lived. Many national servicemen seemed to feel that their experiences could be recalled only with references to television programmes, as though the memories of their own youth were less important than the 'realities' of the television screen.[82]

Television also reinforced the sense that national service should be recalled through the prism of the 'real conflicts' that had come later. Even a commando who had fought at Suez came to feel that his own experience was 'overshadowed' by the Falkands.[83] The British armed forces have become smaller and increasingly prone to define themselves in terms of 'professionalism' – the very quality that national servicemen did not possess. The Special Air Service has assumed a particularly important part in Britain's military self-image and national servicemen often refer to the SAS – as though their own experience can only mean anything if compared to that of 'real soldiers'.[84]

Emphasis on the full-length national service memoir can itself be deceptive. Only a small minority of national servicemen, even of national servicemen who became professional writers, ever produced such memoirs. More commonly, conscription was recalled in passages in books about other things or in brief exchanges in the course of interviews. For many of the most articulate national servicemen, memories of conscription were eventually reduced to one or two anecdotes that were recycled more for their amusement value than because anyone knew or cared whether they were true. Richard Ingrams, the founder of *Private Eye*, liked to tell the story of how he had failed to obtain a commission because his commanding officer had said, when presiding over the Unit Selection Board, 'Shrewsbury's a soccer school – isn't it? What did you play?' and Ingrams had answered 'The cello, sir.'[85]

Auberon Waugh, a colleague and friend of Ingrams, wrote a fictional account of military service in a novel that was first published in 1960. Later he produced a number of autobiographical recollections about his time in a cavalry regiment during the Cyprus Emergency. Waugh's military career came to an abrupt end when – attempting to unblock a jammed machine gun on his armoured car – he fired several bullets into his own chest. This incident was horribly real. Waugh almost died and the consequences of having shot out some of his internal organs would plague him for the rest of his life.

As he lay on the ground, Waugh was approached by his sergeant, Chudleigh, and, summoning up what might have been his last breath for a moment of heroic flippancy, he said, 'Kiss me, Chudleigh.' Waugh's *bon mot* was circulated among his journalistic associates and often provided a title for biographical writing on Auberon Waugh. Waugh himself, however, admitted in his autobiography: 'The story is denied by Chudleigh. I have told the story so often that I honestly cannot remember whether it started life as a lie or not.'[86]

3

The Politics of Conscription, 1945–1949

[P]eople had not spent their energy building up the Labour movement to get a Labour government to enforce military conscription for the first time in this country.

R. J. Davies (Labour MP), House of Commons, March 1946[1]

The chap who thought of this idea ought to be shot.
National serviceman undergoing basic training in the RAF, late 1940s[2]

Constraint was the basis of national service and this was true for the country as much as it was for the men who turned up for basic training. Politicians did not introduce peacetime conscription because they thought it would do young men good. Anthony Eden, the Conservative shadow Foreign Secretary, said: 'I have never heard anyone defend conscription for the sake of conscription.'[3] Rather it was maintained after the war because politicians could see no other way to meet immediate military needs. The matter was not, in any case, at the centre of post-war political debates. Discussion, such as it was, revolved around the length of service rather than its necessity, and, just as conscripts gritted their teeth and said 'two years to push', so politicians made national service palatable partly by insisting that it was a temporary measure – one that was never, at any particular moment, underwritten by legislation designed to last more than five years.

Peacetime conscription was a novelty in Britain. In continental Europe, compulsory military service had been a defining feature of the modern state, but sea power was the key to British defence. The land armies that grew up in nineteenth-century continental Europe were unnecessary in the British Isles because there was no land frontier to defend. If the British fought on land at all, they often did so by subsidizing foreign forces or, in the empire, by recruiting local troops. The British army was small and composed in large measure of men who served for long periods of time. Far from being 'the people in arms', the British army consisted of men drawn from a distinct section of society, usually the poorest, who sometimes spent years serving in remote garrisons overseas, especially in India. Respectable people often regarded soldiers with horror. When William Robertson, the first man in British history to rise from the rank of private to that of field marshal, abandoned his position as a domestic servant to enlist as a private, his mother allegedly wrote: 'I would rather bury you than see you in a red coat.'

The British did not introduce conscription during the Boer War of 1899 to 1902, but in its aftermath a group of politicians and retired army officers campaigned for universal military service and founded the National Service League. The League's leaders argued that Germany posed a military threat to Britain. They also talked about 'national efficiency' and the poor health of many young British men. The League urged the government to introduce compulsory training, only a few months of which would be full-time, to provide the country with a trained reserve in the event of a German attack. The League became more dynamic in 1905 when Lord Roberts, recently retired as Commander-in-Chief, became its leader and Leo Amery, a rising Conservative politician, became its secretary and driving force. The League was well financed and well organized; it claimed a membership of almost 100,000 by 1913, but it failed.[4] No government was tempted to introduce peacetime conscription.

During the First World War, Britain raised a large army but conscription was not introduced until 1916. Indeed, in some ways, deliberate direction of 'manpower' – the word itself was coined during the war – was about keeping men out of the army as much as getting them in because the voluntary recruitment campaigns that took place early in the war had stripped factories of their workers. Sir Auckland Geddes, a member of the National Service League and the first Minister of National Service, later suggested that the main function of such a ministry should be to 'prevent the militant and pugnacious young men of the country flocking in excessive numbers into the fighting services to the detriment of essential civilian activities'.[5]

Between the wars conscription was barely discussed in Britain, partly because for most of this period Germany had no conscription and Britain faced no obvious military threat. When Charles de Gaulle published his book *Vers l'armée de métier* ('Towards the Professional Army') in 1934, it caused a scandal in France because calling for the professionalization of the army was seen as an assault on democracy. The book was published in English under a more anodyne title: *The Army of the Future*. A professional army in Britain was simply taken for granted. The size of the forces was in any case limited by the state of public finances and recruitment was partly sustained by unemployment – though the sense that the army was a last resort for otherwise unemployable men did nothing to improve the esteem in which soldiers were held and, even during the hungry thirties, there were men who preferred starving in Newcastle to eating in the Durham Light Infantry.[6]

Political opposition to conscription came from three forces. The first of these was nationalism. Irish nationalists resented the idea that they might be required to fight for the British empire. Though many Irishmen volunteered to serve in the British army, the government was reluctant to introduce conscription to Ireland, even during the First World War. The second force against conscription was liberalism. The Liberal party opposed restriction on individual freedom and some prominent Liberal ministers resigned from the wartime government rather than go along with conscription in 1916. The third force, and the one that mattered most after 1918, was socialism. The argument that military service was 'democratic' or even part of a revolutionary tradition, which was so often deployed in France, counted for little in Britain.[7] Some members of the Labour party opposed militarism of any sort, including Britain's participation in the First World War. More specifically, Labour politicians worried about the possibility of industrial conscription, i.e. that workers might be compelled to work under government direction or that military discipline might be used to break strikes. Left-wingers had complicated relations with military service during the 1930s. On the one hand, it was they who worried most about the rise of fascism and Nazi Germany; on the other, they were most opposed to increased resources for the military.

The threat of Nazi Germany did eventually force conscription on Britain. In April 1939, the government of Neville Chamberlain (who had briefly served as Director of National Service during the First World War) introduced the Military Training Act, which required single men aged twenty to twenty-two to undergo six months training as 'militiamen'. The Labour party opposed the act. When war broke out in September of the same year, however, there was little opposition to conscription and the first National Service Act, which required that all men aged eighteen to forty-one register for military service, passed through all its stages, including Royal Assent, on a single day: 3 September 1939. This act was extended in 1942 to take in men up to the age of fifty and unmarried and childless women between the ages of eighteen and thirty.

National service in the Second World War extended beyond the purely military. Men of military age were permitted (or required) to work in war industries and could, indeed, be forbidden to join the armed forces. Men and women were directed to take civilian jobs of national importance. Even Princess Elizabeth was – much to the indignation of some courtiers – required to register at the age of eighteen.

Coal-mining illustrated the scale of wartime direction of labour. From December 1943, young men were drafted into the mines by ballot, something that many feared more than military service.[8] The government defined the groups who were exempt from conscription to the mines with the precision that was characteristic of wartime labour policy. These groups consisted of those who had been accepted for duties as aircrew or as artificers on submarines and skilled men who were required by the forces for particular trades.[9]

Conscription during the Second World War was relatively uncontroversial. The government could afford to be generous in its attitude to conscientious objectors, partly because it knew that they would not be numerous. Some men who had initially objected to their call-up eventually changed their mind: at least one of them ended up as a highly decorated veteran of the Special Operations Executive.

Desertion, mainly involving working-class soldiers, was quite common but never turned into a systematic political resistance to conscription. Some deserters rejoined the army under false names – one of them winning the Victoria Cross.

As the end of the war approached, generals and politicians began to discuss whether conscription should be continued after the return of peace. The abolition of conscription would have been difficult when British servicemen were all over the world. In the short term, troops would be required to police areas that the British occupied. In the longer term, it was unclear what kind of military obligations might fall on Britain – though politicians from both sides believed that Britain should remain a 'great power' with influence throughout the world. The loss of India, which seemed inevitable to many by the end of the war, meant that Britain would abandon some of its garrisons but it also meant that it would lose the use of Indian troops – many of whom had served outside the subcontinent. Various expedients were discussed. The British negotiated to maintain some Gurkha soldiers from Nepal; they used prisoners of war from Germany, Italy and Japan to provide labour for years after the end of fighting. Polish units remained with the British army until 1949, and the government contemplated creating a foreign legion, which would recruit from that substantial pool of young men in central Europe who had lost their homes and/or acquired a taste for fighting during the previous five years.[10] People close to the army continued to advocate a British foreign legion in the 1950s.[11] More seriously, the services recruited women – something that they had never previously done in peacetime. None of these expedients was sufficient to produce troops in the numbers required, but there was no formal decision about post-war conscription, perhaps just because ministers took it for granted. An official wrote in October 1946:

> post-war planning in the Services ... assumes that there will be a system of national service or conscription. It was hoped that a decision to this effect would have been taken by the Cabinet and announced by the end of the war. This did not occur, and with the break up of the Coalition Government, the matter lapsed.[12]

Between the surrender of Germany and that of Japan, the government changed. The general election of July 1945 increased the Labour party's representation in the House of Commons from 154 seats to 393, giving it an absolute majority; the Conservative party lost 190 seats, almost half of all those that it had previously held. The result came as a shock to many Conservatives, especially officers in the smarter regiments of the army. The Coldstream Guards, stationed in Italy, organized a mock election to educate their troops. Almost all the officers, largely Etonians, took it for granted that everyone would vote for Churchill and they had to import a Wykehamist from the Scots Guards to try to make the case for Labour, but the other ranks (mainly young, working-class men from the north east) voted Labour.

Labour voters wanted change. This meant better housing, free medical care and no return to the unemployment of the 1930s. Military matters, however, barely featured in the election. Only one Labour candidate in ten, and a handful of Conservatives, mentioned conscription in their election addresses.[13]

Anti-militarism was less influential in the Labour party than it had been in the 1930s. Many of the younger MPs had served in the armed forces during the war and almost the whole party had regarded the war against fascism as worthwhile. Even the emphasis that party leaders still placed on 'collective security' and the United Nations was usually matched by a belief that Britain would need substantial armed forces and perhaps, indeed, that it would have to provide many of the troops that would be required for international 'policing operations'.

Ernest Bevin did most to change the Labour party with regard to conscription. He was one of the most extraordinary figures in British politics. Born illegitimate and orphaned at eight, he had become a lorry driver and eventually leader of the Transport and General Workers' Union. During the war, he was Minister of Labour and National Service and, in the Labour governments of 1945 to 1951, Foreign Secretary. If any coherent thinking underlay the British attitude to post-war military service, it would best be summed up as 'Bevinism' – though Bevin's political outlook, even more than that of most politicians, was often a matter of instinct rather than clearly worked-out thought.

Bevinism meant fervent anti-Communism. As a trade union leader,

Bevin had dealt with Communists since the 1920s and was consequently not prone to illusions about the future behaviour of the Soviet Union. Bevin also believed that Britain ought to be a great power and this meant, among other things, that it would have to maintain large forces.

Bevin's position with regard to military service was odd. On the one hand, his personal links to the trade unions were closer than those of any other minister; on the other hand, as Minister of Labour and National Service, he had been closely associated during the war with the one thing that trade unions most disliked: the direction of industrial labour and, in particular, the conscription of young men for work in mines. After the war, he occasionally spoke as though he regretted that military service did not go with some broader project of social levelling. Addressing boys from Emanuel School in south London, which stood on the awkward frontier between grammar and public school as well as that between officers and other ranks, he said: 'It must be as easy for the miner's son to enter the professions as for the son of the middle-class home to enter the steel plate industry or go down the mines. The broadest possible view of national service must be taken by all.'[14]

However, the need to keep the goodwill of the unions limited the social impact of national service. Post-war military service was separated from the direction of civilian manpower, which the unions disliked. Effectively, military service was to be universal for young men, but all other forms of compulsory service, in factories or mines, for the rest of the population were to be abolished. There was little discussion of conscripting women for either military or civilian purposes once hostilities had ended. Even the Medical Corps, which required no conventional displays of virility from its recruits, did not call up women doctors.[15]

It was Bevin who secured the key decision by Labour leaders in favour of post-war conscription, when Attlee was attending the San Francisco conference which founded the United Nations. The day after German surrender, Bevin presided over a meeting of the tripartite committee that brought together representatives of the parliamentary Labour party, the National Executive of the Labour party and the TUC. He persuaded the committee to support conscription. He did so with several sleights of hand, pretending that conscription would not last for long after the war (he probably knew that it would), that service would limited to one year (he knew that the forces wanted at least eighteen months) and that it would contribute to collective security (he knew that a breach with the Soviet Union was likely and would undermine the effectiveness of the United Nations).

Labour attitudes, however, were complicated by an important minority of dissidents inside the parliamentary party and, perhaps more importantly, by the sense that the party was heir to anti-militarist and anti-conscription traditions – a sense that made some conscripts assume that a Labour election victory would be in their own interests.[16] There were powerful men in the Cabinet who had opposed the maintenance of conscription when it was first discussed in 1945. A few Labour MPs criticized conscription on pacifist or anti-militarist grounds that sometimes harked back to the political debates of the pre-1939, or even pre-1914, period. Speaking on the subject in 1948, Ellis Smith, Labour MP for Stoke, referred to 'Sidney Street, Antwerp, Gallipoli and the responsibility of Mr Churchill when he was a young man, sending forces to Liverpool and Salford because dockers were taking a stand on trade-union rights'.[17]

Most Labour MPs, however, did not regard conscription as a particularly important issue, and those who did often had complicated positions. James Callaghan, who had been a naval officer during the war, was the spokesman for 'ordinary servicemen' who resented those who gained exemption from service or received special treatment while they were in the forces. George Wigg, who had joined up as a private in the 1920s and eventually risen to the rank of lieutenant colonel in the Education Corps, defended conscription but attacked the privileges given to officers in some regiments; he attracted much derision from Tory MPs, who quickly discovered that he carried a chip as heavy as a rifle on his shoulder. Michael Foot was a rare example of a Labour MP who supported conscription, in the way that continental socialists did, because he believed that it would make the army a defender of democracy. Denunciation of government policy on conscription provided some MPs with a means of attacking Bevin's foreign policy. Richard Crossman, in particular, argued that the Anglo-American entente would make war more likely rather than less, and that Britain was being made to adopt conscription in order to fit in with American interests.[18]

Outside the Labour party, conscription was opposed by the two Communist MPs – though the Communist party seems to have adopted a more qualified position in the 1950s (merely calling for a reduction in the term of service) and did not encourage its members to resist their own call-up. The Independent Labour party was the group that remained truest to the anti-militarist traditions of pre-war socialism, and it was the party that campaigned most explicitly against conscription,[19] once putting up a candidate in a local election who was an army deserter.[20] However, it had only three MPs in 1945 and, by 1948, all of these had defected to the Labour party. The Liberal party opposed conscription in parliament – though the Liberal party conference supported it and a number of 'National Liberals', including one who had been a fervent opponent of conscription in the First World War, were now, in effect, Conservatives.

Conservative MPs, with just one exception, voted in favour of conscription, and Labour leaders knew that they could override dissidents in their own party with Conservative support in the House of Commons, but they were reluctant to do so. Instead, they tried to justify military policies in non-militaristic terms and to ensure that their policy was supported by the widest possible section of the Labour movement, which included members of the party and the trade unions outside parliament.

The ministers in the new government who had most to do with the armed forces were Frederick Bellenger, who was Secretary of State for War from October 1946, and Albert Alexander, who served as Minister of Defence from December 1946. The latter post, which oversaw all the service ministries, had been created in 1940 and, until 1946, held by the Prime Minister. Emanuel Shinwell succeeded Bellenger at the War Office in October 1947 and then Alexander at Defence in February 1950. None of them were impressive ministers. They exemplified the contradictions of the party with regard to conscription and the military more generally. Bellenger and Alexander had served as officers in the First World War and the former, in particular, was generally seen as fairly deferential to military leaders – though he had opposed the long-term maintenance of conscription in 1945. Both men came from relatively humble backgrounds but neither had deep roots in the Labour party – they had begun life as, respectively, a Conservative and a Liberal. The result was that they often commanded respect from neither the service chiefs nor their own parliamentary colleagues. Shinwell – the most left-wing of the three and the one with the most anti-militarist past – was curiously more popular with senior officers than either of his colleagues.

At the end of the war, there was a period of uncertainty about Britain's future military burdens. A report by the Armistice and Post-War Committee to the War Cabinet summed matters up in April 1945:

> It would clearly have been desirable for the starting point of our examination to have been a comprehensive review of the post-war defence problem of the British Empire from which could be deduced the size of the forces to be maintained by the United Kingdom, both for the fulfilment of its obligations under the World Organisation and for its essential security tasks in different parts of the world. It is clear to us, however, that no such review is possible at the present time.[21]

In October 1945, Ian Jacob, military assistant to the Secretary of the War Cabinet, explained why the government would find it difficult to make an immediate decision about the future of conscription, but added:

> New scientific developments, and in particular the atom bomb, have caused a feeling of uncertainty about the shape of our future armed forces.
>
> It is evident that for some considerable time the size of the Armed Forces to be retained will be such that they can only be supported by the continuance of National Service on the present basis. The problem will be how to reduce the period spent in the forces by young men called up from something like six years to a reasonable period, say two years.[22]

Jacob anticipated three phases. The first, lasting eighteen months or two years, would bring the forces down to a level that could be sustained by two-year conscription. Then would come a second period, of three or four years, during which the forces would be maintained at the same level to meet 'occupational duties on a large scale and other abnormal commitments'. A third period would begin after about five years, when the 'abnormal commitments' had been discharged but when 'the atom bomb and other developments may be expected to begin to affect the lay-out of our forces'.

This uncertainty persisted for some time. A Ministry of Defence report of 1946 said that in the 'unsettled condition of the world' it was not possible to be sure what forces Britain would need, but that it had certain 'inescapable' commitments.[23] These were the provision of garrisons in bases overseas, the preservation of law and order in overseas territory, the maintenance of a strategic reserve at home and overseas, the protection of lines of communication, the maintenance of air and coastal defences, and the provision of training and administration in the UK for forces throughout the world. The report added that another aim of British policy should be 'showing the flag'. Conscription often fitted into a more general debate about Britain's place in the world that did not necessarily depend on any rational calculation about how it might contribute to military power. The Foreign Office saw willingness to call up young men as a sign of national resolve that would show how Britain had broken with its policy in the 1930s when 'our failure to maintain compulsory military service after the 1914–18 war' gave 'the impression that the British people had lost the will and self-discipline to protect themselves and enforce their voice in world affairs'.[24]

The big question, which was to some extent masked by talk of policing occupied territories and maintaining prestige, was: what power might pose a real threat to British interests after the defeat of Nazi Germany and Imperial Japan? The Soviet Union was obviously the most dangerous military antagonist for Britain, but anticipating the particular kind of threat that it would pose, and the resources that Britain would have to respond to it, was hard. Uncertainty about the matter haunted British defence policy during the first few years after the Second World War. The result of this was that post-war conscription was built on the shifting sands of changing strategic assumptions.

The first uncertainty of post-war planning came from the fact that no one knew how soon the Soviet Union would be in a position to attack the West. It had been devastated by the Second World War, and early British planning was based on the belief that war with the Soviet Union was unlikely until 1957. The first long-term aim of post-war conscription was, therefore, to provide a large reserve of trained men, of the kind that Britain had so conspicuously lacked at the beginning of the previous two wars. In the First World War, the British had been able to shelter behind the French army during the two years that it took them to build up a large army of their own. In 1939 and 1940, the policy had failed and the failure had almost proved disastrous. Now the aim was to lay the basis of relatively quick mobilization by requiring all young men to undertake a period of full-time service with the armed forces. They would then spend six years undergoing less intensive training as reservists. This would allow them to be recalled in time of war. The policy gave little weight to commitments outside Europe and the Middle East. It rested on the assumption that the armed forces would have time to mobilize in the event of war and on the expectation that they would have years in which to build up reserves.

Projections that Britain would have time to train and then recall huge numbers of reservists in the event of war came to seem optimistic. This was partly because the Soviet threat suddenly seemed more imminent. Two events underlined this. In March 1948, the Communist party effectively took over Czechoslovakia. In June of the same year, the Soviet Union blocked land access to west Berlin, forcing the western powers to launch an airlift. The Cold War also meant that the British kept troops in Austria and Trieste for longer than originally anticipated and that, in 1948, they began fighting against Communist forces in Malaya. Britain no longer needed a large reserve that could be called up in the event of war. Rather it needed full-time soldiers who would be available for immediate deployment in the event of Soviet attack in Europe or who would actually be deployed to theatres of war outside Europe.

The second uncertainty concerned alliances and commitments. Immediately after the war, Bevin seemed to hope that Britain might, along with France, be part of a 'third force' that would stand between the United States and the Soviet Union.[25] Even during this period, however, there was debate about, for example, whether Britain needed a military presence in the Middle East and, if it did, whether that presence should be based in Egypt or Palestine. Eventually, alliance with the United States and membership of NATO (founded in 1949) became the pillars of British defence policy, but, even before this, the British were keen to prevent America from retreating into her pre-war isolationism and sometimes saw conscription as a token of British good faith that would strengthen the hand of those in Washington who opposed such a retreat.[26]

The third uncertainty sprang from military technology. The means by which wars were fought – or might be fought – changed more quickly in the five years after the defeat of Nazi Germany than during the war itself and perhaps than during any other period in human history. In May 1945, the officials and officers responsible for post-war military planning did not know about the atomic bomb. In January 1947, the decision that Britain should develop a bomb was taken by a small group of ministers. It is possible to argue that the atom bomb made all other military technologies redundant and that there was something absurd about training men to use bolt-action rifles and bayonets at a time when a single plane could wipe out a city. A Labour MP told his party conference in June 1946 that 'in an age of atomic and germicidal war, it would be better to train scientists' than to maintain conscription.[27] There was, though, no instant change in British military policy. The Soviet Union did not explode its own atom bomb until 1949, and even after that date British planners often discussed atomic bombs as though they were more terrible versions of conventional weapons rather than something entirely new. For example, they anticipated war in which an initial exchange of nuclear weapons might be followed by a period of conventional fighting. Some thought that fear of retaliation might prevent warring countries from using atom bombs at all, as such fears had, supposedly, prevented the use of poison gas in the Second World War.[28] The fact that there had never been a war in which both parties possessed atomic weapons conferred an abstract quality on military planning.

Matters were made more complicated by the fact that the armed forces were really preparing for two different kinds of war. In the long term, they had to be ready for all-out war against the Soviet Union, which would involve the deployment of millions of men and the use of modern weapons. However, the end of the Second World War also meant that British troops were pinned down in all sorts of small-scale 'police actions', in which 'heavy tanks and bombers and long-range projectiles for mass destruction' would be useless.[29]

The fourth uncertainty concerned money. In the immediately post-war years, military planners gave relatively little consideration to how they might pay for the armed forces. The Treasury was not consulted about early schemes for conscription – advice about the economic consequences of such a policy came, if at all, from the Ministry of Labour or the Board of Trade. In an early report, a brief passage about economics was pasted on to the finished document as an apparent afterthought. Calculations about economic effects were skewed by the fact that the high unemployment of the pre-war years allowed officials to argue that, even with conscription, Britain would have more civilians at work in the late 1940s than it had had in 1939.

The war had been expensive: by 1945, Britain owed £3,000 million and was the world's largest debtor. The peacetime projects of the Labour government elected in 1945 would also cost money. Keynesian thinking meant officials were less concerned to contain public spending than they would have been before 1939, but even Keynesians recognized that military spending was of less economic use than civilian spending and that, in particular, spending to maintain troops overseas would be economically damaging. Some Labour politicians tried to focus minds on the economic consequences of conscription and on the way in which economic failure might undermine military power. Douglas Jay, the Labour MP, wrote in April 1946 that if the chiefs of staff had their way 'it would follow that the United Kingdom cannot carry out its military commitments and achieve economic recovery and independence'.[30] Herbert Morrison put the arguments against an extensive and expensive form of conscription in terms of great power status: 'Economic recovery is a matter of operational urgency and on a long view there may be little gain from maintaining large armed forces if the result is that in the economic field we become a second class power.'[31]

The gravity of Britain's economic circumstances was exposed in 1947. In return for a loan in 1946, the US had insisted that sterling should be made convertible in July 1947. However, it quickly became clear that allowing the conversion of sterling to dollars would exhaust all Britain's reserves of foreign currency, and convertibility was suspended two months after it had been introduced.[32] This was also the year in which Hugh Dalton resigned as Chancellor and was replaced by the more austere Stafford Cripps, who had expressed doubts about the wisdom of long-term conscription.[33]

Alongside shifting military strategy went a changing attitude to conscription. Initially, the government simply continued the wartime policy of calling men up for 'the duration of the emergency'. In May 1946, however, it was announced that, from January of the following year, men would be called up for a defined length of time, which would in the first instance be two years, and that the period served would be gradually shortened.

At the same time as it was tinkering with wartime arrangements, the government brought forward a new law to set post-war conscription on a secure footing. Legislation was first proposed in 1946 and was put before the House of Commons in early 1947. It was amended in 1948 and finally came into effect in January 1949. The greatest source of acrimony concerned the length of time men would be required to serve. The chiefs of staff would have liked the period to be set at two years, but settled for eighteen months. Some Labour backbenchers wanted an even shorter period of service. Faced with a revolt by some of its own MPs, in the spring of 1947 the government agreed that it should be reduced to one year. Attlee's willingness to concede on this point may have owed something to the fact that Bevin, the most effective supporter of national service in the Labour party, was away at a conference in Moscow. The whole affair was so embarrassing that Attlee sent a personal telegram to George VI:

> The vote against the Government on the Bill was rather heavier than was expected. Labour Members voting against were predominantly elderly members traditionally opposed to all forms of conscription and Members from Wales. Having regard to the past tradition of the Labour Party on this matter I am not disposed to take the adverse vote too seriously, though there may be some difficulties at the Committee Stage.[34]

However, national servicemen never did serve for just one year. Towards the end of 1948, before the National Service Act came into force, the government effected another volte-face and restored the length of service to eighteen months.

Justifying such rapid changes of policy involved politicians and officials in some uncomfortable contortions. The Secretary of State for War claimed that the initial reduction in the projected length of service sprang partly from discussions with industrialists and concern about the economic effects of calling men up for a longer period.[35] When the length of service was increased again, he painted an implausible picture of the high hopes for international cooperation that he and his colleagues had, so he claimed, once entertained, and argued that these hopes had been dashed in the recent past. Such justifications aroused derision from the Conservative opposition and from journalists who believed that the change was rooted in the internal politics of the parliamentary Labour party rather than the international politics of the United Nations.[36]

In fact, the positions of almost all participants in the national service debates were riven with contradiction. The government had claimed that one year of service would be feasible in September 1948 when, as a response to the Berlin airlift, it had extended the service of all current conscripts by three months – which meant that some of them served for over two years. The position of the service chiefs was also odd because they had asked for longer service in 1947, at a time when they could not easily accommodate the conscripts that they were getting: 200,000 men were being registered for national service in a year when the forces could really take only 150,000.[37] The ministry toyed with expedients that included lowering the length of service even further, creating a labour corps to take men who were not wanted for combatant service or exempting men whose service had been deferred. The forces themselves were pressed to take as many men as possible.

Matters were complicated by the type of conscripts the forces were getting, as well as their number. From early 1947, men were allowed to defer service in order to complete their education or to finish apprenticeships. In the long term, the services would get these men back when their deferments expired, which was usually three years after they had first been given. In the short term, however, deferments removed a large number of the most skilled men from the call-up. The effects of this process were at their worst just as post-war conscription was institutionalized. The army reckoned that it needed 10 per cent of recruits to be in the highest category – defined in terms of fitness, mental ability and education. In 1947, only 4 per cent of them reached this standard. The Adjutant General wrote: 'At the moment . . . we are (I hope) at about the bottom of the trough in regard to average quality.'[38]

The army had the greatest need for conscripts and it was the Chief of the Imperial General Staff, i.e. the country's most senior soldier, who intervened most in the matter. In June 1946, Bernard Montgomery succeeded Alan Brooke in this post. 'Monty' was an extraordinary figure: arrogant, vain and bitterly lonely. Churchill said that he was 'in defeat, unbeatable; in victory, unbearable'. Montgomery himself once began an answer to a journalist with the words: 'As God once said, I think rightly . . .' When Montgomery visited a camp in 1947, the conscripts were taught how to reply if he asked 'Who am I?' The correct answer was: 'Sir! You are Field Marshal Viscount Montgomery of Alamein, Chief of the Imperial General Staff, Sir!'[39]

Montgomery quarrelled with civilian politicians but the most damming remarks about him usually came from soldiers themselves. More than any other man, he seemed to epitomize the transition from the high drama of war to the low comedy of a peacetime army.[40] Montgomery talked, with characteristic grandiloquence, of creating a 'new model army'. This army was designed to conduct the large-scale training of reserves described above. However, Montgomery also believed that conscription should have a social function and that it should teach young men about matters such as wood craft. There was a touch of the head scout about Montgomery, and he took an interest in young boys that aroused comment even among those who did not suspect that there was a sexual element in his behaviour.

Montgomery's interventions were almost entirely counter-productive. He exasperated politicians and his fellow chiefs of staff. He was easy to mock and the fact that national service was associated with him meant that, from the start, it was portrayed as laughable. The Labour MP Richard Crossman wrote that the 'Great conscription muddle' was 'Monty's pet idea, which he sold to Ernest Bevin. It was unnecessary and, without Monty at the head of the War Office, we should never have had it. But Monty thought a period in the forces should be a part of every boy's education.'[41] It was said that 'Montgomery principles' had turned 'regimental officers . . . into a cohort of club-leaders and Rover-Scouts'.[42] When Peter Nichols set out to write a play, based partly on his own experiences as a conscript just after the war, he 'dipped into a couple of Montgomery's books, *Forward from Victory* and *The Path to Leadership*, full of exhortations to his soldiers and, when there were none of them left to listen, to youth-leaders and Mothers' Unions. Sad and frightening and funny all at once.'[43]

In spite of the fact that, or perhaps because, Montgomery's name was so associated with conscription, its most vehement opponents were often those who regarded themselves as defenders of military efficiency.[44] Basil Liddell Hart was the most vociferous of these. Born in 1895, he had been a regular officer and, invalided out after the First World War, he became a military writer, combining his pontifications on grand strategy with an endearing interest in women's fashion. Though he had never held a military rank higher than that of captain, he regarded himself as being at least the equal of the Chief of the Imperial General Staff – 'in pre-war years Monty frequently wrote to tell me how closely he followed my writings'[45] – and perhaps the superior of other strategic thinkers: 'Winston's mind moves in old ruts. Even before the war he could not grasp that technical quality would discount the conscript army on which he counted.'[46]

Liddell Hart disliked conscription and campaigned against it, though he was disappointed that the government had not formally sought his advice: 'it is not practicable to make detailed proposals for the streamlining of military service unless one is actually called in to investigate the matter and has all the official data placed at one's disposal. I have a good deal of experience of such investigations in the past.'[47]

His argument was rooted partly in a belief that new technologies required professional soldiers to operate them and partly in a more historical vision – he despised the French army, which made so much of conscription, and he admired the wartime Wehrmacht, which had roots in the forced professionalization of the Weimar period. His most influential ally in this campaign was Giffard Le Quesne Martel – another apostle of armoured warfare – who had retired from the army with the rank of lieutenant general in 1945. Both men believed in small, highly trained and well-equipped armies.

Away from Whitehall and Westminster, national service was a matter that concerned almost every family with a boy under the age of twenty. Readers of newspaper articles might well have got the impression that peacetime conscription was almost universally unpopular. It was not surprising that the *Daily Mirror* – a left-wing newspaper with a tradition of criticizing the military – ran frequent articles on the hard lives of conscripts and the uselessness of the tasks they were compelled to undertake. However, attacks on conscription were also published in the *Daily Telegraph*, the *Daily Express* and the *Daily Mail*, all conservative papers.

One should not conclude from all this that national service was imposed on an unwilling country. Those who opposed post-war conscription were a significant and noisy minority. Ordinary people disliked it because of the disruption that it caused in the lives of their own sons; army officers disliked it, especially during the Montgomery years, because the emphasis on training often made their lives dull and repetitive and distracted them from what they regarded as 'real soldiering'. However, there was a difference between disliking conscription and believing that it should be abolished or that there was any realistic alternative.

Few people in the late 1940s suggested that Britain could live without large armed forces. Officers argued that increased pay and esteem for regulars might produce enough recruits without the need for conscription but it was not, in fact, clear that service pay was particularly low by historical standards. The real problem of recruiting lay in the fact that, as far as working-class recruits were concerned, full employment made civilian life more attractive and, as far as officers were concerned, the declining fortunes of the gentry made it harder for them to subsidize young men in a profession where pay often failed to cover living costs. In purely military terms, the armed forces would certainly have been better off with a smaller number of recruits who would serve for longer.

The government did toy with schemes – modelled on the American pattern – that might have allowed men to be called up by ballot rather than by universal conscription, but it invariably decided that such schemes would be rendered unworkable by a public sense that they were unfair. Army officers complained about national service throughout the period in which it was in force, but the most senior officers never called for its abolition; indeed, they fought for its retention during the late 1950s. Similarly, the general population often grumbled about national service but public opinion polls in the late 1940s showed that the majority of people favoured its retention – even if that majority was smallest among the age groups that were actually likely to be affected by conscription. All discussion of conscription was rather abstract. The batches of white-faced eighteen-year-olds who turned up every two weeks for basic training did not care about the projections of British strategy years into the future. A national serviceman wrote in 1949: 'Conscription debates in Parliament mean little to a conscript. Arguments about hypothetical needs, based on widely conflicting statistics of manpower, are remote from our personal problems, and the only thing that really interests us – demobilisation time – seems a foregone conclusion, unlikely to be brought nearer.'[48]

4

The Experience of Conscription, 1945–1949

Post-war conscription became associated with regularity, predictability and a certain brutal order. By the early 1950s, most boys approaching their eighteenth birthday knew that they would have to serve in the forces and knew how long they were going to serve. The shrewder among them could probably also hazard a good guess at what rank they would hold and what unit they would serve in. This order, however, did not spring into existence with the end of fighting in 1945. The first peacetime conscripts were called up in circumstances that still owed more to the chaos of war than the bureaucracy of peace.

The Second World War had had a messy end for the British. The intense fighting in northern Europe that had begun with the Normandy landings in June 1944 finished with German surrender on 8 May 1945. There were casualties until the last moment. Those lucky enough to survive unscathed marked the day with drunken celebrations. Alan Sillitoe, trying to get himself recruited into the Fleet Air Arm, recalled that his father got so drunk that he vomited his false teeth into a Nottingham gutter; fortunately the family, which had done well from wartime munitions work, could afford to replace them.[1] A private in the Sherwood Foresters in Italy woke up thinking that he had literally lost his sight; it turned out that he had fallen down some steps and that an equally drunk sergeant, trying to treat his injuries, had put bandages across his eyes.[2]

The end of the war in Europe, however, did not mean an end to fighting. Very few knew that the Americans had tested an atom bomb; most soldiers thought it would take an assault on the home islands to defeat Japan. It was reckoned that taking Malaya alone would involve landing 182,000 British troops.[3] In August 1945, just before the destruction of Hiroshima, British commanders still anticipated months of fighting and hundreds of thousands of further casualties. Further down the chain of command, well-informed officers such as Michael Howard and Denis Healey thought that they might have years of war in the Pacific ahead of them.[4]

The armed forces had been turned upside down by the war. There were 4,653,000 British people in uniform by 1945. Nine tenths of them were men and the great majority were conscripts: 2,920,000 were in the army, 950,000 in the air force and 783,000 in the navy.[5] The experience of servicemen varied hugely. There were men who had not set foot on British soil since 1939 and had spent much of the intervening time on active service, but most servicemen did not leave the British Isles until the summer of 1944 and a million of them had still not done so by the summer of 1945.

The War Office graphs reproduced overleaf reflect the transition from the small and all-regular services of 1938 to the very large and predominantly conscript forces of 1946 and then to the more stable period of peacetime national service in the 1950s, by which time conscripts made up about a third of the services and constituted only a slight majority in the army.

Relations between the various services had changed during the war. The army was still larger than the navy or air force, but it did not have the near monopoly of fighting that it had enjoyed in the First World War. Indeed, between the fall of France and the D-Day landings, there were long periods when most soldiers had little to do except cleaning kit. The RAF, by contrast, had become more important during the war. After soldiers dragged themselves home from Dunkirk, British survival seemed to depend on a small number of fighter pilots during the Battle of Britain and then, after 1940, on the aircrew of Bomber Command who took the war to the Germans. The RAF endured horrifying casualties and its war was one of sudden violence and individual combat, very different from the slogging battles of the army.

The RAF went with a different kind of social order. It was not classless – one of the most celebrated novels about class in post-war Britain, John Braine's *Room at the Top* (1957), revolves around the sexual rivalry between two former airmen, one a sergeant and one a squadron leader. Class distinctions in the RAF were, however, less rigid than those in the other services. Only a minority of airmen

Regulars (male), Conscripts (male) and Women in the Three Armed Services, 1938–1954 (in thousands)

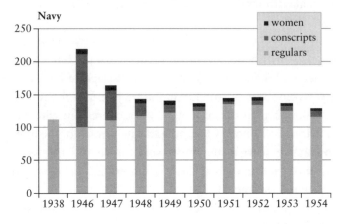

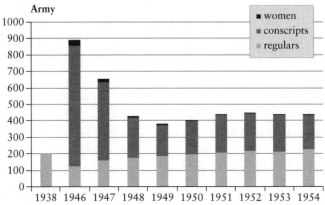

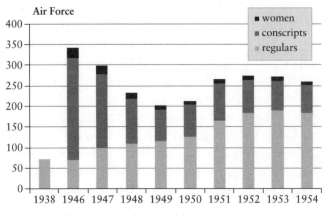

Source: WO 384/16, 'Abstract of Army Statistics', 1955

actually flew but that minority had an influence over the culture of the whole service and flying in wartime fostered a comradeship that partly transcended social origins. One post-war conscript from a working-class family said that the atmosphere of the RAF called his 'mental map of class boundaries' into question: 'Being shot up over Düsseldorf and seeing your mates die night after night didn't leave any taste for affectation.'[6] Pilots who had their hands on the controls of an aircraft did not worry about the issues of authority that haunted army officers. The RAF, unlike the army, did not issue orders that officers and other ranks should not frequent the same pubs. Flying, or maintaining aircraft, required technical skill that sometimes cut across the distinction between officers and other ranks.[7] Other ranks in the air force were better educated than their counterparts in the army; officers were less likely to have the public school education that was traditionally associated with army officers. The social basis of the air force became an obsession for Winston Churchill, a fact reported by his aide and fellow Harrovian John Colville,[8] who felt inspired to overcome the handicaps of his own patrician background and become a fighter pilot.

The air force kept some of its prestige after 1945, but this played a surprisingly small role in the minds of post-war conscripts. Almost all men who served in the RAF had put it down as their first choice among the services; few said that its wartime reputation played a part in their desire to serve with it. The very fact that the air force had had a 'good war' contributed to a decline in morale when peace came. A report of 1949 commented on the depressing 'mental adjustment' required as officers moved from a 'life of constant risk, demanding the exercise of high skill and courage', to ground-based desk jobs.

In May 1947, when this investigation began, such cases of depression were very common, especially among junior officers, and their effect on the morale of stations as a whole was profound. Upon individual NS recruits, however, it appeared to be wholly indirect ... But a milder, more general gloom is still spread from the lack of opportunity to fly, learn how to fly, or to make direct contact with aeroplanes, which is believed to be characteristic of National Service in the post-war RAF.[9]

The war also brought changes in the army. For most soldiers before 1939, the regiment had been their world. A second lieutenant was supposed to think, or at least to pretend, that nothing was more desirable than commanding a battalion of his own regiment as a lieutenant colonel. One officer going to Sandhurst in 1934 had been advised by his uncle, a regular soldier, 'Don't get ambitious – it's fatal.'[10] Regiments mattered less in the war. New units were created that had no history and, in some cases, no future beyond the current conflict. Men were moved around as, and when, their services were needed. From 1943 onwards, most army recruits were recruited into the General Service Corps and were only subsequently posted to regiments.

Before 1939 there had been a sharp gulf between officers and other ranks in the army. The military academies at Woolwich, for engineers and gunners, and at Sandhurst, for other cadets, were fee-paying institutions recruiting mainly boys from public schools. Promotion from the ranks to commissioned status was unusual. Andrew Man, who was to command a battalion of the Middlesex Regiment, joined up as a private and was eventually sent to Sandhurst. But Man was an exception that proved the rule. He was a public school boy whose family had fallen on hard times. Among his Sandhurst contemporaries, the number of Etonians was greater than the number of men promoted from the ranks.[11]

The outbreak of war in 1939 meant the rapid expansion of the officer corps. Men were commissioned from outside the traditional officer class and, eventually, it was decreed that all officers should begin in the ranks. Greater formality was brought to the process of commissioning, which was, increasingly, removed from the control of regimental commanding officers. War Office Selection Boards (WOSBs) were established, partly to mimic aspects of the officer selection exercises used in the German army. Psychiatrists were eventually appointed to selection boards and this 'scientific' selection aroused bitter resentment among some who regarded themselves as defenders of the social order.[12]

War sped promotion. In peace, it had been common for men not to reach the rank of major until they were forty; by 1945, it was reckoned that the average age of majors in fighting units was twenty-eight.[13] The greatest beneficiaries of wartime promotion were not those who had been commissioned during the war (who rarely rose above the rank of captain), but men who had already been regular officers before the war and who were now promoted much faster than would have been normal. Halfway through the war, three quarters of those who held the rank of lieutenant colonel or above had been regular officers or reservists before the war.[14] What marked the successful men out was that they were tough, energetic and possessed of the quality that had been most derided in the officers' mess during the 1930s: ambition. Officers who rose in the Second World War were to dominate the British army for a long time. When he became Secretary of State for Defence in 1964, Denis Healey, himself a wartime major, gathered around him a group of senior officers – Cecil Blacker, Michael Carver, Walter Walker – who had first shown their capacities when commanding battalions in the Second World War and who were, one suspects, similar to the tough lieutenant colonel (known as 'Basil the bastard') who had commanded Healey himself in 1944.[15]

The British armed forces did not return to 'normal' as soon as the Second World War was over. Between Japanese surrender (in August 1945) and Indian independence (in August 1947), they were subject to a unique set of pressures. Britain retained almost all of the imperial possessions that it had held in the nineteenth century. It also held the mandates that the League of Nations had awarded after the First World War and had acquired *de facto* responsibility for areas into which British troops had advanced during the war. The other imperial powers – France, Holland and, for that matter, Japan – were all weak and this created vacuums into which the British were often sucked. Finally, the United States sought to scale down its forces and bring its troops home until fear of Soviet expansion caused President Truman to reverse this policy in 1947.

Nationalists all over Asia, mobilized by participation in the Japanese war effort, as in Burma, or opposition to the Japanese occupation, as in Malaya, did not want European rule. The British began to suppress nationalist discontent and this sometimes meant that they ended up fighting in places, such as Indochina, that had never been part of their empire. Soon the British were present in an area that extended 'from the Persian railhead at Zahedan to New Guinea and the Australian seas'.[16] When the Dutch East Indies were placed under the aegis of Louis Mountbatten, just after the Japanese surrender, Britain acquired responsibility for an area of half a million square miles with 80 million inhabitants. There were also British troops in much of Europe. In Greece, they were sent to suppress Communist insurrection in 1946. In Italy, they tried to contain forces of Yugoslav partisans and they were to remain in the disputed city of Trieste until 1954.

Mike Calvert was the kind of officer who bounced around the periphery of the ramshackle British empire after the war. He had fought with the Chindits in Burma before being invalided to India and was posted to Trieste in 1945. He then moved to China, where he spied, and Malaya, where he helped reconstitute the Special Air Service. He did not adjust well to the atmosphere of a peacetime army and his military career came to an end in the 1950s after he had, among other things, urinated on the billiard table in the governor's residence in Malaya – an incident that he disarmingly described as 'one of those deeds that lost the empire'. He recalled the immediately post-war period in these terms: 'We had a million troops in Abyssinia, Eritrea, Austria, Germany, Indonesia (quite a lot), Indochina, Madagascar (not handed back [to the French]), Iran and Iraq . . . We were the king-pins with no money to do this.'[17]

Under these circumstances, servicemen could not simply be released as soon as the fighting stopped. The Minister of Labour had announced a plan for demobilization before the war had ended. Most conscripts were released according to a formula that took account of their age and length of service. Each was given a number that defined his position in the queue to be demobilized. Between 18 June 1945 and 28 February 1946 a total of 2,082,950 servicemen were demobilized, of whom 1,374,460 came from the army, 414,230 from the RAF and 294,260 from the navy.[18] However, plenty of wartime conscripts still remained in uniform in 1947.

Demobilization was a source of much bitterness.[19] The insistence on equity meant that men were released in accordance with their demobilization number but without regard to where they happened to be. This meant that a man might be retained doing nothing in a camp down the road from his own home because men with higher demobilization numbers were still in the Far East. Soldiers who had put up with things during the war felt differently when the fighting was over and when some of their comrades were going home. Men were piled into overcrowded bases and often separated from the officers under whom they had fought and who might still have commanded their respect. An army report of 1946 spoke about soldiers in the Far East thus: 'Drafts of men roam about the country like droves of armed sheep, but more articulate – the Transit Camp, that slaughterhouse of hope, looming menacingly before them.'[20]

The armed forces in the year or two after Japanese surrender had an improvised and temporary feel. No one was sure what was about to happen and many men had no concern except to extract themselves. As an officer in Burma recalled: 'everything was concerned with running down'.[21] James Notley, a regular officer who had served in India, North Africa and Italy, found himself commanding a holding battalion in Clacton: some of the men were former prisoners of war on their way to demobilization and some were young conscripts called up since the end of the war, whom Notley considered 'nothing like as good as soldiers in Italy'.[22] Edward Grey, an NCO with the Durham Light Infantry, recalled the petty futility of military life immediately after the war. He was in Greece where his regiment began to take in the first group of reluctant post-war conscripts. He thought that, better handled, they could have become good soldiers but nothing seemed to work out. He tried to improve the literacy of his soldiers and asked the Education Corps for materials, but none were sent. Later he built a tennis court, which was promptly taken over by the officers. Grey was relieved to be demobbed in 1946.[23]

Mutinies and 'strikes' broke out in overseas bases, particularly those of the RAF – the Red Air Force, as one colonial governor labelled it. Disturbances started at Jodhpur in India in October 1945 and spread to twenty-two bases by early 1946.[24] It was reckoned that, at one point, around 50,000 airmen across the Near and Far East were involved in a coordinated movement of protest.[25] The fact that airmen were often responsible for webs of communication helped spread rebellion. Demob numbers were illicitly relayed in Morse code from RAF Uxbridge via Gibraltar, Egypt, Karachi, Calcutta, Rangoon and Singapore to bases in Malaya.[26]

John Saville was a university graduate from a working-class Jewish family who finished the war as a sergeant in the Royal Artillery. He was also a Communist but had disregarded the party's order that its members should seek commissions. In 1945, he was serving in India and witnessed a protest at an RAF base near Karachi. He attributed this partly to the fact that airmen 'were often of a more skilled kind with membership of a trade union much more common than the average infantryman or gunner'. Saville's own rebellion came when a captain with white knees (a sign of a man recently posted from England) ordered him to organize training for the men. 'My war is over . . . and you can go and fuck yourself,' Saville replied.[27]

An RAF base in the Far East could give the first post-war conscripts an interesting perspective on military discipline. Peter Nichols arrived at such a base, in Bengal, in early 1946. He was greeted by a 'brown, case-hardened' corporal:

> You billet orderly, Corp? I asked.
> Don't Corp me. I'm Stan, all right? And there's no orderly. Ram [the Indian bearer] takes care of the basha.
> You off duty then?
> I've finished son. We've all finished, we've been here long enough. We've told them we're not working again till our number's up.[28]

Ray Self was not called up into the air force until October 1950 but he believed that 'they' were still haunted by the memory of 1946 and the fear of 'another mutiny'.[29] Self appears to have been unusual among post-war conscripts in knowing about the upheavals of 1946, and the enquiries that the RAF conducted into conscript morale during the late 1940s did not unearth mutinous feelings – though perhaps the fact that such enquiries were conducted at all shows that 'they' were indeed frightened by the prospect of disorder.

Three places epitomized the mood of uncertainty that marked the British armed forces during the late 1940s: India, Germany and Palestine. Between them they accounted for roughly half of the 476,000 troops posted abroad in April 1947, of whom 100,000 were in Germany (this number had halved since the previous year), 72,000 in Palestine and 58,000 in India.[30]

India had been a scene of British military endeavour since the eighteenth century and a stepping-stone in the career of officers from

Arthur Wellesley to Bernard Montgomery. After 1945, however, it was obvious to many that the Raj was dead, and Indian independence was granted on 15 August 1947. This was accompanied by the end of the India that British soldiers had known. What had been a single unit ruled from Delhi was now split into two. Pakistan (itself divided between two non-contiguous geographical areas, one in the north and one in Bengal) was, by the time of independence, almost exclusively Muslim. India comprised the remainder of the subcontinent and had a mixed population, with a Hindu majority.

The Indian army had been separate from the British army but its officers had been almost entirely British. The last years of British India had gone, in an odd way, with the apotheosis of the British-officered Indian army. It had provided much of the manpower with which Britain pursued the Second World War in Asia and the Middle East. British officers had been trained in India during the war – by its end, 290 cadets were being sent to India every four weeks.[31] After the war, however, the Indian army began to change. Indian troops had to be shipped back from places such as Malaya. The Gurkhas, recruited from Nepal, were divided between the British and Indian armies. The Indian army itself was split as troops were divided between India and Pakistan. British soldiers were usually passive spectators to the savage inter-communal riots and massacres that preceded the partition of India.

Some British officers served the new states, particularly Pakistan,[32] for a time and a few British officers were commissioned into the Indian army as late as 1946.[33] However, the number of officer cadets sent to India declined and few of them stayed. Post-war conscript officers would undertake the long sea voyage to Bombay, and then go to Bangalore, where they lived for a few months in a luxury that would have been unimaginable in Attlee's Britain, before being shipped back to serve in British regiments.

Most British officers in the Indian army transferred to whatever positions they could find. Edward Pickard moved from the Frontier Force Rifles to a searchlight regiment of the Royal Artillery. Used to commanding tough Peshwari tribesmen, he was now in charge of a regiment that contained only three regular officers and a few regular NCOs. He recorded in his diary: 'The remainder are mere children . . .

It is a very much changed army to the one I knew pre-war' – though he added sportingly, 'I think it is going to be fun.'[34]

Men who had spent their whole lives under the blazing sun in regiments with a marked sense of their own history now found that they were making do as best they could at squalid camps in Oswestry or Aldershot. Harold Perkin, called up in 1948, served as an education officer in the air force. Three of his fellow officers were refugees from the Indian army: 'bewhiskered old soaks with fiery red cheeks and Edwardian manners'. One of them was serving with the rank of flight lieutenant (equivalent to the rank of captain in the army) but had, apparently, been a full colonel and occasionally appeared at mess nights in the uniform of the Bengal Lancers.[35]

P. J. Wilkinson spent his early years in India, where his father was a civil servant, before going to boarding school in England and to Sandhurst. In 1933 he was commissioned into the 19th Lancers of the Indian army. Like many of his comrades, he was a good linguist who learned Urdu and Hindi. He served in the war against Japan and commanded his regiment for a time before, much to his chagrin, being replaced by a more senior officer who had 'spent the whole war in the India Office and did not know one end of a tank from the other'. As the partition of India approached, his regiment was split, with Hindus being sent to India while he remained in what was now Pakistan. Sikh squadrons were driven away in tears under armed guard. It was, as he recalled laconically, 'a bit of a wrench'. His brother officers were 'concerned' but none committed 'an act of ill-discipline'.

Wilkinson chose to return to the UK rather than serve the Pakistani state. He moved from the cavalry to the artillery and was, initially, posted to the least prestigious element of this, an anti-aircraft unit. Eventually, he persuaded his superiors that his skills and experience might at least warrant posting to a field artillery unit and he was sent to Germany in 1949 – he discovered that his new regimental commander could not even be bothered to learn German.[36]

There was a tragi-comic aspect to the British army's last days in India. In 1946, at a time when some of the most experienced India hands were desperately seeking new jobs in Europe, the authorities took Major D'Arcy John Mander from his office in the control commission in Berlin and sent him to Calcutta, apparently to try to deal with the 'awful slaughter'. Mander was a gallant soldier who had escaped from an Italian prison camp and set up a spy ring in Rome. He spoke fluent German, but had no experience of India.[37]

Fresh-faced conscripts witnessed the twilight of British rule on the subcontinent. John Nye was conscripted into the RAF in 1945 and kitted out at Padgate: 'what a dump it is organization is practically non existent ... you can imagine conditions when I say 300 pass through every week'. He was sent out to Karachi in June 1946, moved to Bombay and then (in March 1947) on to Ceylon before being brought back to Britain in August 1948. As a member of the RAF police Nye spent much of his time conducting fruitless investigations into how RAF stores so frequently came to be on sale in Indian civilian markets, and attempting to suppress riots in Bombay: 'as usual with RAF organization, no one knows what we are doing here'.[38]

Germany also epitomized the confusions of the first two post-war years. The British Army of the Rhine was formed in August 1945. Later it would become a by-word for comfortable, and mind-numbingly dull, postings. Immediately after the war, things were different. The fixed lines of the Cold War had not yet been seared into the German landscape. British troops were still there as occupiers rather than as defenders of the Germans. Technically British troops would remain an occupying force until they were put under NATO command in 1952. In practice the Berlin airlift of 1948-9 probably marked the point at which British relations with the Germans changed for the better. The airlift illustrated the uncertain and often improvised quality of British military life in the period. The Soviet Union cut all land access to West Berlin, which was an island of western influence at the heart of Communist-ruled East Germany. For a moment, it seemed as though there might be a real danger of war. The western allies responded by flying all commodities, including coal, into the city.

In the first few years of occupation, British troops were often regarded with hostility by the local population. Germany was in chaos. Cities had been bombed to an extent that shocked even soldiers from London or Coventry. The country was desperately poor and, until 1948, did not even have a functioning currency of its own. Large numbers of German men were still prisoners of war in Russia and some German prisoners provided labour for British forces in

Africa and the Middle East as late as 1947. British conscripts in a Hamburg NAAFI lost all appetite when they saw starving children pressing their faces against the window;[39] others remembered 'Germans scrabbling for cigarette ends that we dropped in the gutter'.[40] German women, desperately poor, often resorted to prostitution. Venereal disease in Germany was seen as a particular problem.[41]

Roger Alford was called up in November 1944 and commissioned, in October 1946, into the 7th Queen's Own Hussars; the fact that a man who had spent almost two years in the ranks could be an officer in a smart regiment said much about how the army had changed in the previous five years. He was sent to Germany and remembered that 'I had never really considered what life would be like in a regiment which was well trained but did not have a war to fight.' As it turned out, the answer was partly what it would always have been for a peacetime cavalry officer: 'horses, dogs and sport'. However, discipline was difficult because men convicted of offences would have their date for demobilization set back, so the army was left with wartime conscripts who could not be sent home until they had managed to serve a certain period without getting into trouble. One solution was to put persistent offenders in a special unit – the 'Woodpeckers' – who were set to heavy forestry work in the hopes that they would then be too tired to get into fights.[42]

The single posting that best incarnated the frustrations of the British military in this period was Palestine. The British had held the country as a League of Nations mandate since 1919, while also committed by the Balfour Declaration of 1917 to create an independent Jewish state there. An Arab uprising in 1936 had been suppressed with brutality and Jewish guerrillas also attacked British forces. During the war, though, some Jews fought with the British army and Britain was able to use parts of Palestine, notably the Port of Haifa, as military bases. One result of this was that quite large numbers of the men posted to Palestine after 1945 belonged to unglamorous units that were charged with looking after stores and were not well prepared for being shot at. Simply guarding equipment was a problem when so many Jews and Arabs were keen to get their hands on weapons.

After 1945, Jewish emigration increased sharply as survivors from

Nazi concentration camps left Europe. In 1947, the United Nations recommended the partition of Palestine. The British were reluctant to enforce a policy that was opposed by the Arabs and announced that they would consider their mandate at an end on 15 May 1948. However, from 1945 until their final departure, British troops were attacked. Jewish resistance groups, notably Menachem Begin's Irgun, became more violent. On 22 July 1946, the King David hotel in Jerusalem was bombed, with the loss of ninety-one lives. In December of the same year, a group of British soldiers was kidnapped and beaten and, in July 1947, two British sergeants were captured and hanged, apparently in retaliation for the hanging of members of Irgun.

The British intervention in post-war Palestine was brief and, in that the British always knew they were going to leave, futile. The last-minute scuttle out of Palestine, as Arab and Jewish forces attacked each other, looked undignified. Matters were made particularly awkward by the fact that so much equipment had been stored in Palestine and had, therefore, to be moved out at short notice.

There was an anti-Semitic strain to some discussion of Palestine in British military circles.[43] However, this was not universal. Indeed the confusion of British experience in Palestine came partly from the fact that the army itself was divided. Sometimes this was a matter of unit. Drivers from the Royal Army Service Corps said that paratroopers had behaved 'like Nazis'[44] when exacting revenge for Jewish attacks. Sometimes it was a matter of location. Attacks by Jews on the British army were most common in the north of the country but one conscript officer recalled: 'We were in the south where the Arabs were tremendously on top, and we saw the absolute best of the Jewish side there.'[45] Men who had served in Europe during the war were sometimes sympathetic to the Jews because of what they knew of Nazi persecution – though men who had served in the war against Germany were often also particularly resentful of Jewish attacks. Some British conscripts were sympathetic to the Jews because they saw them as more 'European' or more 'civilized' than the Arabs.

Post-war British conscripts often found it hard to fit their experience into the wider political framework and this was especially true of those who came up against the complicated animosities of

Palestine. John Watson was called up into the RAF just after the war and sent first to Egypt and then to Palestine. He became strongly pro-Jewish – partly because he was horrified by the conditions on the refugee ships that brought Jews from Europe and partly because he came to dislike the 'Herrenvolk' attitude of some of his fellow servicemen. However, he also detested socialism and blamed the Attlee government for British policy in Palestine. His life took a sudden turn for the worse when he lost his rifle – it had, apparently, been stolen by one of the Arab guards at his barracks. Now this colonel's son from Wiltshire was charged and put in military prison – where he seems to have endured some harsh treatment. Even this, though, did not make him left-wing in any conventional sense. The worst thing that he could say about the military authorities was that they had behaved like the Soviets.[46]

Most of all, conscripts recalled Palestine as a place where they were shot at by both sides and where there was real uncertainty about who the enemy might be. Jim Parrit was called up in 1946 and sent to Palestine with the Royal Artillery. Arriving in Haifa to escort a train, he was told that it was too dangerous to leave the station but that he and his men could sleep in a NAAFI hut. During the night, Arabs stole their Bren gun; the following morning, the train on which they were travelling was blown up by Jews.[47] Kenneth Lee, who was a gunner in Palestine, talked of 'a stab in the back war' and said that soldiers attacked in the night sometimes did not know whether they were fighting Jews or Arabs.[48]

Service in Palestine aroused a degree of resentment among British conscripts that was only, perhaps, paralleled by that felt for service around the Suez Canal during the undeclared war of the early 1950s. The Palestine Pals and the Palestine Veterans Association were formed in 1997–8 and seem, at least in part, to have been designed as a riposte to 'Israel's boastful Golden jubilee'.[49]

The two or three years after the end of the war were marked by the blurring of all sorts of divisions. Wartime conscripts served alongside men who had been called up after the Japanese surrender. Until 1946, the wartime system of calling men up 'for the duration of the Emergency' persisted. Irate fathers wrote to newspapers complaining that their sons were unable to make plans about their education or careers.[50] In the army, everyone except guardsmen still joined up in the General Service Corps rather than in a specific regiment. 'Potential leaders' were sent to training battalions – notably that at Hollywood in Northern Ireland – but these were designed to prepare men to be both officers and NCOs and the length of service in them was usually six months, so that potential officers were separated from their comrades only after they had spent a substantial period in the ranks.

It was also often unclear where the first post-war conscripts would be sent or what they would be required to do. Failing to call men up when so many wartime conscripts remained in uniform would have been politically impossible. However, a huge military machine, which had just come to the end of a world war, did not always benefit from an influx of untrained men. Indeed, in the short term, the need to train and organize new recruits, at a time when the forces were also trying to maintain a complicated range of military enterprises and to demobilize large numbers of troops, created problems rather than solving them. One officer recalled his service in Egypt in the autumn of 1946 thus: 'The war time conscripts, still awaiting demobilization, were bored with playing soldiers in the desert . . . while the recent arrivals needed convincing that their stint in uniform was necessary.'[51]

Those called up at the end of the Second World War or immediately after it felt, even more than the great bulk of national servicemen who were to come later, that there was something incongruous about their military experience. David Price joined the RAF in January 1946, having been an apprentice in a reserved occupation during the war. He thought that his military service was a waste of everyone's time: 'the war was over and things were running down – the regulars did not want us and I wanted to earn money and progress'. He was sent with two other men to keep 'squatters' away from a deserted base.[52]

Born in 1926, Godfrey Raper was called up when the war was almost over. He took a short course at Oxford designed to prepare men for commissions and then reported to a training unit during the Indian summer of 1945, but he considered it 'little more than a joke' because 'the war was over'. He then attended a succession of courses in a succession of bases, all of which were being closed down. He recalled a brief interlude at a deserted airfield in Lincolnshire that felt like a grounded *Marie Celeste*. It was full of poignant relics of the life that had until recently been lived there: a programme for the film club still fluttered on a notice board.

After almost getting his men killed in an exercise with live ammunition, Raper saw that he would never make a good officer and began the oddly difficult business of getting himself reduced to the ranks. He was sent to a unit in Croydon to be 'deofficered'; it was full of 'headcases', including one who had thrown down his rifle at battle school and said 'I will soldier no more.' Raper was then posted to a holding battalion, apparently designed to make men so miserable that they would welcome overseas postings. Finally, he joined the Education Corps and went to Palestine in November 1946.[53]

A few quick-witted, cynical and well-connected men were able to exploit the chaos of the post-war army. Alan Clark, the future Conservative MP, was the most notorious of these. He later claimed that he had joined up at the age of seventeen, just before the end of the war, and endured the Brigade Squad for men who sought commissions in the Household Division. Actually, he seems to have spent a single day in the Household Cavalry before moving to the army reserve. When called up after graduating from Oxford, he persuaded the authorities that he had fulfilled his military obligations.[54]

The novelist Simon Raven took a more favourable and enterprising view of military service. Born in 1927, he was conscripted in 1945, after having been expelled from Charterhouse for homosexuality:

> There followed a happy time in the rough and ready army of the immediately post-war period. Since the war was too recently concluded for people to worry much about morality, my disgrace at Charterhouse did not prevent my being sent to India as a Cadet and then duly sent back again with a commission in the Oxfordshire and Buckinghamshire Light Infantry, a regiment of sound if hardly brilliant social standing. I was consequently forgiven by the authorities at Charterhouse and allowed to join the old boys' association.[55]

Raven's contemporaries at Charterhouse illustrated the 'rough and ready' element in post-war conscription. William Rees-Mogg had gone up to Balliol but the master of the college 'decided to give my place ... to a demobilized ex-serviceman'. His undergraduate career interrupted, Rees-Mogg was called up and hurled into the chaos of RAF Padgate. He escaped to become an education sergeant – a comfortable posting but not quite the kind of military service associated with a future editor of *The Times*. When he was discharged, his commanding officer provided him with a testimonial: 'Sergeant Rees-Mogg is capable of performing routine tasks under close supervision.'[56]

James Prior, later a Tory cabinet minister, went into the army under the impression that he would be commissioned into the smart '60th Rifles', but he was sent to a depot in Derby 'that had no regimental attachments at all', before being trained, with Raven, in India. Prior was glad to become an officer in the Royal Norfolk Regiment. He remembered the whole experience as marked by 'an extraordinary mixture of grim reality and peacetime frivolity'.[57]

Many men, even if they were not as cynical as Simon Raven, seem to have had a more interesting experience of military service in the mid to late 1940s than they might have had a few years later when the armed forces had established routines for dealing with national servicemen, and when the chaos of the post-war world had subsided. Jeremy Morse had 'officer material' stamped all over him. He had been head boy at Winchester, his father had served with the King's Royal Rifle Corps, and he himself won the Belt of Honour during his officer training. By the mid 1950s, such a man would have been called up into his father's old regiment, put in a potential officers' platoon after two weeks and commissioned after about six months. He would then have spent eighteen months serving with other young men from grand public schools before going up to Oxford. As it was, Morse was called up at the beginning of 1947. He was initially recruited into the General Service Corps and did not begin to wear the badge of his father's regiment until well into his service. He also joined at a time when all conscripts were expected to serve a long period in the ranks, and did not become an officer until he had been in the army for eleven months. He was posted to Palestine, where he got to know the tough Jewish settlers at the local kibbutz: once, out of sheer perversity, he drove down a road that they had mined. At the age of nineteen, he watched British troops move out of southern Palestine just before the Arabs attacked.

Morse was then, along with three other conscript second lieutenants and 180 riflemen, attached to the Royal Army Service Corps – at the opposite end of the military hierarchy from his own regiment – and made responsible for moving supplies out of Egypt: 'I learnt a lot about human nature there, probably more than if I had stayed with my somewhat crack battalion.' His demobilization was delayed by the Berlin airlift and he finally escaped from the army after twenty-five months of service. He did not regret the chaotic circumstances of his military career. He thought it better than 'sitting around on some air-field' and that 'If you're nineteen and you go to Palestine and you go to Egypt and there's a little bit of fighting and nobody gets killed, it's almost perfect, isn't it?'[58]

John Quinton came from a humbler background than Morse, had been educated at a grammar school and was called up in May 1948 before he went to Cambridge. Like Morse he served an extra few months because of the Berlin airlift. Not wanting to be an officer, he joined the Intelligence Corps and became a sergeant. Quinton's service seemed more *The Third Man* than *The Virgin Soldiers*. He was sent to Trieste, where he interrogated refugees from Croatia and Slovenia in primitive Italian. Aged nineteen, he set up a smuggling ring that moved contraband and information across the Yugoslav frontier. One day, a member of the gang staggered into his office leaving a trail of blood. It was, as Quinton recalled fifty years later with the calculated understatement of a successful banker, 'somewhat tragic that ultimately, because of a mistake by my commanding officer, all except one of them were shot dead on the frontier'.[59]

Between 1945 and 1949, the hierarchies and rigid divisions of the armed forces were slowly resurrected. In 1946, psychiatrists were dropped from the officer selection boards. The regimental system, which had been weakened during the war, was restored to much of its former importance and recruitment through the General Service Corps was abolished in 1948.

Divisions between officers and other ranks became, once again, sharply marked after the war. At first, all soldiers were still required to serve a period in the ranks. However, this became an increasingly empty formality. During the war, men had moved up and down the ranks and many officers were promoted after acquiring substantial experience as NCOs. After the war, the qualities regarded as desirable in an NCO were separated from those regarded as desirable in an officer. In 1948 the training battalions that had mixed potential officers with potential NCOs were abolished. From then on, men regarded as potential officers were sent straight from basic training to Officer Cadet Training Units.

During the war, training at Sandhurst and Woolwich had been suspended. All officers passed through one of the Officer Cadet Training Units. By 1945, there were dozens of such institutions scattered around the country and often accommodated in hotels or boarding houses. After 1945, the War Office concentrated the training of conscript army officers at Eaton Hall in Cheshire, and Mons barracks in Aldershot.

Separate training establishments for regular officers were restored. The Britannia Naval College at Dartmouth was reopened for potential naval officers. It continued, for the first few years after the Second World War, to function as a boarding school, taking boys from the age of thirteen, though increasing numbers of cadets were admitted at the age of sixteen or eighteen. Cranwell became, once again, the officer training academy for the Royal Air Force. Sandhurst was reopened in 1946 as the academy for all regular army officers. The abolition of the academy at Woolwich implied that distinctions between technical branches of the army and the more socially prestigious infantry and cavalry units were to be abolished. Sandhurst also ceased to be a fee-paying institution and was, in theory, now open to all boys who could pass a test that was pitched below the level required for university entrance.

In practice, the democratization of the regular officer corps after 1945 was limited. An RAF officer noted that: 'Many people used to regard – and still do regard – the Army as a refuge of the dull-witted sons of the upper class who were quite incapable of any other profession.'[60] The abolition of the Woolwich academy meant a decline in the intellectual quality of the technical arms rather than a rise of that in the infantry and cavalry. The standard of mathematics among Sandhurst students in the post-war period was notoriously low.[61]

The abolition of fees at Sandhurst did not mean that it started to recruit large numbers of boys from state schools. Almost half of its intake came from 150 schools represented at the Headmasters' Conference and a third of them came from twelve schools – Wellington, Eton, Winchester, Haileybury, Rugby, Cheltenham, Charterhouse, Sherbourne, Bedford, Radley, Marlborough and Blundell's.[62]

Some army officers, or former officers, campaigned for the army to become *less* democratic after 1945. One wrote: 'There is scarcely any doubt that practically every officer who has spent the normal short period in the ranks is the worse for it.' He argued that such service eroded the capacity to give orders. He believed that the pre-1914 public schools had produced 'the finest body of regimental officers the World has ever seen', but that their quality had declined because they now instilled 'comradeship rather than leadership'.[63]

A sense of the mood in the British army is given by the fact that some senior officers disliked the change of nomenclature at Sandhurst that involved calling students 'officer-cadets' rather than 'gentlemen-cadets'.[64] Sandhurst did not restore the title 'gentlemen' to its cadets but it did instil a gentlemanly ethos and some of its post-war graduates were more conscious of this ethos than men who had been through the war. Alberic Stacpoole illustrated some features of the new/old officer values. His mixture of snobbery, altruism and institutional loyalty would eventually find its outlet when he became a Benedictine monk. When he was called up for national service, he applied for a regular commission and went to Sandhurst. He was initially disappointed to be commissioned into the Duke of Wellington's, a relatively humble infantry regiment, but 'they grew on me'.[65] In Korea he fought gallantly, winning the Military Cross, but his definition of gallantry was different from that of more senior officers. On one occasion he noticed his company commander – a veteran of the Second World War – running across an area of open ground, where he risked exposure to enemy fire. Stacpoole rang the commander, a man two ranks senior to himself and possessed of much more military experience, on a field telephone, and complained that running 'was not really an officerly thing to do'.[66]

The careers of many regular officers had been shaken up by the war and the effects of this were still visible for years after 1945. Michael Forrester went up the ladders of wartime promotion and down the snakes of peacetime retrenchment. Born in 1917, he obtained a regular commission in 1938. During the war he fought in Crete, where he rallied soldiers and locals to attack the Germans before escaping in a small boat (he won a bar to the Military Cross that he had been awarded in Palestine) and was then wounded at El Alamein. He became an acting lieutenant colonel and commanded a battalion that landed at Salerno, where he won the Distinguished Service Order. He took his men to Normandy, where he was wounded again, and then became military assistant to Field Marshal Alexander. After the war, he was posted as military attaché in Washington and retained his acting rank for a year, but was reduced to being a 'local' lieutenant colonel and then to a simple major. He did not much mind the demotion – his rise had been so fast that he had never commanded a company, the task usually given to majors. At the age of thirty-three and with German shrapnel in his leg, he pushed himself through the ferocious training required of paratroopers, was posted to the Parachute Regiment and eventually rose to the rank of major general.[67]

The war created divisions among regulars officers. Rapid promotion meant that some served under men who had once been their juniors. Officers who had spent years in prisoner of war camps returned to find their regiments being run by tough young men who had made their reputations in 1944. The stoical discipline of officers who had led their soldiers into captivity at Dunkirk or Singapore had nothing in common with the ruthless determination of those who had fought their way out of Arnhem.

National servicemen – national service officers in particular – understood how the fortunes of war had divided their own superiors. James Kennaway and John Hollands, both post-war conscripts, wrote novels that described the bitter, sometimes deadly, animosities between wartime officers.[68] Kennaway and Hollands were writing works of fiction, but their characters had real-life counterparts. A lieutenant colonel of the Northamptonshire Regiment was a 'fierce, bitter man' but one who had commanded a battalion in the Italian campaign, 'knew his profession' and extracted a high standard of work from his sergeants and subalterns, having apparently 'given up' on the majors and captains who had themselves been through the war. Part of the bitterness between the lieutenant colonel and his brother officers seems to have sprung from the fact that he had commanded a company of the

5

Boys: National Servicemen before Call-up

*We were never teenagers as such; now you have got the teen-
age element but we were never teenagers cos you finished
school and within eighteen months, a couple of years you were
in the army ... so those years didn't mean anything.*
    Terrance Atkinson (born in 1936 and called up in 1955)[1]

National service told the authorities much about young men when
they were called up at eighteen; several ministries drew on information they obtained about conscripts. *The Times* published a succession
of letters about adolescents in general and about boys between leaving school and conscription in particular,[2] and the King George's
Jubilee Trust responded to this debate by commissioning a study of
'the influences affecting the upbringing of young people'. The Trust's
report was published in 1955, with sections on life at school, life in
the services and life in the period between the two.[3]

Conscription, however, raised questions as well as providing information. These questions were particularly pressing with regard to
what happened to men in the years before they were called up. During
the war, adolescents had been subject to a degree of formal control.
Those who worked could be required to remain in jobs that were useful to the war effort. Sixteen-year-olds were required to register by the
local education authority and were invited to an interview, which did
at least mean that officials knew what some of them were doing.[4] All
this ended in 1945. Unless boys were caught breaking the law, the
state, and most of the adults who commented on 'youth', had little to

do with them in the years between the day they left school and the day they turned up for their pre-national service medical inspection.

Furthermore, the years of national service were ones in which notions of what it was to be young – especially a young man – were uncertain. Boys of sixteen or seventeen had money to spend, particularly in the second half of the 1950s, but a distinct youth culture could be glimpsed only over the horizon.[5] Rock and roll intruded incongruously into the armed forces. An air force base in Germany made discreet – and, as it turned out, unnecessary – preparations in case servicemen rioted during a showing of the American film *Rock Around the Clock*.[6] Conscripts standing outside their huts on Christmas Island in early 1958 heard Elvis Presley's 'All Shook Up' over the public address system, before a voice intoned, 'The Valiant with the weapon is now lined up for take off', and more appropriately solemn music was played to prepare them for an atomic test.[7] Generally, however, young British men of the late 1950s understood that 'youth' (in its glamorous sense) was something that belonged to other places or other times. Shortly before he was called up, John Sutherland, a grammar school boy from Colchester whose flirtation with rebellion had extended no further than listening to 'trad jazz', went to see the film *Rebel Without a Cause* and tried to imagine how the wealthy, stylish Californians that it depicted might fit into his own milieu: 'these, one gathered, were *sixth formers*?'[8]

John Ferris was a working-class boy who joined up about the same time as Sutherland. He disliked 'trad jazz', partly because he associated it with grammar school boys, 'grammalogues' as he called them. He also disliked rock and roll, which he associated with the least interesting boys from his own class. His life revolved around the modern jazz of Cleo Laine and Miles Davis, but trying to pin down his own form of youthful identity when interviewed forty years later, he could only refer to the 1960s: 'I was,' he said, 'a kind of proto-mod.'[9]

The word teenager was being widely used by the late 1950s, but the youth culture of the time seemed staid by comparison with what came later.[10] Terry Dene illustrated the awkward relations between 'youth culture', as it came to be understood in the 1960s, and national service. Dene, a singer when British rock and roll was an embarrassing imitation of the American model, was called up into the King's Royal

Rifle Corps in 1958. He was, however, far from being a hero to his fellow conscripts and, after being bullied, he was invalided out. His concerts were subsequently disrupted by national servicemen, angry at Dene's apparently light escape from his military obligations.

Most national servicemen, like most of the British population, were working class. A survey of 1950 (the results of which are tabulated below) found that 74 per cent of army conscripts and 62 per cent of those in the air force came from families headed by someone who was 'an operative', either skilled or unskilled.

Occupation of Senior Wage Earner in Families of Recruits to Forces and the General Adolescent Population

Occupation of Senior Wage Earner	General Adolescents' Sample (Males)		Army Sample (Volunteers)		Army Sample (National Service)		Royal Air Force (Volunteers)		Royal Air Force (National Service)	
Operative: Skilled and Unskilled	70		75		74		67		62	
Inspectoral and Supervisory	10		8		10		11		13	
Professional and Technical	6	23	2	13	5	19	7	24	10	32
Clerical Routine and Higher	7		3		4		6		9	
Other Grades, Don't Know and No Answer	3		6		6		7		5	
One Senior Wage Earner	4		6		1		2		1	

Source: Leslie T. Wilkins, *National Service and Enlistment in the Armed Forces: A Report on an Enquiry Made for Several Government Departments into the Attitudes of Young Men Prior to, and on Joining the Armed Forces* (1951), p. 7

The Registrar General divided up the civilian population of England and Wales in a slightly different way. Adult men were grouped into five categories. In 1951, 3 per cent of them belonged to the professional and upper managerial class (I); 15 per cent belonged to the 'intermediate class' (II); 53 per cent were 'skilled workers' (III); 16 per cent were 'partly skilled' (IV) and 13 per cent were unskilled (V). The top 3 per cent took in doctors, lawyers, senior business executives and army officers. The 'intermediate' class contained many clerical workers and most, though not all, schoolteachers. 'Skilled workers' included some clerks – though 75 per cent of those in this category were manual workers. Manual workers, of one kind or another, therefore made up over half the working population. Manual work meant more than one thing. Middle-class people might think that anyone who got their hands dirty belonged to more or less the same social class, but an apprentice-trained carpenter would not regard a street sweeper as being his equal and working-class boys seem to have been particularly sensitive about hierarchies of prestige within their own class. The complicated regulation of work and pay that had emerged from the Second World War, and from the desire of trade unions to maintain different rates of pay for different jobs, sometimes produced a hierarchy of almost surreal complexity – the Ministry of Labour published pay rates for 'buffalo picker manufacture'[11] and 'leather belting and strap butt currying'.[12]

Class was not static. The relative status attached to different jobs changed over time. After 1945, working-class boys (or their parents) tended to want skilled manual jobs. They valued white-collar occupations less highly than they would have done in the 1930s – probably because the principal advantage of white-collar work, job security, counted for less at a time of full employment.[13] Middle-class people, including army officers, often felt that 'the relatively low monetary reward of the white collar worker has stripped his employment of much of the kudos and respect it formerly commanded'.[14]

A man's position in the Registrar General's social categories might change in his lifetime. Men often entered the intermediate class when they were relatively old – having 'risen from the ranks' through promotion or having established a small business. By contrast, men usually entered the top social class at an early age – often passing directly from full-time education into the professional classes when they were, say, called to the Bar. It was unusual for men to be in class I at the very beginning of their military service, though one soldier – Julian Bullard – was elected to a fellowship at All Souls while undergoing basic training. Quite large numbers of men would, however, have understood that they were more or less certain to enter this class at some point in their twenties. Simply being commissioned would put a man in social class I and it seems likely that a large proportion of the 13,900 men who, in 1951, had reached this class before the age of twenty were national service officers.[15]

Official definitions of class emphasized occupation, but income, consumption and lifestyle also played a role in how people thought about the subject, and social change in the 1950s made the relations between these things more complicated. Wages for manual workers rose and some middle-class people came to believe that manual workers earned more than they did. Cars, fridges and televisions became more common and the possession of such items was sometimes seen, in itself, to confer middle-class status.

The armed forces had their own private version of the official class system. The commandant of the War Office Selection Board (responsible for choosing national service officers) divided candidates into four groups – the 'old upper class'; 'professional and business'; 'the sons of working men'; and finally a mysterious group, which did not in his view make good officer material: 'the former middle class'.[16]

Some people defined their own class position in terms that were, according to official or academic definitions, 'wrong'; since officials and academics were middle class, it is not surprising that such 'errors' were most common in the working class. When workers in Woodford (a mainly middle-class suburb of London) were asked what class they belonged to, almost half of them said 'middle' and 3 per cent said 'upper middle'.[17] For much of the population, the most important division was probably not that which separated middle from working class but that which separated 'rough' from 'respectable'. In the 1930s, unemployment had been a common cause of severe poverty. At the time of full employment that began with the Second World War, poverty was more frequently caused by old age or long-term sickness but it was also increasingly associated in the minds of many with large families, crime and an apparently wilful refusal to hold down a steady job. Social commentators made much of 'problem families' who failed to look after their own children.

The division between rough and respectable was often arbitrary and subjective. Many men who went on to have eminently 'respectable' lives came from backgrounds that were in some respects 'rough'. Leslie Thomas spent the later part of his childhood in an orphanage, but he seems to have established himself as a journalist even before he made his fortune with a national service novel.[18] There was, however, one very visible and widely accepted frontier between the rough and the respectable. Conscripts, especially in the air force, were respectable; regulars, especially in the army, were rough.

The class position and self-image of men before call-up was particularly complicated. Most of them had only recently begun work. Furthermore, there was little relation between the incomes of young men and their social status, as perceived by the adult world. A boy in the sixth form at grammar school was likely to be, or be on the path to becoming, middle class, but he earned nothing. An apprentice was on his way to joining the skilled working class but earned little. A boy doing casual labour, on the other hand, might be relatively well paid. At the ages when boys were called up, there was an inverse correlation between the length of time they had stayed at school and the amount of money they earned. Among boys who were called up at the age of eighteen or nineteen in the late 1950s, almost a third of those who had left school at fifteen were earning over £8 per week; among those who had left school at seventeen, only one in ten was doing so.[19] Middle-class comment on working-class boys often made much of the allegedly easy money that could be earned through unskilled work.[20]

A few boys grew up in circumstances that gave them special insights into class. The most privileged were most likely to have such insight – though they often professed to dislike the word 'class', partly because they associated it with 'socialism'.[21] A stockbroker's son who went from Eton to the Grenadier Guards described his background thus: 'fairly classical upper class one ... we have a family estate. It was a beautiful sort of house, built in the late eighteenth century. And, you know, servants and things like that.'[22] David Cainey (born in 1933) was the son of a butler and grew up 'totally aware of class divisions'. When his father's employers 'came out in their carriages', the children of the servants took their caps off. Cainey passed the 11-plus and went to grammar school before being commissioned into the RAF Regiment during national service. He recalled childhood fights with boys from Clifton College (a public school) but insisted that his awareness of difference did not produce resentment. He thought 'I owed them proper respect.'[23]

Sometimes those most conscious of class were close to a social frontier, especially if they felt themselves to be on the 'wrong' side of it. Derek Watkins, born in 1928, grew up in a mining village near Rotherham in which everyone other than his own family was 'Red Labour'. His grandfather was an under-manager of the pit. Watkins went to the village school with the miners' sons, but never felt happy there. During a May Day celebration, a union representative told him to 'fuck off' because his father was a Conservative. Watkins was pleased to escape into the army.[24]

Space was one of the most tangible ways in which class affected people's lives, and one of the simplest ways to sort young men into social categories was by comparing the number of people in their homes with the number of rooms. Most conscripts in the air force, and about half of conscripts in the army, lived in homes with at least one room per person, but 7 per cent of national servicemen in the army and 3 per cent in the air force came from homes in which there were two or more people for every room.[25] Wartime bombing meant that homes in industrial cities became even more cramped. Families shared small houses or squeezed into prefabricated houses – often put up on bomb sites. A Borstal boy was discharged from the Pioneer Corps in 1950. It was recommended that he should not return to his own home, where conditions were bad. His stepsister and her husband were willing to take him in but they lived in a prefabricated house and already had five children of their own.[26]

Physique was also related to social background – a fact highlighted by national service medicals. Men from poor backgrounds were shorter, thinner and less fit than their more privileged contemporaries. A doctor attached as a national service medical officer to the Royal Army Service Corps described some recruits 'from Manchester and

Glasgow' as 'dwarves' because they were under five feet tall and weighed less than a hundred pounds.[27]

Class and region interacted. Northern England, Scotland and most of Wales were dependent on old industries – steel, shipbuilding and coal-mining – that had suffered badly during the depression of the 1930s. The south and the Midlands were more prosperous. A greater part of their population was made up of skilled workers, especially those in new industries, such as motor manufacture. Men who worked in new industries tended to be more mobile (geographically as well as socially) than men who worked in old ones. In Banbury, old trades (such as wheelwright) were the domain of local men; new ones (gas fitter or toolmaker) attracted 'immigrants' who had come into the town from elsewhere.[28]

Gradations within the more privileged classes could also be complicated. This was partly because they were divided by degrees of privilege and partly because the nature of the middle class differed from area to area. Variations were particularly marked in parts of northern England and the Midlands, in which relatively small towns often revolved around a single industry. In Yorkshire, cities that were just a bus ride apart (Doncaster and York or Bradford and Leeds) could have different cultures. John Braine, born in Bingley near Bradford in 1922, evoked the provincial middle class, and especially the sharp variation between one town and another, in his novels of the 1950s, as did John Wain, born in Stoke-on-Trent in 1925.[29]

Describing the parents of men born in the early 1930s in Huddersfield, the left-wing sociologists Brian Jackson and Dennis Marsden commented on the fact that there were two middle classes:

> The first is national, metropolitan in interest, mobile, privately educated. Such are the senior civil servants, doctors, executives, who stay a while and pass through the city; or who belong as natives here, but 'belong' elsewhere too. And then there is that other middle class, very local and rooted, of the self-made businessmen, works officials, schoolmasters clinging to their home town.[30]

Jackson and Marsden's view of the Yorkshire middle class was, on this issue at least, similar to that of the military authorities. An army report of 1956 described northern industrial towns thus: 'The compactness of the economic unit is repeated in each town and in many of the more isolated communities such as are found up the Pennine valleys.' For the army, the middle-class men who came from such communities made poor 'officer material' because they were 'parochial' and prone to be 'ill-at-ease when taken from their environment, and hence they become brusque, awkward and self-conscious'.[31]

Banbury in Oxfordshire presented a revealing contrast with the industrial towns of Yorkshire. Here the typical businessman was 'less concerned with making as much money as possible than he is with maintaining his social status and position'.[32] The wealthy cared about those subtle gradations that marked out aristocrats from 'county' families (who could afford to hunt and maintain country houses even if they had no titles) and county families from 'gentry' (who were poorer and usually obliged to work for their living). Twenty-three local families lived in houses that were styled 'Hall' or 'Park'; sixteen local men had been educated at Eton. A large number had entries in Who's Who (a classic sign of membership of the 'national' middle class) and many had held military rank of lieutenant colonel or above.[33] Oxfordshire produced a particularly large number of national service officers.[34]

Many national servicemen grew up in some distinctive provincial sub-set of the middle class. In Nottingham, a group of men went into the Royal Artillery under the aegis of Peter Birkin, an industrialist and colonel in the Territorial Army. Birkin's protégés were largely drawn from local middle-class families – usually the owners of middle-sized businesses. John Robinson was a typical example. He had left Bromsgrove school and was working for the family wallpaper business when, shortly before his call-up, his father's accountant introduced him to Birkin.[35] Men such as Robinson were often educated at public schools (though never at the grandest institutions) and they were usually (but not always) commissioned during their national service. They were, however, recognizably different from the upper-middle-class boys who would have been commissioned in the smartest regiments. They often spoke with slight regional accents and their higher education, if they had one, involved studying technical subjects at provincial colleges.

The north east was another area with a distinctive regional middle class. George Lightley was born in 1930 and brought up by his grandfather, a colliery manager. He studied agriculture at King's College Durham because 'this was pretty much the only university we knew'.[36] John 'Jack' Burn came from a similar background: his father had been an underground electrician in a coal mine but had inherited a shop and become reasonably prosperous. Burn also went to King's College Durham and probably had slightly wider horizons than Lightley because he read history, French and English, less practical and more prestigious subjects. His father advised him that law was probably not a profession for men from his background – thus sentencing him to a lifetime teaching in the kind of northern grammar school that he had himself attended.[37]

Notions of social class in post-war Britain were intimately associated with the education system. Even though only a small minority of national servicemen went straight from school to the forces, most national servicemen had spent a substantial – often the greater – part of their pre-service life at school. The overall educational level of young men increased during the 1950s – though this did not translate into the national service intake in a simple way because educated men seem to have begun to escape from the call-up towards the end of the decade (see Appendix VIII).

The Crowther Report on education in England and Wales (1959) drew much of its information from a survey of national servicemen. Between August 1956 and April 1958, the army and air force surveyed the educational backgrounds of 7,970 national servicemen.[38] Of the men in the sample, 5,795 had left school at fifteen or younger, 1,181 had left at sixteen, 408 had left at seventeen and 586 had left at eighteen or nineteen.[39]

Until 1944, elementary education was provided by the state – though in practice local education authorities had begun to split their provision into 'primary' (up to the age of eleven) and 'secondary' (from eleven onwards). There were also a variety of private schools, which often styled themselves 'public schools', and grammar schools, which were fee-paying institutions but which had been endowed for the provision of free education to the poor and which now operated under a degree of state control and with state subsidy that required them to offer at least a quarter of their places free to children who won scholarships.

R. A. Butler, President of the Board of Education in Churchill's wartime government, came from a caste of academics and officials in the Indian Civil Service which revolved around the passing of exams. Butler's Education Act of 1944 sought to bring the benefits of exam-based selection to the whole of England and Wales. It created a 'tripartite' system. Children were examined, usually at eleven, and then sent to one of three types of school: grammar schools (for the most academically able), technical schools (for those with a more practical bent) and secondary moderns (for everyone else). Writing in 1954, a sociologist remarked that the 1944 Education Act 'so far as social stratification is concerned, is probably the most important measure of the last half century'.[40]

Social stratification meant something different at different levels of society. Some men talked about schools in terms that derived from their own communities rather than the official language of the Ministry of Education. Ernest Dobson was a miner's son from the Durham coalfield. He attended the mixed school in the village – 'the top school' – but failed the 11-plus by a few marks so that he was unable to attend 'what we used to call the upper standards school'.[41] Studies of national servicemen revealed not only that some boys from secondary moderns were more intellectually able than some from grammar schools but also that some boys from the skilled working class had made a conscious decision not to go to grammar school.[42]

In practice, the system never worked quite as simply as the Butler Act had anticipated. There were few technical schools – only 556 of the 7,970 national servicemen whose school records were examined by the Crowther Committee had been to them. A few private schools failed to survive in the new climate. Generally, however, the big public schools did well; some of them were, in fact, in better shape in 1948 than they had been just before the Second World War.

Public schools were at the top of the military hierarchy. Though only a small proportion of national servicemen had attended them, they provided a disproportionate number of national service officers – 80 per cent of them in the early 1950s.[43] Public schools were also unusual in that a large proportion of their pupils stayed at school until the age of eighteen and then went straight into the forces. Of 276 public school boys in the Crowther survey, 158 had joined the forces at eighteen and a further fifty-two of them did so at nineteen.[44]

Public schools were often militarized. Harrow had almost bankrupted itself in the 1930s by constructing a memorial to its dead of the Great War, and Wellington had been established for the sons of officers – piquantly, its headmaster was killed by enemy action when a confused Luftwaffe pilot dropped his bombs in rural Berkshire. But war seeped into the classroom even at less obviously military schools. Piers Plowright, born in 1937, remembered teachers coming back to his prep school with 'odd twitches and limps and bad tempers'.[45]

Apart from the Quaker institutions, which had their own role in preparing men for the call-up, almost all public schools had an Officer Training Corps (OTC) or, after April 1948, a Combined Cadet Force (CCF). Some boys, particularly in the aftermath of the Second World War, were effectively conscripts, in the sense that they were forced to undergo military training. One school expelled boys who refused to serve as cadets.[46]

Those who thought about 'youth' and national service were often influenced by a sense that 'public school values' ought to be more widely diffused. They assumed that public school headmasters would be particularly qualified to offer advice on conscription.[47] Men from Charterhouse who were posted to the British Army of the Rhine in 1946 were disconcerted to find that their old headmaster – Robert Birley – had been made educational adviser to the Allied Control Commission and enjoyed the honorific rank of major general.

Grammar schools varied greatly. On average 20 per cent of English children and 36 per cent of Welsh ones attended them in 1953, but the proportion differed from one local authority area to another: it was less than 10 per cent in seven of them and more than 35 per cent in ten.[48] About 145 grammar schools (direct grant schools) had a special status. These were schools that preserved a high degree of independence and the right to charge fees. This category encompassed most of the grandest institutions – Manchester Grammar School or King Edward's in Birmingham. About 1,200 schools were 'maintained' grammar schools, which were more directly under state control and enjoyed less prestige than the direct grant schools. Some of the more modest grammar schools were, in fact, more likely to train boys for skilled working-class jobs or low-level office work than for the liberal professions – a fifth of the grammar school national servicemen studied by Crowther became 'craft apprentices' after leaving school.[49] Jim Riordan (born in 1936) wrote of his own education:

> The grammar schools were run along the lines of public schools with houses, prefects (who wore braided jackets), streaming and the ultimate ambition of preparing the elite for entry to Oxford or Cambridge. In truth, in my school [Portsmouth Southern Grammar School] most rose no higher than five-year apprenticeships in Portsmouth Dockyard, as coppersmiths, riveters and electricians.[50]

The class position of grammar schools was complicated. In the suburbs of southern England, a school might recruit from quite a narrow social range. Ronald Hyam welcomed his call-up because it meant 'liberation' from the 'deadly homogeneity' of his grammar school:

> We all came from exactly the same type of background (including most of the staff) and mostly lived in exactly the same kind of 1930s semi-detached or in four-unit terraces. There can surely have been few communities so uniform in living pattern as those lower-middle-class suburban ones ... Agnostic Protestantism, soccer, philistinism – that was our local culture.[51]

Elsewhere grammar schools mixed children from the middle and working classes – two thirds of children at grammar school had parents who had left school at fourteen.[52] Sometimes this meant that grammar school boys talked with one kind of accent at home and another at school; a few of them, at least among those who survived at school until they were seventeen, seem to have defined themselves in terms of their school rather than their family background.[53] However, post-war grammar schools did not open up huge opportunities for working-class children. They were less likely to go to such schools in the first place; those who did were less likely than their middle-class contemporaries to stay until they were eighteen, and those working-class children who reached university seem to have felt ill at ease in their new milieu and often obtained poor degrees. It may be that the main long-term effect of grammar schools was to help some relatively well-off boys to rise within their own class rather than to provide new entrants to that class. Furthermore, one commentator on the middle classes suggested, prophetically as it turned out, that grammar schools would not last because they catered for pupils who were always 'passing through' on their way to greater things and would therefore have no long-term interest in the survival of their old schools.[54]

The division between grammar schools and secondary moderns intersected with class divisions and with differences in the perceptions of class. A survey of the early 1950s asked London boys of thirteen and fourteen: 'Do you think there are social classes in England?' Most of them replied that they did not understand the question, but these answers could be broken down further by social origin and education: 66 per cent of working-class boys at grammar school and 78 per cent of working-class boys at secondary moderns did not understand. Middle-class grammar school boys were most likely to say that they understood the word 'class' and to use it in the same way that adults would. Further questioning revealed that most boys did have some conception of class distinctions, even if they did not use the word. Asked to rank various occupations, almost all of them put member of parliament at the top and road sweeper at the bottom. Understandings of class varied with the boys' social and educational background. Working-class boys were more likely to ascribe prestige to skilled manual work, particularly if their own fathers did such work, and the small group of middle-class boys at secondary modern schools were more likely to define class in terms of style and behaviour than in terms of occupation.[55]

Grammar schools educated many boys up to the age at which they were first called up. They too had military associations and these associations had grown closer during the war, when many boys had proceeded straight from school to the armed forces.[56] Grammar school boys had been especially important in the RAF, but they had also provided an increasing number of army officers. The army had been forced to accept officers from outside its milieu for recruitment. As one wartime officer wrote, 'If he [the recruiter] cannot get Eton, he will get a good Grammar School ... If he cannot get the genuine ex-public school boy, he will get the best imitation in the market.'[57]

After the war, grammar schools continued to prepare boys for military service in direct ways. Many of them had Officer Training Corps and when the Ministry of Labour organized pre-national service information days, one grammar school took its entire sixth form straight from the cricket field to the hall in which the event was taking place.[58]

Grammar school culture, however, did not always fit neatly with that of the armed forces, and this became more obvious as the conventional military hierarchy, and public school dominance of the officer corps, was restored after 1945. Grammar schools were almost always day schools and, for this reason, their pupils found the transition from school to barracks more shocking than did public school boys. Boys from grammar schools were more likely to go to the provincial 'redbrick' universities, which tended to take men before they had performed national service. Oxford and Cambridge, with a higher proportion of public school entrants, encouraged men to complete national service before coming up. Of 1,525 grammar school boys surveyed by Crowther, 671 had entered the forces when they were twenty or older. This compared with just sixty-six (of 276) public school boys who had deferred their call-up. The armed forces, the army especially, also preferred men who came straight from school and believed that such men made better officers than did graduates. The headmaster of one public school wrote in October 1949 about the dangers of letting men go to university before they joined the army: 'I asked a young nineteen-year-old subaltern what he thought of these older national service recruits. "Poor devils," he said, "they've had it."'[59] Max Poulter, who himself held a national service commission between school and Oxford, wrote of his officer training, 'I began to realize that being more mature, well qualified and independent minded was not a recipe for success in the army, which valued the more docile qualities of a public-school prefect.'[60]

Public schools were purely male institutions and often went with a conscious assertion of paternal authority: a boy was often sent to his father's school and it was the father who oversaw his education there. Grammar schools, by contrast, taught boys who were in daily contact with female relations, and during the war a few grammar school boys were brought up in households that contained no men.* Some commentators suggested that the upward social mobility of grammar school boys often went with strong mothers, sometimes ones who had a powerful sense of being in the 'wrong' class, and self-effacing fathers.

The profanity and violence of the forces seemed shocking to grammar school boys, who had often been raised in the urban lower-middle class and who were used to the privacy of their own family. The headmaster of Leeds Grammar School told the National Council of Women at Harrogate in 1949 that heads of 'secondary schools in the north' were worried about military service:

> If the boys come back mentally and morally soiled there is a big price to pay. For that reason the headmasters think that it may be better for them to go to the university first. Then they may be tougher and more mature to stand up to temptations and dangers. That is the opinion of headmasters who are in favour of National Service. They were wondering if the deterioration mentally and morally, and even physically, is worth the price.[62]

A distinct group of grammar school boys from working-class backgrounds passed the 11-plus but never adjusted to the middle-class culture that went with academic education. National service seems to have posed particular problems for these boys. Their distaste for the alien disciplines of an academic school must have been increased if they knew that they were going to have to endure two years of equally alien discipline at the age of eighteen. Things were especially awkward for those who left school just a year before they were due to be called up but did not enter into an apprenticeship or course that would offer them a chance of deferral. An official report commented on those who left school at seventeen, either because they had failed exams or fallen a year behind at some point in their career:

> These boys were found very often to be not much more than average in personality and achievement. One or two who had given up a job or who had abandoned a VIth form course were often ... difficult to

* The war also meant that grammar schools themselves became more feminine institutions because some of them were forced to employ women teachers.[61]

place because they were unlikely to make a good impression on employers ... in varying degree they suffer from the instability of adolescence,
defeatism or a sense of failure.[63]

The majority of boys had not been educated beyond the minimum
school leaving age. In 1952, 222,900 boys left school at fifteen; in the
same year only 35,200 stayed at school until they were sixteen.[64]
Some believed that those who wanted to make a start on practical
training were more inclined to leave school early because of national
service. One headmaster in Scotland commented on the fact that 'the
boys of better quality almost entirely regarded it [national service] as
a gap, with the result that they tended to leave school earlier than
usual'.[65]

A large proportion of boys continued with some kind of training
once they started work. In the late 1940s, about one in six conscripts
deferred their service to complete apprenticeships; ten years later this
figure had risen to one in four and almost a third of national servicemen (not all of whom deferred) had undertaken apprenticeships.[66]
Apprenticeships varied considerably and did not always go with privilege. Among a group of working-class Glaswegian boys, all of whom
had left school at fourteen, the number who undertook apprenticeships was almost half the total number called up for national service.[67]
By contrast, of eighty-five boys registering for national service in a
London suburb, which would have been more prosperous than Glasgow, only twenty-one were apprentices: significantly, sociologists
distinguished the nine 'elite apprentices' (such as draughtsmen or telephone engineers) from the twelve 'other apprentices'.[68]

Some thought that the impending call-up made men less likely to
settle in an apprenticeship.[69] Others believed that obtaining deferment of national service made men more likely to take apprenticeships,
and thus produced a decline in their prestige.[70] The truth is probably
that national service had little direct impact on the number of youths
who embarked on apprenticeships. This increased because the number of skilled jobs was increasing and also because the comparative
scarcity of workers made employers seek ways of binding workers to
them. Having said this, national service did have effects on men once
they had started apprenticeships. Some, exasperated by their low pay

and menial status, had broken apprenticeships even before they were eighteen.[71] Some envied their workmates who had been allowed to leave work for the forces at the age of eighteen[72] and welcomed the call-up as a chance to escape. M. E. M. Herford, a factory doctor who made a special study of young men in the period before their call-up, reckoned that 41 per cent of those he encountered had broken apprenticeships before the age of twenty-two, because they were unfitted to the work. He did not think that national service itself was usually a reason for the break – though it often provided an excuse.[73]

Tom Hewitson, born in 1932, was an apprentice decorator, but he had always wanted to be a soldier and, at the age of eighteen, he deliberately provoked an argument with his employer in order to get sacked and make himself available for call-up – though his father then had an accident and Hewitson was obliged to seek deferment in order to help with the family finances.[74] Some men interrupted apprenticeships in order to go into the forces. Of men called up in September 1951, 2,831 had completed apprenticeships (or less formal forms of on-the-job training) but 1,652 men in such positions joined the forces before completion and a large number of them seem to have made a conscious choice not to defer.[75] Most of those who interrupted an apprenticeship to perform national service eventually went back to complete their apprenticeship, or to work in some related trade.[76]

Men who settled well in apprenticeships and obtained deferment of military service often found that call-up, when it came, was particularly painful. Working-class men who finally joined the forces in their early twenties did so after having acquired professional skills and often at a time when they were 'courting'. National service blocked out two years in which such men might have hoped to earn reasonably good money and to enjoy life before marriage and children.

Not surprisingly, national service was unpopular with boys who had completed apprenticeships.[77] The career of Ken Lynham shows why. He was born in 1937 and educated at technical school before becoming an apprentice fitter in a dockyard. His adolescence was overshadowed by the call-up. He deferred his service until the age of twenty-one. During the last six months of his apprenticeship he worked in the drawing office – 'I was a collar and tie then' – and earned full pay. National service meant his earnings dropped to 'a pound a week'. It also interfered with his life in other ways. He got engaged on his twenty-first birthday: 'national service is coming up, we ought to make a go, we ought to make a commitment', but he could not contemplate marriage until after his service was over. Only men who were willing to sign on for three years (and thus get higher pay) could afford to get married. He remembered that he was 'apprehensive to say the least' before conscription and that it came 'right at a crucial time in life'.[78]

Men who deferred military service in order to complete professional training led anxious lives. Their employer served a double function, and sometimes had a double power, because he provided them with a means of staying out of the forces as well as a means of support. The War Office recognized that employers sometimes used their power to obtain cheap labour.[79] Occasionally employers seem to have arranged deferral even against the wishes of their apprentice; frequently employers simply understood the formal world of qualifications and deferment better than young working-class boys. Harry Sanson, born in 1930, was an apprentice plumber in the north east. He paid his dues to the plumbers' trade union but did not play an active part in its affairs, and his deferral seems to have been arranged almost without intervention on his own part: 'the chap I was working with got us deferred'.[80]

Albert Balmer was allowed to defer his service when he was apprenticed to a coach painter. However, his employer died and he then had trouble in finding another job because no one wanted to take a man who would soon be called up. Eventually he found work as a house painter.[81] Albert Tyas, born in 1929, was an apprentice plumber who became excited by the stories that his colleagues told him about the romance of service in Egypt. When he was called up, he did not fill in the form asking for deferment and went to work 'joyful' about his imminent departure. His 'gaffer' had other ideas and arranged a deferment – the result of which was that Tyas avoided eighteen months of moderate tedium in the peacetime army, and was instead called up in 1950, sent to Korea and captured. He did not get home until 1953.[82]

Life for apprentices could be a war of nerves. If they deferred for long enough they might escape altogether; on the other hand, being called up at an advanced age might be worse than getting it over with early. Jack Gillett became an apprentice pattern-maker in 1946 and deferred his service until his apprenticeship finished at the age of twenty-one. He then enrolled in a City and Guilds metallurgy course 'which would have got me past the magical age of 26' (the maximum age for call-up), but further extension was denied and he was called up in 1952.[83] Brian Bushell was a grammar school boy, born in 1931, who became an apprentice lithographer and deferred his national service. After a year, he decided that he just wanted to get it over with and did not seek to extend his deferment. Patrick Sumner, born in 1936, was from a similar background and was apprenticed as a railway engineer. He repeatedly managed to defer but was then, in spite of pleas from British Rail, called up at the age of twenty-three in 1959.[84]

The one thing that all national servicemen had in common was war. Since no one born after September 1939 was called up, every national serviceman had lived through the whole of the Second World War. War bit into family life and changed relations between the sexes. Richard Faint, a docker's son born in 1936, said that the absence of husbands at the war meant that women started to read newspapers.[85] Fathers were often called up. Sometimes this meant that grandfathers – in many cases veterans of an earlier war – were the dominant male influence on the lives of boys. Long absence made some boys ill at ease with their fathers – 'when this man appeared, I hated him'.[86]

War could be devastating for a family that was already unstable in some way. A Borstal boy who had acquired a string of convictions before, during and after his military service was the son of a waitress and a man who was said by some to be dead. The authorities found it 'very difficult to trace the background and structure of his family relationships . . . one can only surmise that at some time during the war associations with the father finished and the general conditions and standards deteriorated'.[87]

Boys who grew up in industrial areas were likely to have been bombed: a boy born in 1932 was more likely to come close to violent death as an eight-year-old in an Anderson shelter than as a twenty-year-old on patrol in the Malayan jungle. Paul Croxson (born in 1936 and called up in 1954) wept as he recalled, in his seventies, how his father had been caught outside the family shelter and almost killed by a German flying bomb.[88] David Davies, born in 1934, remembered his grandfather opening the door of the shelter so that he could see Bristol burning.[89] Jack Coley said simply: 'when we got out [of the shelter] there was no house'.[90]

Many national servicemen had been evacuated during the war. Almost a million and a half mothers and children were taken out of vulnerable areas in September 1939. Most of them returned quickly but then one and a quarter million moved in the period from September 1940 to the end of 1941. Some children went back and forth from one home to another – sometimes as their own families were bombed out, or as middle-class families in country areas decided that, like the characters in Evelyn Waugh's *Put Out More Flags* (1942), they did not want to share their house with a twelve-year-old from Bethnal Green.[91]

Social observers after the war were sometimes exercised by the effect that dislocation – particularly separation from their mother – might have had on very young children. They believed that this upheaval might account for the 'delinquent generation' of the late 1950s.[92] In fact, the most obvious disturbance seems to have involved children who were already of school age. It was they who were most likely to be separated from their families and to stay away from home for a long time.

Evacuation, the absence of male teachers or even the physical destruction of schools all disrupted education. A report on conscripts in the air force put it thus:

> During the war years there was an unfortunate deterioration of educational standards in the nation's schools, which affects particularly the groups entering NS during the period under investigation, and tends to reduce the general literacy (though not the general intelligence) level.[93]

A national serviceman in the Pioneer Corps said simply: 'The reason I could not read or write was the blitz.'[94]

Some effects of the war were benign. It increased the economic security of some working-class families, particularly among those whose fathers managed to stay out of the forces. Unemployment pretty much disappeared and wages in war industries were relatively high. Alan Sillitoe's father had been unemployed for long periods during the 1930s, and had served three months in prison for a desperate act of petty fraud. The war changed everything. The issuing of gas masks was the first sign of a welfare state: 'At last we mattered to the government, which was arranging for us not to be choked to death during an air raid.'[95] His father got a job and 'couldn't resist going into the terrific anti-aircraft barrage to enjoy the glow in the sky from burning factories that had always refused him a job'.[96] Alan himself, whose work in engineering factories was defined as useful to the war effort, found it hard to get out of jobs rather than into them.

Many other boys were sucked into the war economy at a relatively young age. E. Dorking was born in London in 1930. His parents were poor: his mother took in washing and his father was a betting man who was called up to the army in both wars. Dorking was evacuated to Eastbourne and then to Pembrokeshire, where he seems to have become an agricultural labourer before the official school-leaving age. His educational certificates were lost in the move back to London, and armed with nothing but his wits he set out to find a job. During the last months of 1945, he lived in Birmingham. His aunt, with whom he lodged, took most of his pay but he found it hard to move because he was in a 'reserved occupation', i.e. one considered useful to the war effort. Eventually, he managed to obtain work as a shorthand writer, before being called up into the Ordnance Corps.[97] Any boy called up between August 1945 and mid 1949 was likely to have begun his working life during the war. This often meant fifty hours a week of hard factory work.[98] Not surprisingly, these men sometimes found the slow pace of life in the peacetime armed forces to be depressing.

The effects of war on the middle classes were less direct. Prosperous families sometimes went to live in the country. A few schools were moved to the countryside or amalgamated with other institutions for the duration of the war. Some children were sent to the United States or Canada; this also meant that a small proportion of the men who eventually took national service commissions in smart regiments had been raised outside the ordinary structures of the English class system.[99]

Though the middle class as a whole escaped the effects of war to a greater extent than the working class, two sections of it experienced those effects with special force. The first was made up of those whose fathers worked in the empire. The sons of British civil servants and army officers in India were sent to school in Simla or Dehradun rather than risking the voyage across U-boat infested waters that would have taken them to an English prep school.[100] The second section was made up of regular officers. Officers might serve until a comparatively advanced age and consequently many of them endured long separations from their children during the war. Edmund Bruford-Davies was born in 1928, the son of an officer who had been commissioned just after the First World War. While Bruford-Davies was at Radley, his father wrote him letters urging him to concentrate on getting into Oxford or Cambridge rather than contemplating a military career. These were the kind of letters that many fathers wrote to their sons, but Bruford-Davies senior's were unusual in that they were written from Colditz Castle, where he had been imprisoned after parachuting into occupied Albania.[101] The son disregarded his father's advice and joined the army. He was a prisoner in North Korea when his father died in 1951.

In one sense, national servicemen were lucky. Unemployment had haunted their elders. Just before the Second World War, there had been 4,961 unemployed juveniles in Liverpool alone.[102] Even if they had never experienced it directly, post-war conscripts were still influenced by memories of unemployment. In Scotland, Wales and northern England, many fathers had been out of work and told their children bitter stories about years on the dole or about the insecurity of scraping a living when faced with the constant threat of the sack. In the late 1940s, the RAF found that its conscripts – who had left school at a time when 'no employable man wants employment'[103] – were still concerned with job security:

> Conditions of full employment in civil life have not wiped out the fear of unemployment, and there is also anxiety that competition for work may reduce wages and conditions of labour. Some men actually believe that the National Service Acts are a Government scheme for preventing unemployment or disguising it.[104]

The labour market was so tight in the post-war years that unemployment rates among boys before national service could be as low as

0.5 per cent. Job opportunities were best in the prosperous areas of southern England and those who studied eighteen-year-old youths in a London suburb were slightly disconcerted to find that '50 of the 85 young men felt settled in their type of job, and intended to remain in it, as far as they could foresee, for the rest of their lives'.[105] Even areas that had been associated with the worst of the pre-war depression had little unemployment in the 1940s and 50s. In December 1956 there were just four boys under the age of eighteen in Jarrow and Hebburn who were registered as unemployed.[106]

One effect of full employment was that most young men did not need the Youth Employment Service, which existed to provide them with advice. Instead they relied on networks of 'mothers and fathers, sisters and brothers, aunts and uncles'.[107] A third of all school-leavers in 1951 were said to have got their jobs through such networks.[108] Informal recruitment increased the propensity of working-class boys to disappear from official view between leaving school and being called up.

Among conscripts, there was a small proportion of men who did not fit the general pattern of employment stability. Sometimes unemployment was the result of rebellion against work, or against the type of work that was available. Sometimes the expectation of national service itself created unemployment. The Director of Education in Liverpool wrote to the Ministry of Labour in 1950:

> The Liverpool Youth Employment Committee have, for many years, been gravely concerned regarding the relatively high number of youths aged 17–18 years in the City who are unable to obtain work of any kind. Generally speaking, although by no means always, these young people are of the unskilled type whom employers are unwilling to engage because of their impending call-up for military service and the reinstatement obligations that devolve upon employers.[109]

A few men also changed jobs frequently in the years before national service. Of those called up in September 1951, 4,842 had had only one job before they joined the forces, 2,092 had had two, 980 had had three, 398 had had four and 285 had had more than four.[110] Those who studied the young often condemned the frequent changing of jobs. They regarded it as a sign of instability, 'immaturity' or even psychological problems.[111]

Some thought that national service encouraged instability of employment. In 1949 a magistrate asked: 'Does the unsettling period between leaving school and the Army which prevents many of these boys from taking any but dead-end jobs without prospects for the future, cause or encourage many of the original lapses into crime?'[112]

The Youth Employment Service in 1949 reported the frequency with which boys changed jobs around the age of seventeen: 'Some of them are "drifters" and the knowledge that they will soon be called up makes the "I couldn't care less attitude" to work more pronounced.'[113] A survey of Scotsmen born in 1936 reported that: 'the uncertainty caused by impending National Service did not encourage stability'.[114]

Broadly speaking, those who did not hold down stable jobs in the year or two before national service fitted into one of three categories. The first of these, discussed above, consisted of grammar school boys who had left school at seventeen. They did not have much time to establish themselves in work before call-up and may in some cases have been working-class boys who did not feel entirely comfortable with the middle-class world that went with grammar schools. The second category, sometimes overlapping with the first, was made up of men who – knowing that they had a life of regular employment and pinched respectability ahead of them after military service – made a conscious decision to undertake short-term, unskilled jobs before they were called up.[115] The third category was composed of those who found it difficult to hold down jobs under any circumstances, and for whom the prospect of the call-up added to their difficulties. They had often attended that substratum of schools that existed below the ordinary tripartite categories and they sometimes had criminal records.

A survey of boys in London who endured some period of unemployment found that a third of them in one area had been before the juvenile courts. The great majority (278 youths) had attended 'secondary (ex-central)' schools – known after the Butler Education Act as 'secondary moderns'; in addition to this there were fifteen grammar school boys and fifteen who had attended technical schools. There were also thirteen who had been at approved schools – institutions for boys with criminal records or who were seen as requiring particular care – and thirteen who had been to special schools (for boys who were educationally subnormal). There were ten boys who had been at school in Eire and who presumably belonged to that substantial, and from the point of view of the authorities often troublesome, section of the working class that was still closely associated with Ireland. The report noted the fact that many came from backgrounds 'either at home or at school as a result of which irregularity of employment was not surprising'.[116]

Some men who were eventually classified as unfit had less stable employment records than those who went into the armed forces. Perhaps this was because instability of employment went with the physical deprivation or psychological problems that caused men to be classed as unfit. Perhaps it was because the prospect of call-up could overshadow a man's life even if he was not ultimately obliged to serve.[117]

Instability of employment was not always, from the point of view of boys themselves, a bad thing. Working-class young men did not necessarily see dead ends in the same places as middle-class adults did. Many of them might well have argued that even a few years in an enjoyable job was a rare opportunity to be seized eagerly and would probably have laughed if they had read a sociologist's report on one army conscript who became a professional footballer: 'he is doing well enough financially, but a footballer's life is a short one and it would have been better if he had completed his apprenticeship as a joiner'.[118]

For a lucky few, frequent change of jobs seems to have been a means by which enterprising boys who had not succeeded in conventional education groped their way towards an exit from the working class. John Ferris had grown up as the child of a single mother and spent some of his early years in a children's home and, partly because of his circumstances, was not able to go to grammar school. He left school at fifteen, having been told that his ambition to work in an office was inappropriate for one of his education. He worked for a time as a carpenter's mate, and then held fifteen or twenty jobs, mostly labouring ones, until he joined the army at eighteen. Like many men from relatively underprivileged backgrounds, he signed on for three years of service. After his demobilization, Ferris returned to education and in due course became an academic sociologist.

Some men had a sense of their own class position that did not match the social circumstances of their backgrounds. Arnold Wesker said that his officers found him disconcerting because 'Coming from no upper class I spoke like one – confident, articulate, well read.'[119] Ferris was also articulate and well-read. He conspicuously did not belong to the 'upper class' of Eton and Christ Church men, whom he was to encounter when he was a waiter in the officers' mess of a smart regiment. He did, however, have a clear sense of how he might differ from the classes immediately adjacent to his own. He knew that he did not fit with boys of his own age who had been to the relatively grand Abingdon grammar school but he did not feel entirely at home with his working-class relatives from rural Oxfordshire either. Indeed, he thought of his identity largely in terms of a rural/urban division. He chose to join the Royal Fusiliers (rather than his local county regiment) because he wanted to be in London, and he later began his academic career with a pioneering study of the gentrification of Barnsbury.[120]

In the 1950s, social workers, magistrates and youth leaders regarded one group of young men with particular concern. 'Teddy boys' or 'Teds' first came to public attention in 1953. They derived their name from their 'Edwardian' style of clothing. Commentators believed that there were between 10,000 and 30,000 Teds in London, which was, initially, the centre of the phenomenon. In the late 1950s, Teds were blamed for a succession of violent incidents in London, of which the most notorious was the Notting Hill riot of 1958, when young white men attacked West Indian immigrants.

Teddy boys seem to have been drawn mainly from the unskilled elements of the working class: 'market traders, porters, roadworkers, a lot of van boys, all in jobs that didn't offer much – labourers could cover the lot'.[121] Some suggested that Teds were the residue of young men – with relatively high pay but no long-term prospects – who had been left over when their more able, or conformist, contemporaries had been creamed off by the 11-plus or apprenticeships.

Was there a link between Teddy boys and national service? A

youth-club leader believed that violence by 'the Edwardians' was due, in large measure, to the fact that the lives of men between the ages of fifteen and eighteen were disrupted by the prospect of the call-up. She believed that young men who deferred their service until they were twenty or twenty-one fared better.[122] Others felt that raising the age of call-up had the opposite effect, and in 1955 the Minister of Education warned his colleagues that they would face 'the criticism that by raising the age of call-up they were increasing the gap between school-leaving age and national service, which was now regarded as fertile ground for juvenile delinquency'.[123] In 1962, one statistician suggested that the end of conscription itself was a reason for the fall in juvenile crime.[124]

Certainly by the late 1950s it sometimes looked as if the armed forces regarded Teds as being among their principal enemies. Army barbers cropped their hair and sergeants mocked their clothes.[125] 'Drill pigs' tried to break them: 'I seen the hard Teddy boys on their knees crying.'[126] Chaplains occasionally tried to redeem them: 'We have just had our talk from the Padre, which was so good that two "Teds" are coming to Church.'[127] Middle-class young men, the kind of people who would become officers, tended to regard all rough working-class recruits as Teddy boys.[128] Indeed 'Teddy boy' was a term applied to almost anyone that the army disliked – including the tough young men who spat and swore at British troops in Larnaca or Port Said.[129]

What did young men know about national service before it happened? Popular newspapers carried numerous reports about the life of servicemen – most of which did not suggest that it was attractive. The Central Office of Information made a documentary film in 1955 entitled *They Stand Ready*. Its central figure, John Saunders, was a young man of the 'good working class' (his service had been deferred while he completed his apprenticeship) who is called up to the Royal Armoured Corps. He is posted to Germany, where he becomes a corporal. The tone of the film was one of stoical resignation rather than celebration. National service was presented as a regrettable necessity.[130]

Individuals and associations published guidance for conscripts. The work of Basil Henriques exemplifies the tone of forced jollity in which they were often addressed. Born in 1890, he was educated at Harrow and Oxford. He was a magistrate who published a book on 'the prevention of unhappiness in children'[131] and who also wrote an introduction to Enid Blyton's *Six Bad Boys*. The National Association of Boys' Clubs published his pamphlet entitled *So You're Being Called-up*. In this, he told future conscripts: 'It's rather like going to the dentist; you dread it beforehand, but after it's all over, you are jolly glad you went.'[132]

In the mid 1950s, the Ministry of Labour organized information sessions for men who were about to be conscripted. However, the proportion of eighteen-year-olds who attended them was small and the most common question seemed to be the one that most preoccupied 'the better class' of boy: 'How can I obtain deferment?' Military representatives at such meetings were rarely impressive. Officials complained about a lieutenant colonel 'who passes alright but is not ideal' and a 'rank cockney' sergeant.[133]

Some employers helped prepare men for national service. Such initiatives were most common in large companies with personnel departments and also, not surprisingly, in companies that employed managers with military experience, though companies with Quaker traditions – Cadbury and Rowntree's – were also concerned about national service, perhaps because they were alert to the dangers that it might pose to the welfare of young men.

Most boys, however, did not work for such companies – only 27 per cent of national servicemen in the army (41 per cent in the RAF) had discussed their future with their employers.[134] Boys probably got more information from talking to their colleagues or friends over sweet tea and Woodbines than they did from pep talks by visiting dignitaries. A survey of 1951 found that 62 per cent of boys aged fifteen had discussed national service with 'friends in the forces'; by the age of eighteen, it was 94 per cent. A third of boys who had talked about national service with friends in the forces had received a negative impression from them. Talking about national service did not necessarily mean thinking about it – though the proportion who had 'not thought about it all' dropped from 62 per cent to 24 per cent.[135] Older brothers could be useful. One public school boy was surprised that his working-class comrades turned up at barracks with entire sets of kit that had belonged to their brothers. The boys then laid this on their bed for kit inspection, keeping it separate from the uniforms that they wore every day.[136]

As youths approached the age of call-up, attitudes polarized. The number of the indifferent dropped and the numbers of those who were favourable or unfavourable increased. Overall, 26 per cent of those aged eighteen were favourable to national service while 18 per cent were unfavourable. Even just before registration, however, 56 per cent of boys were still 'indifferent' about national service, or had given the matter little thought: 'National Service seems to be regarded by the majority of young men as something which just happens, about which they can do nothing.' Samuel Osborne was born in 1931 and called up into the Catering Corps at the age of twenty-one. Interviewed in 1987, he explained his feelings about it: 'it were just a sufferance at that time'.[137]

There was another problem. Explaining national service meant knowing what it was for. This was more complicated than it seemed. The middle-aged worthies who often volunteered themselves as guides for young men certainly had a clear vision of national service. They thought that it would instil fitness, leadership and team spirit. Officials at the Ministry of Labour took a more hard-headed approach. They knew that attempts to make national service seem exciting would just prepare boys for disappointment or more probably be greeted with derisive incredulity:

> It was positively harmful to hold up National Service as a 'high and noble destiny' if a young man was going to be engaged on menial tasks much of his time. Not everyone realized that life in the Forces in peace time was very humdrum and bristling with chores. The essential thing was to be frank.[138]

Sometimes there were sinister undercurrents beneath the brisk optimism with which influential men talked about national service. Sir Harold West, a Sheffield industrialist, took a particular interest in the welfare of young men before they were called up,[139] and, as president of the Sheffield and East Midland region of the Economic League, organized courses for apprentices about to undertake national service.

Major General Spurling of Northern Command – who regarded these courses, and West, highly – insisted that the League was 'completely divorced from any particular political activities except in so far as it is relentlessly opposed to Communism'. The Tory Under Secretary of State for War, however, decreed that the League, which campaigned against trade unions as well as Communism, was 'not apolitical' and must play no further official part in preparing young men for national service.[140]

Three problems faced those who talked most about young men before the call-up. First, such people were often associated with bodies that sought to organize young men – the boy scouts, the sea cadets, youth clubs or the 'missions' that public schools had established to bring the virtues of muscular Christianity to the urban poor.[141] However, the majority of conscripts were not associated with any youth organization or any organized leisure activity. The most striking feature of national servicemen was how divorced they were from the very institutions that were meant to represent 'youth'.

Secondly, there was a paradox in the attitude of many influential adults to youth and national service. They approved of military service and, indeed, often assumed that their task was 'bringing home to the public at large and to young men in particular the purpose of national service and its potential value to the man who undertakes it in the right spirit'.[142] At the same time, such influential adults had a strong conception of the life that they regarded as desirable for boys between leaving school and entering the armed forces. They approved of those who undertook apprenticeships or at least held steady jobs. They also believed that night classes and any activity that brought boys into regular and deferential contact with their elders were good things. The truth, though, was that the 'better kind of boy' – who led a structured life and who undertook education or training beyond the school-leaving age – was usually the most hostile to national service. Young men who disliked their work, changed jobs frequently and avoided participation in organized leisure pursuits were usually those who took to the armed forces most easily and it was these boys who often made up the bulk of regular recruits.

Thirdly, influential adults were often confronted with the uncomfortable sense that national service was making the 'problems' of youth worse rather than better. Rates of juvenile crime rose in the 1950s. Some working-class young men seemed to be turning their back on education, training or long-term planning of their lives and it often looked as if the prospect of being called up contributed to this. The King George's Jubilee Trust was forced to concede:

> Universal compulsory National Service for young men is something new. And because it is something that is likely to be with us for years to come, it has profoundly affected the outlook of the boy who leaves school at 15 years of age, and on whom there is no longer any compulsion to continue his education. For him it is more than a breakaway from education; it cuts his life into two almost unrelated parts – before and after National Service; it creates an artificial interlude in which the high hurdle still ahead of him obscures the need to plan and work for the future.[143]

6

Call-up

*I seem to remember, I was having this kind of fantasy or desire
not to go into the army . . . I remember I got my money for the
last term and I had something like £60 and there was a boat
for sale on the Isle of Skomer, and I remember it was £60 something and I was thinking, oh, if only I can get that boat I can
get, you know, I can get it, and live on it. This is a sort of obvious fantasy.*

Stuart Brisley (interviewed 1993)[1]

For most men, escaping the call-up was indeed a fantasy. Their first
contact with the machinery of national service came when they
were summoned to register at one of the 1,200 Ministry of Labour
centres – registration taking place on a Saturday.[2] The arrival of the
first envelope around their eighteenth birthday was itself an unpleasant memory for some. Robin Ollington recalled how, in January 1948,
his mother had shouted that he had better get used to getting up
because 'his papers' had arrived: 'I remember going under the covers
and dreading going downstairs.'[3]

A high proportion of men, at times a fifth, failed to register for
national service at the correct time,[4] but most did so when reminded –
though numbers of defaulters increased in the late 1950s, as men
sought to avoid being called up before national service was abolished.[5] A small group, presumably made up of those with strong
objections to military service, did not register at all: 2,387 men fell
into this category between 1949 and 1960. Most of these were eventually prosecuted.[6]

In the late 1940s, the British state had great powers over its subjects. Compulsory schooling and the National Health Service meant that the authorities had a good idea where any eighteen-year-old was likely to be. The end of the Second World War made conscription easier to enforce: civilian life was more orderly, and military obligations now fell exclusively on young men. Policemen could be paid bounties for arresting deserters,[7] and sometimes questioned boys simply because they seemed 'of military age'. As national service came to an end in 1960, the Ministry of Labour recorded just 105 men with outstanding military obligations who were 'untraceable' or 'in suspense'.[8]

Civil servants had a good idea how many men would be available in each year, though they could not be completely sure until registration had taken place. With regard to the 1952–3 intake, the authorities knew that 352,000 men had been born in 1934. They believed that 42,500 of these had died before they reached the age of eighteen, 1,500 were blind or certified insane, 6,500 had emigrated and 21,500 had joined the forces as regulars. A further 103,500 would have their service deferred. Thus 176,500 men would proceed to medicals. Of these, 29,500 could be expected to fail the medical and 2,500 would be 'conscientious objectors etc'. A further 26,000 men joined the RAF after their medical, presumably because they hoped to avoid posting to one of the other services – 2,000 men also volunteered for the navy at this stage and 2,500 men volunteered for the army. Finally, 1,000 men emigrated after their medical. Overall, 113,000 men born in 1934 would be available for posting as national servicemen. However, 61,500 older men, who had been granted deferments, which were now about to expire, would top up this number.[9]

The power of the state was not, however, felt equally by every young man in the land. Anyone who wanted to go to university or to obtain employment in the public sector or, indeed, to obtain employment of any legally recognized kind knew that he would face the question: 'Have you done your national service?' Most eighteen-year-olds came from families where defying the law would have seemed inconceivable, but escaping national service was easier for men from communities that were suspicious of the police. The Census Office was, in general, confident of its ability to trace young men – though it accepted that a few – 'possibly gypsies or young vagrants'[10] – were invisible. Escape was also easier for anyone with access to work in the informal economy and anyone with family in the Republic of Ireland. Irish origins were a source of useful ambiguity.[11] A man who went to the Republic was safe from conscription into the British forces. When the British government declared an amnesty for wartime deserters in 1953, 400 men who had fled from the British armed forces after the end of the war, a few of whom were national servicemen, emerged from the Republic under the mistaken impression that they would be covered by the amnesty.[12] Inhabitants of Northern Ireland were exempt from national service. Irishmen resident on the mainland for more than two years were liable for conscription, and most accepted this obligation 'without demur',[13] but an Irishman might claim that he was just visiting and the British state was less likely to be able to find out his real date of birth or military record. A study of naval deserters concluded that men went on the run in the summer, when seasonal work was easy to find: 'the affectation of an assumed Southern Irish name and accent enables a man in desertion to obtain registration at a Labour Exchange without difficult questions being asked'.[14]

Some men contrived to live outside the formal economy so successfully that the state was unaware of their existence. Charles Richardson was established as a 'scrap metal merchant' and seems to have conducted his affairs in a way that did not involve much interaction with the official world – except when he was arrested. One of these prosecutions had disastrous consequences for him: 'They noticed in their wisdom that I was nineteen, and wanted to know why I was not in khaki like other nineteen-year-olds.'[15]

Men who lived outside the world of tax, identity cards and fixed abode are, by definition, hard for the historian to trace. Occasionally, a court case gives a glimpse of how some men evaded military duties. Michael Charteris and Donald Muddiman met in Liverpool prison. Charteris was keen to avoid military service and Muddiman, having already been a soldier and discharged on medical grounds, suggested that he should impersonate Charteris, join up under his name and then get discharged again. The scheme failed because Muddiman deserted as soon as he received his first pay and the military police went to the house of the real-life Charteris.[16] Other men were more skilful. In 1954 Paul Squires was prosecuted for driving without a licence. However, he appealed against his conviction, claiming that the man observed at the wheel of his car had, in fact, been his twin brother, an army deserter who could not be located.[17]

No group of fit men in mainland Britain was systematically excluded from conscription. Conscripts were members of all political parties. Regular soldiers were discharged for being Communists but there was no such rule with regard to conscripts;[18] a Conservative MP insisted that men should not be prevented from obtaining national service commissions because they had, in a moment of undergraduate indiscretion, joined the Communist party.[19]

Some believed that black men were discreetly excluded from the call-up. It is certainly true that the armed forces did not want to recruit large numbers of non-white soldiers, but they never enforced a 'colour bar',[20] and, in 1954, about seventy 'colonial immigrants' were called up every month.[21] By the late 1950s, West Indians were a small but noticeable part of the conscript army. Robert Douglas served in the Ordnance Corps with Percy Lewis – 'a diminutive Jamaican who arrived in Britain just in time to be called up'.[22]

Unlike their counterparts in the states of continental Europe in the late nineteenth century, the British military authorities rarely faced problems with men who did not speak the national language. About 3,800 Welsh speakers reached national service age each year,[23] but only 250 of them spoke no English and most of these were excused from service because they worked in agriculture. The Wrexham recruiting office reckoned that only one or two monoglot Welsh speakers entered the armed forces each year.[24] The occasional Gaelic speaker also surfaced in the armed forces – though most of them too would have been excluded as agricultural workers. Those who presented themselves as spokesmen for Welsh interests believed that lacking complete mastery of the English language was a disadvantage for Welsh conscripts and sometimes tied this to a wider sense of Welsh identity: 'Wales is a land of mountains and was, until comparatively recent times, a pastoral country. When attacked by professional armies, the natural tactics of the Welsh were to withdraw into the mountains, driving their beasts before them and resorting to guerrilla warfare. Wales has known little of professional soldiering.'[25] Officials recognized more prosaically that 'Welsh National Servicemen who are to varying degrees bi-lingual can be put at a positive disadvantage in the Army because they tend to think more naturally in Welsh and find it hard to adjust themselves to an environment in which English is the main language.'[26] The navy and air force simply excluded men with imperfect English; the army made sure that there were Welsh-speaking testers to interview them at Ministry of Labour medicals.

Scottish and Welsh nationalists sometimes objected to serving in what they regarded as a foreign army – though the influence of both groups was limited in the period of national service. John Grieve – son of the poet and nationalist Christopher Grieve, who wrote under the pen name of Hugh MacDiarmid – declared himself a conscientious objector in 1950. He did so partly on political grounds – arguing that national service was contrary to the Act of Union – though he also claimed to have an absolute opposition to war. His appeal was refused – partly, it seems, because the tribunal believed that he would be willing to fight against England.[27]

Between 0.3 and 0.5 per cent of men called up claimed to have conscientious objections to military service.[28] Objectors appeared before one of seven local tribunals, composed of up to five people, presided over by a judge or barrister. There were four possible outcomes. Some men were granted release from service without conditions. (This was rare – though it was the only outcome some pacifists would accept.) Some were required to perform military service in a non-combatant unit, such as the Medical Corps. Some were required to work outside the armed forces in some area recognized as being of particular value. Finally, some had their appeals denied and, if they refused to serve, were sent for trial. Between January 1949 and June 1960, 8,284 men passed before tribunals. Of these, 3,275 were set to appropriate civilian work, 1,653 were assigned to non-combatant service in the forces and 197 were granted an unconditional discharge; 3,159 applications failed. Men who objected to a decision could appeal to one of the two appellate tribunals. In 1959, 227 men did so and 102 of them succeeded in attaining some change to the original decision.[29]

Those exempted if they undertook specified civilian work were required to do this for two months longer than they would have served in the forces; the extra period was designed to match the reserve obligations that would have been attached to military service. A few obtained easy civilian postings. A dentist was required to treat school children for two years;[30] an accountant worked in his father's firm – his father was a solicitor and seems to have known the chairman of the tribunal in question.[31] The Friends' Ambulance Unit employed conscientious objectors and service in the FAU could seem remarkably like service in the armed forces. Leaders in the unit were chosen, at least initially, largely from among those who had been prefects at Quaker public schools. Men were put through a period of training that included morning runs, route marches and lights-out at ten. Alcohol was forbidden, but many men, like their contemporaries in the armed forces, began to smoke during this period. Finally, they were 'posted' and the lucky ones got to travel – some to Iran and Southern Rhodesia.

Some men disregarded the verdicts of tribunals and did not attend preliminary medical examinations for national service; a few refused to make any concession to military authority and simply failed to turn up for medicals without making a formal claim to be conscientious objectors. Such men were tried and sometimes sentenced to successive terms of prison as they repeatedly refused to attend medicals. Between 1 January 1949 and 30 September 1960, 4,792 men failed to attend medicals. Of these 1,150 were successfully prosecuted; the remainder, presumably, had a good reason for non-attendance. On first prosecution, penalties ranged from fines, imposed on 291 men, to imprisonment for more than a year, imposed on twenty-one men. There were 342 further prosecutions, which resulted in 125 fines and 217 prison terms, six of them of more than one year.[32] An objector had the right to make a further appeal to a tribunal after he had served three months in prison. The Ministry of Labour did not always find it easy to secure what it regarded as the appropriate punishment for conscientious objectors. Magistrates pointed to legislation that discouraged sending men under twenty-one without previous convictions to prison. Some sent convicted men to Borstal, which objectors disliked because it meant that they were denied the chance of appeal they would have enjoyed if sent to prison.[33] One magistrate remarked that he could see no reason to imprison a man of previously good character and imposed a small fine.[34]

Some men confronted the armed forces even after they had been posted. Private William Moulton, for example, first applied for registration as a conscientious objector in 1948 but his service was deferred, presumably so that he could complete an apprenticeship, and he did not appear before a tribunal until March 1951. The tribunal decreed that he should be registered but compelled to perform 'non-combatant duties only'. He did not accept this verdict and refused to obey orders when he arrived at the depot of the Pioneer Corps. He was court-martialled and sentenced to four months in a civilian prison.[35] Rex Dunham was sent to prison for a year in October 1959 after he had refused the direction of a tribunal that he should take hospital work in lieu of military service. He said that 'he could not obey the dictates of man'.[36]

A few men developed, or expressed, conscientious objections only after having arrived in their units or even after having completed the bulk of their service. Gabriel Newfield decided to present himself as a conscientious objector after having completed his full-time service, which he enjoyed, and at a time when he had only fairly light part-time duties to discharge. The War Office helpfully explained that he would have to serve three months in detention before he could appear before a tribunal. He turned up at his camp and refused to wear uniform, the most common disciplinary offence committed by men who wanted to express objections to service. Eventually, he managed to persuade the military authorities to court-martial him and was sentenced to ninety-six days – the ideal sentence from his point of view. He served his time in the camp prison – reading books and talking on first-name terms with the national servicemen set to guard him. At the end of his time, he appeared before a tribunal, which accepted his objections as legitimate and discharged him.[37]

Newfield was lucky. He served in a unit – the Medical Corps – that was not famous for brutal discipline and that, in any case, contained many conscientious objectors. Furthermore, he was articulate and had held the rank of sergeant during his own service. John Whitely, who became a Quaker while undertaking national service with the

Grenadier Guards, had a harder time.[38] It was often alleged that men who refused to wear uniform had been made to stand naked.[39]

Conscientious objectors were unusual but not, so far as one can tell, unpopular with the public or their own contemporaries. Many of them provided character references, which were usually sympathetic to the individual, if not to the notion of conscientious objection. Harold Pinter's former housemaster at Hackney Downs School wrote:

> I hold Conscientious objectors in no very great esteem and I think that a spell in one or other of the services would do HAROLD PINTER a world of good, but I must in justice to him say that I have always found him reasonable, intelligent and pleasant (all) above the average and that I have no reason whatever to doubt his sincerity.

His headmaster added that Pinter had been prone to 'discard the drab, the unattractive and the difficult' and that any alternative service imposed on him 'should be of a nature which will compel him to exercise much self-control and self-discipline ... which ... will have a high value in moulding Pinter's character'.[40]

Sometimes support for conscientious objectors could be expressed by unexpected people and in moving terms. A manager of a Birmingham engineering firm wrote to the appellate tribunal about a Jehovah's Witness who had cancelled his apprenticeship in order to pursue his religious life: 'he was so earnest in his desires and prepared to make the sacrifice, we felt it unwise to force him to carry on his apprenticeship ... he left with our best wishes for his future.[41]

Ordinary conscripts sometimes resented men who were seen to have evaded service in some dishonest way, but not many imagined that conscientious objection was an easy way out. A few former conscripts seem to have regarded conscientious objectors as 'unmanly' but more common was the one who said: 'I think you would have had to be very brave to be a conscientious objector.'[42] Peter Duncumb was an RAF national service pilot. His brother had been a conscientious objector during the war and had been sent to Burma with the Friends' Ambulance Unit. Duncumb had a high opinion of his brother, who had 'seen more real war than I ever did'.[43]

Some servicemen had doubts of their own about the morality

of war, or at least the kinds of wars for which they were being trained; many felt, especially during the hellish weeks of basic training, that a willingness to stand in the way of the military juggernaut required heroic courage. David Batterham volunteered for parachute training – which meant being trucked to an airfield with a group of tough young men singing 'they scraped him off the tarmac like a lump of strawberry jam' and undertaking the terrifying first jump from a tethered barrage balloon. All the same, he felt that his father, who had been an objector during the war, was braver than himself. He seems to have failed to gain a commission partly because he pointed out to the selection board that pacifism required a degree of moral courage that he himself lacked.[44] Geoffrey Lloyd was another upper-middle-class boy who had flirted with claiming conscientious objection but who eventually, having exhausted all possibilities of deferment, was called up shortly after having been elected to a fellowship of King's College, Cambridge. He was set to scraping caked filth from a urinal with a bayonet and decided that life in the officers' mess would be more agreeable – presumably, unlike Batterham, he kept quiet about his anti-militarist feelings when he appeared before the selection board.[45]

At first, conscientious objection was almost exclusively reserved for those whose objection was religious[46] and for those who stated an opposition to all war, rather than opposition to the particular tasks that they might be set by the British government. Quakers, Christadelphians, Jehovah's Witnesses and Seventh-day Adventists were all likely to be pacifists, as were some Methodists – though there was no theoretical impediment to a member of any Church stating that he had religious objections to war.

In 1952, Richard Pankhurst, the son of the suffragette Sylvia Pankhurst, had his application to be registered as a conscientious objector rejected because he said that he would have been willing to fight against Hitler but objected to participating in the colonial war against Mau Mau in Kenya.[47] Harry Wolfe Lipschitz began his appeal against military service by citing Thomas Masaryk's claim that his race was 'the human race' and went on to say that he was not a pacifist and would have fought against fascism 'because the evils of fascism were greater than the evils of war itself '. His appeal was refused,[48] as was that of a man who said that he would only be willing to serve in an army of 'the world federation'.[49]

As time went on, tribunals became more prepared to respect secular objections and more willing to allow for the possibility that men might object to particular kinds of war, nuclear or colonial. Bernard Crick, born in 1929, avoided the call-up with a succession of educational deferments and foreign research fellowships. However, he returned to Britain in 1955 to find that the government had recently raised the age of eligibility for call-up to thirty-five, and that he was thus still liable. He then drafted papers, in which he said that he had previously been an unconditional opponent of war but that his position had changed: 'while I have no ultimate objection of conscience to being part of a conscript army so long as it appears to be in the undoubted national interest and to be a possible deterrent to total war, yet I would refuse to take part in any lesser wars'.[50] He was not attracted to the public displays of opposition that his friend Gabriel Newfield made and it is not clear whether his claims to conscientious objection were upheld or whether he avoided the call-up in some other way.

David Hockney went before a tribunal in Leeds in September 1957. His objections to service had nothing to do with religion and sprang mainly from distaste for colonial wars. He remembered that the panel asked 'no really wise ... and no really stupid question'. Hockney's case was accepted – perhaps because the panel sensed the iron will that lay under his diffident manner or perhaps because national service was running down. He worked in a hospital and finished his time on a general medical ward, where he acquired an intimate acquaintance with death that few serving soldiers would have had.[51]

The machinery of conscientious objection worked best for those who were articulate and able to express some philosophical position with regard to military service, those who were, as one objector put it, 'the verbally adroit';[52] though the man who told the chairman of the tribunal that his question was 'both ungrammatical and incorrect' did not advance his cause.[53]

It was sometimes taken for granted that conscientious objectors would be educated men: one guide for Christian pacifists described the career of 'Tony' who 'hopes one day to be a classics master in a grammar school' but was, for the time being, a 'bricklayer helping to relieve the housing shortage'.[54] The Friends' Peace Committee Conscription Group told an official committee on tribunals in February 1956 that they should make more allowance 'for the unintellectual boy'.[55] A Sunday School teacher, trying to make a case on behalf of a working-class boy who belonged to the Open Brethren, wrote: 'I know that he is not blessed with great fluency of speech and that although his understanding of things is firmly implanted in his own mind and heart, he has great difficulty in transmitting his mind coherently and lucidly to others.'[56]

Quakers had advantages in dealing with the tribunals. They were a recognized and well-established body with a tradition of objection that extended back into both wars. They had lawyers, publications and an organization. Their argument with the military authorities was conducted in a language that both sides understood. The Quakers went out of their way to help other objectors, and educated men, who found it easy to adapt to the culture of Quakerism, were particularly likely to take advantage of this help. Quaker boarding schools were important in creating leaders who could interact with their counterparts in the Anglican middle class. In some ways, the tribunals functioned like the War Office Selection Boards for potential officers and both favoured school-prefect types who could stand up straight and give clear answers in an unwavering voice. Thomas Green (headmaster of Bootham's, the Quaker school, from 1944 to 1961) told his charges who were due to appear before tribunals that 'one only had to mention Ackworth [another Quaker school], Bootham and Quakers and you would be all right'. Roger Bush remembered: 'Although I could not claim to be a convinced Quaker, the tribunal clearly took the view that ten years at Quaker schools had rendered me unfit for anything other than the alternative service option.'[57]

David Morrish was a good example of the kind of man who was well received by tribunals. He grew up in Plymouth during the 1930s with conventional patriotic opinions. In his late teens, however, he began to question both his Anglican background and his military patriotism. He went to Exeter University partly because it would give him time to sort his ideas out before conscription. He acquired a Quaker girlfriend and began to attend meetings of the Friends. He took a teaching course and then managed to fund his way through two years of a postgraduate degree before taking a fellowship in Wisconsin. When he came back in 1956, at the age of twenty-four, he finally decided that he should face the tribunal as an objector. He recognized that he had a relatively easy time – partly because he was supported by the Quakers, partly because he was willing to serve in the Friends' Ambulance Unit and partly because national service was coming to an end anyway. The tribunal recognized that he could probably have claimed further exemption as a teacher and that he should be given credit for moral courage.[58]

As with many aspects of national service, class mattered when it came to being recognized as a conscientious objector, and some men associated with the Friends came, in a Quakerish way, to worry about the privileges that they enjoyed: 'It was said that Quakers presenting themselves to the board were always nodded through but that if one was a Jehovah's Witness, who apparently hold similar views about killing people, it was more difficult to get exemption. I think this must have been a "Class Thing".'[59]

Jehovah's Witnesses certainly had a more awkward time in front of tribunals than Quakers. Francis Mackay, a part-time labourer who sold Bibles and editions of *The Watchtower*, and was therefore regarded by his own Church, but not by the state, as a minister of religion, told a tribunal that he was not a pacifist because he would fight if ordered by God to do so. He could not imagine the circumstances under which God would give such an order but 'God will take everything into his own hands.' Mackay eventually escaped prison or conscription by taking a job as a coal miner.[60] Other members of his Church did not escape at all. In 1957, when the end of national service was in view, a magistrate complained about his continuing obligation to send Jehovah's Witnesses to prison.[61]

Bryan Reed, a Quaker and a member of the Central Board for Conscientious Objectors, sought to put apocalyptic theology into terms that lawyers might understand: 'As you are no doubt aware, the Jehovah's Witnesses believe in the coming of a theocratic government, but have, in the meantime, no interest in changing one form of temporal government for another.'[62] The chairman of the London local tribunal said that he and his colleagues had difficulty in granting applications of Jehovah's Witnesses because 'they often seemed unaware that the belief of their own Church was that Jehovah had told his chosen people that they might fight for Palestine with carnal weapons'.[63] In 1956, thirty-four out of thirty-nine men prosecuted under the National Service Act were Jehovah's Witnesses.[64]

Apart from those with conscientious objections to national service, certain groups were excused from conscription – technically, their call-up was deferred until they reached an age at which they were no longer liable. The list of 'reserved occupations' was, however, smaller than it had been in the Second World War and it was progressively reduced as the immediate needs of post-war reconstruction were met. Agricultural workers were more or less automatically deferred until November 1951; after this date they could apply for deferment and quite large numbers were granted it. Coal miners, fishermen and merchant seamen were allowed to defer – the last were expected to join the Royal Naval Volunteer Reserve.

After the war in Europe ended, men were no longer compelled to work in mines but until February 1947 they could still volunteer for mining as an alternative to military service.[65] After this date, a man could escape from military service by becoming a miner but he would be called up into the forces if he left the industry before he was twenty-six. A few men took jobs as miners because it provided them with a means of escaping military service. Ken Coates worked in the pits of Derbyshire and Nottingham from 1948 to 1956 because he did not want to join an army that was fighting an imperialist war in Malaya.[66] However, movement was more marked in the opposite direction. As soon as the war ended, many men left the pits and often regarded even long engagements in the regular army as preferable to mining. In 1951, only 1 per cent of national service soldiers had been 'mining workers' but 16 per cent of army volunteers belonged to this category.[67]

In 1951, the government tried to persuade men who had been miners and were now in the forces to return to the pits. It expected to recruit around 1,000 miners per year at national service medicals.[68] Men were also released from the forces if they agreed to return to mining. Not many seem to have taken the offer. At the end of 1951, only three ex-miners in the air force had applied to return to their former profession.[69] Even men serving on the front line in Korea – where ex-miners were valued for their toughness and digging skills – were rarely tempted to go back.

Fathers who worked underground were often keen for their sons to escape from mining and regarded military service as a small price to pay in return for this. David Wilson was the son of a miner from the north east. His father urged him not to go down the pit and he took an engineering apprenticeship before being called up.[70] Ernest Dobson came from a similar background. His father 'didn't want us to go to pit'. However, Dobson's attempt to get a job as a bricklayer failed and for a time he did work in a mine. After a couple of years he resigned: 'the best thing I ever did . . . never felt safe . . . me dad being in all the falls and that'. He worked in a cosmetics factory for nine months before his call-up.[71]

A variety of more esoteric requests were made for exemption from, or deferment of, national service. A group of musicians, notable among whom was Dame Myra Hess, pointed out the damage that could be done to a musician's career by call-up.[72] Winston Churchill intervened to defend the interests of apprentice jockeys.[73] Theological students presented another kind of problem. Men in holy orders were usually exempt from national service but men preparing for ordination were not. The Church of England felt that national service would be an advantage for its clergy and actively discouraged them from seeking to avoid it. Nonconformist churches objected to the imposition of military, or at least combatant, service on theological students. The Catholic Church objected to the calling up of theological students on the practical grounds that it would disrupt their long training programme. The government was keen to avoid too much discussion of the matter and seems to have operated a discreet policy that allowed students to defer until the moment of their ordination and then secure exemption.[74]

Notions as to what constituted work of national importance that might justify deferment of military service changed in the period from 1945 to the late 1950s. During the Second World War, large groups of men had been kept out of the forces because they were doing civilian work that was vital to the war effort. The National Service Act of 1948 aimed to do away with such large-scale exemption. Industrial workers were not exempted and neither at first were men with particular scientific skills. Lord Cherwell, Churchill's scientific adviser, urged the government not to make potential science students waste their time on the parade ground,[75] and some research scientists escaped national service – usually being deferred to the point at which their call-up became impractical. In theory, the maximum age of call-up was raised to thirty-five in the mid 1950s to catch men who had deferred for educational reasons or studied abroad. In practice, the authorities were not very assiduous in pursuit of evaders by this stage.[76] Increasing numbers of deferments were granted for research scientists, for science teachers and eventually for science graduates working in private industry. Deferments were also sometimes granted to skilled workers involved in technological projects seen as being of particular national importance. The service departments sometimes protested about these concessions – though the Admiralty also asked for deferment to be granted to civilian workers on its own projects. In practice, the general improvement in education meant that the forces still received a larger absolute number of science graduates until 1957.[77]

After registration, men were called for a preliminary examination conducted under the aegis of the Ministry of Labour. The length of time between registration and examination varied, partly because the authorities sometimes used delays as a means to slow down the rate of intake of men to the forces. This tactic was employed in the late 1940s,[78] and again ten years later as national service moved towards its end.[79] In some cases, men had waited for over a year after registration without hearing anything further.[80]

Potential conscripts were called to gloomy municipal buildings – exuding 'the faintly salty smell of damp concrete and stale cigarettes' – to be inspected. By 1955 there were ninety-five boards in sixty-one centres across the country, which had, by this stage, examined 2 million men and passed 1.5 million fit for service.[81] Officials, and conscripts themselves, talked of 'medical boards' – though, in fact, the inspections were concerned with more than physical health and no one appeared before a 'board' in a formal way. Men were examined by a doctor and, usually, took a written test. They also talked to a 'military interviewing officer', most of whom were retired officers and rarely men of much charm.[82]

From 1948 onwards, men were classified according to the PUL-HEEMS test – the acronym stood for physical capacity, upper limb function, locomotion, hearing, eyesight (with one rating for each eye), mental capacity (intelligence) and stability (emotional and mental). Functions were graded on a scale of 1 to 8 – though, in fact, the full range of grades was only used for eyesight – so that, for example, the only possible grades for physical capacity were 2, 3, 5, 6, 7 and 8. The only possible grades for mental capacity and stability were 2, 3 and 8. With regard to everything except eyesight, it was suggested that qualities 1 and 2 should imply fitness for 'full combatant service in any part of the world'; 3 implied 'restricted service in any part of the world'; 4 and 5 meant 'full combatant service in temperate climates'; 6 meant 'restricted service in temperate climates'; 7 meant 'service in the United Kingdom' and 8 meant 'permanently unfit for service'. Each man was then given an overall grade of between I and IV. Men in grade IV were hardly ever used, except for doctors and dentists, who could perform physically undemanding tasks as medical officers.

Assessment of intelligence and mental stability depended on written tests. Men were divided into M.2, who were considered 'able readily to assimilate ordinary forms of instruction and to act on their own initiative'; M.3, 'Men of a lower standard but who can be expected to assimilate simple instruction and to discharge their duties without close supervision'; and M.8, men who would require close supervision or be unfit for service. Those who failed to obtain the minimum score were interviewed and, unless there was strong evidence to the contrary, were to be regarded as of 'lower intelligence'. Evidence of intelligence beyond the test might be revealed by 'school record, literacy, the nature of employment since leaving school and wages earned'. In 1950, on one of the occasions when the army thought, wrongly, that it would be able to abolish the Pioneer Corps and thus reduce the admission of 'dull' soldiers, the Ministry of Labour introduced a new test of intelligence (the R 50). Men who performed badly on the tests were interviewed and divided into three categories: 'satisfactory', 'borderline dull' and 'definitely dull'. From November 1950 to April 1951, 71,458 men were tested; 13,786 of these scored less than 25 and were interviewed. Examination of a sample of those who were interviewed showed that 40.1 per cent were put in the first category, 58.5 per cent in the second and 1.4 per cent in the third.[83] The tests were presented to recruits 'in a precisely standard way, known as the patter'.[84] The authorities understood, however, that the examination was not entirely scientific. It was hard for interviewers to distinguish 'intellectual defect' from 'personality defect' or apathy.[85] Medical boards tended to interpret 'sub-normal' as 'bordering on mentally defective'.[86]

Final decisions about men's suitability to serve were made by the medical boards. From 1950 until 1953, tests and interviews were administered by servicemen.[87] Indeed, some of the testers who appraised potential recruits were themselves conscripts who became 'sergeant testers'. Not surprisingly, the quasi-civilian life of attachment to the Ministry of Labour was regarded as an attractive posting.[88] Such positions were reserved for men who had deferred their own call-up and who were, therefore, older than most of the men they would test.[89]

The Wanstead Office employed three sergeants and tested about 4,000 recruits in eight months. One of them recalled that some of those they interviewed were 'pathetic'. Asked what he read, one of them replied: 'Bread, carrots, potatoes – same as everyone else'; another, apparently in the grip of 'serious physical and neurological disorders', told his interviewer that he had been born on 'April Fool's Day'.[90] The testers believed that some men who failed tests suffered from the educational disruption of the war and that others had not had regular schooling because they were the sons of 'bargees and showmen'.[91]

Emotional stability was the most obviously subjective judgement that medical boards were required to make. Interviewers examined men's records at school and work. They looked for evidence of: 'Personality disturbance shown by excessive resentment, suspicion, multiple grievances or false ideas or any difficulties at home, school or work' as well as for physical symptoms – including stammers, bed-wetting or 'silly inappropriate laughter'. They were also to look for evidence of mental illness in the family, broken homes and records of commitment to mental hospitals or convictions for criminal offences.[92]

Sometimes information about young men was circulated without much regard to their privacy. At a meeting to inform the public about national service, two parents told visiting officials that their sons suffered from conditions (a damaged foot in one case and 'underdevelopment' in the other) that they would not wish to disclose at their medical.[93] In both cases, the information was passed to the board. After a medical in 1952, the authorities called in Roger Hall's father, a butcher, to complain about the fact that Roger was a vegetarian.[94]

There were many complaints that Ministry of Labour medical boards passed an excessive number of men as fit.[95] Occasionally recruits with undiagnosed conditions died during their service.[96] More commonly, they were thrown out during later medical inspections, particularly at the beginning of basic training, or because they proved unable to stand the pace of training – though, occasionally, it was also alleged that training sergeants had ignored Ministry of Labour medical classifications and subjected men to demands that were beyond their capacities.[97] Of 1,726 men examined when they first arrived in one command in the first quarter of 1956, forty-two were immediately discharged because of poor eyesight.[98] Terence Morris was discharged from the Ordnance Corps in 1953. He was partially sighted, had attended a school for the blind and carried a blind person's free transport pass: the medical board had placed him in grade II.[99] Dick Langstaff was passed even though he told the doctor that he could not see the test chart let alone read any of the letters on it – he was discharged after twenty-three days.[100] Around 1 per cent of men who passed Ministry of Labour medical boards in 1952 proved unfit to serve within their first few weeks in the forces,[101] some after a single day of service. A War Office report of 1956 suggested that medical boards were so concerned with preventing the 'shrimshanker getting away with it' that they let unfit men through.[102]

Perhaps doctors on the Ministry of Labour medical boards were keen to give young men the benefits of service or to punish those whom they regarded as reluctant to serve.[103] There is not, however, much evidence that unfit men were passed as a matter of policy. Ministry of Labour statistics show three things. First, that the proportion who failed the medical varied from year to year. Second, that the overall trend was up and failure rates became very high in the last three years of national service. Third, that failure rates for men who deferred their service, and therefore underwent their medicals some years after registration, were sometimes higher than failure rates for men who underwent their medicals soon after their eighteenth birthday. For example, among men born in 1929 who underwent their medicals by the end of 1948, the failure rate was 13.5 per cent; in 1950, the failure rate for men born in 1929 was 27.4 per cent – meaning that deferred men were failing in larger numbers than those who had been inspected when they were eighteen. At first glance, this is surprising. One would expect – and officials did expect[104] – that men who had deferred to complete their education or apprenticeships would be fitter than those who entered the forces at the age of eighteen. Increasing failure rates may have owed a little to better techniques of investigation, such as the systematic use of X-rays.[105] More importantly, though, the authorities seem deliberately to have used medical requirements to slow intake during the 1950s when they had less need of recruits.

Sometimes, the forces discussed controlling the national service intake through medical examination in explicit ways. During the Korean War, they took men from categories that would previously have been rejected[106] and, as demand for recruits dropped in the late 1950s, they rejected whole categories of men. Sometimes the variation was achieved in more discreet ways, by changing the numbers placed in each category rather than varying the categories that were accepted. Thus, the proportion of men placed in grade III increased from 5.4 per cent in 1948 to 16.4 per cent in early 1960.[107]

Testing national servicemen revealed some patterns. The 'harvest' was better in the second half of each year than in the first. The autumn entry contained a disproportionate number of men who had deferred their service to complete their education or to finish apprenticeships. Of those entering the armed forces in September 1951, 26.4 per cent had completed an apprenticeship before they joined up,[108] while the overall proportion of men who came to the forces after having completed apprenticeships seems to have been rather less than 15 per cent in that year. The RAF talked of an 'academic flush' at the end of the school summer term[109] and reckoned that the average IQ of men admitted from August to November was 104, while that of men admitted from February to June was 96. One report suggested: 'the actual numbers available for the more highly skilled trades are almost double as many in a good week in November as in a poor week in March'.[110]

Health also varied by region. Army medical statisticians noted, for example, that a conscript from Glasgow was almost three times as likely to have respiratory disease as one from East Anglia.[111] One study of Glaswegians born in 1932 – who had been 'cradled, therefore, in the lean years of the early 'thirties, years when the shadow of unemployment lay heavily over Clydeside, and nurtured largely during the war of 1939–45, years of storm and disorganization' – showed that a third of them, compared to just less than a fifth of the national population, had been rejected for service.[112]

The Royal Air Force aimed to reject about 20 per cent of men who put it down as their first choice but it fixed the level at 25 per cent for certain counties. It had no fixed target for Kent – presumably because this was an area where the RAF believed young men to be healthy and well educated. The army studied scores for general intelligence, education level, mechanical ability and physical ability. Men with the highest educational scores made up 10.1 per cent of the total entry but 13.7 per cent of those from the Home Counties and 4.4 per cent of those from Glasgow and south west Scotland. Those from the suburbs did better than those from the country and small towns who, in turn, did better than those from the middle of large towns.[113]

Some men tried, with varying degrees of determination, to fail their medical and recounted colourful stories of how they had smoked a cigarette with crushed aspirin, gorged themselves on butterscotch or affected a chronic limp. Many thought that they could fail the medical if they were 'diagnosed' as homosexual. Michael Parkinson considered imitating a friend who had gone to the medical wearing his sister's underwear and his mother's perfume.[114] The novelist Paul Bailey said to the examining doctor, 'I think I may be a homosexual.' He was told, 'we have failed you anyway' and sent to see a specialist.'[115] In fact, Ministry of Labour instructions gave no specific guidance on what to do with homosexuals – though it may be that examining doctors would simply have regarded this as one form of 'instability'. The air force specifically ruled out homosexuality as a reason for rejection, even when a national service recruit 'presented to the Recruiting

Officer a doctor's certificate describing his homosexual tendencies with a view to being excused Service'. Regulars would be dismissed for homosexuality but 'there is no authority for exemption from National Service on similar grounds'.[116]

Most youths, even if they were unenthusiastic about military service, did not try to fail the medical. Few eighteen-year-olds wanted to be told that they were unfit, and failing the medical occasionally seems to have undermined their confidence so badly that it disrupted their civilian careers. It was presumably disheartening for a man to hear (in this case fourteen years after the examination) that he was prone 'to attacks of depression often as a reaction to home difficulties' and was also liable to 'psychosomatic complaints'.[117] Results of medicals were communicated to the Post Office, which wanted to know about the health of its employees, and the Australian immigration authorities until the mid 1950s.[118] Even in the late 1960s, men seem to have felt that having failed their medical disadvantaged them with regard to life assurance policies, employment or permission to emigrate to South Africa.[119]

At their preliminary interview, men were invited to say which of the services they wished to join. Their chances of getting what they wanted were, in fact, uneven. The army's need for conscripts was greater than that of the other services and most men would go into the army regardless of their preference. In terms of first preference, the navy was bound to be the most oversubscribed of the services simply because it took so few men. The result was that, for much of the period of national service, only those with a family link to the navy or men who had already served in the Royal Naval Volunteer Reserve stood much chance of becoming sailors.

The air force took more national servicemen but it was still oversubscribed. In May 1951, the number of men registered for national service opting for the RAF was slightly greater than the number opting for the army. When the second preferences of those who had made the navy their first choice (a little less than 10 per cent of the total) were taken into account, almost half of them wanted to join the air force, but it would take only 38 per cent of them.[120] The attraction of the air force sprang in part from the fact that its discipline was known to be less harsh than the army's. Opportunities for technicians were greater in the air force than in the army and consequently it attracted more educated men. Conscripts in the air force were, in general, more educated than those in the army and it took very few men from the lowest educational categories. In the early 1950s almost half of air force conscripts (compared to around a third of those in the army) had some formal qualifications and 42 per cent of airmen (against 16 per cent of soldiers) had stayed at school beyond the minimum leaving age. A little over 40 per cent of airmen (against 12 per cent of soldiers) were educated at grammar school.[121] However, the air force attracted comparatively few men from the highest social categories. The wealthy 24-year-old baronet Sir Henry Shiffner, who served as a clerk in the aptitude testing office at Cardington and occasionally gave his friends lifts across the vast base in his Lagonda, was a rare exception.[122] Public school boys who expected to obtain commissions were unlikely to join the air force, unless they were admitted as trainee pilots. The air force was the natural home of grammar school boys – especially those from the less prestigious schools and those who had left school after the minimum leaving age but before they were eighteen. By the late 1950s, after an increase in the educational level of the overall population, just over half of national service airmen had stayed at school beyond the minimum leaving age of fifteen; just under a quarter of the army sample had done so.[123] The pull of the air force for such men became a circular process – the more of them joined up, the more attractive the air force became to others like them.

The hierarchy of the services was obvious during the official discussions about the distribution of the national service pool. The RAF usually creamed off the best men: when the services, faced with the Korean War, admitted an extra 10,000 men from medical categories that would previously have been rejected, the RAF took only 1,000 – the rest went to the army.[124] There were acrimonious exchanges between officials – as the Ministry of Labour complained about the 'unjustifiable waste of everyone's time' involved in having men interviewed and then rejected by the RAF, and the air force itself complained about 'constant nagging' and the fear 'that the RAF is getting away with something'.[125]

The same hierarchy was impressed on conscripts themselves at the Ministry of Labour centres. After they had undergone their medical examinations, men who had opted for the RAF were interviewed by an air force representative and passed to the army only if they were rejected. Sometimes this meant that the army inspections of those who had put it down as second choice could not be completed by the end of the day.[126]

Recruits were asked if there was a unit they wished to join or a trade they wished to pursue in the forces. Men going into the army after 1948 were recruited into a particular corps and regiment. The allocation was not final. Many corps and regiments took some men after they had completed basic training in other units.

How much choice men had about what happened to them once they were in the forces depended partly on what, and who, they knew. A small number of privileged men had already met the commanding officers of the regiments in which they were to serve. John Robinson was part of the coterie of young men built up around the South Nottinghamshire Hussars (an artillery regiment of the Territorial Army) by Colonel Peter Birkin. On Birkin's instructions, he wrote on his form that he wished to join the Royal Artillery, adding, 'I am a serving member of the South Notts Hussars.'[127]

Most national servicemen, however, had relatively little choice – partly because regular recruits were given preference when it came to choosing units. Some men wanted to serve in the infantry – either because of some local or family tradition or because they wanted to see 'real soldiering'. Since the infantry was notoriously hungry for men, these wishes were, at least in the short term, usually gratified, even if they had skills that would have been of obvious use in a more technical unit.[128] Even within the infantry there were degrees of desirability. The Foot Guards, which were more prestigious than infantry regiments of the line, contained a large proportion of regulars.

Two kinds of units attracted a disproportionate number of national servicemen. On the one hand were corps (such as Education and Pay) that took comparatively small absolute numbers of men and required that some of their recruits had formal qualifications. On the other, were those corps (largely concerned with unskilled labour) that rarely required any educational qualifications but which were seen as unattractive and consequently rarely chosen by any soldier who had any say in the matter.

National Service (NS) Entrants to Army Basic Training Units by Corps/Arm 1954*

Arm/Corps	No. NS entrants	% NS men in entry
Non-Combatant Corps	101	100.0
Royal Pioneer Corps	3,401	94.0
Army Catering Corps	6,039	93.4
Royal Army Pay Corps	2,956	93.0
Royal Army Medical Corps	3,851	93.0
Royal Army Education Corps	752	87.7
Royal Army Ordnance Corps	9,218	87.4
Royal Army Dental Corps	204	87.2
Royal Artillery	13,545	83.3
Royal Signals	10,223	82.1
Infantry	25,842	79.8
TOTAL ARMY INTAKE	106,896	77.7 ⟵
Royal Army Service Corps	8,605	74.4
Royal Electrical & Mechanical Engineers	9,864	72.6
Royal Engineers	6,825	68.5
Royal Military Police	1,170	66.0
Intelligence Corps	222	64.7
Royal Army Veterinary Corps	151	60.4
Royal Armoured Corps	2,631	45.3
Household Cavalry	254	43.1
Foot Guards	1,042	41.1
Army Air Corps	0	0.0

* Derived from figures given in Appendix IX.

77.7% is the number of national servicemen as a percentage of the total army intake in 1954. Every unit with a lower percentage than this was taking a disproportionate number of regulars and every unit with a higher percentage was taking a disproportionate number of national servicemen.

The army was notorious for its inability to allocate men to anything that matched their position in civilian life or their own wishes. One general reckoned that 52,000 craftsmen entered the army in 1952 and that only 6,400 were in a job that matched their skills.[129] Part of the problem sprang from the fact that there were simply not enough skilled jobs in the army and that most soldiers were allocated to 'teeth arms' – infantry, artillery and tank regiments – which had little use for skills acquired in, or useful to, civilian life.

Sometimes, the allocation of men to military roles was laughably inappropriate. Fred Dibnah, the steeplejack, had strong nerves, a good head for heights and some experience of handling explosives. He said that he did not care what he did as long as he could be out of doors. He was put in the Catering Corps.[130] Allocation to the Catering Corps was frequently a source of dissatisfaction – perhaps because the army was cavalier about how it fed its soldiers or because the Catering Corps was considered (along with the Ordnance Corps and the Pioneer Corps) as an appropriate place in which to dump men who were in one way or another too 'difficult' for posting to more prestigious units. In 1954, almost a fifth of all national servicemen went into these three corps, which took very few regulars.* Kenneth Hill was called up in 1947. He wanted to be a driver in the Service Corps or, failing that, a store man in the same corps. His third choice was the Catering Corps, to which he was assigned. He and several other men deliberately failed their catering course in the hope of escaping their fate, but they were told that they would stay until they passed.[131]

Charlie Reading had undergone a five-year apprenticeship in the building trade but was assured that there was no chance of a posting to the Royal Engineers unless he signed on for three years. He refused and was sent to the Catering Corps, where he found himself trained alongside three former bricklayers.[132] An officer at a court martial defending a soldier who had been in trouble for a succession of offences finishing with participation in a riot at a military prison explained that his client had been called up to the Catering Corps:

---

* Figures calculated from 'Abstract of Army Statistics'. In 1954, the Ordnance Corps took 8.6 per cent of national servicemen, the Pioneer Corps 3.2 per cent and the Catering Corps 5.6 per cent.

At this stage he was not aware of what was expected of him, but to his dismay realized that he was to be trained as a cook. This was the direct opposite to what he expected as his trade in civilian life was that of a sawmill apprentice. After a fortnight's training at Aldershot he was posted to Woolwich to be trained as a cook. He promptly complained to a certain army officer of the Army Catering Corps that he had no interest whatsoever in cooking and that he was desirous of a transfer. He was told in as many words not to talk silly and carry on with his work.[133]

John Noble, by contrast, was an apprentice chef who wanted to join the Catering Corps but was told that there were no vacancies. He was offered the chance of being a field cook in the Medical Corps, which in retrospect he regretted not having taken, but:

> they seemed to be manoeuvring me towards the county regiments and they were saying that with the Norfolks and the Suffolks, both being in combat, one in Korea and one in Malaya, very short of personnel they felt that there was where the vacancies lay and that was probably where I would go.[134]

The odd allocation of men to positions in the armed forces owed something to military incompetence. There was also an element of coercion. The services were keen to make men sign on as regulars and often used the prospect of getting a particular posting as an inducement for men to undertake regular engagements. The educated were unlikely to yield to pressure – they understood the rules and many knew that they would soon be assigned to clerical duties. Working-class men – often desperate for positions that allowed them to use their skill and to avoid the infantry – were more vulnerable. Many of them were misled. Leslie Ives, who joined the infantry in 1949, wrote forty years later: 'I believe the Navy and the RAF got the cream – and even later am I right in thinking you had to sign on for 3 years to get in either of these?'[135]

Most national servicemen still lived at home and leaving for their training units meant saying goodbye to their families, often for the first time. Many remembered the awkward exchanges among people who were unused to displays of emotion. Ken Lynham kissed his mother for the first time when he left to join the army at the age of twenty-one.[136] Jack Spall was the son of a bus conductor. He recalled the morning in 1948 when he left to join the RAF: 'I see it clearly. It was sort of in the kitchen before I went off, and he [Spall's father] said "Um, um, well look, um, I've only got one thing to say, um, just be careful of the girls who hang around camp."'[137]

A. E. Fisher also joined the RAF and described the process thus:

On the morning of my departure, father and I had a cup of tea together in the kitchen – he was getting ready to go to work. We left the house together and walked to Westbourne Park Station. There we shook hands, because I was at that awkward stage of one's life when one doesn't hug one's father. A final wave, and I caught the Underground to Euston. There were a lot of young men with brown paper parcels and tense expressions. We were among the early National Service men.[138]

7

Basic Training

No, not worried, just miserable.

Motor fitter from London,
undergoing basic training in the RAF, late 1940s[1]

National service, at least in the army, usually began on a Thursday – so that training units had time to get men settled in before the weekend – and it usually started with a train journey. Every conscript was sent a railway warrant and instructions about the base to which he was to report. The journey itself could be exciting. To many eighteen-year-olds, trains were still glamorous and exotic. Most youths had not travelled much and some had never been more than a few miles from their home. A few had never been on a train and had no idea how to buy a ticket.[2] John Waller had never left West Auckland before he was called up. He asked the station master how he would know when his train arrived at the regimental depot of the Durham Light Infantry and was told, correctly as it turned out: 'there will be a big bastard there shouting'.[3]

Men were collected at stations and taken to their depots. The process did not always run smoothly. Among the young men disgorged from a three-ton truck at the depot of the Buffs in 1958, one was even more disgruntled than the others. It turned out that he was a civilian who had been standing on Canterbury station when the NCOs had swept him up with the recruits.[4]

Once at their barracks, men queued for their kit, packed their civilian clothes to be sent home, and collected a variety of objects with perplexing names: 'eating irons' meant a knife, fork and spoon;

'housewives' meant sewing kits to maintain their uniform. Recruits often remembered the moment when they realized that their civilian life was over. For some, it came when the lorry drove into the barracks: 'The wooden gates slammed and we had entered, for eight weeks, a prison.'[5] For John Barkshire, it was when he sent his civilian clothes home: 'And so your link with the human race outside disappeared in a brown paper parcel.'[6]

The exact timing of the transition from civilian to serviceman was often remembered for years afterwards. One soldier wrote a memoir devoted to the 3 February 1949. This was the day on which he reported to Oudenarde barracks in Aldershot as a trainee driver in the Royal Army Service Corps. Between two in the afternoon and half past nine in the evening, 1,250 recruits had been churned through the army's mill, and several had already gone absent without leave.[7]

The real terror for many recruits came with the first night of national service. The requirement that lights should be turned out at a certain hour rubbed in the loss of adult dignity and freedom. Undressing in front of other men was often a painful experience. Lights-out removed whatever fragile protection against bullies might have been provided by the oversight of non-commissioned officers.

Some men were used to sleeping away from home. Many of those from the upper-middle class had been at boarding school since they were seven. The urban working classes had often been evacuated during the war. Some had spent periods in various forms of institutional care. Some came from families that were so poor that the very notion of privacy would have been meaningless – one recruit said that the first night of basic training was the first time, apart from during a long stay in hospital, he had had a bed to himself.[8] There were, however, some conscripts who had never slept a single night outside their own bedroom. Many recalled that their dominant memory of the first night of national service was that of listening to one of their comrades crying himself to sleep.

Going to bed raised awkward questions about how far men should observe the rituals associated with home life. Should they brush their teeth? Should they put on the pyjamas that had been carefully packed by their mothers or should they jump into bed in their underwear, which seemed, at least until the forces began to issue pyjamas in the 1950s, to be what most recruits did?

Christians steeled themselves to say their prayers on the first night. Well-meaning clergymen had sometimes told them that the armed forces was a lions' den, in which their faith would be tested. Bruce Kent, later to become a Catholic priest, accomplished his act of 'heroic witness' and was disconcerted to find that an Anglican boy in the same hut was also saying his prayers.[9] Some of those who said their prayers were subjected to – usually gentle – mockery.[10] Often they were treated with courtesy.[11] John Hodgson, on his way to ordination, read the Bible during his basic training with the Durham Light Infantry. His comrades expressed bewilderment at first, then began to listen to him: 'Bereft of their home background anything that smacked of home normality was appealing.'[12]

Basic training was relatively short. Sailors spent just two weeks learning to drill on shore before being posted. Most soldiers received six, eight or ten weeks, as did airmen. Those who were sent to theatres of real fighting were usually given extra training. Some were also given specialized training as, for example, vehicle mechanics, which might last for several months. Memories about how long basic training lasted were often vague – partly, perhaps, because recruits were confused and shocked when they underwent it. One thought, forty years after the event, that his basic training had probably lasted six weeks but 'it seemed like six months'.[13]

Conscripts, especially during the early years of national service, were often horrified by the conditions of their camps. Money was short in the aftermath of the Second World War and the armed forces had to mend and make do. Many men believed that their barracks dated back to the Great War, the Boer War or Crimea. Some were put in Nissen huts or the 'Spiders' that were built out from a central point. Heating came from a single stove. There were sometimes no mirrors, which presented problems for men who were expected to be smart on parade. Food – never notable for its quality in any part of the British armed forces – was revolting.

Bathrooms were sordid beyond belief: '20 basins for 120 people, 1 plug between them – the rest stuffed with bog paper.'[14] There was sometimes no hot water. At Catterick, one recruit, an old boy of Stoneyhurst, became so desperate that he went to a Catholic church and asked the priest for a bath; the favour was granted with, one assumes, much urbane Jesuit humour about the 'monastic' quality of army training.[15]

The 'Shinwell winter' of 1946–7 (when Emanuel Shinwell as Minister of Fuel and Power was blamed for having failed to manage coal supplies properly during bitterly cold weather) was a particularly bad time to go through basic training. One soldier believed that army camps could only be kept open if one latrine remained unfrozen and that his own camp, just, met this condition.[16] William Rees-Mogg wrote of his time in the air force: 'For most of those who lived through it, 1947 was one of the most unpleasant years of their lives.' He and his comrades 'burned anything we could lay our hands on, except the snooker table, in an effort to keep the hut warm; we failed'.[17]

Conditions for national servicemen got better in the 1950s. This was partly because of greater prosperity and partly because the armed forces made a conscious effort to improve the lives of servicemen, especially as the end of conscription came into view and they knew that they would have to attract more regular recruits. By the early 1950s, men who had been brought up on the horror stories of their elders sometimes found that the barracks were less bad than they expected. One wrote home: 'It might surprise you – it certainly did us – but we actually have two white sheets to sleep on.'[18]

The first days and weeks of national service involved a succession of unpleasant experiences. Sometimes men were victims of real violence; more frequently they suffered humiliating abuse. One recruit recalled that 'verbal brutality felt physical'.[19] Ill-fitting uniforms chaffed and heavy boots blistered feet. Most men felt that they did not get enough food – though, purely in terms of quantity, servicemen were usually better fed than civilians. No one got enough sleep. Many fell ill. Servicemen were injected against various diseases – a bored national service member of the Medical Corps might give 25,000 injections in the course of his service.[20] The injections often produced a short-term fever. In theory, recruits were given time to recover; however, this rule was frequently disregarded. In any case, reporting sick was complicated and unpleasant and carried the terrifying risk that a conscript might have to endure part of his training again.

Just as conditions for all conscripts improved during the 1950s, conditions for each individual conscript improved during his training. The first two weeks were the worst. Generally, it was during this period that recruits were not allowed out of barracks. The anticipation of their first forty-eight-hour leave became an obsession that made some men feel physically ill. In 1955, the mother of an eighteen-year-old airman wrote about her son's basic training unit:

> His letters bring out the atmosphere of stress and anxiety in which these young men live, heightened by threats of penalties, especially the loss of leave. 'One man in our hut is so worried that he started getting up at three am to put on his equipment ... Without exception everybody's *one* idea is how soon they will get leave. In the lavatories the writings are not obscenities but "In two weeks and four days I get my forty-eight hours".'[21]

After the first leave, things began to improve. Most recruits spent much of their first free weekend travelling to and from home. They found that it was relatively easy for men in uniform to get lifts, probably the first concrete advantage of military service that they discerned. A night in their own bed meant a return to a gentler world, and, reflected in the eyes of their civilian friends, they caught a first glimpse of their own military identity:

> Mac commented on the changes in me – the short hair, the slim fitness, and the distracted air, as if I were slightly out of touch. I felt slightly out of touch – or different – although it was not a bad feeling. It was as though I was no longer just another lad, making his way, but that I was involved in something big, and adult, that people respected.[22]

When men returned to barracks, discipline seemed easier. The most problematic recruits, the ones who suffered worst and who were most likely to draw the wrath of the NCOs on to the whole platoon, had often been discreetly removed: discharged from the forces or, in the army, transferred to the Pioneer Corps. Those that remained were knitted into a brutal solidarity. The NCOs began to seem more human. Michael Heseltine remembered that, eventually, his sergeant told a joke; it was not a funny joke but it illustrated a new climate in which it might be conceivable for both the sergeant and the men under his command to smile.[23] Also, the next batch of recruits arrived after two weeks and the sense that other people were even greener, and had even longer to serve, was reassuring.

The shouting and abuse seemed less terrifying once recruits had had time to draw breath and think things through. During his first ten days in the Royal Artillery, Anthony Hampshire asked himself: 'why are they treating me like this? I am not a criminal.' After this, the 'light went on' and he began to understand that training was a kind of 'game'.[24] Another recruit, recently escaped from a monastic order, looked back on training thus: 'In the army it can be fun to obey blindly as long as your life isn't in danger, and there are fellows around who can share the contempt you feel for authority.'[25]

Training got easier as recruits progressed through their courses. They got fitter and they mastered the rituals of military life. The hardships of their training had advantages. Men slept soundly at night and exercise gave them an appetite that made army food seem palatable: 'braised heart and mash with thick gravy, bread and butter and jam and fruit and a pint mug of sweet tea which I filled up twice.'[26]

Men often began to enjoy the very absurdities of their routines. To their own astonishment, they threw themselves into the competition to be 'best platoon'. The passing-out parade and the evening of drunkenness that followed were memorable events. One soldier remembered how one of his inebriated comrades was hung by his heels from the barrack-room window – to prevent him from vomiting on the floor that the platoon had spent the day polishing.[27] If the first day of basic training was usually the most miserable day in a man's military career, the last day of it was sometimes the happiest:[28] from then on, for many, national service was just a matter of counting days. The drama of basic training – the utter misery of its early stages and the perverse pleasures of its denouement – often overshadowed every other aspect of men's service, even for those who were posted to theatres of real fighting.[29] Ian Martin, who served during a particularly violent stage of the Cyprus Emergency, wrote:

> It was the most intense and exciting period of my life, and in many ways everything since then has been one long anti-climax. Anyone who can survive the first few weeks of basic training in the British Army

(at least as it was then!) can survive anything: nothing in the rest of one's military service or subsequently can ever be so bad again.[30]

The world of national servicemen during the first stages of their basic training was a small one. Their lives revolved around their hut, their base and the immediate area. The Royal Fusiliers were trained in the Tower of London, which had its own sinister romance, but they were not allowed out for several weeks – so that they looked long-ingly at the bright lights of the city during their rare moments of leisure. Towns such as Aldershot or Catterick were, in effect, just large army camps, so it made little difference to men trained there when they were finally allowed out of their barracks.

The world of basic training was also small in terms of contact with the wider military world. After the abolition of the General Service Corps in 1948, soldiers were assigned to a particular regiment or corps. Between 1948 and 1951, infantry regiments were grouped together to operate training depots. After 1951, infantrymen were trained at the depot of their own regiment. Most infantry regiments had regional associations. Among 133 recruits being trained at the depot of the Royal West Kent Regiment in March 1953, all but thir-teen lived in Kent – ten of them were the sons of men who had served in the regiment.[31] For all the talk of regimental identity, men were quite often transferred in accordance with the army's needs or, less frequently, their own desire. It was possible for a conscript to move through several different regiments during his first few months in the army.

Regimental identity was weaker in the artillery, signals, engineers and tanks. Soldiers here belonged to a 'corps' before they belonged to a regiment. In the first instance, men in a corps joined a 'training regi-ment', which existed solely for the purpose of processing recruits. Men in the navy and, especially, the RAF had wider horizons. They belonged to a service rather than a regiment or a corps.[32] The Admir-alty valued tradition but it also knew that no national serviceman was likely to join the navy unless he already had some attachment to those traditions – either because he came from a naval family or because he had joined the Royal Naval Volunteer Reserve. As for the air force, recruits did not need instruction in its history because much of it had

taken place in the skies above their heads when they were children –
though the daily life of most national service airmen was very different
from that of a Spitfire pilot and some of them grew exasperated by
endless references to 'the few'.

During their first weeks, most national servicemen saw only a small
part of the spectrum of military hierarchy. Senior officers usually
spent their time at training depots shut in offices wrestling with the
paperwork that was generated by the waves of recruits and this was a
dispiriting experience. Martyn Highfield had served in the Far East
during the war and reached the rank of major (at the age of twenty-five)
in 1945. He returned to Britain, dropped a rank (he would claw his
way back to major by the time he retired) and went to Oswestry,
where the Royal Artillery maintained a whole brigade of training regiments: 'we took 400 men in on a Thursday and discharged them
thirteen days later on a Wednesday. There was not much to do in this
initial two-week period except drill.' Highfield spent eighteen months
from 1948 presiding over what he called 'this sausage machine process'.[33] Ken Perkins was another captain in an artillery training
regiment in the late 1940s. Perhaps because he himself came from a
humble background, he sympathized with the recruits, who resented
'brutal and pointless discipline', and recognized that 'a good deal of
what the national serviceman was required to do seemed open to
question and he had the inclination to seek answers'.[34] Perkins sought
every possible relief from boredom and eventually got back into
action by volunteering as a spotter pilot.

Cecil Blacker was a more successful soldier than Highfield or Perkins and would rise to the rank of full general; he had had an exciting
war in Europe and had won the Military Cross. After 1945, he turned
away from serious soldiering for a time to devote himself to show
jumping, but, in the late 1950s, he accepted command of a training
regiment in Catterick. It was not a job that he enjoyed. He recognized
that 'a kind of love–hate relationship grew up between the military
and civilian worlds' and that his own role was largely confined to trying to ensure that 'regimental friendliness got down to the teenagers
shivering in the Nissen huts'.[35] Blacker was not very successful at per-
colating 'regimental friendliness' because even keen soldiers got the

impression that the training regiments at Catterick regarded handling national servicemen as an 'irksome chore'.[36]

Soldiers were interviewed by a personnel selection officer who was meant to help direct them to an appropriate posting during their military service, but many of them remembered this as a formulaic encounter that gave little sense that they would have any real choice. Most men's contact with officers was confined to the second lieutenant who was in nominal command of their platoon. However, these officers (often national servicemen themselves) touched the lives of private soldiers remarkably little: 'At this time, I couldn't begin to tell you the name of my platoon commander ... [he was] ... a bit of a nonentity to me';[37] 'I found officers to be uncaring, snobbish or real upper class twits, but harmless.'[38] Every now and then, there was an awkward moment when the civilian world seemed to cut across military hierarchy and, for example, a private realized that he was going up to the same Cambridge college as his officer.[39]

Officers themselves did not always know what they were meant to be doing in training depots. Cyril Williams wrote, shortly after he was commissioned: 'As we are in the Holdings section no one really wants us; we are given to trainee squads but we have very little to do and it is very boring indeed when we are with them.'[40] NCOs were the real powers in the lives of trainees. The NCOs at training depots were usually regulars. They had more experience than the junior officers who were nominally above them. Some national servicemen were told, more or less explicitly, to disregard anything that the officer said.[41]

Sergeants – with handle-bar moustaches and booming voices – loomed large in the mythology of national service, but even these men did not necessarily have much to do with the daily life of new recruits. Corporals and lance corporals gave most of the orders. These were not elevated ranks – many regulars were made junior NCOs comparatively quickly so that they could be used to train conscripts. Indeed training national servicemen came to be a consuming activity for much of the regular army, and not one that did much to improve the morale or quality of regular soldiers. John Chapple, who began military life as a conscript and finished it as a field marshal, said that virtually all regular NCOs were involved in training and that this 'treadmill' meant that no one ever got 'above a certain standard'.[42]

In basic training, corporals and lance corporals were small, malevolent gods. Leslie Ives, who trained with the York and Lancaster Regiment before joining the Green Howards, wrote: 'out with your battalion a lance corporal's whims are not taken too seriously but in basic training he is a very superior being'.[43] Recruits often came to hate their corporals. Sometimes they drew a distinction between sergeants – relatively remote figures who might even seem fatherly and who were often believed to have distinguished war records[44] – and their corporals – sadistic, peacetime soldiers who compensated for their numerous inadequacies by inflicting misery on recruits: 'Our corporal is a b ... but our sergeant is not too bad until he loses his temper.'[45]

A former airman, presumably an officer, who had served at a 'square bashing camp' explained the problems of basic training thus:

Authority has thought fit to entrust the body and soul of the new recruit, during his first eight weeks of service, to the tender care of an unintelligent and often semi-literate corporal 'drill instructor'. During this conditioning period the bewildered and frightened newcomer is thoroughly bullied, but fails to complain to Authority for fear of dire consequences. This fear is one of the first and most important things instilled into the impressionable mind: fear of the sergeant, fear of the officers, who are portrayed as demi gods, fear of the guard room, but, above all, fear of the corporal himself.[46]

The air force itself recognized that 'The NCOs in charge of men in initial training fail in many cases to carry out their duties in a satisfactory manner.'[47] The kind of behaviour that aroused fear among recruits emerged in court martials. A corporal in a training regiment of the Royal Signals at Catterick was tried in January 1955. He admitted that he had called a national service private a 'horrible little man' and that he had 'straightened him up the best way I could by placing one hand on his back and lifting his chin with my other hand'. The recruit said that he had been throttled by the collar until he almost blacked out. The corporal was acquitted.[48] A trained soldier of the

Coldstream Guards was court-martialled in March 1953. He had held a red-hot poker close to the bare stomach of a recruit: the recruit turned away and was burned. The trained soldier was convicted.[49]

Army pay, even for regular sergeants, was low and NCOs sometimes exploited recruits in direct ways. Some soldiers were encouraged to buy presents for their sergeant. A sergeant sold recruits padlocks to protect their possessions against thieves and repossessed the locks after the ten weeks of training was over – he was eventually busted down to the ranks.[50] T. C. Sparrow's NCO sold the recruits an electric iron and 'needless to say' sold it back again to the next intake.[51] The *Daily Express* (not an anti-military newspaper) ran an advice column about 'Your Son and the Call-up'. One parent asked why soldiers were made to pay to have their name and number engraved on metal identity disks. The newspaper replied: 'The army pays. If the man is charged for this job, then there is a private "racket" going on.'[52]

To survive basic training, recruits were first required to pay obsessive attention to the cleaning, polishing and correct arrangement of kit. Every article of kit – including blankets, razor, shaving brush and eating irons – had to be laid out for inspection in a particular way. Men were introduced to the button stick – designed to allow them to get the correct shine on the buttons of their uniform without getting polish on the uniform itself. Piers Plowright recalled 'all those army smells', of which polish was the most important. His sergeant's hand was stained with a mixture of nicotine and Blanco.[53]

Drill came next. Recruits learned to march, stand to attention and present arms. Drill mattered most to infantry regiments and especially to the Brigade of Guards, for whom it was a *raison d'être*. Men who went into the air force particularly resented drill and disliked the brief period in which they were treated as though they were infantry soldiers. The most telling complaint airmen made about their training was that it was too much like the army's.

Conscripts were introduced to weapons. Almost every recruit learned to fire a Lee Enfield .303 Number 4 Rifle, which had been used in the British army since 1941, and which was itself a modification of a rifle that had been used since 1895. They also learned something about the Bren gun, an effective light machine gun, and the Sten gun, a sub-machine gun that was mainly dangerous to those who used it. Many national service memoirs repeat the story of the recruit whose Sten gun stuck so that it continued firing as he turned, spraying bullets all around, to ask his instructor what to do.

Boots became the subject of a surreal drama. The required sheen could often be achieved only by 'burning' them, which would also ensure that they ceased to be waterproof and were thus useless for serious military purposes. Burning boots was forbidden, though every sergeant in the British army must have known that it was done. Peter Burke – looking back on his own training at Catterick through the prism of his career as a cultural historian – wondered whether boot burning was not a form of initiation into the differences between formal and informal rules in the army. It taught men that they might be required to do things that were in theory forbidden. Burke wondered whether such training might have affected, say, attitudes to the interrogation of prisoners.

The most sinister aspect of basic training involved the bayonet. Soldiers were taught:

> If your second opponent is out of range, punch forward 'on guard', advance on him, and thrust again. If he is so close that you have no room to come 'on guard', withdraw from the first thrust, point your bayonet at him, make another thrust, and advance. If there are more enemy, kill them in the same way.[54]

National servicemen charged at straw dummies with fixed bayonets. Bayonet training became a staple of writing about national service: 'UP into his guts . . . And HATE him.'[55]

The playwright Arnold Wesker recalled his time in the RAF: 'The central dramatic moment for me during training was the unacceptable order to snap a bayonet into the end of our rifles and run screaming at a hanging sack of straw.'[56] Wesker refused to charge and then, after some subtle bullying by his officers, agreed to do so. The dramatic tension of the moment was resurrected in his play *Chips with Everything* (1962).

A few found bayonet training a useful way to let off steam[57] or simply found it absurd. Mostly, though, even hardened soldiers came to hate it. A marine commando recalled being told 'imagine he is a six foot Russian bastard bearing down on you'. He and his comrades trained with bayonets until their 'fingers bled'.[58] Michael McBain believed that bayonet training in the moat at Fort William, inflicted on the potential officers in his own intake, was the worst aspect of his training.[59]

The function of bayonet training was psychological as much as military. It hardened men to the prospect of killing in a way that shooting at distant cardboard cut-outs on the rifle range could not. John Arnold enjoyed shooting and was good at it but he wondered 'could I really shoot a fellow human being?' Since he was sent to learn Russian, he never got the chance to find out. Bayonet practice, by contrast, did not lend itself to abstract musing about the morality of killing and Arnold said that his faith in human nature was strengthened by the fact that his fellow recruits 'all hated bayonet practice'. Bayonet training could be so traumatic that it haunted men even on the front line. Benjamin Whitchurch, who was only 5ft 3in tall and who had had to make a special request to stay with his company when it went to Korea, had some nasty memories as he fumbled with trembling fingers while the Chinese overran the position that his regiment were trying to hold: 'the order came towards the end of the battle to fix bayonet, the one thing I dreaded because . . . I had always been killed in training'.[60]

Perhaps the most brutal testimony to the effectiveness of bayonet training in inuring men to violence came from the fact that conscripts so often used the weapons against themselves or each other. During his training at RAF Bridgnorth in 1959, one airman wrote to his family that he had attended the funeral of a comrade who had been killed by a bayonet thrust – he did not say whether the death was suicide, murder or an accident.[61] A Scots Guardsman was detained after stabbing himself with his bayonet. His suicide attempt was apparently provoked by having been put on a charge for having a rusty bayonet.[62] In Glasgow during the early 1960s, gangs fought with bayonets that had been liberated from Highland regiments by enterprising national servicemen.[63]

The armed forces took men from almost every kind of background. Later they might be divided by rank, but for the first few weeks of their service everyone served on the lowest rung of the military ladder as a private, aircraftman or naval rating. There was supposedly no privilege, privacy or patronage on the first day of national service. For some children of the Butler Education Act, being called up into the armed forces was like being put through the 11-plus backwards. Suddenly they found themselves back with boys they had known at primary school. One former conscript described the army as a 'huge 18+ comprehensive school ... [which] had a very unifying effect on the nation'.[64]

The impact of this mixing can, however, be overstated. Middle-class men often commented on the social heterogeneity of the intake into the armed forces – perhaps because, sometimes for the first and last time in their life, they found that men of their own background were in a minority. Working-class men, however, meant something else when they talked about the way in which the early stages of national service threw different kinds of men together. For them, the striking element of this mixing was regional rather than social: 'Included in our ranks were Jocks, Taffies, Paddies, Geordies, Scouses, Brummies and Cockneys.'[65] Even within the training depot for the Home Counties Group, recruits commented on regional origins: 'They came from far and wide, some from all over Kent, others from London, Sussex, Surrey and Middlesex.'[66] Regional accents were still marked in the 1950s and many youths had barely moved outside their home town before they were called up. Not surprisingly, they defined themselves by where they came from – 'I'm a Scouse Pa' what are you?'[67] – and spent the first few days of national service trying to find men who shared their origins.[68]

Regional origin was often the main identifying feature that men discerned in their fellow recruits during basic training and often formed the basis of the nicknames by which they called each other. Sometimes an apparent reference to regional origin was a reference to social position too. Some men from the south associated Liverpool and Glasgow with a criminal lumpen proletariat,[69] and an educated soldier might be called 'Oxford', even if his education amounted to having five GCEs and a less pronounced West Country accent than most of his comrades in the Dorset Regiment.[70] In many cases, though, working-class conscripts seemed unaware of, or uninterested in, the fact that their barrack rooms contained men who were more socially privileged than themselves. This may have been in part because middle-class men refrained from saying anything that would draw attention to their social origins and sought to 'slip out of their middle class backgrounds'.[71] It may also have been because working-class men simply had no reason to care about social differences unless those differences had some direct impact on their lives.

Middle-class conscripts, and working-class men whose education had brought them close enough to see the middle-class world, were interested in class. Educated boys were most likely to be aware of class, which was a matter of near obsessive discussion in the literature of the 1950s. In addition to this, schools and universities were themselves important – to some eighteen-year-olds *the* most important – gatehouses on the social frontiers. Educated recruits found that they had a succession of ready-made categories into which they could put each other – ones that implied understanding if not mutual respect. Brian Goodliffe remembered that there were seven men from his own school (Charterhouse) with him as he went through basic training for the Royal Artillery at Oswestry.[72] He identified almost every middle-class soldier he subsequently met partly in terms of the school they had attended – Whitgift, Bancroft's, Tonbridge, Harrow, Wellington, Haileybury, Marlborough, Downside. The narrator of David Lodge's autobiographical novel of national service (conscious of his own grammar school and redbrick-university origins) sums up a particularly smug fellow recruit as 'Oxford . . . PPE . . . hockey blue'.[73] A Harrovian recalling the other 'potential officers' he encountered in basic training said that grammar school boys were 'on the same ladder but a couple of rungs down'.[74]

To see how social class looked on the various steps of the social/ educational ladder, it is worth examining the Rifle Brigade. This was a prestigious regiment that recruited boys from grand public schools, who would generally obtain commissions, and also working-class Londoners, who would stay in the ranks. There were limits to the social mixing of the Rifle Brigade and some conscripts had been picked for commissions before they even arrived at the regimental depot.[75] However, unlike the guards, of which more below, the Rifle Brigade did not separate potential officers and ordinary private soldiers from the very beginning of their service and they allowed at least some grammar school boys into potential officers' platoons.

Someone at the top of the ladder would have a clear view of the social hierarchies involved in all this. Christopher Hurst was called up into the Rifle Brigade in 1948. He understood the prestige of his regiment and also the fact that a man such as himself would probably obtain a commission. He wrote: 'It never occurred to me, any more than it evidently did to those who controlled our destinies, to wonder whether I was truly "officer material".'[76] Hurst, however, also admitted that it would have been hard for a man like himself to serve in the ranks in the Rifle Brigade because so many of the officers were fellow Etonians.

A rung down on the ladder was Stanley Price, a doctor's son with a place at Cambridge who had been to the Perse school, which in social terms was 'basically a direct grant [grammar] day school'. At first, everyone, 'toffs and toughs', trained together. The former included the Gordon-Lennox twins, who parcelled up their civilian clothes and sent them to the Duchess of Richmond, their mother. 'Blimey,' said the corporal, 'blokes here sending their clothes home to a boozer.' Price was then put in the potential officers' platoon, of which he wrote: 'If the first four weeks were an initiation in filth and squalor, the next six weeks were an introduction to the subtle gradations of the British class system.'[77] Men from the upper-middle class, or those whose education had put them on the verge of entering that class, were struck by the importance of school for potential officers in the regiment 'and the school, I was rapidly informed, was Eton'.[78]

Ordinary grammar school boys of the kind who did not have places at university were rarely so interested in the subtle gradations of the upper-middle class. Derek Seaton was such a man and his understanding of the class system in the British army was not sufficiently good to appreciate the prestige attached to the Rifle Brigade – he had wanted to go into the Coldstream Guards, because his girlfriend liked the uniform. He did, however, understand that broad social divisions mattered when it came to choosing who might be commissioned:

In those days the British Class System reigned supreme ... and all University graduates were automatically offered such a course [as potential officers], as were children of aristocratic families or of the landed gentry or of (Conservative Party) politicians. Grammar school boys – I was one – were allowed at least to 'have a go' to make up the numbers and, after all, the aforementioned had to have someone to beat – or is my prejudice showing?[79]

Divisions within the officer class, as opposed to the broad separation between the officer class and other ranks, mattered little to men such as Seaton. Indeed a notable feature of national service writing was that men from lesser public schools often recall their first encounter with Etonians,[80] but that those whose own social origins lay a long way from the public schools never mentioned the subject.[81]

For the working-class boys who made up the majority of entrants into the Rifle Brigade, rankings of regiment, class and public school meant almost nothing. Ron Cassidy was called up in 1951 – 'ambushed into it by the government', as he later put it. He came to enjoy the army, signed on as a regular and eventually rose from the ranks to become a major. However, he did not even mention the potential officers' platoon when recalling his national service, and presumably he would have understood that the prospect of an immediate commission was never going to be held out to a man such as himself. As for the prestige of his own regiment, he thought vaguely that it might be 'akin to the fire brigade'.[82]

It was rare for units to include anything like a genuine social cross-section of young men. A large part of the 'rough' working class was put in the Royal Army Ordnance Corps, the Catering Corps and the Pioneers. Large numbers of grammar school boys were conscripted into ground trades in the air force and this was their natural home as much as the Rifle Brigade was that of the Etonians. Graham Mottershaw wrote from his RAF training unit: 'the talk consists of filth and blasphemy which surprises even a vulgar person like me; more sensitive and sheltered natures must suffer hell'. However, his hut was hardly filled with the lumpen proletariat. Out of twenty-one men in it, seven had their school certificate – a high proportion in the England of the late 1940s.[83]

Finally, such social mixing as did occur in basic training was short. Most regiments separated 'potential officers' after a few weeks. Even men who subsequently failed one of the officer selection boards would often be made NCOs and given some position, usually as a clerk, that would keep them apart from ordinary private soldiers.

A retired officer suggested that the decision to 'segregate national service officers ... into special squads [had the] disastrous result of giving both groups just enough time to notice and dislike each other's superficial faults without giving them the further time required to appreciate the virtues which lie beneath them'.[84] This was unfair. The working classes seem hardly to have noticed the public school boys among them, and middle-class boys appear to have regarded their brief sojourn among the working classes with a wistful nostalgia. Bruce Kent was a public school boy called up soon after the war when the rigid hierarchies of the army were not as well established as they would later become. All the same, he described his experiences thus: 'For me the classless society of Hut 53 lasted only six weeks. Pip Permaine the trainee butcher and Ray Spain with the Brylcreemed hair, my first mates – where are you now?'[85]

In the smartest of all regiments, the classes did not mix for even a few weeks. The Household Division ensured that potential officers were placed in Brigade Squad and separated from other ranks from the beginning. Generations of Etonians have repeated that the training to which they were subjected was 'as hard if not harder' than that given to ordinary soldiers – Alan Clark, who spent precisely one day as a full-time soldier, was particularly eloquent on the subject.

Many public school boys believed that they were particularly well equipped to survive the early stages of national service. They had all lived away from home. They were used to institutional life, cross country runs and all-male company. Most of all, public school boys usually had some military experience as members of the Officer Training Corps. Knowing how to drill and handle a rifle, they were less likely to be humiliated in the first weeks of training. A few men had extensive military experience before they even received their call-up papers. R. D. Cramond had volunteered for training as a pilot with the RAF in June 1944, when he was seventeen and a half. He had been sent to Oxford for six months of pre-officer training, but failed to qualify for air crew duties because of poor eyesight. He then went to Edinburgh University and joined the university branch of the Territorial Army, which was run by Colonel Buchanan-Smith, who had helped devise the War Office Selection Board. The TA arranged for him to do his basic training before he was even called up, and by this time he was being paid as a sergeant rather than an ordinary recruit. When he arrived at his regimental depot, he was twenty-two years old and reckoned that he had eight years of training.[86] 'Mac' McCullogh, who served with the Tank Corps from 1959 to 1961, not only had been a member of the CCF at school but also, through the good offices of his brother-in-law, who had been an officer in Malaya, had been allowed to train with 22 SAS, before he was called up.[87]

Most importantly, perceptions that public school boys had of basic training were influenced not so much by what had happened before as by what happened afterwards. Joe Studholme recalled his induction into the King's Royal Rifle Corps thus:

> being flung into a platoon which was completely mixed, you know, some people like me, public school boys, and then a lot of wonderful cockneys from the East End and, you know, and Yorkshiremen and people, for whom it was the most frightful shock, to come away from home probably for the first time into a barrack room. Whereas we took it green, I mean it was, you know, slightly more uncomfortable than life at a public school, but not that much.[88]

Perhaps he was right to say that the spartan conditions of public school had hardened him to army life, but the fact that the regiment had decided to try to get him a commission before he even left Eton may also have helped to sustain his morale.[89]

For such men the horror of the first few days in the armed forces was made much more bearable by the knowledge that it was likely to be shortlived. One recalled that an 'initial period of unpleasantness' seemed a preliminary to joining his 'rightful sphere' among 'fellow gents in the officers' mess'. He was 'always comforted by the thought, which we had had instilled in us at school, I mean I assumed that I would be commissioned eventually'.[90]

*

Who did worst in basic training? Middle-class men who wrote about basic training were often struck by the suffering of men who came from their own social background. Famous accounts make much of young men with sheltered upbringings who were incapable of mastering military skills or getting on with their rougher comrades. Percy Higgins – the doomed young man in David Lodge's *Ginger, You're Barmy* – is a 'slender, willowy boy whose physical appearance suggested . . . aristocratic inbreeding'. He is unworldly and slow-witted. Tom Stacey's account of training with the guards revolves in part around the tragedy of 'Teardrop' – a middle-class man who is savagely bullied and eventually invalided out.[91]

There were times when middle-class men were attacked during training – particularly during the dangerous period between being identified as a probable officer and going to an Officer Cadet Training Unit.[92] But it would be wrong to assume that basic training for national service always saw baying mobs of proletarian thugs hounding bespectacled grammar school boys. Boys from the middle or lower-middle class were not necessarily more vulnerable than their working-class contemporaries. Physically most of them would have been more robust than boys who had been born to poor families in the depths of the inter-war depression.

William Purves was called up in 1950. He described himself as coming from a 'sheltered background' in a small town in lowland Scotland. He was the only child of a school mistress and a farmer and had, until his call-up, worked in a bank. He was sent to the training depot of the Highland Light Infantry. At first, it looked as though he might suffer the same fate as Percy or Teardrop. He found himself with fifty-nine Glaswegians who were 'tough characters', and he reckoned that he never managed to sleep an entire night during the first two weeks of his service without being turned out of his bed. Eventually, though, he and his comrades arrived at a *modus vivendi*. Perhaps the Glaswegians had discerned in Purves the core of steel that would eventually cause him, as a nineteen-year-old second lieutenant in Korea, his uniform caked in his own blood, to rally two platoons and lead a retreat after every other officer had been killed or wounded. He became the only national serviceman to win the Distinguished Service Order and later one of the most powerful Taipans in Hong Kong.[93]

Educated men had advantages even if they did not belong to that particularly privileged group that benefited from public school background or the anticipation of potential officer status. Men who read easily and understood the formal language of official communiqués were more likely to know what was going on. The armed forces needed educated men (partly because such people were so rare among regular soldiers) and quickly found uses for anyone who was at ease with the written word. When Len Woodrup arrived at an air base in 1951, he and other men with educational qualifications were put in a separate room and set to marking the tests that were set for the other conscripts.[94]

Those who suffered worst during training were probably those from the least privileged backgrounds. For many such men, the early stages of their military career – which, for the uneducated, almost always meant the army – was a time of terrible confusion. Brian Goodliffe recalled that one of his fellow gunners in the early 1950s had never left his home area – he did not know the name of the county he lived in or which political party was in power.[95] The poor education of many NCOs actually made it more difficult for the least educated conscripts to follow them. Educated men might laugh at the laboured formality of military patois – never say 'pull the trigger' when you might say 'depress the mechanism' – but some conscripts found such language incomprehensible.

Accents presented problems for some working-class men. The educated sometimes worried that their speech would mark them out in the eyes of their less privileged comrades and sometimes laughed at their own inability to understand others – Paul Foot said that his own escape into a potential officers' unit began when after 'about five days some men came round talking in an accent I could understand'.[96] On the whole, however, a mastery of received pronunciation was an advantage in the forces. The BBC had ensured that every recruit could understand 'Oxford English', even if they could not speak it, and almost every NCO had to be able to speak in some version of 'correct' English, in order to be understood by officers. Men with strong regional accents found life harder. Glaswegians were often literally incomprehensible to their comrades,[97] and felt isolated if they served in units dominated by Englishmen: 'hard men from Glasgow, kept together in mess and billet, distrusting everyone else for a while due to being in a strange element'.[98] Brian Vyner underwent his basic training at Barnard Castle, where, 'in typical army fashion', 'public school boys from down south' were mixed with Glaswegians: 'We could not understand them but they could understand us. We settled down better than them.'[99] Derek Johns said that the frequent fights between recruits from Newcastle and those from Glasgow sprang in part from the fact that they could not understand each other.[100]

Dirtiness was a trigger for abuse. Class distinctions – and especially the crucial one between the more-or-less respectable working class and those beneath them – revolved partly around hygiene. Few recruits in basic training had much chance to bathe frequently, but failure to wash at all marked men out in the forced intimacy of a barrack room. Some national servicemen remembered spectacular examples of filth – such as the man, 'from a remote Scottish croft', who did not change his underwear during the whole of his basic training. Apparently, or so his roommates came to believe, he was used to being sewn into his clothes at the beginning of winter and not getting undressed until the spring.[101] The disgust that recruits felt for some of their comrades matched the feelings of NCOs, for whom dirtiness was next to 'idleness' in the hierarchy of military sins. Some soldiers were forcibly washed. One national serviceman recalled of a comrade in the infantry: 'we had to scrub him because he stank'. After five weeks, the awkward recruit 'disappeared'.[102] Forcible washing revealed the ambiguities of bullying during national service. Often those who did the washing thought of their action as a matter of simple group interest and perhaps even as an act of solidarity that went with 'helping the weakest men to keep up'.[103] One soldier remembered: 'a tall gangling half-wit called Norris who never washed would be stuck under the showers by a lynch mob and scrubbed with floor-mops: a wonderful instance of the way persecution can be gloried when it is undertaken for the common good'.[104]

A few soldiers had relatively benign memories of being made to wash.[105] Most victims felt differently. Being dragged across a barracks through a crowd of jeering men, publicly stripped, pushed under a stream of cold water and vigorously scrubbed with stiff brushes was painful and humiliating. When a national serviceman and former Borstal boy was convicted of housebreaking, after having deserted from

Catterick, his mother told the court that 'he had trouble over four soldiers who were throwing water over him and scrubbing him down with a broom'. This case gave rise to questions in parliament and an admission that other recruits at Catterick had been scrubbed with brushes.[106]

There was also ambiguity about exactly who was responsible for such forcible washes. Ernest Dobson, who served with the Durham Light Infantry, said that one of his fellow recruits was picked on by sergeants and washed in cold water every day.[107] Usually 'scrubs' were carried out by other recruits,[108] but NCOs (corporals especially) seem to have encouraged, and sometimes ordered, such practices. Derek Blake was a grammar school boy who enjoyed his training with the RASC. He did not think that there was bullying in his unit but

> the type of person who took a lot of stick was the person who was, how shall I put it, unhygienic and we took matters into our own hands ... we used to take 'em down to the ablutions and give 'em a scrubbing. That was usually at the behest of one of the NCOs ... he would imply that we should deal with matters ourselves.[109]

John Harlow recalled that, in a training regiment of the Royal Artillery, the two biggest recruits were told to scrub the neck of one of their fellow soldiers with a 'yard brush', which they did until it was 'red, raw'.[110] Sometimes the forcible washing of recruits was condoned by the military authorities. A War Office report on problematic conscripts described the case of 'Private R', who had been transferred from the infantry to the RASC and was 'a miserable specimen, thin with a lopsided head ... [and] had boils and carbuncles'. R was also 'very scruffy at first' and 'often had to be scrubbed'.[111] In 1957 (perhaps at a time when the brutalities of national service were beginning to be seen as less acceptable), a corporal and a lance corporal in a training battalion of the Ordnance Corps were convicted by court martial of ill-treating a recruit. They had forced an eighteen-year-old national serviceman to undress, thrown cold water over him (it was December) and scrubbed him down with a hard broom. The two accused said that they had acted on the orders of a senior NCO and in accordance with normal custom. The prosecuting counsel (a major) said: 'The court might think it was a "regimental scrub" which was known in most regiments but in this case it went beyond the bounds of reason.'[112]

In 1959, a corporal in the Signals Corps was charged after a national service recruit was tied and held under a shower. An initial enquiry had ended with a light sentence being imposed on the corporal. Some of the men training with the victim had apparently written to their MPs to complain about the failure to hand down a more severe punishment (which may, once again, be a sign of the changing climate as conscription ended). It appears, though, that other private soldiers had been involved in the original brutality.[113]

Large numbers of national service memoirs allude to suicides – usually in basic training: 'there were several suicides during my time, and the RSM of my basic training regiment seemed to glory in the fact'.[114] According to Simon Bendall, a conscript in the artillery: 'There were many rumours of recruits found hanged in the washrooms after only a few days in the army.'[115] Colin Metcalfe, called up into the Signals, remembered: 'Probably most intake units had a "suicide wood" in the neighbourhood where an unhappy rookie . . . had supposedly topped himself. We had one.'[116]

Benjamin Whitchurch, in the Gloucester Regiment, said that a man committed suicide while he was at Bulford camp – though not someone he knew directly.[117] Edwin Haywood, who served in the Royal West Kent Regiment, said that there were 'lots of attempts at suicide' during training and that one or two succeeded. He recalled a man who had hanged himself from a toilet cistern.[118] Men often tried to kill themselves in toilets: the only places in which they could hope to get a few minutes of privacy.

It is possible that a small number of cases were magnified by rumour. Tony Betts, in the RAF, found that men at each of his successive camps would tell stories about the chap who had jumped 'from that water tower over there'.[119] Some memoirs, however, are very specific. Ray Self was called up in May 1950. On the first night at RAF Padgate he was woken by the man in the next bed, who said: 'there is a guy hung himself in the shithouse'. He went in and found a man hanging by a rope from the toilet cistern. It was 'quite a stunning thing for me at the age of eighteen to find a dead body'. The commanding officer told the men not to write home about the incident, because he did not want questions in parliament. Self believed that suicides at Padgate took place at a rate of about one a week and that men frequently drank Jeyes Fluid or threw themselves from towers – though he himself never saw another suicide victim. He thought that suicides were covered up.[120]

If Self was right, then there was indeed a considerable cover-up, because the RAF authorities said in 1957: 'They strongly reject the suggestion that Padgate has been the scene (and cause) of many suicides. Of the hundreds of thousands of men who have passed through the station, three have taken their lives since 1944 and each of those it is claimed had a "psychopathic history".'[121]

There was probably uncertainty about some deaths. Accidents were common in the armed forces and there must have been occasions when it could not be determined whether a recruit had killed himself deliberately or not. Suicide was a crime until 1961 and it may have been that the armed forces gave the benefit of the doubt to men who might have tried to kill themselves, or that the forces attempted to cover up suicides to spare the feelings of relatives.

There is, however, quite strong evidence that suicide was more common in the armed forces than in civilian life – partly because some aspects of military service were so unpleasant and partly because some men in an institution that revolves around killing are likely to have the means and inclination to kill themselves. Suicides among regular servicemen seem to have been frequent. A report on the inquest on a sailor who had jumped in front of a train at Portsmouth in January 1947 revealed that: 'Three young men belonging to the Navy have committed suicide within the last fourteen days for no apparent reason.'[122] A soldier from the Royal Artillery stole a number 113 bus from outside Edgware tube station with the intention of crashing it.[123] National servicemen sometimes described the suicides of regulars with ghoulish jollity. One remembered a major serving in Sierra Leone who shot himself with a Bren gun – 'a difficult achievement'.[124] Another wrote to his parents about a regimental quartermaster who had shot himself – using a mirror to ensure that he did not miss.[125]

Whatever the authorities may, or may not, have tried to do, not all national service suicides were covered up. The question was discussed in parliament, particularly with regard to the camp at Catterick. Some national servicemen were also the subject of inquests, which yielded heartbreaking details. In 1951, John Booth, who was eighteen years old, gassed himself at his home in Manchester. He had left a note saying: 'I cannot go on any longer and I do not want to go back into the army.' It emerged that the medical board had failed to notice that he had 'claw feet' and this made it agony for him to wear boots. He had been excused boots for twelve days at Colchester and 'given treatment' when the problem recurred.[126] On Christmas Eve 1954, William Delaney, aged twenty-one, gassed himself at home three days after he had been discharged from Woolwich military hospital, to which he had been admitted after taking an overdose of aspirin. His commanding officer in a training regiment of the Royal Engineers said that he was an 'average soldier' and not in any trouble.[127]

In February 1956, an open verdict was recorded on Gordon Pilling of the South Lancashire Regiment who had drowned in a river. The coroner concluded that there was no evidence of bullying or horseplay. His training supervisor said that Pilling had not complained but that he had had trouble laying out his kit properly and had been 'checked for it before'. Pilling's father said he had arrived home two days before his death in a distressed condition: 'His main worry was a kit inspection.'[128] A fellow private recalled that the night before his disappearance Pilling had seemed to be in a trance and had sat on his bed looking at his kit. John Hall of Leeds was found dead on a railway line a week after he was conscripted into the army, a note beside his body: 'I am sick of being called names I wouldn't call my worst enemy and I am sick of the food I can't bear to look at it. I just can't stand it any longer I would rather be dead.' The coroner revealed that the letter 'also contained allegations of bullying at the barracks' (of the Ordnance Corps), but that 'he had gone into the matter carefully and found no evidence of this'.[129]

Stanley Mackie was found hanging at the West Kirby RAF camp four days after he arrived. His commanding officer, an NCO and fellow recruits all maintained that there was no bullying at the camp. One of his comrades told the inquest: 'Mackie appeared to be worrying about everything: cleaning of brass, webbing, filling of forms and parades. He always thought he was going to do something seriously wrong. He took everything seriously. He would never laugh. We had to tell him to laugh.'[130]

8

Making Men

*That two years matured me physically, and I do not just mean
my body. The way you bear yourself involves more than the
body. I mean a kind of manhood. In the old phrase, I went in
a boy and came out a man. But not a very nice man.*

Peter Burns[1]

*The Services are not curative institutions and cannot 'make
a man' out of a mental defective, a chronic neurotic or a
psychopath.*

Instructions to Ministry of Labour and
National Service medical boards[2]

A man as opposed to what? Were men the opposite of boys and was
national service, therefore, a means of instilling adulthood? Were men
the opposite of women and did national service mean taking conscripts away from female influence? Some of the more astute conscripts
noticed that 'men' was used as a synonym for 'other ranks' and wondered whether the opposite of a man might be an officer,[3] especially
when they saw pink-cheeked nineteen-year-old subalterns standing
next to forty-year-old sergeants.[4]

Was sexual experience a necessary part of being a man? This question often became, in retrospect at least, one that national servicemen
posed themselves because so many of them had read Leslie Thomas's
The Virgin Soldiers (1966). National servicemen are relatively unusual
in applying the word 'virgin' to men rather than women and often

unusually reflective about the significance of male sexual inexperience – though they sometimes admit that, when it came to the discussion of sex, the frontiers between fact and fiction were even more porous than they were with regard to other aspects of military life.

National service coincided with changes in relations between, and within, the sexes. Demobilization in 1945 was accompanied by a celebration of marriage and domesticity – though there were more divorces than ever before. Prosecutions for homosexual offences between men became more common in the 1950s: Hugh Trevor-Roper talked of a 'Jehad',[5] and a more recent historian has described the period as one of 'heterosexual dictatorship'.[6] Some of the people who had been adults during the Second World War – soldiers who queued outside brothels in Benghazi or women who had caroused with American airmen in dance halls – probably regarded the official sexual morality of the post-war years with private amusement, and some of those who were born in the post-war baby boom came to deride this age of apparent prudishness. Former national servicemen themselves would become ruefully aware that they had grown up before the 'permissive society' that they associated with the 1960s.

Though the period of national service is often seen as one of 'repression', it was a time when sexuality – male sexuality, in particular – was much discussed. Alfred Kinsey's *Sexual Behavior in the Human Male* was published in 1948: it was set as a discussion topic for national service officer cadets.[7] The Wolfenden Report on homosexuality and prostitution (1957) drew on information about national servicemen, of which more below.

Military service, even more than most forms of male initiation, involved competing and conflicting notions of what adult masculinity might involve. Sometimes masculinity meant something purely physical and was investigated in intrusive ways. An army report described Private C of the Royal Army Service Corps (RASC) as an example of a soldier who was 'of adequate intelligence but physically immature': 'He mixes with the others, but is a bit effeminate; his only sport is table tennis. When he came in he was twenty, but physically very immature, with voice not properly broken and diminutive genitalia.'[8]

However, often definitions of 'manhood' had nothing to do with

physique and sometimes little to do with qualities that later generations might regard as particularly sexual. Sometimes those who talked
most of 'manhood' were suspicious of the more Heathcliffian male
characteristics; 'dark', with reference to complexion, sometimes featured in reports on 'problem' servicemen. For some, 'manhood' meant
restraint, self-discipline, chastity and, in the English sense of the word,
gallantry.

Defenders of national service presented the transformation from
boy to man as a unified and gradual progression in which physical
and emotional 'maturity' developed together until a deep-voiced,
barrel-chested, demobilized soldier strode up the road to his family
house, ready to marry his childhood sweetheart and buy his proud
father a pint of bitter. Individual national servicemen, however, sometimes felt the transition as something that happened quickly – the
result of a single experience rather than of prolonged exposure to
military institutions. Often that single experience was one of violence.
This might be the 'ordinary' violence of basic training. It might, however, be the violence of real combat.

The small number of conscripts who went into battle sometimes
presented this as a rite of passage to manhood and occasionally pin-
pointed the moment more precisely. For William Purves, an officer in
Korea, his first sight of a dead body was 'really my sort of growing
up – sort of changed me from being a boy into being a man'.[9] A private who served in Malaya recalled: 'after the first kill, I do not know
if we all come grown up as men, but it come natural to us that we was
going out to kill a bandit'.[10] Men sometimes compared war to sex: 'an
unbelievably violent emotional release . . . a moment of discharge, in
every sense'.[11] A first experience of sex and a first experience of mortal
combat could be closely associated; some national service officers
underwent different forms of initiation into adult masculinity during
the leaves that they enjoyed in Japan soon after they had led men on
battlefields in Korea.[12]

The emphasis on battlefield experience as a mark of manhood
raised awkward questions for all concerned. It suggested that most
national servicemen were not 'men' at all. Manhood for the returning
fighter might be something that separated him from society, rather

than integrating him into it, and it might be possible for a soldier to be initiated into the bloodiest kind of combat without becoming, in other senses, 'a man'. D. F. Barrett served in Korea with the Middlesex Regiment and believed that his comrades had changed from being 'boys to young men' in just eight weeks. One of them was Private Nixon, who had repeated brushes with death and who was once separated from his own unit for twenty-four hours after being stunned by a shell while helping to carry a wounded man away from the battlefield. Nixon must have been at least nineteen years old but he 'looked twelve' and in England was often refused service in pubs.[13]

Once the initial humiliations of induction into the armed forces were over, for most national servicemen manhood came to mean something that was social as much as physical. An RAF report described national service as offering 'a kind of initiation into virility'. 'Virility', in this context, meant a capacity to live independently: 'Many have had no previous opportunity to leave home, and believe it will be a valuable lesson in independence. Others have left home regularly for boarding school, but have been economically dependent.'[14]

Most conscripts were indeed living away from home for the first time. Activities were invented at weekends to ensure that youths could not escape to their parents too frequently. In financial terms, independence was more limited. National service pay was low: after compulsory deductions for 'barrack room breakages' a private rarely had more than a pound a week to spend for himself. Working-class men, for whom the ability to earn money was almost a defining feature of adult masculinity, bitterly resented the drop in pay that came with the call-up.

The armed forces intersected with the domestic culture of post-war Britain in odd ways. A senior army officer believed that men in the north were more dependent on their families than those in the south and that consequently they 'matured' later.[15] Most national servicemen polished floors and ironed uniforms – things that might, in the civilian world, have been regarded as 'women's work'. Airmen surveyed about the matter made interesting remarks: 'Maybe, I will make a good housewife some day'; 'they are making us into "pansies" rather than men'.[16] Occasionally, conscription offered touching glimpses of the home lives into which it had intruded. A 'white-collar' recruit said that the effect of his own call-up was that 'Dad will have to do the washing up now.'[17]

Mothers played a large role in the thinking of the military authorities and anyone reading service department documents might sometimes suppose that the 'over-protective mother' was a greater threat to British interests than the Red Army. In 1949, an admiral wrote that it would be best to get recruits 'at sea or abroad where they would be removed from the temptation to run home to mother'.[18] Mothers did indeed sometimes shelter deserters – one absconded conscript hid in his mother's house for a year.[19] One woman, insisting that this was not her own case, appealed for an amnesty for deserters in 1958, saying that there must be 'quite a lot of decent boys among them and there must be many broken-hearted mothers'.[20] The War Office tried to post all soldiers at least thirty miles from their home: 'to ensure that NSM [National Service Men] took an integral part in unit and Army life, which they could not do if they were so close to Mother that they could be home every day after normal duty'.[21]

Regular officers believed that overseas service was a good thing because it got men away from their families and from the other 'mollycoddling' institutions of civilian life:

> If he [the national serviceman] has a real grumble he makes it to the right person, who makes it his business to put it right. It does not occur to him to write to a Member of Parliament, for there is no necessity to do so, and there is no need to upset parents with exaggerated grouses and they are both at any rate too far away to be of any use.[22]

Simon Raven, who joined the King's Shropshire Light Infantry as a regular officer in the early 1950s, having himself been a conscript in the mid 1940s, was a particularly articulate exponent of army misogyny. He was enthusiastic about the benefits of getting soldiers abroad away from the 'post-war apparatus of welfare and complaint' where men 'demanded compassionate leave if their mothers broke a little finger', and he praised foreign postings where men 'ceased to be civilians who wore uniform for eight hours a day and hurried home in the evenings to their mothers or their girls'. He was especially keen on Kenya, where 'mothers, MPs and the *Daily Mirror* were meaningless'.[23]

The *Daily Mirror* did indeed present itself as part of an alliance with the mothers of Britain to protect their conscript sons. This presentation was so successful that Barry Reed's mother wrote to the *Mirror* to complain about the absence of supplies for national servicemen in Korea – which was all the odder because she did not read the paper and because, as the wife of a prominent businessman and the mother of a public school boy who was on his way to winning the Military Cross, she had little in common with its usual readers.[24] In 1953 the *Mirror* complained about the fact that the Jubilee Trust enquiry into, among other things, national service contained no women members: 'Can anyone be more interested in the welfare of young men than their mothers?'[25]

Press discussion of national service often involved reference to mothers. A Panglossian series of articles in the *Evening News* on 'Your Son and the Call-up' provoked a torrent of complaints from mothers which in turn caused the reporter to write: 'It is the weak vessels who are habitual complainants ... In very many cases their capacity for thought and action had been reduced by dependency on possessive mothers.'[26] An article in the *Daily Mail* in 1953 said: 'Too many Mums influence their boys against National Service before they even march through the barrack gates.'[27]

Paranoia about the influence of mothers often went with a more generalized hostility to the welfare state, left-wing journalists, questions in parliament and anything else that might undermine the ability of the armed forces to impose brutal conditions on recruits, or the willingness of recruits to endure those conditions. The small number of female Labour MPs – Barbara Castle, Bessie Braddock, Edith Summerskill – took an interest in the fate of national servicemen and were regarded with particular dislike by regular officers.[28] Recruits in the Loyal Regiment were told not to write to Braddock;[29] at drunken mess nights, officers in the Royal Fusiliers described 'with medieval relish' the ways in which they wanted Summerskill to die.[30]

There was, though, an underlying social reality. Mothers had become more influential. For one thing, all women now had the vote (which had not been the case when senior officers first entered the armed forces in the 1920s) and they were more prone than men to vote Conservative, which may be why even Conservative ministers took their complaints seriously. In addition to this, there really were a large number of 'mothers' boys' in post-war Britain. The mortality rate for middle-aged men was lower than it would have been fifty years previously but it was higher than that for women. The disparity had been increased by the two world wars, and was particularly marked among the poorest section of the working class, the group that gave the military authorities most cause for concern. Among a group of men born in Glasgow in the early 1930s, one in ten had no father by the early 1950s.[31] War had meant that fathers had been absent from many families while boys were growing up. All of this had a class dimension. Officers were mainly drawn from those who had been educated at boarding schools, where they had been raised by men, even if their father was not physically present. It was working- and lower-middle-class sons who lived with their mothers. An army report concluded that men with dead fathers who lived with their mothers tended to be against national service while those with dead mothers tended to be more favourable.[32]

Occasionally, the armed forces made conscious efforts to win mothers over. One commanding officer wrote to the mothers of boys who arrived in his unit for basic training,[33] and in 1952 a War Office document about the need to increase regular recruiting suggested: 'The great and at times dominating influence of the soldier's womenfolk must be intensively studied with a view to winning over the women so that they become favourably disposed to the Army and the Regiment. Womenfolk are of two main categories: (i) mothers; (ii) wives or potential wives'. It was suggested that officers might address the occasional letter to women in category (i) – though with regard to women in category (ii) it was 'inadvisable to correspond'.[34]

Official notions that boys would become men by breaking away from their 'dependence' on home, and especially on their mothers, sometimes missed the point. Some young men did not have a 'neurotic' or 'weak' attachment to their home, but rather a rational sense that it was more tolerable than life in the services. An airman undergoing basic training told an enquiry into morale: 'I miss my parents very much. But there is one thing the RAF has done for me. It has taught me to appreciate my home and parents more than I ever did before entry.'[35]

Other men were worried about leaving their families not because they were dependent but because they thought that their relatives might be dependent on them. Those whose mothers had been widowed or otherwise damaged by the war were particularly concerned by the effects of their absence: 'I am most deeply worried about leaving my mother . . . She has . . . lost two sons and I know that when I am away her health suffers through worrying about me, the only son that she has left'; 'I do get worried about my mother . . . You see she is expecting to go into hospital any time'; '[I am] worried about my family, especially my mother who has not got over an attack of war nerves. She is very highly strung with a son of twelve to support.'[36]

Working-class boys sometimes sent money home from their pitifully small wages.[37] Even in the RAF, whose recruits tended to come from comfortable homes, some men were concerned about the effect of the loss of their earnings on their parents. A sheet-metal worker from Glasgow said that his mother was no longer getting his pay and that her husband did not earn much.[38] The RAF noted that, 'At the age of call-up, men of low civil status are earning a relatively high proportion of their total life-earnings, and passing through a brief period when it is customary for men to contribute materially to the budget of those who reared him.' Concern about families was felt among 3 per cent of white-collar workers but 7 per cent of apprenticed industrial workers and 11 per cent 'at the vanboy-general labourer level'.[39]

Sometimes national service was seen as an experience that could be understood only by other men and this sometimes created a complicity with male relations: 'there was a lot of father to son you know . . . you had a feeling that you had to do your bit after your father and uncles had actually had to fight'.[40] However, the feeling that military experience could only be shared with other men did not necessarily go with a tough-minded misogyny. John Whybrow usually addressed his letters from Korea to both his parents, but, when he was recovering in a Japanese hospital after losing a leg, he wrote to his father saying, 'I hope that this will be the hardest letter I shall have to write you' and added: 'the thought of Mums of course is pretty hard to bear'.[41] Another conscript remembered his return from Korea thus:

My mother suspected much – she thought that I looked old and thin (this after five weeks of sunbathing and eating well on the Empire Fowey on the voyage home). My father thought I was a strong silent hero and would not have been surprised if I had won a medal (he made sure when the time came that I applied for each of my campaign medals, one from the nation and one from the United Nations).[42]

Men might become closer to their mothers precisely because they valued a relationship that was removed from the brutality of military life. Neal Ascherson went into the marines partly to fit in with his father's wishes, but he did not feel that his father was a natural recipient of military confidences: 'I didn't talk to my father about Malaya, but I did tell my mother some of the more horrific things which weighed on my conscience.'[43] Another marine officer who saw active service wrote in his diary: 'Why is it I have never been able to disclose my deepest thoughts and fears even to my mother?'[44] When Richard Ingrams returned from Malaya, he came upon his mother having tea with her own mother. He regarded it as a civilized and quintessentially English scene – the exact opposite of everything that he had endured in the army.[45]

From the beginning, national service was associated with sex. In August 1947, Lord Moran (Churchill's doctor) expressed the fear that conscription would be a 'demoralizing experience', especially for those who served abroad. Referring to those who advocated licensed brothels he wrote: 'if we accept such doctrines for a whole generation, we shall ultimately undermine the foundations of the national character ... conscription itself, apart from its medical consequences, interferes with the building up of character, which in the past has been no small part of English education'.[46]

A few months earlier, a deputation headed by the Archbishop of Canterbury had visited the Secretary of State for War to discuss the 'moral welfare of national service men' and 'the desirability of giving sex instruction in the army'.[47] A subcommittee on sex education in the army that met in 1948 and 1949 included representatives from bodies such as the Catholic Marriage Guidance Council and the Association of Social and Moral Hygiene. Its report stressed the importance of marriage 'in relation to the position of the family in a civilized community'.[48]

The armed forces were Christian, particularly Anglican. The social world of an Anglican clergyman – respectable but not commercial and more at home in the countryside than in the city – was similar to that of most army officers, many of whom, most notably Bernard Montgomery, were the sons of clergymen. Army chaplains ('padres') fitted into military hierarchy because they held officer rank.*

The military associated Christianity with the inculcation of 'manly morality', and frequently evoked it in matters of sexual morality. An army guide of 1947 suggested:

> The task of the Regimental Officer is to help the Padre by trying to per-suade his men that what he says is right, sensible and up-to-date and not just old-fashioned 'clap trap'. The following paragraphs give quite shortly certain aspects of the attitude of Christianity towards sex which should help Officers to deal with this subject ... the sexual appetite was implanted in man for the lawful use in Wedlock.[49]

In spite (or because) of the fact that Anglicanism was so strongly associated with formal military hierarchy, many recruits felt particu-lar disdain for the Church of England. Catholic chaplains were sometimes admired for their rapport with working-class recruits and (in theatres of war) their willingness to endure the rigours of the front line. Nonconformist and evangelical bodies that operated outside the formal structures of the armed forces were sometimes seen as dispen-sers of 'real' faith, and the Salvation Army was remembered with affection by even the most secular of conscripts for the practical help that it provided. However, conscripts understood that, so far as Angli-canism was concerned, there was 'institutional religion in the army but it was not that devout'.[50]

Religious ceremonies were, in theory, optional in the armed forces during the period of national service – a fact that some officers regretted – though recruits quickly learned that attendance at church parades might be less unpleasant than the alternative, which usually meant peeling potatoes.[51] 'Chaplain's hour' in which a padre talked to recruits was, by contrast, enforced during basic training. Most sol-diers seem to have welcomed this because they valued a period of

---

* Naval chaplains did not have a rank.

relative comfort and peace in which they could be reasonably sure that they would not be shouted at. Some simply used the hour to catch up on sleep.

A few men became more religiously observant in the course of their service,[52] and religion sometimes became important to men who served in theatres of active warfare, especially Korea, where casualties were relatively high. Some men participated in religious discussion groups during their service – though they often saw these as a means of escaping from the culture of the armed forces rather than as part of military life.

More commonly, however, men who were already devout began to rethink or even lose their faith and this seems to have happened even faster than it did to ordinary young men in the 1950s. Army padres were often unthinking and conventional. Christians who came into contact with them were unimpressed and, in fact, those men whom the Church of England had encouraged to perform military service before ordination often had a particularly low opinion of military chaplains.[53] A letter by a 'former National Serviceman' in 1955 described the belief that service 'is a positively beneficial influence on the lives of young men' as a 'new but very dangerous heresy'. The writer went on to talk about four chaplains he had met in the army: one described the Pope as a 'dago priest', one attributed the phrase 'opium of the people' to the Bishop of London, one threatened to have agnostics buried in unconsecrated ground and one 'looked very ill at a drum-head service and made a confused sermon about how to be a Christian with a hangover'.[54]

Cyril Williams, a national service artillery officer who served in the Canal Zone, was a disciplined and loyal soldier, but even he felt that there was something odd about the coexistence of violence and army religion. He wrote:

> The service [on Remembrance Day] went well but it struck me as rather mad as only twelve hours earlier we had lain in an ambush to get some Arabs and were under orders to shoot at sight and the next morning here we were parading very piously at 'God Box'.[55]

On a day-to-day basis, sex in the armed forces meant not Christianity but the clap. The War Office kept statistics on the rates of venereal disease among soldiers in various postings. Immediately after the war, rates were high in Germany, Austria and Japan. These rates reflected the poverty and chaos of conquered countries but they also said something about the conduct of the British army itself and in particular the culture associated with long-service regular soldiers. Senior officers feared that conscripts would be 'corrupted' by this culture. In November 1947, a War Office conference was told:

> On the subject of service in the BAOR [British Army of the Rhine] by young NS soldiers Commander in Chief said the VD figures were now stationary, and he hoped would soon show an improvement. He was making every effort but there were still some units which he did not consider fit to take NS men. The main trouble was the bad influence of low-grade regular soldiers.[56]

VD rates among British soldiers in Germany and Austria dropped, as the number of soldiers present in those countries declined and as order returned to civilian society. Later, venereal disease became associated with postings to the Far East. Rates elsewhere were lower – though they were always higher in foreign postings than in the UK and always by this stage higher outside Europe than inside it.[57]

The forces sought to prevent VD by showing conscripts explicit films about its physical consequences. Men about to visit foreign cities were given blood-curdling lectures about the dangers that they would encounter. One doctor doing his national service in the navy was told to warn men going ashore at Algiers that drinking absinthe would make them go blind and that the local women had the 'pox':

> I had never heard of absinthe until I read it up in Ship's regulations and . . . I had no real idea of VD rates ashore. I felt vaguely uneasy about these tactics because I was anxious not to arouse anti-racial feeling . . . however scaring the men like this seemed to be the thing to do, or so I was informed.[58]

Long-service soldiers had heard lectures of this kind many times before and one told a conscript: 'they give the same bloody lecture every time a troop ship docks, no matter which country it is'.[59]

A middle-class man who did his national service as an army clerk remembered his arrival in Japan thus:

Most of our time was spent in travelling between one camp and the other, and being lectured and lectured on one single solitary lonesome subject time and time again until we were fed up to the teeth with hearing about VD – and it all did no good at all to the people at whom it was aimed. Last year over 30% of the British troops returning home from the Korean theatre were suffering from it.[60]

Servicemen returning from an evening out were required to report any sexual encounters and to take appropriate precautions. They were also issued with 'prophylactic kit': condoms, cotton wool, antiseptic cream. Peter Featherby recalled that being given two condoms was 'a rude shock to a young eighteen-year-old'. By the time he was commissioned, he reckoned that precautions against VD were probably a waste of time.[61]

Condoms were so widely circulated that some servicemen must have handled them on many occasions before they had a chance to put them to their intended use. Airmen on a base in Germany in the late 1940s were required to carry a contraceptive and 'mentioned instances of where their parents had discovered this and put the wrong construction on the possession of this offending article'.[62] David Morgan, a corporal in the RAF, remembers being asked by a comrade whether he could give him 'some durex'. Morgan had never had sex but he was pleased to find that 'at least I could pass as someone who might have need of . . . condoms from time to time'.[63] Boys inflated condoms and bounced them around their barracks; they filled them with water and placed them in the beds of their comrades. A national service officer on a troopship in the Mediterranean inflated two gross of condoms and threw them over the side so that soldiers could fire at them with revolvers. A naval pharmacist later asked how a ship that had not docked in any harbour had managed to use so many contraceptives.[64] In Korea, soldiers of the Middlesex Regiment deployed condoms to protect the muzzles of their guns and had almost forgotten the original use of these devices until their company commander said – just before a church parade – 'Get those bloody French letters off those weapons.'[65] George Thomas, a Welsh Labour MP, expressed the concern that Methodists felt for the moral welfare of national servicemen in 1954. He alluded, among other things, to the recent court martial of a British officer in Kenya, who had been accused of murdering civilians, but the single thing that best seemed to epitomize the dangers facing 'young men, who are raw in the ways of life, and who are just approaching their manhood' was that 'all that a boy of 18, who left school only three years earlier, has to do is to ask for a contraceptive and it is given to him'.[66]

Conscripts understood the hypocrisy of official attitudes to sex. Military morality emphasized chastity outside marriage. Almost all the forms of sexual recreation in which young men were likely to indulge, sometimes even masturbation, were condemned.[67] Young soldiers were discouraged from getting married and particularly from marrying girls that they met while serving away from the British Isles. Yet the theoretical emphasis on chastity went with the practical expectation that some servicemen would frequent prostitutes.

Many servicemen felt that military chaplains had no moral interest other than sex, or the suppression of sex. A future Archbishop of Canterbury recalled of his service in the RAF: 'The talks were usually moralistic and the most embarrassing were about sex, a subject on which the Chaplains were definitely out of touch with the earthy culture of working-class people.'[68] Another airman, not a devout one, wrote that his padre had said, 'If you can't control your sexual urges, then get married, that's what marriage is for (and not a word about the ethics of loose living).'[69] Sometimes it came to seem as though the whole Anglican Church was just another part of the 'prophylactic kit' to prevent servicemen from catching venereal disease. A national service officer, struggling to keep his religious faith in the barbaric world of the marine commandos, wrote in his diary: 'If one undergoes temptation to have sexual relations with a woman and refrains chiefly because of fears of VD, it is surely the most frightful hypocrisy to call it religion ... Which is reduced to a mere cover for weakness.'[70] A short story about national servicemen in the army said of the padre: 'the only reason we had one was to look after complaints and give the VD lecture every three months'.[71]

Military attitudes to sex produced all sorts of oddities. They meant that men were solemnly instructed about the dangers of loose women at a time when they were unlikely to catch sight of any woman. Alan Fisher remembered that at the end of basic training, 'Like a monk released from a monastery, I had become shy of girls.'[72] Eighteen-year-old boys who might blush if a female shop assistant said 'good morning' were given 'education' that was designed for battle-hardened regular soldiers who had whored their way around the world. Sometimes all this had the paradoxical effect of making national servicemen more aware of their sexuality. David Morgan felt curiously aroused by the rumour that 'they' had put bromide in the tea: it implied that he might be gripped by uncontrollable sexual urges.[73]

How much sexual experience did conscripts have when they joined up? In 1947, a subcommittee of the Army Education Advisory Board believed that the young conscript 'may have had, but more probably had not had, sex relations'.[74] Conscripts themselves often expressed the belief that the majority of their comrades were virgins.[75] Sociologists who studied a group of eighteen-year-olds registered for national service in London in 1948 divided them, with Kinseyesque precision, into three categories:

> Fifteen ... could be regarded as approaching 'adulthood', i.e. having heterosexual voluntary seminal emissions with or without coitus, their rate of masturbation having fallen; 43 were 'adolescent', i.e. masturbating frequently, and without heterosexual emissions; 20 may be considered 'children' as no history was obtained of any emissions – which may have been due to delayed development, or denial to the doctor at the interview.[76]

Most observers who interested themselves in such matters assumed that teenagers became more sexually experienced during the 1950s. However, the armed forces seem to have worried about the sexual experience of conscripts less. In any case, by the late 1950s, it was quite rare for men to join up when they were just eighteen years old, and the particular sexual threats presented by the chaotic conditions of post-war Germany had declined.

Sometimes conscription had a direct impact on relations between young men and women. A few men were married when they were called up or got married during their military service; some got married precisely in order to 'regularize' relations before they went into the armed forces. The proportion of married conscripts increased during the 1950s – partly because the average age of conscripts went up and partly because the age at which most people got married went down. In 1950, 2.1 per cent of national servicemen serving in the ranks were married.[77] By 1957, the proportion had risen to 10.1 per cent,[78] and, by October 1959, it had reached 17 per cent.[79] The armed forces, however, did not encourage marriage. National servicemen, unlike regulars, had no right to married quarters. Neither those adults who set themselves up as moral guides to young people nor the majority of conscripts themselves saw very young marriage as a good thing. A grammar school boy in the air force commented on an unpopular man in his barracks: 'an entirely immoral, thieving type, already married at the age of eighteen'.[80] Men who married very young, or even entered into close relationships with women, were seen as 'immature' and 'dependent'.[81] Early marriage was also often associated with 'rough' backgrounds. Sometimes – like joining the armed forces as a volunteer – it was rooted in a desperate flight from an unhappy home background, though very few working-class boys would have been in a position to set up a new home if they married at eighteen. Significantly, the proportion of regular soldiers who married young was higher than that of national servicemen who did so. In early 1954, only 1.9 per cent of national service other ranks under the age of twenty-one were married. The figure for the same age group among short-service soldiers was 7.8 per cent; for long-service regulars, it was 2.8 per cent.[82] An experienced officer was quoted in a pamphlet on sex education in the army: 'Many soldiers are from broken homes and are pathetically anxious to have happy married lives. This, I believe, is one of the reasons so many soldiers make impatient marriages with Germans.'[83]

Boys who were 'courting' (usually skilled workers who were saving up to establish an independent household) were particularly hostile to conscription. By contrast, men who were already married often welcomed it – perhaps because the forces seemed to offer an escape from the claustrophobia of a hasty marriage just as marriage had seemed to offer an escape from some previous life.[84]

National servicemen, or for that matter men who had their national service ahead of them, made unattractive suitors for many girls. They were poor, at a time when increasing numbers of civilian workers were relatively well off – 'most girls didn't bother with uniformed soldiers because they knew we didn't have a great deal of money to spend'[85] – and they lacked the glamour that might have attached to servicemen in a real war. Any man who had completed his service and had years of uninterrupted earning ahead of him was likely to seem more attractive than a spotty youth in an ill-fitting uniform. American servicemen – better paid, more smartly dressed and associated with the glamour that went with films and popular music – were often more attractive to young British women than British soldiers and airmen. Revealingly, though, many young conscripts do not even seem to have reached the stage at which they might regard Americans as rivals. Only when older reservists were recalled for service during the Suez crisis did the American authorities confine their servicemen to base in order to avoid fights over girls in dance halls.[86]

Men who had girlfriends when they were called up worried that they would lose them and this anxiety was made all the more intense by the fact that a girlfriend might provide practical and emotional links with the civilian world.[87] Occasionally, jealousy had tragic consequences. Jimmy Wands, a 'softly spoken' doctor's son from Edinburgh, went home on leave from basic training in the RASC to find that his fiancée was seeing a married man. He shot the girl and her lover before shooting himself.[88] More commonly, rejection produced storms of collective misogyny. Some men pinned up the letters in which their girlfriends ended affairs – so that every member of their unit could write letters of abuse to the woman concerned.[89]

Some men who commented on young women in the 1950s saw their lack of interest in British conscripts in moralistic terms. John Wolfenden, chairing his famous committee on 'vice', remarked that 'good-time girls' congregated around American servicemen.[90] Women could, though, be in an awkward position. In the 1950s, they were expected to get married relatively young and they might in the normal course of events expect to know the man they would marry from a very young age. National service, however, cut across the normal routines of courtship – imposing pressure to get engaged or married but also making it less likely that engagements or marriages would last. Anne Collins had been going out with a boy three years older than

1. The Labour government of 1945 decided to continue conscription into peacetime.
Here Clement Attlee, the Labour Prime Minister, meets a national serviceman in Berlin.

2. A conscript arrives at the guards depot.

3. Induction interviews for national servicemen.

4. Trainee guardsmen clean their kit. Note how they sit, in the approved fashion, astride their beds.

5. Bayonet training.

6. An airman's 'eating irons'. Note the national service number stamped into the spoon and fork.

Sgt. J. Evans'
No. 5 COY. IRISH GUARDS

Brigade Squad.
GUARDS DEPOT, FEBRUARY, 1951.

7. The Brigade of Guards put potential officers in Brigade Squad and separated them from ordinary recruits from their first day of service. This photograph shows training staff and seventeen potential officers. Of the latter, seven were Etonians.

8. Leave: Glamorgan.

9. Leave: Libya.

10. Most national servicemen never heard a shot fired in anger, but in Korea some saw bitter fighting. This photograph shows one of the most famous national service veterans, John Whybrow, who went up to Cambridge with an artificial leg and the Military Cross.

11. Even in Korea, not all national servicemen fought. Here, two national servicemen from the Royal Army Service Corps operate machinery in a field bakery.

12. Korea: shower parade. A national service officer bathes on the front line.

13. Malaya: a photograph, taken by a national service officer, of Iban trackers who led British soldiers through the jungle.

14. Malaya: members of the Royal Army Pay Corps athletics team in Singapore. Leslie Thomas (author of *The Virgin Soldiers*) is front left.

herself since she was thirteen. A relatively independent and educated woman who went to art college until she was eighteen, she nevertheless understood that 'you had to husband hunt' and that, for example, a single woman was unlikely to be granted a mortgage. Her boyfriend deferred his service to complete his apprenticeship and she felt that this prolonged a painful period of uncertainty ('you're holding fire all the time'). The couple had an understanding that they would marry when the man came out of the services but, as things turned out, they were married very quickly when he was posted abroad. She did not see her new husband for two years, and the relationship had floundered within a few months. She got divorced, and married an older man who had completed his service. The memory of her brief first marriage was still painful when she was interviewed about it over forty years later.[91]

As far as some British women were concerned, national servicemen were almost invisible. The proportion of conscripts who had some established relation with a woman increased as the average age of national servicemen rose in the late 1950s, but this was partly counteracted by the fact that the number of men being called up dropped so sharply during the same period. One of the last men to be called up remembered going to a dance during his Christmas leave of 1960, when he still had two years left to serve, and meeting girls who refused to believe that national service still existed.[92]

For many women, national service was always 'in the past' because it was something that they heard about only from boyfriends or husbands who had come out of the forces before they began courting. Sometimes details of their husbands' military careers filtered through slowly. Marion Jack met Archie when they worked together before he was called up, but they did not go out together until after he returned from Korea, where he had served with the Highland Light Infantry. They married in 1956, by which time he was twenty-two. After his death, she told an interviewer that her husband could have escaped from national service because his mother was sick but that he had insisted on going. He had a small scar where a bullet had 'swished' over his head.[93]

Peter Beadle, who had killed guerrillas as a private in Malaya, tried to sum up the long-term effect that this had on him:

You become hardened, you become very hardened. That is something my wife can't understand with me today, because I am such a nice person. I have got no feelings for hardly anybody, I don't know if it is through Malaya, me training or me mates I was with. To this day, I am a very hard person.[94]

Middle-class women seem to have known less about their husband's service than working-class ones – perhaps because they lived in a culture that valued emotional restraint or perhaps just because middle-class men married later, by which time their national service was more remote. Some men did not even tell their wives about actions in which they had been involved or decorations they had won. Robert Gomme was a corporal in Korea, where he was part of a patrol that once killed an enemy soldier – like many men in this position, he devoutly hoped that he had not fired the fatal shot. However, he remarked that his wife could discern no long-term effect of his military service, except for the fact that he knew how to press his trousers, something that he had been taught in basic training.[95]

Educated women sometimes found it hard to take national service seriously – especially, perhaps, because so many of them heard about it when the anti-military culture of the 1960s was already coming into view.[96] Some came to assume that stories of national service were a byword for the tedium that they associated with the dreariest kind of man. Margaret Forster wrote one of the foundational texts of the Swinging Sixties – *Georgy Girl* (1965) – and she married Hunter Davies, a fashionable plebeian writer (born in 1936) who had avoided national service on medical grounds. In Forster's novel *Dames' Delight* (first published in 1964) a woman student at Oxford, trying desperately to sustain conversation with a public school boy, asks him about his national service in the Brigade of Guards, and is rewarded with a few minutes of excruciating tedium.

Whatever their previous sexual experience, conscripts probably had a fairly clear sense of how they expected sexual relations to be conducted. This was not a direct product of Christian morality; even the most optimistic military authorities recognized that religion had little impact on the morality of servicemen. Rather it went with a general sense of what might be considered respectable and with a dose of that greatest of all post-war virtues: deferred gratification. First, young men generally believed that female virginity was a 'good thing' and even those of them who believed in and/or engaged in pre-marital sex often hoped that their future wives would be virgins.[97] Secondly, conscripts usually believed in romantic love. They thought sexual relations ought to be accompanied by intense emotions. Thirdly, they believed in marriage, they thought that they themselves would even-tually marry and they assumed that most women they encountered would also wish to marry.

Most conscripts read novels of one kind or another and went to the cinema. They expected sex to take place as part of a story and that the story would have a beginning, which was probably a meeting, an end, which was probably a wedding, and a middle, which might, if they were lucky, involve sex. One of David Lodge's novels, in part about a group of national servicemen, is entitled *How Far Can You Go?* Young men in the 1950s understood that the most attractive, enter-prising or ruthless of them might get furthest with the largest number of girls, but most assumed that they were travelling on broadly the same set of tracks towards more or less the same destination.

All this meant that the first days of national service came as a vio-lent shock. Stanley Price, later a novelist and playwright, wrote: 'Some of us, probably a majority – no doubt all virgins – had been condi-tioned to see sex as the culmination of romance. Now we were faced with it as merely a component in a vast litany of filth.'[98] The era of whispered confidences was over as conscripts endured barrack-room boasting or watched a bored medical officer tap a lurid colour photo-graph with his ruler to illustrate the effects of advanced gonorrhoea.

The sexual culture of the army was deeply shocking to respectable civilians. A regular soldier was discharged and sent to Borstal after having had sexual relations with a horse. His sentence was, appar-ently, more severe because the horse belonged to his colonel.[99] The relatively small number of women in the armed forces also sometimes made national servicemen aware of their sexual naivety. At a time when women in most of the civilian world were, or at least affected to be, demure and chaste, women in the armed forces often behaved with rumbustious vulgarity. R. D. Laing remembered a nurse in the army hospital to which he was posted as a national service doctor.

The commanding officer asked her disapprovingly, 'Do you know when you have had enough to drink, sister?' and she replied, 'Oh yes, I always fall flat on my fucking face.'[100] One national service private was sent to wake up women soldiers. He was equipped with a pick-axe handle and told, probably by a corporal who was shaking with suppressed laughter, that he was not allowed to touch the girls but could bang on their beds. As he walked down the hut, the girls showed him their breasts. It was, as he recalled many years later, 'a growing up for me'.[101]

Servicemen frequently encountered commercial sex.[102] Officers knew about this but regarded prostitution in the UK as posing no particular problems.[103] Men whose service took them to the Mediterranean, Africa or the Far East were introduced to brothels or prostitutes by the regular soldiers with whom they travelled. The Gut, the winding street in Valletta, was particularly notorious. Quite large numbers of men, however, were spectators rather than participants. Some men reacted to offers of sex with revulsion, which was probably born partly from the dire warnings they had been given about venereal disease, partly from disgust at the squalor of their surroundings (a squalor that was often evoked in markedly racial terms) and partly from their distaste for the sexual morality of regular soldiers.

National servicemen were encouraged to think of women in moralistic ways. Commanding officers, army doctors and padres emphasized varying kinds of moral and physical 'cleanliness' and repeatedly insisted that the type of girl one might want to marry was different from the type of girl who might consort with servicemen. A guide to regimental officers warned that soldiers knew the wrong kind of German girl: 'The ones he meets are the counter-parts of the girls in England who used to go with the American negroes stationed there, and would have run after the German soldier had our positions been reversed.'[104] A report on two national servicemen who were 'low-grade, minor criminals' in an ordnance depot suggested that one of them had got a comparatively light sentence for attempted rape 'because the girl was no better than she ought to have been'.[105] One conscript wrote: 'I'll say this about my National Service – it taught me two things. I acquired a taste for Carlsberg and I learnt how to tell a tart from a good girl.'[106] Other national servicemen had more complicated feelings about the differences between 'tarts' and 'good girls'. *The Virgin Soldiers* was a shocking novel partly because it portrayed the hero's relationship with a Singapore prostitute as one of romantic love while his relations with a sergeant's daughter, who is herself loved by a war hero, revolve around physical desire.

Leslie Ives was, so he claimed, a real-life 'virgin soldier' – though, as a working-class boy who had seen active service in Malaya with an infantry regiment, he was the kind of man that middle-class conscripts often imagined to be sexually experienced. His relations with women would not fit neatly into either the official army morality of chastity, marriage and 'good girls', or the unofficial army morality of ruthless whoring. In Malaya, Ives got to know a 'taxi dancer' called 'Shirley': 'My fellow leave mates dared me to take her out in the conventional sense.' He took her to the cinema:

> no doubt I got amorous (as in an English back-row cinema situation) which she no doubt tolerated in a patient sort of way. She was probably surprised that I did not seek her professional favours over night – but I resisted the temptations – much to the amusement of my mates who had hatched this little plot to presumably relieve me of my virginity no doubt.[107]

National service raised questions about what constituted 'sexual experience in the full sense of the word'. The phrase was presumably used by sociologists to mean penetrative sex with a woman. Behind all discussion among military officials lurked a more basic description which meant 'having done something that might give you the clap'. National servicemen might, however, acquire more than one kind of sexual experience. It was possible – for men who served in some places overseas – to have a purely physical experience of sex with a woman, or with many women, that did not involve an exchange of emotions or even of words. A soldier seeking 'immediate treatment' after a night out in Germany in 1945 might as required fill out a brief questionnaire about his night's encounter on 'platform 3, Hamburg Main Station' with a woman whose name he did not know.[108]

Equally, it was possible to get to know women well. This might involve a relationship, like that of Ives with his Singapore bar girl, that was physically chaste. Men who served with the Medical Corps often got to know prostitutes, as they provided them with condoms or treated them for infection. Such acquaintances may have been intimate and friendly without becoming sexual in any conventional sense. John Cowell, a devout but undemonstrative Catholic serving in Cameroon, treated various forms of venereal disease and became friends with local girls, including Lucy, who cleaned his hut, but does not seem to have slept with them.[109] Piers Plowright, also a Christian and, according to his own account, without sexual experience, seems to have had friendly relations with prostitutes when he served with the Intelligence Corps in Malaya.[110] In Kure, Japan, a prophylactic centre was in the same hut as the education centre – so that girls coming for treatment often passed by the classroom and got to the know the 'schoolie'.[111]

Finally, 'sexual experience' might be a matter of words rather than deeds. 'Fucking' was the single word that was most associated with national service – in his advice to conscripts Basil Henriques wrote wearily that outside observers might suppose that there was only one word in the English language. A national serviceman with a special interest in language claimed that during his training he had heard 'fourteen fucks' (he means uses of the word) in sixty seconds.[112] Stuart Crampin counted as a single airman used 'a certain seven-letter word' 111 times in one hour.[113] An army chaplain recalled hearing the word 'fucking' used thirty times as he walked a hundred yards across a camp.[114] Returning patrols in Korea, fearing that they would be shot at by their own side and not trusting to the official passwords, sometimes uttered an 'Anglo-Saxon word familiar to all soldiers' to make it clear to the sentries that they were British.[115]

The word 'fuck' was never used on radio or television until the 1960s, never used on the film screen and rarely printed – which is why early books on national service often resorted to 'mucking' and 'mugger'.[116] However, military language in itself was not shocking to national servicemen. There were few conscripts who did not know what the words meant. What was new was the relentless ubiquity of obscenity. In working-class communities, men might swear at work or in the pub, but they observed certain restraints. Coal miners would avoid swearing in front of women, children and their own relatives – even if the relative in question was a son in his twenties who was already a coal-face worker himself.[117] In the army, by contrast, swearing was everywhere. Recruits were particularly struck by the way in which the formal religiosity of the forces went with the relentless profanity of the NCOs. A corporal, seeing a soldier who had failed to remove his beret in church, shouted: 'Oi! You take off your hat in the house of the Lord, cunt!'[118] A sergeant instructed his charges on their duties at a funeral service: 'PRESENT ARMS – and when you get inside that church you will sing like fuck.'[119]

Men talked about sex with other men and learned to affect a worldly air even if they lacked real experience. Middle-class servicemen, in particular, seem to have assumed that going into the forces was, in itself, a form of sexual initiation that required them to talk in brutally explicit terms. Some saved up dirty stories for the first night in the barrack room with the same care that they packed their kitbags. Frederic Raphael said of his contemporaries in Cambridge that one could spot the former national servicemen because they 'smoked a lot and said "fuck a duck"'.[120]

The playwright Peter Nichols recalled his own complicated form of sexual education during national service. He was still a virgin when he came out of the air force in his early twenties and like many of his comrades combined sexual knowledge with a lack of sexual experience: 'we'd never touched a naked girl but we knew all about buggery, bestiality and necrophilia'.[121] However, while his contemporaries learned to cover up their inexperience with the tough, foul-mouthed manners that were associated with the experienced heterosexual man, Nichols had spent much of his service with an entertainment unit that was dominated by the heroically camp Kenneth Williams. Nichols later wrote: 'My two and a half years' National Service didn't make a man of me. I came home with a deep sun-tan, a yellow silk kimono with blue dragons and a taste for Ravel, Delius, Aldous Huxley and Virginia Woolf.'[122] While other conscripts were saying 'fuck' and 'tart', Nichols, a heterosexual, adopted the knowing innuendo of a middle-aged drag queen – 'Have you heard? Monty's coming out.' All the same, Nichols entitled the early parts of his autobiography 'Boy' and the later parts 'Man'. The chapter on national service marked the transition.

*

Middle-class national servicemen often believed that their working-class comrades were more sexually experienced than themselves.[123] Even before Penguin Books won the legal right to publish *Lady Chatterley's Lover* (in 1960), the writings of D. H. Lawrence exercised an influence over the ways in which educated young men thought about sex. They assumed that it was 'natural' and important but also that it went with the supposedly greater spontaneity and even virility of the working class – though it was also sometimes suggested that homosexuality was a feature of the 'rough' working class and of regular soldiers who were often associated with this class.[124] The novels of John Braine and Alan Sillitoe, both rather Lawrentian authors, contributed to the sense that young men of proletarian origin were more sexually adventurous than their middle-class contemporaries. Sillitoe was one of the few national service autobiographers/novelists to be explicit about his sexual experience before joining up.

Middle-class conscripts sometimes acted as scribes for soldiers who were less literate than themselves and this meant that they found something out about other men's sex lives, though what they found out might be more complicated than it seemed at first glance.[125] John Boorman, with a film-maker's instinct for a good story, describes writing letters for an illiterate recruit, who shouted obscene instructions across the barrack room as everyone laughed and roared approval. Boorman then wrote carefully worded letters full of tender expressions of affection and read them out quietly to the illiterate who thanked him and said: 'You can be, you know, a bit more loving next time.'[126]

National service army officers were expected, as one report put it, to be 'masculine in outlook' and to have 'likes and interests characteristic of men'.[127] The War Office provided curiously little detail of what such likes and interests might be. Candidates concluded that talking about 'rugger' was a safe bet for anyone who wanted to get past the War Office Selection Board for potential officers. The navy seems to have taken a broad-minded view. William Donaldson claimed to have been commissioned after giving a practice lecture on 'the ballet as a career for young men'.[128]

Officers were meant to cultivate, or at least affect, a form of masculinity that went with a Tom Brown version of public school virtues – Christian, gentlemanly, clean-cut, chaste and self-restraining. Lieutenant Colonel Andrew Man was himself the son of an army chaplain – though, having come to a commission after some time in the ranks, he might have had a more realistic view of army morality than most officers. He took a particular interest in the welfare of national servicemen and told a passing-out parade of officers: 'A gentleman is one who behaves as a gentleman whatever his upbringing and background, whether he is rich or poor, and who strives to carry in himself the principles of Christianity and in so doing lay the foundations of leadership.'[129] The aggressive masculinity that went with boasting of sexual conquest seems to have been less common among officers than it was among other ranks, at least during the early stages of military service, and many servicemen welcomed their escape into a potential officers' squad precisely because it got them away from their comrades 'with one track minds'.[130]

Many would have said that friendship or comradeship was the most important aspect of their time in the armed forces. The more reflective of them, though, often paused for thought. Relatively few kept in touch with their former comrades after demobilization unless their military careers fitted into some other aspect of their civilian lives.

Ronald Hyam recalls with particular affection his relationship with Graham: 'From Graham I learned the art of honesty within mateship . . . before Graham I would never have called anyone mate; after Graham it was a term of endearment to be prized.'[131] 'Mate' suggests the ambiguities of relations formed during national service: it was a short interlude and usually composed of even shorter postings. Tony Betts was another conscript with good memories of his time in the RAF but he recognized that the 'comradeship' that he valued was always temporary because 'everyone was poised to move on'.[132]

'Mateship' oiled the social mechanisms of the barrack room and could be easily transferred from one base to another. It did not, however, imply real intimacy:

> It made you part of something that was the same wherever you went, made you one of the blokes. It was the same wherever you went. You always promised to write to your mates at the last place and you never

liked the look of your new mob and in a week or so you were still putting off the letter to old Chalky White or Nigger Brown or Dusty Miller
or Dinger Bell or Jack Frost.[133]

The hero of Robin Chapman's national service novel is struck by
the fact that men in the potential officers' platoon really know each
other (because they have been at school together) and consequently
refer to each other by their Christian names rather than by nicknames
or the 'ever ready "mate"'.[134] Factory workers in the late 1950s often
said something that might easily be said of national service: 'Mates
are not friends.'[135]

For all the breezy masculinity of the term, some homosexual men
seem to have valued 'mateship' and felt that the armed forces might
offer the chance of relations – especially ones that crossed social
classes – that might not be possible in other circumstances. The most
famous long-term friendship to spring from national service was
probably that between the working-class Glaswegian Bill Douglas
and the middle-class Peter Jewell, first formed in an army camp in
Egypt and celebrated in Douglas's film *My Ain Folk* (1973). Tom
Wakefield's novel of 1983 about a homosexual love affair begins in an
army camp in the 1950s and is entitled simply *Mates*.

Homosexuality posed particular problems for defenders of national
service. In 1954, Arthur Lewis, a Labour MP, asked the Minister of
Labour whether he would 'permit a National Serviceman . . . to claim
exemption on conscientious grounds where the person signing on has
grounds to believe . . . he may be liable to corruption from the practice of homosexuality in the Armed Forces.'[136] Lewis was probably
making a deliberate attempt to annoy the guards officers on the Conservative benches, but concern about homosexuality was widely felt
among observers who were favourable to national service and close
to the armed forces. A youth leader advised conscripts: 'I want to put
you on your guard about coming up against men who want be on
terms of close personal affection with a member of their own sex.'[137]

An army pamphlet advised:

Many young men joining the army are without experience of sex, some
are without much interest in it, and a great many are very ignorant or

misinformed on the subject ... I have heard many say that they think they 'must be undersexed'. They may withdraw from an attempt to develop a normal sexual life, and lead a life of masturbation, with consequent feelings of guilt and inferiority ... Some imagine that they must be homosexual, and from a desire to develop some form of sexual relationship, may fall victims to those already fixed in that line of conduct.[138]

The government became concerned with homosexuality partly because of a case – that of Lord Montagu in 1954 – that had involved the seduction of airmen. John Wolfenden (headmaster of Shrewsbury and Vice Chancellor of Reading University) had close links with the armed forces and had already provided the army with much advice on education, including sexual education. In 1954, he was chosen to chair the Home Office Departmental Committee on Homosexual Offences and Prostitution (to give it its full name), which finally reported in 1957 and laid the way for the eventual legalization of homosexual acts between consenting adults in Britain. The Wolfenden Committee received information from all three services. The matter seems to have worried the air force more than the army or the navy – perhaps because of the Montagu case or perhaps because the air force took a more 'modern' and interventionist attitude towards practices that had been quietly tolerated in the other services.[139]

The experts who testified on the matter did not believe that 'real homosexuality' was common in their forces – though they admitted, in response to questions from the committee, that officers at court martials were not well placed to distinguish between 'real inverts' and mere 'perverts'. They thought that most servicemen who indulged in homosexual practices were young and confused as to their real nature. The witness for the air force suggested that homosexuality increased among servicemen posted overseas – because the heat aroused lustful thought or because of the absence of women. He also believed that homosexuality was most common among poorly educated servicemen.[140] John Wolfenden, whose son Jeremy – a flamboyant and highly educated homosexual – had recently finished national service, responded with an arch allusion to 'aircraftman Shaw' (T. E. Lawrence).[141]

The navy and the air force believed that homosexuality was uncommon among men in front-line units. The navy insisted that the practice was almost unknown on warships – though, the Admiralty's own brutally frank appraisals of disciplinary offences suggested that 'pseudo-homosexuality' had replaced bed-wetting as the most common means by which sailors, presumably regulars, sought to get themselves discharged from the service.[142]

The air force believed that homosexuality was 'almost entirely confined to ground trades. This may be a reflection of the fact that air-crew are all selected volunteers with a paramount interest in flying.'[143] Both the RAF and the navy believed that medical servicemen might be disposed to homosexuality. The navy representative thought that 'the kind of people who go in for this tend to be people like mental nurses, and people who do what might be called women's work'; while the RAF representative said: 'I do not know whether we should be able to say whether homosexuals are naturally attracted to medical work, or whether medical work makes them homosexual.'[144]

The army, by contrast, was forced to admit that homosexual offences did involve in large measure the most prestigious and 'masculine' regiments: 'There is also reason to believe that persons afflicted with homosexual tendencies are strongly attracted towards soldiers and particularly towards men of the physical requirements and standard of deportment required by the Guards Brigade, to which the majority of soldiers in this district [London] belong.'[145] The army assumed that homosexual practice among guardsmen presented a particular problem. When national service came to an end, the guards sought to improve the 'moral tone' of the brigade in order to make regular recruiting easier: one regiment dismissed forty soldiers in a week.

Only a small proportion of homosexuals in the armed forces can have been sufficiently careless or unfortunate to be found out. In the summer of 1955 only four out of 400 men in Colchester military corrective establishment had been sentenced for 'indecency',[146] and speculation by senior officers about the incidence of homosexuality must have been based on limited information.[147] Having said this, it does seem that particular kinds of homosexual subcultures flourished in the armed forces, and that military values often went with disdain for much civilian morality. Homosexuals convicted by civilian courts during the 1950s frequently said that they had acquired their taste for sex with other men during military service in the Second World War, and the Chief Constable of Liverpool told the Wolfenden Committee that men were often prosecuted because of 'things they learned and got into when they were serving together during the war, and even after the war, when they went on national service'.[148]

An air force memorandum suggested that:

> the 500% increase from 1939 to 1953 in homosexual offenders (mostly civilians) appearing before UK civil courts and the increased incidence within the Service are not unconnected with the growth of the armed forces, which provide conditions favourable to the spread of homosexuality. The non-selective flow of National Service entrants since 1947 must also be a contributing factor to this spread both in and out of the Service.[149]

Air force statistics suggested, in fact, that most homosexual offences involved regulars rather than conscripts, and that the proportion of regulars among offenders was even higher than the proportion of regulars in the RAF as a whole.[150] However, each offence, by definition, involved more than one person and military authorities were particularly concerned by the idea that homosexual relations might involve men of different ages and ranks – presumably these differences often ran parallel to the divide between conscripts and regulars.

Concern for the 'protection' of national servicemen played a part in the deliberations of the Wolfenden Committee and particularly in the thinking of John Wolfenden himself. He was keen that the age of homosexual consent should be fixed at twenty-one because:

> we have a good deal of evidence that young men doing their period of National Service are at present very much tempted – if that is the right word – by others . . . it has been put to us that the age for men might be higher than the age for girls.[151]

What did ordinary servicemen make of homosexuality? It was talked about – some said that it was impossible to bend over in a barracks without exciting ribald remarks or gestures. The Virgin Soldiers refers to homosexuality among soldiers in Malaya in a matter-of-fact way and, perhaps because so many are influenced by this work, some authors of national service memoirs assumed that some reference to homosexuality, even if only to comment on its absence, was a required part of the genre.[152]

In spite of the fears that their elders expressed for their welfare, not all conscripts were threatened, or even discomfited, by homosexuals in the forces. Indeed, an air force report complained about the attitude of 'amused tolerance' taken towards homosexual or effeminate behaviour.[153] Peter Birkin was a colonel in a Territorial Army regiment, the South Nottinghamshire Hussars. He acted as a patron for many middle-class Nottingham men as they were called up – helping them to get into the 'right sort of unit' so that they would later be able to undertake their part-time service with his regiment. Birkin was a homosexual and it seems reasonable to assume that his interest in young men was in part one of physical attraction – he often met his protégés at the local rugby club. None of those who benefited from Birkin's patronage appear to have known about his sexuality at the time, but none seem to have been worried when they found out about it many years later.

Day-to-day life in the military often meant dealing with men who appeared homosexual and who rarely seem to have excited either fear or disapproval. One conscript wrote home to his parents that he had made friends with a man from Bournemouth who was known as 'Mary': 'I do not know why.'[154] David Morgan recalls 'Terry', a camp regular at his air base in Germany, who was accepted by his comrades without fuss. Godfrey Raper in the Education Corps in Palestine indulged in 'homosexual banter' in the office with a comrade. He added 'people used to flirt' but 'nothing happened', not even, he believed, masturbation.[155] John Cowell recalled a sergeant in the Medical Corps who was known as 'Flossie' and invariably referred to as 'she' but who, in spite of this, was respected.[156]

Men who had accepted their own homosexuality before they were called up appear to have adjusted well to the armed forces, sometimes better than their heterosexual comrades. Reg Martin was born in 1935 and, by the time he went into the army at nineteen, had had a number of homosexual experiences. He joined the Royal Army Medical Corps and found training relatively easy. He had attended and been expelled from a succession of boarding schools so he knew how to march and how to fit in with strangers – 'I mean it was a regiment. I was born into.'[157] The forced intimacy that shocked some of his comrades amused him:

> I used to lie there absolutely amazed by the different ways people could take their clothes off without . . . without people seeing them take their clothes off. It's . . . absolutely amazing the contortions people get into in taking a shirt off, or taking their pants off or something. And they'd stand there, as though, like little Miss Prims, you know. And the older the person would be, the more prim they would try to be . . . I found this absolutely amazing considering we were all males in one room.[158]

He commented with amusement on the fact that men from the Gorbals and the East End were often homesick: 'They're not the big hard nuts that they would like you to believe.'[159] He got to know (female) prostitutes in Darlington, near his camp at Catterick. He sold them penicillin, for the treatment of venereal disease, for five shillings a time and sometimes slept on the floors of their rooms while they 'did business' behind a curtain: 'And they were always trying to find a boyfriend for me. And I'd say, "I've got a camp full" . . . I would have said that, oh, fifteen per cent of the camp was gay.'[160]

Martin himself had numerous sexual encounters during his time in the army – including, apparently, affairs with a surgeon and with a national service second lieutenant. The military hospital offered a convenient place in which to conduct his 'secret liking of people':

> you could do what you like in that linen cupboard, you know, it's nice, warm and cosy and you have plenty of towels and everything. And you would be very happy for at least an hour. And that's what most people did. Sometimes we got caught, because you'd have an emergency, you know.[161]

The nursing sisters seem to have been tolerant even when they opened the linen cupboard to find Martin and his friends in the throes of passion. He was never prosecuted for any sexual offence.[162]

Few men born in the 1930s were as worldly about sexual matters as Reg Martin. Roy Strong wrote in 2013:

For someone who is now in his seventies it is difficult to communi-
cate ... what it was like to come to sexual maturity in the middle of the
1950s. If I had been born in 1945 instead of 1935 I should probably
have lived the life of a gay man in a society which by 1980 accepted
such orientation ... If I had gone to boarding school or done National
Service [he failed the medical for reasons unrelated to sexual orienta-
tion] I would have found out much that I was only gradually to piece
together.[163]

Homosexual acts were punishable under military law. This in itself
could be revealing to otherwise inexperienced young men and sometimes the punishment of homosexuality aroused more comment than
its practice. Michael Perry, serving as a clerk in the Royal Army Medical Corps, said that he learned much about homosexuality from his
access to a manual of military law. He believed that there was 'mild
homosexuality' on his base and this involved mutual masturbation
but not 'buggery or sodomy'.[164] Antony Copley, later to become a historian and to write, among other things, on the history of homosexual
law, remembered that a petty officer on his ship was arrested for making advances to a national service rating; Copley thought that the
rating had been used as bait to trap his seducer. The petty officer was
sent home to Britain as a prisoner and an obviously broken man, but
for some reason proceedings against him had to begin on his own ship
and he was therefore brought back to the Mediterranean and to a
vessel that was then moored in Port Said, in November 1956, in the
middle of the Suez operation.

Of his own time in the navy, Copley recalled:

I was aware of my own homosexual feelings during my national service
and enjoyed the company of the working class ratings and NCOs with
whom I served. Two memories stand out. Whilst I was still a rating,
sailors from Victoria barracks were invited to one of the Russian cruis-
ers in Portsmouth for the visit of Khruschev and Bulganin. Charmingly,
I was very openly approached by one of the Russian sailors. And all
this was almost certainly on the same day that Commander Crabbe
was losing his life under its hull. The other memory remains very vivid.
On a formal naval visit to Naples in the spring of 1957 I took shore
leave to visit Capri and the garden of Axel Munthe. On arrival I fell

into the company of a PTI Royal Marine Corporal. We spent the day together, visited the garden, swam in the sea, spent time in a night club. Nothing happened, or was said, that was explicitly sexual, but so it was. Unfortunately the marine had overstayed his leave and was confined to barracks back in Malta. I made discreet enquiries and established that no serious punishment had been imposed. We never met again. Friendships of this nature in the Navy were all but impossible at the time.

Perhaps life in the services was most traumatic for those who had homosexual feelings that they had not yet understood or accepted. A man born in 1936 recalled his innocence in an autobiographical account written during the 1980s: 'It now seems strange to me that this situation [physical chastity] continued during National Service in the navy, throughout my time as a university student and indeed until I was in my early thirties.'[165]

A man born in 1931 and brought up as a Scottish Presbyterian did not have sex until he was twenty-seven. He recalled that his national service in the air force from 1952 to 1954 was marked by 'the usual unrequited lust/love for men I knew' and added:

> From the comments of my working-class Royal Air Force acquaintances, I at least learned that sex could happen outside marriage. I knew that homosexuality existed because it was an offence. Because I worked as a clerk, I learned that some men were moved into the Squadron after time in the glass-house for sex with other men.[166]

Christopher Hurst was called up into the Rifle Brigade in 1948. National service expanded his knowledge in two different ways. On the one hand, he continued to have the kind of experiences that a man of his background might have had if he had proceeded straight to Oxford. He fell in love with a Sebastian Flytish officer cadet who was doing his military service between Ampleforth and Christ Church and who was 'not so much handsome as beautiful in the manner of a Dresden china shepherd: tall, fair and with a peach-bloom complexion'.[167] When Hurst was commissioned and sent to Cyprus, he read *Swann's Way* – 'I kept finding thoughts and feelings articulated which I instantly recognized but had never seen or heard expressed in words before'[168] – and he talked to Sigmund Pollitzer, an aesthete who had moved to Cyprus partly to escape from English prudery and repression: 'This was my first conversation ever about homosexuality with an adult homosexual.'[169] Alongside all this, however, Hurst also discovered a different kind of sexual style among ordinary soldiers. He was struck by the case of Sergeant Major Banks, who was busted down to the ranks after making 'a very unmistakable sexual proposition' to a corporal while drunk. Banks could not have been compared with a Dresden shepherd and he suggested a form of homosexual identity that had nothing to do with reading Proust or talking about art. He was a smartly turned-out and tough-minded NCO whose weather-beaten face and husky voice made him seem older than his thirty-one years. He also had the name 'Gladys' tattooed on his arm. He looked, as Hurst recalled thirty years later, 'anything but a "poof"'.[170]

Asked whether national service was a good thing, a conscript undergoing basic training in the RAF said: 'it makes a man out of him and if he has anything wrong with him they will see him OK'.[171] Servicemen coming to the end of their time in the forces – especially those who had seen active service – were sometimes less sure that they knew what 'making men' might mean. Peter Mayo was very masculine in some ways. An athlete and climber, he underwent the brutalities of commando training in the Royal Marines without complaint. He became an officer and was 'a Christian and a gentleman' of the Tom Brown variety (he had been head boy of Rugby). At first, he disapproved of the licentious behaviour of his comrades in arms – though he seems to have become dubious about aspects of Christian morality, especially sexual morality, during his time in the marines: 'the five wise virgins must have been quite intolerable'.[172] He led his marines ashore at Suez and saw violent action. He was grazed by a bullet and a sergeant died next to him: 'My hands were covered with his blood and I shall never forget the sweet, hot smell of it.'[173]

Returning from Port Said, he was shown some pornographic pictures – the stokers on the troopship had bought them from Egyptians and passed them to a sergeant who had then handed them up to the officers' deck. In a curiously thoughtful passage of his diary, Mayo wrote:

They were quite nauseating and degrading, and perverted, but they had of course the effect of arousing desire and lust, and a sneaking feeling that such disgusting excesses could be rather fun in a sensual way, if the intellectual horror were overcome. It only served to bring home my own gross inexperience. I suppose my inhibitions are the result of my upbringing.[174]

On arrival back in England, Mayo made the following entry in his diary: 'Letter from mummy. She is terribly pleased that her little boy is home again safe and sound.'[175]

9
Officers

Is that hurting?
Yes.
Yes, what?
Yes, a little bit.
Yes a little bit WHAT?
Yes, a little bit, sir.

> Conversation between conscript private
> and army dentist (officer), 1946[1]

Post-war conscripts began their military careers, at least nominally, on the lowest rung of the ladder (as privates or as the equivalent ranks in the air force or navy). Unlike regulars, national servicemen could not proceed straight to officer training academies.[2] However, unlike wartime conscripts, they were divided quickly, and almost definitively, into those who would be commissioned and those who would stay in the ranks. Within a few weeks of reporting for duty, most men knew whether or not they would be officers, and many of the best-connected national servicemen knew before they even received their call-up papers that they were likely to be commissioned.

All three services commissioned conscripts. Getting into the navy at all was hard, and public schools seem to have discouraged their boys from undertaking their national service in the navy because they believed that commissions were easier to obtain in the army.[3] Some national service naval officers were recruited because they had degrees in engineering and the rest were often self-confident or highly educated. The navy valued academic distinction more than the other services and two of its national service officers – Jeremy Wolfenden and Peter Jay – vied for the distinction of being recognized as 'the cleverest man in England'. National service officer cadets in the navy were known as 'upper yardmen' – a Hornbloweresque title that evoked the days when thirteen-year-olds had climbed the rigging. They were selected after a short period of basic training and sent to train on ships at sea: training that included some hard exercises in navigation.

National service naval officers were almost always drawn from relatively privileged backgrounds, but they often commented that social class counted for less in the navy than in the army. This was in part because many regular naval officers had been educated at Dartmouth and were thus less preoccupied by the hierarchy of public schools that so interested army officers. It was also because naval officers generally lived on ships and were not required to indulge in the expensive entertainments that were sometimes expected of officers in smart regiments. Most importantly, officers who might be required to guide a destroyer into Valletta harbour, for example, placed a higher value on technical competence than social polish.

The RAF commissioned larger numbers of men than the navy. It also ran officer selection in a more systematic and centralized fashion than the other two services. From 1951, the air force identified potential officers at their Ministry of Labour medicals. They were defined in largely educational terms and included 'all recruits with the basic educational qualifications of School Certificate or its equivalent'.[4]

Between 1951 and 1955, potential officers among ground crew were all sent to RAF Hednesford, where they underwent the same basic training as ordinary recruits. During the first four weeks, 'every effort [was made] to avoid giving to the recruits any suggestion that presupposes that they will be commissioned'. Eventually men were invited to fill in forms stating whether they wanted a commission, and, if not, why not. After six weeks, potential officers were interviewed and some were sent to the air force selection board, which would determine whether or not they should be commissioned.[5] From 1955, potential officers were spread around a variety of bases, those identified as suitable being sent to a ground crew officer selection centre. The RAF also interviewed graduates before they were called up to determine whether they were suitable for a commission, and offered them a chance of being sent to another service if they were not.[6]

At first commissions were rare for national service airmen. In 1950, over 50,000 conscripts were posted to the air force, of whom the vast majority were ground crew. Of these, 700 were commissioned, and a further 300 were trained to fly as officer cadets.[7] That year there were just 811 national service officers in the air force.[8] Officer numbers expanded quickly in the next few years – perhaps because of the active approach that the service took to commissioning and perhaps too because the RAF, drawing many of its recruits from grammar schools, was particularly affected by the Butler Education Act of 1944. By 1953, there were 3,393 officers and 73,637 other ranks among national service airmen.[9] After this, the proportion of officers declined again – though it never fell back to its 1950 levels.[10] Apart from the small group of men who actually flew planes, RAF officers rarely led glamorous lives: many were posted to departments concerned with secretarial work or catering.[11]

Many national service airmen who could in theory have been officers did not put themselves forward for commissions – in 1951, 50 per cent of those who were educationally eligible for commissions did not wish to be considered for them.[12] In part, this reticence was due to the fact that a large proportion of airmen had left school at sixteen: such youths met the minimum education qualifications for a commission but may in practice have believed that they were unlikely to get one or that they would not feel comfortable as officers. Of those who chose not to apply for commissions in the mid 1950s, 20.4 per cent said that they felt personally inadequate to hold a commission. Another 27.5 per cent cited their belief that holding a commission would be too expensive – an odd view in light of the fact that an RAF officer would not usually have expensive social obligations and recruits tended to overestimate how much officers were paid.[13]

Some who went into the RAF were in effect trading the chance of a commission for a relatively comfortable and interesting life. A senior officer in the service recognized that graduates – he seems to have meant graduates in technical subjects – who were not preselected for commissions 'still prefer the RAF to other services (not always from the highest motives admittedly)'.[14] A study of airmen revealed a group who deliberately turned away from obtaining commissions in favour of acquiring skills in trades that might be useful for their future careers. This was particularly true of men who had served apprenticeships before joining up. Investigators were struck by the fact that some skilled workers were uninterested in social status, or at least in the kind of social status offered by the officers' mess. About a third of men who did not apply for a commission hoped, instead, to learn a trade; more than one in ten of them wanted time for study.[15]

Aircrew, especially pilots, were different. Flying was attractive to many young men; it offered the prospect of serving in the 'teeth arm' *par excellence* and all pilots were potential officers. The chance of a flying commission was the one thing that attracted upper-middle-class men into the air force. The selection of pilots was more scientific than that of officers in any other part of the armed forces. Medical standards were ruthlessly enforced. No one with slow reactions, poor eyesight or a nervous disposition was allowed to fly a Meteor, even if his father was Air Chief Marshal. Men rejected for flying commissions usually understood that they had been through a rigorous but necessary process.[16]

Most national service officers were in the army. In August 1954 there were 5,869 officers and 207,022 other ranks among national servicemen in the army.[17] Given that no one could be commissioned until he had spent at least six months in the ranks, that some men took considerably longer and that others, officers especially, were released early so that they could go to university, it seems likely that something between 3 and 4 per cent of all national servicemen were commissioned at some point.[18]

After a few days in the army, recruits were interviewed by a personnel selection officer (PSO), who advised them about, among other things, whether they should seek a commission. Some young men were identified as potential officers, or other rank 1 (OR1), at this stage.

Educational level was the most important element in determining who became an OR1 – but the army did not make decisions on educational grounds alone. In 1951, about a third of all graduate national servicemen from England were not rated OR1.[19]

Most army units separated OR1s from the bulk of their comrades after a certain time (usually about two weeks). Sometimes, the OR1s were sent to a special squad in the same training depot or to a separate unit that might exist to train potential officers for a whole corps. For the first three years after the war, training regiments for 'leaders' mixed men who were expected to be commissioned with men who were expected to serve as NCOs. From 1948, the separation between a potential officer and those destined to stay in the ranks was sharper. Special units were often officially described as being for 'junior leaders' but recruits knew that they were really for potential officers.

Soldiers identified as potential officers received the same basic training as other privates, though the atmosphere in units for potential officers could be competitive, and the most ambitious demonstrated an enthusiasm for spit and polish that exasperated their comrades.[20] Some NCOs who commanded potential officers resented the privileges that their charges would enjoy,[21] but most were helpful, occasionally because they were running sweepstakes on the results.[22]

After a few weeks, men would appear before a Unit Selection Board (USB), usually convened by the commanding officer of their training unit, to determine whether they should be put forward for a commission. Almost all men who attended an USB were OR1s. In the early 1950s, the army encouraged USBs to reject larger proportions of men partly in order to ensure that more of those who got through this stage managed to pass the later tests.

To men from the officer class, USB was a joke. Neal Ascherson recalled the exchange with his commanding officer in the Royal Marines:

> 'I want you to think carefully: suppose you had the choice of playing football with your commando group or playing tennis with an extremely attractive blonde. Which would you do? Think very carefully about your answer.' So in order to show respect I thought very carefully about this and said: 'I think I'd probably play football with my men, sir'. He said: 'That's the right answer.'[23]

Less privileged men found things more awkward and many of them felt that the USB was, even more than other parts of the officer selection process, linked to social class.[24]

Those found satisfactory at USB spent three days being assessed at the War Office Selection Board (WOSB). Candidates were required to undergo tests of initiative and 'leadership', involving improbable exercises in which they were required to cross 'rivers' with the aid of planks and oil drums. They were also required to give 'lecturettes' – ten-minute talks that were designed to display self-confidence and articulacy. Apolitical, middle-brow topics – Gilbert and Sullivan[25] or bee-keeping[26] – were favoured: 'one candidate gave a compelling account of the social history of whisky, which was much praised by a conducting officer with a face ravaged by his own research into the topic'.[27] Candidates were interviewed by a committee, which enquired into their backgrounds, interests and reasons for wishing to become an officer.

Those responsible for officer selection, especially at regimental level, regarded the process as an art rather than a science. They made much of 'leadership', 'style' and 'enthusiasm' – qualities that did not lend themselves easily to measurement, or even definition. They trusted experienced officers to judge candidates according to their own instincts, and were sceptical of formal tests. Smart regiments were centres of resistance to attempts to democratize the army. Bernard Fergusson was proud of the fact that the Black Watch, which he commanded, contained many officers whose fathers had served in the regiment. He also believed that having been captain of the boats at Eton was adequate proof of officerly qualities, and was angry that the War Office did not share this view.[28]

Some regiments seem to have ignored the results of intelligence tests or even tests of medical fitness, if men from the 'right' background did badly. W. J. R. Morrison, called up in 1949, did not regard himself as 'much of a soldier'. He had done badly in the practical tests that were administered to recruits and was described at this stage as a 'potential clerk' but, like most public school boys, he was posted to a potential officers' platoon. He sailed through WOSB: 'When it subsequently came out that I had played for English Public Schools earlier in the year I was home and dry. We only discussed rugby as far as

I remember.' He eventually won the prize for best cadet in his officer training – still, he thought, because of the rugby.[29] John Scurr scored badly in an intelligence test when he first arrived in the Durham Light Infantry. However, when those conducting the tests found out about his education, and thereby, implicitly, about his social background, they gave him another test and then put him in a potential officers' platoon.[30] Piers Plowright also did badly in an intelligence test during his basic training but the 'kindly sergeant' in charge of the process said that he was probably officer material anyway and sent him to a potential officers' unit. Plowright thought that the decision was mainly to do with class and that 'speaking well' and having been to public school were the key attributes sought.[31]

Those who succeeded at WOSB were sent to one of the two Officer Cadet Training Units. Those destined for the infantry, the Ordnance Corps, the Military Police, the Intelligence Corps, the Royal Army Service Corps (RASC), the Pioneer Corps and the marines (technically part of the navy) were sent to Eaton Hall in Cheshire, as were men destined for the Royal Electrical and Mechanical Engineers (REME) until late 1954. Eaton Hall was the family seat of the Duke of Westminster. A nineteenth-century building knocked about a bit by various forms of military occupation, it was still more comfortable and attractive than most barracks. Over the staircase hung a large grubby painting – *The Adoration of the Magi* by Rubens – that was often the target of high jinks by the cadets. One of the instructors wrote that 'the trappings of by-gone elegance help to lift training above the normal routine of "learning to be an officer" into the realms of "learning to lead men"'. Cohorts of about sixty cadets arrived every fortnight for most of the year.[32]

Officers in the Royal Artillery, the Royal Engineers, the Armoured Corps, REME (from late 1954), the Signals Corps and the Pay Corps were sent to Mons in Aldershot. The Armoured Corps and the artillery spent their whole sixteen weeks at Mons; other corps and regiments spent six weeks there and were then sent for more specialized training. Mons took more students than Eaton Hall – about 600 at a time when Eaton Hall had 480.[33]

Mons was reputed to have a harsher training regime than Eaton

Hall – perhaps because it was in a town where everything revolved around the army. For much of the national service period, Mons was also the home of Regimental Sergeant Major Brittain, known for having the loudest voice in the British army. Brittain was the most famous of the sergeant majors who drilled cadets as they passed through Officer Cadet Training Units – so famous that even soldiers who never got anywhere near being officers had heard of him.[34] The others were Copp (of the Coldstream Guards) at Eaton Hall and Lynch of the Irish Guards (who succeeded Copp). Former cadets often made a cult of these NCOs. Oxford undergraduates formed a Copp dining club. Autobiographies recall a selection of bons mots – 'there's nothing in the world I like better to see than a young ensign fairly cutting about in front of his platoon' (Lynch); 'I've had enough of your San Fairy Ann attitude' (Copp) – the more erudite cadets guessed that this was a rendition of 'ça ne fait rien' that had been picked up from an Abbeville tart in 1916 and passed down through generations of men in the sergeants' mess.[35]

There was, however, an element of artificiality about the relation between officer cadets and their NCOs. The power of the latter was only temporary. The metaphor of theatre – so often applied to national service – was especially apt with regard to officer training. Kevin O'Sullivan said that Catterick, where he went through basic training, was 'kitchen sink drama' but that Eaton Hall was 'high comedy' – 'an arena for the theatrical display of military values' in which Lynch was the 'producer, director and compère'.[36] The performance of RSMs was not, underneath its outward forms, an entirely dignified one. Visiting dignitaries at Mons often paid homage to Brittain, but he was a parade ground soldier: though he had joined the army in 1917, he had never seen active service. Privately some cadets despised Brittain: 'big, fat, noisy, vulgar man'.[37] The end of Brittain's career was sad and must have taught him, if he had ever had any doubt on the subject, about the ruthlessness of the officer class. Shortly after his retirement, he was evicted from his army quarters.[38]

National service officers were taught tactics, map-reading and the handling of weapons. Occasionally they had an uncomfortable glimpse of what real war might be like: one was told by his instructor that his revolver, the symbol of officer status, was useless for real fighting and that on the battlefield he should pick up a 'dead man's rifle'.[39] Cadets were required to play sports and often were made to box. The last of these ordeals was remembered with horror by many men. A report on officer training in the Signals recognized that compulsory boxing was controversial but that it was 'a guide as to the character of the participants and whether an individual possesses "guts"'.[40]

Outright failure at cadet school was rare. In 1950, 7.94 per cent of cadets at Eaton Hall were held back for further training and 2.61 per cent were returned to their units; even then, some would come back and take commissions later.[41] In 1955, fifty-eight candidates were returned to unit from both cadet schools. Of these thirty-five were 'lacking officer qualities in most respects', and twenty-three lacked some technical ability.[42] For most cadets, 'failure' by this stage usually meant failure to get into a prestigious regiment. An instructor at Mons remarked that the worst cadets would be sent to the Catering Corps 'where their powers of leadership would not be strained'.[43]

As the military authorities themselves recognized, the award of commissions favoured certain categories of men. The first distinction was regional. Men from the south of England were most likely to be commissioned: 66 per cent of national service officers came from this region, which contained 40.5 per cent of the total national population. The north of England, by contrast, provided 28.5 per cent of national service officers while containing 49 per cent of the population. Scotland had just over 10 per cent of the country's total population and provided just over 5 per cent of national service officers.[44] Recruitment into the Territorial Army exposed the scale of the problem. The TA took most of its officers from those who had held national service commissions but, unlike the regular army, it had to work on a regional basis so that most soldiers were posted close to their home. This created problems when some areas contained more officers than others. A study of 1952 showed that the Territorial Army could meet less than half of its requirements in Scotland. By contrast, the eastern and southern areas (excluding Cornwall) had a surplus of officers. London and its seven surrounding counties needed only a little more than a quarter of all TA officers but produced almost half of them. Surrey, the 'stockbroker belt', was the most 'over-officered' county in the United Kingdom – its production of officers accounted for almost seven times its needs. Most northern and Midlands counties, by contrast, were 'under-officered'.[45]

A report by the Chief Education Officer of Northern Command suggested that the regional basis of recruitment was partly a matter of tradition and culture. Men from the south were most likely to have relations who had already been officers. The north was sometimes associated with 'pacifist', which in this context presumably meant nonconformist, beliefs. The middle classes of the north were also believed to be more 'inward looking', less interested in events outside their own region and more likely to have a 'technical' rather than 'general' education.[46] The army believed that national service itself had begun to erode this difference as boys from the north were increasingly likely to gain military experience and then influence their younger relations. Welshmen were under-represented among those who were commissioned. The army defined Wales as part of the 'north' and admitted that the chances of obtaining a commission for a Welshman were about one quarter less than the chances of any other 'northerner'.[47]

Accents mattered in the army. Personnel selection officers seem to have discriminated against men who were held to have 'strong' regional accents. The officer-training wing of the Signals Corps, which attracted some men of relatively plebeian origin, engaged an expert on speech from Leeds University to teach its cadets how to talk. Some national servicemen believed that having a Yorkshire accent could get a man removed from a potential officers' squad.[48]

Scotsmen were less likely to be commissioned than men from England. The army itself believed that the under-representation of Scots sprang from the nature of the Scottish education system, the fact that fewer men attained the necessary educational levels and the fact that there were few Scottish public schools.

It also seems, however, that some Scottish soldiers (at least those from outside Glasgow) escaped from the constraints of the English class system. Scottish accents did not disadvantage candidates for commissions in the way that regional English accents did.[49] The very fact that public schools in Scotland were rare may have meant that attendance at an academic day school in Scotland was more accept-able than attendance at a grammar school would have been in England or Wales. William Purves was offered a commission in the smartest Scottish regiment of the line in spite of the fact that he came from a comparatively humble background. Ronnie Cramond, commissioned into the Royal Scots, claimed that he was one of three Scottish cadets who arrived at Eaton Hall in November 1949 and that he, a bursary pupil from George Heriot's School in Edinburgh, joined fifty-seven others – 'all from the Guards Training Depot and virtually all from top English public schools such as Eton, Rugby, Winchester'.[50]

Regional origin, by which the army set such great store, related to social class. Indeed, the expression of a regional identity was itself a statement about class because the grandest members of the *grande bourgeoisie* thought in national, rather than regional, terms and based their lives around institutions – Oxford, Cambridge, the Inns of Court, the Stock Exchange – in the south east of England. The most secure members of the officer class wore their regional affiliations lightly – a man might serve in the Welsh Guards when his brother held a commission in the Scots Guards.

A public school education was the single most important asset for a potential officer, and the kind of education that a man had received mattered more than its extent or academic distinction. The War Office divided schools into three categories: public schools, grammar schools and 'others'. Young men from public schools stood by far the best chance of being commissioned. There were some straightforward rea-sons why public school boys were at an advantage. Almost all of them had been members of the Officer Training Corps or Combined Cadet Force. Housemasters wrote references for the selection boards and gave advice to boys about, for example, the relative advantages of the guards, the 'RB' (Rifle Brigade) and a 'county regiment'.[51] Officer selection panels sought qualities that tended to go with a certain type of schooling – enthusiasm for team games and a display of 'social graces'. Simply getting on with other potential officers was important, so anything that provided men with a common culture was useful. David Bentata recalled: 'Eaton Hall came at just the right time in my life. My main sport was long-range .303 rifle shooting and I was keen as mustard to be in the army, and to gain a commission, since I felt that was what my education at Blundell's had prepared me for.'[52]

It was no secret that family background mattered. Sons of generals or cabinet ministers were rarely rejected.[53] Having a father or brother who had been an officer was an advantage.[54] A colonel who chaired WOSB compared the selection of officers to the breeding and care of cavalry chargers, an image that itself says much about the social assumptions of the British army:

> The commanding officer of an ABTU [Army Basic Training Unit] once wrote concerning one of his potential officers. 'He's all right. I knew his father who was in the regiment, and his grandfather was in it before that.' The selectors found themselves in agreement with this verdict, but, and this is important, not without examining form as well.[55]

Officer selection procedures were not, however, rigged in a blatant way. It was possible for men who appeared to have all the right connections and attributes to fail. There were public school boys, and even the sons of regular officers, who served out their whole two years as privates.

An army study of June 1954 examined the qualities of men who had the minimum qualifications to be officers.[56] Men from the south of England, who were also the ones most likely to be commissioned, were young (two thirds of them were younger than nineteen and a half), only one tenth were graduates and over half of them had studied 'arts'. In the north, more than half of men were aged over twenty, one fifth were graduates and over half had studied science. Of northerners, around a quarter had attended public schools against four in ten of southerners. In the south around a quarter of men had fathers who had been officers; in the north the figure was one in ten.[57]

If northern grammar school boys with scientific degrees from red-brick universities were commissioned at all, they tended to go into units that required particular technical expertise. The Medical Corps was one of these, and the figures for Scotsmen commissioned look even lower when one remembers that almost a quarter of all Scottish national service officers were in fact doctors or dentists.[58] REME drew a larger proportion of its officers from the north than any other corps of the army. Some educational courses led directly into technical branches of the army: almost all graduates in forestry from the University of Aberdeen in the 1950s seem to have been commissioned in the Royal Engineers.[59] A manager at ICI told a War Office enquiry into national service that engineers from the company had an easier time than chemists because the latter did not have a specialty that was of particular use to the forces and were rarely commissioned.[60] Generally, the army seems to have assumed that men with scientific qualifications were suited for particular technical functions but that the overall 'officerly' qualities required by the artillery, Armoured Corps and infantry (the most prestigious units in which to be commissioned) were more likely to be found among eighteen-year-olds from public schools.

The brigadier commanding the War Office Selection Board wrote in 1953:

a) There is a general tendency in the North towards earlier specialization, which does not foster officerly qualities. So many technicians from the North have no interests whatever outside their own narrow line of study.

b) Deferrents for technical training are higher in the heavy industrial areas of the North and Midlands. The effect of this is that by the time they come into the Army many men are too set in their ways to be adaptable to Army Life.[61]

Occasionally, the army broke down the education of its recruits by the kind of subject they had studied as well as the level attained. In the second half of 1951, 1,068 graduates were called up, of whom 685 had degrees in science. Of the remainder, 293 had degrees in arts subjects and ninety in economics or commerce. These men were distributed in a revealing way. Both the graduates who went into the Foot Guards had studied arts, as had eighteen out of twenty-eight in the infantry of the line. Science graduates were concentrated in REME, which took 219 of them, and the Royal Engineers, which took 236.[62] Among those who entered the army having left school at eighteen, 2,181 had specialized in arts, 1,667 in science and forty-three in economics. Men who had studied arts dominated all the prestigious 'teeth arm' units – even those, such as the artillery or the tank regiments, that might have been supposed to require some technical competence.[63] National service officers were themselves struck by the disdain for technical expertise. One said, in retrospect, that more recognition should have been given to the fact that every man in the armoured corps was a 'technician of some kind'.[64]

Viscount Weymouth remembered being told that having achieved the lowest possible score on mechanical tests did not preclude a commission in the Life Guards, which was, supposedly, an armoured regiment: 'it was soon to be impressed upon me that the Household Brigade was virtually independent from the rest of the British army. The tests that were devised for others did not necessarily apply to ourselves.'[65]

Some men asked not to be officers. A. B. Carter, in the Royal Electrical and Mechanical Engineers, was sent to a potential officer wing but changed his mind, 'and several other minds' and 'went non-desirous'.[66] David Baxter and David Lodge both asked to be released from potential officer status. Both recalled that the army was disconcerted by this request and that many of their contemporaries imitated them once they had made a stand. Baxter relished the fact that refusing a commission required the very qualities – initiative and leadership – that army officers were meant to have: 'Our small attempt to decide the conditions of our service measured the inertia of our fellow potential cadets: now that the idea occurred more than half of the course resigned in the morning.'[67]

Outright rebellions, in which men such as Baxter asked to be removed from potential officer squads, were rare. It was, however, relatively common for men to express themselves 'non-desirous' of having a commission – though the proportion of men who did so diminished in the early 1950s, as the army sought to encourage men from outside the 'officer class' to seek commissions. The proportion of non-desirous men increased again in the late 1950s – perhaps as the end of national service came into view and the hierarchies of the army began to seem less important.[68]

Some men, who did not regard themselves as rebels against the army, decided that an officer's life was not for them. Jack Burn was a graduate (from King's College Newcastle) who had served in the University Training Corps. Some men from his background did become officers and he himself was encouraged to apply for a commission, but he was told by friends that mess bills were hard to sustain on the pay of a national service subaltern and that he would be better off as a sergeant in the Royal Army Education Corps (RAEC).[69] John Kelly was from a similar background. He remembered the two public school boys in his basic training unit who displayed ostentatious enthusiasm to be commissioned, but he distinguished them from the majority of the platoon who were 'ordinary lads' and from his own associates who were destined for non-commissioned rank in the RAEC: 'we graduates must have seemed oddities . . . with little interest in applying for commissions'.[70] T. C. Sparrow knew about the Education Corps because of a talk at school (Prince Henry's Grammar School in Evesham), which had identified it 'as being particularly suitable for those with a grammar school education'. He was, against his wishes, identified as a potential officer but, after seven weeks in the army, he persuaded the authorities that the Education Corps was his proper destination.[71] Investigating the reasons why there were so few officers for the Territorial Army outside the Home Counties, the military authorities found that 'Potential Officers were being allowed or persuaded to go into the RAEC, sometimes finishing as only sergeants.'[72]

Men of high education frequently expressed the wish not be commissioned. And, once again, this often overlapped with regional and social differences. In Scotland, graduates made up 26 per cent of potential officers but 41 per cent of potential officers who expressed themselves 'non-desirous'.[73] Graduates may have rejected commissions because those who did national service after university also tended to be grammar school/redbrick university men who were ill-at-ease with the army for social reasons.

Among those who wanted a commission but failed to obtain it, some were stoical. A few returned to their own regiments as clerks and thus saw their own papers: 'an NCO of above average intelligence but does not appear to take the army seriously'.[74] David Batterham found out that the selection board had regarded him as a 'half-convinced conscientious objector'.[75] Tony Dipple regarded his WOSB verdict – 'I had no personality and could not express myself' – as fair.[76] David Henderson had been company sergeant major in the cadet force of his grammar school. He was rated as a potential officer but failed the War Office Selection Board: 'obviously I did not fulfil all the requirements'. He had another try later in his military career and was told that he 'did not have a wide enough interest in things'. He accepted the decision, signed on as a regular and rose to the rank of sergeant. He felt no bitterness towards officers – even when one of them wounded him with a grenade: 'Sir, I think I have been hit . . . I think that I had better lie down, sir.'[77]

Rejection for a commission could, however, be painful and could raise questions in a man's mind about his own status and background. A. R. Eaton joined the Royal Artillery and was pleased to be put in a potential officers' course, on the strength of his Queen's Scout Award – though he also said that life 'with the toffs' was less fun than in his original unit and that there were 'no scraps on the floor'.[78] His father was keen for him to 'get on in the army',[79] but Eaton's letters home reflect a growing sense that his family background, which seems to have been comparatively humble, might be a bar to a commission:

> I don't care what Dad says. You have to have one or more of three qualifications before getting the remotest chance of reaching Mons. The most important is the name of your school – a grammar or tech is almost useless. It has to be something good like Brentwood or Harrow or something. Secondly, the recent army record of brothers and fathers – if they have been commissioned of course. Also your own trade or your father's trade – a builder is no good.[80]

After facing his Unit Selection Board, he wrote: 'Not much good news this time, I'm afraid. I've rather let the family down by failing to get WOSB . . . CO refused to put me forward after last interview . . . He said I just wasn't the officer type – but I should make an extremely good NCO.'[81]

The fact that 'good NCO' could be a damning verdict says much about the class divisions of the armed forces. A conscript in a cavalry regiment heard that he had been turned down on account of 'NCO tendencies'.[82] Peter Mayo was perfect officer material: a rugby player and a Christian, he had been head boy of a major public school and was called up into the marines before he took up his classics scholarship at Cambridge. The only other middle-class man in his hut would have been mortified if he had seen Mayo's diary entry about him: 'There is one other RMFVR [Royal Marine Forces Volunteer Reserve] bloke in the hut called Terry J . . . very nice really but slightly authoritative, if that's the right word, and he occasionally lays on the "good man" act a bit thick. He would make a very good NCO.'[83]

John Green wrote to his parents in enthusiastic terms about the early period of his army training: 'It's all rather fun here, if you treat it as a big game'; 'There is a good chance of a commission'; 'If you play rugger here you can get away with anything.'[84] He was put in a junior leaders' platoon and approved of his new companions: 'The people here, i.e. the ORIs, are very nice all grammar and public school types – one chap in my room has a BA and has just finished a three years research studentship.'[85] Green, however, failed WOSB and went to Malaya as a private. His letters home suggest a new view of the army and his own social position:

> Why do 90 per cent of officers always treat private soldiers as if they were some sort of obnoxious silage? Really some of them I would be ashamed to be seen with in England – they are really revolting in their manners. Still I shan't meet them in civilian life.[86]

In principle, men who failed WOSB were returned to their original unit and to the ranks. There was often an uncomfortable period in which the army tried to decide what to do with them. Paperwork was sometimes lost.[87] Robert Miller said that he became a 'non-person' after failing WOSB. He worked in the kitchens of his regiment for a while before being sent to train as a clerk.[88]

The army was not indifferent to the fate of men who failed to become officers. The commanding officer of the 14/20 Hussars protested against having all men who failed to become officers returned to his unit:

> The great majority of these boys are naturally disappointed and somewhat disgruntled. They therefore need careful handling and individual

attention, if the best is going to be got out of them ... In fairness to these young men, who must obviously be above the general National Service standard.[89]

Such men were actively encouraged to make their military careers in particular units, or particular jobs, that required a degree of education and that offered some protection from the discomforts and humiliations inflicted on ordinary soldiers. The Education Corps, where those responsible for teaching soldiers were given the automatic rank of sergeant, was an obvious destination for rejected officers. The Intelligence Corps was another – a brigadier from the corps said in 1960 that it would appeal to educated men (the minimum requirement was a GCE in English language) who had failed WOSB: 'they would find the atmosphere congenial both in the matter of trades and the type of soldiers serving in the Corps'.[90]

Piers Plowright was such a soldier. Educated at Stowe and waiting to take up a place at Oxford, he failed WOSB and was then posted away from the Fusiliers, into which he had initially been called up, into the Intelligence Corps, which was 'quite often home for brightish lads not likely to be officers' and which contained 'a lot of failed officers'[91] as well as grammar school boys. Plowright was sent to Malaya, where he enjoyed his time as a sergeant in Field Intelligence, though he had a twinge of regret when he came across the 'very pukka' officers of the King's Dragoon Guards: 'I felt a bit inferior because I had failed to be an officer.'[92] He then went up to Christ Church, where he felt it 'odd to be back with the officer class again'.[93]

Even men who returned to their own units after failing officer selection often ended up in a clerical position that removed them from ordinary regimental duties and that usually brought with it a corporal's stripes. Some saw refusing such jobs, or the promotion that went with them, as a form of rebellion. Having left a potential officers' squad, David Baxter became a clerk but he refused any promotion above the rank of private. Andreas Whittam Smith failed WOSB and then decided that 'if you cannot be the top, be the bottom' – a double or quits attitude that underlay a successful later career. He refused to be a 'poncey little pay corporal' and served out the remainder of his time as a private.[94]

A few national service officers later expressed regret that they had not stayed in the ranks. P. J. Kavanagh felt that the potential officers' squad at the Armoured Corps training regiment was less friendly than the platoon into which he had originally entered. He wrote: 'I've often wished since I'd said "No" and gone back to my friends; perhaps only because it would have been something to preen myself on. I can only admit it never occurred to me. Chiefly I wanted to get out of the eye of those infernal Policemen.'[95]

At the other extreme were men who tried to become officers more than once and, occasionally, more than twice.[96] This was true of those who had been graded 'watch' at WOSB, and of those who failed their cadet courses but were allowed to retake part of the course or to return at a later date. The commandant of Mons wrote of men 'whose failings cannot satisfactorily be eradicated by a prolongation of training at OCS but who may well make good if they are given a position of responsibility in their own unit'.[97] Men serving in the UK or Germany would be allowed back after eight months, or eleven months if serving with the Education Corps. Men serving overseas could be allowed back after nine months, or twelve months if serving with the Education Corps. It was therefore, at least theoretically, possible for a man to return to officer cadet school when he had served three quarters of his two-year term.

Some men tried to get a commission even after the full-time element of their national service was over. One went through officer training school but was returned to his unit as unsuitable and trained as a clerk. He then reapplied to go before WOSB and returned to the cadet school, where he failed again after six weeks. He finished his national service as a lance corporal but then joined the Officer Training Corps at university and was eventually commissioned, four years after his first attempt, as an officer in the Territorial Army.[98] Rodney Giesler had wanted to become a naval officer but failed the medical to get into Dartmouth naval college. He went instead to Pangbourne, a public school that specialized in preparing men for naval careers, but was then called up into the army. He failed to obtain a commission and insisted, perhaps a little too emphatically, that this was much for the best, that he had had a more interesting time in the ranks, that national service officers were 'dreadful little pip squeaks' and that officers from smart regiments had, in any case, recognized his 'cut glass accent'. All the same, Giesler went to some trouble, after his full-time service was over, to transfer into the Royal Naval Volunteer Reserve and eventually get a commission in it.[99]

Background and contacts mattered most when it came to choosing regiments in the army. The smartest cavalry regiments were a world of their own.[100] In 1948, an officer cadet in the Royal Armoured Corps (which incorporated the cavalry regiments) reckoned that a fifth of men in his unit were fellow Etonians but that even Etonians apparently stood little chance of getting into the cavalry without family connections.[101] Even, and perhaps especially, men whose fathers were regular officers understood that anyone without a private income should avoid the cavalry.[102] Alan Bexon was a grammar school boy from a middle-class background in Nottingham who joined the 14/20 Hussars. He might have been commissioned but it was made clear to him that he would not be allowed to stay as an officer in the cavalry without independent means and he decided that he preferred his regiment to the prospect of a commission.[103]

There were hierarchies between and within corps. The Royal Horse Artillery (RHA) was most prestigious for officers in the gunners, partly because of its association with the glamour of the cavalry, and only officers who passed out high at Mons could hope for commissions in the RHA. At the bottom of the scale stood units such as the Royal Army Service Corps, seen as relatively easy in which to get a commission.[104]

Prestigious regiments had traditions of recruiting officers from privileged backgrounds. They were marked by a sharp distinction between officers and other ranks but by a relaxed egalitarianism among officers themselves. Christopher Hurst, an Etonian who was called up into the Rifle Brigade but then commissioned into a lesser regiment, wrote disapprovingly about the atmosphere of the Lancastrian Brigade training centre, to which he was briefly attached:

> Few of these officers were 'gentlemen' – the county gentry, wherever they hailed from, normally preferred to be with their own kind in the Guards or cavalry, or in the Green Jackets and a small number of more select light infantry or county regiments, or Highland ones (the Black

Watch, especially) if they were Scots. My Barton Stacey friend John Wilberforce, for example, went into the King's Own Yorkshire Light Infantry, a battalion of which his father commanded till his death in action.[105]

Simon Raven's half serious analysis of the 'English gentleman' was partly based on his own experience – first as a conscript in the Oxford and Buckinghamshire Light Infantry and then as a regular officer in the King's Shropshire Light Infantry, which he recalled thus:

> unsmart by 'Brigade' [i.e. the Brigade of Guards] standards ... below the Rifle Regiments but above most Heavy Regiments of the line ... all the regulars (though not all the National Service officers) had been to important public schools, and some of them could boast a vague country house in their family background.[106]

One result of this hierarchy was that some regiments ran a surplus of potential officers and exported men to be commissioned in lesser regiments after they had completed their basic training. This was true of the guards. The Rifle Brigade and the King's Royal Rifle Corps were also difficult regiments in which to get a commission. One national serviceman, who later became a regular and rose to the rank of field marshal, undertook his basic training with a rifle regiment before being packed off to the artillery for the remainder of his service.[107] Denys Whatmore had initially been sent for basic training to the Highland Light Infantry but persuaded the personnel selection officer to have him transferred to the King's Royal Rifle Corps. He and all his contemporaries were warned that they would have to transfer to other regiments on being commissioned – a decision that aroused particular resentment from the two Etonians in the cohort.[108] The Signals Corps, by contrast, exported almost no officers – only nineteen of 131 men from the corps who passed WOSB in 1956 went to other units.[109]

Regiments were allowed – indeed expected – to take account of regional origins and family associations when they chose officers. In theory, the choice was made at the end of officer training and took account of the cadets' performance as well as the needs of each regiment. In practice, all sorts of personal negotiations took place outside official procedures.

Many were commissioned into particular regiments as a result of intervention by family or friends. Anthony Howard described the circumstances under which he became an officer in the Royal Fusiliers: 'In my case it was real jobbery. I had a friend who knew very well the colonel of the Fusiliers (she was the mother of an Oxford friend). She put in a word for me with the colonel of the regiment.'[110]

The expectation that men would have family links with a particular regiment was so strong that Howard's friend Michael Holroyd invented a 'Bunbury-style' uncle to ease his own entry into the Fusiliers – a ruse that may have worked partly because, as an Etonian, he obviously came from the 'right background'.[111] Less privileged men were made to understand that the Fusiliers was not for them.[112]

John Nott engineered a transfer from the RASC to a more socially acceptable regiment through his aunt, a friend of the Adjutant General.[113] John Barkshire wanted to join the Duke of Wellington's Regiment because it was famous for the quality of its rugby: 'a cousin of my father's was a very great friend of somebody who had recently commanded the regiment and he got me in'.[114] Barry Reed was a seventeen-year-old when his uncle, who had commanded a battalion of the Middlesex in the war, suggested that he might join this regiment. Over lunch at the East India Club with the colonel of the regiment, it was agreed that, providing he passed WOSB, Reed would be commissioned into it. The commanding officer of the regiment received other requests to keep an eye on 'good young men' who had some family connection with the Middlesex.[115]

The process by which men were commissioned and then matched up with particular regiments involved informal guidance, pressure and unspoken understandings. John Chynoweth was a grammar school boy and graduate of the London School of Economics. He was disappointed to be called up into the RASC, and felt that his degree in economics might condemn him to a job in managing stores. He managed to transfer to the infantry and to get commissioned into a 'good county regiment', but was told that 'my grammar school education and lack of private income would of course rule out the guards and the cavalry'.[116]

The authorities repeatedly denied that private incomes were required of officers,[117] and men from humble backgrounds did occasionally manage to get commissioned in county regiments, though not in the guards, the cavalry or the Rifle Brigade. Some regiments, particularly the humbler ones, made allowances for national service officers, who were not expected to appear in mess kit or to entertain lavishly; life was less expensive in units serving overseas, especially if they were on active service.[118] All the same, officers in smart regiments were required to spend money. Those commissioned into the 12th Lancers – an armoured car regiment patrolling the jungle roads of Malaya – were told that two mess jackets ('to be bought from Rogers'), boots and spurs were essential.[119]

The army's view of class was not explicitly linked to money. Many officers would have claimed to regard the son of a country parson whose family had scraped together enough money to pay the fees at Marlborough as a more desirable comrade than the son of a wealthy industrialist – though, in practice, English public schools ensured that the sons of industrialists often learned to act as if they were the sons of country parsons. Privileged boys rarely discussed money and it was left to grammar school outsiders to suggest that one needed £300 a year to contemplate a commission in the guards,[120] or that it took £6,000 of education, spread over two generations, to create an officer in the Rifle Brigade.[121]

In theory, regiments did not offer national servicemen commissions until they had finished their officer training. In practice, regiments had often made contact with potential officers long before this. Smart regiments, in particular, chose some of their officers before they even joined the army. In 1954, the Rifle Brigade and the King's Royal Rifle Corps admitted that they had offered provisional commissions to seventeen men, nine of whom were still at school.[122]

The Household Division (i.e. the five regiments of Foot Guards and the Household Cavalry) more or less openly recruited its officers from school. The official history of the Grenadier Guards was explicit about the regiment's policy:

> regimental headquarters kept files on potential officers, some of whom were put down for the Regiment at birth. Since everyone had to do National Service, there were plenty of applications to join the

Regiment . . . The Lt Colonel Commanding the Regiment . . . examined the candidates' housemasters' reports and interviewed them at schools such as Eton.[123]

When the guards were pressed about their officer recruitment, they explained:

There is no deliberate policy to exclude those who were not at public schools from commissioned rank in the Brigade of Guards nor is any test that is different from that applied for admission to all other regiments carried out.

The Guards spend much of their service in London. A single junior officer finds life in London on his pay most difficult and dull and can have a much better time on it elsewhere. A married officer finds it almost impossible to live on his pay in London at all. This deters candidates from applying who have not got private means. Since people who can afford to do so usually send their sons to public schools, this virtually confines entrants to those educated at public schools. The remedy is of course a substantial London Allowance.[124]

This was a disingenuous – and, given the number of officers from county regiments who were enjoying free accommodation in Korea, tactless – letter. There was no formal rule that officers should have private incomes but guards officers were sometimes required to buy expensive clothes or to join the Guards Club. The regimental history of the Grenadiers explains:

mess bills on Queen's Guard [i.e. for those undertaking ceremonial duties in London] were large, making life difficult for those who had no private income . . . Fathers sometimes sought the guidance of the Lieutenant Colonel on what allowance they should give their son. He would reply 'Give him a car and enough money to run it.'[125]

A few brave fathers ignored the suggestion that they pay their sons an allowance and some guards officers, especially those who served outside the UK, managed without private incomes. Martin Morland, who was commissioned into the Grenadiers, said: 'I think they quite like sort of reasonable young men to go into what sounds like a snooty outfit where you have to be rich . . . You didn't actually need a private income – you just stayed away from nightclubs and didn't have a fast car.'[126] Morland's definition of 'reasonable young men' seemed to mean those whose families belonged to the *noblesse de robe* rather than the *noblesse d'épée* (his father was an ambassador) and those who had not been to Eton (he had been to Ampleforth). 'Reasonable young men' were certainly expected to be well-connected: Martin Morland and his brothers were introduced to the Grenadiers by the future Duke of Norfolk, who had married a cousin of their mother's.

Regardless of explicit financial requirements, guards officers were always drawn from a narrow social circle. One Etonian wrote to his old housemaster that Caterham – the guards depot – would be 'rather like starting school again'.[127] There were times when almost half of the men recruited to the Household Division as potential officers were Etonians, as were twenty-five out of thirty-eight national servicemen who held commissions in the Grenadiers in the early 1950s.[128] Potential officers were recruited directly into Brigade Squad, which meant, in effect, that commissions were reserved for men who had some contact with their regiment before they were called up. There was little chance that anyone who joined a lesser regiment could transfer to the guards and no chance that anyone who joined as an ordinary guardsman or trooper (without being in Brigade Squad) could be commissioned into the guards.[129]

John Milne found out about the impassable frontier that divided guards officers from other soldiers when he was called up in 1948. He asked to be posted to the Scots Guards: 'that's the toughest regiment there is, it'll do me no harm to go in there'. However, after around three weeks in the regiment, he was identified as a potential officer and told to leave: 'Because there was at that time a rule in the guards, once you've been a private in the guards, you cannot be an officer in the guards. And I was classified as a potential officer, therefore, "Sorry young man, off you go."' Milne completed his basic training with the Royal West Kent Regiment and was commissioned into the Gordon Highlanders.[130]

Men who joined the guards often had a family link with a regiment – one assumes that guardsmen made up the 2 per cent of potential officers who, surveyed about how their parents would feel if they were commissioned, answered that they would 'take it as a matter of course'.[131] Hugh Currie joined the Coldstream Guards in April 1948 after his godfather had introduced him to the colonel of the regiment.[132] Tom Stacey's father secured him an interview with the colonel of his own regiment – the Scots Guards – during his last holiday from Eton.[133]

Personal and family links connected smart schools with smart regiments and grand families. Bruno Schroder, of the banking family, went from Eton to the Life Guards because his grandfather had been a colonel in the regiment. His aunt had married Geordie Gordon-Lennox, who recruited his fellow Etonians for the Grenadiers.[134] Later Schroder employed Richard Abel Smith, son of Henry Abel Smith,[135] a colonel who had apparently had a *tendresse* for the mother of Viscount Weymouth and who had tried to recruit Weymouth himself into the Horse Guards.[136]

The preponderance of public school boys in the guards was not in itself surprising: the same would have been true of many regiments. More striking was the absence of some schools. Wellington was the most military school in the country, but, precisely because so many of its boys were the sons of professional officers who lived on their pay, they were rarely rich or used to a grand social life. Relatively few boys from Wellington went into the guards. Monmouth was the only institution in Wales that might have been defined as a public school and it had an association with the Welsh Guards – its headmaster had been chaplain to the regiment during the war. However, no boy from the school seems to have been commissioned into the guards.[137]

There was a certain democratization of the officer corps in the 1950s and this was reflected in an increase in the number of northerners being commissioned between 1951 and 1954. Egalitarianism was not an end in itself for the military authorities during this period and, indeed, the main changes in officer recruitment occurred after the Conservative victory in the 1951 election: a victory that meant, among other things, that an Etonian ran the War Office. In part, the social change in the officer corps may have been a by-product of educational change. As the Butler Education Act made its effects felt, increasing numbers of grammar school boys had the educational qualifications to become officers and thus the number of grammar school officers would have increased even if the proportion of eligible candidates from such backgrounds who were commissioned stayed the same. The last few years of national service recruits were largely composed of men who had deferred their service and, because public school boys mainly went into the forces at the age of eighteen, this meant that conscript officers after about 1957 were more plebeian. The last national service officer – Richard Vaughan – was born into a prosperous working-class family (his father was a cabinet maker) and had left grammar school at sixteen to train as an accountant before being commissioned, in early 1961, into the Pay Corps.

The army also had pragmatic reasons for democratizing its officer recruitment because it needed to recruit more northerners to create an appropriate officer corps for the Territorial Army. Finally, the armed forces seem to have come to value technical skill (of the kind often possessed by grammar school boys) rather more. As national service came to an end, they realized that there were a few technical jobs that were particularly hard to fill and their final bids for national service officers revolved largely around men who had degrees in technical subjects.[138]

The democratization of the officer corps as a whole did not touch the smartest of regiments. The Household Division remained a law unto itself. Auberon Waugh appeared before the War Office Selection Board after having been through Brigade Squad as a trooper in the Horse Guards. He recalled:

> No winds of change were blowing through the regimental offices, but at WOSB we were given to understand that it was by no means automatic nowadays for ex-public schoolboys to be appointed to a commission. The interviewing officer let it be understood that he much regretted this new arrangement but I thought I detected a note of dishonesty in the sentiment and I launched into a deeply insincere harangue about the virtues of the new people coming up from the grammar schools and provincial universities.[139]

At least so far as his own regiment was concerned, Waugh had no reason to be worried. Commissioning policy in the household regiments was untouched by democratization. Welsh Labour MPs, who kept a suspicious eye on the officer intake of the Welsh Guards, extracted the admission that, between 1953 and 1963, the regiment had not commissioned a single officer who had not attended public school.[140]

The association of certain regiments with a certain social milieu or with particular families was so strong that men could feel compelled to obtain commissions. This was reflected in the case of Peter Basset, whose father had been an officer in the Welsh Guards during the war and who was himself destined for this regiment. Shortly before the end of the course at Eaton Hall, a sergeant major read cadets a list of their postings. Basset was told that he was going to the Middlesex Regiment. He insisted that there must be a mistake and, when the sergeant major repeated the posting, 'his face went as white as a sheet'. It was revealed that Basset had been the victim of a joke – he was, indeed, to go to the Welsh Guards.[141] However, the joke seems to have shaken Basset and shortly afterwards, during a Christmas ball, he shot himself. He had apparently left notes suggesting that he had let his family down, and a fellow cadet told an inquest that he 'was worried about getting back into the Welsh Guards, and said it would be a way of thanking his father for all the kindness shown to him'.[142]

The case aroused much interest – it seems to have inspired a scene in Andrew Sinclair's autobiographical novel of national service in the guards.[143] A tribute to Basset was published in The Times by Field Marshal Alanbrooke – the fact that an eighteen-year-old cadet should have his obituary written by one of Britain's most eminent generals probably illustrates the burden of expectation under which Peter Basset had laboured.[144]

Basset's friends and family grieved but they did not rebel against the army. Twenty years after Peter's death, his mother edited a collection of religious writings 'which have helped me through some sad times'. The book was dedicated 'To my husband Ronnie and my son Peter'.[145] Peter Basset's elder brother remained as a regular officer in the Scots Guards. Shortly after the suicide, the cadets were paraded in front of a sergeant major – a 'foxy faced bastard' – who had given Basset a hard time. He said that they needed to put the death behind them and move on. Spontaneously the cadets shuffled half a pace forward towards the NCO, but the moment passed and order was restored.[146] The cadets went home for Christmas and most of those who had been contemporaries of Basset's were commissioned into their regiments within a few weeks.

Two weeks later, a second cadet – George Ellis, who had been a friend of Basset's – also shot himself. He left a note that was read to the inquest at the request of his parents:

> I have had every care lavished on me. All my life I have been unable to look after myself and I have had to rely on one asset – my personal charm – to get me through life. My body and mind are quite immature and I am not fit to live, let alone lead men. The reason for my decision has nothing to do with Eaton Hall or home. It is my fault alone. I have been in positions of authority and I am not fit to do it and I am thankful that I will not get men killed. God bless my parents.[147]

The captain of Ellis's platoon said that the cadet was a 'little serious but well liked by his comrades' and that he had intelligence but 'lacked drive', mainly because he was young, 'mentally and physically'.[148] Ellis's father could explain the death only as being an example of suicide spreading 'like measles'.

The cases aroused more discussion than most national service suicides – partly because of the social position of the victims. Eaton Hall, 'which through no fault of its own has recently come into the news', was opened to the press in January 1954.[149] The suicides were the subject of questions in parliament – though the government insisted that the cases revealed no problem with officer training.[150] Many men who passed through Eaton Hall heard stories about Basset and Ellis, and some believed that there had been later suicides.[151]

National service officers themselves discussed suicide by their comrades. John Bingham shared a room at Mons with a man who hated the course and had been carried on to it only because of his public school background:

> Then, one weekend, halfway through the course, G. went on a visit to his home. He never came back. He took a shot-gun, walked through the garden into the trees and there, in a patch of bluebells, he killed himself. He had only a few weeks more to do at OCTU.[152]

Bingham thought that men such as G. should be 'weeded out . . . or placed in low pressure positions', but he opposed 'a general softening up of training'.

'G.' sounds remarkably like John Julian Hurd – son of the Conservative MP Anthony Hurd and brother of the future minister Douglas Hurd, who had himself recently completed national service as an officer in the Royal Artillery. Julian Hurd had gone home to celebrate his mother's birthday. She wrote in her diary: 'a lovely morning – all rather late getting up – J decorated my chair with a charming bunch of flowers'. The next day she wrote: 'Julian shot himself in the wood this afternoon.' Anthony Hurd told an inquest: 'He was a boy who read and liked the classical philosophers, poetry and the Bible, a boy who thought deeply for himself, and I can only feel that he must have found the conditions of his recent life unbearable.'[153]

Julian Hurd's mother wrote in her diary that her son had 'died from what might be called an overdose of beauty after having been starved of it for so long'. Anthony Hurd met the commandant of the Mons Officer Cadet Training Unit. He refused the offer to visit Mons, thinking that such an occasion would degenerate into a ritual inspection. He sought a meeting with Harold Macmillan, when Macmillan was Minister of Defence, to discuss the interests of national servicemen.[154] He does not seem, however, to have made any direct reference to his son: in all his public statements, Hurd *père* focused on the conditions of working-class men who served in the ranks.

A national service officer was generally commissioned about six months after being called up. If he was sent to the Far East, he spent a month travelling there and back and probably a bit of time hanging around and/or undergoing further training. The War Office reckoned it got eighteen months of 'useful service' from officers who served in Britain or Germany, that this figure dropped to between twelve and fifteen months for men who served overseas and might fall as low as nine months for men who served in Malaya.[155]

Almost all national service officers (97.4 per cent in one survey, against 87.4 per cent of other ranks) said that they had enjoyed their service.[156] This may simply have reflected the fact that officer selection was designed to pick men who were likely to express positive views of the armed forces. In the summer of 1956, *The Times* interviewed a group of undergraduates who had just finished their national service as officers. There were 'no chronic malcontents' and only one of them 'felt that most of the talk about the "good effects" of national service was nonsense'. All the same, the former officers agreed that there was much time wasted in the army, though they thought that this was a problem for other ranks – none of them suggested that they themselves had wasted their time. They also felt there was not enough real training and that insufficient effort was made to explain the purpose of national service: 'the National Service Act, uninterpreted, makes the intelligent man rebel and the unintelligent man try to get through their two years with as little effort and trouble as possible'.[157]

For a few national servicemen, becoming an officer was socially useful. John Sutherland described his own time as a second lieutenant in the Suffolk Regiment as conferring 'brevet membership of the upper classes' which seems in part to have helped him overcome the disadvantages of Colchester Grammar School and Leicester University.[158] Christopher Farrell was probably more typical of grammar school officers than Sutherland. He came from a middle-class family in Huddersfield and, looking back as a successful, 26-year-old salesman for a large company, he described the public school boys that he had met during his national service thus:

> It was a different kind of education altogether. They're just as intelligent as I am, but I don't suppose they've got GCE in more than two subjects. They concentrated much more on sport. I share rooms with three public school boys now, and they had a well known cricketer for their coach, and he used to belt them with a cricket bat when they did anything wrong. That's the sort of thing we should have had more of at Marburton College. My old man doesn't believe in public schools. He'd probably say that I'm snobby about this, but he doesn't know. As far as I can see, it's no good coming to London unless you've been to public school.[159]

Many of an officer's duties in a peacetime army were not, in fact, so different from those of a prefect in a public school. Officers inspected parades and imposed punishments, usually doing both under the thinly disguised guidance of their sergeants, who were almost always regular soldiers. Auberon Waugh was probably not exaggerating much when he wrote: 'If any trooper complained of the food, one would taste it delicately from his plate, roll the revolting substance round in one's mouth and say "absolutely delicious!", just as nannies had always behaved with sour milk in my childhood.'[160]

Shortly after he was commissioned, P. J. Houghton-Brown wrote to his mother about the novelty of his status. He had to get used to being saluted and having someone else to press his trousers: 'I must cultivate the army way of making a small job last a long time. This afternoon I had a little to do, did it in a quarter of an hour, and have been trying to keep out of people's way ever since.'[161] Officers endured the arcane rituals of the mess and watched in fascination or horror as nights degenerated into well-rehearsed drunkenness. Bruce Kent recalled the majors in his tank regiment who were 'painfully interested in Mess games'.[162]

On active service, officers and other ranks might mix quite closely – 'you slept with your sergeant, if you see what I mean'.[163] Relations might also be reasonably close in the commandos, where officers and other ranks underwent some of their training together, and where officers sometimes drank with the men under their command. Some regiments, though, insisted on the sharpest possible divisions. An officer of the Coldstream Guards – on an exercise in the desert – was rebuked for letting his men see him bathing.[164]

A few relations were so close that the division between officers and other ranks could not shake them. Identical twins performed their national service in the Queen's Royal Regiment in Malaya: one as an officer and one as a private. The NCOs of the regiment, who could not tell the two men apart, saluted them both when they were out of uniform; the senior officers were said to disapprove of the fact that the brothers socialized together.[165] More commonly, officers got sudden, and poignant, glimpses of life on the other side when they encountered someone they had known in a former life. D. F. Barrett was commanded in Korea by an officer with whom he had undergone basic training.[166] Men from humble backgrounds who had been commissioned, and men from privileged backgrounds who served in the ranks, would occasionally have awkward conversations with men whose rank was different but whose social background was similar. John Hodgson was a grammar school boy from Barnard Castle who became an officer in the Durham Light Infantry, which was, to his father, 'a social leap beyond his comprehension'. When Hodgson took a draft of men out to Suez, he found that one of them was an old friend from childhood football games.[167] A private in the Rifle Brigade who had spent a year at Eton before being expelled attracted the occasional perplexed glance from national service officers who thought that they recognized him.[168]

National servicemen on both sides of the divide were less likely than regulars to regard the separation of officers and other ranks as natural. The army carried out a survey into how regular and national service officers were regarded by their commanding officers. Given that senior officers were always regulars, it is not surprising that they tended to rate regulars slightly more highly but there were only two areas in which the two kinds of officers were seen as very different. Regulars performed better when it came to 'getting on with other officers'; national servicemen performed better when it came to 'being approachable for the men'.[169]

Most men, however, were struck by the social portcullis that cut across their life when officers and other ranks were divided. After he had been commissioned, Bruce Kent caught a glimpse of 'Paddy' – a friend of his from basic training and a fellow Catholic: 'I felt like Black Beauty watching poor old Ginger on his way to the knacker's yard. Our eyes met in recognition and that was that.'[170] John Peel claimed that his sister's fiancé, a second lieutenant, insisted that Peel, a private, should call him 'sir' during family gatherings.[171]

The fact that officers enjoyed the services of a 'batman' or 'soldier servant' was often denounced as an example of 'outdated' class privilege in the armed forces – though, in truth, officers sometimes found that their batman was the only non-commissioned serviceman they got to know.[172] One of the few friendships to flourish across the ranks was that between Anthony Howard and his batman, who was charged, among other things, with waking Howard from his afternoon siesta if the commanding officer undertook an inspection. The servant in question was John Ferris – a boy from a tough working-class background who had signed for a three-year engagement. He was hardly a typical fusilier – though he had left school at fifteen, he eventually became a lecturer in social policy at Nottingham University – and Howard, a left-wing journalist, was hardly a typical infantry officer. Howard and Ferris liked and respected each other and remained friends after they left the army, but there were limits to how far men from such different backgrounds could really know each other, and Ferris – the working-class sociologist – seems to have been more aware of these than Howard.

Even the annual ceremony when officers waited on their men at Christmas did not really mean that the system of ranks had been challenged. Peter Nichols recalled his experience in the air force:

> We were served our dinner by the officers, the cruellest insult service life had to offer. These public-school boys not much older than ourselves looked as embarrassed as we felt, and carried out this repellent ritual with a show of bravado while we sat at wooden mess-tables muttering 'thank you sir'.[173]

In any case, as the more socially astute national servicemen noticed, officers ate their 'dinner' in the evening and were not, therefore, inconvenienced much by having to serve meals at noon. In Egypt in 1953, officers of one regiment served the other ranks before retiring to their own mess, where they resumed their normal lives: 'The dinner ended up with a nut fight but a cease fire was ordered when a subaltern hit the 2 i/c on his bald head.'[174]

There were many men who enjoyed their time as national service officers and some who stayed on or returned to the army after university as regulars: two of them rose to the rank of field marshal. However, many national service officers never quite accommodated themselves to the ways of the regular army. Simon Coke enjoyed being an officer in the Coldstream Guards, but, when he was offered a regular commission with the regiment, he refused because he had come to dislike the 'anti-intellectualism and relative snobbery of the regular officers'.[175]

Even men who enjoyed their service often came to feel uncomfortable with the life of an officer, which seemed so archaic. W. S. B. Loosmore was commissioned as a national service doctor and sent to

Malaya. He had an unusually interesting time. He found a four-foot cobra in his 'thunder box',[176] limped back from a rugby game with a team from 22 SAS[177] and once noted in his diary: 'I never thought that I would find myself suturing a Gurkha bottom in full evening dress on a Saturday evening.'[178] All the same, the rituals of army life began to grate. His commanding officer once sent him a note drawing his attention to mess rule 283, which specified that decanters should be passed 'distal to the glass, not proximal to it'.[179] Most of all, though, he was anxious that he might have come too close to the world of the regular officer: 'I am worried because this army nonsense does not seem to me to be such nonsense as it once did. I must be losing my sense of values.'[180]

IO

Other Ranks

Your rank?
Well. That's a matter of opinion.
Exchange between officer and Private James Bailey
(Carry on Sergeant, 1958)

In the regular armed forces, the army especially, other ranks knew their place. They and their officers were separated by a system that a national serviceman described as 'social apartheid'.[1] They wore different kinds of uniform, ate in different places, travelled in different classes on the railway. If they were brave, they received different medals. If they were ill, they were treated in different wards. If they were captured, they went to different prison camps. One national service officer conducting an equipment inspection discovered that his camp had pokers (other ranks, for the use of) and pokers (officers, for the use of): the former had loops on the end and the latter had knobs.[2] For many regular servicemen, the division seemed natural. Other ranks were drawn almost entirely from the working class – often its most underprivileged element; officers were drawn from the upper-middle class and landed gentry. Other ranks had almost all been educated at elementary school and left at the earliest opportunity with no qualifications; officers were almost invariably educated at public school to the age of eighteen.

National service blurred the social boundaries of the armed forces. The very notion that a serviceman might be a 'potential officer' was disturbing to a culture in which it had previously been assumed that men were born on one side or the other of the divide between commissioned and non-commissioned status. The air force, in particular, sometimes treated 'Potential Officer Material' (POM) as though it were a social category in itself, which bore only a tangential relation to officer status. Increasing the 'POM requirements' was used to 'regulate the flow of high ability candidates' for skilled jobs rather than as a means of getting more officers.[3]

Some working-class national servicemen did recognize that their natural place was in the ranks – though the mere fact that they commented on the distinction suggests that they did not take it entirely for granted. Leslie Ives was a good soldier in a 'good regiment' (the Green Howards) and he endured the rigours of jungle warfare in Malaya with stoicism. All the same, he never held any rank above that of private: 'My mates and I had about as much chance of becoming officers as becoming king.'[4]

For other conscripts, used to more subtle and flexible social structures in their civilian life, the sharp divide between officers and other ranks seemed incongruous. Karl Miller recalled that 'the Army had yet to develop a middle class, and the sergeants' mess was no approximation to one.'[5] To put things more precisely, the armed forces lacked much sense of the densely inhabited social borderlands that encompassed men whose origins ranged from the upper end of the working class to the middle of the middle class.

The population of these social borderlands increased during the period of national service. This was partly because the Butler Education Act meant that a growing proportion of young men had stayed on at school beyond the minimum leaving age. Some of these were highly qualified – part of the joke in the exchange quoted as the epigraph to this chapter comes from the fact that Private James Bailey (B.Sc. Econ.) would have been better educated than any officer in his training regiment, though connoisseurs of educational snobbery would recognize that he had been to the 'wrong' kind of university. More commonly, however, grammar schools produced youths educated to the age of sixteen and equipped with the General Certificate of Education – young men who were too well educated to fit comfortably in the ranks but not usually well educated enough to be seriously considered for a commission. The post-war years also saw an increase in the number of apprentice-trained, skilled workers and these too – men with a strong sense of the dignity and autonomy that ought to attach to skilled work – were often uncomfortable in the forces.

The complicated hierarchies of civilian life intersected with, and exacerbated, some divisions of military society. Rank, the thing that mattered most to the regular forces, cut across education, the thing that mattered most to middle-class conscripts, and skill, the thing that mattered most to many working-class ones. The role and status of NCOs was affected by the fact that so many educated men earned a stripe in return for doing white-collar jobs in the forces. The relations between the services – and within the various elements of each service – were changed by the fact that so many men valued postings that offered the opportunity to practise a skill rather than to display conventional martial virtues. Finally, the existence of national service meant that the most important division in the armed forces – one that overlapped with divisions of education, skill and respectability – often came to be that between conscript and regular.

The status attached to 'other ranks' varied from one service to another. Gulfs between officers and 'men' were sharpest in the army, especially in the smartest of regiments. Cavalry regiments, in particular, were effectively run by NCOs, and other ranks had little to do with officers.[6] Relations in the navy varied with ship. On a minesweeper, relations were of necessity less formal and distant than they would be on an aircraft carrier.

It was in the air force that the 'social apartheid' of the forces was most likely to break down, and relations between officers and other ranks were largely determined by how close they got to an aeroplane. After the war, many RAF officers never left the ground, and ground officers, who lacked any obvious technical skill, seem to have had little respect for other ranks and to have commanded even less from them.[7]

Things were different when it came to men who actually flew. The rough camaraderie that had grown up during the war sometimes persisted after 1945. One airman remarked: 'I found the ex-flying type of officer much friendlier and less rank conscious than the non-flying types.'[8] Even those who never served as aircrew (and the great majority did not) might occasionally talk to pilot officers on terms that implied some degree of mutual respect. Radio operators and men in control towers, by definition, spent much of their time talking to pilots, who were almost always officers, and this created a strange democracy of the airwaves. Alan Sillitoe noticed that his working-class Nottingham accent mutated into something more 'neutral' as he spoke on the radio.[9] Don Wallace, called up in 1952 and rising to the rank of corporal, wrote that 'Control tower work was probably the next best thing to being in air crew, as we were involved with flying procedures and talking to the pilots, either face to face or instructing them over the R/T.'[10]

Flying could be a leveller, even for men who were not meant to fly. While private soldiers spent much of their forty-eight-hour leaves dozing in railway carriages or hitching lifts to get home, airmen could sometimes scrounge trips in aeroplanes. This involved a degree of complicity between officers and other ranks. Harold Evans once got from Wiltshire to Manchester in the gun turret of a Lancaster bomber on a 'training flight' that had been fixed up by an officer who also lived in Manchester.[11] Jimmy Reid, a card-carrying Communist, was surprised and disarmed when the commander of his base offered to get him flown up to Scotland to attend a wedding.[12] At a time when junior officers in the army might insist that a private in their hockey team should return to base in the back of a truck rather than sitting in the same car as themselves, an air vice marshal occasionally turned up at aerodromes and offered to give non-commissioned national servicemen a joy ride in a Harvard trainer.[13]

The distinction between conscripts and regulars sometimes overlapped with that between NCOs and privates, or men who held the equivalent rank in the other services. Most national servicemen ended their military careers as privates and most NCOs were regulars – this was especially true of senior NCOs, sergeants and warrant officers. Indeed the need to train and organize national servicemen speeded up the promotion of regular NCOs, especially from the rank of corporal to that of sergeant.[14]

In 1949, an army report concluded that something between 10 per cent and 30 per cent of conscripts had become NCOs by the end of their service. The careers of the majority of them stopped at the rank of lance corporal.[15] Most men obtained promotion late in their service, and therefore the army expected that the proportion of NCOs among conscripts would drop as service was reduced to eighteen months.

The proportion of national servicemen who became NCOs was changed, first, by the Korean War. This had a direct effect on some regiments. In the summer of 1950, over half of the 1st Battalion of the Middlesex Regiment were national servicemen, but among these only two men had reached the rank of full corporal.[16] The regiment's posting to Korea brought rapid change. The intensity of fighting required NCOs with quick wits rather than with the more ponderous qualities of regulars who were used to presiding over parades and kit inspections. D. F. Barrett, one of the men eventually promoted to corporal, wrote in December 1950: 'the situation within the platoon is that our Regular Army mentors are literally fading away before our eyes'.[17] Even in Korea, however, there were limits. Barrett believed that it was impossible for men in his own regiment to rise beyond the rank of corporal.

The effects of Korea were felt even by conscripts who never went to the Far East. In response to the war, national service was extended to two years in September 1950 and this meant that men had more time to get promoted. Furthermore, the average age of conscripts increased in the 1950s, partly because the age at which most men were registered crept up and partly because increasing numbers of men came into the forces after having deferred to complete apprenticeships or to complete their education. In the late 1940s, almost all conscripts had been eighteen (because those who deferred had not yet completed their apprenticeships). By February 1956, about a quarter of all national servicemen (but almost half of all national service corporals and over half of national service sergeants) were over twenty-one.[18]

By the mid 1950s, when they made up about half of the army, national servicemen comprised almost a tenth of sergeants and between a quarter and a third of corporals. They were times when most lance corporals were conscripts. On the whole, men did not get promoted to these ranks until relatively late in their service. Most national service lance corporals held the rank for around a year and most corporals did so for about nine months. The excruciating slowness of army bureaucracy could mean that: 'in the case of national servicemen it often happens that, by the time a promotion is finalized, the soldier has left the Army'.[19]

The army made NCOs out of some unpromising material. The authors of a War Office study were disconcerted to find that 8 per cent of national servicemen who had been referred to psychiatrists during basic training because of perceived defects in personality or intellect subsequently became NCOs. A big, breezy man who had worked in a timber yard and was semi-literate became a lance bombardier. The army found it curious that men graded 3 for 'emotional stability' had been promoted more frequently than those graded 2 and that NCOs included those who had been deemed to 'lack even the normal aggressive vigour which would have been thought necessary for the control of men by an NCO, even in peacetime'. The authors of the report discounted the possibility that 'unstable men and negative weaklings are more likely to be chosen as NCOs' – though their own survey suggested that the 'colourless stable' group performed better than some ordinary soldiers and that a simple ability to stay out of trouble was enough to get a man promotion in some non-fighting units.[20]

In the early stages of training in the army, some men were rated as Other Rank 4 (OR4), which meant that they were seen as potential NCOs. Between 1952 and 1957, the proportion of recruits in this category increased from about one fifth to just under a third. (See Appendix VIII.) The army did not break down this figure into regulars and national servicemen – though the great majority of those joining in any particular year would have been the latter.

There was, however, not a simple relation between initial rating and promotion, and the number of men who actually became NCOs remained more or less stable as the number who had been rated OR4 increased. This is all the more surprising because, as national service was run down in the late 1950s, an increasing proportion of conscripts would have been close to the end of their service and ought, therefore, to have been ripe for promotion. The reason for this disparity seems to lie partly in the fact that many national service NCOs had a particular kind of trajectory. Most regular NCOs rose slowly through the ranks, passing from lance corporal to corporal to sergeant. Many national service NCOs, by contrast, were relatively well-educated men – who had probably been rated as potential officers (OR 1) rather than potential NCOs (OR 4) when they first arrived in the army. The social origins and educational level of national service NCOs and national service officers were not always very different. The RAF increased the number of conscripts it commissioned in the early 1950s and, at the same time, reduced the number of its national service sergeants. This seems to have meant in effect that they commissioned men doing jobs, especially in education, that in the army would have attracted a sergeant's stripes. In 1953 there were just forty-one national service airmen who held the rank of sergeant or above; at roughly the same time there were almost 3,000 national service sergeants in the army.[21]

In the army, a large proportion of national service NCOs, sergeants especially, held their rank because they did some particular job that brought an automatic promotion, rather than because they had risen through the ranks. Few of them exercised direct authority over other servicemen in the way that a platoon sergeant would, and many of them were in non-'teeth arm' units. Of the 1,101 national service sergeants in the army in late 1958, 187 served with the Medical Corps, seventy-six with the Royal Electrical and Mechanical Engineers, 134 with the Pay Corps and 554 (i.e. just over half of the total) with the Royal Army Education Corps (RAEC).[22]

The Education Corps was, unsurprisingly, the best educated element in the army. Of men admitted into the corps in the first six months of 1956, forty-seven were graduates, seventeen had some higher education, eighty-four had A levels and seventy-three had GCEs. Men of education level 5 and below – who made up the great majority of recruits in every other unit – were entirely absent.[23] Men were not usually admitted directly from civil life. Rather they joined other units, usually infantry regiments, transferred at the end of their basic training and were sent to the RAEC depot at Beaconsfield for a few months of further training in how to teach and how to behave as an NCO. Shortly after passing out, members of the RAEC were promoted to acting sergeant.

Educational sergeants taught all sorts of soldiers – from sullen army apprentices at Arborfield to head-hunting Dayak tribesmen in Malaya.[24] Most of them were attached to regiments. This itself could be a strange experience. They lived and ate with other sergeants but their new comrades were older than them and owed their stripes to years of experience and/or performance on the battlefield. Eighteen-year-old conscripts sometimes felt awkward in the presence of their elders – though they seem on the whole to have been treated with amused courtesy. T. C. Sparrow was attached to the Green Howards, where he met Clarence 'Lofty' Peacock, who had joined the regiment in 1936, after having served six years with the Coldstream Guards. Peacock had won the Military Medal in Palestine in 1938 and the Norwegian War Cross in 1940. He had also won the Distinguished Conduct Medal and had, in Germany in 1945, effectively rallied an entire company at a time when almost every officer had been killed or wounded. After the war, he had served in Malaya, Cyprus and Hong Kong, and he was said to be the most decorated regimental sergeant major in the army. Peacock greeted Sparrow with the words: 'They're promoting them straight from the cradle nowadays.'[25]

The job of members of the Education Corps was to instruct soldiers in reading, writing and arithmetic. They also sometimes taught current affairs and more obviously military skills, such as map-reading. Many of their pupils were regulars – partly because educational levels among regulars were lower than those among conscripts and partly because the forces had an interest in educating regulars but were reluctant to waste time in schooling men who would be with them for only two years. The army required men to acquire certificates of education before they could obtain promotion and, indeed, required those who were already NCOs to pass exams if they wished to retain their rank. Sometimes 'schoolies' found themselves teaching the very sergeants with whom they messed. Not surprisingly, tests were often discreetly rigged in the candidate's favour.

A large number of national servicemen also became corporals or lance corporals because they served as clerks. Clerks were usually men who were too well educated to stay in the ranks but too plebeian, obviously lacking in martial qualities or rebellious to become officers. Some of the best-known national service writers – David Baxter,

David Lodge, Leslie Thomas – were clerks and several novels were written under the table during the substantial periods when there was not much to do in an army pay office.

A few clerks had dramatic lives. Patrick Wye was called up into the RASC in 1951. He was trained as a clerk and hoped that he might get a posting to Vienna. As it was he was attached to an army unit that was assigned to support army pilots who had, in turn, been attached to the navy. Wye ended up on board the aircraft carrier HMS *Ocean*. He joined it in Malta, celebrated his nineteenth birthday in the Mediterranean and then sailed to Korea, where he kept records of flying missions.[26] Frank Stokes was also a clerk in the RASC. He was sent to Egypt to work in an office processing claims for damages caused by British forces. He was the only non-officer in his department. He wore civilian clothes, lived in a scruffy hotel in Cairo and occasionally slept in the office when he was 'duty officer'. He visited Haifa on behalf of the Levant Claims Commission and, like other British soldiers, moved out of Cairo quickly in 1951, when the Egyptians abrogated the treaty regulating their relations with the British. He met Armenians, Greeks and Jews and felt that he had had a 'national service like no other'.[27]

For most conscripts, clerking was more mundane and could, indeed, seem rather absurd to men who had been brought up on films about commandos and fighter pilots. One man spent his entire time in a tank regiment filing documents without once seeing the inside of tank.[28] Robert Miller was trained as a clerk after failing to become an officer. He was taken aside and told that his pre-service experience – working for the Foreign Office – qualified him for a 'special job'. This turned out to mean writing to officers who had been posted away from the Royal Artillery reminding them to pay their subscriptions for the upkeep of the regimental band.[29] Not surprisingly, the great majority of conscripts, and even two thirds of grammar school boys, wanted to avoid clerical work.[30]

Clerking probably began to seem more attractive as the realities of military life began to dawn on recruits. Clerks sat in warm offices and enjoyed predictable and on the whole undemanding military careers. One recalled that being a clerk in a training company allowed him to 'see behind the façade of the Army and to join that privileged and small band who live between the layers of the Army's structure'.[31] He added: 'Life in the barracks had settled into a very comfortable routine of 9–5. We had established our place in the Army hierarchy, we knew just how far we could manipulate the system to our advantage, we knew who to be wary of and who were our allies.'[32] Alan Watson served as a corporal with the aptitude testing section at RAF Cardington. He and his twenty-five colleagues put their fellow recruits into a variety of categories, but they also understood they themselves belonged to a particular caste:

> Our backgrounds were fairly similar ... mostly ex grammar school boys with a few graduates doing their deferred national service. So social homogeneity and the nature of the work generated a particular group identity. That suited us well but also meant that we tended to be looked upon as if we were practitioners of some arcane rites (that is, the testing processes), were unreasonably privileged and not 'real airmen.'[33]

The British armed forces were huge organizations spread across the globe and nothing moved without documentary authorization. Clerks sat at the centre of paper webs that let them understand, and sometimes control, events thousands of miles away. Men who had never fired a rifle after basic training might have an oddly intimate acquaintance with violence. A clerk sitting in Shropshire compiled records about, among other things, the deaths of servicemen – mostly, in fact, the product of accidents.[34] *The Virgin Soldiers* contains a scene, apparently based on a real incident, in which a clerk in Singapore reconstructs the life of a dead soldier from the pages of a pay book, stuck together with blood, which he has, against regulations, carried with him into the jungle.

Clerks could be powerful. David Baxter noted how every man in his battalion depended on the goodwill of a pay clerk and how the sergeant in charge of his office had a 'social round like a duke'.[35] A conscript recalled his service in the Ordnance Corps in Eritrea, where a warrant officer in the ledger office 'really ran the Depot' with the aid of a corporal 'who had the form filling all sewn up'.[36] Robin Ollington, in the depot of the Warwickshire Regiment, learned to forge the signatures of his officers and was thus able to authorize payments when they had all gone to the races. One day a regular attacked

Ollington, who had been sent to arrest him for desertion. When the regular emerged from detention, the regiment was making up a draft of men for Hong Kong. Ollington switched a couple of bits of paper and his enemy was dispatched to the other side of the world.[37] A clerk in Malaya intercepted a message that some soldiers might be eligible for leave: 'it transpired that I was the only person interested'.[38] A national serviceman in the RAF records office ran a lucrative criminal enterprise – hinting to men that he could arrange their posting to places near their home if they paid him a few pounds.[39]

An intelligent man in an office might come to understand the workings of the armed forces better than senior officers. In early 1955, Bernard Barr, a lance corporal in Japan, was stenographer at a meeting of officers to discuss how they would run down forces in Pusan in Korea. A brigadier presided over the meeting and most of those attending were majors and 'half colonels'. Barr reckoned, however, that his own position had given him a better understanding of what was going on than most of those present at the meeting had. He also seems to have produced a crisper summary of the meeting than the New Zealand major who had acted as its nominal secretary was able to do.[40]

Some clerks exercised a cruel Pinteresque control over their officers. Ageing captains could stay away from the horror of seeking civilian employment only if they kept their paperwork at bay and they could manage this only if some supercilious nineteen-year-old showed them how to do it. Sometimes clerks ran their own world with little interference from their nominal superiors: 'Officers generally figured very little in our lives, but occasionally they gladdened our hearts by doing something that was monumentally stupid.'[41]

Like clerks and army teachers, men in the Intelligence Corps were often given non-commissioned rank and, independently of rank, the corps had special prestige in the eyes of some national servicemen – perhaps just because those whose lives had revolved around the 11-plus were fascinated by the word 'intelligence'. Seeking to find out why some men did not want commissions in the army, the War Office asked a sample of educated men whether they would prefer a 'special job' as a sergeant in the Education Corps or a private in the

Intelligence Corps to being an officer: a significant minority of candidates said they would prefer a 'special job'.[42]

Intelligence was, like the Education Corps, a place in which grammar school boys often mixed with those from public schools who had failed to become officers. Paul Croxson had left grammar school at the age of sixteen and spent two years training as a librarian before being called up into the RASC. He asked to be posted to the Intelligence Corps and repeated this request even when he was told that there was no chance of its being granted. Eventually, to his surprise, he was sent to Intelligence, which was 'paradise after the Service Corps'. He believed himself to be the least well educated of the recruits in his new unit, and marvelled that their instructor sometimes referred to them as 'gentlemen'. They were taught cryptography and, as part of the course, were made to do the *Daily Telegraph* crossword. He went to Germany and was assigned to trying to work out Warsaw Pact orders of battle by listening to radio call signs.[43]

Some members of the Intelligence Corps were trained in 'interrogation techniques' that came close to torture,[44] and some were posted to areas – Cyprus and Malaya – in which it was said that the security forces sometimes extracted information from captured guerrillas by means that would not have been sanctioned by the Geneva Convention. There is no evidence that members of the Corps were themselves involved in such interrogations, which seem to have been carried out mainly by policemen or by soldiers from ordinary regiments. Indeed members of the Intelligence Corps – usually young, highly educated men who felt ill at ease with conventional military values – often disapproved of the brutality they saw or heard about.

The elite of those who worked in intelligence, which did not just mean those who were members of the army Intelligence Corps, were those who learned Russian. This programme recruited from all three services. It was ferociously difficult. Men who failed to learn fast enough were returned to their unit and even among those who passed there was a division between those considered good enough to be 'interpreters' and those who were merely allowed to become 'translators'. The rewards for those who survived the course were high. Drill was almost forgotten. Students escaped the ordinary drudgery of service life. They were taught by Russian émigrés – 'refugees and dissidents who had been existing in London bed-sitters until this opportunity to teach their wonderful language arose'.[45] Some of them performed Russian plays under the direction of actors who had worked with Stanislavsky.

John Ockenden passed out of his linguists' class at Bodmin and was sent, still as a private, to provide translation services for the War Office in London, where he was allocated to a shadowy agency – MI3(d) – and charged with briefing English and American officers. He wore civilian clothes, commuted from home and entered the War Office by an obscure entrance – the one opposite Horse Guards Parade being apparently reserved for men holding the rank of brigadier and above. Since he and his comrades had no official existence, they had to go to the London Assembly Centre at Goodge Street underground station to receive their pay. The great drama of his military career came in March 1953 when Stalin died and he read black-edged editions of *Pravda* as his superiors tried to guess the meaning of sinister troop movements around Moscow. Ockenden drew the relatively unknown Khrushchev in the office sweepstake over who would succeed Stalin.

The Russianists subverted conventional military culture in several ways. This was partly because soldiers, sailors and airmen trained together and their sense of being associated with other linguists was often stronger than their sense of belonging to their own service. More importantly, it was because of rank. Some Russianists were commissioned, but in practice rank did not count for much among the linguists. For them hierarchy had more to do with their scores in language tests than with the pips on their shoulder. Officer training, when it did occur, was fairly cursory. John Arnold and some of his comrades were put through a truncated course at Mons – where, he claimed, they were taught how to attack but not how to retreat.[46]

Some men tried hard to get on the Russian course and even walked out of potential officer squads in their enthusiasm to do so. An air force study of men who were educationally eligible for commissions but did not want them found that many wanted instead to be Russianists. Of 198 men who were asked, eleven wanted to be 'interpreters' or 'learn a language'.[47] As time went on, and perhaps as the purely military aspects of national service came to seem less relevant, many men – even among those who had been officers in smart regiments – expressed regret that they had not learned Russian.

Most of all, perhaps, the Russian course subverted class hierarchies or at least those that mattered in the armed forces. The Russianists understood that they came from different backgrounds. Indeed the difference between the naval coders, generally upper-middle class, and the air force conscripts, largely lower-middle class, was an object of sub-Nancy-Mitford satire in the house magazine of the Russianists. Airmen, apparently, said 'serviette' and wrote home: 'Bill what was in the same form as me at grammar school, was in the last intake.'[48] In reality, however, more than any other servicemen, the Russianists led lives that revolved around educational ability rather than social class. A study of working-class grammar school boys found that one had rejoined the forces after national service specifically because he wanted to get on the Russian course. He seems to have found being a Russianist comfortable because it placed him in 'a kind of social no man's land'.[49]

The linguists were the least martial of all national servicemen; most of them barely touched a gun during their service. Their lives were more like those of hard-working undergraduates than those of soldiers. In other ways, however, the linguists were more closely associated with real warfare than were other servicemen. Their comrades in 'teeth arm' units spent most of their time drilling and polishing kit and, except in Korea, even those on 'active service' often barely saw their enemy. Linguists, by contrast, were in constant contact with the armies of hostile forces. Those in Europe listened to Warsaw Pact radio traffic, translated Russian documents or thought about Soviet military plans. Some of them were uncomfortably aware of the one thing that most conscripts barely thought about: what would happen in a real war. John Waine went straight into the Russian course after just five days kitting out at Padgate. He never even endured basic training, but felt 'This wasn't playing at soldiers. This was for real.' The Russian émigrés who taught Waine talked about the 'liberation of the Soviet Union' and he himself felt 'should there ever be military action on Soviet territory, one would be there'.[50] Russianists piled into the Cambridge Arts Cinema on Saturday mornings to watch Soviet films – including documentaries featuring real footage of the Wehrmacht and the Red Army. Occasionally, they went on exercises, in which they were, for example, required to translate a diary that was badly written in Cyrillic, dropped in a river and stained with blood.[51]

Russianists represented a very small proportion of national servicemen (probably one in 400) – though they were significant because they enjoyed great prestige among other educated men of their generation. Some of them became famous in later life and produced influential, often highly colourful, accounts of their experiences. They were also, with the possible exception of RAF pilots, the only group of men who always looked back on their national service as having been worthwhile.

Skilled working-class men made up a large proportion of conscripts and, towards the end of the 1950s, they probably made up the majority of them. Skilled men, more than any other group, saw national service as an unwelcome interruption of their lives. This was partly because such men tended to defer and hence to enter the forces relatively late, and partly because conscription often interrupted careers at a point when a man might expect to start earning good money. It was also for less tangible reasons. In civilian life, a skilled worker would be treated with respect and exercise a certain control over his working day. The call-up, however, stripped away all the hard-earned privileges of a time-served craftsman. Tools were often a symbol of these privileges, because craftsmen owned their own tools, but conscription hurled them into a world where they did not even own their clothes. A pattern maker remembered that he spent his last afternoon before joining the army cleaning and greasing his tools before hiring a taxi to take them home and stash them in his parents' spare bedroom.[52] A national service airman in the late 1940s objected to the fact that the RAF provided cheap tools: 'Why can't we buy our own, then we'd be proud of them and look after them.'[53]

Not surprisingly, skilled workers had strong views about what they wanted to do in the forces and the first desire for many was to stay out of the army. The navy took a few hundred lucky men from among 'apprentices who were completing their deferment since these would, in general, be eligible to enter into the artificer trades in which there is at present a severe shortage'.[54]

For most, the air force was a more realistic option. The RAF attracted men who wanted to work with machinery, many of whom were skilled workers. In the late 1950s, 48 per cent of RAF conscripts, compared to 32 per cent of those in the army, had undertaken craft apprenticeships; 78 per cent of those in the RAF, compared to 41 per cent of those in the army, had undertaken vocational courses since leaving school.[55] Relations between the RAF and its skilled conscripts were not always smooth. The sheer number of skilled men joining meant that appropriate jobs could not be found for them all and many had unrealistic views about the possibilities that would be open to them. In addition to this, the RAF noticed, more than any other service, that there was a conflict between a military hierarchy based on rank and a civilian status based on skill. A report of 1948 put it thus:

> Many aspects of life in the RAF are resented, not because they are irksome but because they involve either a threat to or a direct assault upon the status of the men concerned. Unfortunately the rank system does not exactly parallel the status system. This means that in the eyes of the man and his fellows it is possible to be of lower rank yet of higher status, than another. There are many examples – the most obvious is that of the skilled fitter who may be an LAC or Corporal yet must take a heavy load of responsibility when compared with the Sergeant or even the Warrant Officer who is doing an office job.[56]

The clash between 'status' and 'rank' was often one between national servicemen from the skilled working-class and regular NCOs who lacked any specific skill.

The RAF tried to improve its handling of skilled men. It put them in front of panels to determine what skills they had and whether those might be of use during their service. Many men hoped to get into the RAF because it seemed to offer the best chance of pursuing their civilian occupations. Sometimes this became a self-defeating process as the RAF attracted more skilled men than it needed and those who had invested high hopes in their posting were disappointed, particularly when the RAF reserved certain positions for men who signed on as regulars. Nonetheless, the proportion of postings that required technical skill was higher in the air force than in the army. From the early 1950s, the RAF organized recruits into three categories. 'E' stood for 'engineer' and described men with some specific technical skill, which usually meant apprentice-trained workers. 'N' stood for 'non-engineer' and designated men, presumably for the most part grammar school boys, who did not possess a specific skill but who were of generally high intelligence and/or educational level. 'O' stood for 'orderly' and designated men who could perform unskilled jobs.[57]

Within the army, there was a hierarchy of units and postings for other ranks, which was not the same as that for officers. For an officer, the most prestigious posting was usually to an infantry regiment. Many working-class men, by contrast, saw the infantry as the military equivalent of unskilled labour – something that would be an anathema to anyone who had undertaken an apprenticeship. In October 1960, the public relations office of Northern Command issued a press story about Private Birkin, who was then serving with the Sherwood Foresters in Singapore: 'It did not take him long to decide that Army life was the one for him and he signed on for 22 years.' Birkin wrote an indignant reply:

> You could not have insulted my intelligence more by saying that I would sign on for 22 years in an infantry mob. I hate the army as an institution but if I were to sign on at all it would be in a corps. I am a National Service man and proud of it.[58]

The Royal Electrical and Mechanical Engineers (REME) was probably, so far as most skilled workers were concerned, the best unit – one described it as the 'elite trades thing of the army'.[59] Precisely because such units were attractive to working-class men, regulars, who usually had first choice of unit, sometimes snatched up places in them. However, conscripts often came to dominate military postings that required particular skills, usually ones that had been acquired in civilian apprenticeships. In 1954, national servicemen composed 92 per cent of telegraph mechanics in REME, 88 per cent of line mechanics in the Signals and 80 per cent of draughtsmen in the Engineers.[60] The ideal for many working-class conscripts was to wear an overall rather than a uniform and to operate a machine rather than be ordered around by a sergeant. Unlike their officers, other ranks held technical specialism in high esteem; nothing was more damning than the verdict that a conscript was fit only for 'general duties'.

Few men learned new trades during national service, and unions lobbied to prevent the 'dilution' of skilled work by men who had been trained in the forces. One 'trade' was particularly coveted by working-class conscripts: at times, around 40 per cent of recruits told the authorities that they wanted to be drivers. 'Lorry driving is the most popular occupation with all Service intakes, and is particularly popular with the army samples.'[61] Some young men from the less respectable end of the working class had worked as drivers' mates or 'van boys' before they were called up, and a few of them had already picked up an ability to drive before they were old enough, or wealthy enough, to take a driving test.

For an unskilled but ambitious working-class boy, driving might fit into practical plans for the future. In the 1950s, some considered lorry-driving to be the ideal job. It offered the chance of travel without having to live away from home and it offered the chance to work outdoors without having to endure the hardship of physical labour.[62] Most of all, lorry-driving meant escaping from the factory or the warehouse. A survey of industrialists in the north Midlands in 1954 discovered that 'many men who had taken up motor driving in the army, found it difficult to settle down to their pre-service job, refusing to be confined within four walls and seeking a lorry driving job or some out-door equivalent'.[63]

The sharpest social distinction in the armed forces was often that which separated conscripts from regulars. Just under half of the army and about two thirds of the Royal Air Force was composed of regulars for most of the period of national service. Regular servicemen were often drawn from tough backgrounds and they frequently behaved in ways that offended civilian notions of respectability. Some regular officers used the term 'old soldier' as a by-word for laziness, poor educational standards and delinquency,[64] and contrasted the regular other ranks unfavourably with conscripts. Peter de la Billière, a future lieutenant general who joined up as a private in 1951, wrote:

At that date the quality of the regulars tended to be very low: people volunteered for the army only if they could find no other employment, and many of those who did join up could not read, write or even sign their names. The National Servicemen, on the other hand, embraced all types, and included many with first-class brains.[65]

The commanding officer of an infantry battalion believed that the difference between conscripts and regulars sprang from the fact that the former had plans for their career: 'This is a great advantage, particularly over the regular soldier, who so often has drifted into uniform and who often has so few ideas about his future.'[66]

The gulf between conscripts and regulars was particularly marked in the toughest of units – the marines and the Parachute Regiment. Both recruited comparatively few conscripts, but for this reason they could afford to be selective and appear to have chosen mostly conscripts with a relatively high level of education – sometimes the kind of men who could have become sergeants in the Education Corps or even officers. They seem to have done so in part because they needed a certain number of relatively educated men who could read maps, operate radios and handle paperwork.

A regular officer in the marines remembered: 'In many cases it [national service] rather overshadowed some of the regular marines, who on the whole were not as well educated as the NS men.' He said that conscripts were often ex grammar or public school boys who were going to university and that they were 'very high calibre'.[67] A. R. Ashton, a national serviceman who served in the ranks with the Royal Marines Commandos, was from a minor public school. He was encouraged to join partly because his friends told him that it had 'none of that army bull'. He remembered his national service comrades as being 'accountants, printers, management trainees, all from broadly middle or lower middle class backgrounds'.[68] By contrast, Keith Jessop – a working-class boy who, as a rock climber and later diver, had attributes that one might usually associate with commandos – had difficulty in persuading recruiters to accept his application to undertake his national service in the marines.[69]

The small number of national servicemen who became paratroopers were also relatively well educated. It was, presumably, only during national service that paratroopers might be expected to take time off from assault courses and 'murderball' to attend art classes in Farnham.[70] Owen Parfitt believed that there were only four or five other national servicemen in the 1st Battalion of the Parachute Regiment in 1956. The conscripts behaved well because they did not want to do anything that might damage their education or work prospects when they were demobilized. They were different from the regulars – some of whom were 'aggressive criminals'.[71] A group of senior officers from the Parachute Regiment said that they had used national servicemen to fill posts in signals and intelligence. They contrasted the conscripts with the regulars who were, as they drily recalled, 'very live wires' requiring 'careful handling'.[72]

Young conscripts were sometimes more tolerant than senior officers of regular soldiers. Some found regulars to be glamorous or interesting. This was true of men who had fought in the Second World War. Sergeants were relatively old men by army standards and had usually, at least in the first few years after 1945, done some serious fighting to earn their stripes. In Singapore, Peter Burke heard that two of the sergeants in his regiment had trained together and then endured a Japanese prison camp together.[73] Burke caught extraordinary glimpses of the life of a regular soldier. He talked to Sergeant Jacques – a kindly and eccentric figure who still used the archaic term 'volunteer' rather than regular. Jacques epitomized the odd mixture of smartness and delinquency that often characterized long-service men. He had once hidden in the loft over a barracks in Germany 'where the unit forgot about him'. He had come down only to eat his meals and had spent most of his time polishing his kit – with the result that he seemed a model soldier when he finally came down.[74]

Old soldiers could evoke the Kiplingesque long-service army that had provided garrisons for the empire. Such soldiers were often heroically indifferent to the concerns of 'getting on' and 'staying out of trouble' that were so important to post-war civilian life. The soldier who had cheerfully remained a private for his whole career or, more probably, been repeatedly 'busted down' from a higher rank for disciplinary offences was a stock figure in national service memoirs. Such men really existed. Private Pannell was a regular with the Royal West Kents who, by the age of thirty-seven, had repeatedly been promoted and repeatedly busted down. When his platoon was ambushed, it was Pannell who rallied the men. He won the Distinguished Conduct Medal.[75]

Serving in North Africa in the late 1940s, Frank Dickinson met Sergeant Shakespeare, who was busted down for chasing a soldier when drunk. Shakespeare had been in the army since the 1930s. When his comrades asked him what he had been before that, he answered: 'a baby'.[76] Dickinson also got to know two regulars – Jasper and Yorkie – who had served together for years and owed loyalty to no one except each other. Jasper eventually deserted and was recaptured at Port Said. Dickinson saw him on a glass house detail and flicked him a packet of cigarettes. Jasper winked in reply.[77]

Jasper and Yorkie talked in the patois of the old army, which derived partly from the languages of the countries in which they had served. Leslie Ives remembered words 'from Hindustani – or other languages that the old sweats used to quote words and phrases from'.[78] Peter Nichols, serving in the RAF, was also struck by the private language of the long-service regular: 'From Hindi he had got dekko, tikh hai and turda pani, from Arab bint and shufti, and from the air force increment, inventory, requisition and promulgation.'[79] Robin Ollington served at the regimental depot of the Warwickshire Regiment in 1948 shortly after the regiment returned from Palestine:

> Suddenly as the overseas outposts of Empire went, all these old soldiers came back to England to us and you had, in the sergeants' mess, these wonderful groups of men who did not even speak English. They spoke these wonderful pidgins – army, Indian, African – and they could talk to each other.[80]

The glamour that was attached to some regulars in the late 1940s dissipated as the Second World War and the Raj began to seem more distant memories. The phrase 'old soldier' was itself deceptive. By the mid 1950s, few regulars could trace their military careers back before 1945. Most regulars, especially those – the great majority – who held the rank of corporal or lower, were relatively young. At the end of national service, the average age for a corporal in the British army was just under twenty-eight, for a lance corporal it was just under twenty-four – though men in their twenties who had been knocked around by life might seem old to eighteen-year-old conscripts.

Relations between national servicemen and regulars were sometimes tense. The very existence of conscription could create animosity. Some national servicemen found regulars helpful or sympathized with them: 'a large majority of them hated it as much as we did'.[81] Some conscripts, however, came to dislike anyone associated with military authority, and some regulars came to resent the complaints about service life and the implication that no one with a choice in the matter would ever sign on: 'Regulars became more hostile as Nat[ional] Service was phased out and conscripts became a minority. It is fair to say that the reverse was true when my service began and regulars were definitely treated as "inferior".'[82] W. Findlay, who served with the Signals, said that there was 'no problem' with the regulars 'but we did tend to look down on them as "thick"'.[83] G. T. Kell, who served with the Medical Corps, recalled:

> there were a few regulars. Some of these were sad lonely misfits. A private in his thirties had little rapport with teenagers. These regulars were institutionalized. They didn't have the responsibility of an NCO and in many cases they had no trade qualifications. Yet they were quite happy taking orders.[84]

In the eyes of many national servicemen, regulars were idle, poorly educated and from 'rough' backgrounds. Conscripts often regarded those who volunteered for regular service with pity or contempt. 'They don't do it if they have a good home'; 'They join up just to get the easiest and laziest life going.'[85] Ray Self said: 'Most regular RAF men I mixed with had come out of orphanages, no initiative, very institutionalized.' He remembered a corporal in his early forties who read *The Dandy*.[86] Bernard Parke, another airman, recalled: 'There was rather a gulf between the regulars and the national service men . . . the latter thought the others to be thick.'[87]

The gulf between national servicemen and regulars in the air force was particularly marked.[88] In a service that depended on technical expertise rather than physical toughness, it often seemed that there was no job – except flying – that could not be done better by a national serviceman than a regular, and regular airmen lacked the delinquent glamour that attached to some long-service soldiers. An air force report of 1951 commented thus:

> Regular and National Service airmen. Apart from certain exceptions . . . this consciousness of difference is general. Is it due to differences of manners and morals? This is sometimes suggested (for example, by one airman who wrote, 'I dislike the company of regulars. I was not brought up to only occupy my mind with drink, women etc.'). . . . One acute example of incompatibility was observed, between NS and Regulars, where a Corporals' Mess was used exclusively by Regulars, the NS Corporals messing with the NS men, and in this case it seemed probable that the principles of selection of the two groups had been so different as to produce antipathy between them.[89]

In Gordon Williams's autobiographical novel of national service in the RAF, a conscript sums up the world of the regular: 'Ritchie knew the type, long service wallah compensating for lack of real possessions by buying small, expensive items like fountain pens and lighters and leather writing cases. Things that could be easily carried. Same reason Jews bought a lot of jewellery.'[90]

Saying what regulars thought of national servicemen is harder because most non-commissioned regulars left no records of their private thoughts. Albert Shippen, a wartime NCO in the Durham Light Infantry who stayed in the army until 1948, suggested that national servicemen were superior to the regular soldiers who stayed on in the army beyond the war: 'A lot of them were tradesmen. They weren't what you would call army barmy. They didn't demoralize you in any way. They used to make you think a bit more.' Shippen enjoyed his conversations with national service educational sergeants and believed that national service as a whole was 'one of the best things that ever happened to the British army and without them we would not have survived'. He thought that '75 to 80 per cent' of men in administrative functions where 'more intelligent people were required' were national servicemen and that 'regulars just didn't have the ability to do these things'.[91]

In practical terms, the gap between national servicemen and regulars narrowed during the early 1950s. In February 1950, the minimum regular engagement was reduced to three years. In September of the same year, the period of national service was increased to two years. By the mid 1950s, there were 196,000 conscripts and 193,000 regulars in the army, but as a War Office report put it:

> Nearly half of those who are counted as Regulars are on a 3-year engagement. Men who do not re-engage serve for a period which approximates more closely in length to the present period of National Service than to what is normally understood as the period of service of a Regular soldier.[92]

If we assume that most three-year men were relatively young, then something between a quarter and a third of men of national service age who joined the army signed on for three years.[93] The Ministry of Defence recognized that many regulars would not have signed on at all if it had not been for the threat of conscription. In 1955, 85 per cent of regulars were drawn from men of national service age and the ministry estimated that reducing the length of national service by just three months would lose them 3,000 regular engagements per year.[94]

Many men of national service age 'converted' in that they signed up for three years before they were called up; others 'transferred' to three-year engagements after receiving their papers. In the air force, the total number of transfers and conversions between March and May 1950 was 1,449, it increased to 2,346 in the next quarter and then went up to 7,427 and 7,662 in the two quarters after that (i.e. just after national service had been extended) before dropping back to 6,992 from March to May 1952. For a time, the number of those of national service age who entered the air force on three-year engagements was greater than the number who did so as two-year conscripts.[95] Men signed on for three years partly to get higher pay and partly because they were often given to understand that signing on for an extra year would give them a wider choice of trade.

The advantages of three-year engagements, however, were inversely proportional to the success of recruitment. The more men that accepted such engagements, the less likely each individual serviceman was to get the posting he wanted. The proportion of three-year men who did something related to their previous occupation seems to have been only minutely higher than the proportion of ordinary national servicemen who did so – though it may be that three-year men would otherwise have been in a particularly weak negotiating position.[96] In addition to this, the ambiguities created by short-service engagements did not always improve the morale of the forces. Three-year men continued to think of themselves as conscripts and were often described as such by the military authorities. Two-year conscripts, on the other hand, often became even more prone to define themselves in opposition to regulars. The air force suggested that men justified not signing up for three years by denigrating regular service ever more vigorously. The fact that three-year men often started off in the same position as ordinary conscripts highlighted the extent to which 'volunteers' were less free than conscripts.

Bill Butler wrote of his service in the Sherwood Foresters:

> Apart from the Pioneer Corps there was nothing less attractive than the infantry, it seemed. We were a mixture of those who knew no better, those of little education, some who had had a brush with the law and a sprinkling of regulars who signed on for three years or more. The latter were regarded as completely beyond the pale by National Servicemen.[97]

A significant number of working-class conscripts seem to have believed that postings to the air force and navy were reserved for men who had signed on for an extra year. This was not true – though it is likely that officers who conducted interviews at national service medicals may have found it convenient to let men think that it was. The culture of national service encouraged men to count days and to construct a hierarchy of servicemen around the length of time that men had served and that they had left to serve before they were released. Under these circumstances, a man who had signed on for a whole extra year could seem pitiable and incomprehensible. Two-year conscripts were shocked that men would give up their freedom for such pitiful messes of pottage. Robin Hems, a national service corporal in the Scots Guards and himself from a poor background, believed that some signed on for three years because they smoked and needed the extra pound a week to buy cigarettes.[98]

Some men felt that they had no choice but to sign on for three-year engagements. This was especially true of skilled workers who wanted to avoid an assignment to the infantry or to 'general duties'. A firm of shipbuilders in Gateshead reported:

> Some of the apprentices complain that they are being blackmailed into serving three years. This is a very difficult position for the more intelligent apprentice as, having obtained his Higher or Higher National at the age of twenty-one, there is no hope of him having a position of real seniority if he merely goes for two years' service. He will often find himself in the charge of longer-term servicemen who have much lower standards of mentality than himself, and he is apt to regard his service with a rather jaundiced eye.[99]

The aviation company BOAC was favourable to national service and closely associated with the RAF (the head of its personnel department had been a wing commander). Though it was not obliged to do so, it agreed to hold open jobs for men who signed on for three years,[100] and was not hostile to men signing such engagements: 'Generally it is not worth enlisting for more than 3 years if you intend to return to BOAC, but there is something to be said for a 3-year engagement.' However, it also warned its employees attending national service medicals that 'The Service Interviewing Officers will probably try to persuade you to volunteer for more than two years, but remember that you have a completely free choice whether you do so or not.'[101]

The RAF made a deliberate choice to 'blackmail' – or at least press – certain kinds of men into taking three-year engagements. A minute of 1957 read:

> If he [the recruit] really wants a particular trade then he must think in terms of regular service, the benefits of which should be emphasized. Indeed he should be left with the feeling that he will indeed be fortunate to get the trade he wants as an NS recruit.[102]

Even the institution of three-year engagements, however, did not really help the armed forces to recruit long-term regulars. Most men who did sign for three years left as soon as their time was up. Few national servicemen could be persuaded to sign on for longer periods as the end of their service approached. Indeed, the culture of conscription, and the emphasis on military service as something to be endured for the shortest possible time, seem to have made fewer men contemplate long-term careers in the forces – even men who subsequently said that they regretted not having stayed on often left as soon as their two- or three-year engagement expired. Senior officers despaired at the impossibility of getting their best conscripts to stay on. Peter Jeffreys commanded a regiment that was seen to have done well in Korea and which contained a large number of national service NCOs: 'The tragedy is that not one single NCO was I able to persuade to become a Regular soldier.'[103]

The Queen's Hard Bargains

Rather more than usual has been heard lately of what have been called 'the Queen's hard bargains' – those national service men of bad character or poor physique whom the services must accept as part of their annual quota.

The Times, 16 July 1953

National service is sometimes now recalled as though it was primarily an instrument of social discipline. It was, however, never intended for this purpose. Far from seeing conscription as a means to reform delinquents, commentators often worried that it might corrupt young men.[1]

Having said this, the armed forces took a certain number of conscripts whose behaviour was, in one way or another, seen as awkward. Officers applied a variety of loose terms – dullards, morons, bad hats and psychopaths – to these youths. Broadly speaking, 'hard bargains' were characterized by one or more of the following: poor educational level (particularly illiteracy), a criminal record, psychological instability and an inability to adjust to collective life. In 1954, the War Office carried out an enquiry into the fate of men who had been regarded as 'problems' when first recruited. The language of the report says much about the way in which the army regarded some recruits:

> Among the National Servicemen who are sent to the visiting psychiatrist as part of the initial intake procedure are some who cannot be classed either as dullards suitable only for discharge or employment in the Pioneer Corps, or as suffering from a psychiatric disorder calling

for rejection or treatment, but yet present a problem in that they do not appear likely to train well, adjust well, or make a very positive contribution during their period of service. Immaturity, mild neurotic traits, low intelligence, psychopathic tendencies normally below the level that denotes a criminal, a poor background, a timid inadequacy, a weak resentment against life in general and military service in particular – these are some of the qualities which in varying combinations and in varying strength define the larger part of this section of recruits.[2]

The report drew on gradings that men had been given relating to their intelligence, educational level and psychological stability. It also cited remarks by commanding officers about individual soldiers, which suggested a more subjective, and often derogatory, way of seeing recruits. Attention was drawn to physical deformities, poor hygiene and effeminacy. One soldier was said to stammer and bite his nails.

The RAF and navy could take their pick of conscripts and not surprisingly the men they picked were unlikely to be criminal or educationally subnormal. In 1956, conscripts made up a little over 10 per cent of the navy but they accounted for only eleven of the 783 sailors who were in detention.[3] Most 'hard bargains' ended up in the army. A few delinquent conscripts were found in unexpected places. An officer cadet at Eaton Hall admitted to stealing from his comrades – too embarrassed to return the money, he had then put it on the collection plate at Chester Cathedral.[4] Neal Ascherson claimed that he had been at Eaton Hall with a deserter from the French Foreign Legion who sometimes suggested that they supplement their income with smash and grab raids: 'let's try Woolworths'.[5]

A few of the most problematic soldiers found a niche in fighting regiments. An 'ammunition number' on a gun team, for example, was a labourer who did not need the mechanical or mathematical abilities required of men who operated guns. One artillery unit contained a 'contentedly asocial' former farmhand with low ratings for intelligence and education. He was 'below average on the guns' but happy as a groom in the stables, where he was 'cheerful' though lazy: 'He lives in the harness rooms (didn't particularly want a bed), is never in the unit except for meals.'[6]

More commonly, such men were allocated to non-fighting corps.

The Catering Corps was one of these: a Borstal report on a man of 'mental capacity III', who was anxious about his health and came from a chaotic family, suggested that 'he should do well in the Army Catering Corps'.[7] The Royal Army Service Corps – responsible in large measure for transport – was another common destination. Many of its recruits came from the most deprived parts of the working class and included some criminals. A study of 200 Borstal boys convicted in the mid 1950s – the subjects of the study had been born between 1932 and 1938 – found that a large proportion of them had performed their military service in the RASC.[8]

There were, however, gradations within the RASC. Some were defined as 'tradesman' because they possessed, or were able to acquire, particular skills. Even those with low ratings on intelligence tests could become competent drivers.[9] Sometimes men from this unprestigious corps acquired the one thing that many national service recruits most coveted: a driving licence. One assumes that it was in part because of this that so many Borstal boys born in the 1930s later acquired convictions for 'taking and driving away'.[10]

At the bottom of the hierarchy was the Royal Pioneer Corps (RPC). It provided unskilled labour for the army – which mainly meant lugging stores from one part of a camp to another. During the war, it had taken in conscientious objectors, who did not wish to fight, and refugees from central Europe, whom the authorities did not trust to carry a gun. By 1945, this had changed and the RPC was recognized as the natural home of men who were unable to master even the skills of an infantry soldier. Discussion of men who were rated in the lowest medical categories and/or illiterate often blended into discussion of the Pioneer Corps. The military authorities themselves were never enthusiastic about its existence and sometimes considered abolishing it entirely. Those who urged its maintenance often saw it as primarily a means to prevent certain kinds of men from bringing down the standard of other units. An officer noted: 'I know that . . . you are taking steps to eliminate dullards, but I feel that it would be optimistic to hope for 100 per cent success . . . we would do better to take this type of man into the RPC.'[11]

The RPC was run down in the late 1940s but in 1951, as the country began to rearm, the army needed a reservoir of unskilled labour, particularly in remote bases where local workers were hard to recruit. Men came into the Pioneers by three routes. In each intake (of which there was one every fortnight), thirty men, including six regulars, came in the normal way (as they would come to any other unit). It was from these men that almost all NCOs were drawn. In addition to this, there was a 'special entry' reserved for men who had been rated M3 for mental capacity, which amounted to ninety men per entry, reduced to seventy per entry in 1954. Finally, transfers from other units of men who had initially been rated M2 but then been downgraded amounted to fifty or sixty men per intake, but was increasing by 1954. The army anticipated that the RPC would in due course amount to 7,700 men, of whom 1,880 would be 'normal standard' and the remainder (5,820) 'low mental category'. In April 1954 the strength of the RPC was made up of 3,638 men who had come in via 'normal entry' and 4,973 who had come via special entry. 'Normal entry' included transfers; so really the 'normal category' contained only 1,694 men and the 'low category' 6,917.[12]

The Pioneer Corps was run down again during the late 1950s – as fewer men, especially those from the lowest medical categories, were called up. By this time, the only national servicemen joining the corps were those who had been rejected by Army Basic Training Units and they were 'as a class, probably the worst category of men now joining'.[13]

The expectations of men in the Pioneer Corps were reflected in the case of a man of 'low mental ability' born in 1928 who came from a family of criminals. He himself had three convictions for larceny and had served time in both an approved school and a Borstal. He had been unable, even in the acute labour shortage of the Second World War, to hold down a job for more than nine months. But in the Pioneer Corps, in which he undertook his national service from 1948 to 1950, he was apparently seen as 'very good, clean, honest, reliable and a hard worker'.[14]

Only one conscript who served with the corps left a first-hand account of his experience. Royston Salmon had wanted to go into the RASC but was sent to the Pioneers when the interviewing officers discovered that he was illiterate: 'A lot of men who cannot read or write go into the Pioneers.' Salmon learned how to read and write while he was in the army, an achievement that he recognized as being unusual.[15]

Generally, however, the Pioneer Corps was described only from the outside, by men from other units who were attached to it. Usually these outsiders regarded the Pioneers with affectionate contempt. While awaiting a posting to officer cadet school from his infantry training regiment, W. J. R. Morrison was put in a holding company with men who were due to be sent to the Pioneer Corps. He remembered that he was one of only two literate men in his barracks but that he enjoyed his brief time there; one of his new friends taught him how to pick locks.[16]

George Gardiner was attached to the Pioneers as a 'sergeant tester', responsible for conducting intelligence tests:

> Most of our work with each fortnightly intake was to sift out those who should never have been called up at all, either because they were too dim to be of any use even to the army or on psychiatric grounds, and recommend their discharge. Then the slow bureaucracy of the army got to work, and many absconded while waiting for their discharge papers to come through. They were then brought back by the military police, while their discharge procedure had to start all over again. There were regular suicide attempts.[17]

Jeff Nuttall was a sergeant from the Education Corps attached to an ordnance depot, mainly so that he could teach the regular NCOs in the unit rather than because anyone thought that the ordinary conscripts had any educational potential. He wrote:

> When I was at Weedon the central pavilion was the billet for the Royal Pioneer Corps detachment whose job it was to lug cases of FLN rifles around the depot and send them off to Kenya and Cyprus. They had long ago stripped the roof of lead so that rain poured straight through into many of the rooms. They were rough simple lads. They slept in their clothes, many of them, handing in perfectly clean pillowcases and pyjamas for laundering every week.[18]

For ordinary national servicemen the Pioneer Corps was a black hole, 'said to be a fate even worse than the infantry'.[19] They understood that being posted to the corps was humiliating but they knew

almost nothing about its internal workings. Accounts of basic training in other units often refer to some particularly inept or slow-witted
recruit who was in due course removed from his original unit and sent
to the Pioneers: 'a fate worse than death in our eyes then!'[20]

The Pioneers were considered low even by the standards of those
recruits identified as 'problematic' at the basic training units. Only
one of the eleven examples of such recruits described in a report of
1954 had sunk as far as the Pioneer Corps and he was described thus:

> a showman's son who spent his childhood and youth travelling with
> the fair, had no education, and was completely illiterate. For over a year
> he had been greasing guns at a REME unit next door, and is considered
> one above the labouring class by his Adjutant. He is popular, well
> behaved and plays football. On his second primary education course he
> won the prize as best student. Being basically under the average intelli-
> gence he will not progress further in the Army, but he has made a fair
> showing, considering the bad start.[21]

Illiteracy was the most obvious failing that made men bad soldiers
in the eyes of the army. The War Office estimated that 1 or 2 per cent
of conscripts were unable to read or write. This seems, however, to
have involved a fairly rigorous definition of illiteracy. Army educationalists sometimes defined 'illiteracy' as meaning a reading age of
seven[22] or five,[23] but the army's own tests were simple: men who were
unable, even with help, to complete a form on entry to the forces were
classed as illiterate.[24] The army almost never accepted illiterates as
regular soldiers. Complete illiteracy in the army diminished as time
went on. This was partly because education improved, especially as
the generation who had been schooled primarily in peacetime began
to be called up. It was also partly because the army became more
selective and began to exclude men whose education might present
problems. In October 1952, the Secretary of State for War told parliament that 850 of the national service men admitted to the army in the
year up to the end of June 1952 (or 0.7 per cent of the total intake)
were illiterate, 'although of sufficient mental capacity to be accepted
for service'.[25] This seems, in fact, to have been a slight underestimate.
The army's own figures suggested that men defined as illiterate made
up just over 1 per cent of the intake in 1952, and that their numbers

declined after this until they reached 0.84 per cent of the intake in the first eight months of 1954.[26] In the first half of 1956 a total of ninety-two such men joined the army. All of them were national servicemen. One was in the artillery, two in the infantry, four in the Ordnance Corps, seventeen in the RASC and sixty-eight in the Pioneer Corps.[27]

Illiterates were classed by the military authorities as educational level 8, and some men at this level had attended special schools for the educationally subnormal. Level 7 was made up of men who had completed schooling to the normal age but then performed badly on the tests administered when they were first recruited to the armed forces. The proportion of such men among national service army recruits dropped from 20.7 per cent in 1952 to 18.4 per cent in the first eight months of 1954.[28] The army sometimes talked about a group of 'semi-literate' or 'sub-literate' men who constituted part, but not all, of those classed as educational level 7. A minute of early 1954 suggested that there were 3,250 sub-literates in a year's intake.[29] Army educationalists also talked about a third group of men, who had reading ages of less than twelve; they believed that 'nearly two-thirds of the Army, Regulars and National Servicemen alike', belonged to this category in 1951.[30]

Some defined illiteracy in looser terms and used it to encompass a larger number of soldiers. Senior officers gave figures that ranged from 10 to 30 per cent for the proportion of illiterates in the post-war army.[31] Assessments were complicated by the ire of a few officers – who denounced the intellectual limits of some soldiers in lurid terms[32] – and by the more relaxed attitude of some sergeants, whose own education was limited and who tended to use the word 'scholar' to mean anyone who had any schooling. When Tom Bingham arrived at his training unit, the sergeant asked him: 'Are you a scholar?' Bingham, still smarting from his failure to win the highest entrance award at Balliol, said: 'Not really.' 'Well, can you read and write?' asked the sergeant.[33] Peter Burke, another Oxford scholar, recalls that a sergeant asked the men of his training platoon whether there was anyone who could not read and write and received no response. The sergeant then said, 'It's nothing to be ashamed of – I am not too good with letters myself', at which point half a dozen men, about a fifth of the group, put their hands up.

Men of both level 7 and level 8 were more common among

conscripts than among regular recruits. The average educational standard of regulars was lower than that of national servicemen but they were also a more homogeneous group, containing fewer men at both the highest and lowest levels. Army officers sometimes complained about 'illiteracy' among regulars and suggested that it was higher than among conscripts. The army usually reserved places at its Preliminary Education Centres for regular soldiers, which suggests that a large group of regular recruits were regarded as educationally unfit for service until they had received additional instruction. Furthermore, the instructors of the army Education Corps (mainly national servicemen) spent much of their time introducing regulars (often NCOs) to the rudiments of spelling. The apparent discrepancy may arise from different definitions of 'illiteracy' and a comprehensive definition might include many men at educational level 6, most of whom were regulars. One suspects, too, that regular officers – whose own prose style was characterized by laboured formality rather than clarity or concision – were as intolerant of poor spelling as they were of dirty buttons on parade.

Illiterates leave little evidence about their experience but War Office reports give occasional glimpses of their life. Men of educational levels 7 and 8 were most common in Caernarvonshire, where they made up 44 per cent of those called up, and least common in Peebles, where they accounted for 6 per cent. Welsh 'illiteracy' seems to have sprung in part from problems with the English language.[34] The War Office noted that illiterate men 'took care' to marry literate women and therefore gained a useful guide who could lead them through the written world.[35] Some men seem to have acquired similar guides during their time in the forces. David Fisher, an educational sergeant in Korea, took to hanging around when company orders were pinned up because he knew that some of the men would have trouble reading them.[36] Many educated men wrote letters for their friends during basic training but one was still writing letters for a comrade when they had both reached Malaya: 'He is a case, has been in the army eight months and on the run as many times.'[37]

Defenders of conscription sometimes implied that it might serve an educational purpose, but few men learned to read or write in the army. In April 1953 a twenty-year-old national serviceman – Private

James Reid Chittick – was court-martialled for desertion from the Ordnance Corps. His defending officer pointed out that he had initially been happy in the army but had felt out of his depth because he could not read or write and had become the butt of jokes from his comrades. The defending officer suggested that the army should take part of the blame because Chittick had been unable to do more than write his name after nine months – he was sentenced to six months.[38]

Violence raised awkward questions for those who commanded national servicemen. It was, after all, the *raison d'être* of the armed forces. National servicemen were judged on, among other things, their 'levels of aggression', and having too low a level could be seen as a problem. Those sent to a psychiatrist were rated on a three-point scale (OT1, OT2 and OT3). OT1 men were 'natural fighters'; OT2 were normal; 'OT3 is the rating given to approximately 10 per cent of those referred to psychiatrists at the ABTU who are so timid or so unstable as to be a positive or potential liability in the battle area.' A follow-up report on men who had been seen by a psychiatrist revealed the ambiguities of the army's attitude to aggression. The report's author admitted that men who were rated OT3 had actually performed better than men with 'normal' levels of aggression, which may have been because 'problem' cases tended to be kept away from combat units and thus assigned to duties that might be well suited to a pacific temperament. However, commanding officers felt that a degree of fighting spirit was desirable, even in soldiers who were never likely to get near the front line. One soldier was, by the standards of soldiers who had been seen by an army psychiatrist and who were 'semi literate', highly successful in that he had risen to the rank of lance bombardier. However, his commanding officer said that he had been 'too kind' to serve as a regimental policeman and that he 'mucks in too much for an NCO'. By contrast, aggression, even aggression that involved breaking rules, could be presented in a positive light. A report on a private in the RASC read thus: 'He now – says his CO – has some spirit, and was even in a recent fight.'[39]

Fighting was common in some units. Officers sometimes turned a blind eye to violence in the ranks and perhaps assumed that it was a natural part of working-class life. Leigh Parkes recalled that a Borstal boy in his hut 'glassed' another soldier during the drinking session that followed their passing-out parade at the end of basic training, and that 'we potential officers made ourselves scarce'.[40] A middle-class national serviceman in Cyprus in 1958 wrote that there had been a fight in his camp between the Royal Ulster Rifles and the Royal Scots Fusiliers:

> sternly dealt with by the CO, after he had made a short sharp angry speech to the whole battalion about 'disgraceful hooliganism', which he appears to think should be left to the Greeks and Turks, since he specifically encourages 'toughness' in dealing with them as opposed to in the camp itself. At the moment I could do with a lot less toughness all round![41]

There were, however, limits to the violence that soldiers were allowed to use. They might fight each other in private, but open riot, striking a superior or the use of weapons got them into trouble. Matters were bad in the Pioneer Corps – perhaps because it contained both violent men and men whose mental or physical limitations made them vulnerable to bullying. In the summer of 1953, Abdul Guraimer Sumer – a 21-year-old national service pioneer from South Shields – was sentenced to eight months for inflicting grievous bodily harm with a knuckleduster. A subsequent search of the joint Ordnance Corps and Pioneer Corps camp at Nesscliffe revealed a stock of illegal weapons including rubber coshes, a home-made extending spring cosh, lavatory chains that could be used as knuckledusters and a bicycle chain.[42]

Ian Fleming's novel *From Russia with Love* (1957) describes Donovan Grant – illegitimate, poorly educated and insanely violent – who is called up (in the late 1940s) and posted as a driver to the Royal Corps of Signals, just the kind of non-'teeth arm' posting that was often given to men with criminal propensities. He is rebuked after almost killing a man in a boxing match and then recruited by the Soviet secret service, which recognizes the military usefulness of psychopaths.

The British army was always worried by men who enjoyed the violence that soldiers were supposed to deploy as a duty. A psychiatric report of 1951 concerned a twenty-year-old gunner who sounds like a real-life version of Donovan Grant. He had lost his mother at a young age and run wild. He had grown up a 'sturdy, dark-complexioned young man with a sullen expression and aggressive manner'. He had convictions for theft dating back to the age of eight and had served time in approved school, Borstal and prison. He had left school at fourteen and, though he was of average intelligence, 'he has no wish to better himself, and learns nothing from the experience of punishment. His civilian offences are pointless from the material standpoint and he gets a thrill out of outwitting authority.' He had undergone tough physical training as a paratrooper but then been excluded from this unit because of theft. He was a boxer but 'his aggressive instincts are canalised into fighting (not boxing) his opponents into defeat'. He was thrown out of the army.[43]

Glaswegians seem to have had particular problems with the army, or it had particular problems with them, partly because of the city's reputation for violent crime. A report of 1952 dealt with 'National Servicemen of Bad Character' performing their part-time service after their ordinary two years had elapsed. The four examples of problem cases that the report cited were all from Glasgow. Two of the men were said to have attended only five days of camp in 1952 – the normal obligation would have been two weeks – after having been arrested for larceny and assault with a broken bottle.[44] When nine men were sentenced for riot at a military detention centre in 1959, five of them came from Glasgow (the remainder came from London, Liverpool and Edinburgh).[45] A report on a problem conscript in the RASC finished with the words: 'the more he keeps away from Glasgow the better'.[46]

National servicemen, unlike regulars, were under no obligation to state whether or not they had a criminal record when they joined the forces. The Ministry of Labour and the Prison Commission were keen that such a record should not, in itself, rule men out of military service – either because they thought that such a ban might impede rehabilitation or because they did not want men to benefit from their crimes. The issue was discussed most frequently with regard to the treatment of Borstal boys who were called up. Borstals – the name came from the Kent town in which the first institution was located – had been established early in the century to provide 'training' for young criminals – from 1948, the upper age limit was set at twenty-one.

Borstal sentences could be up to three years, and some boys would have been retained until they reached the age of twenty-one – though most were released before they had served their full sentence. Some youths were allowed to defer their military service because their Borstal governors believed that they would benefit from a period of resettlement in civilian life before they joined the forces.[47] There were, however, boys who went straight from Borstal into the army. Slightly fewer than 2,000 boys were sentenced to Borstal training every year.[48] In 1955, 1,044 men released from Borstal were eligible for national service; some of those not called up may have belonged to that category of people with such mental or physical disability that they were not even summoned to pre-national service medical inspections. About half of the Borstal boys – compared to around a fifth of the general population – were rejected for service by medical boards.[49] Sometimes this seems to have been because juvenile delinquents were drawn largely from the very poor and often suffered from physical ailments; sometimes rejection appears to have been on psychological grounds and to have sprung from an understanding that 'psychopaths' should not serve in the armed forces. A group of boys at an approved school who had murdered one of their teachers in March 1947 were released from prison in March 1956. They seemed willing to reintegrate into civilian life – one of them had arranged to train as a hairdresser while he was on parole – but the Home Office and Ministry of Labour decided that they would not call them up.[50]

It seems that, in an average year, 600 Borstal boys entered the armed forces as national servicemen[51] and that the total number of such young men in the forces at one time would not have much exceeded 1,000 – this amounted to about one conscript in every 300. Almost all of these would have gone to the army and a very large proportion would have been in just a few units. Not all juvenile criminals would have been Borstal boys. A substantial number would have been sent to approved schools, which were designed for younger boys and not, unlike Borstals, reserved for those who had been convicted of a crime. Others would have been bound over by magistrates, fined, put on probation or, in a few cases, sent to adult prisons. One study on the 'military value of the ex-juvenile delinquent' looked at sixty-seven men – fifty-one conscripts and sixteen regulars. Only eighteen of these had been to Borstal; seven had been 'bound over' by magistrates, forty-seven had been put on probation, forty-six had been to approved schools and eighteen had endured some other form of punishment, such as a fine or imprisonment; most had, in fact, been punished in more than one way.[52] If this study was representative, then we might assume that the number of juvenile criminals entering the forces was about four times greater than the number of Borstal boys, but this would still be a small proportion of all national servicemen.

Why, then, was there so much talk about criminal national service-men? In part, the answer probably lies in the innocence of most conscripts. Eighteen-year-olds from respectable backgrounds were liable to be shocked by even quite modest displays of misbehaviour and it may be that many of them overestimated the number of hard-ened criminals, even former inmates of high-security prisons, in their midst.[53] The Borstal boy in the barracks during basic training is a recurrent theme in national service memoirs.

Some Borstal boys adjusted relatively well to the army – perhaps because only the most promising of them were passed fit, or perhaps because the army's own disciplinary machinery kept men away from the civil courts. All the same, almost half of Borstal boys released straight into the forces had been convicted of another offence within a few years and a third of one sample were discharged before they had completed eighteen months of service.[54] Some men lasted a lot less long. A 'mentally defective' Borstal boy born in July 1927 was called up in 1945 but discharged after thirty-seven days – including fourteen days on which he had been on leave and four days on which he had been absent without leave.[55]

The authorities, both civil and military, were much exercised by the problem of criminals undergoing national service. In early 1949, a magistrate wrote to The Times suggesting that conscription brought innocent but impressionable young men into 'close contact with hard-ened young ruffians with long records, some of whom have even been released from Borstal to join the Army'.[56] The criminal convictions of national servicemen were not revealed to the army and this gave rise to some extraordinary assertions about the level of criminality among them. One official suggested that national service Borstal boys accounted for a large proportion of the 3,000 army court martials every year and that 5 per cent of national servicemen had criminal records when they entered the forces. He admitted that the second of these figures was a 'guess'.[57]

The Secretary of State for War wrote in 1954:

I have recently had brought to my notice an example of the very serious consequences of men of bad character 'ganging up' in a unit in the Middle East. These men embarked on a campaign of crime. This took various forms, of which the most serious were threatening and striking non-commissioned officers, desertion and arson. The men even went so far as to intimidate other members of the unit by threatening that, if their activities were reported, the families of the men who reported them would suffer. If a junior non-commissioned officer reported a man he would later be assaulted, usually after lights out, and on more than one occasion while he was asleep in his tent. When this happened other occupants of the tent were too frightened to give evidence.

The majority of the men in this unit came from one large city and there is no doubt that the methods they used were those of the city gang which causes the civil police so much trouble. Such a situation could hardly have arisen if the previous records of the men concerned had been known to the authorities. When these men were ultimately brought to trial by court-martial it was found that the majority of them had previous civil convictions, including convictions for crimes of violence. The regular soldiers among them had not declared their civil convictions on enlistment.[58]

The Secretary of State wanted commanding officers to be informed of the previous civil convictions of national servicemen.[59]

The crimes committed by national servicemen were in the main relatively trivial – Private Brian Hatcher, who strangled his nineteen-year-old wife while on weekend leave from Aldershot, was an exception.[60] Sometimes national servicemen directed violence against themselves. This was true of those who attempted suicide but also of those who sought to acquire injuries that would render them unfit for service. Driver Alexander Russell, aged eighteen, of the RASC was a 'hard bargain' national serviceman who, in the words of an army psychiatrist, 'appeared to have difficulty in adjusting to Army conditions'. He eventually placed his foot in front of a railway engine. He was court-martialled for 'maiming himself'.[61]

Not all who committed crimes in the army were retarded or aggressive. Some had been embarked on successful careers that were rudely interrupted by the call-up. Clarence Da Costa of the Royal Signals had come to England from Jamaica in 1956 and rose from being a dishwasher to being part owner of a Soho club. He was, however, called up and, when he found that one of his partners had absconded with £200 of his money, he deserted to sort things out. He was recaptured and court-martialled for desertion, having also acquired a civil conviction for possession of 'Indian hemp'. The press reported that Da Costa, one of the relatively few black men to be conscripted, was known in Soho as 'Tony the Toff' and was a 'bongo-drummer' and drug addict.[62] Private Michael Follet worked as an illegal bookie while performing his national service. He earned £2 9s a week as a clerk in the Royal Electrical and Mechanical Engineers but often did not bother to collect his pay. He sometimes spent £100 in a few days on 'greyhounds, hire cars and girls'. He was an enterprising man – though perhaps also a psychologically unstable one since, believing that he owed money to someone in a position to make his life unbearable, he eventually committed suicide.[63]

Punishments inflicted on soldiers were mainly carried out in their own units. The most common punishment was confinement to barracks and/or fatigues. Men who committed civil offences could be prosecuted in the civil courts and sent to Borstal or prison, in which case, theoretically, they were obliged to return to finish their military service at the end of sentence. In addition to this, special detention centres were established. The most notorious of these were the one at Colchester – nominally a unit for training of delinquents rather than an institution of pure punishment – and the one at Shepton Mallet, which was a military prison. In June 1955, there were 400 inmates at Colchester. Ninety-seven men had been convicted for stealing, forty-two for civil offences, such as larceny, and thirty-nine for military offences, such as insubordination or striking an officer; some men had committed more than one offence.

Time served in detention did not count towards national service obligations so men who had very poor disciplinary records could end up serving for more than two years – though the army was sometimes keen to be rid of its hardest cases: the Kray twins, Charles Richardson and Bruce Reynolds (the man who planned the Great Train Robbery of 1963) prided themselves on having been dishonourably discharged after having spent most of their national service in detention or on the run.

A few men spent their entire youth in a running battle with military authority. Among a group of 253 Scottish men born in 1936, two deserted and spent most of their two years in prison; a third, presumably having committed a more serious offence, was retained in the army for two and a half years to complete his sentence.[64] An army clerk in Korea came across men who had served for four years before the forces finally discharged them.[65] In June 1960, Private Terence Bush of the RASC – described as a 'persistent absentee and deserter' – was sentenced to twelve months' imprisonment by a civilian court for having organized a conspiracy to escape from military detention at Blenheim barracks. Bush was, by this time, twenty-five years old. He had a 24-year-old wife and two young children. He had first been called up for national service at the age of eighteen in 1953 and had been arrested and returned to his unit three times.[66]

The most common offences, committed by 192 of the 400 inmates at Colchester, were absence without leave and desertion.[67] The former implied a relatively short period away from barracks; the latter something more calculated. In practice, the difference between these two offences was not so great. During the war large numbers of men had deserted and remained at large for long periods of time – often until 1945 or even until the general amnesty for wartime deserters that came with the coronation in 1953. National servicemen were less enterprising. They were almost all young. Few of them had a loyal woman or a network of criminal associates who could provide them with shelter and few were as lucky as Private David Halladay, who inherited £26,000 after five months in the Catering Corps, and promptly moved to Paris.[68]

For some men, desertion fitted into wider patterns of criminal behaviour. One man, discharged from Borstal into the army in September 1948, was absent without leave twice in his first month of service and then 'quietened down for a few weeks', before being charged and acquitted of a civil offence, convicted of taking a German girl into barracks and, finally, charged with stealing lead piping.[69] Another man (born in 1928) had been convicted of eight civil offences by the time he was twelve. He was called up in April 1946 and deserted after eight days.[70]

Signalman Charles Connor went absent without leave in 1951. When a policeman saw him in civilian clothes and with a woman, Connor escaped – breaking a window and slipping out of his jacket as the policeman grabbed his arm. When Connor was eventually captured, he joined an attempted break-out from military prison and was prosecuted for 'mutiny'. His defence counsel read out a letter from his mother. She told the court that her son was her only support and that his father, who had been ill, had died in January:

> Please allow me to acquaint you with certain facts regarding my son, which I sincerely hope will vindicate him in some small way. Charles was called to the forces early in December but unfortunately could not take to the idea of soldiering and after only six days' service he went absent without leave. Since then until his final escapade, he has been on the run with occasional spells of captivity, certainly the mark of a bad soldier but, believe me, he was a perfect son to me and he showed it. But the charge of mutiny frightens me, sir. How can a man be guilty or even charged with an offence he does not know the meaning of? How on earth can the military authorities expect a soldier of a few days' standing to distinguish between mutiny and ordinary absconding?[71]

Most men who left their units had no long-term plans to evade their military obligations; they were just seeking to sort out some short-term problem. David Baxter, who left his depot to spend a long weekend cruising art galleries and bookshops in London, felt that he needed a few days away from the barracks to keep his sanity.[72] Sapper Roy Newall, a 21-year-old national serviceman who was apparently 'pampered by his parents', went absent in 1957 because he wished to attend to his sick mother and his prized chrysanthemums – he got six months.[73]

Family circumstances presented problems for many recruits, and army psychologists were always on the look-out for 'over-protective mothers' – though some of the most troubled recruits had no mothers at all. Some men, however, rebelled precisely because they wished to take responsibility for their families. Aircraftman Cicero Banks left a base near Doncaster almost every day and hitch-hiked forty-six miles to his home in Bradford. There he attempted to 'keep a restraining hand' on his father, who had taken to beating his mother up. Banks was eventually placed in the guardroom for being absent without leave and escaped twice. He was sentenced to seventy days' detention.[74]

Even long-term deserters were not seen as posing the kind of threat that their predecessors had presented during the war. In 1944 it had been reckoned that 7.08 per cent of those arrested for all crimes were deserters;[75] by 1950 this figure had dropped to 0.9 per cent.[76] Scotland Yard reported in 1949:

> During the war the deserters from all Allied Armies here did account for a fair proportion of the crime but that is not the position now. The deserter of today is the misfit in the conscripted army and when he deserts becomes absorbed into industry by the use of fictitious documents.[77]

Parliament was told in 1950 that 1.114 per cent of regulars and 0.771 per cent of national servicemen had deserted in 1948.[78] Numbers must have dropped, because by July 1958 there had apparently been only 8,881 post-war desertions from the armed forces: 752 from the navy, 3,273 from the RAF and 4,856 from the army.[79] In the air force, regulars were significantly more likely to desert than conscripts and this also seems to have been the case in the navy. A large proportion of national service desertions came from the units that took conscripts seen as awkward. In the year to March 1951, 835 national servicemen deserted from the army: 117 of these were from the Pioneer Corps and nineteen from the Catering Corps. By contrast, there were only eighty-four deserters from the Royal Artillery, which was far larger.[80]

Occasionally, enquiries by outsiders afford a glimpse of what life might have been like for some of the men who deserted. Gunner Shillingford was called up in March 1950, having, to the surprise of his doctor, been given a medical classification of grade 1:

This youth was mainly illiterate. He could not read or write properly before he went into the Army. He had never had regular employment owing to ill health. He was at some racing stables for six months. He occasionally drove a lorry for his father, but owing to his ill health he had never had regular employment.

Shillingford collapsed on the parade ground a few days into basic training and then, having heard bad things about his next camp, he went absent without leave, for the first of many times. His father, a veteran of the First World War, wrote to the commanding officer outlining his difficulties; the commanding officer called Shillingford before him and told him that he would be better off dead. Shillingford deserted again and lived in fields, eating grass and begging coppers to buy food. At some point in his military career, it appears he learned to write and used this new skill to forge an entry in a Post Office savings book. Eventually his father found him and took him back to the authorities, but he was sentenced to another period of detention, which meant that he had now been in the army for more than two years.[81]

Throughout national service, the military authorities showed great distaste for conscripts with criminal records. In the late 1950s, a senior officer wrote to the Secretary of State for War that the presence of delinquents among national servicemen was deterring respectable boys from enlisting:

> Now that we are committed to building up an all regular Army, and the importance of regular recruiting has become paramount, I consider that we should once more seek agreement to the exclusion of the real bad hats – Borstal boys, Approved School boys, and those who have served prison sentences – from the call up.[82]

The suggestion that conscripts were bringing crime into the army is odd. It is true that national servicemen were, in theory, called up without regard to their criminal convictions and that regulars, by contrast, were required to 'attest' to any convictions when they joined up and could therefore be turned away by the forces. In practice, however, the forces did exclude a large proportion of national servicemen with criminal records. As for regulars, there was no way of ensuring that they told the truth and, unsurprisingly, men with long criminal careers often lied about them. At court martials, it frequently emerged that regular soldiers had criminal convictions they had not disclosed when they joined up. In one court martial, all fourteen accused had civil convictions – only two of the soldiers had attested to these when they joined.[83] All the evidence suggests that regulars were more likely to be criminal than national servicemen. Long-service regulars made up half of all inmates in military detention, at a time when they constituted about a quarter of the army.[84] Furthermore, in private, senior officers recognized that serious social problems were much more often associated with regular recruits than with conscripts.

National service provided the military authorities with an alibi. They sometimes blamed crime on conscripts, and the suggestion that some of those called up were criminal, illiterate or psychopathic helped to reinforce an image of regular army recruits as clean-cut, clean-limbed paragons of healthy living.

If national servicemen had indeed produced a disproportionate number of problem soldiers into the army, then the quality of the intake ought to have improved as conscription came to an end in the late 1950s and early 60s. In fact, the opposite seems to have happened. Among men joining as regulars from July 1960 to June 1961, 18 per cent admitted that they had criminal convictions.[85] Some units found that the switch to all regular recruitment brought them more problem recruits. Not surprisingly, these were especially numerous in the Pioneer Corps. It had abolished national service recruitment by 1958 but an intake of 172 short-service regulars in that year included four bed-wetters, and thirteen who had to be discharged on medical grounds. One had refused to eat anything except bread, butter and jam since he was seventeen years old and was discharged after forty-two days. Another had repeatedly gone absent without leave and spent time in a civilian prison, he suffered from claustrophobia and lacked 'military respect'; the authorities concluded that he was a psychopath rather than a malingerer. A third had been in and out of mental hospital and treated with electro-convulsion therapy. A fourth had a bone missing from his leg and had spent four years in an orthopaedic hospital as a child. In addition, 150 men had deficiencies in their kit and there were virtually none with the ability to become NCOs.[86]

More disturbing for the army were regular recruits to infantry regiments, which were often prestigious in the eyes of their officers but unattractive places for working-class boys who wanted – if they wanted to have anything to do with the armed forces at all – to learn a trade. The Brigade of Guards had particular problems in recruiting in the immediate aftermath of national service. They reduced ceremonial duties in London – partly to attract soldiers who might prefer to see more active service and partly, one suspects, to get men away from the temptations that life in the capital might offer. *The Times* sent its defence correspondent to a prestigious infantry regiment, the Green Jackets, in March 1961, as it moved to all-regular recruiting. The journalist reported that a fifth of all recruits were not up to the standards that the regiment required: 'the Green Jackets recruit mainly in the East End of London and are drawing now on the children of the Blitz, many of whom lacked security in childhood'. Many were 'pathetic cases', a category that included 'mental dullards, the bed-wetters, the grossly unstable, the physically unco-ordinated, the bad influences'.[87]

There was one important difference between conscripts and regulars which may in part account for the different way in which the two groups of men were seen by the authorities. Regulars were more likely than national servicemen to commit almost every kind of crime and also more likely to have psychological or educational problems. They were, however, less likely to rebel against the very idea of military discipline. Regulars had, after all, chosen to join up, they often came from backgrounds which had some long association with the army, and they served for relatively long periods, during which they came to accept the idiosyncrasies of military authority. An MP who inspected the Military Corrective Establishment (MCE) at Colchester in 1955 remarked that all new arrivals were placed in A Company and that those who behaved well could earn transfer to B Company, in which they might enjoy certain privileges:

> I noted a marked difference between the attitude to the MCE of the bona fide Regular soldier and the average National Service man. The majority of Regular soldiers accepted their punishment philosophically . . . In the end they bore no particular grudge against the Army about their treatment in the MCE.

On the other hand, the National Service man regarded the MCE with smouldering indignation ... and he left with a bitter grudge against the system which condemned him to that form of training.[88]

A Glasgow solicitor acquired some expertise in defending conscripts from the city who had come into conflict with the military authorities. One of his clients was Private Bates of the Royal Pioneer Corps. Bates had been called up in August 1949 and had, by March 1951, accumulated fifty-six days in military custody for various offences (absence, losing equipment and driving without authority) as well as thirty days in a civilian prison for assault. He was accused – with men from the Pioneer Corps, the RASC and the Catering Corps – of rioting at a detention centre in May 1951. The solicitor told the court martial:

my client and many of his kind cannot appreciate the difference between a country in a state of war and a country in a coterie of countries where there is grave international disquiet. While in a state of war Bates might make a good soldier. I say with confidence in a state of comparative peace, as we are in now, Bates is bad military material, because quite frankly in questioning him I found that his attitude is that he regards himself – and it is a peculiar attitude that one finds difficult to understand – not so much as a man who is mobilized under the National Service Act but rather as a reluctant recipient of a sort of nationalized press gang.[89]

Bates got three years.

12

Korea

Men were dying ahead. A battalion attack against a heavily fortified enemy position was in progress. This was war. All at the same time, I was excited, afraid of being afraid and, more than anything else, curious.

Peter Holmes[1]

Peter Holmes was a national service second lieutenant with the Royal Leicestershire Regiment. He had arrived in Korea in October 1951. Having celebrated his nineteenth birthday a few weeks earlier, he was, just, old enough to be sent to war. He did not, however, expect to see much fighting. The regular officers told him that he was unlucky to have missed out on the regiment's previous posting to Hong Kong. They thought that the conflict in Korea was pretty much over. On the night of 4 November, Holmes and his brother officers were called to a conference: 'Anyone know Major W? . . . Well, he was killed an hour ago.' The officers learned that the Chinese had begun an intensive bombardment and were obviously planning to attack; they did so before the conference was over. Holmes told his sergeant to get the platoon packed up and ready to move in half an hour. Suddenly, there was an explosion. A private in another platoon, fumbling in the dark as he attempted to pack his kit, had accidentally pulled the pin out of a grenade. He threw it away, but threw it uphill and it rolled back down to the platoon commander's tent. It killed one man and mortally wounded another. The platoon commander, Holmes's near contemporary at Eaton Hall, lost a leg.[2]

Holmes himself was ordered to mount an attack that he believed to be suicidal. He envied those men who were going in first because they would at least die quickly. The night before the attack was 'the longest and most miserable that I have ever spent'.[3] The attack was cancelled at the last moment, but fighting was still intense. The regiment had sent 550 men into action on 5 November; two weeks later, 339 were capable of walking out, the rest had been killed or wounded. Sixteen out of thirty-five men in Holmes's platoon were still more or less unscathed.[4]

Holmes led thirty-three patrols as his regiment probed the enemy defences. On the first of these he was ordered to advance until he was shot at. Two men from his platoon refused to go and Holmes read them a formal warning that they would be considered in breach of King's Regulations if they persisted in their defiance. They did persist and both got five years.[5] Holmes himself had won the Military Cross – the citation spoke of 'coolness, buoyancy and courage' – by the time he went up to Cambridge. He later became a mountaineer, author and chairman of Shell, then the largest company in the world.

Private Saunders of the Royal Norfolk Regiment left less of a mark. His letters to his mother and 'uncle' (presumably stepfather) survive. He wrote from a troopship between Aden and Colombo:

> I understand why you never came to see me off, I felt the same way as the ship started to pull away from Southampton, so in one way I was glad you didn't come because it would have been harder for both of us when it came to saying goodbye.[6]

On 13 November, the War Office telegraphed his father to say that Saunders had been killed by a mine three days earlier. He was buried in Allied plot 23, row 5, grave 1607. His effects were divided between his parents. Each received £6 10s 2d from his back pay. An inventory of his personal effects, four in total, was sent to his mother and she was invited to chose two of them.[7] Saunders had been nineteen.

The war that brought Holmes and Saunders to Korea began in 1950. At the end of the Second World War, Korea, which had been ruled by Japan for forty-five years, was effectively divided. Communist forces (supported by Russian soldiers coming through Manchuria) ruled north of the 38th parallel. In the south, authority was initially exercised by the United States Army Military Government in Korea, which ruled with the aid of local officials, some of whom had previously served the Japanese occupation. Syngman Rhee, who had spent much of his life in the United States, formed a right-wing Representative Democratic Council and called for a united and independent Korea. In 1948, the Americans allowed elections in the American zone. Syngman Rhee's movement won these, promulgated a new constitution and installed Rhee himself as president. His rule was marked by brutal repression, corruption and further recourse to policemen and others who had collaborated with Japanese rule. Kim Il-Sung ruled the North with Russian and Chinese support.

In June 1950, the North Korean army invaded the South. The United Nations Security Council denounced this invasion and resolved to resist it – a resolution that was possible because the USSR was boycotting the UN in protest at the exclusion of Communist China. In practice, however, the US itself was the only power in a position to provide South Korea with immediate help. Forces from Japan, where General MacArthur ruled as pro-consul, were hastily shipped to Korea. However, American soldiers, poorly prepared for this kind of operation, and soldiers of the South Korean army (the ROK), often poorly prepared for any kind of fighting, were forced back. They abandoned Seoul, the capital city, and took refuge in a small area, about a tenth of Korea, in the Pusan peninsula in the south of the country. The Americans built up their forces and then counter-attacked. MacArthur organized a daring landing of troops at Inchon, some way behind what were then North Korean lines, in mid September 1950. American and South Korean forces retook Seoul, crossed the 38th parallel on 1 October and seemed for a moment poised to overrun the whole of North Korea. What stopped them was mobilization by Chinese forces, which began to fight with the North Koreans in an increasingly open fashion.

The British Cabinet first discussed United Nations action in Korea on 27 June 1950. It was a small item on the agenda, which came below measures to restore the white fish industry.[8] British leaders believed that they should support the United States and the United Nations, and there was not much difference on this issue between

Attlee's Labour government, which took the initial decisions, and the Conservative party, which returned to government in October 1951. However, the British were reluctant to treat Korea as a general war against Communism. In any case, the British armed forces were already overstretched and in no position to provide great help.

In the summer of 1950, British reservists were called up. The first British soldiers to arrive, however, did not come from the UK itself but from the garrison in Hong Kong. On 14 August, a national service lance corporal with the Middlesex Regiment wrote in his diary that one of his comrades had met a drunken naval officer who said that ships were being assembled to take troops to Korea: 'At first we laugh at his story . . . The next question is "Who is going?" He tells us that it is the 1st Middlesex.'[9]

The lance corporal was better informed than his superiors. On 19 August, in the middle of an army swimming gala, Andrew Man, commander of the 1st Battalion of the Middlesex Regiment, was summoned to be told that his regiment was to be sent to Korea. Alongside it would go the 1st Battalion of the Argyll and Sutherland Highlanders. The two regiments were to be under Brigadier Basil Coad. The Middlesex were primarily national servicemen – Man reckoned that 55 per cent of his soldiers were conscripts. The Argylls were mainly regulars and seem to have been even less well informed than the Middlesex: 'Word started to accumulate that we were going to Korea. We didn't know what Korea was.'[10] They were seen off with a speech by Lieutenant General John Harding (commander of British Far East Land Forces), who told them to 'shoot straight and shoot to kill'.[11]

The total number of British servicemen in Korea was small. At first, the British 'Brigade' amounted to two depleted battalions. In March 1951 there were 15,000 British soldiers in Korea – at a time when there were 35,000 in Malaya, 45,000 in the Middle East, 63,000 in Germany and 244,000 in the UK.[12] The authorities never released figures for the number of national servicemen who served in Korea. No one could be sent there until they were nineteen and it would have made little sense to send men who were close to the end of their service on such a long journey. These circumstances must presumably have restricted the number of conscripts who were sent. The Ministry of Defence claimed in 1953 that most soldiers in Korea and the Far East were regulars – though its statement on the matter was rather guarded.[13]

British casualties in Korea were higher than in any other theatre during the whole period of national service: 830 men were killed in action, three died from 'terrorist action' and seventy-five died of their wounds. Of those killed, 280 were national servicemen and a further 1,056 conscripts were wounded;[14] almost all the casualties were soldiers.[15] By the standards of fighting in Normandy in 1944, let alone that of the Somme in 1916, British losses in Korea were relatively small. Even those men unfortunate enough to be posted to front-line units were likely to survive. Thirty-three men of the 1st Battalion of the Norfolk Regiment were killed in Korea and 108 were wounded, but there were 700 men in the battalion, most of whom survived without lasting physical damage.[16]

In spite of this, Korea was, in some ways, *the* national service war. It had a direct and malign effect on all conscripts because, as a result of Korea, the government extended the length of national service from eighteen months to two years. This changed the nature of conscription. Conscripts had been fighting in Malaya since 1948 but the extra six months made it easier to post men to areas of active conflict – particularly in the Far East. Men were no longer being called up just to train for a hypothetical war; from now on, a significant minority would fight in real wars.

Even those who would never go abroad felt the effects of the extension of the term of service. Robin Ollington was a clerk on a base in Warwickshire when the commanding officer told the men that national service had been extended by six months. All the regulars cheered, 'like school'.[17] The division between regular and conscript was slightly blurred by Korea. National servicemen were now to receive the same pay as regulars for the last six months of their service. A new three-year regular engagement was also created and some men signed on for three years because they had been given to understand that doing so was the price of avoiding transfer to a unit that was on its way to Korea.[18]

It was in Korea, more than anywhere else, that the idea of national service as an amusing or trivial experience was punctured. The national service officer in John Hollands's autobiographical novel reflects on his posting to Korea at the end of officer training: 'it was no longer a matter of taking three weeks' leave, sewing two pips on his tunic and drifting about a depot saying, "Carry on, Sergeant"'.[19] Far from being a comic interlude in serious lives, Korea sometimes came to seem the only utterly serious part of some men's lives. Houston Shaw-Stewart was a figure out of P. G. Woodhouse. As a boy at Eton, he was beaten for, among other things, donning a false beard to go to the cinema. His adult life revolved around shooting, sociability and riding to hounds. As a national service officer, he switched from the Coldstream Guards to the Royal Ulster Rifles because he hoped to go foxhunting in Northern Ireland. His plans were foiled when the regiment was sent to Korea. There, in January 1951, his company commander was shot dead standing next to him. Shaw-Stewart rallied the soldiers and led a counter-attack at great risk to his life. He received the last Military Cross to be awarded by George VI.[20]

Many national servicemen saw Korea as the 'real war', against which their own experiences ought to be measured. Tom King, an acting captain in Kenya and later Secretary of State for Defence, recalled: 'The "Koreans" were the ones who really had a hard war and had lost people. You could tell that; they were a bit wild, quite a lively lot.'[21] Divisions of units into men who would, or would not, go to Korea came to assume huge importance in the memories of national servicemen. David Batterham believed that his incompetence at mathematics, which had prevented him from being made a 'surveyor' in the Royal Artillery, might have saved his life by preventing him from being sent.[22] Brian Sewell was pulled out of a regiment going to Korea so that he could attend the War Office Selection Board. He was commissioned and spent the whole of his service in the UK but said later that he would rather have been a private in Korea.[23] John Boorman was taken out of a unit on its way to Korea and drafted into the Education Corps. He recalled: 'the atavistic death that comes from exclusion from the tribe'.[24] Neal Ascherson claimed that every officer to pass out of Eaton Hall with him (apart from his fellow marines) was sent to Korea.[25] Eaton Hall itself was changed by Korea. Veterans of the war arrived as instructors and brought a whiff of real violence to the lives of cadets – Major Leith-Macgregor, who had won an

MC and provoked a mutiny in Korea, was a particularly stern disciplinarian.[26]

British soldiers in 1951 knew little about Korea. It was not the kind of place that featured in the textbooks boys had read at school; it had never been part of the British empire and had not been an obvious battleground on the maps into which so many boys had stuck pins during the Second World War. Ordinary soldiers had only the haziest notions of where it might be – one fusilier, having spent six weeks on a troopship getting there, still thought that he might be able to go home by train for a one-week leave.[27] 'Even the grammar school kids would have been hard pressed to locate Korea', which was 'a land only previously known to geography teachers'.[28]

The military authorities made little attempt to explain to British troops what they were doing in Korea and few of them understood much of the political context of the war. Their information, such as it was, came from 'Crown News' – the newspaper produced by the army – or from the thick weekly editions of the *Daily Mirror* which families sometimes sent out, and which arrived weeks after the events they described. In any case, the lives of soldiers were dominated by their own struggle to survive in the small plot of land they were required to defend. Even the broader military details of the war meant little to them. Peter Holmes wrote: 'Dates lost meaning. Life merely progressed from one incident to the next.'[29] Peter Farrar was an unusually well-informed conscript – he was an educated man who had been briefly assigned to the Russian course and who had an air-mail edition of the *Daily Telegraph* sent out to his position on the front line. All the same, he responded to an interviewer's question about the politics of the war with exasperated courtesy: 'the people who ask, very rightly, these kinds of questions find it very difficult . . . to imagine how narrow and limited this little mental world is. The Royal Fusiliers stuck there on those bleak hillsides in Korea.'[30]

The political context of the war was complicated. There were several occasions when the fighting seemed about to end. This was the case at the very beginning, when it looked as though the North Koreans would win and then, a few months later, when it looked as though MacArthur's forces might take the whole of the peninsula. In July 1951, cease-fire negotiations began and it seemed possible that they would bring the conflict to an end within a few weeks. As it was, fighting continued until July 1953. The Duke of Wellington's Regiment endured 126 casualties in May 1953, almost two years after negotiations between the two sides had started. There was no peace treaty. Fighting ended with an armistice, which fixed the frontier between North and South more or less where it had been before the war in which over a million people, mostly Koreans, had died. British soldiers often blamed their own allies for the continuation of a pointless struggle. Farrar was unsure whether most of his comrades knew who Kim Il Sung or Mao Tse Tung were but they did know the name of Syngman Rhee – they blamed him for the failure of armistice negotiations and sometimes sang an obscene song about him.[31]

Korea was an abjectly charmless place. Its landscape was bleak and its climate almost unbearable for soldiers who had little shelter. Spring and autumn were tolerable but the summer was very hot and winters were bitterly cold: tears froze on cheeks in the open air and toothpaste had to be thawed before use.[32] The country was poor to start with. Japanese occupation, the Second World War, a corrupt government and foreign armies sweeping across the land in 1950 had done nothing to improve it. A national service officer wrote:

[D]riving about that inhumanly stark, clay-brown countryside was a strange experience. Ravaged by a sequence of advancing and retreating armies, it was nearly deserted ... Sometimes you'd see white-robed figures picking hopelessly among ruins, or dead and neglected in a paddy field, but mostly the local population kept out of sight, waiting for this terrible thing to pass. Except for the hordes of orphaned children; they besieged you everywhere pleading for jobs.[33]

Large military hospitals, battle training courses and centres for leave were all in Japan. Soldiers did not go to Korea for any purpose other than fighting. Men were horrified by the squalor of the place when they first arrived. One national service officer said that his dominant memory of arriving in February 1951 was 'the deadly stench of corrugated iron gone rusty'.[34]

Relations with the local population were poor. The language was impenetrable: one American soldier, attempting to extract information through an interpreter, complained that it took eight minutes to say 'perhaps'. It was not, however, clear that being able to speak to each other would always have made things easier. Many Koreans had had enough of foreign occupation. Soldiers from the Gloucestershire Regiment encountered a woman who turned out to be a university professor and to speak fluent English. They asked whether there was anything that they could do for her. 'Leave my country,' she replied.[35]

In cultural and racial terms, the North Koreans, against whom the British were fighting, seemed indistinguishable from the South Koreans, who were their allies, and some conscripts arrived in Korea not knowing whether they were fighting for the North or South.[36] Even the qualities that the British admired in their allies/enemies seemed inhuman ones. Soldiers spoke of the Korean stoicism and capacity to bear pain. A Conservative MP said in January 1951: 'those of our men who were prisoners in Japanese hands during the last war all say that, of all the guards they most feared, none were worse than the Koreans.'[37] His remarks were designed to alert the British authorities to the prospect that British prisoners of war might be ill-treated, but the men who had collaborated with the Japanese were at least as likely to be in the South Korean forces as in those of the North, and some United Nations soldiers regarded North and South Koreans as pretty much the same.[38] British prisoners were often held by Chinese soldiers and sometimes recognized that there was an element of truth in the claim that their guards were there to protect them against the Koreans as much as to prevent them from escaping.[39] Most British soldiers saw Koreans, of both North and South, as being brutal and sometimes felt in retrospect that they themselves had been debased by association with the brutality of the latter. George Brown, a national serviceman with the King's Liverpool Regiment, recalled seeing the porters who carried water being hit with a rope. He and his comrades thought it funny at the time but he looked back on it as shameful.[40]

The poverty of the Koreans attracted pity rather than sympathy. Desmond Barnard was a national serviceman with the Royal Norfolk Regiment. He and his comrades threw what food they could to pleading children but felt that things were hopeless: 'the whole country was devastated'.[41] Occasionally, enterprising, or desperate, prostitutes managed to get close to the front line, but, generally, British soldiers did not even develop the relations of commercialized sex that marked their lives in Hong Kong or, when they went on leave, in Japan. Probably the only Koreans they saw as human beings were the boys who shared the quarters of British units – 'every company had a sort of adopted boy'.[42] Some of these boys were official soldiers of the ROK and some had simply attached themselves to allied armies to scavenge food; it says much about the state of Korea that English soldiers could often not tell the difference between these two categories.

The sense that Korea was a uniquely unattractive posting quickly took hold. A few men sought to stay with units that were being posted to Korea, even if it meant lying about their age or physical qualities. Mostly, though, men feared being sent there. Patrick Preston was enjoying a comparatively comfortable life as a national service sergeant in the Education Corps in Singapore but he had heard enough of Korea to make him grateful that he would not have to go there:

> Talking of warfare, the situation in Korea appears to be very serious again, apart from the possibilities of giving birth to general conflict. More and more troops, both United Nations and Communist, are killed in the senseless struggle for a heap of ruins and a smoking pile of typhus infested bodies.[43]

Those soldiers who did go to Korea were quickly and painfully disabused of any illusions they might have had about the power and importance of their own country – the sense of British control that marked the wars of decolonization was conspicuous by its absence in Korea. Even the film that the British government made to justify national service recognized that Britain's contribution in Korea had been relatively modest. The United Nations assembled a coalition of sixteen countries to fight in Korea, but the resources of the United States dwarfed those of its allies. Men got off the troopships to be greeted by military bands made up of African-Americans (themselves an object of curiosity for British soldiers) and sometimes passed under banners saying 'Through this gateway pass the best godammed fighting men in the world: the United States Army'[44] or 'welcome to the sector of the rough, tough, rugged, American Marines'.[45] Rations were often issued by Americans so that, from the moment of their arrival, British soldiers were eating American food, which seemed plentiful to men who had been brought up in wartime Britain.[46] They also came up against a cavalier disregard for British military hierarchies. Black American drivers ignored officers and asked privates: 'Say, are you guys for the war?'[47]

Americans could be contemptuous in their attitude to British troops. When Basil Coad, in command of 27 Brigade, arrived, an American officer said: 'Glad you British have arrived – you're the real experts at retreating.'[48] Most shocking to ordinary national servicemen, however, was the fact that so many Americans did not realize that there were any British soldiers in Korea. A conscript there was told by his girlfriend, studying in America, that the people she met did not know about the British presence.[49] The fact that MacArthur had praised the valour of the French force, which was even smaller than the British, was particularly galling and British soldiers were sometimes asked whether they were French.[50]

British equipment and clothing was so poor that the British contingent was sometimes known as the 'Woolworth's Brigade'. Soldiers resorted to black-market dealings to obtain American material. American soldiers valued alcohol, which was hard for them to obtain by legal means. Some British soldiers bought carbines for liquor and one officer claimed that a jeep could be acquired for a bottle of gin.[51]

At the highest level, there was a difference of opinion between American and British strategists. The Americans, MacArthur in particular, were more aggressive and more inclined to widen the war. British officers resented what they took to be the high-handed American approach. They believed that British lives were sometimes squandered in pursuit of relatively unimportant objectives. Andrew Man, commander of the 1st Middlesex, believed that the Americans were too prone to stick to valleys – which made movement, especially for motor vehicles, relatively easy – and too hesitant about tackling more difficult objectives in the hills.[52] Much of this thinking filtered down to national service subalterns and even to ordinary privates. Benjamin Whitchurch recalled that 'that stupid man MacArthur' had decided to 'chase Commies' thus bringing the Chinese into the war and prolonging it – a prolongation that meant, among other things, that Whitchurch himself was taken prisoner.[53]

For older soldiers, the Far East was almost synonymous with the British empire. Brigadier William Pike said: 'You must remember that when we started soldiering, we just assumed the Empire would go on and on.'[54] National servicemen learned the realities of British imperial decline at an earlier age. From the end of July 1951, British soldiers fought as part of a 'Commonwealth Division'. They were thus part of an international entity, which was fighting as part of another international entity (the United Nations), which was in turn subordinated to the realities of American power. British soldiers did not feel like the senior partners in this arrangement. Australian, New Zealand and Canadian soldiers were usually older than their British comrades, and a British national service officer believed that 'the lowliest gunner' in the New Zealand forces earned more than himself.[55]

Most of all, the life of a British soldier in Korea was dominated by fighting. At first, men were sometimes sent into battle almost as soon as they got there. D. F. Barrett arrived at the front line less than a month after he had first heard the rumour in Hong Kong that his regiment was being posted to Korea:

> At full light, the source of the strong smell of rotting flesh is self-evident, coming as it does from bodies buried in shallow graves all over our hill, some of which have been partly exposed by the heavy rains. Hands, feet and the occasional head are springing up like corn all over the hillside, coupled with lumps of rotting flesh that was once a man.[56]

Some were caught up in dramatic retreats before they had even reached the front. William Purves arrived in Pusan with the Bren gun carriers for his regiment. Within a few days, they had all been burned to prevent them from falling into North Korean hands as British forces pulled back.

Both sides dug in, so that the conflict began to resemble the First World War. The extreme cold of the Korean winter created special hazards. Many men improvised petrol heaters out of empty shell cases and these frequently exploded; British military hospitals in Japan devoted much of their energy to treating burns.[57] Uniforms were full of lice, which were dormant in the cold but would wake up and torment soldiers during a forced march. Summer produced different kinds of problems. Trenches became infested with insects, snakes and vermin. Some soldiers lay on their bunks and took pot shots at rats with their sten guns.[58]

Face-to-face conflict came when one side or the other attacked and this could be terrifying. Dennis Matthews was a national serviceman operating a Vickers machine gun with the Royal Northumberland Fusiliers at the Imjin River in April 1951. The Chinese attacked in such numbers and with such determination that all his training was undermined. Usually, a Vickers machine gun was set up to give a 180 degree angle of fire, but, at the Imjin, the machine gunners needed a 360 degree angle of fire because they realized that the Chinese were as likely to be behind them as in front of them. Even a rate of fire of 450 rounds per minute did not stop the attacking forces. The regiment headquarters pulled back and Matthews thought that the men operating the Vickers guns were being sacrificed to cover a retreat. Eventually, the machine gunners were allowed to withdraw. Matthews was not quite sure how the order had originally been given but it was passed down to him as 'every man for himself'. Matthews and three other men survived by avoiding the most obvious track, which was under fire, and going into the hills.[59]

The Gloucestershire Regiment (the Glosters) had an even harder time than the Ulster Rifles. They tried to defend their positions as other troops behind them were pulled out and as tanks, which might have provided some relief, failed to get through the narrow passes that led to the front line. The Glosters ran low on ammunition, sustained heavy casualties and eventually faced the certainty that they would be overrun. A national service private recalled the terrifying sequence of events. The ostentatious calm of their commanding officer as it became increasingly obvious that they would not be relieved, the destruction of equipment to prevent it falling into enemy hands, the order to fix bayonets and Anthony Farrar-Hockley – the adjutant of the regiment – shouting: 'if you want to live, smash your weapons; if you want to die, go on fighting'.[60]

Denys Whatmore, a national service second lieutenant with the Hampshire Regiment, who fought with the Glosters, left an extraordinary account of how he and a few comrades evaded capture. The platoon under his command was sent to try to hold an advance position. His first battle was strange because the tracer bullets were 'very beautiful'. The Chinese began to blow bugles 'and that was a bit nerve wracking because they got closer and closer'. He called up supporting mortar fire but two men in his own platoon were wounded by bombs that dropped short of their target. There was 'quite a fight' for half an hour. A Chinese machine gun got on their right flank and began to fire with deadly effect. Whatmore's batman was killed. Whatmore fired his own sten gun until it jammed, then used his dead batman's rifle and then his own pistol until he ran out of ammunition. Finally, he fired a flare gun. Chinese soldiers came close enough to throw a grenade but it fell short of its target. Whatmore threw a grenade of his own, which seemed more effective. By this time, all his soldiers were shouting that they were out of ammunition and the telephone line to company HQ was cut.

Whatmore pulled his platoon back – a dangerous exercise because it meant moving into fire from the machine guns of his own side.[61] By the time he got back to a more secure position, he had only thirteen of his original thirty-six-man platoon. Some of the others were wounded and had been evacuated but many were dead: the remnants were 'sombre but not downhearted'. The platoon were sent to the top of a hill – later known as 'Gloster Hill' – on which the battalion would make its last stand. Large numbers of Chinese troops went past them so they were surrounded. British and Filipino tanks tried to reach them but one was destroyed thus blocking the way for the others. American jets dropped napalm on the Chinese – the British were so close that they could feel its heat. It became clear that the Glosters were in a 'tight fix'. Whatmore heard the regiment's bugler play behind him and the surviving members of the battalion cheered.

Eventually, the Glosters were given permission to try to fight their way out and the commanding officer devolved decisions about how to do so to company commanders. Captain Mike Harvey, commanding Whatmore's company, asked his officers whether they wanted to surrender or fight. They all wanted to fight. Harvey then decided that they would go forward into the enemy lines rather than back towards their own. As it turned out, this was a wise move because the Chinese forces had encircled their position and, in doing so, left relatively few men in front of the British. Escape was not easy, though. The Glosters had to leave their wounded behind. Whatmore borrowed a jagged tin to drink from a puddle. The few Chinese they encountered were curiously slow to react – it may have been that they did not realize that these unkempt, desperate-looking men were British soldiers

Whatmore and his comrades now had to return to their own lines by doubling back and going through a steep gorge with fire coming from both sides. They crawled along a stream bed. Many men were hit. A tracer bullet passed six inches in front of Whatmore's face and burned in the mud. Men shouted from behind that 'they are coming for us with knives', but Whatmore had no means of knowing whether this was true. They reached their own lines as American tanks supported a retreat by South Korean troops and at first the tanks fired on them. Eventually they made contact with the tank crews and managed to climb on to their vehicles. By this stage, there were forty-six men left of the ninety-six who had first sought to fight their way out. Whatmore's own platoon had now dropped from the thirteen men who survived the first part of the battle to three. Whatmore had lost one of his boots and his shirt in the scramble. The survivors of the battle were reunited with members of their regiment who had been held in the rear. Some of the soldiers were in tears. They all slept in their muddy clothes. The following day Whatmore and his men got new uniforms and a bath but 'some Korean pinched my watch'. Recovering from the battle, Whatmore celebrated his birthday: he was twenty. Later he went back to find the bodies of some of his men. They were badly decomposed and a swarm of bees was nesting inside a nearly severed head. He also found his own beret.[62]

Men who were captured went through the hours of uncertainty about whether they would be killed as their private possessions – watches, wallets, photographs – were pillaged. Eventually they endured weeks of marching that took them from the front line to the camps in which they were to be confined. Men suffered badly from the meagre and unfamiliar diet, which often gave them dysentery. Sometimes American planes attacked the columns in which they marched. A total of about 1,000 British servicemen were captured in Korea – most of them belonged to either the Royal Ulster Rifles, many of whom had been captured in January 1951, or the Glosters, captured in April 1951.[63] Captivity was relatively short – prisoners were released with the armistice of July 1953, so no one was imprisoned for more than three years. Most captured British soldiers seem to have displayed great courage. They often met attempts to give them political 'education' with derision.[64] There are no complete figures for the proportion of national servicemen among prisoners but, by the end of September 1952, 119 conscripts had been captured and six were known to have died in captivity.[65]

Men recalled Korea in horribly graphic terms. John Hollands, a national service officer who won the Military Cross, wrote an auto-biographical novel, *The Dead, the Dying and the Damned*. He explained its title thus:

> The Dead are those who died well and cleanly, through one swift stroke of a bullet or a piece of shrapnel; the Dying are those unfortunate enough to join their comrades only after minutes or perhaps hours of hopeless agony; and the Damned are those who survived, the men who did the killing and who have yet to be judged for it.

Peter Holmes recalled deaths that were 'sad and macabre' but, from the point of view of the victim, 'easy'. An officer was decapitated by shrapnel so that his 'body seemed to stand up for ages with blood spouting out'. Many, however, did not have 'easy' deaths. Holmes watched the 'six hour death of Corporal F ... whose stomach had been blown away by a grenade'.[66] Soldiers remembered men who were wounded in the groin or who had their skin burned off by the explosion of their own phosphorus grenades.

Just before going out on patrol, Holmes told his men briskly that 'the morphine was in my top left pocket and it was to be used'.[67] P. J. Kavanagh, another national service officer, was haunted by the memory of a time when his own nerve had failed as he tried to inject morphine into a dying man – 'his scream a white wall of cold fire'. The moments during which Kavanagh fumbled with the needle before handing it to a medical orderly were 'an eternity of agony for the dying man'.[68] Often the most horrible injuries were the results of battlefield accidents rather than enemy fire. D. F. Barrett watched British planes accidentally drop napalm on soldiers from the Argyll and Sutherland Highlanders. He once saw a man who had been travelling perched on a tank and had become trapped under the revolving turret. The tank was driving along a potholed road with the injured man still attached, as the crew sought someone who could relieve him, presumably by amputating a limb.[69] Not surprisingly, his comrades came to take comfort from their belief that army doctors would finish off badly wounded men,[70] though there is no evidence that the medical officer of his own regiment, himself a national serviceman, ever did such a thing.[71]

When the lines were more or less static – which they mainly were in the two years after the summer of 1951 – soldiers would emerge from their trenches at night. They repaired the wire in front of their positions – wire that might give them a few vital minutes if they were attacked. They also patrolled in no man's land. Sometimes these were 'listening patrols', designed to find out what was happening on the other side; sometimes they were 'fighting patrols' to engage the enemy. Taking prisoners, who could be interrogated, was particularly prized, though soldiers were under no illusion about the need for violence. They hoped that their prey would come quietly; 'if not, well obviously the other thing happens', as one national serviceman put it.[72]

Robert Gomme, a national service corporal with the Royal Norfolk Regiment, was on such a patrol. He and a few conscripts explored a ruined village on a freezing night in the winter of 1951–2: 'alone in a lunar landscape, only the squeak of snow under our boots broke the silence'. They came across a group of enemy soldiers and waited silently. Gomme had assumed that they would try to grab a prisoner but other members of the patrol opened fire. They killed two men and carried one of the bodies back. The following morning, a burial party managed to dig a grave for their victim in the frozen ground. The corpse had yielded no information – the dead man had no regimental badges or documents and carried nothing but a mud-stained Chinese atlas, which Gomme still had forty years later.[73]

Soldiers had disconcertingly close encounters in no man's land. Francis Cheesman was a conscript in the Royal Fusiliers who was mentioned in dispatches and who attributed his success on patrols to the fact that he came from a long line of poachers. Like many British soldiers, he respected the Chinese, who 'were doing the same job as we were'. Interviewed in 2000 – 'I can see it as if it were yesterday' – he recalled how a 'Chink' stood up suddenly in no man's land and raised his hand 'like a Red Indian'. Cheesman could not shoot because one of his own comrades was in the line of fire. The Chinese soldier waved and the British soldiers let him go. For a time, they wondered whether the single soldier was a scout for some larger force and whether they were about to be attacked. As they waited, Cheesman felt oddly calm and wrote his name and number in the sand before his patrol moved back to their lines.[74]

On 23 November 1952, the Duke of Wellington's Regiment sent a two-man 'lying up patrol' to investigate digging conducted by the Chinese. As was often the case in Korea, the patrol brought together men from very different backgrounds. Ian Orr was a nineteen-year-old national service second lieutenant; Thomas Nowell was a sergeant and about ten years older than Orr. Nowell had been kept out of the forces during the war because he was a miner but he joined up as a regular soldier as soon as he was allowed to do so – presumably, like many men, he thought that almost any life was better than working in a pit. He was a tough professional soldier who became a sniper. Nowell and Orr left their own lines in darkness and made their way to what Nowell described as 'Chinaman's land' and hid themselves near the area in which they believed the Chinese were constructing a tunnel. It was very cold and neither man could move much, even to eat their rations, for fear of the crackling noise that their frozen clothes would make. They were so close to their enemy that, at one point, a Chinese labourer relieved himself on top of Nowell. The two men lay still all day and, when darkness fell again, they made their way back to their own lines – a delicate operation because no one had told them the new passwords that had been issued to their comrades. When they got back, Orr and Nowell had breakfast and then separated – they came from different companies and do not seem to have known each other well. Nowell stayed in the army and served at Suez. Orr, having won the Military Cross, went up to Cambridge.[75]

William Purves, a national service officer, led a patrol of men from the King's Own Scottish Borderers. He climbed up into the attic of an apparently empty house and saw a girl asleep. He had not seen a woman for a 'year or so' and thought her very beautiful. He also realized that his patrol must be much further behind enemy lines than he had previously thought and that it would be better not to let 'the jocks' know that they were so close to a young woman. He went downstairs and ordered his men to return. He did not rate very highly their chances of getting back, and in retrospect believed that the Chinese had probably seen his patrol but held their fire in order not to expose their own position.[76]

Other patrols did not escape so lightly. Thomas Henson, a national service officer with the Norfolk Regiment, was leading one through no man's land at night when they were attacked at such close quarters that it was impossible to use their weapons. For a time they grappled in the dark – gripped, as Henson recalled it, by 'blind rage' rather than 'fear' or 'exhilaration'. Henson himself managed to shake a Chinese soldier off his back and one of his men was bitten on the hand. At some point, the two sides drew far enough apart for weapons to be used and the British threw grenades into a field in which the Chinese were hiding – setting the millet on fire. At the end of the encounter, only four of the Norfolks were 'capable': three were dead and 'five or six' were wounded. The radio operator had lost his aerial. He wept as he scrabbled for it in the dirt, but managed eventually to transmit a call for help. Henson won the Military Cross. The language in which he described the incident sixty years later – 'terrific full marks to the Bren gunner there' – evoked the school boy that he had been just a year before this incident.[77]

Divisions of rank, and the divisions of social class that often went with rank, changed in Korea. The stiff formality of the parade ground was a long way away. Everyone was frequently dirty and bedraggled. Men lived rough and ready lives. When Barry Reed was about to be discharged from his national service as a second lieutenant in the Middlesex Regiment, he realized that he had no idea about the etiquette of an officers' mess – he had spent most of his time in Korea, where he had been decorated for gallantry but rarely had to worry about which way to pass the port.[78]

Some national service second lieutenants in Korea appreciated the oddity of their position. As boys of nineteen or twenty, they were making decisions that might mean life or death to thirty men. Peter Holmes commanded a platoon that was mainly made up of

working-class national servicemen. His sergeant – a former para-
trooper who had won the Military Medal in the Second World
War – was often 'the real leader of the platoon in those early days'.
As for Holmes himself:

> At Eaton Hall we had been given the following instructions on 'the
> Officer and Men relationship'. We were told 'not to seek popularity or
> relax discipline, to be efficient ourselves, to give our men a sense of
> unity, to put their interests before our own, to explain things to them,
> to do things with them, to share their hardships, to be their champion
> but also their chief critic, to know their names and use them, to set a
> good example ... to devote all our energy and resource to attaining the
> highest possible state of morale in our men', in summary to strike a
> mean between the severity of Frederick the Great and the subtle
> approach of Lawrence of Arabia ... On the whole I felt it would be
> easier just to get to know them as well as I could.[79]

Sometimes, in the heat of action, distinctions might almost disappear. When a signaller – Bailey – brought him the order to launch
what seemed to be a suicidal attack, Holmes had just made some
cocoa. He shared the half-filled cup with Bailey 'fifty/fifty' and said
that he regarded this as 'the most generous act of my life'.[80] The two
men would have come from very different classes, but they experienced briefly the absolute equality of young men who thought
that they had only a few hours to live. Holmes formed some lasting
friendships with other national service officers who served in Korea.
While he was on the battlefield, however, he was closest to the other
ranks in his own platoon. He came to have particular regard for
his sergeant, his signaller and Private Abrahart, a 'hard-boiled repro-
bate' who had seen 'every gaol in the empire' but who was good on
patrol.[81]

Some officers, often the most conservative and military minded,
remained in touch with men that they had commanded in Korea –
usually through regimental associations. For many officers, however,
their own departure from the front line marked the end of their contact with their troops. John Whybrow was a second lieutenant in the
King's Shropshire Light Infantry. A grammar school boy waiting
to take up a scholarship at Christ's College, Cambridge, he was

himself on a social frontier – culturally a member of the upper-middle class but socially a little below the level of men who would usually have been commissioned into a respectable regiment of the line. In his diary, Whybrow mocked himself as the 'KYO' (Keen Young Officer). He recalled exchanges with his soldiers – some of them men from the north east who had been transferred from the Durham Light Infantry:

> KEEN YOUNG OFFICER: Well chaps, nice morning, any complaints?
> CHORUS: Ay, when do we get out of this f. . . hole!
> KYO: Sleep all right?
> CHORUS: What – with awnly wun f. . . camp bed in the f. . . tent!
> KYO: Right-ho, we'll see what we can do for you.

Whybrow was wounded in action – his commanding officer drily remarked that his 'dash and bravery' had 'outweighed his common sense' – and sent to Japan for treatment. He returned to the front line, at his own insistence, and led an attack on a Chinese bunker. The attack was a disaster and he was badly wounded – one of his legs would be amputated. His men, at great risk to themselves, got him back to their own lines.[82] Whybrow was evacuated to Japan for treatment. His father sent a penknife to each of the men who had saved his son's life. Writing a brief memoir decades later, Whybrow was able to give the name, rank, number and status (regular or national service) of all the soldiers who had saved him. He saw the corporal who had rallied the platoon and organized his rescue at Buckingham Palace when they were both decorated – the corporal got the Military Medal, awarded to other ranks, and Whybrow got the Military Cross, given to officers. After this, however, Whybrow did not meet his soldiers again.[83]

Some veterans of Korea recalled a solidarity that had transcended social class and that was felt with a poignancy made all the more intense by the sense that it would not survive away from the front line. P. J. Kavanagh wrote that he valued:

> Above all the sense of experience shared and a kind of equality, even in the rigid British army, most of all that. There isn't any room for the old class fear, at least for a while. In spite of the schoolboy rubbish,

comradeship existed . . . Once you've had a glimpse of that, whatever the circumstances, and felt how it made your bones lie easy, the absence of it worries you, you've got a sense of deprivation.[84]

Jim Jacobs remembered the egalitarianism of life in Korea: 'Life was hard, but equally so for all . . . The majority of our officers and NCOs appeared to be fellow members of the human race, and, for the most part, treated us as men not boys.'[85] In *The Dead, the Dying and the Damned*, John Hollands attributed the following thoughts to a conscript private:

> on the second morning [after leaving the front] there was a very distinct difference in the attitude of the officers and NCOs. Before, while in the line, most of the officers had been friendly, always ready to exchange a joke or two, but now they had suddenly become snobbish, demanding that every second word spoken to them should be 'sir', and swaggering around the company lines criticizing every little point as though they owned the place.[86]

In a curious sense, the experience of soldiers in Korea fitted in with the image that the British army had of itself. After the upheavals of the Second World War, many officers had been keen to restore and strengthen the regimental system, and it was probably in Korea that regiments counted for most: 'The loyalty of the soldiers is first to their platoon (pretty strong) but above all to their Battalion, which carries a name and a flag.'[87]

Each battalion held a particular plot of ground and, given that all strategic decisions were ultimately taken by the Americans, British officers could not expect to exercise authority much above regimental level. The names associated with Korea – the Durham Light Infantry, the Middlesex, the Northumberland Fusiliers, the Duke of Wellington's Regiment – were those of ordinary county regiments. The cult of the Glosters epitomized a certain view of the British regimental system, and the fact that the cult annoyed men from other regiments showed, perhaps, that regimental loyalty really meant something in Korea.[88] The Glosters were a family regiment, closely associated with a particular area. Their commanding officer – John Carne – was a 'good regimental officer'. He was a dutiful and, when the occasion demanded it, heroically brave man but he seems to have had no ambition beyond commanding a battalion of his own regiment.

Ordinary soldiers seem to have felt that the regiment was a real presence in their lives. Regimental solidarity mattered and some men attributed the relatively high survival rates of British soldiers in captivity to the fact that men from the same regiment stuck together – they contrasted themselves with the American soldiers, for whom the regiment was an administrative formality that bore no relation to geographical origins.

Two lieutenant colonels, Andrew Man, of the Middlesex Regiment, and Peter Jeffreys, of the Durham Light Infantry, wrote accounts of how the men in their battalions had performed. Both officers thought highly of the national servicemen who had made up more than half the men under their command. Jeffreys wrote: 'Before going into action I was apprehensive that the qualities of toughness and self-assurance would be lacking in the very young men that we had brought.' The fact that conscripts had proved good soldiers, however, raised awkward questions about regulars: Jeffreys admitted that he had been disappointed by the behaviour of regular sergeants and corporals.[89]

The opinions of national service officers who served in Korea are also revealing. Sometimes they respected the regular NCOs who served under them – especially when such men were veterans of the Second World War or when those men, like the corporal whose action saved Whybrow's life, proved themselves in battle. Sometimes, though, they saw regular soldiers as too rooted in the routines of peacetime soldiering. A former national service officer who had served in Korea wrote newspaper articles suggesting that his own regiment had laid excessive emphasis on drill and not enough on fitness, fieldcraft, shooting and signals – the things that mattered on the battlefield. He believed that casualties could have been averted 'if old soldiers like Sergeant X had spent less time on the drill square in Germany bullying and shouting at the men they were to let down in action'.[90]

National service officers were not always very favourable about regular officers either. Peter Holmes wrote that one of his fellow officers was 'a man with much better than average intellect for a regular officer'. Another, who had attended the same public school as Holmes himself, was 'typical Sandhurst' and 'stupid in a pleasing sort of way'.[91] In spite of all this, Holmes had a higher opinion of his own regiment than most others – partly because so many of its officers had done serious fighting between 1939 and 1945. He reported the view of another national service officer that most majors in other regiments were 'imbued with an odious mixture of stupidity, arrogance and out-dated social views'.[92]

Two national service officers – both, like Holmes, decorated for gallantry – had more favourable views of the army. William Purves was admired by regular officers – at least one of them believed that Purves had saved his life – but Purves himself remarked that the national service officers 'flourished' in Korea but that the regulars 'did not do so well – it must have been a blow'.[93] Barry Reed, who rose to the rank of major in the Territorial Army, said that a regular commission was seen as a career for men who 'can't do anything else', but that 'national service people on the whole were all going to do other things'.[94]

What scars did men bring back from Korea? Some were physical. Peter Holmes carried nothing but a sliver of shrapnel in his hand.[95] He gave no outward sign of having been troubled by his brushes with death in Korea. John Whybrow bore the physical consequences of the war (he had lost a leg) with stoicism, but he remained physically frail until his death in 2007. He appears to have made a conscious decision not to let his injuries overshadow his life.[96] He travelled around Europe before going to Cambridge. Barry Reed gave up his place at Cambridge and went straight into business – he seems, in retrospect, to have felt that this was the only result of his service in Korea that he regretted.[97] William Purves was wounded while leading a fighting retreat. He was taken to an American field hospital because the British medical staff were overwhelmed with the casualties and eventually evacuated to Japan. He woke up on a train still in his blood-soaked uniform and with his pistol strapped to his waist. He had shrapnel in his arm for the rest of his life. He claimed to feel sorry for those who had had less exciting experiences: 'sadly a lot of people hated their national service'.[98]

The psychological effects of service in Korea were hard to measure. Many veterans, looking back from the 1980s or later, commented on the fact that the cultural expectations around men who might have been damaged by combat were different in the 1950s. Whybrow wrote: 'I did not, at any time, at least not consciously, suffer from post-combat trauma or stress symptoms.'[99] His contemporaries at university commented on his cheerfulness.[100] However, for all his considerable courage and optimism, Whybrow also suffered from severe, sometimes crippling, bouts of depression and anxiety for the rest of his life.[101]

Denys Whatmore said that there was no offer of counselling and that he had not the slightest need of it – 'that may not be true for those who were taken prisoner. I wondered after the Gulf War [of 1991], I truly wondered has the army changed or have people changed'. Whatmore recalled having nightmares for 'one, two or three weeks. I distinctly heard bugles and woke up saying here they come, this was the only effect for me.' He never had nightmares again, though he found it hard to settle back into his civilian life as a minor civil servant and he eventually rejoined the army.[102] Dennis Matthews, a survivor of the Battle of the Imjin River, said that 'I used to grind my teeth in my sleep, I think it was maybe some form of nightmare.'[103] Edwin Haywood talked of nightmares and lack of sleep that lasted for two years after his return from Korea.[104] Some men found life unbearable. Joseph Roberts, who served in the Black Watch, kept his composure for some years and then, when he was married and his eldest daughter was about to be born, 'I came home one evening and went to pieces, ended up caked out for about three years.'[105] Benjamin Whitchurch had endured battle and captivity but, most of all, he seems to have been haunted by the fate of his comrades. He met the mothers of Blondy Martin and Ginger Bishop but did not want to describe the circumstances in which their sons had died.[106]

Stephen Martin interviewed national service veterans of Korea in the mid 1990s and found that some of them were only just beginning to seek treatment for post-traumatic stress disorder:

A lot of people say they're nightmares: I say they're not nightmares. They're like I'm there and I'm back. Most of the time I'm getting chased, mind, I'm in a crouched position and I'm getting chased, and that's when I'm not reliving the minefield thing, you know, sommat like that. All I'm trying to do in me mind I think is *justify*. I'm just trying to work it out and get it clear in me mind so's I can tell people you know. So it's not hurt us any that way; it must have hurt us a little bit, but I can't, unless I tell them nobody knows about it like, you know.[107]

Maynard Winspear presented a relatively benign account of his national service. He joined the Duke of Wellington's Regiment specifically because he wanted to go to Korea. He was thrown out of a potential officers' platoon for playing a practical joke. He repeatedly laughed during the taped interview in which he describes his experiences. He left the army in December 1952 and returned to find work in his home area, but his landlady eventually asked him to leave her house: his propensity to shout in his sleep was disturbing the other tenants.[108]

13

Imperial Emergencies

Few questioned why they were in Malaya, and there was not much effort to explain the politics of the situation to the troops. Two soldiers I can remember had views that led them to believe that we had no right to be there, but I am certain that it did not affect their soldiering. The British Army in Malaya in the early 1950s never suffered from the malaise which at that time (even before Dien Bien Phu) was affecting the French Army not very far away in Indo-China.

Former national service lieutenant
in the Manchester Regiment[1]

There would be a real argument for national service if the conscripts refused to fight in colonial wars, as the French youth are doing. But they don't. They go off cheerfully to Cyprus, Kenya, Malaya – anything to escape the tedium of Aldershot or Salisbury plain.

A. J. P. Taylor, writing in the *New Statesman*, 1955[2]

Peacetime conscription coincided with the end of the British empire. When the first men were called up in 1945, the British still ruled a quarter of the globe. By the time the last men were demobilized in 1963, the British empire was on its way to being just a few dots on the map. Boys who had been educated at public schools to run the empire sometimes realized during their national service that there was soon going to be no empire to run.

After 1945, troops fought to contain various kinds of rebellion, and the boundaries between civilian and military authority were sometimes blurred. General Sir Gerald Templer, sent to Malaya in 1952, combined the authority of a civilian high commissioner with that of a military commander. General Sir George Erskine, sent to Kenya in 1953, did not displace the governor but was granted greater powers than would usually have been given to a soldier. Field Marshal Lord Harding was sent to Cyprus in 1955 to replace the civilian governor.[3]

How far did this militarization of the empire affect conscript soldiers? National service meant that men who would not normally have come into direct contact with the empire spent time in Britain's overseas possessions, but this never affected more than a significant minority of conscripts. A large proportion of men never left the United Kingdom, and most probably never left Europe.[4] In 1956, at a time when there were 190,000 conscripts in the army alone,[5] just 19,684 national servicemen were serving in Cyprus, Kenya, Malaya and 'other active service stations abroad'.[6]

Furthermore, the fact that men had been brought up in an imperial culture, or even that they themselves sometimes expounded elements of that culture, does not mean that they were committed imperialists. In July 1954, the magazine of a minor public school reported a speech given by Major General Whitfield to school cadets: 'When the time for national service came they should all seek to become officers and NCOs. At all times they must try to keep alive the vision of the greatness of the Commonwealth and Empire.'[7] Whitfield, however, had been born when Queen Victoria was on the throne and commissioned just after the First World War. Younger men, even those from Whitfield's old school, were beginning to use the phrase 'white man's burden' with a degree of irony.[8] Antony Copley was to become a historian and admirer of Indian nationalism. As a national serviceman, he wrote a passage in his formal journal (to be read by his superior officers):

> The British Empire is not a great ideal just for its own sake. It is a great example to the rest of the world of countries working together in a spirit of mutual aid. Consequently the closer the various colonies and dominions can work together with the motherland, the greater and more successful will the example be.[9]

His private diary recorded more complicated feelings. It contained little direct mention of the empire, but it did reflect his disquiet with British behaviour in Cyprus and about the Suez expedition.[10]

Leslie Thomas came from the opposite end of the social spectrum from Copley, but he too had been bombarded with imperialist propaganda even before he was called up and sent to Malaya. He had grown up in a Barnardo's home. Its housemaster – 'the gaffer' – was a ferocious Tory who believed that the races of the world could be arranged in a clear hierarchy: the English, followed closely by the Scots and the Gurkhas, followed, quite a long way down, by the Welsh and then the rest of the world. 'The Labour Party,' he would say with dire tone, 'is full of conscientious objectors. They wouldn't fight for the Empire. Ask to see their medals, and they couldn't show them to you ... Churchill fought for the Empire. So did Eden. They've got the medals.'[11]

The boys liked the gaffer but his propaganda provoked them into vigorous support of Attlee in the 1945 election. A number of them were confused by repeated references to 'the Empire', which they took to mean the Kingston Empire, a cinema that they were forbidden to visit because it was 'too late and too lewd'.

Many men wanted colonial postings – the West Indies were particularly coveted – but their desires were expressed with regard to travel and climate rather than politics. Few conscripts described their experiences as being part of an imperialist project and many related their encounters with empire in light-hearted tones. A national service officer who was posted to Tanganyika gave his memoirs the subtitle: 'A Cheerful Happy Gallop through Experiences in Africa with the King's African Rifles'.[12]

Equally, few conscripts opposed empire in an active way. Men who were hostile to national service generally denounced the effects that it had on the conscripts themselves rather than on the populations of the countries to which they were sent. Anthony Howard and Michael Holroyd disliked the philistinism and brutality of the army but they had benign memories of Brigadier Bernard Fergusson. Neither mentioned that he had once helped to protect an officer accused of murder in Palestine.[13] A few national servicemen felt that their participation in colonial wars had been wrong but this feeling seems to have developed, or at least been expressed, mainly in retrospect.

What often did differentiate conscripts from their elders – and particularly from senior officers – was their sense of the transience of empire. Unlike settlers or regular soldiers, they had no long-term stake in the countries to which they were sent and perhaps their relative powerlessness gave them a more detached view of Britain's future prospects. For many, the empire was already dead. A clerical corporal at the Commonwealth HQ in Kure, responsible for clearing up the aftermath of the Korean War, noted ruefully that only the locally recruited Japanese staff were given a holiday on 'Empire Day'.[14]

Most conscripts had grown up in a country that was almost racially homogeneous: the *Empire Windrush*, which brought West Indians to Britain in 1948, was mainly known to national servicemen as a troopship that transported men to the Far East. Sometimes the first encounters with non-European peoples – at Aden or Port Said – produced torrents of abuse from British servicemen. Even liberal-minded national servicemen used language that would seem shocking to a modern reader, and which sometimes shocked them when they reread their diaries or letters. However, the racial thinking of conscripts was more complicated than it might seem at first glance. Some of them used the word 'wogs' in real or implied inverted commas; often they treated such language as though it were another aspect of military jargon to be mastered. One wrote home from a troopship docked in Colombo: 'Egyptians are wogs, Koreans are gooks, but what the Malays are I don't know.'[15]

When the Suez Canal was closed and troopships were sent around the Cape of Good Hope, conscripts were even more shocked by the oppression of apartheid than they had been by the squalor of Aden. Jack Burn, on his way to Malaya, was on the first troopship to stop at Cape Town since 1945. The Gurkhas on the boat were taken off separately and the city was full of signs saying 'whites only'. Burn recalled that 'even then' he was 'appalled'.[16]

The armed forces were based partly on racial differences. Non-Europeans served under British officers but the reverse was almost never true. British officers in colonial units were often given higher rank and higher levels of responsibility than would have been the case in a British regiment. This produced odd results because officer cadets who were not considered up to the standards required of officers in smart English regiments were sometimes posted to colonial regiments. A man who had been judged inadequate to command thirty guardsmen outside Buckingham Palace might, instead, command a hundred askaris in Nigeria.[17]

However, the racial segregation that often marked British communities in the empire meant little to conscripts who were mostly working-class young men. They sometimes disliked the European settlers, especially in Kenya, and in many parts of the empire national servicemen seem to have thought of themselves as living in intimate and amiable relations with the local population.[18]

Relations between the races were probably worst in a place – Egypt – that was not formally part of the empire. Egyptians resented the British presence in numbers that greatly exceeded those allowed for by the Anglo-Egyptian treaty of 1936. Furthermore, the very fact that there were so many British troops in, or passing through, Egypt created numerous occasions for violence. A conscript on a troop train heading to Eritrea in 1948 recalled the scene as it was attacked by a crowd of Egyptians:

> A brown hand gripped to the window sill as a boarder tried to scale the window ledge. A bayonet was jammed through the hand and deep into the woodwork. The victim hung for a few seconds before wrenching free and falling to the sand. A violent act for boys, many recently out of school, but they were learning.[19]

In the late 1940s, the Egyptian government allowed the British to employ local workers. Egyptians did menial jobs for low pay but their presence inside British camps meant that at least some British soldiers met locals on terms that did not imply automatic hostility. E. A. Dorking was sent to the Canal Zone with the Ordnance Corps in 1949. He said that the Arab foremen who brought labourers to work in the ammunition dump were respected because the camp would have been hard to run without them. Dorking himself – though only a corporal – had an Arab 'batman' – Hussein – to perform his own domestic chores.[20]

Relations between the British and Egyptians deteriorated after October 1951, when the Egyptian government abrogated the treaty of

1936. Servicemen were now confined to the area immediately around the Suez Canal. Egyptian workers were withdrawn from British bases, which deprived soldiers of the servants who made their lives easier elsewhere and also removed all chance of friendly relations with the local population. Camps were dusty, hot and fly-ridden. Only one soldier in a hundred lived in permanent buildings and almost four in ten of them lived in tented camps. They were also victims of frequent, small-scale attacks by Egyptian nationalists or by raiding parties who hoped to steal stores. Soon soldiers were living behind barbed wire and were allowed out only if they were armed. The Labour MP Richard Crossman suggested that the prospect of being sent to the Canal Zone was the single biggest obstacle to regular recruiting for the army.[21] Barbara Castle, another Labour MP, claimed that soldiers had, in effect, become inmates of a concentration camp that they guarded themselves.[22]

There were moments when the British and Egyptians fought small battles – most notably in early 1952, when the Lancashire Fusiliers stormed the Bureau Sanitaire, used as a base by nationalist policemen who were believed to have orchestrated attacks on the British. Outright confrontation, though, was rare. The British attributed most of their fifty-five casualties in Egypt to 'terrorism'.[23] Ordinary soldiers were influenced by rumours about what had happened to men who fell into Egyptian hands:

> We didn't know what it was all about. You see, all sorts of tales used to come back, and whether they were true or not, you didn't know. Once, I remember somebody coming back and saying that they had found this squaddie on the road, and Egyptians had cut off his private parts and shoved them into his mouth.[24]

Conscripts rarely understood what they were doing in Egypt – they were fighting people with whom they were not at war and occupying a country that was not a British possession. One of the fusiliers who stormed the Bureau Sanitaire recalled: 'I didn't know what it was all about – the attack on the barracks. Funnily enough the army didn't get down to politics, what it was all about.'[25]

Relations between British soldiers and the Egyptians were marked by bitter mutual hostility. A national service officer wrote about a route march: 'All the men looked very sorry for themselves but as soon as we went through an Arab village they changed completely and started singing and making wisecracks at the local Arabs – a very heartening display of spirit.'[26] He was told to shoot Arabs who were seen loading stolen ammunition. It was, he thought, 'Rather caddish not giving them a chance but they had to be taught a lesson.'[27] In February 1953 he said that three Arabs had been shot stealing stores – 'none of this ever gets in the papers'.[28] The next month, there were 'a dozen shootings per week' and 'The best score was at Geniefa where thirteen local Arabs were caught in a searchlight, five were killed and the rest wounded.'[29] When his unit stopped people, 'The main idea was to cause as much inconvenience to the local Arabs as possible ... all good fun.'[30]

National servicemen posted to the British empire were often involved in police actions directed at the local population. Three conflicts attracted particular attention: Malaya, 1948 to 1960; Kenya, 1952 to 1960; and Cyprus, 1955 to 1959 – all described by the British with the ambiguous term 'Emergency'.

Malaya saw the first and longest of the colonial Emergencies. The country was made up of nominally independent sultanates that were in practice required to take advice from British officials. The population of the peninsula consisted partly of ethnic Malays, partly of those of Indian origin (mostly Tamils), partly of aboriginal inhabitants of the jungle and partly of ethnic Chinese. Some of the latter were wealthy businessmen, but most worked as labourers on rubber plantations. During the war, the Chinese had increasingly resorted to 'squatting', i.e. farming on land that did not legally belong to them. They had suffered badly under the Japanese occupation of 1942 to 1945 and they had also provided the most important elements of organized resistance to the Japanese – resistance that was sponsored by both the British and the Communists. In 1945, Chin Peng, a Communist leader, was awarded the Order of the British Empire for his wartime work.

After the war, the British imposed a new order on the sultans who had collaborated with the Japanese. Most political power was now vested in a Malayan Union. The power of the British was more explicit, though so too was the intention that Malaya should be given independence and that all those who lived there should be given citizenship. In 1948 the Malayan Union became the Federation of Malayan States, a body that saw a partial restoration of the status of the sultans. Active resistance to British power came mainly from the ethnic Chinese and from the Communist party, which drew most of its support from them. There was violence against the colonial authorities from 1945, and in June 1948, after three rubber planters had been killed, the British declared a state of emergency. The Malayan Communist party was banned and its leaders retreated to the countryside. Here they formed the Malayan Races Liberation Army (MRLA),* under the leadership of Chin Peng. Nominally a movement of the whole Malay nation but in practice dominated by ethnic Chinese, it began a guerrilla war, largely directed against rubber plantations.

British soldiers usually described the guerrillas against whom they were fighting as 'bandits' – though the authorities encouraged the use of the phrase 'Communist Terrorist' or CT. In 1954, a British military source described the MRLA as a 'rigidly disciplined fighting force composed partly of fanatical Communists and partly of bandits de carrière'.[31] The truth seems to have been more complicated. The MRLA's power was limited by the fact that it had so little appeal outside the ethnic Chinese – who constituted a minority of the population in Malaya and not a powerful minority. In addition to this, the MRLA was itself often divided. Not all the Chinese in Malaya were Communist. Some joined the MRLA for reasons linked to local circumstances and rivalries as much as to global ideological struggle.[32]

Some British soldiers attributed atrocities to the MRLA – blaming them for killing prisoners or British rubber planters or, more realistically, Chinese rubber tappers who had failed to cooperate. A conscript claimed that one of his comrades had discovered some belongings of his own brother, recently killed in action, in the possession of a captured MRLA fighter and that he (the British soldier) had then killed

---

* This was the translation that the British gave to the movement's name. Its founders claimed that it would have been better rendered as Malayan Peoples Liberation Army.

two captives.[33] This personal hatred was, however, fairly rare. Many soldiers knew that the MRLA had emerged partly out of anti-Japanese resistance and the single book about Malaya that they were most likely to have read was Spencer Chapman's *The Jungle is Neutral*, which described the author's experiences of fighting with Chinese guerrillas against the Japanese. A few British soldiers felt respect for the courage and self-sacrifice of their opponents,[34] and were more likely to express their disdain for MRLA turncoats who informed on their former comrades. Some national service autobiographers referred to Chin Peng with grudging admiration.[35]

For a time, the British government seems to have felt that the insurgency in Malaya might present a real threat. Perhaps their fear sprang partly from ignorance – the war had depleted the numbers of Chinese-speaking specialists in Malaya. It did not help that some of the first regiments sent to Malaya were drawn from the Brigade of Guards. Guardsmen – wedded to drill, smart turn-out and unquestioning obedience to orders – were not well suited to the demands of jungle warfare: one report noted that a guards battalion had failed to kill a single 'bandit' for the first nine months they were in Malaya.[36]

Attacks against the British reached their highest level in the early 1950s. Two events were particularly important. First, in early October 1951 the British High Commissioner, Sir Henry Gurney, was assassinated when travelling along a jungle road. The attack was almost accidental; the guerrillas did not realize that such a prestigious target would drive into their ambush. All the same, it was a damaging blow to British prestige. A few weeks later, on the Ulu Caledonian estate, 11 Platoon of D Company of the Royal West Kent Regiment was ambushed. An officer, ten other ranks and all three of their Iban trackers were killed. It was the worst single 'battle' of the Emergency. One national serviceman from the platoon, who had been held back at camp, described arriving on the scene of the ambush: 'There were the dead laying in all sorts of twisted positions. There were pieces of hair and skin and bone stuck to the side of the truck, the truck itself was like a sieve . . . not a square foot of it without a bullet hole in it.'[37]

Initially, the British responded to the insurrection with 'counter-terror'. They tried to make the Chinese frightened of supporting the guerrillas. They destroyed property, burned villages and forced squatters, suspected of supplying the MRLA with food, to move. Soldiers and policemen conducted large-scale sweep operations in which they tried to capture people who sympathized with the guerrillas. Intelligence about the guerrillas was poor and brute force was sometimes used as an alternative to good information. The authorities did little to prevent brutality and issued a succession of edicts, some of them retroactive, allowing various forms of violence, notably the shooting of people who were trying to escape: seventy-seven such people were killed from July 1948 until April 1949.[38]

The British remained ruthless for the remainder of the Emergency, but their violence became increasingly controlled and targeted. Lieutenant General Sir Harold Briggs, appointed as commander in 1950, established committees to bring civil and military powers together. The forcible resettlement of squatters into 'villages' in which they could be guarded and watched was conducted in a more systematic and extensive way. The collection of intelligence improved.

The Conservative election victory of 1951 brought Oliver Lyttleton in as Colonial Secretary. He took a particular interest in Malaya – partly because he had business interests in the region and partly because, as a former officer in the Grenadier Guards, he knew about some of the problems that soldiers had faced in the early part of the Emergency. Lyttleton decided that military and civil power in Malaya should be conferred on a single man and appointed Sir Gerald Templer to this post. Templer was the quintessential 'soldiers' soldier'. The son of a regular officer, he had been educated at Wellington and Sandhurst before being commissioned into his father's old regiment. He was keenly interested in military tradition and much given to ostentatious exercises in blunt speaking. Templer continued resettlement policies so that, eventually, around half the entire Chinese population had been forcibly moved. Supplies to some villages were reduced to levels just above starvation to eliminate all chance that inhabitants would pass food to the MRLA. However, Templer also began to declare some areas as 'white' – meaning that guerrillas had been more or less eradicated and that restrictions could be lifted.

Guerrillas were forced to take greater risks to retain contact with the civilian population and Templer stopped sending large groups of soldiers to sweep through areas. Instead troops generally operated in small patrols, moving quietly in the hope of tracking down a guerrilla camp or laying ambushes for MRLA fighters when they came to collect money or food from sympathizers.[39] Increasingly, the MRLA retreated into the jungle – sometimes trying to grow their own food there. Templer had succeeded in creating a kind of reverse Maoism. It was British soldiers who moved among the civilian population like fishes in water – one of the reasons why a posting to Malaya could be relatively agreeable – while the insurgents were cut off from sources of supplies and information. The British now found it relatively easy to identify their enemies, who were in the jungle with guns in their hands and red stars on their caps. The army was less concerned now with the messy business of separating enemy fighters from potentially sympathetic civilians. Increasingly, violence in Malaya happened in places where no one outside the army was likely to see it.

In terms of the absolute number of casualties, Malaya was the second most deadly conflict of the national service period, after Korea: 331 servicemen were killed in action there and at least 119 of these were national servicemen.[40] In spite of this, Malaya was – from the point of view of many soldiers – a 'good war'. This was partly a matter of timing. The Second World War was still close enough to confer an air of legitimacy on British military action, especially because Malaya had been the scene of fairly brutal fighting against the Japanese. The Emergency had been declared by a Labour government, at a time when the Communist threat seemed real. The more restrained use of force after 1950 was driven by military logic rather than by a sense that earlier policies had been morally wrong.

British attitudes to Malaya are best exemplified by reaction, or lack of reaction, to a single incident at the beginning of the Emergency. In December 1948, a patrol primarily made up of national servicemen from the Scots Guards arrived at a village, Batang Kali, inhabited by Chinese labourers on a rubber plantation. They separated women and children from adult men and drove the former away. When the women were finally allowed to return to their huts, they found the bodies of twenty-four men.

There was an enquiry into the event by Sir Stafford Foster-Sutton, Attorney General of Malaya, which concluded that all the dead had been shot while trying to escape. No papers from the original enquiry survived, though Foster-Sutton continued to insist that his conclusion had been correct.[41]

The official account was implausible. The owner of the estate on which the dead men had worked did not believe that they had links with the guerrillas.[42] It did not seem likely that the bodies of men who had been shot while trying to escape should be clustered in small groups rather than spread out; it was also remarkable that fourteen, mostly inexperienced, soldiers should have fired with such accuracy that they killed all the victims outright. A Communist MP denounced British behaviour at Batang Kali in the House of Commons, but no action was taken against any soldier.

In 1970, the *People* newspaper published a long article about Batang Kali. It did not spring from anti-militarism. On the contrary, the paper had denounced a Labour MP who had suggested, when discussing American behaviour in Vietnam, that the British army might not have entirely clean hands. At this point a former national serviceman, William Cootes, who had been at Batang Kali approached the *People* and told them that he had seen a massacre; eventually, four members of the patrol gave sworn statements to the newspaper – a fifth said that he would be willing to talk to any subsequent enquiry. All of them said that the civilians at Batang Kali had not been shot while trying to escape. They talked of 'sheer bloody murder' and 'killing in cold blood'.[43]

The soldiers had understood that they were to 'wipe out a village' – the incident happened soon after they were told that three Hussars had been 'burned alive'. The patrol had been under the command of two relatively junior non-commissioned officers[44] – one man said that the absence of an officer on the patrol had itself suggested that something sinister was going to happen.[45] Cootes said that he had been told he would be shot if he refused to participate in the killings.[46] However, other guardsmen recalled being told that men who did not want to participate in the killings would be excused – though no one exercised this option. Cootes said that the soldiers were relieved that 'we had got away without having to shoot the women'.[47]

One explained: 'I did not want to kill anybody, but was too frightened to move and make myself look a coward in front of the others . . . I was also aware of the strict discipline of the Guards.' Another did not ask to be excused but did volunteer to guard the women, who were being held in a lorry some way away, and thus removed himself from the scene of the killing. A third soldier said that he fired into the ground to avoid hitting villagers. Cootes described how he and some of his comrades had taken seven men to the river: 'We were just looking at each other waiting to see who was going to shoot first. I remember an old man about 80 staring at me constantly.' When they heard shooting from other groups, they opened fire 'instinctively almost' and 'Once we started firing we seemed to go mad.' The river turned red with blood, and a man's brains spilled onto Cootes's boots. He said that some of his comrades were excited and some stayed quiet. He himself thought 'we must all be out of our minds to do a thing like we had just done'. When the killing was finished, the soldiers burned the village but left the bodies untouched. Cootes found some puppies inside one of the burning huts and took them back to his camp.[48]

The two NCOs who had commanded the patrol – Douglas and Hughes – were also interviewed. Unlike most of the men under their command, both were regulars. Their relation was odd because Douglas was technically the senior of the two, although he was only twenty-two years old while Hughes was thirty-one and had fought in the Second World War. Both insisted that the victims at Batang Kali had indeed been shot while trying to escape. Douglas had apparently shot a youth early in the operation. He believed that he had killed him outright, but Hughes said that he himself had finished off the badly wounded boy – an act that he considered 'humane'. Douglas had not killed a man before and was violently sick. Hughes, who had killed men in Greece and elsewhere during the war, said, 'it was always like that the first time'.[49]

Some members of the patrol remembered being advised afterwards – either by an officer or by one of their NCOs – that they would face serious charges if the truth came out and that they should devise a story to cover what they had done. They told an enquiry in Kuala Lumpur that they had shot men trying to escape. One of them remembered that an official told him that he hoped that they would 'get away with it'.[50]

In response to the *People's* report, Denis Healey, the then Secretary of State for Defence and not a man who felt unqualified admiration for the guards, referred the matter to the Director of Public Prosecutions. Soon after the election of a Conservative government in June 1970, however, the Director of Public Prosecutions decided that there was not enough evidence for a prosecution. The decision to abandon prosecution had been taken in consultation with the Attorney General, a former guards officer.[51]

Officers discussed the possibility that Douglas, who was still serving with the army, might bring a libel action against the *People* but decided that this might not be a wise idea: 'if . . . the court's decision was adverse . . . the reputation of the Scots Guards, and the Army, would receive a further blow and the opportunities afforded to the *People* for further publicity greatly enhanced; it might even reopen the possibility of criminal proceedings'.[52]

The commanding officer of the Scots Guards interviewed a number of officers and NCOs who had been in Malaya in 1948. He was 'absolutely confident' that no general order had been given to shoot civilians. He believed that it was impossible to establish 'even the outline of what happened, let alone the details'. He stressed that the battalion had not been in Malaya for long at the time of the killings and that there were then no clear rules about the circumstances under which soldiers should open fire: 'There is some danger that the jungle operations in these early days might be compared with the comparatively organized days of the Briggs and Templer plans.' He emphasized the difficult circumstances when 'The requirements of this emergency over-rode the unpreparedness of the National Service Soldiers on the ground.' He concluded that there was no evidence that events at Batang Kali had 'happened in any way other than described in the Regimental History'.[53]

The former conscripts who had been on the patrol at Batang Kali were haunted by what they had done. Some wept as they described it twenty years later. However, the incident had not aroused much discussion at the time and, even many years later, was often treated in a fairly cursory fashion. A British civilian in Malaya, interviewed forty years after the events, recalled simply that the Scots Guards had 'rounded up a considerable number' and then shot them while they were trying to escape. He believed that the region was 'very quiet after

that'.[54] There was no sense that the incident might raise wider questions about the conduct of soldiers, in particular national servicemen.
David Erskine's history of the regiment, published in 1956, said that
the victims at Batang Kali were killed as 'a result of their own folly'
and that 'it was many months before there was any further trouble
around Batang Kali'.[55] Tom Stacey was a national service officer with
the Scots Guards who served in Malaya shortly after Batang Kali. He
wrote a hostile account of his time in the army but it concerned his
experience of basic training. Only the most attentive readers would
have noticed a single sentence at the end of his essay that might
have hinted at Stacey's disquiet about things his regiment did in
Malaya.[56]

Malaya was a military victory for the British. The MRLA was
destroyed. Its leader went into exile. Malaya became an independent
state – in 1957 – while the Emergency was still in force. The British
had in effect become the allies of the post-colonial state. There was no
question of coming to terms with guerrilla leaders, and British veterans of Malaya – unlike those of, say, Palestine or Kenya – never saw
men they had fought against come to power. One man's account of
national service in Malaya was published with an introduction by a
former chief of staff of the Malaysian armed forces.[57]

Success in Malaya became associated with the mystique of General
Templer, who went on to become Chief of the Imperial General Staff.
The Malaya campaign also aroused smugness about the supposed
British mastery of counter-insurgent warfare, which was increased by
French and American failures in Indo-China. Even when referring the
Batang Kali case to the Director of Public Prosecutions, Denis Healey
remarked that the army deserved 'the highest praise', for 'the success
of the operation [in Malaya] was historically almost unprecedented in
a guerrilla war of this nature'.[58]

Though high as an absolute number (at least by the standards of
post-war Britain), casualties in Malaya were low as a proportion of
men who served there. British soldiers did not dread being sent there
in the way that they dreaded a posting to Korea. The worst fighting in
Malaya was concentrated in a short period in the early 1950s. Even
then, it was possible to have relatively little contact with the enemy.[59]

Some who served in Malaya found questions about whether they 'hated' the enemy to be incongruous because they had never actually seen an MRLA fighter. For many, their most important encounter in Malaya was with the jungle itself rather than any of its human inhabitants. They remembered the heat and humidity, the difficult terrain, the mosquitoes and hornets and leeches. Sometimes they were also struck by the beauty of what they saw.

David Loewe, a national serviceman with the West Kents, never saw the enemy – though he heard shots as his comrades fired. His most dangerous encounter came when he was dismantling his 'basha' (shelter) one morning and heard rustling on the ground. He investigated and found a krait, a venomous snake. He had apparently slashed the snake's belly with his machete the previous evening and then slept more or less on top of the wounded reptile.[60]

Fighting in Malaya was almost entirely confined to the rubber plantations or jungle. Once they were back from patrols, British soldiers were relatively safe from attack. They could lounge around their bases in shorts, go swimming on the beach, visit leave centres in the highlands and go drinking in the cities. Kuala Lumpur and Singapore rarely saw violence. Most British soldiers killed by the MRLA died 'in action' – out on patrol and with a gun in their hand. They did not, unlike their comrades in Palestine, Egypt or Cyprus, fear kidnapping or bombing. A sergeant with the Hampshire Regiment thought that the absence of terrorists in the cities made the Malayan campaign different from other counter-insurgencies. He believed there was little danger while off duty: 'I don't think anyone was apprehensive.'[61]

British forces in Malaya had a long administrative 'tail', partly because of the complexity of handling the paperwork relating to national servicemen who were constantly coming and going. A large group of servicemen, therefore, never entered the jungle. Peter Burke worked as a national service army clerk in Singapore. The closest he came to real fighting was when he escorted an officer to collect the regiment's pay. This meant that he enjoyed the curious frisson of walking into a bank with a loaded sub-machine gun.[62] Patrick Preston, a national service sergeant with the Education Corps, was in Malaya in 1951: 'Bandits seem to be killed every day, but there's still enough of them to cut the throats of the rubber planters and tappers and shoot up transport columns.' His own life in Singapore, however, was 'cushy': 'neither the war against the bandits nor the war against the Communists affect me in the least'.[63]

Many national servicemen wanted a posting to Malaya. They liked the climate and the exoticism of the place. The polishing and drill that dominated the life of soldiers in Britain or Germany was almost completely absent in Malaya. Relations between officers and other ranks were less formal in the jungle than they would have been on an ordinary base.

Most British soldiers felt that they had behaved well in Malaya. John Noble was proud of his regiment – the Suffolks – and insisted that its behaviour was 'still governed by the correctness'.[64] Having said this, British forces were in Malaya to kill, and perhaps because Malaya was perceived at the time as a 'clean war', soldiers used the word 'kill' in an uninhibited way. Officers of the West Kents drank a bottle of champagne that their commanding officer had offered for the first kill;[65] a newspaper reporter told English readers that there were five hats hanging in the mess: 'each one represents an enemy whose troublesome days are over'.[66] Regiments counted up their totals as if they were cricket scores.

A guerrilla captured with a gun was almost invariably hanged and British soldiers sometimes gave evidence against men they had taken prisoner. David Henderson's patrol heard moaning the morning after they had conducted an ambush and found a wounded man, who was taken away by the Malay police. Henderson and his comrades later gave evidence against him. The defence counsel pleaded for mitigation on the grounds that his client had an aged mother to support but the judge interrupted to warn that hanging was 'the only possible sentence'.[67]

There were times when soldiers committed illegal acts of violence in Malaya, notably the killing of guerrillas who had surrendered or been wounded, and national servicemen sometimes talked about such acts, of which they did not necessarily disapprove, though they often attributed them to Dayak trackers or Fijians.[68] However, British soldiers did not always see killing in legal or political terms. The distinction between legal and illegal kills could seem arcane and irrelevant to those who pulled the trigger. Sometimes, this meant that they expressed a tough-minded 'realism' about the need to kill, but at other times individual soldiers seem to have felt disturbed even about 'legitimate' kills. A hanging, which was entirely legal, or an ambush of armed men could make British soldiers feel uncomfortable, even if they did not put their concern into a broader political context. Peter Beadle, a private and three-year 'conscript' with the West Kents, described his first kill, in 1953, thus:

> we lay there and all thoughts were going through my mind that we got to kill somebody and all of a sudden the word come along the line that the two Communists were coming, they was armed and we was armed. When they was about ten yards away, they was challenged. They turned to run, but we all fired, all fired at once, and the two bandits were killed. I do not know if I hit him or if my bullet went in the air or where they went. When I looked down my rifle it was shaking like a leaf it was. But ... the thought of killing someone at eighteen and a half, that's only eighteen and a half years old, and I looked at my mate and I said to him 'Bob what do you think of that' and he said 'that was frightening wasn't it' and I said 'yes mate it was'.[69]

Most kills sprang from ambushes conducted by British troops, who lay in wait for men known to be coming down a particular path, or from attacks on guerrilla camps. The number of weapons seized was, at least in the later stages of the campaign, roughly equal to the number of men killed, which suggests that most of those attacked had been armed.[70] There was, however, a huge disparity in firepower. Guerrillas were usually outnumbered and almost invariably outgunned. This could in itself make men feel uneasy about the circumstances in which they killed. The targets of Peter Beadle's first ambush were armed with a sub-machine gun, dropped by the British for the anti-Japanese fighters in 1942, and a rifle, captured from the Scots Guards. These two men were attacked by a platoon that was equipped with three Bren guns, three sub-machine guns, nineteen .303 rifles and some M.1 American rifles: 'you imagine what they [the bodies] looked like'.[71] Another victim of the West Kents took five bullets to the body, which did not kill him, 'before a sixth shot had blown off the top of his head'.[72] One conscript arrived in Malaya to see his new comrades dragging 'one or two terrorists off the battle wagon'. They had been 'cut up with Bren guns' and were being 'treated like loose meat'.[73]

Visibility in the jungle was limited and men shot at close range. British soldiers sometimes followed trails of blood left by those they had wounded; they were close enough to hear their enemies gasping for breath and to get some sense of individual motives – as when, for example, a man who had almost reached cover turned back and faced near certain death as he attempted to reach a wounded comrade.[74] There was none of the anonymity that sometimes attended large, confused confrontations on battlefields in Korea. Men knew that they had killed particular individuals and, indeed, identification was a crucial part of the process. Dead bodies were strung on poles and carried out of the jungle; hands were sometimes cut off so that fingerprints could be taken. Piers Plowright was serving as a national service NCO in the Intelligence Corps in Malaya in 1957. He did no shooting but one day was called on to identify two people who had been killed a few hours previously. He had never seen a dead body and was keen not to 'seem sissy'. Forty-five years later, he had a 'sort of frozen frame memory' of a man and a woman. The dead woman – 'clearly pregnant' – was 'sort of snarling'.[75]

Officers often led attacks and were sometimes the first to fire. They were, therefore, particularly likely to be clear about who they had killed. Geoffrey Barnes was one such officer. Educated at a minor public school and waiting to go to Cambridge, he was called up in 1951 and in due course commissioned into the Royal West Kent Regiment. He had applied for a regiment that was due to go to Malaya because 'I might as well try to be a proper soldier.'[76] In Malaya, he commanded 11 Platoon – reconstituted after the mortal ambush a few months previously. He was conscious of 'the debt of last October's ambush',[77] and – after months of jungle service, more than one ambush and more than one killing – Barnes wrote: 'those members of our old 11 Platoon who had been cut down ... [h]ad yet to be fully avenged'.[78]

The platoon was made up mainly of national servicemen. The oldest of them was twenty-six and Barnes himself celebrated his nineteenth birthday in Malaya. He was an enterprising and energetic soldier. He selected the best sharpshooters – 'my killer squad'[79] – for an ambush and he put his men in soft rubber shoes so that the guerrillas would not be able to spot the characteristic tracks made by

British army boots. He contrived to display an impressive nonchalance about physical danger – when a bullet, accidentally discharged by a soldier on parade, passed between his legs, Barnes put on his best David Niven voice and said, 'Sergeant Philips, please have a word with this man.'[80] He was a popular and, beneath his gruff manner, humane officer. When a soldier was killed on patrol, Barnes went through his possessions to ensure that nothing was sent back that might distress his parents. He was deeply moved by the death of a private, a devout Methodist who had been contemplating ordination. At the end of his first term at Cambridge, Barnes received a card 'From the Boys of 11 Platoon wishing you all the best at Christmas'.[81]

Barnes's relations with imperialism and militarism were not straightforward. He liked the army but he never seems to have contemplated a career as a regular soldier, and he noted, in a characteristically reflective aside, that his desire to see 'proper soldiering' had not been strong enough to make him volunteer for a unit on its way to Korea. He had grown up partly in Malaya, spoke 'kitchen Malay' and was interested in the country – he would later study anthropology. However, his formative memories were not of deferential servants or military parades but of the terrifying collapse of imperial power that he had seen as he fled through Singapore in early 1942 with his mother and brother. He knew all too well that the Chinese, who made up the bulk of the MRLA, had suffered under Japanese rule – a Chinese labourer had been beheaded on his father's plantation. Barnes *père* had been interned by the Japanese: imperialists who had no embarrassment about the exercise of power.

Barnes wrote or spoke as though killing was natural and inevitable. He reported the opinion of his company commander about a dead 'bandit': 'He would have killed you at the drop of a hat if he had had the chance. I am afraid that's the way it is.'[82] However, the very frequency with which he rehearsed these arguments suggests that they never quite convinced him: 'I still felt a futile regret at the few seconds of firing that had smashed the life from the CT's body. He had not had a chance.' Barnes was particularly affected by an early moment of bloodshed. Going into an MRLA camp, he shot and wounded a guerrilla, Chew Wai Lam. Barnes subsequently prevented his Dayak tracker, Reban, from killing Chew with his parang (machete). He was later told by a police superintendent that Chew had provided some 'low level intelligence information', but that he was likely to be hanged. Barnes found it 'somewhat depressing' that a man should be nursed back to health and then killed.[83] He subsequently gave evidence at the trial and Chew was indeed sentenced to hang.

Later Barnes's platoon attacked another camp. They were met with machine-gun fire and pinned down for a time before managing to dislodge the enemy with grenades and mortar fire. Barnes left three different accounts of what happened next. The first came from a letter to his parents, which he cited in his autobiography: 'We . . . started the long job of carrying the dead chappie . . . onto the estate road . . . Everyone seemed pleased, although I honestly expected them to be peeved with us for not getting more bodies, as we should have done.'[84] The second came in an interview that he gave to the Imperial War Museum in 2001: 'Chap I had shot wasn't quite dead, bits of his lung tissue . . . oozing out, he was expiring rapidly . . . so he was dispatched.'[85] The third account came in Barnes's autobiography, which was also published in 2001:

> [T]he CT was clearly dying. In the unlikely event of surviving hours of rough travel on a litter to the nearest road he could only face the prospect of months in hospital until he was able to stand trial. He then faced the virtual certainty of a sentence of death . . . Recalling the case of the bandit we had captured in January, and the advice that I had been given for dealing with similar matters in future, I made my decision. He was now unconscious. I put my carbine close to his head and squeezed the trigger. Click! Empty magazine . . . 'Let me do it, Sir' said H . . . who was standing nearby. I nodded.[86]

Under military law, Barnes and his men had committed a crime – though he was right to say that their victim faced nothing except an agonizing journey out of the jungle, followed by the gallows if he survived. Barnes sometimes affected a brisk tough-mindedness about violence. However, the fact that he chose to recount the incident so many years after the event, and that he recounted it in such different ways, suggests that he was troubled by what he had done. He could never quite rid himself of the view, expressed to his company commander, that killing in ambushes was 'rather like murder'.[87] Even the letters that he wrote to his parents capture some of the disturbing incongruity of life for an officer in Malaya:

> It is amazing how one day you can be covered in mud and sweat and often up to your waist in water, and the next you are all dressed up in Mess kit listening to a band playing under a perfect night sky; and one day you have killed a man ... and the next you find yourself playing with your company commander's children![88]

Barnes was unusually articulate and frank when it came to describing the act of killing. He was not, however, the only man who seems to have felt uncomfortable. Raymond Hands was a platoon commander with the Suffolk Regiment in Malaya in 1951 and 1952. Like Barnes, he was seen by his own troops as a particularly humane officer.[89] Going into a Communist camp, he fired first but only wounded his target, who was then killed by a corporal. Hands then shot a 'girl' carrying a gun and finally shot Liew Kon Kim, a leader of the MRLA. The platoon carried the bodies out of the jungle, which was 'unpleasant' and 'hard work', and then they went to the beach and swam. Hands was awarded the Military Cross – the citation said that he had 'demonstrated the highest example of dash and personal bravery under the most adverse conditions'.[90] All the same, shooting a woman, even a woman who was carrying a gun, cannot have come easily to a nineteen-year-old from Stratford upon Avon. Hands did not tell his wife about his Military Cross until after he had married her and his sons did not find out about it until they cleared out a trunk many years later. It is hard to know whether such reticence showed that Hands was modest about his courage or uncomfortable about the killings.[91]

The Kenyan Emergency was declared in October 1952, in response to violence from part of the Kikuyu tribe and from the smaller Embu and Meru tribes, which were aggrieved at the expropriation of their land and their relatively underprivileged position in Kenyan society. A movement that became known as Mau Mau began to resist British authority and sought to bind people with blood-curdling oaths that attracted much attention from the white population of Kenya and from some in Britain. Mau Mau did not mobilize the whole black population of Kenya or even the whole Kikuyu tribe, who were bitterly divided among themselves.

The British sought to contain Mau Mau by forcibly moving Kikuyu to villages where they could more easily be controlled or to detention camps, by 'screening' Africans to detect Mau Mau sympathies and by hunting down Mau Mau fighters in the forests. According to some estimates, 150,000 suspects were detained without trial and over a million people were forcibly moved.[92] Loyalists were armed and organized into a Home Guard – though its members were not always properly controlled by the British or, for that matter, protected from violence by British soldiers. As in Malaya, the British used informers and turncoats to provide information or guide soldiers to enemy camps, and eventually armed 'counter gangs' of surrendered Mau Mau to hunt their former comrades.

General Erskine arrived as Commander-in-Chief in Kenya in June 1953. He brought a new degree of determination and effectiveness to British operations.[93] The most notable of these was Operation Anvil in April 1954, during which the British, wishing to cut Mau Mau supply lines, sealed off Nairobi and screened the entire population. Members of the Kikuyu, Embu and Meru were allowed to remain in the city only if they could prove their loyalty.

Overall, the number of national servicemen who went to Kenya was small – in 1954, only 2 per cent of all British soldiers were serving in East Africa at a time when more than three times as many were serving in the Far East.[94] British soldiers in Kenya were an unrepresentative sample of the army as a whole. Many of the troops there were either black Africans serving with the King's African Rifles (KAR) or settlers serving with the Kenya Regiment. The officers and some of the NCOs in the KAR were British. This meant that the proportion of privates who served in Kenya was lower than it would have been in other places. In March 1951, officers made up a tenth of the British army but a quarter of all British soldiers serving in East Africa.[95] The proportion of privates would have increased as British regiments were sent out to deal with Mau Mau: the Lancashire Fusiliers, the first British regiment to arrive, contained seven national service officers and 292 other ranks.[96] However, the proportion of officers and NCOs, and thus of regulars, among soldiers in Kenya would still have been higher than it was in other theatres. Between the autumn of 1952 and July 1954, just over 4,000 national servicemen served in Kenya and at the end of this period there were 160 national service officers and 2,293 other ranks there.[97]

The army in Kenya operated in the city as well as the forest, and screening operations meant that it was frequently in contact with civilians as well as obvious Mau Mau fighters. Soldiers admitted that this had led to abuses. The commanding officer of the Lancashire Fusiliers confined 'a few men, mostly with bad records', to headquarters because he did not trust them to maintain 'the highest level of discipline to ensure that exemplary standards are shown by all men in dealing with the African population'. Some soldiers from the regiment had written to a Labour MP, though it was not clear whether they wrote to complain about the way their comrades had behaved or the way they had been punished.[98] A national serviceman with the Northumberland Fusiliers said that his regiment became known as the 'Nairobi bandits' because of their propensity for stealing possessions from suspects, though he thought that they were no worse than other regiments.[99]

Even when the British came up against Mau Mau groups in the forest they were rarely involved in straight fights. The disparity between the firepower of the two sides was even greater than it was in Malaya. Casualties on the British side were almost indecently low in view of the number of Mau Mau suspects who were killed. Brian Thompson, a national service officer attached to the King's African Rifles, remembered that a section under his command once carried out an 'ambush' that involved firing 117 rounds and four mortar bombs at what appeared to be a group of unarmed women who were carrying food which might, or might not, have been destined for a Mau Mau group.[100]

The number of Mau Mau suspects killed was much larger than the number of weapons seized, which suggests that at least some of them must have been unarmed – though sometimes any object that might have been used to kill was defined as a 'weapon',[101] and Simon Raven claims that a national service officer in his regiment was charged with planting weapons next to the bodies of dead suspects: 'proven self-defence is an absolute get out in this game, even with pinko magistrates umpiring.'[102] The Colonial Office regarded with incredulity claims that 430 Mau Mau 'fighters' had been killed outright while resisting arrest or seeking to escape.[103] Some men who served in Kenya said that they had seen things they preferred not to discuss.[104] Some gave chilling detail. A soldier with the East African Service Corps remembered 'going down to have breakfast at Karatina, where the 23rd KAR were, and there were 27 dead bodies laid out, most of them with bullets through the head'.[105]

So far as the army was concerned, the most damaging incidents occurred in June 1953. At a roadblock, Major Gerry Griffiths, of the King's African Rifles, shot two Kenyans, whom he alleged to have been Mau Mau supporters, with a Bren gun. The two men died horrible deaths – attempting at one point to haul themselves under the path of trucks on the road in order to end their agony.

A little later, soldiers under Griffiths's command conducted a search in an area of forest around Chuka. They had two men, apparently surrendered Mau Mau, with them to act as guides and both were brutally treated. One had an ear pierced with a bayonet so that wire could be threaded through it and he could be treated like a dog on a lead. The other had an ear cut off after Griffiths had threatened him with castration. Both guides were shot and reported as having been killed while trying to escape. The patrol also shot a number of villagers who appear, in fact, to have been members of the loyalist Home Guard.

Griffiths was court-martialled for the shooting of the two Kenyans at the roadblock but acquitted on a technicality. Subsequently, General Erskine arranged for an enquiry into the conduct of the army to be carried out under Lieutenant General Sir Kenneth McLean. Its terms of reference were restricted: it investigated the conduct of the army only since the arrival of Erskine. It examined allegations that had emerged during the court martial of Griffiths: that officers offered rewards for kills, that regiments kept scoreboards and that a 'competitive spirit' was fostered. The outcome of the enquiry was anodyne. A succession of military witnesses, some of them national servicemen, testified. Witnesses were generally asked at the end of their evidence whether they knew of any fact that might damage the honour of the army, to which they always answered 'no'. Occasionally odd details emerged. A national service officer attached to 23rd Battalion the KAR said that he had seen no one tortured or burned but that he had seen men 'given a few clouts'.[106]

Two young officers – one with a short-service commission and one performing national service attached to the KAR – had been present during the incident at Chuka. The short-service officer said: 'I went out having a good idea cruelty might happen knowing Major Griffiths as I did.'[107] Asked why he had done nothing to prevent the violence, he replied: 'I will not say I thought he would put me on a charge but I certainly would have expected to be told off.'[108]

After the McLean enquiry had finished, Griffiths was court-martialled again – this time for the violence at Chuka. He was convicted of grievous bodily harm and sentenced to five years.* The short-service officer admitted that he had perjured himself in evidence to the McLean enquiry. The national service officer who had served under Griffiths was not asked to explain his conduct further. He was the senior of the two subalterns present at the incident and the prosecuting counsel in the second Griffiths court martial was keen that he should be questioned, but the president of the court martial said that the officer could not be made to appear, because he was no longer in Kenya or the army.[109] This was a strange response, because the officer was still a member of the Territorial Army, and thus subject to military discipline, and because soldiers in other cases were often retained abroad so that they could give evidence in court martials. The War Office was reluctant to discuss the involvement of national service soldiers in the Griffiths affair. When an MP asked whether Griffiths had commanded national servicemen, officers suggested that the minister might answer 'no' on the grounds that a national service officer was different from a national serviceman.[110]

The Griffiths case was, so far as the army was concerned, straightforward. Since Griffiths had been convicted and since the details of his behaviour were so terrible, there was no point in denying that anything was wrong. Other soldiers were shocked by the case. A national

---

* Norman Skelhorn, who as Director of Public Prosecutions would decide to abandon the investigation into Batang Kali, represented Griffiths when he sought leave to appeal against his conviction.

service officer fighting in the Malayan jungle wrote to his parents: 'that Kenyan officer got off on a technicality – he was as guilty as hell. His CO has also finished his career through this.'[111] It was, however, reasonably easy to limit the damage. The Secretary of State for War told the Cabinet that an official inquiry would show the incident to be 'exceptional'.[112]

Whereas the killings at Batang Kali in Malaya had involved one of the most prestigious regiments in the British army, the Griffiths case involved a mainly Somali company of the KAR. Griffiths was bitter and unsuccessful. Having risen to command a battalion with the acting rank of lieutenant colonel in the war, he was now, at the age of forty-three, serving with the substantive rank of captain. He was also a Kenyan settler and had a personal grievance with Mau Mau – who had, apparently, killed his horse. Regular soldiers implied that the battalion in which Griffiths had served was poorly led and that units in Kenya had particular problems. They argued that soldiers drawn from among the settlers had not attended 'our officer training academies' and that the King's Africa Rifles suffered from the fact that it could not attract high-quality officers and NCOs:

> A large number of all the Platoon Commanders are either Kenya Regiment or National Service boys of nineteen or twenty. It seems to me that under the circumstances things could more easily get past in a KAR battalion than would be conceivable in a British battalion.[113]

Individual soldiers in Kenya were sometimes disturbed by what they saw or did. One result of conscription was that concerns about military brutality reached the civilian population of Britain and were then sometimes transmitted out again to soldiers in the field. David Larder, a national service officer in the Glosters attached to the Devons, wrote to the *Daily Worker* describing how he had shot a Mau Mau suspect and then, as ordered, cut off his hands for identification purposes: 'What have I become?' He later wrote that the suspect he had shot was unarmed and had no possessions other than a Bible and an English primer.[114] Larder was court-martialled for disobedience.[115] After returning to Britain he was eventually allowed to appear before a tribunal for conscientious objectors. Officers giving evidence to the McLean enquiry believed that Larder might have

334

circulated evidence about the army's behaviour – though they also claimed that there was no evidence – other than his own account – to suggest that Larder really had cut the hands from corpses.[116]

The *Daily Herald* carried the headline 'Is your son a murderer?'[117] At the McLean enquiry, a Methodist chaplain with the Devonshire Regiment was told: 'We have heard suggestions made that particularly from the North of England a lot of parents are writing to their boys saying "what are you doing ill-treating these Africans?".' The chaplain replied: 'We have had one or two people who had letters from England rather suggesting that the battalion has started an orgy of killings and brutalities, which is completely the wrong picture.'[118]

Violence by troops in Kenya was widely discussed. Sometimes it aroused indignation. Roy Fuller's novel *The Father's Comedy* (1961) described a national serviceman who has rebelled against the brutality of his own officer in Kenya: 'Don't you know this verb "interrogate"? It means threaten, beat, shoot, burn.'[119] Sometimes, though, violence was reported in almost flippant terms in regimental magazines: 'The company commander was considerably relieved when he arrived as he had pictured Sgt Channing signalling from the Canal Zone, after many months, that he had got a human "Gyppo" trophy in the bag.'[120]

The novelist Simon Raven served as a regular officer with the King's Shropshire Light Infantry in 1956. He alluded to 'one or two incidents of a sufficiently bloodthirsty nature to annoy Dr Edith Summerskill'.[121] A national service NCO with Raven's regiment, William Fitt, described one such 'bloodthirsty encounter'. His patrol killed two men and one woman they believed were Mau Mau – there were no casualties on the British side. Fitt and his comrades 'had to carry the results out'. A woman's foot had been blown off. Having bound her wound with leaves, she insisted on walking, but eventually collapsed.[122]

It is hard to assess how widespread disquiet about brutality was among national servicemen who served in Kenya. This is partly because so many soldiers wrote or recorded accounts of their time in Kenya after they had become aware that British actions there might be open to criticism, and it is difficult to disentangle how they might have felt at the time from how they came to feel – or to think they 'ought' to feel – later.

William Fitt was the NCO with the Shropshire Light Infantry who described the Kenyan woman trying to walk out of the forest with a wounded foot. He disliked the white settlers – 'racism in the raw' – and knew that Barbara Castle had criticized British conduct, which made him and his comrades 'wonder'. However, his overall view was positive: he loved Kenya and thought that national service did him 'a power of good'.[123] Brian Thompson's memoir of his national service in the KAR mixes frank accounts of brutality against 'suspects' with farce; he is one of the former officers to derive comic effect from the fact that he served with Sergeant Idi Amin.[124] He also recalled a moment of almost surreal oddity. He once looked through the sight of his rifle at a Mau Mau fighter, 'naked except for a battered brimmed hat': 'It was one of the most intimate and unsettling moments of my life.'[125]

Simon Maclachlan was commissioned into the Royal West Kent Regiment as a national service officer but, wanting to avoid service in Germany and believing that working with African soldiers would be interesting, he volunteered for the KAR and arrived in November 1953, just after the first of the Griffiths court martials. Maclachlan had been raised partly in Ireland and felt vague sympathy for the idea that the British should be 'kicked out', but he knew little about the political roots of Mau Mau and what little he understood of Kenya came mainly from reading the works of Elspeth Huxley. Interviewed in 1987, he recalled a 'sort of hunting mentality . . . one is a bit horrified at one's attitude'. Overall, however, his dominant feeling immediately after his service appears to have been regret that it was over. He missed the beauty of Kenya and felt that life in England was 'slightly more pedestrian'.[126]

The war in Kenya did not yield the clear-cut outcome that some soldiers associated with Malaya. In purely military terms, Mau Mau was destroyed but Kenyan independence was then granted and Jomo Kenyatta, who had been imprisoned during the Emergency, became the leader of the independent country. One national serviceman who served with the Royal Engineers in Kenya from 1953 to 1955 said that the operation was futile because Kenyatta came to power – 'rightly so in my opinion'.[127]

*

Conflict in Cyprus began in April 1955. The island had been ruled by the British since the late nineteenth century. Most of its population were Greek and around a third were Turks. Colonel George Grivas led the EOKA movement in a violent campaign to secure 'Enosis' – union with the Greek mainland. Not all Greek Cypriots supported violence, or even Enosis, but for reasons of prudence or principle few were prepared to help the British fight EOKA. The British were able to use Turkish policemen – but their effectiveness was limited by lack of contacts in that part of the population that supported EOKA. When, in 1958, the Turks themselves began violent demonstrations in favour of partitioning the island, the British resorted to bringing their own policemen out.

This was a conflict on a small island rather than in a large and thinly populated country. There was no realistic prospect of large-scale population movements to cut guerrillas away from their base. Furthermore, especially after the British lost the capacity to keep garrisons in Egypt, Cyprus was strategically important to them and was flooded with troops. Michael Harbottle, who served as a company commander there in the mid 1950s, reckoned that 15–20,000 troops were hunting around 170 committed EOKA guerrillas.[128] Later, there were 40,000 servicemen on the island, which meant that they came to make up almost a tenth of the entire population.

Under these circumstances, both insurgency and counter-insurgency acquired a special dimension. The direct encounters between armed men that sometimes characterized fighting in Malaya or Kenya were rare in Cyprus. EOKA specialized in hit-and-run attacks. The British responded with large-scale searches. These operations were laborious and, from the point of view of ordinary soldiers, dull, and they did not often produce results. They also meant that British soldiers were as likely to be dealing with aggrieved unarmed civilians as they were with EOKA guerrillas. The official history of the Suffolk Regiment, which had been devastatingly effective in Malaya, noted that 'there was little to show for the huge and sustained effort' of the regiment in Cyprus.[129]

Cypriot guerrillas sometimes retreated to the Troodos mountains but even the most remote parts of the island were never that far from towns. Furthermore, much of the fighting took place in towns and villages themselves. This meant that British servicemen, and their families, could not be safe even when off duty. It also meant that violence by the British army was often directed against civilians who were EOKA sympathizers, or simply Greeks, as much as it was against armed guerrillas.

Attacks produced spirals of retribution. In July 1958, an armoured car detachment of the Horse Guards ordered a boy to take down a pro-Enosis slogan. He refused, a riot broke out and the troops killed two civilians. Three days later, two soldiers from the regiment were killed by EOKA in reprisal for this incident. In August 1958, EOKA gunmen shot the wives of two British soldiers (killing one, Catherine Cutcliffe, and seriously wounding the other).

A soldier wrote to his father:

> I suppose you heard on the radio about all the trouble we had in Famagusta last Friday. About the two women being shot, one dead and the other very ill. The troops were called out ... they gave the Greeks a hell of a time. The troops just went mad. There was no order for the first two hours. The officers could not control them. I suppose you heard what the Mayor of Famagusta said, '250 injured', and I'll bet most of them had their heads split open. The lads all had riot sticks. In the first two hours they hit every Greek male they could lay their hands on.[130]

An army storeman wrote that, after the attack on the two women, he issued batons to any soldier who wanted one and that a sergeant had returned to barracks with the butt of his sub-machine gun bent and 'covered in bits of skin, hair and blood'.[131]

Ordinary soldiers, national servicemen in particular, were more aware of violence than their comrades in Kenya or Malaya. This was partly because the constant threat of attack imprisoned them on their own bases. Officers, who could wear civilian clothes and carry pistols, moved with a reasonable degree of freedom, but other ranks enjoyed no such privileges. Relaxation meant drinking beer in their own NAAFI or being driven to a beach where they could bathe under armed guard. David Lance spent eighteen months as a national serviceman at an RAF wireless station, but thought he saw more of the island when he returned fifteen years later for a two-week holiday than during the whole of his military posting.[132] The confinement of British servicemen – soldiers especially – could itself become a source of violence as men took out their resentments on the local population during the brief periods when they were released from their camps. A national service naval officer wrote in his diary:

> A few days ago I visited Kyko camp ... We may be at the mercy of the inconstant sea but they are subjected to inconveniences through sun and rain. In summer all water, washing or drinking, is too hot to serve either purpose. In winter they are bitterly cold. The rain dissolves the camp into mud. They walk through mud, they sleep in mud. Can one wonder if they are a little rough in handling suspects?[133]

Beatings of civilian crowds in towns and villages were more visible. than killings in the jungles of Kenya and Malaya.[134] Albert Balmer, a national serviceman in the Royal Artillery, remembered an occasion when a suspect was being brought back to headquarters on a truck that contained a sergeant and six gunners:

> At intervals one gunner would shout a warning, to make the sergeant look away; as soon as he did a gun butt would come back and hit the prisoner. When the prisoner got to his destination he was bundled out of the vehicle, falling and breaking a leg. An enquiry took place, but what the outcome was I don't altogether know. No one in our battery, as far as I know, received a reprimand of any kind.[135]

I. W. G. Martin, a national service corporal attached as an interpreter to the Royal Ulster Rifles, was particularly bitter in his denunciation of the violence inflicted by his comrades:

> When I arrived two platoons from B Coy and the RUR riot squad were smashing up every single thing in the place: books, cups, plates, chairs, table, furniture, mirrors, etc. (damage estimated at £2000), everyone except me was thoroughly enjoying themselves, especially the RUR officers of course, one of whom said he hadn't enjoyed himself so much in years and didn't today's events make me change my mind? ... To keep up the farcical pretence of no ill-treatment, etc., everyone in authority has perjured themselves again and again: and any attempt by

me or anyone else to tell the truth could never succeed . . . last night at one of the worst villages in the Famagusta area: 'B' Company went in strength to search coffee-shops, together with myself and a UK police sergeant: . . . they started proceedings (at least the officers did and the other ranks soon followed suit) by throwing chairs at people in order to get them into the coffee-shops . . . You can of course get away with anything in this country as long as you don't leave any bruises, but just 'poke people around a bit'.[136]

After he left the island, he received a letter from a comrade that described brutality in even more blunt terms:

> After you left, things got particularly bloody and disgusting: what happened the day Mrs Cutliffe got knocked defies description, there was wholesale rape and looting and murder. Two men were beaten to death by the Grenadiers in the 'Snakepit' in Karalos, four more died in Varosha and a thirteen year old girl raped and killed in a cage in 51 Brigade, also a ten year old boy was strangled by a Company Sergeant Major in the Military Police. It appears that the RUR did not kill anyone; it was not for want of trying, though.[137]

The fact that Cyprus was more accessible than Kenya or Malaya, and the fact that EOKA had powerful allies on the Greek mainland, meant that events on the island could not easily be concealed from the outside world. Some national servicemen also had a stronger sense of the Cypriots as being victims of injustice. British soldiers might regard Cypriots as different from 'white people', but they were not as different as the populations of Africa or Asia. The educated classes in Britain had a tradition of sympathy for Greek nationalism and some of the most privileged servicemen sent to Cyprus, including many of those trained as interpreters, who therefore witnessed interrogations, were classicists. People in Britain at the time knew more about what was happening in Cyprus than they had known about Kenya or Malaya. On their return, some men were asked, 'Was it as bad as the papers said?'[138]

Simon Coningham was a national service officer with the West Kents in Cyprus. His regiment were mainly in the hills and he led long patrols through beautiful countryside. His memories of service were relatively benign, though he heard rumours about reprisals, in particular about the commanding officer of another regiment who told his men 'you have got two hours' (to take revenge) after an attack. He himself came across only minor examples of brutality. Once he saw a British policeman deliberately scrape the shin of an adolescent detainee with his boot. Coningham objected and was later warned that alienating the 'civil power' would not advance his military career, hardly a threat that was likely to strike terror into a national serviceman. He also recalled operations in which his regiment penned together all the adult men of a village while they conducted searches and interrogations. As the day grew hot, women brought water for their sons and husbands but the soldiers turned the women away.[139] None of this was very savage by the standards of twentieth-century counter-insurgency and the 'caging' operations were legitimate from the army's standpoint. All the same, there was something disconcerting about the very fact that the actions of the West Kents were so open. Perhaps, indeed, the low-level humiliations applied in a village square could seem more troubling than the more extreme – but discreet – violence that the same regiment had meted out in the Malayan jungle a few years previously.

National servicemen sometimes thought that there was a grim inevitability to the violence. An officer with the Wiltshire Regiment wrote to his parents: 'I cannot quite see how we are not going to get hateful to these people.' A little later his convoy was stoned and he regretted that there were 'not enough of us to stop, and beat the hell out of them as we wished'. After one of his soldiers was killed on patrol: 'The platoon was very upset; it would have gone badly for any terrorist we caught at that time.'[140]

More than in other colonial conflicts, violence in Cyprus seems to have divided British troops. Some relished it but others were horrified by the sentiments of their comrades:

The only unsavoury incident that I heard reported during this period occurred when a Scots regiment picked up two unidentified suspects, and, it was rumoured, subjected them to unpardonable interrogation methods, in this case up-ending them with hands bound into a fountain. When I heard of this, I became angry and disturbed; a fierce

341

argument broke out in the tent between those who thought it acceptable – all's fair in love and war – and those, like me, who felt that this was precisely what the Allies had stood against in the Second World War.[141]

The cycles of violence and revenge that marked the Cyprus Emergency were felt even in Britain. David Baxter, in a military hospital recovering from a fever and about to be posted as a clerk to Dorset, described the mood when a member of his corps was killed in Cyprus, supposedly shot in the back while doing his Christmas shopping:

> The desire to have guns and kill could be felt like a heat-wave anywhere in the barracks. I felt it in the sick bay and, having nothing else to do, indulged a wish to be posted to Cyprus where there was hate and action so that a man need not be responsible to himself, for he could lose himself in the heroic pace of a general hate.[142]

Reviewing Baxter's book, a journalist recalled two Oxford undergraduates talking of the joys of 'Cyp-bashing' and the 'time one of Jack's men shot a woman by mistake'.[143]

Owen Parfitt, a conscript in the Parachute Regiment, saw a Turkish policeman beating up suspects shortly after a soldier had been shot: 'At the time, you think: My God, this is wrong; but you're so incensed about the incidents that have gone on.' He remembered Greek Cypriots coming out of church and spitting on the body of a soldier as it lay in the gutter. He also described a time when he and his comrades had pretended to be about to shoot a suspect: 'I'm not proud of it; perhaps I will talk about it when I've had a couple of drinks.'[144]

Some conscripts, however, seem to have assumed that violence was condoned by the military authorities. Albert Balmer recalled being addressed by a general who said that 'they' (EOKA) were 'bastards, bastards, bastards', and offered to defend any man who was accused of shooting a Cypriot.[145] A marine remembered angry attacks on Cypriot crowds with batons, which 'really did tear into the mob', and a 'terrorist' arrested just after a bomb attack: 'our sergeant major, a hard man, grabbed him and smashed his nose, moved his nose around his face . . . it was quite sickening that'. He once saw some of his comrades interrogating a suspect: 'he wasn't a pretty sight . . . I wouldn't say torturing him but they was giving him a rough time.' However, the Marine felt that there was nothing he could do. He feared a complaint would get him 'put inside' and then he would have to do another six months of service.[146]

The guilt expressed by some servicemen about military behaviour in Cyprus was incongruous. Britain had selfish reasons for wanting to stay on the island – it was an important strategic base – but British soldiers were holding the ring between Greeks and Turks and the variety of Greek nationalism preached by EOKA was hardly liberal. Much British misbehaviour on Cyprus involved beatings and humiliation rather than the more lethal violence of earlier colonial conflicts. The most important thing to distinguish Cyprus from Kenya and Malaya was time. Violence in Malaya was at its worst in 1950 and 1951 – shortly after the Second World War, at the height of the Cold War and around the time that national service finally settled into the pattern of two-year service. Violence in Kenya was at its most intense a few years later, but still at a time when some British people – though perhaps not many conscripts – might have believed that Britain had an empire to defend. Violence in Cyprus reached its peak in 1958 – after the humiliation of Suez, after the last wave of decolonization had begun and, perhaps most importantly, after the end of national service had been announced.

Was the attitude of conscripts to colonial violence different from that of regular soldiers? Both conscripts and regulars killed. There is little evidence either that the army systematically entrusted the most brutal fighting to regulars or that national servicemen were deliberately 'blooded' to initiate them into a culture of violence. Most men recognized that they were not forced to participate in illegal acts of violence – though their lives might not have been comfortable if they had refused. Often men seem to have had contradictory feelings about violent action. Few of them rebelled against it, but many – even, and perhaps especially, those who participated in the most notorious killings – felt uncomfortable about what they had done. The short-service officer who was present at the scene of the Griffiths atrocities may have been telling the truth when he said that he and his national service comrade were 'sickened' by what they had seen – which does not necessarily mean that they had not also been complicit in at least some of the violence.[147] There was, though, one important difference between regulars and conscripts. Regulars served in successive campaigns and saw each incident as part of a wider pattern – which was why they felt exasperated at the growing criticism of their actions by civilians. One officer asked about events in Kenya replied:

> [A] certain number of them [the other ranks of his regiment] served in Malaya, and they cannot see any difference in killing a German, or a bandit in Malaya, and a Mau Mau in Kenya. We refer to them as the enemy in our reports, and that is how we regard them.[148]

Regulars were conscious that they were part of a tradition that linked them to earlier conflicts – one thinks of the NCO at Batang Kali who vomited after shooting a man, and was 'comforted' with the assurance that it was always like that 'the first time'. National servicemen, by contrast, were almost always killing 'for the first time'. Violence was something that cut uncomfortably across their civilian lives and, increasingly, as time went on, conscripts seem to have felt that the morality of the civilian world was more compelling than that of the army.

14
Suez

Late one evening, a voice at the other end of the billet: 'Eden's a bloody warmonger. He doesn't know what it's like'. It was a moment, a relatively brief moment as it turned out, when history broke through the routine boredom and farce of National Service.

Memoir of national service in the
air force by David Morgan[1]

In some lucid intervals not devoted to the Suez crisis, I have been trying to think over matters discussed with the Minister on 20th November ... about the future of National Service.

Note by official in the Ministry of Defence, 1956[2]

Suez was a brief and, in retrospect, disastrous military operation. A coup in 1952, partly provoked by British behaviour in the Canal Zone, brought the army to power in Cairo. Colonel Gamal Abdel Nasser, an exponent of Arab nationalism, established himself as the most important figure in the regime. For a time, it seemed that the British would accept the new order. In 1954, they signed an agreement with the Egyptian government that committed them to withdraw from the country and they had completed this withdrawal by June 1956. British bases were to be maintained jointly by the British and the Egyptians and the British reserved the right to return if the canal was threatened.

However, Nasser then nationalized the Suez Canal, which was owned by an Anglo-French consortium. The British and French interpreted this as a threat to their links with the Far East and also to their increasingly important oil supplies from the Persian Gulf. They planned a military expedition to reassert control of the canal. To provide them with an expedient to justify the invasion, they came to a secret deal with Israel: Israeli forces were to attack Egypt and the British and French would use this attack as an excuse to intervene and 'separate' the two sides. The operation was hampered on the British side by the scarcity of equipment and properly trained troops. In spite of these problems, in purely military terms 'Operation Musketeer', as it was christened, should not have been difficult – the British, French and Israeli forces were superior to the Egyptian. Politically, things were more complicated. There was division inside Britain. Much of the left never felt that the invasion was justified and Gaitskell, the leader of the Labour party, denounced it. Anthony Eden, who had succeeded Churchill as Prime Minister in the previous year, had come to see Nasser as a second Hitler and felt that failing to stand up to him would be 'appeasement'. However, Eden was sick and crushed by years of Churchill's elephantine condescension. Furthermore, he had misled the House of Commons when he said that there had been no collusion with the Israelis over Suez. Pleading ill health, he resigned in January 1957. Most importantly, Suez divided the western alliance. It was undermined when Eisenhower – the President of the United States and the former commander of Allied forces in the Second World War – denounced it and effectively ordered Britain back into line.

Everyone understood that Suez meant the end of an era, but they did not agree about what that era had been. For some, the humiliation of being overruled by America meant the end of Britain's pretensions to great power status. For some, the attempt to intervene in another country meant the end of Britain's pretensions to moral superiority. Many were shocked by what they saw as the incompetence of the British forces and the contrast with what they believed to have been British military prowess in the Second World War. Anthony Howard remembered the landing as being 'like a comic version of D-Day'[3] and, indeed, Howard's company waded up to the beach purely to provide newsreel footage – the rest of the battalion just disembarked in the harbour.[4]

Some believed that national servicemen had come close to

rebelling – or perhaps even, in discreet ways, had rebelled – during Suez. A. J. P. Taylor, who had the previous year bemoaned the political passivity of national servicemen, wrote to his son – serving in the RASC – and offered to stand by him if he was court-martialled for disobeying orders. His son wrote back saying that 'he and his mates' were resisting government policy more effectively by loading stores so slowly that they would impede the operation.[5] Andrew Sinclair's novel *The Breaking of Bumbo* (1959) revolves around a moment when a national service subaltern is expelled from his guards regiment after having incited his men to mutiny: 'Do you think it's *right* for us to go and get killed, just to get back a bit of sand that belongs to the Egyptians anyway? . . . We've won every bloody battle for the Establishment in three hundred years. It's time we asked *why*.'

It is possible that Taylor *fils* and his comrades worked with deliberate slowness – though one suspects that the RASC did not function with Prussian efficiency at the best of times. Equally it is possible that Sinclair did deliver a speech like Bumbo's – though one suspects that it was delivered, not to guardsmen in November 1956, but to his fellow undergraduates at Cambridge some time after Suez. Sinclair was not drummed out of the army and was, indeed, an officer in the Coldstream Emergency Reserve when his novel was published.

Rebellion by conscript soldiers during Suez was rare and rebellion for political reasons by ordinary national servicemen was almost unknown. The Conservative party had won the general election of 1955 and would win the next one in 1959. Since young men voted Labour more than the old and women, national servicemen would have been to the left of the country, but the difference was not marked. The majority of conscripts were too young to vote and they did not on the whole belong to a politicized generation. Most men who expressed political opinions of any kind adopted those of their parents. The mid 1950s was a time when young people were conservative (and often Conservative in the party political sense) in ways that would be inconceivable ten years later. A national service officer in Cyprus wrote to his mother in November 1956:

> I have just heard the news that they have at last landed. Jolly good thing too. High time we showed a firm hand, and did something about it.

The Labour Party's attitude makes me angry. I would have loved to have gone myself, and I think all of us would.[6]

Almost everyone came to recognize that the Suez expedition had been a mistake and some left-wingers looked back on the episode as a formative moment in their own political development. However, the civilians who protested against Suez were never more than a minority of the British population. Furthermore, national servicemen were often cut off from contact with the civilian world, so many of them knew nothing of the demonstrations against Suez. Soldiers who protested almost invariably did so because of the effect that the expedition had on themselves, rather than because of some broader political belief.

Those most likely to express hostility to Suez seem to have been the educated men who worked in clerical jobs – these were also the servicemen who were in the best position to listen to radio broadcasts and read newspapers immediately before the operation. Alan Watson was serving, mainly with other grammar school boys, as a personnel selection assessor at RAF Cardington. His unit was riven by fierce division: 'If the rest of the armed forces were anything like Aptitude Testing, then this would have been a difficult war.'[7]

The rest of the armed forces, however, were not like Watson's colleagues. Many recalled their opinions of Suez with amusement or embarrassment or did not recall them at all. Francis Holford was a lance corporal in the Buffs and serving in Cyprus at the time of Suez. A public school boy who had failed to obtain a commission and had a place at Cambridge, he explained the unthinking Conservatism of many young men in the 1950s: 'the first kind of real social life I got was joining the local Billinghurst Young Conservatives when I was in the sixth form. Because that was about the only social life . . . that and the Young Farmers that's all there was really.' He said that he had no 'political' views on Suez, meaning it seems that he did not oppose it. He thought that a pilot who was said to have damaged his plane to avoid bombing the Egyptians was 'a bit off'. Holford thought that he voted for the first time 'around 1958' and that he voted Conservative: 'because you know I was brought up that that was . . . the only way to vote, and to vote any differently was probably unpatriotic'.[8]

Even men who would later become active on the political left often supported Suez at the time. Michael Harbottle was a regular army officer who eventually rose to the rank of brigadier and founded an improbable organization called 'Generals for Peace'. However, he admitted that he had had no feeling that Suez was wrong: 'everyone in the army felt about time Nasser was given a punch on the nose, that feeling of justification stayed with me for quite some time'.[9] Paul Foot, who later became a campaigning journalist and member of the Socialist Workers Party, was called up into the army in the summer of 1956. At this time he still held the conventional views of his class – he came from a prominent Liberal family and his father was Governor of Jamaica. He admitted that there had been debates among his fellow conscripts over Suez, but 'I am ashamed to remember what role I played. Every officer was absolutely 100% in favour of the operation', which was opposed by 'only the slightly more radicalized of the soldiers'. Foot admitted that he found reading his diary from the period painful.[10]

Antony Copley did read the diary that he kept of his time as a national service naval officer and was slightly surprised to discover there was nothing on 'politics and Suez' between September (when his ship was being fitted out for the assault) and 1 November, at which time he noted: 'we are sailing into a war, a war I do not believe in but do not as yet sufficiently disbelieve in to try to leave the Navy'.[11] Copley also noted that he had not, at first, known that his ship was sailing to Port Said. Only when they were out of the harbour, did the captain tell them their destination.

Bruce Kent, conscripted and commissioned in 1948, had left the army by the time of Suez and would eventually become a radical priest and leader of the Campaign for Nuclear Disarmament. Interviewed in 1989, he said: 'I would have done absolutely anything that I had been ordered to do ... I reflected *Daily Telegraph* values – so apolitical.' He said of Suez: 'I remember thinking it good that Nasser and company had got their comeuppance', but most revealingly he asked his interviewer, 'Was it 52 or 53?'[12]

Even national servicemen who disapproved of Suez usually expressed their disagreement within the limits of military discipline. John Barnes wrote to his parents in November 1956: 'I should think you will all be rather shocked by Israel's action against Egypt. Don't you think Sir Anthony has put us in a rather sticky position?'[13] Barnes seems to have assumed that his parents would share his view, itself a revealing sign of how unrebellious national servicemen were. He did not try to hide his opinion – he knew that letters were being censored – but he did not seem to have considered disobeying orders. He became a non-commissioned officer, remembered his time in the navy with affection and admired his commanding officer.

Peter Jay was a national service midshipman who had been born to the purple of the British left. His father had been a Labour minister, Gaitskell had been his next-door neighbour and Richard Crossman once told his mother with characteristic tact, 'I shan't mind if that beautiful son of yours get killed by the Cypriots.'[14] Jay was bitterly opposed to Suez and came close to rebellion. He denounced the expedition to Rear Admiral Sir Anthony Miers[15] and in the pages of his own official journal – his superior officer wrote 'fine stuff' after a strongly worded attack on British policy.[16] Jay's most damning assessment of Suez was written, again in his official journal, in December 1956:

> [C]onsidered in the light of the advance of human civilization from puerile pugilists to adult arbitration, in terms of peace, posterity and the survival of posterity, in terms of the fight against Communism and for the hand of the uncommitted countries, in terms of England's traditions of moderation and moral uprightness, can one honestly condone an act of petty indignation and selfish irresponsibility which may at one blow have struck out the credit for peace so dearly earned on many battlefields and seas? I prefer to forgive it as a tragic blunder of a great man whose patience was tried beyond breaking point and whose reason was wracked with every worry known to age and responsibility. It is a human tragedy as well as a tragedy for humanity.[17]

However, Jay did not resign his commission, and in the end accepted his father's view that 'it was the duty of a member of the Armed Forces to obey orders'.[18]

The Suez crisis came and went quickly. No one had much chance for reflection and soldiers who were on the whole confined to bases were in a particularly poor position to know what was going on.

Anthony Howard was older than most national servicemen and considerably more politically aware – he had been president of the Oxford Union. At first, he did not take the whole thing seriously because he 'could not believe that the British government would be so stupid'. While he was on the ship to Suez, the adjutant of his regiment approached him and said: 'you're not very keen on this enterprise, are you? If it is any help to you, one or two of us [the regular officers] think the same.' The adjutant then told Howard that if he were to incite his platoon against taking part in the expedition, he, Howard, would be discreetly smuggled home and discharged on medical grounds – pretty much what happens to the fictional Bumbo in Sinclair's novel – but the other ranks would get seven years for mutiny. Howard had probably never really contemplated disobeying orders and he had not told the commanding officer of his disquiet. He led his men on to the beaches and even, much to his own distaste, fired a few shots.[19]

Fighting at Suez was, for a brief period, intense but confusing. There was something incongruous about a 'war' that involved living in the middle of an enemy city. Men in the Royal Fusiliers were rebuked for giving their rations to Egyptian children.[20] It was hard to know who was the 'enemy'. The British believed that some of the men firing at them were not in uniform and that Egyptian soldiers had changed into civilian clothes. After a day's fighting, a national service officer wrote in his diary: 'there seemed to be the understanding that "wog" meant an armed wog, all the others being termed "civvies"',[21] but he was uncomfortably aware that his men were not sure whether some of those that they had shot were armed or not. The British never knew how many Egyptians they had killed – some of them reported dark rumours of mass graves – and they did not in the short term have much idea of how bad their own casualties had been either.

In fact, the number of British dead at Suez was small, but one national serviceman came to epitomize the tragic futility of the operation. Anthony Moorhouse was the son of a wealthy businessman (a manufacturer of jam) and an officer with the West Yorkshire Regiment. On the 11 December 1956, a week before his twenty-first birthday, he returned alone in an army Land Rover to a building that he and his men had raided the previous day. He was acting without orders and there was no obvious reason for him to go back. He was overpowered by the crowd and abducted. For some time, the British tried to find him and/or negotiate his return but, on Christmas Eve, Nasser told a UN representative that Moorhouse was dead. He had been hidden in a trunk or cupboard and, because his captors had been prevented from returning to him by the British searches, he had suffocated. It was a horrible and squalid death and his only lasting memorial was to inspire the character of Mick Rice in John Osborne's *The Entertainer* (1957) – a play that seemed to epitomize the association between Suez and indignity.

Most commanders in combat units at Suez did not worry much about the political views of their soldiers. The brunt of the fighting was borne by the Parachute Regiment and the Royal Marines Commandos, units that contained a smaller proportion of national servicemen than most ordinary infantry regiments. General Sir Michael Gray, a company commander in the Parachute Regiment in 1956, said that he did not 'recall any feeling about the political influences that were going on in the United Kingdom'.[22] Alun Pask was a national service paratrooper who went to Suez. He and his friends knew nothing about the mood in Britain or opposition to the expedition. They did not understand why it was suddenly curtailed: 'there we are, all psyched up and ready to go, and then the rumour came: "Cease-fire." "Christ! What the hell's happening?" we thought.'[23]

A. R. Ashton was a national service marine. His unit was sent to Malta 'ostensibly for training' but had 'no inkling' of what was really happening. General Sir Hugh Stockwell, the commander of the British and French land forces, visited them on 27 September and invited them to 'gather round' à la Montgomery, but their first real information came when they heard a BBC broadcast piped from the governor's palace: 'we felt aggrieved that, like cuckolded husbands, we were the last to know'.[24] Only when they were on the boat to Suez did they receive proper briefings – first from their own lieutenant and then from a more senior officer: 'we knew a little by now of the raging political controversy that was occupying the political stage at home.'[25] Ashton's commanders suspected that national servicemen might disapprove of the expedition. Nicholas Vaux was a lieutenant in 45 Commando during Suez. Interviewed in 1992, by which time he had risen to the rank of major general, he said that his unit was more or less evenly divided between national servicemen and regulars and that many of the former were 'very intelligent and well educated'. He thought that 'any disquiet on political grounds would have been confined very much to the national service element' but that he had not seen any concrete manifestation of such disquiet.[26] Ashton was certainly an intelligent and well-educated man and he wrote movingly about the carnage at Suez. He saw a corporal weeping after he had lost most of his section and a trail of blood 'a foot wide and thirty feet long',[27] where a wounded soldier had been dragged to safety:

> All during one's formative years one had been brought up to respect human life and value property: now suddenly we were plunged into a complete reversal of these values. Buildings shattered; vehicles burning; homes ransacked and looted, bodies of young men bleeding to death in filthy gutters. The man who described war as a mass nervous breakdown was not far wrong.

None of this, however, translated into political opposition on Ashton's part. On the contrary, he and his comrades were 'straining at the leash' before the operation. After it, they thought 'thank Christ it's over' but they also 'had a feeling of unfinished business'.[28]

Other national service marines had similar feelings. Peter Mayo was an upper-middle-class second lieutenant in the corps. He understood rather earlier than Ashton that war was coming. On 22 September, he wrote in his diary that his life might end 'with an Egyptian (or Russian) machine-gun bullet through me'. Like many men of his background, he was curious and anxious. On 31 October he had a 'tautening feeling' and hoped that the young marines would 'hold up'. On 2 November he wrote: 'I wish I were happier about the cause we are to fight for. The legal rights of the case are fairly plain. But, even so, where does it all lead?' Mayo's young marines did 'hold up', and, for all his doubts, Mayo never came close to suggesting that he or his men should not fight. After having been debriefed with other officers in Malta, he noted on 4 December that he had learned 'quite a lot that is still secret'. He regarded the operation as a military failure but felt, like Ashton, that it 'should have gone further'.[29]

Antony Copley opposed the expedition and was disgusted by much of what he heard:

> Reports creep in about action ashore. Our losses total just over a hundred but no one is perturbed by hundreds of 'gyppos' lying dead about the street. S [a regular midshipman] laughs hollowly about the smell of flies over pus-running bodies – why cannot they see the tragedy of it all? Listen to our smart jargon, 'gyppos', 'wogs' . . . I am ashamed of my country and ashamed of myself.[30]

Copley, however, never disobeyed orders, and like many servicemen he felt that the British had made things worse by not even finishing the job: 'Butler [a British commander] is a complete British moron. Why in the hell didn't he at least press on to Ismailia?'[31]

Overt rebellion by politically aware national servicemen was rare, but grumbling was common. Particularly important were reservists, men who had undertaken their service some time before but were recalled to the forces in 1956. Discontent seems to have been greatest, not in the front-line units, but in those concerned with logistics. The reservists in such units were often relatively old men who had been dragged away from jobs and families. They were not as disciplined as infantry soldiers and, unlike marines or paratroopers, they felt no thrill at the idea of combat.

Nick Harden was called up as a national serviceman in 1956 and posted to Maidstone, where he joined a field engineering regiment that was short of men. He found the base in 'utter chaos'. There were three classes of men there. Some were regular soldiers, usually in the army since they were boys, who were willing to accept discipline. Some were national servicemen, who often felt that it was *de rigueur* to complain – though Harden admitted that he actually enjoyed his service. The third were reservists: 'If the national servicemen were resentful of army discipline, they were angels compared [to the reservists].' For three or four weeks, his unit was not told where they were going but then they were suddenly moved and Harden, a Liverpudlian, realized that they were arriving at Liverpool docks. Once they were on the ship, an education officer told them that Nasser was a 'usurper': 'we were all fairly politically naive – so he could tell us anything really'. Harden remarked that this was an 'untold story of Suez', but he also made it clear that there were limits to the rebellion of the soldiers. For one thing, the engineers were more awkward than the combat troops, and particularly than the marines, alongside whom they were stationed when they arrived in Malta. Furthermore, few men translated their discontent into political form or did anything that would impede military operations – rather than just demonstrate their contempt for the more ostentatious manifestations of army discipline. Harden himself felt 'no resentment at all'. He recalled that 'Occasionally someone would stand up [in discussions about the expedition] and then they [presumably his comrades] would say "Communist" or "Bolshevik".'[32]

There were mutinies provoked by Suez. A group of reservists from the RASC were court-martialled after incidents at a base at Minden in Germany in early October 1956. The men, all apparently expecting to be sent to the Middle East, had been insubordinate and gone to the sergeants' mess shouting 'We want the CSM [company sergeant major]'. Four reservists, including a corporal and lance corporal, were convicted by court martial.[33] Men from the RASC were also court-martialled after events at Platres in Cyprus on 1 October 1956. The commanding officer said that the unit had mobilized in a hurry and arrived in Cyprus between 6 and 9 September 1956. A group of reservist NCOs 'created a disturbance' and he, the commanding officer, 'was faced with the problem, therefore, that the majority of the unit had a loyalty to a faction calling themselves reservists . . . Many of the reservist NCOs were loathe to take disciplinary action against a fellow reservist.' One of the reservists had written a letter, which was not published, to the *Daily Mirror*. Men presented grievances that were similar to some that had been published in the *Daily Sketch*. There seemed to have been communication between reservists in various units. A letter was intercepted from 54 Company of the RASC saying 'there will be a mutiny here as well as Cyprus if they are not careful'.[34]

One should not take this apocalyptic talk at face value. Few protests had much explicit political content. A group of men on parade sang 'The Red Flag' but this was part of a general display that the soldiers were 'truculent, cheeky and obviously thought they were on top', more than an expression of Marxist principles. One reservist told the regimental sergeant major: 'it is the government we are after and Antony Head [the Secretary of State for War]', but other soldiers disassociated themselves from his remarks.[35] Discontent sprang from the conditions of British soldiers rather than any interest in the case for or against the Suez operation in itself. Many of the grievances were simply to do with the rapid mobilization of men under awkward conditions.

The reference to left-wing newspapers suggests paranoia on the part of some officers about political rebellion in the army. In truth, though, the most severe resistance to military discipline did not involve *Daily Mirror*-reading national servicemen; it did not even involve the kind of trade unionist mentality that had been seen in the air force at the end of the Second World War. On the contrary, the typical 'mutineer' was usually from one of the least prestigious units – the RASC or the Catering Corps – and was often a reservist who had formerly been a regular soldier. Some men already had a number of disciplinary offences on their record, and sometimes the ill-discipline that accompanied mobilization around the Suez expedition was not that different in type from the ill-discipline that occurred in such units much of the time.

Women – often conspicuous by their absence in the lives of national servicemen – were important during the Suez crisis because many reservists were married. When seven men were prosecuted for mutiny, it emerged that two of them had got married in the very week they were recalled to the army.[36] One woman was found guilty of removing £3 and 15 shillings from a gas meter; her husband was a lance corporal who had been recalled to the RASC and had not, apparently, passed on his pay to his wife.[37] One reservist prosecuted for mutiny during Suez had received a letter from his wife saying that she had pawned her wedding ring because he had failed to provide money: 'I expect you have either gambled it, or spent it out enjoying yourself, drunk most of the time, because from what I hear . . . all you blokes are on is one long holiday.'[38]

'Mutiny' was a loose term. It could be applied to any act of collective insubordination. For this reason, good officers used it sparingly. They sought to assuage or negotiate when dealing with minor discontents, to isolate the few men who might be determined enough to mount real resistance and to avoid confrontation with large groups of soldiers. Many officers understood the difference between disquiet and disobedience and their own duty to prevent the first from turning into the second. Ill-discipline in prestigious infantry units during Suez was treated differently from ill-discipline in the RASC. There was trouble in the King's Royal Rifle Corps at Derna in Libya in the last week of September 1956, and eventually, as the official report put it: '[A] spontaneous voicing of dissatisfaction with existing conditions arose.'[39] This was, however, presented as a manageable and, indeed, managed problem: 'The following morning the Commanding Officer saw all those involved and addressed them and, as far as is known, the whole matter was quietened down and no further trouble arose.'[40] The fact that the news had spread outside the regiment at all was presented as an unfortunate accident.[41]

Similarly, a protest which involved about 150 men in the Grenadier Guards about 'bull' was treated as relatively minor. The men were told that kit would not be inspected and the authorities considered that there was: 'no sign of indiscipline or lack of morale in the battalion.'[42]

The fact that at the time discontent rarely took an explicitly political form, and did not actually impede the operation, does not mean that it was not significant for the participants. G was recalled to the Royal Engineers after having completed his full-time national service. His regiment, concerned with port operations, was largely made up of dockers and was 'pretty bolshie'.[43] They threw stones and booed when they were addressed by 'General Somebody or Other'.[44] Like many soldiers they seemed to have little idea where they were going when they embarked.[45] At the time, G and his comrades were bitterly aggrieved at their treatment but did not consider mutiny and did not see their actions as related to political opposition to the war. At the end of the operation, they were given a £5 bounty and tempted to burn their uniforms. G spoke of his unit having 'contempt for officers', but he understood little of the political context and was surprised to discover that there had been demonstrations against Suez.[46]

Like many of those involved in Suez, G became more consciously left-wing as time went on and he did come to express outright opposition to the operation. He seems to have been influenced partly by the

15

Ending National Service

The Queen's Shilling was, by 1957, wholly optional. National Service was winding down. Deferment (with the prospect of never having to serve) was there for the asking. You could get medical disqualification with a hiccup – fake or real. It was reverse Kitchener: Your Country Didn't Need You.

John Sutherland (born October 1938)[1]

National service did not end with a bang but with a series of whimpers. The last men went into the armed forces in November 1960 and emerged, having been kept in for an extra six months, in the early summer of 1963. However, interest in national service evaporated as soon as men stopped being called up and it is not clear that anyone, including the military authorities, knew exactly when the last conscript finished his service. In any case, national service had been winding down long before its formal end. No one born after September 1939 was conscripted, which meant that no one was called up at the age of eighteen after 1957. With various expedients, the Ministry of Labour slowed the rate of conscription from 1955.

The number of men drafted to the forces in 1956 – before the formal announcement of the end of national service – was 130,032, which compared to 170,384 men who had been drafted in 1952. The number drafted in 1959, the last full year of conscription, was just over 61,000. Conscripts got older, partly because the government raised the age of registration every year from 1955. Since the call-up age could not increase indefinitely, this in itself made it obvious that national service would have to end reasonably soon. Conscripts also became more plebeian – partly because educated men were increasingly keen to avoid service and the government was increasingly prone to let them do so. The notion of universal liability, which underwrote the long-term legitimacy of national service, had in effect disappeared. Conscripts themselves appreciated that conscription was a 'dying dinosaur'.[2] One man, called up in October 1957, remembered: 'it felt slightly as if they weren't sure they wanted us and having got us were not sure what to do with us'.[3]

The National Service Act of 1948 had stipulated that no one born after 1935 was to be called up. This had been changed by Order in Council in 1953 to allow men born up until the end of 1940 to be conscripted. Further extension would have required new legislation.[4] Few expected such legislation, and ministers discussed the possibility of abolishing national service years before they made a formal announcement in 1957.

For a time, between the Korean War and Suez, it seemed that conscription had settled on stable, though not permanent, foundations. The length of service was set at two years; the need for servicemen was established both by the state of relations with the Soviet Union and by the engagement of British troops in Kenya and Malaya. The Labour party had lost the general election of October 1951 and Winston Churchill formed a Conservative government. Conservative MPs had, with only one exception, voted in favour of the bill to introduce national service and Churchill personally had made much of the issue. The service ministers in the first years of the second Churchill government were unlikely to ask awkward questions about the armed forces. Harold Alexander, who was Minister of Defence from 1952 to 1954, had been Churchill's favourite general in the war and accepted a post in the government because 'I simply can't refuse Winston.'[5]

The apparent stability was deceptive. Two years of service suited the forces well and it was retained after the end of the Korean War, which had been its ostensible justification, but it made conscription in Britain more onerous – especially, as critics pointed out, in comparison with the countries of continental Europe. Two-year service also underlined the fact that the purpose of conscription had changed. Men were no longer being trained to provide a reserve; rather they were being held ready to fight a potential war in Europe or being used to fight real wars in Asia. The implication of this was that national service would cease to be necessary if relations with the Soviet Union improved and/or if Britain reduced its commitments overseas.

The fact that the Labour party was now in opposition meant that left-wing backbenchers could afford to be vociferous. Freed from the responsibility of government, Labour MPs complained about conditions and length of service and hinted that national service as a whole might be unnecessary, but did not feel obliged to propose specific alternatives. Emanuel Shinwell, who, as Secretary of State for War, had introduced two-year service, now called for the length of service to be reduced, and suggested that the call-up be allowed to 'peter out' by 1954.[6]

In public, Conservative ministers dismissed attacks on national service but they were in an awkward position. Conscription did not fit easily with the prosperous consumerist society of the late 1950s, for which the Conservatives were happy to take credit. In 1955, the Conservative party did 'not regard the current two years period as necessarily having come to stay'.[7]

In private, ministers sometimes recognized the difficulty of continuing national service. In 1952, Montgomery had lunch with Shinwell. Afterwards, he sent Churchill a note about their meeting. He believed that Shinwell attacked national service because he needed money – 'his son has cost him a good bit lately' – and such attacks made good journalistic copy. Montgomery gave Shinwell a firm talking to and believed that he had left him 'less of a Labour politician and more of a good British citizen'.[8]

The Prime Minister – a connoisseur of Montgomery's style – must have relished the note's pomposity and gracelessness. In private, though, Churchill had already begun thinking about how to respond to Labour attacks on national service. He asked Antony Head, the Secretary of State for War, to prepare information that he, Churchill, could use against Shinwell,[9] but he also asked his officials how justified Shinwell's views were,[10] and prevented Head from making a speech justifying two years service on the grounds that doing so would raise an issue that was unlikely to do the government any good.[11]

Head was a loyal defender of army interests. Born in 1906 and educated at Eton and Sandhurst, he was commissioned into the Life

Guards and for much of the inter-war period had been a dashing officer – whose regimental duties did not distract him from a career as an amateur jockey and adventurer. After distinguished service in the war, during which he rose to the rank of brigadier, he left the army and entered parliament in 1945. He became Secretary of State for War with Churchill's return to government in 1951.

Head had always understood that national service was a temporary expedient rooted in the 'short-term virtue of being the only way to provide enough men to fulfil our immediate overseas commitments'.[12] Almost as soon as he moved into the War Office, he asked:

> Was any assumption ever made about the duration of National Service? This admittedly is a very long term thought but supposing by 1956 or 57 we got some kind of a settlement with the Russians and a certain amount of disarmament took place, and consequently a decrease in the size of the army, would National Service then be retained?[13]

By 1955, Head was seeking to build up the regular army so that, if possible, 'we should have a chance of turning over soon after 1958 from National Service to an all Regular Army.'[14]

Britain's strategic circumstances had changed between 1952 and 1955. After the death of Stalin in March 1953, the prospect of war in Europe seemed less likely. The technology of warfare also changed. The Americans tested the first thermonuclear (hydrogen) bomb in November 1952 – it was much more powerful than the atom bombs that the Americans had stocked since 1945. The Russians exploded their first hydrogen bomb in 1953 and the British, largely excluded from American secrets, worked hard to develop their own version. The means by which nuclear weapons might be delivered changed too. The government authorized the development of the Blue Streak missile in 1955, though, as it turned out, the project was too expensive and the British resorted to buying American weapons.

At least at first, however, strategy had little direct influence on decisions about the future of national service. The service chiefs did not know how they would fare without conscription and how its end would affect voluntary recruitment. Even the navy, which took hardly any conscripts, worried about abolition – fearing that its own supply of skilled workers might be eroded if the other services were forced to make greater efforts to recruit such men.[15] One official wrote of attempts to estimate future recruiting: 'What we in the War Office are after . . . is some sort of agreed guess produced by a suitable body in lieu of the many and varied guesses that have been bandied about.'[16]

An all-regular force of well-paid, well-equipped servicemen might attract recruits. New problems, however, would be created. Promotion would be slower for regulars when the army no longer needed so many senior NCOs to lick its national servicemen into shape.[17] Furthermore, particular functions in the forces – the army especially – would be hard to fill. Infantry regiments, which subjected men to stiff discipline and left them with no skill that was useful in the civilian world, would find the end of national service difficult. As late as July 1960, officers reckoned that, by the second half of 1962, the infantry would fall short of its needs by 7,000 men: only the guards, the Parachute Regiment and the Scottish and Irish regiments – the last of these, in any case, drew many of their recruits from an area in which national service had never been applied – would be able to fill their ranks.[18]

The social changes of which Conservative politicians boasted in the late 1950s made it harder for the forces to recruit. Full employment and the welfare state meant that civilian life was more attractive. Better education had created a group of respectable and relatively well-paid men – the kind who rarely joined up. Some officials looked hopefully to the most economically depressed regions because they believed that unemployment had spurred recruitment in the 1930s. The only sure consolation, however, came from the knowledge that the birth rate had increased in the 1940s and that therefore, in due course, the pool of young men available for recruitment would increase in size.[19]

Some ministers also worried about the impact that the abolition of conscription might have on Britain's allies. Debate was provoked by the German decision in 1955 to set service for their own conscripts at one year, but some argued that attempts to persuade the Germans to reverse this decision would make it difficult to reduce the British term. Alec Douglas-Home, Secretary of State for Commonwealth Relations, was concerned that Australia and New Zealand had not been consulted about the end of national service.[20] The First Lord of the Admiralty, Lord Hailsham – always prone to inject a note of hysteria into any debate – suggested that the end of national service would mean the break-up of NATO.[21]

From the political point of view, the case put by the forces was awkward. On the one hand, they insisted that they needed conscription but, on the other hand, they did not need all the young men who were liable to be recruited. They pushed for some form of selective service,[22] at a time when politicians knew that national service could survive only if the fiction of universal liability was maintained. Ministers grew exasperated by the insistence of the services that they would need conscription for the foreseeable future. Head admitted that selective service based on a ballot would be best from the point of view of the army but did not think it a 'tenable political position in the long run':

> [T]o take this course would be to admit that national service was with us in perpetuity as the only means by which the Services could be provided with the necessary technical assistance . . . unless the Services disciplined themselves by preparing for the end of national service, they would never let it come to an end.[23]

The case against conscription was usually stated in economic and/ or political terms: it was expensive and unpopular. MPs appreciated that their constituents – including 'highly respected citizens who are known to be moderate in their views'[24] – were against conscription, and party leaders understood the dangers of ignoring such sentiment. Anthony Eden, who became Prime Minister when Churchill retired in April 1955, told the Cabinet in December 1955 that he hoped national service could be ended 'during the lifetime of this parliament'. It illustrates the political delicacy of the subject that a civil servant did not record his remarks in the official minutes of the meeting.[25] The following year, Eden wrote to the Minister of Defence that he could see the military case for national service but did not think that it would be politically acceptable after 1958 unless international tension rose and that he did not think that selective service would be regarded as fair.[26]

In fact, there had been a change in conscription policy in October 1955. In a bid to reduce the rate at which men were called up, while preserving, at least ostensibly, the appearance of universal obligation, it had been decided to reduce the number of registrations from four to three per year. The result of this was that the age at which men were first registered rose by three months every year. In addition to this, there was to be an increasingly long wait between medical examination and the receipt of the enlistment notice.[27]

In the summer of 1956, a Cabinet committee was convened to discuss the future of national service. It was chaired by the Lord President of the Council, the fifth Marquess of Salisbury, a self-consciously unintellectual figure with right-wing opinions and a pronounced lisp. One suspects that his aunt, Gwendolen Cecil, might have been thinking of him when she wrote, in her biography of her father the third marquess, that the 'general mediocrity of intelligence which the family displayed was only varied by instances of quite exceptional stupidity'. Iain Macleod, the Minister of Labour and National Service, was very different: charming, subtle and famously described by Salisbury as 'too clever by half'. Macleod disliked 'conscription' – a word that he insisted on using instead of 'national service'.[28] He proposed that the maximum age of call-up should be lowered so that all deferred men (i.e. those who undertook apprenticeships or further education) would in effect be excused. Eighteen-year-old school leavers, of the kind who provided the army with many of its officers, would continue to serve, at least, as Macleod no doubt muttered *sotto voce*, if they were too naive to see the advantages of deferment.[29] In economic terms, Macleod's plan made sense because it would have spared all skilled workers. It was not, however, as Macleod quickly conceded, politically feasible, because it would not have been seen as fair and because, in any case, the surplus of young men registering was too high to be absorbed by excusing those who had been deferred.

The Salisbury Committee's report, presented to the Cabinet in January 1957, concluded that national service should not be regarded as 'permanent and essential' but that it would be needed until at least 1965 and that the relatively small number of men needed during this period should be chosen by ballot. Macleod dissented from the report because he thought that keeping a small number of conscripts would cause more trouble than it was worth.[30]

The Salisbury Report was extraordinary. The proposed date for ending national service was later than any of the provisional dates that officials and ministers had discussed during the previous six years – this was all the odder since Head, now Minister of Defence, seems to have acted as spokesman for the forces when he himself had previously complained about their reluctance to end conscription. The method proposed for selecting conscripts was the one favoured most by service chiefs but least by the electorate.

The committee's deliberations may have been influenced by the fact that they took place against the backdrop of the Suez crisis. Service chiefs were more powerful when the country was at war. Extra troops were needed during the operation. One civil servant claimed in November 1956 that 'a delay of at least a year had been imposed on the planned reduction of the Army'.[31] Officials were distracted from long-term planning and Eden, who had been pressing for an end to national service, was weakened.

In the medium term, however, Suez made an end to conscription more likely. This was partly because it exposed some of the fantasies on which British pretensions to military grandeur had been based. Of more immediate importance was the fact that it brought two particularly determined ministers to the fore. Conservatives under Eden had sometimes called for 'the firm smack of government': the armed forces were now to find out how firm government felt.

The first and most important man whose career advanced after Suez was Harold Macmillan. He became Prime Minister in January 1957, after Eden's resignation. Macmillan had fought with the Grenadier Guards during the First World War and still liked to play the guards officer. He cultivated a manner of ostentatious calm and patrician assurance. He also talked frequently about Britain's position as a great power. A national service naval officer expressed the conventional wisdom thus:

> Mr Macmillan is an efficient statesman and a man to inspire confidence. [He] gives me, and I have no doubt most other people also, complete confidence in his ability to negotiate the difficulties that lie ahead; he has taken the right step of putting the mind of the country at ease, by showing us in reassuring terms that Britain is not a fast fading power.[32]

Macmillan was in fact a clever, neurotic man. He had the long-term sense of historical change that sprang from a classical education and the short-term sense of Britain's military weakness, and dependence on America, that came from having served as pro-consul in the Mediterranean during the Second World War. He also had an instinct for seizing political advantage. More than any other politician of his generation, he seemed to evoke the Edwardian world of hierarchy, tradition, duty and national greatness; yet, more than any other politician of his generation, he understood the post-war world of consumerism, rising living standards, 'instrumental' voting by a prosperous working class that understood its own material interests and hard-headed diplomacy by American politicians, who understood theirs. Most of all, Macmillan wanted to ensure that the Conservatives took the initiative on national service before it began to damage them electorally and had expressed this desire even when he had been Minister of Defence in 1954.[33]

The second important figure was Duncan Sandys, appointed by Macmillan as Minister of Defence in January 1957. Sandys owed some of his political success to the fact that he had married one of Winston Churchill's daughters, though the marriage was breaking down by the late 1950s. He was a brusque, aggressive man who despised conventional pieties – some believed that he was the 'headless man' in the Duchess of Argyll divorce case. He wanted to maintain British imperial power but was not much moved by the traditions of the British armed forces. His relations with Macmillan – who described him as 'cassant' – were uneasy, though one assumes that the Prime Minister, a calculating man, found it convenient to have such a figure to impose his policies on the armed forces and to take the blame for the offence that they would inevitably cause. Certainly, Macmillan gave him greater powers than had been conferred on any previous Minister of Defence.

The main product of Sandys's tenure at Defence was the White Paper of 1957. The Sandys Review, as it became known, was drafted in breathless terms: 'It is now only a matter of a few years before there will be missiles steered by electronic brains capable of delivering megaton warheads over a range of 5,000 miles or more ... sensational scientific advances in methods of waging war have fundamentally altered the whole basis of world strategy.'[34] It also included some hardheaded statements. First, British power depended on an economy that was being undermined by excessive military spending. Secondly, Britain could no longer expect to fight a major war on its own. Thirdly, there was no real defence against nuclear weapons, and security must, therefore, depend on deterring war rather than planning to win it.

The Sandys review anticipated that the forces could be reduced to a total of 375,000 men – excluding, as the official documents sometimes put it, 'boys, women and Gurkhas'. Conscription was to be abolished. Sandys had taken a more direct and brutal approach to reductions in the armed forces than any previous Conservative minister had done. He had summoned the chiefs of staff in February 1957 and told them to plan for forces of 370,000 men. The chiefs responded, as official notes laconically record, by 'expressing serious concern' and Sandys reminded them of who made the decisions – stating that he 'had no desire to implicate the Chiefs of Staff in the government's decision to cut the armed forces'.[35] The Sandys review anticipated wider changes to the armed forces, which included a reduction in the number of regular soldiers.

Iain Macleod was very different from Sandys but, when it came to national service, the two men were functional allies. Macleod announced in April 1957 that men born after October 1939 were unlikely to be called up. It would, in fact, have been possible to cover all the remaining need for conscripts simply by relying on men born in the last quarter of 1938 or before, who had either been deferred or who were just about to register at the time that the abolition of national service was announced.[36] The government, however, did not want a cohort of conscripts entirely composed of deferred men, because it would have taken too many skilled and educated workers out of the civilian economy and because it would have made it difficult to respond to 'contingencies'. The Ministry of Labour, therefore, proposed, from April 1958, to divide the call-up lists into two – one for men who had been deferred and one for men who were registering for the first time. The last conscripts were drawn from a mixture of these two lists.[37] From the point of view of individual conscripts, this arrangement made it harder to predict whether or not they would be called up. The days in which every fit man knew that he would be registered around the age of eighteen and required to serve either then or three years later were over. By April 1959, there were 70,000 men (24,000 of whom had already been deferred) waiting for call-up or medical examination. At this stage, men coming off deferments could expect to wait four or five months before joining up; this period was expected to increase to six months by the end of 1959 and perhaps to nine months the year after. The complexity of the process did not hide the fact that the numbers being conscripted were falling: 'as the number of men in the A register [i.e. that for deferred men] grows, and the delay lengthens, it will become increasingly difficult to give information without also conveying that a man is not likely to be called up before the end of 1960'.[38]

Even when the political decision had been taken, ending national service was more easily said than done. Some Conservatives feared that they would be blamed if they did not succeed in ending conscription at a pre-announced time: 'if only a handful of men have to be conscripted after the end of 1960 we will be regarded as having failed'.[39] The Prime Minister himself was not sure that an all-regular force would be achieved by 1962.[40] The Labour MP George Wigg bet Sandys that he would not manage to attract enough regular recruits by the time that national service was abolished and, since Sandys and Wigg were both notably lacking in sportsmanship, they were still squabbling about who had won the bet in late 1961.[41]

The scale of the call-up changed during the late 1950s, partly as the Ministry of Labour sought to reduce the number of men being posted to the forces without admitting that there had been a change in policy. Workers in industries deemed to be of particular national importance were added to the list of men who were allowed to defer their service until the age at which they ceased to be liable, as were teachers with first- or second-class degrees.[42] Some men who had served apprenticeships were allowed to extend their training after formal qualification in ways that also made it increasingly unlikely that they would serve at all. Deferment on compassionate grounds was granted on more generous terms.

In 1959, the Ministry of Labour reduced the rate of medical examination to the 'lowest practicable level'.[43] There were, at one point in 1959, 62,000 men who had been born in 1937 and who were still waiting for medical examination. Most strikingly, the proportion of men who failed their medical rose; by 1959 it had reached a third.[44] Officials from the Ministry of Labour insisted that there had been no change of the medical standards applied and, indeed, that they investigated medical boards where failure rates seemed unusually high. It may have been that medical boards became more exigent without encouragement. It may also be that the armed forces were themselves applying stricter standards to men when they arrived at basic training units and the Ministry of Labour boards were simply seeking to ensure that they did not pass men who would be thrown out of the army after a few days.[45] Most of all, potential recruits themselves seem to have been increasingly ingenious and insistent when it came to drawing attention to 'past ailments' or 'minor aches' that might make them unfit for service.[46]

Even before the announcement that national service would be ended, some sensed that the call-up was not being applied with much zeal and that a determined man stood a good chance of avoiding it. As early as 1955, *The Times* argued that conscription was being abolished by stealth:

> Indefinite deferment [is] the Ministry of Labour's euphemism for exemption from national service . . . It only remains for the Ministry to bring out one of its handy careers booklets for those who do not wish to serve in the forces to mark the end of universal national service.[47]

The fate of the most educated men, who also tended to be the most socially privileged, was always a matter of particular concern to the great and the good. In 1956, the master of a Cambridge college made discreet enquiries about whether 'the most likely course was a gradual reduction or a complete wiping out' of conscription.[48]

The Secretary of the Careers and Appointments Board at Nottingham University wrote:

> Some of the more mathematically minded have been endeavouring to prove to their own satisfaction, if not yet perhaps to anyone else's, that the number of other less qualified and equally eligible young men, coupled with the slow rate at which the call-up is at present being implemented, makes it unlikely that their turn will ever come.[49]

20. Another lucky national serviceman: the playwright Michael Frayn (second right) displays a brisk military demeanour while playing cards with fellow Russianists.

21. The men behind *Private Eye* (founded in 1961) often claimed that their irreverent attitude to authority sprang from their experience of national service. One of those men, John Wells (third from left), is shown travelling to the Far East on the *Empire Orwell*. John Moore, later Secretary of State for Transport, is on the right. These men were officers – conditions for other ranks on troopships were less agreeable.

18. Cyprus: gunners with donkey.

19. A few lucky men had extraordinary experiences of national service. The photograph shows John Adair – the only national serviceman to serve with the Arab Legion.

16. Cyprus: two national servicemen in playful mood.

17. Cyprus: British forces sometimes behaved with brutality in colonial wars, but ordinary conscripts often thought of themselves as living on friendly terms with local populations.

15. Cyprus: a national serviceman with a Bren gun.

22. The *Empire Windrush* was mainly known to national servicemen as a troopship. It caught fire and sank off Algiers in 1954. One national serviceman, returning from Malaya, had a last unwelcome encounter with foreign food when he was served frogs' legs at a Foreign Legion barracks after his rescue.

23. The navy: a cook doing national service in the late 1940s.

24. The air force: the writer Gavin Lyall training on a Tiger Moth aircraft. Lyall later flew Meteor jets – though the increased sophistication of aircraft made it hard to train conscripts to fly. In spite of his own experiences, Lyall does not seem to have felt that national service was a very exciting topic. His wife, Katharine Whitehorn, wrote that the 1950s was in a 'damp patch between the battleground of the 40s and the playground of the 60s'.

25. Men mixed more easily in the units such as the Pay Corps than they did in, say, the guards. Here Richard Vaughan, the last national service officer, drinks with other ranks at a demob party.

26. A skiffle group of national servicemen play at Belfast barracks. The youth culture of the 1960s was just visible over the horizon as national service ended.

27. Demob.

The 'mathematically minded' students had a point, especially because graduates in scientific subjects were almost certain by this stage to be excused service. The treatment of science graduates reflected the way in which intentions to enforce a genuinely universal service had been abandoned even before the formal abolition of conscription. A Ministry of Labour report conceded that:

> The history of deferment arrangement for the next ten years is one of gradual whittling away of the original intention that science and engineering graduates should not be given special treatment where national service was concerned. The concept of universal national service as applicable to those graduates gradually receded into the background . . . In 1949 just under 100 graduates were granted indefinite deferment for employment on priority projects, and about 600 were called up. In 1959, which was the last year in which newly qualified graduates were called up, about 600 were made available for national service, and over 3,000 were granted indefinite deferment.[50]

The proportion of graduates among national servicemen had increased during the early 1950s as universities expanded. There were some reasons to suppose that it would increase even faster in the late 1950s – because intakes were increasingly dominated by men who had deferred their service, a category that included all graduates. In fact, the proportion of graduates reached 5 per cent in the autumn of 1955, but then declined to 3.3 per cent in the autumn of 1957, before increasing to 3.9 per cent in 1958 and 1959. If all other figures had remained constant, this would have meant that the chances that any individual graduate would be called up would have dropped by between a quarter and a third. However, other figures did not remain constant – the number of graduates increased while the total of all men called up dropped. The drop in the chances that any individual graduate would be called up was, therefore, sharper. Presumably, this was because the government now gave so many exemptions to educated men. By 1960, officials knew that only a small proportion of the 15,000 men who would graduate from university in that year, and who were still technically liable for national service, would be needed.[51] Finally, the government announced that no man whose deferment ended later than June 1960 would be called up – this meant in effect that most students who graduated in that year, and a large proportion of those who had completed some other form of training, were excused.

The educational and social background of national servicemen changed in interesting ways in the late 1950s. In the army, which took most men and measured education in the most systematic way, the proportion of men educated to eighteen or beyond increased until the end of 1954 and generally declined thereafter – though it rose again in 1958 and 1959. The proportion of graduates peaked, as has been shown, in 1955. The proportion of men who had left school at sixteen rose for most of the 1950s and peaked in the second half of 1958. The proportion of men in educational class 5 (i.e. those who left school at fifteen but had undertaken some further training) peaked at 37 per cent in the first half of 1960. At its very end, national service seems to have fallen particularly hard on the skilled working class.

There was one simple reason why the proportion of relatively privileged men in the national service intake dropped during the late 1950s. Men had the right to request early call-up if they wished to get their military service over in time to go to university. The right was most commonly invoked by men with places at the universities of Oxford and Cambridge. However, no one who reached the age of eighteen after September 1957 was liable for national service so, after this date, many of the most privileged young men had either already entered the forces or made a decision that they were going to try to avoid doing so.

There was also a broader social shift that affected national service. Military patriotism was one of those aspects of public school culture that grammar schools sometimes tried to imitate. By the late 1950s, however, the balance of power between grammar schools and public schools had changed. There were more children at grammar school than ever before and a higher proportion of them than ever before were getting to university. Clever sixth-formers began to wonder whether there was any reason to admire or imitate their contemporaries at more socially prestigious institutions. Claude Scott was a pupil at Emanuel School in south London from 1945 to 1955. In 1952–3, he resigned from the school's Combined Cadet Force. He was not a pacifist or even particularly left-wing – he just thought that square-bashing was a waste of time. There was a small scandal and Scott's parents were called into school to be warned that such subversive behaviour would ruin his career. He held firm and avoided the CCF, just as, because of educational deferment, he avoided national service.*

John Sainsbury (not a member of the grocery family) was from a similar background to Claude Scott's but a county scholarship had plucked him from Hitchin Grammar School and paid for him to go to Eton. Sainsbury was called up in 1957. Interested in military matters, he was keen to serve – though he was slightly annoyed to discover that all his old friends from grammar school had contrived to avoid service.[52]

For some boys from the grander public schools, military service began to seem pointless and one or two of them might have started to question whether some of the other pieties to which they had paid lip-service at school might also be open to question. A Winchester housemaster wrote in 1957 that his protégés no longer got anything from national service: 'The best of them will be positively encouraged to get exemptions and the others will feel that they're tail-enders and the Govt will dispense with their services if a pretext can be found for doing so. No spiritual kick at all and no fun either.'[53] Even regular officers now sometimes advised their sons to defer in the hope of avoiding call-up, and Oxbridge colleges, most of which had encouraged men to discharge their military obligations before coming up, were now preparing for a surge of eighteen-year-olds.

The uncertainty that surrounded the end of national service was a matter of morality as well as calculations about careers and educations. By the late 1950s, the culture of official patriotism that had once surrounded military service was increasingly questioned or mocked. The farce of Suez and the brutality of soldiers in Cyprus (more widely reported than that in Kenya or Malaya) both undermined the prestige of the military.

Things the British armed forces did not do could matter as much as things they did do. In October and November 1956, west Europeans

---

* In 2005, after a successful career in business, Scott became a governor of his old school – which had in the meantime abolished the CCF.

listened to the broadcasts from Budapest in which the Hungarians begged for help against Soviet invasion. Briefly, it seemed possible that Hungary would win its freedom. The more earnest kind of national serviceman was entranced. Waiting with his commando unit to go to Suez, Peter Mayo wrote in his diary: 'wonderful news from Hungary. The rebels appear to have won.'[54] One of David Lodge's characters, attending a pro-Hungarian demonstration, thinks for a glorious moment that he will put his national service training to good use by volunteering to fight with the Hungarians.[55] The Red Army, however, put the Hungarian rising down. The West did not lift a finger. There were sound reasons for the brutal realpolitik of NATO leaders, but their inaction made it harder to persuade idealistic nineteen-year-olds that the British armed forces existed to defend freedom. Antony Copley wrote in his diary, just before his ship arrived at Port Said: 'I am afraid Hungary will once again retreat into the night of despair. Can we risk the destruction of the world for their sake? I am all for peace and have not the self-sacrifice to support a policy of assistance to Hungary.'[56]

The result of running down national service was that the number of men being released began to exceed the number being called up. This, in turn, further diminished the need for men – because a larger proportion of servicemen were approaching the end of their service, when they were most useful, and because fewer men were diverted to train new intakes. From 1957, the forces began to institutionalize the practice of early release for men who were no longer needed. The navy and the air force were most keen to release men, partly because they had a relatively large number of regular recruits and partly because so many of their men performed specialized tasks and could not easily be transferred if the particular function for which they were trained ceased to be necessary. The army opposed early releases. It feared that they would undermine the whole principle of national service, which it still needed, and, knowing how many men preferred the air force or the navy, it was reluctant to countenance anything that might make these services seem even more attractive. However, a few hundred airmen and sailors were released early in the late 1950s, and by 1960 the army itself released men before their time was up. The policy was quite open – though the authorities were understandably reluctant to give it too much publicity.[57] The forces were probably glad to be rid of some of their delinquent conscripts. James O'Donoghue, the last of the Glaswegians who had given the services such trouble, did not report for duty until January 1961 and was put on a charge on his first day. He was discharged early after having spent his last months of duty tending an officer's garden – he celebrated his release by methodically putting weed killer on every plant.[58]

Setting a date for the end of call-up was awkward. No one wanted to be the last conscript. There was a danger that the whole system might come to an end 'in a most ragged and unsatisfactory manner',[59] if men knew the precise day on which it would cease to operate – especially since, as officials recognized, they would not have the resources to track down and prosecute evaders once the machinery of national service had been put in moth balls. In the summer of 1960, officials decided that the last men would join the forces on 17 November rather than at the end of the year: 'the object being to catch unawares the man at the end of the entry queue who thinks that the normal timing of call-up will be followed and that he has, therefore, time to take evasive action'.[60]

Ministry of Labour medical boards ceased to operate in July 1960 and staff at the Ministry were transferred to other duties after issuing the last enlistment notices on 3 November 1960. Throughout this time, however, the authorities sought to avoid explicit discussion of the end of national service.[61]

The Ministry of Defence planned a television programme to mark the end of national service. A major would go to Aldershot and watch the last 300 men arrive at their barracks. He would pick one likely looking candidate – 'Private Bloggs' in the television treatment – and take him back to London to be interviewed. Admiral Louis Mountbatten, Chief of the Defence Staff, would then make a speech about the value of the service performed by conscripts since 1939; the speech was to be recorded because Mountbatten had a dinner engagement on the night when Private Bloggs's comrades were beginning to polish their boots.[62] The Minister of Labour wrote sharply to the Minister of Defence:

I am very anxious that photographs should not be taken of the last National Servicemen to report for duty, for the reasons I explained to the Cabinet. These men will not be at all pleased to be the last to be called up. I should have thought that much the best course would be for propaganda on behalf of the services to concentrate on the new volunteers, rather than on the last conscripts.[63]

The last cohort of conscripts may have been spared publicity, but they understood that they were special. Recruits to the Pay Corps were cheered by their new comrades as they marched across the NAAFI on their first night in the army. The last men to be called up were exasperated by their bad luck – some reflected that a single bad result in the finals of their professional exams would have earned them a deferment and almost certainly complete escape from service. They were all in their early twenties. This meant that the wrench of being dragged away from civilian life was harder than it might have been for earlier conscripts – one recently married man went quickly absent without leave. However, there were also ways in which the last national servicemen had a relatively easy time. The fact that they had almost all undertaken some form of training or education, which had kept them out of the forces when they reached the age of eighteen, meant that they were more socially homogeneous and more civilized than those men who had been called up a few years earlier. They also appreciated that there were likely to be limits to the strictness of discipline now that conscription was winding down. The last squad in the Pay Corps were older than the regular lance corporal who was set to give them orders. Because they were mostly men with some education, a large proportion of them were considered as potential officers, but many said that they preferred to stay in the ranks.*

Richard Vaughan did go for a commission – on the grounds that 'if you can't beat them, join them'. His life as a second lieutenant in the Pay Corps was relatively agreeable. Posted to Salisbury, he was allowed to work in civilian clothes on some days of the week. After

---

* The proportion of highly educated men in the national service intake was actually dropping by this stage but it may be that the Pay Corps got more than its fair share of the educated.

three months, he was sent to Germany, where discipline was more 'regimental', but where he personally maintained friendly relations with the national servicemen under his command. The men called him 'sir' on the base, but he was on Christian name terms with them when he attended their parties.

Vaughan's most delicate task came in October 1962, when he was told that national service for the last few cohorts of men (about 9,000 of them in all) was to be extended for six months.[64] Some said that this was because of the construction of the Berlin Wall. Vaughan himself was told that it was simply because regular recruiting had not filled the army's requirements. It may be that the last national servicemen – being skilled men – were hard to replace with regulars or that the service chiefs, having argued against the abolition of conscription, wanted to make a point to the politicians. Vaughan did not relish the prospect of having to tell the national service other ranks, but it turned out that they already knew; as was often the case, news had travelled via barrack-room gossip faster than it was transmitted through official channels.

Vaughan was demobbed in May 1963, having risen to the rank of full lieutenant. He opted to be discharged in Britain rather than Germany, which meant that he travelled home in uniform on a plane full of his comrades who were already wearing civilian clothes. At Gatwick they were met by the press and Vaughan gave the first of many interviews. As a result of this, he arrived late at his regimental depot in Winchester and found that all the offices were shut. After a festive night out, he slept at the depot and was eating breakfast when the commanding officer summoned him and said that a car would take him to Southern Television, where he would be interviewed as the 'last national serviceman'. He never completed the normal paperwork of discharge and never returned his uniform, which, at the behest of journalists and television producers, he would squeeze into for many years to come.[65] Vaughan was not, in fact, the last man out: about fifty national servicemen remained in Germany until the end of May. These men, however, had all been detained for disciplinary or medical reasons and would not, one assumes, have provided a favourable account of their time in the army.[66] Since Vaughan was, and is, articulate and cheerful, it probably suited the War Office to have him defined as the last conscript.

National servicemen passed into oblivion quickly. For one thing, there were relatively few of them. Of men born in 1938, just over 147,000 had entered the forces, as either conscripts or volunteers, by 1960. However, most of these men would have joined their units in 1956 or 1957 and been out by the time the last men were called up in late 1960. Of men born in 1939, only 63,8000 had entered the armed forces by the time conscription ended. The machinery for dealing with national servicemen was being run down long before the last conscript received his call-up papers. By 1957, there were not enough national service officer cadets in the army to justify two schools to train them. Since the estate around Eaton Hall was unsuitable for the heavy machinery that was needed to train gunners and tank soldiers, it was decided that from April 1958 all officer training would take place at Mons. Field Marshal Montgomery, who had always brought his own unique brand of melancholy farce to national service, inspected a passing-out parade at Mons, in pouring rain, in August 1960. He said that 'he was very sorry that National Service was coming to an end . . . he did not agree with political leaders who said that the armed forces would get all the men that they needed. A cross section of the youth of Britain was needed in the armed forces.'[67] Montgomery gave the stick of honour for the best cadet to Peter Duffell, muttering, as he did so, '*I* never won it.'[68]

National service had weighed heavily on the public consciousness at a time when many families expected their own sons to be called up, but it almost disappeared from sight as soon as this threat passed – the angry letters in newspapers about the iniquities of the call-up ceased. The detailed histories of the last national servicemen dropped out of the collective memory of the Ministry of Labour. In 1976, when the Law Commission finally proposed to repeal the legislation of 1948 that had made the call-up possible, the Ministry suggested that the documents relating to post-war conscripts should be thrown away and added that 'the call-up ended in December 1960, with the result that whole term service effectively ceased at the end of 1962'.[69] The 9,000 men who had been held in the forces for an extra six months in 1963 had been forgotten.

For men born in the late 1930s, conscription was in an odd way more disruptive than it had been for their elders. Their late teenage years were overshadowed by uncertainty. Even men who had been registered and/or undergone their medical could not be sure when, or if, they would finally be called into the forces. Employers were under a legal obligation to give a man back his job after he returned from the forces, but, as the end of conscription approached, they were sometimes tempted to avoid employing men who looked likely to be called up – especially if they had a chequered employment record. This could create a vicious circle in which some men were increasingly reluctant to settle before national service and, at the same time, employers were increasingly reluctant to engage them. A Ministry of Labour official noted: 'Although very few employers dismiss men because they are waiting to be called up, they tend to be reluctant to engage a man with National Service liabilities who for one reason or another has lost his former job.'[70]

Leigh Parkes was born in June 1939 and left school (Haileybury) in 1956: 'national service was hanging over one's head and one did not really know what was happening, but when I left school I was under the impression that I was going to do two years national service'. He thought of teaching in a prep school and decided that it was not worth starting on a career. He began work in his family's lace company but 'I got fed up with not knowing what was happening, so I wrote to the army, asking them to make their mind up whether to call me up or not.' Two weeks later he was summoned for his medical.[71]

Philip Naylor illustrates the ways that national service could disrupt a boy's life. He was born in July 1939 and educated at a grammar school. He was, however, consigned to the 'C' stream and left early. He then went through a succession of apprenticeships while deferring his national service. However, 'By the spring of 1959 my enthusiasm for foundry work had fallen to zero ... despite the boss's reminder that I'd soon find myself in the Army.' He left but found it hard to find another job – 'the first question asked of a twenty-year-old was "Have you done your national service?"' He took a few temporary jobs and went hitch-hiking around Europe. Finally, fed up with the uncertainty, he decided 'to jump before I was pushed' and signed on as a regular in the Royal Engineers. Though his whole youth had been haunted by the prospect of conscription, he was among the very last men to have any legal liability, and could probably have avoided it altogether if he had waited.[72]

Sometimes, by the late 1950s, it seemed as though educated men were only called up if – through perversity, naivety or a sense of duty – they drew themselves to the attention of the authorities. Peter Duffell, born in August 1939, was not even registered until he was almost nineteen and then waited a further sixteen months without hearing anything. Finally, he wrote to *The Times* to complain,[73] and was promptly called up. Since he switched to a regular engagement and became a lieutenant general, he must have regarded this as a benign outcome; his twin brother, who was taken in the same intake, may have felt differently.

James Flynn was born in May 1939. He was a student at London University in 1959 and would almost certainly have succeeded in deferring his service until the abolition of conscription if he had not failed his exams. At this point he decided that he had an objection to some, but not all, wars. The tribunal rejected his appeal to be regis-tered as a conscientious objector in September 1959 on the grounds that he was not an unconditional opponent of all war. Flynn himself

> thought it desirable that I should be adequately trained should I ever consider it necessary to fight. I therefore attended the medical and expressed a preference for the infantry. I wished to go into the infantry as I felt that as an infantryman I would be responsible only for the action in which I was engaged: whereas in an administrative post or on general duties I would be responsible for the efficient running of the army and therefore for any action the army undertakes.[74]

The army, however, decided that Flynn was medically unfit for front-line service and posted him to the Ordnance Corps as a clerk. At this point Flynn 'refused to soldier' and stopped shaving, a serious offence in the army. He was eventually court-martialled. His appear-ance at the trial aroused amused comment in the press.[75] He was dressed in civilian clothes, bearded and to all appearances a 'beatnik', a word that already evoked a youth culture that would soon make men who had done military service seem staid. He was sentenced to six months in prison and went on hunger strike, which he abandoned when he was forcibly fed. After this, he disappeared from view – presumably the army was happy to get rid of him once his sentence had been served.

Though the last years of national service were uncomfortable for many conscripts, in some ways they were even worse for regulars, particularly for regular officers in the army. The tone of civil–military relations changed. When the first peacetime conscripts had been called up, the army still had some of the prestige that went with victory in the Second World War and with the military traditions of the empire. John Hoskyns was the son of a soldier killed at Dunkirk and joined up himself at the age of eighteen in 1945. He believed that the army was 'the only institution in Britain of which people did not feel slightly ashamed'.[76] This was never true but it was, at least, plausible enough for soldiers to convince themselves. In the late 1950s, however, the army itself became infected with self-doubt. Hoskyns resigned his commission in 1957 – he was one of the rare regular officers to make a successful career in the civilian world.

The end of national service was part of a broader change in the position of the armed forces that affected other democratic countries too. Missiles and nuclear bombs seemed to make conventional military skills redundant, and the wars of decolonization, particularly during their later stages, sometimes pitted soldiers against civilians. All of this was seen most dramatically in France, where conservative soldiers, who disliked the new kind of warfare, were labelled 'military Poujadists', and where their dissatisfaction produced the 'generals' putsch' of 1961 – an episode that divided conscript soldiers from regulars.

There was no military putsch in Britain, but the last national servicemen often knew that their own brief military careers coincided with an unhappy period for the army. Those who regarded themselves as defenders of the interests of the army had implied that peacetime conscription was a burden for the forces and looked forward to the day when well-trained, well-paid and dedicated professionals would comprise a lean, flexible and 'hard-hitting' army. At least in the short term, this did not happen, and the end of conscription went with an undignified period when middle-aged officers scrambled to hold on to their jobs.

The Sandys Defence Review, which had anticipated the end of national service, also shook up the organization of the army. The importance of the regimental system was challenged, which was a shock to soldiers who thought of regiments as being like families and who were, indeed, in many cases the sons of officers from their regiment. The end of national service also raised awkward questions about why the forces were so unattractive to regular recruits. The Grigg Committee – which looked into the matter in 1958 – portrayed an army that had become remote from civilian society and that was, in particular, rooted in the culture and hierarchy of public schools.[77] There was nothing that professional officers hated more than 'professionalization', which implied that tradition and unspoken codes were to be swept away by a new emphasis on expertise and formal training.

The changes of the late 1950s were all the more painful because the early part of the decade had been, in an odd way, the golden age of the British infantry. In Korea, Kenya and Malaya, small groups of soldiers had fought their enemy at close quarters. Old-fashioned virtues of courage and discipline counted for something when a single officer with a revolver in his hand might lead an attack. One man epitomized the qualities and traditions of the regular officer corps. Major Archibald Wavell came from a line of soldiers that could be traced back to the Norman Conquest. His father was a field marshal. Archibald Wavell himself, born in 1916, had been commissioned into the Black Watch in 1936. During the war, he served in Burma with the Chindits – winning the MC and losing his left hand. For a time, it seemed unlikely that he would ever fight again and, after the war, he was posted for a time to the Education Corps. Wishing, however, to return to active service, he secured a posting back to his old regiment in Kenya. Here he was killed leading a patrol that attacked a Mau Mau camp on Christmas Eve 1953. He was unmarried and the earldom that he had inherited from his father died with him – though it was clear that his death marked the end of a line in a more general sense.

During his time with the Education Corps, Wavell had commanded some of the most 'unsoldierly' soldiers in the army – almost all national servicemen. A lesser man might have taken out his frustrations on these conscripts, but Wavell was an unusual kind of officer. Scholarly and self-aware, he valued education. He befriended some of his soldiers and stayed in touch with them when they went to university.[78] Perhaps Wavell's death was just a piece of bad luck but, given how few British soldiers were killed fighting in Kenya, one wonders whether there was a degree of self-destruction in Wavell's decision to lead an attack on a Mau Mau camp. Perhaps he felt that the country had no place for a man such as himself or perhaps the war in Kenya was being fought in ways that offended his own notions of chivalry.*

A few years later some regular soldiers felt that the army they knew was being destroyed. General Sir Gerald Templer, the man given most credit for British success in Malaya, was Chief of the Imperial General Staff in 1957. He was said to have come to blows with the Minister of Defence over the proposed changes in the army and to have told Sandys: 'You're so bloody crooked that if you swallowed a nail you'd shit a corkscrew.'[79]

Large numbers of soldiers with years of service behind them were made redundant. The axe fell particularly on majors and senior NCOs. The Adjutant General drafted a letter of brisk condescension: 'As always, a younger generation is coming up to carry on the tasks and traditions that have been yours, and which will remain with those still carrying on.'[80] The last paragraph of this letter was changed after it was pointed out that around half of departing NCOs were under thirty-five and not pleased to be regarded as an 'older generation'. In fact, however, former NCOs did not do too badly in civilian life. Most of them were not proud. They were drawn mainly from the working class, often its least privileged sections. They were used to taking orders and enduring petty humiliations. Many sought comfortable jobs that required an air of authority but not much physical exertion – their presence in the porter's lodge of colleges at Oxford and Cambridge offered some middle-class men their last glimpse of military life.

Officers found things harder. They remained unemployed for longer

---

* The McLean enquiry into military brutality was hearing evidence on the day that Wavell died.

and were, initially at least, more reluctant to use the services of Labour Exchanges – in July 1957, 13.4 per cent of officers who left the army in the previous year were unemployed; the figure for other ranks was just 1.2 per cent.[81] Their difficulties became the subject of concern that was sometimes tempered by amusement. Macleod told the House of Commons in 1957 that officers were not as well informed as NCOs and that they were sometimes unrealistic: 'For example, in planning for the future an officer should obviously think not only of where he will live but of what he will do there. It does not follow that Camberley or Cheltenham are the best springboards for an industrial career.'[82]

Army careers had always ended awkwardly. Only a minority of officers – perhaps just one in four – made it past the rank of major. Those who could not hang on in the army were too old to adjust easily but too young, and in most cases too poor, to retire. Many officers had been born into army families. Sometimes they had spent their early years in some corner of the empire where their father had been garrisoned, before being packed off to prep school and then to one of the institutions – Cheltenham, Wellington, Marlborough – that specialized in educating the sons of officers. Few of them had skills that were of obvious use in the civilian world. Deprived of the clerical corporals who had so often provided them with discreet assistance, some would have had trouble in reconciling a set of accounts or writing a properly punctuated letter. Friends of the armed forces had been pointing out for some time that two years at Sandhurst and twenty years in the army did not necessarily make a man very employable in any post except 'bursar of a prep school or secretary of a golf club'.[83]

Leaving the army was particularly hard for officers in the late 1950s. For previous generations, the transition to civilian life had been made easier by the fact that there were, especially in the inter-war period, not many officers in total – so that relatively few men were chasing the kind of employment that might be available to them. Previous generations of officers had also sometimes had modest private means which, added to their army pension, allowed them to maintain the trappings of respectability in the kind of small town to which they usually retreated.

The men who left the army in the late 1950s found the move more painful. Income tax and death duties had eaten the family money that might once have supported them. Even before they retired, majors and lieutenant colonels were struggling to pay school fees – always a problem for men who had been brought up to regard state education as little better than the workhouse. The educational standards of officers, never glittering at the best of times, had declined since 1945, at a time when more civilians were well educated. Officers felt that they no longer enjoyed the mystique that might have attached to their predecessors in the days when the army was smaller and more socially privileged. Brigadier John Faviell, of the Conservative Research Department, was speaking for many of his former comrades when he wrote: 'Nor can the status of Regular officers and NCOs be raised, particularly in the Army, unless they cease to be regarded as individuals belonging to a bygone age, and as ordinary if not rather inferior State servants.'[84]

The Sandys Review hit a particular generation. Between the end of 1954 and the end of 1960, the total number of officers in the British army dropped almost a quarter (from 28,755 to 21,017). But this was not evenly spread across the age range. The number of those aged forty to forty-four dropped by just under a third (from 5,662 to 3,857); the number of those aged between thirty-five and thirty-nine dropped by over half (from 5,810 to 2,681).[85] These were men who had been commissioned between 1936 and 1945, when Britain still had a large empire. Most of those who were over forty would have passed through Sandhurst and Woolwich when these were still fee-paying institutions training 'gentlemen cadets'. Saddest of all, though, these men had once been real warriors. Even the youngest of them would have been in the army in time to see some action in the Second World War – probably in the brutal fighting between the Normandy landings and the fall of Berlin. The oldest would have served all through the war – young enough to be on the front line but old enough to exercise some modest degree of command. Men who spent the last years of their army careers shuffling paper had once led soldiers in battle. Some of them had been promoted quickly, at least in terms of acting rank, and then found that they were forced to drop in the hierarchy or see their progression frozen after 1945. Some had the heart-breaking experience of retiring with the same rank that they had first earned as a 28-year-old in Normandy or Burma.

Trevor Hart Dyke was slightly different from the run of officers who retired in 1958 – he was older than most of them, having been born in 1905, and he had reached the relatively high rank of brigadier, which meant that he could probably just about live on his pension for the remaining years of his life. His memoir, however, catches the melancholy that afflicted many officers. Born in British India – his father commanded a Baluchi regiment – he was educated at Marlborough and Sandhurst and 'always earmarked for a military career'. He was commissioned into the Queen's Royal Regiment and rose quickly during the war but then reverted to his substantive rank of lieutenant colonel. He finished his career in Berlin:

> By the time my three years in this post expired national service was abolished and any small prospect of promotion went by the board ... How fortunate one was to have served the Empire in its zenith, to have contributed to its victory in World War II, to have enjoyed at little expense, comradeship and sport in many lands, and above all, had the privilege of commanding four battalions in war or peace. But I sometimes envy those old comrades of mine who lie in so many lands and never lived to see the decline and fall of our great British Empire, which we were so proud to serve.[86]

What were such men to do? A few clung on in the army – often by accepting postings in non-combat corps that they would once have disdained. The Education Corps was entirely staffed by officers as national service ended, and this also opened up a few opportunities for regulars. Perhaps such men were just hoping for a few more years of pensionable service; perhaps they guessed that postings away from 'teeth arms' were more likely to give them skills that might be transferred to civilian life.

About 8,000 officers had to retire early between 1957 and 1962, in addition to the 17,000 who would have retired during that time in the normal course of events. Retirement for officers was concentrated in the period from 1958 to 1960. In spite of the emphasis that the army had sometimes placed on its roots among the landed gentry, few took up farming. About 15 per cent planned to go abroad, mostly to the white dominions. About the same number hoped to go into teaching, and the proportion of public school bursars who were ex-officers increased sharply in the 1960s.[87] Most sought careers in industry or commerce. They did not, however, seek to set up on their own account – a fact that the military authorities, perhaps aware of how unworldly many officers were, regarded with relief. Most took comparatively junior positions in large companies – often in personnel departments, where one suspects their style did not improve the quality of British industrial relations.[88] They rarely commanded high salaries in the civilian world. About 7 per cent of retired officers accepted salaries of less than £600 a year; about a third were paid between £600 and £800; just over a quarter managed more than £1,000. To put these figures in context, John Drummond, a former national service officer who joined the BBC as a graduate trainee, regarded £625 a year as a low starting salary.[89] Roy Strong, who began work at the National Portrait Gallery at the age of twenty-four in 1959, regarded a salary of £700 a year as 'near penury'. The 'affluent workers' in Luton car factories were generally earning over £1,000 a year by the early 1960s.

It was galling for a middle-aged major who felt that his whole life was behind him to share a mess with national service officers whose whole life was ahead of them and who relished the prospect of becoming civilians again. Imagine, for example, the feeling in the Royal Fusiliers – a regiment smart enough for its officers to resent menial civilian employment but not so smart that many of them would have large private incomes or family estates to fall back on. Two of the national service officers in the regiment – Anthony Howard and Michael Holroyd – must have aroused particular resentment among their older comrades. Both had a mixture of social polish and intelligence that would serve them well in civilian careers.

Holroyd played a small part in the post-Sandys defence cuts. After eighteen months in the army, he was made an acting captain – just one rank below that held by many men who had served for twenty years or more – and set, with another national service officer, to help decide which officers should be pensioned off:

Majors and colonels of all conditions would send us their forms giving reasons why they should stay or go. Sometimes they wrote in desperation, petitioning us not to fling them back into the civilian life they had never known; either that, or they would describe the joys of managing an egg farm in the Hebrides, a toy shop at Staines or their qualifications for taking the cloth. It was ironic that the breed of person who had made much of one's life so uncomfortable over the past two years should apparently (and to some degree literally) be at one's mercy.[90]

Howard was more sympathetic about the plight of the regular officers whose careers came to an end during the late 1950s. For him, ex-officers were the 'new unemployables': 'By next June [i.e. of 1958] some at least will have hung up their marching boots and have trodden in civilian shoes the down-hill road to a Bayswater third-floor back.' He reckoned that 7,400 majors stood 'no better than a 50 per cent chance of survival' and would recall the day when their father had advised them not to join the army. He urged generous pensions: 'even Victorian England realized that there were obligations towards old retainers'.[91]

For regular officers, one suspects, the pity of Howard would have been even more painful than the mockery of Holroyd. Men who had served for a quarter of a century and fought their way through a world war now found that they were being described as 'unemployable' by a man who had not even been born when they first joined the army and who had been an undergraduate at an age when some of them had been leading a company in battle. Most painfully of all, regular officers realized that their own fate was bound up with national service itself. They had complained about the paperwork and routine training that went with the continual admissions of new cohorts of conscripts but, in truth, that routine had itself become the *raison d'être* for many officers. Howard described the mess night of his regiment with a strangely elegiac disdain:

> Pointing a denunciatory finger at the ranks of flunkeys and lackeys the Commanding Officer demands to be told how, if those politicians succeed in getting rid of national service, all this will go on.
>
> At once the world seems lost; for the fact is, of course, that it won't. One of the things that twelve years of post-war national service has

done is to enable the professional army officer to keep himself in that state of life to which he has always been accustomed. Since 1945, the army has been enabled to live in the past by being offered every year a tribute of 120,000 men. Once that tribute is withdrawn it is difficult to see how the roulette ball will be kept rolling, the swords clanking and the beagles yapping. Without batmen to sweep up the broken glass, agricultural defaulters to repair the crushed rose bushes, fatigue men to clean down the drink-sodden cars, it is doubtful if the fun and games, the slap and the tickle would retain their traditional appeal. For the first time, in peace, the British army may soon have to face the terrible problem of living in the present.[92]

16

A Cold-blooded View

Let me have cold-blooded factual view.
Note by Winston Churchill asking his officials
for advice about national service, 1952[1]

To be cold-blooded about it, one should begin by saying that national service was never intended to have a benign effect on young men or on British society. It was an expedient designed to provide the forces with men at a time when it was hard to recruit regulars. Judged in these terms, it was a success. From the end of the Second World War to the late 1950s, most British servicemen were either conscripts or regulars of national service age on three-year engagements, who were widely regarded as conscripts in all but name.

Without these men, the British armed forces, and Britain's place in the world, would have been very different. It is hard to say whether the balance of power between the Soviet Union and the western alliance in Europe would have changed if Britain had had smaller forces. The American contribution to the western alliance overshadowed that of its allies, and in any case nuclear weapons overshadowed conventional forces. It is, however, certain that, without conscription, Britain could not simultaneously have kept forces in the Middle East, Africa and Asia, and could not have attempted to reanimate its empire after 1945. More generally, the sense that the British governing classes had that they were still presiding over a 'great power' owed much to their capacity to deploy conscripts. The decisions behind all this, however, were not entirely 'cold-blooded', and one effect of national service was to blur the focus of British strategic thinking and to prevent a clear audit of the resources to sustain a strategy.

There were really four different rationales for peacetime conscription. First, it was maintained because Britain needed to police areas that had fallen under its aegis during the last stages of the war. Second, it was maintained in order to train large numbers of reserve troops who could be deployed in a future conflict. Third, it was maintained to provide full-time soldiers who might be ready for immediate deployment. Finally, it was used to provide men who actually did serve in Britain's various wars of decolonization.

Like the owners of an ancient manor house, politicians and generals built on top of existing structures without completely demolishing them. Thus soldiers continued to be required for reserve training, even when national service was being justified mainly as a means of providing men for immediate deployment, and the use of national servicemen in colonial conflicts was an addition to, rather than a replacement for, the deployment of forces that might be ready to fight the Red Army in Europe.

The end of the Second World War left Britain with military commitments all over the world at a time when its capacity to pay for such commitments was particularly low. A cold-blooded analyst might have said that the solution to this was retrenchment, which would have included a quick withdrawal from colonies and a brutal appraisal of the forces that Britain could spare to support its allies. The ability to draw on conscript soldiers was one of the reasons why Britain was able to avoid such retrenchment – it is easier to deploy men if they cost only 28s a week and if the majority of them are too young to vote. British planners were not forced to present a realistic balance sheet of what their defence policy cost – such a balance sheet would have allowed, in particular, for the 300,000 fit young men who were taken out of the economy at any one time, during a period of labour shortage.

In the early 1950s, Britain spent around a tenth of its gross national product on defence. This was high when compared both to other periods of British peacetime history and to other democratic European countries of the time. It looks even higher when we remember that this was also the period when the effects of national service bit

most deeply and that, indeed, Britain was conscripting a larger proportion of its population than its allies.

The Macmillan governments of 1957 to 1963 did to some extent
rethink British defence policy and Britain's place in the world. The
decision to end national service was part of this rethinking. Iain
Macleod – the minister who most disliked conscription and also the one
who did most to dispose of Britain's remaining colonial possessions –
was the most radical proponent of change. At the other extreme was
Lord Salisbury – the minister who did most to resist the abolition of
conscription – who resigned from the government in 1957, ostensibly
in protest against the release of the Cypriot leader Archbishop Maka-
rios but in reality because of a more general disenchantment with
British retreat from world power.

There were, however, limits to the radicalism and extent of British
rethinking. As is frequently the case, this can be highlighted by comparing Britain with France. The French too rethought their place in
the world and in particular their defence policy between 1958 and
1962. Their rethinking produced the dramatic and, for many, painful
decision to abandon French Algeria.

The British transition was less dramatic. Withdrawal from Algeria
provoked mutiny, assassinations and executions. Macmillan's reforms
meant mainly that pensioned-off majors – forced out of the army by
the Sandys Defence Review – grumbled over their pink gins in golf
clubs. In some ways, the very success of the post-war British armed
forces concealed the extent of British decline. British soldiers left
Malaya and Kenya on their own terms and in their own time. There
was no single dramatic humiliation that forced the British to face
the fact that they were no longer a great power; even Suez could
be presented as an unfortunate mistake rather than a symptom of
something larger.

The end of national service was accompanied by other reductions in
defence commitments. Overall, however, conscription in the 1940s
and 50s had established a precedent that continued to influence British
defence policy. It was assumed that the armed forces should consume
a large share of British resources. Throughout the period from the
Second World War to the abolition of national service, the service chiefs
and their political allies used conscription as a bargaining chip – insisting

that its abolition would have to be accompanied by the provision of new resources in other areas. Not surprisingly, regular soldiers were particularly keen on raising regular pay. Simply reducing the defence budget across the board was ruled out.

The result of all this was that in the early 1960s, British spending on defence (as a proportion of gross national product) was only slightly smaller than that of France, which was fighting the Algerian War, and was larger than that of West Germany, which had the Red Army on its doorstep. The simple fact of conscription was not what set Britain apart – most countries in continental Europe had it and, indeed, retained it for longer than Britain. The important point was that Britain's relatively brief resort to conscription took place at precisely the time when relative economic decline might have been expected to make governments aware of their reduced capacity to act as a great power.

In one sense, conscription was just one aspect of a British illusion of great power status – an illusion that few people outside Britain, and perhaps few people outside the British governing classes, believed in or cared about. However, the prospect that Britain's rulers could have adjusted to a more modest position in the world after 1945 is itself fanciful. The British empire had created a political culture that took 'greatness' for granted and victory in the Second World War had reinforced this, even as it eroded the resources with which great power might be supported. Leaders of both political parties shared this culture as did most of the officials who advised them.

Oliver Franks – wartime civil servant, British ambassador to Washington and one of the men behind the foundation of NATO – summed up this kind of thinking in his Reith Lectures of 1954:

> There are some who suggest that the future of Britain lies in making a break with the past and giving up the traditions of greatness. The thing to do is to withdraw from world affairs and lead a quiet life on our island, democratic, contented and reasonably industrious. This is impossible. Geography and history alike forbid it. For us there is no middle way. Nor do most of us really think there is, except in the world of make-believe.[2]

*

Policies designed to secure Britain's military power were, in fact, part of the post-war 'consensus'; indeed 'consensus' – a word most commonly applied to welfare or economic policy – exercised the greatest influence over foreign policy and defence. National service was part of this consensus. It was to a large extent discussed outside the arena of party politics, or at least outside the arena in which the major parties confronted each other. Some Labour left-wingers opposed it and almost all Tories supported it, but the matter was never the object of a straight conflict between the two parties. Indeed it was a Labour government that established national service and a Conservative one that abolished it. Consensus did not mean complete harmony. The parties jostled to see who could extract electoral advantage from the issue, even when they did not come into direct conflict. There were also disagreements that pitted service chiefs against civilians and officials from different ministries against each other. The Ministry of Defence, concerned with what it perceived as military efficiency, was frequently at odds with the Ministry of Labour, concerned that conscription should seem as fair as possible. The disagreements about national service were, however, usually resolved in the private corners of English public life. The making of policy with regard to national service illustrated the propensity of the great and the good to exercise subtle influence. In 1955, Henry Fairlie popularized the term 'Establishment' to describe 'the whole matrix of official and social relations within which power is exercised'. The management of national service illustrates the operation of this matrix. Bishops, professors, heads of Oxbridge colleges and public school housemasters proffered advice and sought inside information.

Industry, or at least a certain kind of industry, fitted into the national service consensus. Large employers – especially those that were state-owned or that derived much of their business from state contracts – found conscription relatively easy to deal with. Some of them continued to make pension contributions – even occasionally to pay money – to employees who were in the forces.[3] Often it seemed that large companies, agencies of the state and business associations all involved similar kinds of people who were united by a shared social and political vision as much as by the pursuit of economic interests. This unity of vision was exemplified by the British Association for

Commercial and Industrial Education, run by Major Scott, which often discussed national service. One group, however, were conspicuously excluded from this world. Official inquiries paid almost no attention to the interests of small businesses and particularly not to the self-employed or the proprietors of family businesses, men who could sometimes have their enterprises destroyed by a call-up notice.[4]

Organized labour became an important, if sometimes junior, partner in post-war consensus politics. Trade union leaders were consulted about national service – their influence was particularly important during the Attlee governments of 1945 to 1951. After 1951, there was less direct consultation, but even Conservative ministers tried not to offend the unions and recognized that, for example, the training of conscripts in new trades could not be undertaken against their opposition. Theoretically, men of national service age working in industries – such as coal-mining – that conferred effective exemption from national service would be called up if they went on strike but, in practice, the authorities avoided anything that might look like 'industrial conscription'.[5]

Trade unions, understandably, focused on the impact that conscription had on their own members and this meant that they devoted most energy to the effects it had on adult men. The shipbuilders' union, for example, agreed to allow more apprenticeships in their industry, thus increasing the pool of skilled labour, only if their employers pressed the government for deferment of national service for those workers who were already qualified.[6] For some young men – trying to negotiate the passage, via apprenticeship, into the tightly regulated world of skilled work – it could feel as though their employers, their union and the armed forces were just different faces of the same leviathan of adult authority.[7] Generally, trade unions began to turn against conscription in the 1950s but their turn was probably less sharp than that of the political left generally.[8] Those who called for outright abolition of national service in the mid 1950s believed that most members of the Labour party supported their cause but that it was impeded by the power of the trade union block vote.[9]

Bringing national service into the picture of post-war consensus makes it seem less benign. Civil servants, politicians and trade unionists may all have consented in the making of policy, but young men conspicuously did not consent to be called up. Some men had tolerable, even enjoyable, experiences of national service and this may have disposed them to look on the post-war consensus favourably.[10] However, for many, their most important contact with 'the state' came through the drill sergeant rather than the National Health Service.

The political framework of their military service was opaque to most conscripts, partly because the regular officers, who exercised immediate control over their lives, often regarded civilians, even Conservative politicians, with disdain and sometimes espoused ferociously right-wing opinions.[11] The armed forces, the army especially, were intrinsically political institutions. Their primary purpose was to fight Communism, and many officers considered that one of the army's potential functions was to suppress internal unrest and, if necessary, to break strikes,[12] which, indeed, they occasionally did.[13]

In spite of this, officials and politicians insisted that open political propaganda must not be directed at conscripts. The chairman of the Army Education Advisory Board said any publication addressed to conscripts should 'keep within the Army's constitutional limits' and not be a 'political or anti-Communist tract'.[14] In March 1953, the Director of Public Prosecutions was asked whether an offence had been committed when men registering for national service were handed a pamphlet entitled 'Cut the Call-up'. Since the men concerned were not yet servicemen and since they were being asked to petition for a reduction in service rather than refuse to serve, the answer to this question was 'no'. The DPP added that the pamphlet was a 'mild and perfectly legitimate form of protest'.[15]

It would be naive to suppose that servicemen, in any country or at any time, share a clear view of the political structure in which they are meant to fit. Post-war conscription in Britain, however, posed particular problems. During the Second World War, servicemen had at least known the enemy that they were meant to be fighting. Some of them probably understood their struggle as part of a broader fight against fascism and perhaps as a means to build a new social order at home. Post-war conscripts, by contrast, were required to serve in forces that were fighting, or preparing for, several different conflicts at the same time. The Communist guerrillas in Malaya were different from the soldiers of Communist North Korea and both were different from the nationalists in Kenya or Cyprus – the latter were strongly anti-Communist. Men who considered registering as conscientious objectors were in an awkward position because so many of them objected to some, but not all, of the uses to which the armed forces were being put. Some national servicemen seem to have thought about the political significance of their actions – at Suez or in Malaya – only years after the event.

Most national servicemen had grown up in a period when there were no great ideological divisions, in Britain at least. They were mostly young and the forces provided them with little in the way of political education. Many of them went overseas without having much idea of what they were being sent to defend. Leslie Ives remembered two lectures on the troopship taking him to Malaya. One, inevitably, was about VD. The other

> seemed to imply that we were leaving good old England at exactly the right time, as general conditions and austerity measures were going to worsen there. A great deal of political unrest was forecast and the prophecy was made that we might never recover our pre-war influence and standing in the world.

Years later, Ives recalled that the political lecture was 'still a puzzle in terms of what impact it was supposed to have on us'.[16] The one group of men with a clear understanding of why they were doing national service were Communists, who had been told that their 'duty was to become a conscript and spread the gospel of peace, brotherhood and socialism among working-class conscripts'.[17]

The political significance of national service was rendered all the more intangible by the fact that most conscripts never fought and that one conflict for which they were supposedly being prepared was so terrible as to be almost unthinkable. War with the Soviet Union – what military planners sometimes referred to as the 'great war' rather than the 'cold war' – would have meant the use of atomic weapons. By the spring of 1955, a committee set up to consider the matter concluded that a single megaton bomb would wipe out any British city except London; ten such bombs would kill half the British population.[18]

Some conscripts were trained to deal with the aftermath of nuclear attack,[19] but the training was so strange that it often made the prospect of nuclear war seem more remote. Some conscientious objectors cited nuclear war as their reason for refusing to serve, but systematic opposition to British nuclear weapons began only in the late 1950s, as national service was ending. A few conscripts dipped their toes into the anti-militarist culture that was beginning to develop but they rarely associated this with any broader reflection on their own military role: one supported CND during his leaves but was a well-behaved sergeant when he was in uniform.[20] Some of those who joined the anti-nuclear Aldermaston marches had served in the British armed forces without apparent disquiet. The majority of servicemen seem hardly to have thought about the matter. Bernard Palmer said that his duties as an officer in the 'queasy post-Hiroshima' days of the late 1940s never made war seem 'more than a remote lark'.[21]

The fact that all-out war would have been so destructive, and so unlike anything that had gone before, also made it seem unreal. The Royal Engineers managed, by burning large amounts of oil, to contrive a plausible mushroom cloud that hung over one exercise in North Germany. The local population viewed it with understandable alarm but British soldiers were amused.[22] War 'games' did indeed seem to be almost 'playful'. When an officer asked one man what side he had been on during a war game, he replied: 'The winning side, of course.'[23] Practising for war could expose the absurd routines of a peacetime army. A national service NCO in Germany was charged with destroying secret documents if the Russians attacked. During an exercise, he tore open an envelope marked 'secret' and found details for the birthday party of an officer's son.[24]

Army officers introducing themselves to conscripts were advised to tell them the British preferred the term 'national service' to 'conscription': 'because that is what it is – service to the Nation. Each national serviceman contributes towards giving the Nation a strong and efficient army.'[25] Judged in an international perspective, however, the most striking thing about national service is that it was not actually very national. Unlike Third Republic France or Imperial Germany, the British state never tried to instil patriotism through conscription. The military authorities were reluctant to call up those from, as a War

Office report put it, 'a social group that is poorly integrated in the Nation. For example barrow boys, Gipsies, the racing community, Liverpool Irish, foreign communities in London, the Glasgow Communities from which the "gangs" are recruited etc.'[26]

Conscription was never applied in the part of the United Kingdom where the largest number of people were likely not to feel themselves British: Northern Ireland. In Scotland and Wales, there was a small amount of overtly nationalistic opposition to fighting for a 'foreign' government. More important was a general sense that conscription did not fit with the social structure of either Wales or Scotland – though Welsh dislike for the armed forces, rooted in chapel-going respectability, was very different from the antipathy to army discipline that was associated with some working-class Scotsmen. Sometimes the single word that aroused most terror in the War Office was 'Glasgow'.

National service raised questions about what the word 'national' might mean in Britain. Many conscripts conceived their identity in largely regional terms and the importance of 'county' regiments probably increased this propensity. However, Britain was a small and relatively homogeneous country and few national servicemen, at least among those from England, thought of their regional identities as being at odds with their national one.

In formal terms, the loyalty of the services was to the sovereign rather than to a nation. Monarchy became intertwined with the lives of some conscripts because George VI died in 1952. Geoffrey Barnes recalled hearing the news in the Malayan jungle. His radio operator crept up and muttered: 'King's dead.' He thought at first that this meant Sergeant King of his own regiment. When he understood, he gathered his platoon and toasted the new queen with 'dark army rum'.[27] Men were pulled out of their units to attend the coronation of Elizabeth II in 1953. The East Yorkshire Regiment put its representatives for the coronation parade on a boat at Singapore. They spent four weeks at sea, followed by six weeks drilling in preparation for the day, then four more weeks on the boat back to Singapore.[28] In Korea, soldiers fired salvoes of shells containing red, white and blue smoke before sitting down to eat ice cream provided by the Americans. For some officers in the Household Division, the coronation was the most significant event of their post-1945 military careers. A national serviceman in the Life Guards stationed in Germany reckoned that two thirds of the regiment had been sent back for the coronation.[29]

Not many national servicemen were republicans, but many felt that there was something odd about the emphasis on archaic ceremonial that they associated with the forces. Asked how he felt about fighting for crown and country in Korea, Jim Laird said: 'The Crown didn't come into it – when the Bull stopped – only survival, and possibly anger.' He was flown back to a British military hospital in June 1953 – arriving to find the nurses absorbed in watching the coronation on their 'new, miracle television sets'. Laird had suffered wounds that would leave him paralysed from the chest down.[30]

Some have justified national service on the grounds that it produced social benefits: that it made men better disciplined, more mature or better able to mix with others. Such arguments had a powerful appeal. Arnold Wesker wrote a bitter play about his national service, but forty years later was gripped by a 'dark, heretical suspicion that conscription kept crime and violence to acceptable levels'.[31]

The argument that national service had social benefits is, however, usually a retrospective one. At the time, many commentators believed that such social effects as it had were negative: that it increased instability and juvenile delinquency among boys before they were called up and encouraged them to waste time while they served. The young men whose behaviour was 'best' from the authorities' point of view – i.e. those who stayed in the same job, completed apprenticeships, undertook further education – were usually most hostile to the call-up. Those men who might have been 'improved' by service, such as illiterates or juvenile delinquents, were often excluded from conscription – usually on 'medical' grounds – or put in special units. Furthermore, national service was necessary, at least in part, because the services found it hard to recruit regulars and because those men who did volunteer for service were often poor and badly educated. Far from being an institution that took 'bad lads' and exposed them to the brisk regularity of military life, national service often took 'good boys' and exposed them to a world of profanity, petty crime and almost pathological enthusiasm to avoid hard work.

National service did not create a more homogeneous and disciplined society – on the contrary, it worked partly because Britain, mainland Britain at least, was already relatively homogeneous and disciplined. Changes in British society in the 1960s would have made it increasingly difficult to call men up, even if the government had wished to do so. Would that substantial group of men of Irish origin living in mainland Britain have been called up during the Northern Irish Troubles? What would the forces have done about non-white immigrants? Black Britons were not excluded from national service but, given how rare such men were, it is significant that they were quite common among those that officers regarded as 'difficult'. The British army recruited 2,000 West Indians in 1960, partly to make good the shortfall that sprang from the imminent end of national service. However, the authorities decided that 'coloured' soldiers should not make up more than 2 per cent of the strength in any corps.[32]

The most enduring myth of national service is that it mixed men from different social classes. Richard Pole remarked that national service introduced him to 'a wonderful cross section' of society. Pole's account of his own service was self-deprecating but his use of the term 'cross section' seems to have involved no deliberate irony. This is striking because he was an officer in the Coldstream Guards – a regiment that separated potential officers and other ranks from the first day of their service. Like many officers in the regiment, he was an Etonian. His father, uncle, grandfather and father-in-law had all been Coldstream officers, as had the men who married both his sisters.[33]

Sometimes, social class impinged on the workings of conscription in farcical ways. When Iain Macleod proposed measures that would in effect have excluded skilled workers from the call-up, he worried that this might provoke objections from the unions that represented the unskilled, but other ministers were concerned for a different reason. They feared that it would produce a lost generation of latter-day Raymond Asquiths and Julian Grenfells as upper-class boys died heroically at the front while the working classes skulked in their factories:

> There was a danger that if men were granted deferment from national service on grounds of technical skill and usefulness to industry the

future Reservists would include a large proportion of the future governing class of the country and if there were to be another war this would lead to the same destruction of the country's elite as there was after 1914.[34]

The survival of rigid class distinctions in the armed forces, the army especially, was striking because civilian society was more mobile in the decades after 1945. This mobility was associated with the Butler Education Act of 1944 and with an increased sense that social position ought to be determined by 'intelligence', which was held to be susceptible to scientific measurement, rather than by birth or by those qualities – accent, manners and access to powerful patrons – that might be associated with birth. Grammar school boys never fitted neatly into the armed forces. Indeed, a report of 1958 into how the army might recruit more regulars as national service ended suggested that a new rank be created for men who had left grammar schools at the age of sixteen or seventeen because such men did not have much in common with either officers or privates: 'The Services should study the possibility of creating an entry (other than as an officer) which will give grammar school boys who hold the General Certificate of Education at Ordinary level suitable status, remuneration, and employment.'[35]

One should not overstate the mobility of post-war British society, but there was at least a chance that a bright boy from a relatively humble background could – with hard work and a great deal of luck – conquer the commanding heights of the British ruling class. He might become an ambassador or a Chancery QC. The only area that was entirely closed to him was the officers' mess of a smart regiment. A boy born into a modest background in 1935 stood a better chance of becoming a cabinet minister than a second lieutenant in the Grenadier Guards.

Some men resented the social exclusivity of the forces and contrasted it with the 'meritocratic' values that they believed to govern their civilian lives. The word 'meritocracy' was coined in 1958 by Michael Young to describe the generation of people produced by the grammar schools who believed that 'IQ + effort = achievement'. Young did not regard meritocracy as a good thing. On the contrary, he thought that distinctions rooted in apparently objective measurement of ability would be more insidious than ones based on ancestry or inheritance. Some national servicemen, however, used the term as one of approbation. In an autobiographical afterword to his national service novel, David Lodge wrote:

> The rising meritocrats produced by free grammar schools and free university education were apt to find that the old-boy network, the lines of power and influence that connected London, Oxbridge and the public schools, the possession of the right accent, manners and style, still protected the interests of the hereditary upper-middle class. Nowhere was this more evident than in the peacetime Army.[36]

Karl Miller also presented the army in opposition to the meritocracy of the scholarship-boy educational elite from which he came: 'it was apparent that the Army was something other than meritocratic, or at any rate that authority rested ... on a highly specialized conception of merit'.[37]

The notion that the armed forces had an entirely rigid social structure should, however, be qualified in three ways. First, the social categories of civilian life were never absent from the forces and they were especially visible during national service. Peter Burke referred to the multiplicity of hierarchies that he encountered when – as a lance corporal who had already won a scholarship to Oxford – he was posted to a locally recruited regiment in Singapore. He found himself 'at the bottom of the rank hierarchy but at the top of the educational and race hierarchy'.[38]

Even those at the top of the various hierarchies understood that their positions were complicated. Inherited privilege and the academic skills that were valued by meritocrats were not mutually exclusive, and one effect of national service was to take academically clever boys from privileged backgrounds into the officers' mess. Simon Raven remarked that regular and national service officers in his own moderately smart regiment could be distinguished by the fact that the former judged men by what (public) school they had attended while the latter judged men by what (Oxbridge) college they were due to attend. No institution in Britain illustrated the celebration of undergraduate cleverness better than the television programme *University Challenge* (which was first screened in 1962). Its presenter, Bamber Gascoigne, was a meritocrat – he had won scholarships to Eton, Cambridge and Yale – but also a member of a privileged family, with especially close links to the Grenadier Guards, the regiment in which he performed his national service.

Secondly, the officer corps was not completely homogeneous or immutable. The smartest regiments always drew their officers from a small social pool, but things were different in the Pay Corps or the air force. Officer recruitment in the army changed over time: it had been more 'democratic' during the war and it became more democratic again during the 1950s – partly because of the need to ensure that there were enough officers for the Territorial Army in the industrial north and partly because the number of men with the educational qualifications to be officers increased.

Thirdly, an emphasis on the distinctions between officers and other ranks – or even between the social status of officers in different kinds of regiments – can be deceptive because it implies that this was the only way in which social class counted for national servicemen. In reality, class pervaded all aspects of national service. It even partly accounted for the fact that Quakers, usually middle class, were better treated than Jehovah's Witnesses, often working class, when they applied to be recognized as conscientious objectors.

The separation of officers from other ranks mattered for those men who had some reason to suppose that they might be officers or whose educational or social background gave them reason to feel that they might be the equal of officers. The men who talked most about 'class', and certainly the ones who did so in the most resentful terms, were often lower-middle class rather than working class. This was related to both educational change, which opened up the possibility of social ascension, and military service, which often marked the limits of that ascension. Social hierarchies are most visible for those who regard them as least 'natural', but they exercise most power over those who accept them as a fact of life. It is also notable that lower-middle-class authors were often conscious of their disadvantages – relative to the officer class – but rarely conscious of the ways in which, say, a pay corporal might be privileged in relation to most soldiers.

Sometimes, the picturesque manifestations of class that were associated with officer status in smart regiments obscured the more mundane ways in which class structured the lives of most conscripts. Consider, for example, RAF Hednesford. Because, in the early 1950s, all airmen with the educational qualifications to become officers (regardless of whether or not they were really likely to be commissioned) were concentrated at this one camp, most of the recruits who did their basic training there would have belonged to that section of the population (about a fifth of it) that had been educated at grammar schools until at least the age of sixteen. Some of the men who passed through this camp had a particularly acute understanding of the British class system.[39] One of these was a sociologist, who, in an autobiographical essay on his national service, gave Hednesford the name of Goldthorpe, after a leading sociologist of class.[40] However, men who were trained at Hednesford usually thought in terms of their own exclusion from more privileged classes – they said relatively little about the social homogeneity of their own milieu in training or the privileges that they might have enjoyed relative to less well-educated recruits.

For most servicemen, officers lived on the far side of an impassable frontier. Distinctions among other ranks, on the other hand, could be important. The formal measurement of intelligence and academic ability did not always divide officers from other ranks – and certainly did not divide officers in smart regiments from those in more humble ones – but it did frequently divide different kinds of non-commissioned servicemen from each other. Indeed, some officers were explicit about the distinction between the qualitative tests, which should be applied to the kind of men who might become officers, and the more scientific measurements, which might be used for those who were lower down the social scale: 'Let us keep the psychiatrist on this valuable work of sorting out the men in the mass, but let us continue to put our faith on the experienced regimental officer for the selection of candidates for both temporary and regular commissions.'[41] The tests administered at Ministry of Labour medicals determined whether men would serve in the RAF or the army – men who had sat the 11-plus had by this time come to recognize the puzzles, like 'Chinese ideograms',[42] of an intelligence test. The testing of intelligence and education level in the forces was even more extensive than that conducted as part of the

11-plus and this helped to change educational policy in Britain. In 1959, the Crowther Report on education concluded – largely on the basis of information about national servicemen – that a substantial number of intelligent boys had not attended grammar school, and this contributed to a move towards 'comprehensive' education.

Most of all, the forces were meritocratic, in a brutal way, to their least privileged recruits. 'Scientific' measurement of intelligence certainly mattered when it came to men who had fewest choices about their military careers. Anyone who scored low on intelligence tests or fell into the lowest educational category was likely to be assigned to the army, likely to be assigned to one of the least popular corps and likely to be given 'general duties' rather than a particular trade. One entire corps – the Pioneers – was kept largely for men who scored lowest on intelligence tests. Indeed, Young's definition of 'meritocracy' referred to the army:

> The flower of that experiment of the 1940s was the Pioneer Corps. When this indispensable body of hewers and drawers was confined to men with IQs below the line required to get them into the Intelligence Corps, the rise in efficiency was spectacular. The morale of these dull-witted men was better. They were no longer daunted by having superior people to compete with.[43]

Young's laboured satire was not far from the tone of real War Office reports:

> National service intakes include an appreciable proportion of men who are sub-standard mentally. For political and other reasons, they cannot be excluded from the call-up. These men are generally unhappy in units of arms other than the Royal Pioneer Corps, since they tend to be relegated to fatigues and other dull duties and their morale suffers. They can, however, develop a very high standard of morale and self-respect if kept together and are capable of a high output of useful if elementary work.[44]

The closing stages of national service coincided with other social changes that appear at first glance to be at odds with each other. On the one hand, this period saw what might be called the death of the British *ancien régime*. Life peers began to dilute the power of hereditary aristocrats in 1958, which was also the last year in which debutantes were 'presented' at court. The clubbable world of the City of London was shaken by the first 'hostile take-over'.

On the other hand, this was also a time when certain kinds of social privilege seemed more secure than ever before. The Conservatives won an electoral victory in 1959, partly because they had promised to end national service. In 1945 Evelyn Waugh had published his elegy for a dead social system, *Brideshead Revisited*. Conscripts read it with amused interest: Peter Nichols entitled the section of his diary dealing with his return from Malaya on the lower deck of a troopship 'Bulkhead revisited'.[45] In 1959, Waugh published a second edition of his novel, but this time he believed that he had been burying an 'empty coffin'. One assumes that part of Waugh's optimism sprang from the fact that his son was performing national service in the Household Cavalry, where he was relieved to find that 'the toffs were still on top'.

There were broader reasons for the British upper-middle class to feel secure in the late 1950s. The truth is that the new world of meritocratic modernity and the old world of inherited privilege were not mutually exclusive. Indeed, the decline of some of the more colourful and obviously archaic aspects of the British class system concealed the degree to which class divisions survived. The end of national service did not end blatant inherited privilege in the armed forces (or at least in the most socially prestigious regiments of the army) but it did mean that the majority of men no longer had to have any contact with that world of blatant privilege. It may also be that their brief contact with such a world actually strengthened the belief of many men that their own privileges – earned through educational achievement – were deserved and in keeping with the 'classless' society that some discerned in the 1960s.

What difference did national service make to individual men? It was intended to make as little as possible. The authorities expected that men would simply go back to whatever they were doing before and employers were required to hold jobs open. The men born in the 1930s usually valued job security – perhaps because of what they knew about the experiences of their fathers – and few of them were prone to take risks. About three quarters of national servicemen went back to their previous jobs.[46] A draughtsman returned to his desk to find that his possessions were still in the drawer where he had left them two years previously.[47] A journalist reported on the men of one infantry regiment:

> It is an odd interlude in a man's life. Take Private Don Bangs. A year ago Bangs was a barrow boy with a pitch in Kentish Town Road, NW and in another year he will be a barrow boy again. Yet in the meantime he is living in a camp with a monkey and six headhunters and spending his time stalking Chinese bandits in Malaya.[48]

Whether national service made much difference to the long-term career of the average conscript is hard to say. It interrupted careers and took men away from civilian work and/or training for around two years. In general, the national servicemen who anticipated changing their professions after their service aimed to move up the social scale – though the social scale itself was changing in ways that made clerical work less attractive. Men who had done unskilled, semi-skilled or clerical jobs often anticipated doing something different when they left the forces; large numbers of men hoped to move into skilled work. The group who anticipated obtaining 'professional or managerial' jobs was smaller – though it was higher than the proportion of recruits whose fathers had held such jobs.[49]

On the whole, the men who were called up between 1945 and 1960 did relatively well in financial terms. They benefited from economic expansion – the British economy did grow even if it did so less quickly than those of some of Britain's rivals – and full employment. It also seems likely that they benefited from the low birth rates of the 1930s – there is more 'room at the top' if there are fewer men to fill it.

The question is not whether conscripts – or the British economy – did well or badly but whether they did better or worse than they would have done if there had been no conscription. There can be no definitive answer here,[50] but there is some suggestive evidence. First, towards the end of national service, relatively few men were called up. When they came out of the forces, they had to compete with those slightly younger than themselves who had not been called up, or with their own contemporaries who had avoided the draft through educational deferments. There is little evidence that former conscripts felt that their military experience was an advantage in these circumstances – rather the contrary: 'the older National Service Man was regarded as being "tainted" when in competition with younger men who had escaped service'.[51]

Secondly, students of social mobility have concluded that it improved during the post-war period but that it improved most dramatically for those born in the 1940s rather than in the previous decade.[52] This would suggest that men born too late to be called up did better than those who had been conscripted. This is all the more striking because birth rates rose in the 1940s – so men born in that decade did not have the scarcity value of those born in the 1930s. A correlation is not a cause. It may be that other forces for social mobility were so powerful that they outweighed both the effects of birth rates and the effects of conscription, but the correlation does at least suggest that we should regard the claims that conscription was economically beneficial with scepticism.

Surveys conducted by the forces themselves did not suggest that military service made men more productive in the civilian economy. An army survey of industrialists in the mid 1950s concluded that some industrialists believed that some workers showed more initiative after national service, but that this improvement might just have been due to the passage of time. Other employers believed that national service made men more prone to waste time and to wait for orders. Given that the report in question was commissioned specifically to help defend national service, this is hardly high praise.[53]

The RAF was particularly interested in skilled industrial workers, who made up a disproportionate part of its own national service intake, and its internal reports painted a bleaker picture of the economic effects of national service. They suggested: 'The NS man is critical of Service life because he believes it makes skiving too easy.'[54] Another RAF report from the same period drew attention to 'the currency of such words as "fiddle", "racket" and "wangle"'.[55] A decade later, a prosperous worker recalled his national service thus: 'Nice sort of life in the RAF – easier going . . . nice to have someone thinking for you all the while – but not enough freedom.'[56]

Some men gained in professional terms from national service but they were probably not those for whom it fitted neatly into their civilian careers but, rather, those who felt its 'disruptive' effects. Educational segregation and full employment in the 1950s meant that some men's social destiny seemed fixed before they were twenty. A man who had failed the 11-plus – or passed it but left school at sixteen – was likely to remain in the same relatively menial occupation until he retired. For a few of these men, two years in the forces provided time to read and think and, in some cases, decide to return to education.[57]

Men born in the 1930s often considered themselves fortunate. Having grown up with the depression, war and rationing, they came to adulthood in an era of economic growth and expanding opportunities. National service did sometimes play a small part in this sense of being blessed – it was one of the uncomfortable features of their youth from which men escaped. One man anticipated that his national service would come to seem 'an extensive Lent' because 'everything, however absurd and wasteful, will seem so jolly after the asceticism of this place'.[58]

Sometimes a restrained scepticism about military culture was the most important long-term effect of national service. Philip Bell, historian and clerical corporal, said that the phrase 'planned like a military operation' always struck terror into his heart.[59] Robert Gomme, also a corporal, who served on the front line in Korea, became a civil servant. Looking back forty years later, he was uncertain about what his national service meant and doubted that claims about its maturing effects were well founded. The most enduring legacy of his service seems to have been a strong dislike for the military metaphors that his colleagues were prone to use: 'it's a minefield', 'ranging shot' and 'smoke screen'.[60]

Attitudes to sex, families and masculinity also owed more to a reaction against military values than an adoption of them. Some have suggested that British men espoused a more 'soft-edged' masculinity after 1963 and that this was related to a decline in martial culture that went with the end of national service.[61] However, it was often former national servicemen who illustrated this softer-edged masculinity. The 'companionate' marriages that so struck sociologists during the mid 1960s must largely have involved husbands who had undertaken military service. Conscripts may have been exposed to a self-consciously brutal, misogynistic world in the armed forces but very few of them adopted its values. On the contrary, national servicemen often seem to have come out of the armed forces valuing 'domesticity' more highly than when they went in. Self-mocking references to 'virgin soldiers' suggest that at least some national servicemen had an ironic and thoughtful attitude to their own masculinity.

Many men came to look back on their national service in relatively favourable terms. Sometimes this was because it fitted into a bio-graphical trajectory. More often, it was because time in the armed forces was an interlude that was exciting precisely because it took men away from the things they might have done in the ordinary course of their lives. A national service pilot, who had gone through the thrilling and dangerous experience of learning to fly when he was eighteen, did not sit in the cockpit of an aeroplane after leaving the air force until he and his grandchildren undertook a brief joy ride from Duxford aerodrome fifty years later.[62] Working-class men often looked back on service in Singapore or Hong Kong as the great adventure of their lives.

There is, however, a contrast between the benign way in which national service is often remembered and the mood evoked by documents of the time. An air force survey of 1948 concluded:

It has been our impression that the very fact of compulsory service in the absence of an obvious threat of war, arouses strong resistance in many men. This seems to be overcome at first by logical and reasonable arguments and by the excitement and career possibilities of the prospect. We are not satisfied, however, that these factors dispose finally of the resistance aroused, and it may be that this is partly responsible for the swing away from co-operation which we witnessed in so many conscripts.

Finally it must be stated that of all those whom we interviewed, by far the larger number thought conscription a waste of time. Many officers agreed that 'a small nucleus of high morale, regular service men, well paid and equipped, would serve the country better and cost less than the present RAF', with its 'rabble of discontented and unhappy conscripts'.[63]

Letters and diaries of servicemen themselves, even those who later described national service in relatively positive terms, often capture feelings of frustration, boredom and the sense that life was passing them by.[64] Some of J. M. Lee's school friends had interesting postings: to Kuala Lumpur – 'the most beautiful city I have ever seen' – or Austria – 'amongst the best British stations in the world'. In spite of this, Lee's friends did not regard his own exemption from national service on medical grounds as misfortune: 'Believe me all the RAF or army does is to make us worse characters, to coarsen our minds, vilify our language and narrow our understanding.'[65]

Every national service career ended with a written summary as an officer wrote a testimonial on the serviceman: 'of sober and honest habits and is recommended for any position of trust'.[66] Presenting a verdict on national service as a whole is more awkward. Even those who might be expected to have the clearest views on it did not always agree with each other. Conservatives who were veterans of national service dominated British politics from 1982, when John Nott asked that his fellow national serviceman Cecil Parkinson join the Falklands 'War Cabinet' to counteract the influence exercised by those older men who had served in the Second World War,[67] until 1990, when John Major (born in 1943) defeated Douglas Hurd and Michael Heseltine for the leadership of the Conservative party. However, the shared experience of military service, in itself, did not give these men much in common. Nott had switched to a short-service commission and led a Gurkha platoon on active service; Parkinson had considered registering as a conscientious objector before, regretfully, serving out his time in the air force.[68] Heseltine talked much about his period in the Welsh Guards but had extracted himself as quickly as possible; Hurd had served out his full time but remarked drily of those in his constituency party who called for the reintroduction of conscription: 'my recollections of National Service must be different from theirs'.[69]

Some aspects of national service – basic training, bull, the jokes, the obscenities – feature in almost every account, but there were also huge differences in experiences and in the effects that it had on individual men. There was no 'outcome' to national service. There was no single conflict that ended in victory or defeat. There were none of the collective events – bonfires, parties, mutinies – that had marked the end of the two world wars. National service was 'ending' almost as soon as it began because individual men were demobilized every two weeks.

Men went back to work – in the tight labour markets of the 1950s, some of them started jobs on the Monday after they were demobilized – marriage and families. It was not until they retired in the 1990s that most of them had much time to reflect on their youth, which is partly why national service was so little discussed in the three decades after it ended.

If they looked back, some national servicemen finished their accounts with clear verdicts. Peter Sharp wrote:

> I count my two years in the Service as a wonderful experience. I would not have missed it for worlds. National Service may seem tough at the beginning – but it should be tough. Rigorous training, they say, teaches you not only Service discipline, it teaches you self-discipline. I think that is true. I'm all for it . . . I went in as a boy. I came out a man.[70]

By contrast, Tom Stacey wrote one of the most notorious denunciations of national service:

> The considered hatred I still retain for the Army which I saw . . . will stay with me until I or others have changed it, or at least until it is openly shown me that it cannot carry out its important duties in a manner which does not affront humanity.[71]

Anyone reading these two passages might be surprised to hear that they come from autobiographical essays that were published in the same volume. They might also be surprised to hear that Sharp was a working-class NCO in the RAF and that Stacey was a guards officer or, for that matter, that Stacey was standing as a Conservative candidate in a parliamentary election just a year after the last conscript left the army.

More commonly, national servicemen end their accounts with a joke. Paul Foot – whose service, after the first hellish weeks of training, seems to have been rather agreeable – said that he felt like asking the Queen for his two years back.[72] Perhaps only a joke can capture the incongruity of peacetime conscription. Arnold Wesker's play *Chips with Everything* played a joke on the audience itself. The air force band on stage played 'God Save the Queen'. The gambit must have made theatre goers, used to standing when the national anthem was played, feel uncomfortable. Now, even the mood of this play has become hard to recapture – not just because Wesker became more favourable to national service and less favourable to this particular play, but because there are hardly any occasions on which ordinary people stand for the national anthem. The culture in which national service existed belongs to a different age.

Appendices

APPENDIX I: THE DEMOGRAPHY OF NATIONAL SERVICE

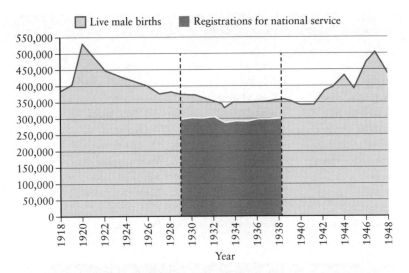

The graph shows live male births in England, Wales and Scotland from 1918 to 1948. The years 1929–1938, in which most national servicemen were born, are highlighted and the numbers who actually registered for national service are shaded. The comparative scarcity of men born from the late 1920s to the early 1940s partly explains why the armed forces needed conscription. It also probably explains why national servicemen sometimes felt overshadowed by the generations above and below them.

APPENDIX II: RANKS IN THE BRITISH ARMED FORCES

Officer ranks in the British armed forces		
Army	Navy	Air Force
Field Marshal	Admiral of the Fleet	Marshal of the Royal Air Force
General	Admiral	Air Chief Marshal
Lieutenant General	Vice Admiral	Air Marshal
Major General	Rear Admiral	Air Vice Marshal
Brigadier	Commodore	Air Commodore
Colonel	Captain	Group Captain
Lieutenant Colonel	Commander	Wing Commander
Major	Lt Commander	Squadron Leader
Captain	Lieutenant	Flight Lieutenant
Lieutenant	Sub-Lieutenant	Flying Officer
Second Lieutenant	Midshipman	Pilot Officer

Other ranks in the British armed forces		
Army	Navy	Air Force
Warrant Officer Class 1	Warrant Officer	Warrant Officer, Master
		Aircrew, Master Technician
Warrant Officer Class 2		
Staff Sergeant, Colour Sergeant	Chief Petty Officer	Flight Sergeant, Chief Technician
Sergeant	Petty Officer	Sergeant, Sergeant Technician
Corporal	Leading Hand	Corporal, Corporal Technician
Lance Corporal		
		Junior Technician
		Senior Aircraftman
	Able Rating	Leading Aircraftman
Private	Rating	Aircraftman

This refers to RAF ranks instituted in 1951. The complexity of RAF ranks sprang from the need to reflect levels of technical skill.

Deaths in British armed forces by theatre of operations and service, 1 January 1948–31 December 1960					
	Navy	Marines	Army	Air Force	Total Deaths in Theatre
Korea	46	28	1,031	30	1,135
Malaya	5	27	893	276	1,201
Palestine	0	2	176	17	195
Cyprus	4	13	274	67	358
Egypt/Suez	1	12	267	69	349
Kenya	0	0	69	25	94
Other (including UK)	2,457	154	8,185	5,393	16,189
Total	2,513	236	10,895	5,877	19,521

Deaths in British armed forces by theatre of operations and cause of death, 1 January 1948–31 December 1960						
	Killed in Action/ Enemy Action	Terrorist Action	Died of Wounds	Aircraft Crash/ Flying Accident	Other Cause	Total
Korea	830	3	75	31	196	1,135
Malaya	300	9	31	173	688	1,201
Palestine	8	119	1	0	67	195
Cyprus	1	109	0	17	231	358
Egypt/Suez	10	43	2	23	271	349
Kenya	4	4	2	21	63	94
Other (including UK)	85	15	10	2,880	13,199	16,189
Total	1,238	302	121	3,145	14,715	19,521

These figures were communicated to Dr Roger Broad by the Armed Forces Personnel Administration Agency in June 2005. The Agency stresses that they may not be accurate. The figures for deaths in Kenya are certainly strange, because the Secretary of State for War told parliament on 31 January 1956 that eleven national servicemen had been killed in action in Kenya.

APPENDIX IV: BRITISH MALE SOLDIERS BY ARM/CORPS AND LOCATION, 1954

British male soldiers by arm/corps, December 1954

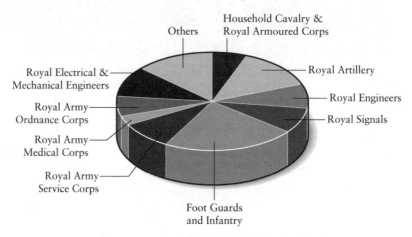

British male soldiers by location, December 1954

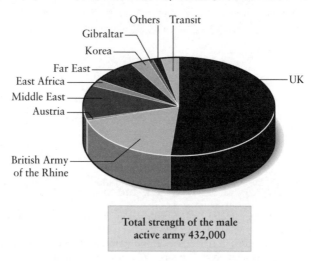

Total strength of the male
active army 432,000

Source: TNA WO 384/15, 'Abstract of Army Statistics', December 1954.

APPENDIX V: MEN REGISTERED FOR
NATIONAL SERVICE, 1948–1960

Men registered for national service, 1948–1960, in thousands

							Deferred and Exempted		
Year of birth[1]	Year of survey[2]	Total registered[3]	Total posted to forces[4]	Unfit[5]	Awaiting medical[6]	Applied for deferment[7]	Applied for deferment – Agriculture[8]	Complete apprenticeship[9]	Agricultural work[10]
1929	1948	299	183.4	28.7	3.9	0.5	0.0	41.4	18.4
1929	1949	297.4	195.7	29.9	2.1	0.3	0.0	34.3	17.4
1929	1950	298	213.2	36.5	5.8	0.4	0.0	5.9	16.0
1929	1951	298	225.9	37.5	1.4	0.1	0.0	0.6	14.9
1929	1952	298	229.6	38.0	1.0	0.1	0.0	0.1	14.1
1929	1953	298	231.2	38.2	0.5	0.0	0.0	0.1	13.7
1929	1956	299	234.9	38.2	0.0	0.0	0.0	0.0	13.3
1930	1949	301.7	171.5	30.9	3.9	0.6	0.0	52.2	19.9
1930	1950	302.8	183.9	33.1	2.5	0.5	0.0	39.1	18.5
1930	1951	302.8	208.2	39.1	7.5	0.4	0.0	5.9	17.3
1930	1952	302.8	222.1	40.4	1.8	0.2	0.0	0.7	15.8
1930	1953	304	224.9	41.6	0.8	0.1	0.0	0.3	15.5
1930	1956	303	231.0	41.2	0.3	0.0	0.0	0.0	14.4
1931	1950	295.9	154.2	36.6	3.3	0.6	0.0	51.8	19.2
1931	1951	297.7	168.6	38.9	3.0	0.3	0.0	41.1	17.5
1931	1952	297.7	193.4	44.4	9.3	0.4	0.0	6.2	16.2
1931	1953	300	209.2	48.0	1.9	0.3	0.0	0.7	15.5
1931	1954	301	211.9	47.5	0.9	0.0	0.0	0.5	15.2
1931	1956	302	218.7	50.3	0.5	0.0	0.0	0.0	14.2
1931	1957	302	219.2	50.7	0.3	0.0	0.0	0.0	14.1
1932	1951	298	146.8	43.6	3.0	0.4	0.0	53.0	18.4
1932	1952	301.4	161.4	47.1	3.3	0.4	0.0	42.2	16.7
1932	1953	302	187.6	53.7	8.6	0.5	0.0	5.7	15.8
1932	1954	303	202.4	55.2	1.8	0.3	0.0	0.9	15.2
1932	1955	303	204.8	56.0	1.4	0.0	0.0	0.4	14.8
1932	1956	305	210.1	58.7	0.7	0.1	0.0	0.1	14.2
1932	1957	306	212.0	60.6	0.6	0.0	0.0	0.1	13.8
1932	1958	306	212.4	60.9	0.3	0.0	0.0	0.0	13.8
1933	1952	277.1	145.7	35.5	3.1	1.7	0.0	52.1	5.2
1933	1953	281	158.4	38.7	3.2	0.4	0.9	42.6	5.0
1933	1954	281	184.2	44.4	8.5	0.6	0.6	7.0	4.5
1933	1955	282	198.8	47.5	1.9	0.3	0.4	1.1	4.3
1933	1956	283	203.5	49.5	1.0	0.2	0.3	0.2	4.0
1933	1957	286	207.0	51.9	0.8	0.1	0.3	0.1	4.0
1933	1958	287	208.8	52.9	0.7	0.0	0.2	0.1	4.0
1933	1959	288	209.8	54.4	0.1	0.0	0.3	0.0	3.8
1934	1953	285.5	148.7	32.4	3.3	0.5	1.3	56.0	6.3
1934	1954	287	161.3	35.3	4.8	0.5	0.8	44.3	5.4
1934	1955	287	187.0	41.5	9.9	0.7	0.6	9.0	5.1
1934	1956	289	203.7	46.5	1.7	0.5	0.4	1.4	4.6
1934	1957	292	207.6	50.0	1.2	0.3	0.4	0.3	4.6
1934	1958	292	209.9	51.2	1.0	0.0	0.3	0.1	4.6
1934	1959	293	211.6	53.0	0.6	0.0	0.1	0.1	4.5
1934	1960	293	212.1	53.7	0.2	0.0	0.0	0.0	4.7
1935	1954	282	138.0	34.2	3.5	0.5	1.1	60.2	6.9
1935	1955	285	149.8	38.1	3.6	0.6	0.8	50.6	6.1
1935	1956	287	176.4	47.3	9.8	1.1	0.5	10.6	5.5
1935	1957	290	192.5	54.0	1.8	0.7	0.4	1.6	5.3
1935	1958	290	196.6	55.5	1.7	0.2	0.4	0.5	5.3
1935	1959	291	199.4	57.8	1.0	0.1	0.1	0.1	5.3
1935	1960	292	200.4	59.1	0.7	0.0	0.0	0.1	5.5
1936	1955	289	136.0	36.9	3.9	0.7	0.8	65.4	6.6
1936	1956	296	147.8	44.1	3.1	0.6	0.6	56.3	5.9
1936	1957	295	172.8	53.4	10.5	1.6	0.4	11.1	5.5
1936	1958	297	189.5	58.7	2.8	0.6	0.4	2.2	5.5
1936	1959	299	195.4	62.0	1.6	0.3	0.1	0.5	5.6
1936	1960	299	197.2	63.4	0.7	0.0	0.0	0.4	5.6
1937	1956	292	124.8	40.6	3.6	0.8	1.1	70.2	8.1
1937	1957	295	136.5	45.4	3.4	0.8	0.7	59.2	7.7
1937	1958	297	160.7	56.1	13.2	1.3	0.5	14.7	7.7
1937	1959	298	180.0	63.2	3.8	0.7	0.3	2.8	7.5
1937	1960	299	184.1	65.4	1.1	0.1	0.0	2.2	7.6
1938	1957	289	84.9	40.0	26.7	5.6	1.3	70.2	9.5
1938	1958	299	117.1	52.1	4.6	0.8	0.9	63.3	9.3
1938	1959	301	132.4	59.3	30.9	1.7	0.4	16.7	9.0
1938	1960	301	147.2	65.2	16.3	0.2	0.1	11.6	9.4
1939	1958	135	22.6	14.2	28.1	6.1	0.6	32.5	4.8
1939	1959	220	53.4	26.7	41.5	0.7	0.4	46.9	7.6
1939	1960	221	63.8	33.0	37.8	0.6	0.1	33.2	8.3

Men registered for national service, 1948–1960, in thousands

Year of birth	Year of survey	Coal miners[11]	Seamen[12]	Complete school certificate[13]	Complete higher education[14]	Hardship, approved schools, etc.[15]	Post-apprentice training[16]	Articled clerks[17]	Science[18]	Emigrant[19]
1929	1948	8.4	5.3	0.1	7.0	1.9	0.0	0.0	0.0	0.0
1929	1949	7.8	3.0	0.0	6.0	0.9	0.0	0.0	0.0	0.0
1929	1950	6.9	4.1	0.0	4.6	1.6	0.0	3.0	0.0	0.0
1929	1951	6.5	4.7	0.0	3.1	1.0	0.0	2.3	0.0	0.0
1929	1952	6.4	4.3	0.0	1.9	1.3	0.0	1.2	0.0	0.0
1929	1953	6.3	4.2	0.0	1.6	1.2	0.0	1.0	0.0	0.0
1929	1956	6.1	3.3	0.0	0.1	0.5	0.0	0.0	0.6	2.0
1930	1949	8.7	3.8	0.5	7.6	2.1	0.0	0.0	0.0	0.0
1930	1950	7.8	4.4	0.1	7.4	1.1	0.0	4.4	0.0	0.0
1930	1951	7.5	5.4	0.0	5.9	1.7	0.0	3.9	0.0	0.0
1930	1952	7.6	5.8	0.0	4.1	1.5	0.0	2.8	0.0	0.0
1930	1953	7.5	5.8	0.0	3.8	1.3	0.0	2.4	0.0	0.0
1930	1956	6.9	5.0	0.0	0.4	0.6	0.0	0.0	0.7	2.5
1931	1950	8.5	4.2	1.0	9.1	1.9	0.0	5.5	0.0	0.0
1931	1951	8.2	4.5	0.0	9.0	1.3	0.0	5.3	0.0	0.0
1931	1952	8.2	5.7	0.0	7.2	2.3	0.0	4.4	0.0	0.0
1931	1953	7.8	6.1	0.0	4.9	2.4	0.0	3.2	0.0	0.0
1931	1954	7.8	5.9	0.0	4.6	2.7	1.0	2.8	0.2	0.0
1931	1956	7.6	5.4	0.0	1.0	0.8	0.0	0.2	0.9	2.4
1931	1957	7.4	5.3	0.0	0.6	0.8	0.0	0.0	1.1	2.5
1932	1951	9.4	4.3	0.9	9.9	2.0	0.0	6.3	0.0	0.0
1932	1952	9.1	4.3	0.0	9.7	1.6	0.0	5.6	0.0	0.0
1932	1953	8.7	5.7	0.0	7.5	3.5	0.0	4.7	0.0	0.0
1932	1954	8.5	5.9	0.0	5.1	1.0	1.3	3.5	0.2	1.7
1932	1955	8.4	5.7	0.0	4.5	0.9	1.0	3.1	0.2	1.8
1932	1956	8.3	5.5	0.0	2.1	1.0	0.2	1.0	0.7	2.3
1932	1957	8.2	4.3	0.0	1.0	1.1	0.0	0.3	1.2	2.8
1932	1958	8.5	4.1	0.0	0.7	1.1	0.0	0.1	1.3	2.8
1933	1952	10.6	3.7	0.8	10.2	2.1	0.0	6.4	0.0	0.0
1933	1953	9.9	4.8	0.0	9.7	1.5	0.0	5.9	0.0	0.0
1933	1954	9.4	5.8	0.0	7.7	1.2	0.8	5.0	0.1	1.2
1933	1955	9.2	5.9	0.0	5.3	1.0	0.8	3.7	0.3	1.5
1933	1956	9.0	5.8	0.0	3.4	1.0	0.5	2.2	0.6	1.8
1933	1957	8.6	5.5	0.0	2.1	1.1	0.2	1.2	1.0	2.1
1933	1958	8.6	5.2	0.0	1.1	1.2	0.0	0.3	1.4	2.5
1933	1959	8.5	5.1	0.0	0.4	1.3	0.0	0.0	1.6	2.7
1934	1953	11.2	5.7	1.0	10.4	2.0	0.0	6.7	0.0	0.0
1934	1954	10.8	5.5	0.0	10.1	1.3	0.0	6.1	0.0	0.8
1934	1955	10.4	6.3	0.0	8.2	1.2	0.7	5.2	0.1	1.1
1934	1956	10.1	6.5	0.0	5.6	1.1	1.0	4.0	0.4	1.5
1934	1957	9.8	6.4	0.0	3.8	1.2	0.7	2.7	1.0	2.0
1934	1958	9.6	6.0	0.0	2.5	1.3	0.3	1.3	1.5	2.4
1934	1959	9.3	5.8	0.0	1.4	1.4	0.1	0.3	2.1	2.7
1934	1960	9.2	5.6	0.0	0.8	1.4	0.0	0.2	2.3	2.8
1935	1954	10.9	5.1	1.2	10.9	1.8	0.0	7.2	0.0	0.5
1935	1955	11.1	4.8	0.0	11.0	1.2	0.0	6.6	0.0	0.7
1935	1956	10.9	6.2	0.0	9.1	1.3	1.1	5.9	0.2	1.1
1935	1957	10.3	6.8	0.0	6.5	1.4	1.4	4.8	0.8	1.7
1935	1958	10.2	6.4	0.0	4.3	1.4	0.9	3.0	1.5	2.1
1935	1959	9.8	6.1	0.0	2.9	1.5	0.4	1.6	2.3	2.6
1935	1960	9.5	6.0	0.0	2.4	1.6	0.2	1.2	2.5	2.8
1936	1955	11.5	4.9	1.4	11.2	1.9	0.0	7.4	0.0	0.4
1936	1956	11.7	5.0	0.0	11.7	1.2	0.0	7.3	0.0	0.7
1936	1957	11.4	6.8	0.0	10.0	1.8	1.4	6.6	0.3	1.4
1936	1958	11.4	6.9	0.0	7.2	1.6	1.7	5.4	1.1	2.0
1936	1959	10.7	6.7	0.0	5.0	1.8	1.1	3.6	2.2	2.4
1936	1960	10.4	6.5	0.0	4.5	1.8	0.4	3.3	2.2	2.6
1937	1956	12.4	4.4	1.7	12.5	2.6	0.0	8.7	0.0	0.5
1937	1957	12.4	4.4	0.1	13.1	2.0	0.0	8.5	0.0	0.8
1937	1958	12.7	5.4	0.00	11.5	2.4	1.5	7.6	0.4	1.3
1937	1959	11.8	5.7	0.0	8.4	2.7	1.6	6.3	1.4	1.8
1937	1960	11.5	5.5	0.0	8.1	2.7	1.0	6.1	1.5	2.1
1938	1957	12.2	4.9	2.5	14.4	6.5	0.0	9.8	0.0	0.5
1938	1958	13.6	5.2	0.2	15.9	5.0	0.1	10.0	0.0	0.9
1938	1959	12.5	6.2	0.0	14.2	5.3	1.3	9.4	0.5	1.2
1938	1960	11.9	6.7	0.0	13.8	6.3	1.2	9.0	0.6	1.5
1939	1958	5.4	1.7	1.1	9.2	4.1	0.0	4.5	0.0	0.1
1939	1959	9.0	3.2	0.0	15.5	5.7	0.0	8.7	0.0	0.4
1939	1960	8.6	3.5	0.2	15.5	6.4	0.4	8.6	0.0	1.0

All figures have been derived from issues of the *Ministry of Labour Gazette*, 1948–1960. There is a slight inconsistency in this table. The *Gazette* frequently stops recording data for one full year group in the course of a year. Thus, in 1957, its May issue records men of the 1931 class but its November issue records only the men of the 1932 class and younger. I have always used the last available figure and thus my numbers for 1957 involve men born in 1931, who had been called up by May 1957, and men born in 1932 or later, who had been called up by November 1957. The chances that a man's status would change diminish as he gets older, so it is unlikely that figures for the 1931 class would have changed much between May and November 1957 – though figures for the 1938 class would have changed a good deal. The Ministry of Labour was not entirely consistent in its policy about when to stop recording the fate of age cohorts. Thus, for example, the entries for 1955 refer only to men born in 1932 or later but the entry for 1956 then goes back to record men born in 1929, 1930 and 1931 - though almost all men in this age group would have ceased to be liable for national service.

[1] Years of birth. Ranging from 1929 until 1939 (in the last of these years, only men born until September were liable to call up).

[2] Years in which men's status was examined. Thus one row in the table will show what had happened in a particular year (say 1950) to all men born in a particular year (say 1930).

[3] Men registered for national service. Except during the last years of national service, everyone registered by their nineteenth birthday and, consequently, this figure should remain roughly the same for most birth years. The number of men born in 1930 who were registered for national service in 1950 should be roughly the same as the number of men born in 1930 who were registered for national service in 1956 – the last year in which statistics were collected for this birth cohort.

[4] Men who had joined the forces as either conscripts or regulars. This number should increase for each birth cohort over time as deferments expired and fit men were posted.

[5] Men classified unfit. No one underwent medical examination until they were liable for immediate call up – i.e. until any deferments had expired. The percentage of men failing the medical, therefore, is calculated by expressing the number of men classified as unfit as a percentage of the sums of those posted plus those found unfit. Some of these figures are displayed in the graph in Appendix VI.

[6] Men awaiting medical or available for posting.

[7] Men who had applied for deferment other than those in agriculture.

[8] Men who had applied for deferment to work in agriculture (after agricultural workers lost the general right to defer in 1952).

[9] Men deferred to complete apprenticeships. This number usually diminishes for each birth cohort over time as men completed apprenticeships.

[10] Men deferred to perform agricultural work. This number dropped in 1952 when agricultural workers lost the automatic right to defer but then increased as discretionary deferments were granted on ever more generous terms.

[11] Men deferred to work in coal mines. It was expected that these men would defer until the age at which they ceased to be liable for call up. In practice, numbers for each birth cohort usually decline over time. This is presumably because some men preferred to take their chances in the forces rather than to endure underground work.

[12] Men deferred as seamen. Here too it was assumed that men would defer until they ceased to be liable.

[13] Men deferred to complete their schooling.

[14] Men deferred to complete higher education. This number usually diminishes over time for each birth cohort as men graduated. The total number of men at university at any one time increased over time.

[15] Men who avoided national service for a variety of unrelated reasons. This number increased sharply in the late 1950s as the authorities became less prone to press men into the forces.

[16] Men deferred to complete training after apprenticeships. This category was created in 1954.

[17] Men deferred as articled clerks in professions such as accountancy and law. These men were sometimes deferred until quite an advanced age – twenty-four or twenty-five.

[18] Men deferred to work on scientific work of high priority. Such deferments had been common during the war, but post-war conscription was initially intended to be universal. Gradually, however, the number of scientific deferments increased and were extended to science teachers and, eventually, all graduate teachers.

[19] Men who had emigrated. Emigration rates were high in the late 1950s and the age of liability for national service was increased to catch men who had gone abroad and returned.

Note: There was one additional category made up of men waiting to take university places. This category was only used once and is not shown on this table. Its absence explains the fact that the figures for 1939/1959 do not quite add up.

APPENDIX VI: FAILURE RATES IN
NATIONAL SERVICE MEDICALS

Percentage of those taking medical who failed, by year of birth

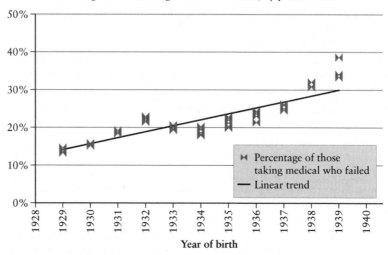

Year of birth

The graph above shows the percentage of men who failed the medical by birth year. There are multiple data points for each birth year because each data point represents the number of men who had failed the medical by a particular year, expressed as a percentage of those who had taken the medical by that year. The data points for birth year 1939, for example, stand for the percentages in 1958, 1959 and 1960.

There are variations from year to year, but the general trend is up. At first glance this is surprising. One would expect men born in 1938 and brought up in an age of full employment and the welfare state to be healthier than men born during the depths of the inter-war depression in 1929. It seems likely that the changes over time sprang from the use of the medical as a means to regulate intake into the forces.

If figures were to be broken down more precisely to allow for the men examined in a particular year (rather than the cumulative total for that year) then variation would be even sharper. Among those born in 1929 who were examined in 1950, the failure rates was 27.39%; among those examined a year later, as the effects of the Korean War were felt, the rate was 7.3%.

APPENDIX VII: PERCENTAGE OF MEN, REGISTERED FOR NATIONAL SERVICE, POSTED TO FORCES, BY YEAR OF BIRTH

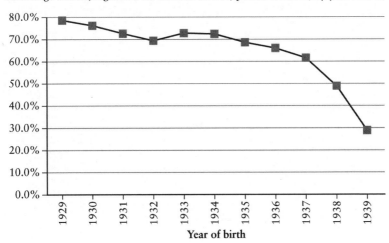

Percentage of men, registered for national service, posted to forces, by year of birth

APPENDIX VIII: INTAKES TO ARMY
BASIC TRAINING UNITS, 1949–60

	Retained	Discharged	% Potential Officer	% Potential NCO	% Educational Level 1	% Educational Level 2
Intakes to Army Basic Training Units, 1949–1960: educational level, potential officers, potential NCOs						
1949 2H NS	53,083	937	7.1	19.8	0.8	3.7
1949 2H Regular	5,502	564			0	0.7
1950 1H NS	62,829	833	4.5	22	0.1	2.5
1950 1H Regular	6,633	732			0	0.7
1950 2H NS	56,505	454	6.9	23	1.1	3.8
1950 2H Regular	9,364	588			0.1	0.6
1951 1H NS	52,130	423	4.1	20.4	0.3	2
1951 1H Regular	8,030	616			0	0.8
1951 2H NS	65,230	447	6.5	20.1	1.6	4
1951 2H Regular	7,099	574			0	0.8
1952 1H NS	61,434	385	2.8	19.2	0.5	1.2
1952 1H Regular	20,550	474			0	0.3
1952 2H NS	63,887	502	7.1	21.6	1.6	2.6
1952 2H Regular	18,359	556			0.2	0.7
1953 1H NS	59,522	450	3.5	19.9	0.8	1.2
1953 1H Regular	18,046	551			0.1	0.3
1953 2H NS	52,589	396	9.5	22.4	3.5	4.1
1953 2H Regular	15,139	344			0.3	0.7
1954 1H NS	54,065	465	4.9	21.9	1.2	1.4
1954 1H Regular	15,882	481			0.2	0.4
1954 2H NS	52,831	432	9.8	24.6	4.7	3.2
1954 2H Regular	14,828	443			0.4	0.4
1955 1H NS	51,949	869	4.4	24.1	1.1	1.1
1955 1H Regular	15,158	608			0.1	0.3
1955 2H NS	54,244	750	10	26.1	5	2.7
1955 2H Regular	13,612	544			0.4	0.4
1956 1H NS	49,578	942	4	25.8	1	1.1
1956 1H Regular	16,461	661			0.1	0.2
1956 2H NS	37,510	985	8.5	27.9	4.8	2.6
1956 2H Regular	14,976	585			0.2	0.3
1957 1H NS	41,019	281	3.7	29.8	1.2	1.5
1957 1H Regular	25,188	740			0.1	0.2
1957 2H NS	33,911	722	6.5	30.8	3.3	2.5
1957 2H Regular	8,679	440			0.2	0.4
1958 1H NS	36,451	889	3.1	31.5	1.2	1.4
1958 1H Regularv	12,133	550			0	0.1
1958 2H NS	28,590	782	4.9	22.5	3.9	3.5
1958 2H Regular	13,616	680			0.1	0.3
1959 1H NS	26,300	738	3.6	32.1	2	2.9
1959 1H Regular	12,985	719			0.1	0.3
1959 2H NS	21,300	666	5.8	33.7	3.9	4.6
1959 2H Regular	10,448	596			0.1	0.3
1960 1H NS	26,229	851	2.9	31.9	1.5	2.4
1960 1H Regular	10,261	575			0.1	0.2

The point at which each category peaks for national servicemen is shaded

Intakes to Army Basic Training Units, 1949–1960: educational level, potential officers, potential NCOs

	% Educational Level 3	% Educational Level 4	% Educational Level 5	% Educational Level 6	% Educational Level 7	% Educational Level 8
1949 2H NS	8.6	5.8	10.3	45.4	24.8	0.6
1949 2H *Regular*	6	7.2	15.1	57.2	13.7	0.1
1950 1H NS	7.2	5.8	13.4	46.9	23.6	0.5
1950 1H *Regular*	3.8	7.2	15.5	59.5	13.3	0
1950 2H NS	9.3	6.6	13.9	43.9	21.1	0.3
1950 2H *Regular*	4.3	5.5	18.9	59.9	10.7	0
1951 1H NS	6.7	6	15	47.2	22.5	0.3
1951 1H *Regular*	4.7	5.7	19.4	58.8	10.6	0
1951 2H NS	6	4.8	18.9	43.5	20.6	0.6
1951 2H *Regular*	4.4	4.3	19.3	58.7	12.5	0
1952 1H NS	3.8	4.3	19.7	46.4	22.9	1.2
1952 1H *Regular*	2.4	3.1	17.6	60.8	15.8	0
1952 2H NS	6.7	6.1	22.3	41.2	18.5	1
1952 2H *Regular*	2.9	4.1	19	58.3	14.8	0
1953 1H NS	3.2	5	22.4	45.1	21.4	0.9
1953 1H *Regular*	1.6	4.1	18.6	59.7	15.6	0
1953 2H NS	6.6	8.3	19.9	37.7	19	0.9
1953 2H *Regular*	2.4	6.4	20.1	56.5	13.6	0
1954 1H NS	3.1	7.4	24.7	42.5	18.9	0.8
1954 1H *Regular*	1.8	5.9	20.6	57.5	13.6	0
1954 2H NS	6.3	9	22.5	37.3	16.4	0.6
1954 2H *Regular*	2	6.8	20.5	57.9	12	0
1955 1H NS	2.6	6.2	22.7	46.7	19.3	0.2
1955 1H *Regular*	1.1	6.3	20.3	58.4	13.5	0
1955 2H NS	6.2	8.7	21.1	39.4	16.6	0.2
1955 2H *Regular*	1.5	6.9	21.1	57	12.7	0
1956 1H NS	2.6	6.6	22.7	46.5	19.3	0.2
1956 1H *Regular*	0.7	5.7	20	60.8	12.5	0
1956 2H NS	6.3	9.4	23.4	37.8	15.4	0.3
1956 2H *Regular*	1.1	5.8	21.2	58.9	12.5	0
1957 1H NS	3.4	9.3	31.8	37.2	15.5	0.1
1957 1H *Regular*	1	5.4	21.6	58.2	13.4	0.1
1957 2H NS	6	10	32.9	32.2	13	0.1
1957 2H *Regular*	1.5	7.3	24.4	54.7	11.5	0
1958 1H NS	2.8	8.1	34.7	37	14.7	0.1
1958 1H *Regular*	0.5	4.3	21.9	58	15.2	0
1958 2H NS	6.8	11.2	33.6	29.1	11.8	0.1
1958 2H *Regular*	0.9	5.3	23.2	55	15.1	0.1
1959 1H NS	4.7	9.9	35.2	32.6	12.5	0.2
1959 1H *Regular*	0.7	4.6	22.8	54.4	16.8	0.3
1959 2H NS	7.5	9.8	36	27	10.8	0.4
1959 2H *Regular*	0.9	7.2	25.3	51.4	14.5	0.3
1960 1H NS	6	10	37	31.3	11.5	0.3
1960 1H *Regular*	0.8	4.3	25.1	54.7	14.6	0.2

1H refers to the first half of each year and 2H refers to the second half. The proportion of men in the highest educational categories was usually higher in the second half of each year – when school leavers and men finishing apprenticeships entered the forces. The intake was divided into national servicemen (NS) and regulars. Figures for potential officers and potential NCO's were, however, given for both categories together.

Potential officers (OR1s) were identified when they first arrived in the army. Almost all of these were drawn from the top four educational levels and most were drawn from the top three. Only a minority of OR1s actually became officers. The proportion of OR1s in the intake peaked (at 10%) in the second half of 1955. There is a marked correlation between the number of potential officers and the number of men in the top three educational levels.

The number of men identified as potential NCOs increased towards the end of national service and seems to bear some relation to the number of men in educational level 5, i.e. the skilled working class.

Educational Levels

Educational Level 1 refers to graduates. One would expect this to increase consistently because the proportion of the men going to university increased and also because the last intakes of national servicemen were largely composed of men who had deferred and all graduates would have been deferred. However, the proportion of graduates in the intake actually peaked in the second half of 1955. Presumably this is because educated men became better at avoiding service and the authorities became more likely to tolerate such evasion.

Educational Level 2 refers to men with some higher education. It seems to have been used, in the early stages, to refer to men with university entrance scholarships – John Masterman, who chaired the Army Educational Council at that time, took such matters seriously.

Educational Level 3 refers to men who left school at eighteen with qualifications that would make them eligible for university entrance. Most public school boys would have belonged to this category and the army seems to have particularly valued such men as officers. The proportion of men in this category peaked in the second half of 1950 – presumably because, after this date, increasing numbers of men deferred to go to university.

Educational Level 4 refers to men who left school at sixteen with the General Certificate of Education. This category included a large number of grammar school boys. It peaked in the second half of 1958.

Educational Level 5 refers to men who had left school at the earliest possible age (fourteen until 1947 and then fifteen) but who had acquired some additional education (at night classes, for example) or performed well on tests when they entered the forces. This would include large numbers of apprentice-trained workers. They increased as a proportion of entrants until almost the end of national service. In its last stages, conscription fell heavily on the skilled working class. When first discussing ways to end the call-up, Iain Macleod, the Minister of Labour and National Service, had wanted, in effect, to exempt skilled workers. The fact that he failed, and that these men continued to be conscripted when men with the highest education levels were frequently escaping, suggests the extent to which national service was structured by social class.

Educational Level 6 refers to men who had left school at the earliest possible age and acquired no further education. This meant, in large measure, unskilled workers. Most regular soldiers were drawn from this category. The proportion of national servicemen in this category peaked in the first half of 1951.

Educational Level 7 refers to men whose performance on tests was below the level expected of men with the minimum period of education. It included many who were regarded as semi-literate. The proportion of national servicemen who belonged to this category peaked in 1949, when the intake included many whose education had been disrupted by the war and when the effect of professional deferment was to remove many of the ablest working-class boys from the intake.

Educational Level 8 refers to illiterates: men unable to fill in a form even with help. The proportion of men of Educational Level 8 in the intake peaked in the first half of 1952, when the needs of the Korean War had forced the army to take men who would normally have been rejected.

Source: WO 384/12-40, editions of the 'Abstract of Army Statistics'.

Intakes to Army Basic Training Units by arm/corps, 1954

Arm/Corps		1H TOTAL	2H TOTAL	1H Potential Officers	2H Potential Officers	1H Potential NCOs	2H Potential NCOs	1H Educational Level 1	2H Educational Level 1	1H Educational Level 2	2H Educational Level 2	1H Educational Level 3	2H Educational Level 3
Household Cavalry	NS	157	97	9	21	38	43	0	3	1	5	6	14
	Regular	159	177	4	13	15	19	2	0	1	0	3	17
Royal Armoured Corps	NS	1,835	796	207	272	248	104	14	50	16	17	67	88
	Regular	1,638	1,544	59	62	332	314	0	2	0	0	17	23
Royal Artillery	NS	7,141	6,404	643	1,548	1,597	1,618	79	408	109	204	282	690
	Regular	1,473	1,240	56	78	334	452	0	3	3	4	16	19
Royal Engineers	NS	3,513	3,312	405	743	830	744	125	346	148	328	301	375
	Regular	1,733	1,409	46	65	490	384	6	6	17	10	73	52
Royal Signals	NS	4,898	5,325	321	656	854	1,238	119	426	93	169	131	333
	Regular	1,044	1,180	20	20	247	298	2	0	0	7	7	15
Foot Guards	NS	478	564	57	74	30	51	1	4	1	8	31	50
	Regular	770	724	18	11	50	45	2	1	0	3	17	9
Infantry	NS	12,755	13,087	485	960	1,739	1,513	22	76	53	70	233	476
	Regular	3,427	3,124	139	181	517	433	0	4	5	5	55	54
Royal Army Service Corps	NS	4,681	3,924	211	460	905	1,087	53	210	23	91	75	351
	Regular	1,541	1,416	29	17	586	644	1	0	1	2	6	6
Royal Army Medical Corps	NS	2,112	1,739	36	43	550	486	31	75	54	84	88	81
	Regular	164	126	1	1	78	50	0	0	4	2	8	7
Royal Army Ordnance Corps	NS	3,890	5,328	116	302	1,432	2,180	25	91	35	75	75	201
	Regular	676	652	16	25	344	302	2	6	1	0	9	10
Royal Electrical and Mechanical Engineers	NS	5,330	4,534	303	622	1,347	1,409	67	253	166	515	262	445
	Regular	1,884	1,834	42	29	682	658	1	1	4	13	22	30
Royal Army Pay Corps	NS	1,539	1,417	85	114	331	264	73	69	57	33	42	31
	Regular	99	123	13	14	42	38	2	1	0	1	9	3
Royal Army Veterinary Corps	NS	107	44	4	3	22	15	4	4	0	1	0	3
	Regular	36	63	0	1	3	10	0	0	0	0	1	0
Royal Army Education Corps	NS	47	705	22	181	24	521	41	429	4	63	1	109
	Regular	40	65	22	24	18	41	20	30	11	10	8	23
Royal Army Dental Corps	NS	61	143	2	4	23	47	0	0	1	4	0	13
	Regular	18	12	0	1	6	2	0	0	0	0	1	0
Royal Military Police	NS	577	593	5	18	555	566	0	2	1	9	13	18
	Regular	320	283	6	7	314	276	0	0	1	0	9	7
Royal Pioneer Corps	NS	1,836	1,565	1	2	113	138	0	0	0	0	1	3
	Regular	101	115	0	1	30	35	0	0	0	1	0	1
Intelligence Corps	NS	134	88	9	6	124	72	7	30	10	5	26	28
	Regular	50	71	2	12	48	59	0	4	10	4	13	17
Army Catering Corps	NS	2,913	3,126	14	32	291	335	0	0	0	5	6	7
	Regular	239	191	2	5	57	50	0	0	0	0	2	0
Non-Combatant Corps	NS	61	40	0	0	0	0	4	6	8	0	12	5
	Regular	0	0	0	0	0	0	0	0	0	0	0	0
Army Air Corps	NS	0	0	0	0	0	0	0	0	0	0	0	0
	Regular	471	479	7	6	74	71	0	1	1	0	6	3

Intakes to Army Basic Training Units by arm/corps, 1954

Arm/Corps		1H Educational Level 4	2H Educational Level 4	1H Educational Level 5	2H Educational Level 5	1H Educational Level 6	2H Educational Level 6	1H Educational Level 7	2H Educational Level 7	1H Educational Level 8	2H Educational Level 8
Household Cavalry	NS	10	16	41	10	81	46	18	3	0	0
	Regular	4	13	56	45	79	86	14	15	0	1
Royal Armoured Corps	NS	173	159	448	107	835	262	282	112	0	1
	Regular	62	72	217	156	1,079	1,102	263	189	0	0
Royal Artillery	NS	831	845	1,216	1,050	3,083	2,096	1,532	1,100	9	11
	Regular	66	71	132	186	909	740	347	217	0	0
Royal Engineers	NS	329	306	1,192	871	1,030	811	387	275	1	0
	Regular	196	134	519	467	846	688	76	52	0	0
Royal Signals	NS	446	625	1,563	1,614	1,820	1,512	722	645	4	1
	Regular	55	52	275	340	658	717	47	49	0	0
Foot Guards	NS	22	44	137	146	194	233	91	79	1	0
	Regular	24	17	158	121	438	427	129	144	2	2
Infantry	NS	635	813	2,550	2,456	6,447	6,488	2,772	2,680	43	28
	Regular	110	160	324	245	1,924	1,789	1,007	865	2	2
Royal Army Service Corps	NS	383	444	945	735	2,231	1,441	953	648	18	4
	Regular	58	54	285	247	1,113	1,029	77	78	0	0
Royal Army Medical Corps	NS	159	172	607	426	846	716	327	185	0	0
	Regular	19	20	56	37	73	58	4	2	0	0
Royal Army Ordnance Corps	NS	230	396	790	1,145	1,880	2,428	846	976	9	16
	Regular	25	39	123	109	473	450	43	38	0	0
Royal Electrical and Mechanical Engineers	NS	395	448	2,173	1,588	1,730	952	531	330	6	3
	Regular	186	215	776	754	848	799	46	22	1	0
Royal Army Pay Corps	NS	155	156	731	712	453	394	28	21	0	1
	Regular	32	49	49	57	7	12	0	0	0	0
Royal Army Veterinary Corps	NS	2	2	24	12	54	15	23	7	0	0
	Regular	1	5	4	16	28	37	2	5	0	0
Royal Army Education Corps	NS	0	104	1	0	0	0	0	0	0	0
	Regular	1	2	0	0	0	0	0	0	0	0
Royal Army Dental Corps	NS	20	39	35	66	5	20	0	1	0	0
	Regular	3	3	10	4	4	5	0	0	0	0
Royal Military Police	NS	66	113	300	279	196	171	1	1	0	0
	Regular	40	35	138	120	130	120	2	1	0	0
Royal Pioneer Corps	NS	3	4	72	78	288	223	1,111	983	361	274
	Regular	2	0	4	5	66	71	29	37	0	0
Intelligence Corps	NS	86	24	5	1	0	0	0	0	0	0
	Regular	21	36	5	7	1	3	0	0	0	0
Army Catering Corps	NS	28	53	507	579	1,797	1,869	575	613	0	0
	Regular	5	9	43	38	167	127	22	17	0	0
Non-Combatant Corps	NS	12	11	12	11	12	6	1	1	0	0
	Regular	0	0	0	0	0	0	0	0	0	0
Army Air Corps	NS	0	0	0	0	0	0	0	0	0	0
	Regular	24	22	104	88	287	321	49	43	0	1

The table shows intake into the basic training units of the army in the first and second half of 1954 broken down by arm/corps. The table distinguishes betwen intakes in the first and second half of each year (1H and 2H). The intake was divided into national servicemen (NS) and regulars. Admission to basic training is not an entirely reliable guide to entrants to the army. The Parachute Regiment at this stage took all its entrants from men who had already undertaken basic training with other units. The Education and Intelligence Corps would also have taken many men who had initially been admitted to the army as members of other units. Most men seeking long-service regular commissions would have gone straight to Sandhurst without undertaking basic training.

Unlike the consolidated figures for the whole army provided earlier, this table divides potential officers and potential NCOs into regulars and national servicemen. Regular entrants to household regiments were required to enter Brigade Squad (nominally as private soldiers) before proceeding to Sandhurst. In other units the majority of potential officers among regulars would, presumably, have been men on three-year engagements, who would not have gone to Sandhurst.

Only the Army Air Corps was reserved exclusively for regulars. However, regulars had more choice with regard to postings than conscripts and, not surprisingly, they chose prestigious units: the Foot Guards, Household Cavalry and Armoured Corps were the only units with more regular entrants than national service ones in a single year. Regulars were also disproportionately represented in units that offered the prospect of learning a trade – especially the Royal Electrical and Mechanical Engineers.

National servicemen were a large proportion of entrants in the least attractive units – the Ordnance Corps, the Pioneers and the Catering Corps. These units also contained a large proportion of men in educational level 7, which included many semi-literates.

The Education Corps was primarily composed of national servicemen and these men were overwhelmingly admitted in the second half of each year – i.e. when men left school or university.

Source: TNA WO 384/15 and 16, 'Abstract of Army Statistics', December 1954 and March 1955.

Officer selection in army, 1951/1952			
	Scotland	North	South
Number of men at Educational Levels 4 and above	1,000	7,500	7,500
Number of OR1s (potential officers)	470	2,400	4,000
Rejected by Unit Selection Board	54	450	450
Declaring self non-desirous	40	250	250
Non-OR1s put forward to War Office Selection Board	45	260	390
Candidates at War Office Selection Board	421	1,960	3,690
Men successful at War Office Selection Board	200	750	1,880

Numbers of OR1s (potential officers) in national service intake			
	Scotland	North	South
1951/2	470	2,400	4,000
1953	589	3,139	4,432
1954	624	3,426	4,289

Percentage of candidates declaring themselves 'non-desirous'			
	Scotland	North	South
1951/2	8.5	10	6
1953	6	7	4.5
1954	5	5	3

Percentages rejected by Unit Selection Boards			
	Scotland	North	South
1951/2	11.5	19	11
1953	14	22	15
1954	19	25	17

Pass rates at the War Office Selection Board			
	Scotland	North	South
1950/51	41%	36%	48%
1951/2	50%	40%	53%
1953	57%	45%	53%
1954	53.5%	48%	54.5%

Note: 1950/51 and 1951/52 have been averaged by the War Office. For these purposes, Wales was in the North.

Source: TNA WO 291/1510, AORG, 'The Different Officer Potentials of Various Regions of Great Britain', L. J. Holman, 1956.

Notes

ABBREVIATIONS

AORG – Army Operational Research Group
IWM – Imperial War Museum
IWMSA – Imperial War Museum Sound Archive
LHCMA – Liddell Hart Centre for Military Archives
NAM – National Army Museum
NAMSA – National Army Museum Sound Archive
TNA – The National Archives, Kew

A PERSONAL PREFACE

1. Robert Blake, *The Unknown Prime Minister: The Life and Times of Andrew Bonar Law, 1858–1923* (1955), p. 282.
2. Roger Bush, *FAU: The Third Generation – Friends Ambulance Unit Post-war Service and International Service, 1946–1959* (York, 1998).
3. Geoffrey Strickland, 'The Torture Lesson', *The Spectator*, 17 March 1984.
4. TNA WO 32/17501, correspondence on this matter and in particular Soames to Emery, 12 May 1960.
5. IWMSA 26098, Benjamin Whitchurch.
6. IWMSA 18825, Joseph Roberts, reels 4, 5 and 7.
7. Andreas Whittam Smith, interviewed by Louise Brodie, *An Oral History of the British Press*, 2007, British Library Sound & Moving Image Catalogue reference C638/08, track 1. © The British Library.
8. Peter Duncumb, interview, 11 January 2013.

INTRODUCTION

1. NAM 2001-07-1187-46, Andrew Man, 'The National Service Soldier in Korea', paper drafted May 1951.
2. NAMSA 2000-04-52, John Arnold, reel 1.
3. Mary Morse, *The Unattached* (1965), p. 16. A researcher arriving in 'Seagate' in 1960 struck up a conversation with a twenty-year-old man about subjects including his service in the navy.
4. Alan Sillitoe, *Life Without Armour* (1995), p. 106.
5. I. C. Taylor, 'National Service in Aden', *The Pharmaceutical Journal*, 263, 7076 (1999), pp. 1018–19.
6. IWM 614, W. H. Butler, Memoir, 'Derby to Derna (an Account of National Service Experiences)', p. 96.
7. Clive Emsley, *Soldier, Sailor, Beggarman, Thief: Crime and the British Armed Services since 1914* (Oxford, 2014), p. 176.
8. D. R. Hurd, 'Soldiers at Salisbury', *The Spectator*, 9 August 1951.
9. TNA HO 345/13, Departmental Committee on Homosexual Offences and Prostitution, 25 May 1955.
10. IWM 7178, C. B. L. Barr, diary entries, 25 and 26 April 1954.
11. Michael Ware, *Gap Year: A Saga of National Service* (2000).
12. Brian Thompson, *Clever Girl: Growing Up in the 1950s* (2007, this edn 2008), p. 63.
13. P. J. Kavanagh, *The Perfect Stranger* (1966), p. 95.
14. David Scholey, interviewed by Kathy Burk, *NLSC: City Lives*, 1992, British Library Sound & Moving Image Catalogue reference C409/085, track 1. © The British Library. Scholey did national service before going up to Oxford because he 'wanted to experience university as an adult'. It turned out that the version of adulthood fostered by a cavalry regiment was not the same as that of an Oxford college, even Christ Church, and Scholey was sent down after failing his first-year exams.
15. Ministry of Education, *15 to 18* (1959), Crowther Report, II, p. 127. In a sample of national servicemen studied from 1956 to 1958, 8 per cent had stayed at school until the age of eighteen. The figure would have been even lower just a few years earlier.
16. King George's Jubilee Trust, *Citizens of Tomorrow* (1955), pp. 17–18.
17. Early release was granted systematically to men who had held university places before the extension of national service in 1950. See TNA WO 32/15743, note on meeting between AG and DPA on 14 August 1951. Early release was quite regularly granted to men after this date.

18. Raymond Leppard in Ronald Hayman (ed.), *My Cambridge* (1977), pp. 97–114, at p. 97.

19. Bill Rodgers, *Fourth Among Equals* (2000), p. 22.

20. Registrar General, *Statistical Review of England and Wales for the Year 1952* (1955), text, p. 10.

21. Leslie T. Wilkins, *The Social Survey: National Service and Enlistment in the Armed Forces. A Report on an Enquiry Made for Several Government Departments into the Attitudes of Young Men Prior to, and on Joining the Armed Forces* (1951), p. 8.

22. David Lodge, *Ginger, You're Barmy* (1962, this edn 1984), p. 32.

23. IWM 15595, David Batterham, letter to parents, 15 June 1953.

24. Gwylmor Prys Williams, *Teenagers' Problems: The Contemporary Social Background and Youth's Reaction to It* (1958), p. 3.

25. Noel Annan, *Our Age: The Generation that Made Post-war Britain* (1990, this edn 1991), p. 3.

26. Nottingham PRO, papers of Professor J. M. Lee, DD 393/1/3, typed note 'The Henry Mellish Grammar School Bulwell Nottingham. The Sixth Form Leaver of 1949'.

27. Barry Supple, *Doors Open* (Cambridge, 2009). Supple talks of his contemporaries as a 'blessed generation' because they benefited from welfare and education and avoided war. The reason why Supple, born in 1930, did not perform national service is given in a footnote on p. 112 of his book.

28. This is the title for a screenplay that Osborne wrote about his early life and also of a chapter in his autobiography *A Better Class of Person* (1981).

29. Brian Corby, interviewed by Paul Thompson, NLSC: *City Lives*, 1992, British Library Sound & Moving Image Catalogue reference C409/012, track 2. © The British Library.

30. IWM 15595, David Batterham, 'National Service Recalled'.

31. T. Ferguson and J. Cunnison opened their study of boys from Glasgow who had been born in 1932 and left school at fourteen with *The Young Wage-earner: A Study of Glasgow Boys* (Oxford, 1951). They followed this up with *In Their Early Twenties: A Study of Glasgow Youth* (Oxford, 1956), which dealt with the same group of men at a time when some, but not all, had been called up. Finally, they published an article that was specifically devoted to the military experience of their subjects: 'The Impact of National Service', *British Journal of Sociology*, 10, 4 (1959), pp. 283–90. R. F. L. Logan and E. M. Goldberg, 'Rising Eighteen in a London Suburb: A Study of Some Aspects of the Life and Health of

Young Men', *British Journal of Sociology*, 4, 4 (1953), pp. 323–45, was based on a sample of men registering for national service. In Scotland a large-scale study of intelligence among children began in 1921. By 1947, this study had come to focus mainly on children born in 1936 and its results were published in J. S. Macpherson, *Eleven-year-olds Grow Up* (1958). In 1969, James Maxwell published *Sixteen Years On: A Follow-up of the 1947 Scottish Survey*, which contained a chapter on national service.

32. This is true of Dennis Marsden, discussed below. John Partridge was due to study classics at university when he was called up in 1953 but 'after two years military service he felt discontented with the course of study that he had chosen, so he changed his degree to social science'. Biographical note in John Partridge, *Life in a Secondary Modern School* (1966). So far as I know, the only sociologist to write about his own experience of national service is David Morgan: David Morgan, *'It Will Make a Man of You': Notes on National Service, Masculinity and Autobiography* (Manchester, 1987).

33. Madeline Kerr, *The People of Ship Street* (1958), pp. 29 and 188.

34. Essex University, Affluent Worker Survey, interview 44.

35. Ibid., interview 13.

36. So far as I can tell, the only explicit reference comes in one quoted interview that begins: 'When I came out of the RAF'. John Goldthorpe, David Lockwood, Frank Bechhofer and Jennifer Platt, *The Affluent Worker: Industrial Attitudes and Behaviour* (Cambridge, 1968), p. 34. The original of this interview can be found at Essex University, Affluent Worker Survey, interview 12. The interviewee had been an RAF medical orderly.

37. Dennis Marsden undertook national service after finishing his degree at Cambridge and it helped to transform him from a chemical engineer into a sociologist. It is not clear what unit he served with, what rank he held or where he was posted – see *Guardian* obituary, 23 September 2009. Brian Jackson undertook his national service before Cambridge. His biographer says almost nothing about national service but does reproduce a photograph of him 'with native servant' while in the forces. Kit Hardwick, *Brian Jackson: Educational Innovator and Social Reformer* (Cambridge, 2003).

38. Brian Jackson and Dennis Marsden, *Education and the Working Class: Some General Themes Raised by a Study of 88 Working-class Children in a Northern Industrial City* (1962, this edn 1966), p. 184.

39. Margaret Stacey, *Tradition and Change: A Study of Banbury* (1960); N. Dennis, F. M. Henriques and C. Slaughter, *Coal is Our Life: An Analysis of a Yorkshire Mining Community* (1956); W. M. Williams,

The Sociology of an English Village: Gosforth (1956); Michael Young and Peter Willmott, *Family and Kinship in East London* (1957); eid., *Family and Class in a London Suburb* (1960).

40. There is, for example, an autobiographical current in Peter Hennessy's work, which is made explicit in his *Distilling the Frenzy: Writing the History of One's Own Times* (2012).

41. Tony Judt, *The Memory Chalet* (2010), p. 119.

42. Tony Judt, *Postwar: A History of Europe Since 1945* (New York, 2005), p. 360.

43. See, for example, Becky Conekin, Frank Mort and Chris Waters (eds.), *Moments of Modernity: Reconstructing Britain, 1945–1964* (1999). National Service is not mentioned in the index to the book – though one of the contributors, Peter Bailey, says in passing that his association with the Coventry jazz scene ended when he was called up and posted to Singapore: Peter Bailey, 'Jazz at the Spirella: Coming of Age in Coventry in the 1950s' in ibid., pp. 22–40.

44. The most eminent social historian to have written about the British armed forces is Joanna Bourke, but Bourke's work – particularly *An Intimate History of Killing: Face to Face Killing in Twentieth-century Warfare* (2000) – is to some extent an exception that proves the rule. She has written about soldiers in the two world wars and Vietnam but not about the less obviously dramatic lives of peacetime conscripts. Her interest in military life involves mainly the most violent aspect of that life – i.e. the battlefield. Similarly, her interest in masculinity involves its most violent manifestations – rape and killing. Furthermore, she tends to be interested in individual experience when faced with existential matters of life and death. The relatively banal lives led by most national servicemen and the schools, regiments and social classes that often seemed to define those lives would not fit neatly into her analysis.

45. David Lance, interviewed by Michelle Winslow, *An Oral History of Oral History*, 2003, British Library Sound & Moving Image Catalogue reference C1149/01, track 1. © The British Library.

46. Lol Coxhill, interviewed by Andy Simon, *Oral History of Jazz in Britain*, 1996, British Library Sound & Moving Image Catalogue reference C122/339–340, track 1. © The British Library. Coxhill remarks, of his time in the air force, that it was 'just national service, spent half my time on a pig farm so the only person in danger was me; carried saxophone around with me'. The interviewer does not follow up these intriguing remarks. John Brooks, interviewed by Bernard Attard, *The Jobbing System of the London Stock Exchange: An Oral History*, 1990, British Library Sound & Moving Image Catalogue reference C463/25, track 1.

© The British Library. Brooks remarks that national service gave him 'a bit of time to think' between Eton and going into the City. Brian Winterflood, interviewed by Bernard Attard, *The Jobbing System of the London Stock Exchange: An Oral History*, 1990, British Library Sound & Moving Image Catalogue reference C463/09, track 1. © The British Library. The son of a bus conductor, Winterflood tells of being replaced by the Honourable Charlie Wilson 'when I came out of the services'. The interviewer does not ask what he was doing in the services, or what the Honourable Charlie Wilson was doing for that matter.

47. Gordon Martin, interviewed by Louise Brodie, *NLSC: City Lives*, 1996, British Library Sound & Moving Image Catalogue reference C409/134, track 2. © The British Library.

48. Samuel Stouffer et al., *The American Soldier: Adjustment During Army Life* (Princeton, NJ, 1949).

49. W. G. Runciman, *Relative Deprivation and Social Justice: A Study of Attitudes to Social Inequality in Twentieth-century England* (1966).

50. Eugen Weber, *Peasants into Frenchmen: The Modernization of Rural France, 1870–1914* (1976). For a specific study of military service see Odile Roynette, *'Bon pour le service': L'expérience de la caserne en France à la fin du XIXe siècle* (Paris, 2000).

51. See, for example, Emmanuel Le Roy Ladurie and André Zysberg, 'Anthropologie des conscrits français (1868–1887)', *Ethnologie française*, 9, 1 (1979), pp. 47–68.

52. Peter Burke, Brian Harrison and Paul Slack, 'Keith Thomas' in eid. (eds.), *Civil Histories: Essays Presented to Sir Keith Thomas* (Oxford, 2000), pp. 1–30.

53. Raoul Girardet, who had already published *La Société militaire dans la France contemporaine (1815–1939)* (Paris, 1953), edited *La Crise militaire française, 1945–1962* (Paris, 1964) as a response to the Algerian War.

54. Robert Bonnaud, *Itinéraire* (Paris, 1962); Antoine Prost, *Carnets d'Algérie* (Paris, 2005); Alain Corbin, *Historien du sensible: Entretiens avec Gilles Heuré* (Paris, 2000).

55. Raphaëlle Branche, *La Torture et l'armée pendant la guerre d'Algérie* (Paris, 2001) and Claire Mauss-Copeaux, *Appelés en Algérie: La parole confisquée* (Paris, 1999).

56. David Anderson, *Histories of the Hanged: The Dirty War in Kenya and the End of Empire* (New York, 2005); Caroline Elkins, *Imperial Reckoning: The Untold Story of Britain's Gulag in Kenya* (New York, 2005).

57. John Comaroff cited in Caroline Elkins, 'Alchemy of Evidence: Mau Mau, the British Empire, and the High Court of Justice', *The Journal of Imperial and Commonwealth History*, 39, 5 (2011), pp. 731–48.

58. See, in particular, B. S. Johnson (ed.), *All Bull: The National Servicemen* (1973); Colin Shindler, *National Service: From Aldershot to Aden – Tales from the Conscripts* (2012); Tom Hickman, *The Call-up: A History of National Service* (2005).

59. Sources for Trevor Royle's *The Best Years of Their Lives: The National Service Experience, 1945–63* (1986) can be found at the Imperial War Museum. Sources for Keith Miller's *730 Days Until Demob!: National Service and the Post-1945 British Army* (2003) can be found at the National Army Museum. Sources for Adrian Walker's *Six Campaigns: National Servicemen at War, 1948–1960* (1993) can also be found at the National Army Museum.

60. E. Tonkin, cited in Laura Tisdall, '"That Was What Life in Bridgeburn had Made Her": Reading the Autobiographies of Children in Institutional Care in England, 1918–1946', *20th Century British History*, 24, 3 (2013).

61. Julian Critchley, *A Bag of Boiled Sweets* (1994, this edn 1995), p. 31. This story is unlikely to be true for several reasons. First, the Green Jackets did not exist as a regiment at the time Critchley was called up. Second, Critchley's school, a sort of second-flight public school, as Paul Foot put it, was not very grand by the standards of the rifle regiments, which often rejected Etonians. Third, as a national serviceman with a special interest in the matter noted, about 16 per cent of grammar school boys were circumcised.

62. TNA WO 32/15604, note signed Dalton, 25 August 1954.

63. NAMSA 2001-02-397, Barry Reed, reel 1. Asked whether he had an allowance, Reed replies that he cannot remember but that, if he did have one, it would have been very small.

64. *Daily Mail*, 4 September 1953.

65. TNA WO 296/41, transcripts, Alan Tuppen interview on BBC television news, 3 February 1970.

1. DEFINITIONS, FACTS AND UNCERTAINTIES

1. Mike Baker, *The Last Intake: The Story of a Serviceman in Singapore and RAF Changi* (1995), p. 46.

2. TNA WO 384/1, 'Abstract of Army Statistics', 1950/1951.

3. IWMSA 18825, Joseph Roberts, reel 2.

4. IWMSA 14865, Godfrey Raper, reel 1.

5. Jeremy Morse, interviewed by William Reader, *NLSC: City Lives*, 1988, British Library Sound & Moving Image Catalogue reference C409/007, transcript p. 5/track 1. © The British Library.

6. *Army List*, August 1948, p. 893.
7. Ibid., December 1949, p. 598.
8. Hansard, 23 September 1948.
9. Tom Stacey in Peter Chambers and Amy Landreth (eds.), *Called Up: The Personal Experiences of Sixteen National Servicemen, Told by Themselves* (1955), pp. 47–66.
10. *Army List*, December 1949, p. 426. Emergency officers were still being commissioned into the Scots Guards up to 30 July 1949 – though this was also the date on which all the first national service officers in the regiment were commissioned.
11. Alan Sillitoe, *Life Without Armour* (1995), pp. 93 and 97.
12. IWMSA 21676, Alan Sillitoe. © Whistledown.
13. IWMSA 13645, interview General Forrester, Brigadier Flood, Brigadier Dawney, reel 1.
14. Henry Askew interviewed by Cathy Courtney, *NLSC: City Lives*, 1992, British Library Sound & Moving Image Catalogue reference C409/082, transcript p. 25/track 1. © The British Library.
15. IWMSA 13645, Forrester et al.
16. TNA WO 32/21720, Proceedings of McLean Court of Enquiry, 28 December 1953, evidence of Private MacCash of the Black Watch.
17. TNA DEFE 7/509, note for Mr Martyn, illegible signature, 13 November 1953.
18. Ministry of Labour and National Service, *National Service* (1955), cmd 9608.
19. Stephen Martin, 'Did Your Country Need You? An Oral History of the National Service Experience in Britain, 1945–1963' (PhD thesis University of Wales, Lampeter, 1997), p. 273.
20. Roy Ramsay, *Green on 'Go': National Service and the TA* (Harrow, 1989).
21. *The Times*, 19 November 1960.
22. See, for example, Mark Garnett's article on Gow in the *Oxford Dictionary of National Biography*, http://www.oxforddnb.com/index/47/101047318.
23. TNA WO 32/17657, Combined Record Office, 15 January 1959. 'It has been the rule of this Office, since National Service began, not to give substantive rank to National Service Men, but I can trace no War Office instruction to this effect, except by inference, in that War Office authority exists for National Servicemen to become substantive cpls in RMP.'
24. Peter Hennessy, *Having It So Good: Britain in the Fifties* (2006, this edn 2007), p. 80.

25. TNA DEFE 10/332, National Service Working Party, 26 April 1951. Indeed the Ministry of Defence trusted the Ministry of Labour's figures more than it trusted those provided by the service departments under its own aegis.

26. TNA LAB 6/684, 'The Arrangements for Bringing Call-up to an End 1957–1960 and Methods Used to Estimate Numbers of Men Available', appendix.

27. TNA WO 384/1, and subsequent volumes of the 'Abstract of Army Statistics'.

28. TNA DEFE 7/509, figures attached to note for Martyn, 13 November 1953, illegible signature. 'This is based on information supplied by the Ministry of Labour and National Service. The figures are for postings and not of those who actually served for the periods mentioned. The differences are unlikely to be large and where they occur will be due mainly to premature release and to men undertaking regular engagements after call up. It is most unlikely that details of the numbers who actually served will be available in the service departments.'

29. TNA LAB 6/415, 'Enquiries as to Men Who May Be Liable for Call-up to the Forces in 1947 and 1948 under the National Service Acts', no date or signature. According to The Times, doctors and dentists could be called up until the age of thirty under the Acts of 1947 and 1948: The Times, 26 November 1948.

30. TNA WO 384/1, 'Abstract of Army Statistics', figures for June 1950.

31. Ibid.

32. Sidney Rosenbaum, 'Heights and Weights of the Army Intake, 1951', Journal of the Royal Statistical Society, 117, 3 (1954), pp. 331–47.

33. Adrian Walker (ed.), Six Campaigns: National Servicemen at War, 1948–1960 (1993), introduction, no pagination.

34. Hansard, 1 August 1963.

35. Ibid., 31 January 1956.

36. Ibid., 1 November 1949.

37. Manchester Guardian, 10 January 1952.

38. NAM 2006-12-77-82, Malcolm Edward Barker, 'The Letters and Diaries of a National Serviceman with the Queen's Royal Regiment (1st Battalion) in BAOR 1952–1953'. Barker kept a press cutting of 1952. The article alluded to nine people killed by shell fire, drowning and a jeep crash during a recent exercise. Barker also kept an 'unfinished commentary' of his own. He believed that casualties on the exercise were higher than officially admitted.

39. TNA WO 384/1, 'Abstract of Army Statistics'.

40. Karl Miller in B. S. Johnson (ed.), *All Bull: The National Servicemen* (1973), pp. 256–66, at p. 258.
41. Brian Goodliffe, *Recollections of Gunner Goodliffe: Life of a National Serviceman in 1952 and 1953, from His Own Diaries* (Harrow, 2009), pp. 28–9.
42. TNA WO 32/16277, minute DAAG to USS, 30 July 1951.
43. TNA WO 32/16277, PS to USS, 10 September 1951.
44. TNA AIR 20/8671, note signed Stephens, 20 September 1955: 'From time to time we are approached by Mr Wigg with enquiries usually about Service statistics.'
45. Hansard, 18 June 1952, question by Fenner Brockway.
46. TNA DEFE 70/96, 'Departmental Committee on Homosexual Offences and Prostitution'. Undated memorandum by the War Office: 'The venereal disease rate is low but as soldiers may now avail themselves of the easy facilities for private treatment, it gives no indication of the extent of prostitution.'
47. Harold Evans, *My Paper Chase: True Stories of Vanished Times, an Autobiography* (2009, this edn 2010), p. 89.
48. NAMSA 1995-05-93, Robin Ollington, reel 1.
49. TNA WO 291/1215, Army Operational Research Group, 'The Testing of National Servicemen at Ministry of Labour Recruiting Centres', March 1952.
50. Rosenbaum, 'Heights and Weights of the Army Intake, 1951'.
51. IWM 66/211/1/43, Trevor Royle, J. G. Inglis, carton 1.

2. NATIONAL SERVICE WRITING

1. David Lodge, *Ginger, You're Barmy* (1962); Alan Sillitoe, *The Key to the Door* (1961); Andrew Sinclair, *The Breaking of Bumbo* (1959); Leslie Thomas, *The Virgin Soldiers* (1966); Gordon M. Williams, *The Camp* (1966); Christopher Wood, *'Terrible Hard', Says Alice* (1970); David Baxter, *Two Years to Do* (1959).
2. *Daily Express*, 28 July 2013.
3. IWMSA 21681, Ray Self. © Whistledown, 2000.
4. IWMSA 21676, Alan Sillitoe, reel 1. © Whistledown, 2000.
5. Terence Blacker, *You Cannot Live as I Have Lived and Not End Up Like This: The Thoroughly Disgraceful Life and Times of Willie Donaldson* (2007), p. 33.
6. Michael Holroyd in B. S. Johnson (ed.), *All Bull: The National Servicemen* (1973), pp. 136–48, at p. 144.

7. John Ferris, interview, 25 July 2012.

8. IWM 12505, T. J. Hunt, 'Midshipman's Workbook'. The officer correcting the logbook wrote on 31 November 1957: 'You must spell accommodation right and "commencement" is a terrible word; why not say "start".'

9. Leslie T. Wilkins, *The Social Survey: National Service and Enlistment in the Armed Forces. A Report on an Enquiry Made for Several Government Departments into the Attitudes of Young Men Prior to, and on Joining the Armed Forces* (1951), pp. 23 and 27.

10. TNA WO 32/10994, Claude Luke to Eric Merrill, 5 July 1957, enclosing an example of a letter from a soldier in Korea that included a reference to having read 'Stargazers last knight' and 'took interest in this book'. The soldier's letter was treated as evidence of poor educational standards in the army.

11. Wilkins, *National Service and Enlistment*, pp. 23 and 27.

12. P. J. Kavanagh, *The Perfect Stranger* (1966), p. 60.

13. Alan Sillitoe, *Life Without Armour* (1995), pp. 102–6.

14. Ibid., p. 110.

15. IWM 4102, Peter Burke, diary entry, 3 March 1956.

16. Frank Dickinson, *Them Days 'ave Gone* (Ely, 2008), p. 121.

17. TNA WO 32/18704. This file contains documents on army libraries.

18. IWM 15595, David Batterham, letter to parents, undated.

19. See, for example, Nottingham PRO, papers of Professor J. M. Lee, DD 393/1/1, letter from Graham Mottershaw to Lee, undated, about RAF camp library in Somerset.

20. *Guardian*, 24 July 2013.

21. Karl Miller in Johnson (ed.), *All Bull*, pp. 256–66, at p. 256.

22. NAM 2006-12-77-82, Malcolm Edward Barker, 'The Letters and Diaries of a National Serviceman with the Queen's Royal Regiment (1st Battalion) in BAOR 1952–1953'. Introductory note to booklet of transcribed letters: 'With the idea of one day writing a book about his experiences as a National Serviceman he began keeping a diary in shorthand ... but soon switched to writing lengthy, detailed letters to his mother and sister, with the idea that they keep them.'

23. NAMSA 2003-03-626, Lt General Peter Duffell, reel 1.

24. Nottingham PRO, DD 393/1/1, covering note with papers deposited by Professor J. M. Lee.

25. IWM 4102, Burke, diary entry, 1 April 1956.

26. Ibid., 20 February 1956.

27. Ibid., 7 May 1956.

28. Ibid., 4 May 1956.
29. Ibid., 25 June 1956.
30. Geoffrey Barnes, *With the Dirty Half-hundred in Malaya: Memories of National Service, 1951–52* (Royston, 2001), p. 28.
31. NAM 2000-08-55, D. F. Barrett, diary entry, 23 August 1950.
32. IWM 3368, L. G. G. Smith, letter, Christmas 1951.
33. NAM 1995-01-164, Robert Gomme, 'Korea: a short memoir'.
34. IWM 2118, Peter Mayo, diary entry, 9 December 1956.
35. John Hollands, *The Dead, the Dying and the Damned* (1956), p. 405.
36. John Crook, *Hilltops of the Hong Kong Moon* (1997), p. 8.
37. IWM 15316, P. J. Houghton-Brown, 'National Service, June 1955–June 1957', no pagination.
38. IWM 1594, B. E. Turberville.
39. IWM 2918, F. N. E. Starkey, diary entries, 20 August 1947, 10 September 1947, 6 July 1948.
40. IWMSA 12919, Michael Randle, reel 1.
41. TNA LAB 6/468.
42. Michael Billington, *Harold Pinter* (1996), pp. 23–4.
43. Tom Stacey, an officer in the Scots Guards, wrote an essay in Peter Chambers and Amy Landreth's collection *Called Up: The Personal Experiences of Sixteen National Servicemen, Told by Themselves* (1955). He had earlier published a book, *The Hostile Sun*, that drew on his experiences as an officer in Malaya. Andrew Sinclair, an officer in the Coldstream Guards, published his national service novel, *The Breaking of Bumbo*, in 1959.
44. The association of certain kinds of national service writing – Lodge and Sillitoe in particular – with 'angry young men' is made by John Sutherland in *The Boy Who Loved Books* (2007, this edn 2008), p. 191.
45. 'Afterword' to the 1982 edition of *Ginger, You're Barmy* (1982, this edn 1984), p. 216.
46. Cecil Blacker, *Monkey Business: The Memoirs of General Sir Cecil Blacker* (1993), p. 119. Cecil Blacker is the father of Terence Blacker, whose admiring biography of a very unmartial national serviceman is cited above.
47. Chambers and Landreth (eds.), *Called Up*, p. 181. Those who had already published books were Tom Stacey and Gabriel Woolf; the vociferous journalist was Robert Robinson.
48. Ibid., p. 83.
49. *The Isis*, 23 February 1955. It was said that Bingham had written three contributions to a forthcoming anthology entitled 'Two-Year Warrior' – only one of these contributions was eventually published.
50. Johnson (ed.), *All Bull*.

51. David Lodge entry in *Dictionary of National Biography* for (Arthur) John Harvey Blackwell, http://www.oxforddnb.com/view/article/68443, accessed 16 October 2013.

52. Lodge, *Ginger, You're Barmy*, p. 213.

53. Peter Burns/Alan Burns in Johnson (ed.), *All Bull*, pp. 81–9, at p. 81.

54. John Nott, *Here Today, Gone Tomorrow: Recollections of an Errant Politician* (2002), p. 41.

55. Peter Nichols, *Feeling You're Behind: An Autobiography* (1984), p. 70.

56. Ibid., p. 128.

57. Ronald Hayman, *Arnold Wesker* (1970), p. 9.

58. Arnold Wesker, *As Much as I Dare: An Autobiography (1932–1959)* (1994), p. 256.

59. Antony Copley, interview, 27 February 2013.

60. NAM 2004-02-106, Simon Bendall, 'diary'; this passage is taken from a note rather than a diary entry.

61. Cited in John Blair, *The Conscript Doctors: Memories of National Service* (Edinburgh, 2001), p. 14.

62. IWMSA 27184, John Akehurst, reel 1.

63. The training film, made in 1943, was entitled *The New Lot*. It was remade in 1944 as a commercial film, *The Way Ahead*.

64. Geoffrey Rosbrook, a national service gunner, can be seen 'leaning on the desk smoking a cigarette' in the NAAFI scene. See *The NAAFI Review*, spring 1955 and Rosbrook's own papers in IWM 15608.

65. IWMSA 26097, Terrance Atkinson, reel 2.

66. Jeff Nuttall in Johnson (ed.), *All Bull*, pp. 17–25, at p. 22.

67. IWM 1941, H. Atkins, unpublished memoir, p. 137.

68. David Baxter, interview, 15 March 2012.

69. David Lodge, *How Far Can You Go?* (1980, this edn 1981), p. 51.

70. Stanley Price, 'A Sergeant's Tale' (1990), unpublished typescript.

71. Stanley Price, *Somewhere to Hang My Hat: An Irish-Jewish Journey* (Dublin, 2002), pp. 167–73.

72. Berwick Coates, *Sam Browne's Schooldays: Experiences of a Typical Squad of Postwar National Service Recruits* (Bognor Regis, 2009), pp. 3 and 5–6.

73. 'Shiner' Wright, *Jack Strop, VD and Scar* (Edinburgh, 2002, 'refined edition' 2010), p. 4. Italics and bold in the original.

74. Barnes, *With the Dirty Half-hundred*, p. 2.

75. Blair, *Conscript Doctors*, p. 76.

76. Cited in Huw Bennett, *Fighting the Mau Mau: The British Army and Counter-insurgency in the Kenya Emergency* (Cambridge, 2012), p. 226.

77. Harry Fancy, *'Remembered with Advantage': The National Service Memoirs of Lance Corporal (Unpaid) Harry Fancy* (Marple, 2009).
78. IWM 714, D. Lord.
79. A. M. Carr-Saunders, D. Caradog Jones and C. A. Moser, *A Survey of Social Conditions in England and Wales* (Oxford, 1958), pp. 247–8.
80. IWM 2918, F. N. E. Starkey, diary entry, 5 September 1948.
81. *The Times*, 29 April 1959.
82. IWMSA 27811, Richard Wilson, reel 2.
83. IWM 675, A. R. Ashton, 'National Service: Royal Marine Commando Memoirs' (1990).
84. The two most celebrated SAS authors – 'Andy McNab' and 'Chris Ryan' – are both the sons of national servicemen. Many national servicemen say that they served with the SAS. This may be pure fantasy in some cases and 'served with' is itself an ambiguous term. However, some national servicemen did hold commissions with the SAS – see the *Army List* for 1954.
85. IWMSA 21688, Richard Ingrams. At the end of an interview by Charles Wheeler in 2000 for a BBC radio programme on national service, there is a revealing comment. After the formal interview is over, Wheeler says: 'Yes, Tony Howard told me that cello story.'
86. Auberon Waugh, *Will This Do? An Autobiography* (1991, this edn 1992), p. 105.

3. THE POLITICS OF CONSCRIPTION, 1945–1949

1. *The Times*, 5 March 1946.
2. TNA AIR 77/608, 'Morale of the National Service Airman on Entry and During Initial Training: Report I of an Investigation into the Morale of the National Service Man in the RAF', January 1949.
3. *The Times*, 7 December 1948.
4. R. J. Q. Adams, 'The National Service League and Mandatory Service in Edwardian Britain', *Armed Forces and Society*, 12 (1985), pp. 53–74; R. J. Q. Adams and Philip Poirier, *The Conscription Controversy in Great Britain, 1900–1918* (Columbus, OH, 1987); Keith Grieves, *The Politics of Manpower, 1914–18* (Manchester, 1988).
5. *The Times*, 8 November 1938.
6. TNA CAB 139/505, Lampton to Chilver, 4 December 1957. As the end of national service approached, officials often speculated on what might stimulate recruitment and whether unemployment in the inter-war years

had done so – though they were unsure how much correlation there had been.

7. Kevin Morgan, 'Militarism and Anti-militarism: Socialists, Communists and Conscription in France and Britain, 1900–1940', *Past and Present*, 202 (2009), pp. 207–44.

8. Alan Sillitoe, *Life Without Armour* (1995), p. 76.

9. TNA LAB 6/682, 'Outline of the History of National Service', 1960.

10. Len Scott, *Conscription and the Attlee Governments: The Politics and Policy of National Service, 1945–1951* (Oxford, 1993), p. 80.

11. *Daily Express*, 12 November 1955, 'Blueprint for a New Army' discussed proposals by the Army League that included a foreign legion and an imperial gendarmerie. Julian Amery, 'How to Strengthen the British Army', *East and West*, 1957, in King's College London, Liddell Hart Archives, LH 15/5/163. On Amery's views about conscription and the use of non-British troops, see David Mitchell, 'The Army League, Conscription and the 1956 Defence Review' (PhD thesis, University of East Anglia, 2012).

12. TNA DEFE 7/146, 'Future Manpower Planning in the Services', attached to letter from Jacob to Newling, 8 October 1946.

13. Scott, *Conscription and the Attlee Governments*, p. 41.

14. *Portcullis*, magazine of Emanuel School, summer 1947.

15. Mrs F. Lucas Keene, letter to the *British Medical Journal*, 19 June 1948, expressing the opinion of the Medical Women's Federation that women doctors ought to be called up.

16. Nottingham PRO, papers of Professor J. M. Lee, DD 393/1, letter from Graham Mottershaw to Lee, 24 April 1951: 'Much as I deplore many of the socialist government's schemes, I have a better chance of release under this government than I would have under the Conservatives.'

17. *The Times*, 2 December 1948.

18. Ibid., 18 December 1946.

19. Ibid., 16 July 1946. In the Battersea by-election of 1946, the ILP candidate was said to have made opposition to conscription the main plank of his platform. He was not elected.

20. TNA LAB 6/569, letter from Gibson, 25 July 1949, apparently written to tribunal for conscientious objectors about James Greig.

21. TNA DEFE 7/146, 'Compulsory Military Service', 12 April 1945.

22. Ibid., 'Future Manpower Planning in the Services', attached to letter from Jacob to Newling, 18 October 1946.

23. Ibid., 'The Introduction of a Permanent Scheme for Compulsory Military Service' (draft), attached to note from W. F. Lamb to Neden, 25 June 1946.

24. Ibid.
25. John Kent, 'Bevin's Imperialism and the Idea of Euro-Africa, 1945–49', in Michael Dockrill and John Young (eds.), *British Foreign Policy, 1945–56* (1989), pp. 47–76.
26. TNA DEFE 7/146, telegram, Field Marshal Wilson in Washington to chiefs of staff, 23 November 1945. Ibid., Jacob to Ismay, 24 November 1945.
27. Victor Yates, cited in *The Times*, 14 June 1946.
28. Brigadier A. H. Head, 'The Army We Need', *The Spectator*, 17 December 1948.
29. TNA DEFE 7/146, 'The Introduction of a Permanent Scheme for Compulsory Military Service'.
30. Scott, *Conscription and the Attlee Governments*, p. 53.
31. Ibid., p. 54.
32. C. C. S. Newton, 'The Sterling Crisis of 1947 and the British Response to the Marshall Plan', *Economic History Review*, 37, 3 (1984), pp. 391–408.
33. Scott, *Conscription and the Attlee Governments*, p. 113.
34. TNA PREM 8/598, Attlee to Alan Lascelles, secretary to the King, 3 April 1947. Attlee was being disingenuous in blaming the rebellion on the elderly Welshmen. As he must have known, the key leader had been the young, clever and English Richard Crossman – see *Manchester Guardian*, 5 May 1947.
35. *The Times*, 23 May 1947.
36. Ibid., 1 December 1948.
37. TNA AIR 20/8993, 'National Service Act: Control of Intake in Relation to Services' Requirements', from Ministry of Defence, 14 October 1947.
38. TNA WO 216/305, AG to S of S and CIGS, enclosing report on quality of national service intake, 22 February 1947.
39. IWM 7778, K. S. J. Hill.
40. Alastair Horne with David Montgomery, *The Lonely Leader: Monty, 1944–1945* (1995), p. xxi.
41. Richard Crossman, 'The Great Conscription Muddle', *Sunday Pictorial*, 14 August 1949, in LHCMA, LH 15/5/114.
42. *Manchester Guardian*, 1 October 1949.
43. Peter Nichols, diary entry, April 1975, cited in introduction to *Privates on Parade* in id., *Plays: One* (1987), no pagination.
44. *New Statesman*, 18 December 1948.
45. LHCMA, LH 13/32, Liddell Hart to Lt General Francis Tuker, 1 March 1948.

46. Ibid., Liddell Hart to Frank Owen, 24 October 1949.
47. Ibid., Liddell Hart to Pyman, 22 December 1949.
48. *News Chronicle*, 25 February 1949, in LHCMA, LH 15/5/114.

4. THE EXPERIENCE OF CONSCRIPTION, 1945–1949

1. Alan Sillitoe, *Life Without Armour* (1995), p. 84.
2. Alan Allport, *Demobbed: Coming Home after the Second World War* (2009), p. 13.
3. Christopher Bayly and Tim Harper, *Forgotten Wars: The End of Britain's Asian Empire* (2007), p. 13.
4. Denis Healey, *The Time of My Life* (1989, this edn 1990), p. 68.
5. Figures given in Alex Danchev, 'The Army and the Home Front' in David Chandler and Ian Beckett (eds.), *The Oxford History of the British Army* (Oxford, 1994), pp. 298–315, at p. 302. According to the War Office, the active army on 30 June 1945 contained 2,930,884 soldiers, TNA WO 73/183.
6. Harold Evans, *My Paper Chase: True Stories of Vanished Times, an Autobiography* (2009, this edn 2010), p. 88.
7. Jeremy Crang, *The British Army and the People's War, 1939–1945* (Manchester, 2000), pp. 59–61.
8. John Colville, *The Fringes of Power: 10 Downing Street Diaries, 1939–1955* (New York, 1985), p. 278, 30 October 1940; see also ibid., p. 433, 30 August 1941. Churchill said: '"They have saved this country." He was referring to the RAF pilots, the majority of whom had come from the Secondary Schools [as opposed to public schools].'
9. TNA AIR 77/608, 'Morale of the National Service Airman on Entry and During Initial Training: Report I of an Investigation into the Morale of the National Service Man in the RAF', January 1949.
10. Cecil Blacker, *Monkey Business: The Memoirs of General Sir Cecil Blacker* (1993), p. 22.
11. NAM 2001-07-1187-46, papers of Andrew Man, Royal Military College, 'Roll of Officers and Gentlemen Cadets', August–December 1929.
12. Alan Lascelles, *King's Counsellor: Abdication and War – The Diaries of Sir Alan Lascelles* (edited by Duff Hart-Davis) (2006), p. 116, entry for 23 March 1943. General Bernard Paget was apparently 'incensed' about the use of psychiatrists who 'subject these boys to a string of impertinent Freudian questions'.

13. Crang, *The British Army*, p. 52.
14. Ibid., p. 53.
15. Healey, *The Time of My Life*, p. 59.
16. Bayly and Harper, *Forgotten Wars*, p. 137.
17. IWMSA 9989, Lt Colonel Mike Calvert, reels 2 and 7.
18. *Ministry of Labour Gazette*, 1946, p. 92.
19. Allport, *Demobbed*.
20. Cited in Bayly and Harper, *Forgotten Wars*, p. 221.
21. IWMSA 26546, Martyn Highfield, reel 14.
22. IWMSA 18565, James Notley, reel 10.
23. IWMSA 16719, Edward Grey, reels 9 and 10.
24. Hansard, 27 November 1946, answer by Mr de Freitas.
25. On these disturbances see TNA AIR 23/2899.
26. Sillitoe, *Life Without Armour*, p. 116.
27. John Saville, *Memoirs from the Left* (2003), p. 67.
28. Peter Nichols, *Feeling You're Behind: An Autobiography* (1984, this edn 1985), p. 74.
29. IWMSA 21681, Ray Self. © Whistledown, 2000.
30. Len Scott, *Conscription and the Attlee Governments: The Politics and Policy of National Service, 1945–1951* (Oxford, 1993), p. 46.
31. TNA WO 32/11578, minutes of meeting chaired by Major General Watson, 5 June 1945, minutes dated 16 June, signed Major Woolley.
32. TNA WO 384/11, 'Abstract of Army Statistics'. In 1950, there were 59 British officers and 43 other ranks in India; there were 156 officers and 30 other ranks in Pakistan.
33. This was, for example, the case of George Cooper, who was born in 1925, commissioned into the Royal Engineers in 1945 and then into the Bengal Sappers in 1946. NAMSA 1989-05-258.
34. IWM 2856, Colonel Pickard, diary entries, 19 November 1946 and 10 August 1947.
35. Harold Perkin, *The Making of a Social Historian* (2002), p. 79.
36. NAMSA 1991-09-1, Col. P. J. Wilkinson, reel 2.
37. IWMSA 12401, D'Arcy John Desmond Mander, reel 1. See too the obituary for Major D'Arcy Mander, *Daily Telegraph*, 16 April 2001.
38. IWM 3438, J. T. Nye, letter, to 'all', 1945, otherwise undated; letters to Mum, Dad and Dick: from Bombay, 6 August 1946; from Bombay, 3 September 1946; from Colombo, 16 March 1947.
39. Geoff Weekes in Ken Drury (ed.), *Get Some In: Memories of National Service* (Great Dunmow, 2006), pp. 13–16, at p. 14.
40. IWM 7778, K.S.J. Hill.

41. Lord Moran, 'VD and Conscription', *The Spectator*, 8 August 1947.

42. Roger Alford, *Life and LSE* (Sussex, 2009), pp. 153–63.

43. For anti-Semitic documents circulated among conscripts in Palestine, see NAM 2006-07-58, papers of Sergeant Herbert Hiscock.

44. IWMSA 14786, Godfrey Raper, reel 3.

45. Jeremy Morse, interviewed by William Reader, *NLSC: City Lives*, 1988, British Library Sound & Moving Image Catalogue reference C409/007, transcript p. 6/track 1. © The British Library.

46. IWM 2717, John Wells Watson, letter to sister, 15 March 1948.

47. George Webb, *Epitaph for an Army of Peacekeepers: British Forces in Palestine, 1945–1948* (Fleet Hargate, 2005), pp. 36–7.

48. IWMSA 9485, Kenneth Lee, reels 1 and 2.

49. Eric Lowe, *Forgotten Conscripts: Prelude to Palestine's Struggle for Survival* (Trafford, 2006), p. vi.

50. Letter from Ivan Yates, *The Times*, 23 January 1946.

51. Ken Perkins, *A Fortunate Soldier* (1988), p. 18.

52. IWM Trevor Royle, 66/211/2(1/74), David Price.

53. IWMSA 14786, Godfrey Raper, reel 1.

54. Ion Trewin, *Alan Clark: The Biography* (2009).

55. Simon Raven, *The English Gentleman: An Essay in Attitudes* (1961), p. 12.

56. William Rees-Mogg, *Memoirs* (2011), p. 82.

57. James Prior, *A Balance of Power* (1986), p. 10.

58. Jeremy Morse, interviewed by William Reader, *NLSC: City Lives*, 1988, British Library Sound & Moving Image Catalogue reference C409/007, transcript p. 8/track 1. © The British Library.

59. John Quinton, interviewed by Paul Thompson, *NLSC: City Lives*, 1988, British Library Sound & Moving Image Catalogue reference C409/001, transcript p. 12/track 1. © The British Library.

60. Wing Commander Walker, winning essay, Trench Gascoigne Essay Competition 1947, *Journal of the Royal United Services Institution* May 1948, pp. 177–86.

61. TNA WO 32/15144, head of department of mathematics, RAMS, to director of studies, RAMS, signed Sisson, 9 May 1954.

62. *Journal of the Royal United Services Institution*, February 1948, discussion on 'The Supply and Training of Officers', 19 November 1947, chaired by Lord Hankey, contribution by Major General Pratt (president of RMA selection board), pp. 45–68, at p. 60.

63. 'Lictor', 'The Production of Army Officers', *Journal of the Royal United Services Institution*, November 1948, pp. 584–9.

64. TNA WO 32/11848, note signed Lambert and circulated on 8 April 1957.
65. IWMSA 12498, Alberic Stacpoole, reel 1.
66. IWMSA 19853, Anthony Denys Firth, reel 3.
67. Obituary, *Daily Telegraph*, 27 October 2006.
68. James Kennaway, *Tunes of Glory* (1956); John Hollands, *The Dead, the Dying and the Damned* (1956).
69. IWMSA 27184, John Akehurst, reel 4.
70. IWM 12515, Sir Peter Holmes, 'Korean War Diary'.
71. TNA WO 71/1024. During a court martial for mutiny, held in Korea from 30 June to 3 July 1951, the defence counsel cross-examined Major Leith-Macgregor about the long-term consequences of his brutal treatment by Italians when he had been a prisoner of war. The implication seems to have been that Leith-Macgregor had been brutalized by his experiences. Note too the way in which violence in Malaya and Kenya was often initiated by soldiers who regarded themselves as having been 'blooded' in the Second World War (see Chapter 13).

5. BOYS: NATIONAL SERVICEMEN BEFORE CALL-UP

1. IWMSA 26097, Terrance Atkinson, reel 1.
2. T. Ferguson and J. Cunnison, *The Young Wage-earner: A Study of Glasgow Boys* (Oxford, 1951); eid., *In Their Early Twenties: A Study of Glasgow Youth* (Oxford, 1956). Letter from Bryan Thwaites to *The Times*, 13 December 1951. Letter from B. Faithfull-Davies to *The Times*, 11 December 1951.
3. King George's Jubilee Trust, *Citizens of Tomorrow: A Study of the Influences Affecting the Upbringing of Young People* (1955).
4. Alicia Percival, *Youth Will Be Led: The Story of the Voluntary Youth Organizations* (1951), p. 161.
5. Mark Abrams, *The Teenage Consumer* (1959).
6. David Morgan, 'It Will Make a Man of You': Notes on National Service, Masculinity and Autobiography* (Manchester, 1987), p. 71.
7. John Blair, *The Conscript Doctors: Memories of National Service* (Edinburgh, 2001), p. 195.
8. John Sutherland, *The Boy Who Loved Books* (2007, this edn 2008), p. 149.
9. Interview with John Ferris, 25 July 2012.
10. T. R. Fyvel, *The Insecure Offenders: Rebellious Youth in the Welfare State* (1961, this edn 1969), preface, no pagination.
11. Ministry of Labour and National Service, *Time Rates of Wages and Hours of Labour* (1946), p. 72.

12. Ibid. (1947), p. 82.

13. R. F. L. Logan and E. M. Goldberg, 'Rising Eighteen in a London Sub-urb: A Study of Some Aspects of the Life and Health of Young Men', *British Journal of Sociology*, 4, 4 (1953), pp. 323–45, at p. 330: 'The families of these lads seemed ... to be seeking higher social status and security for their sons through the skills of engineering, rather than through the old-fashioned snobbery of white-collared jobs.'

14. TNA WO 32/10994, cutting from *Northern Echo*, 11 April 1957. The newspaper was reporting views expressed by Colonel Gould.

15. *Census 1951: General Report*, p. 149.

16. TNA WO 32/15743, 'Note on Shortage of Officers in the North', briga-dier commanding War Office Selection Board, 27 March 1953.

17. Michael Young and Peter Willmott, *Family and Class in a London Suburb* (1960, this edn 1976), p. 101.

18. Leslie Thomas, *This Time Next Week* (1964, this edn 1991).

19. Ministry of Education, *15 to 18* (1959) (Crowther Report), II, p. 155.

20. Ferguson and Cunnison, *In Their Early Twenties*, p. 4.

21. On the propensity of upper-middle-class people to talk in class terms while disparaging the use of the word 'class', see Margaret Stacey, *Trad-ition and Change: A Study of Banbury* (1960), p. 145.

22. Henry Askew, interviewed by Cathy Courtney, *NLSC: City Lives*, 1992, British Library Sound & Moving Image Catalogue reference C409/082, track 1. © The British Library.

23. David Cainey, interviewed by Andrew Vincent, *Millennium Memory Bank*, 1998, British Library Sound & Moving Image Catalogue refer-ence C900/00543, track 1. © BBC.

24. IWMSA 18217, Derek Watkins, reel 1.

25. Leslie T. Wilkins, *The Social Survey: National Service and Enlistment in the Armed Forces. A Report on an Enquiry Made for Several Govern-ment Departments into the Attitudes of Young Men Prior to, and on Joining the Armed Forces* (1951), p. 6.

26. Hermann Mannheim and Leslie T. Wilkins, *Prediction Methods in Rela-tion to Borstal Training* (1955), pp. 188–9.

27. Blair, *The Conscript Doctors*, p. 22.

28. Stacey, *Tradition and Change*, p. 31.

29. John Wain, *The Contenders* (1958).

30. Brian Jackson and Dennis Marsden, *Education and the Working Class: Some General Themes Raised by a Study of 88 Working-class Children in a Northern Industrial City* (1962, this edn 1966), p. 19.

31. TNA WO 291/1510, AORG, 'The Different Officer Potentials of Various Regions of Great Britain', 1956, by L. J. Holman, Appendix D, 'Shortage of Officers from the North', by CEO [Chief Education Officer] Northern Command.

32. Stacey, *Tradition and Change*, p. 31.

33. Ibid., p. 71.

34. TNA WO 32/15743, 'NS Officers – Geographical Distribution', Appendix B, 'Estimates of NS Officer Production by Counties in One NS Cycle', attached to note, 18 September 1953, signed Colonel Houghton-Beckford. Oxfordshire's production of officers accounted for 260 officers for every 100 that were needed by the Territorial Army in the county; this compared with Wiltshire, which produced 95 per cent of its needs. Oxfordshire's surplus sprang partly from the fact that so many 'officerly' young men were at Oxford University, but this alone did not account for it. Cambridgeshire produced 176 men for every 100 that were needed for the Territorial Army.

35. IWMSA 26563, John Robinson, reel 1.

36. IWMSA 19632, George Lightley, reel 1.

37. IWMSA 29062, John 'Jack' Burn, reel 1.

38. Crowther, II, p. 109. The sample was adjusted in various ways.

39. Ibid.

40. David Glass (ed.), *Social Mobility in Britain* (1954), p. 4.

41. IWMSA 19993, Ernest Dobson, reel 1.

42. *Manchester Guardian*, 9 September 1953, 'Old School Tie no Passport to RAF Commissions?' The article reported on findings of Air Ministry psychologists: 'Normally the desire for social status played a part in the decision of an individual offered an opportunity to go to a grammar school or become an officer. The apprentice, however, seemed more interested in acquiring and practising a vocational skill than in raising his social status.' Some of the apprentice-trained men interviewed by the RAF had not sat the 11-plus – 'success in the examination . . . would have conflicted with their desire to become artisans'.

43. TNA WO 32/16277, note for Under Secretary of State, illegible signature, 15 September 1951.

44. Crowther, II, p. 109.

45. IWMSA 24570, Piers Plowright.

46. Quaker Meeting House, temp mss, 914, ECM/9, Central Board for Conscientious Objectors Executive Committee, minutes, 16 January 1952. The board was told that Graham Anderson was to be expelled from the City of London School for refusal to join the CCF. It seems

likely that the school relented after representations by the boy's father, ibid., 30 January 1952.

47. TNA DEFE 13/53, Anthony Hurd to Macmillan, 2 February 1955. Hurd believed that the headmaster of Bradfield College would be a useful person to consult about national service.
48. Harold Loukes, *Secondary Modern* (1957), p. 26.
49. Crowther, II, p. 150.
50. Jim Riordan, *Comrade Jim: The Spy Who Played for Spartak* (2008), p. 28.
51. Ronald Hyam, *My Life in the Past* (privately published, 2012), pp. 77–8.
52. Crowther, II, p. 14.
53. A. N. Oppenheim, 'Social Status and Clique Formation among Grammar School Boys', *British Journal of Sociology*, 6, 3 (1955), pp. 228–45.
54. Roy Lewis and Angus Maude, *The English Middle Classes* (1949), p. 238.
55. H. T. Himmelweit, A. H. Halsey and A. N. Oppenheim, 'The Views of Adolescents on Some Aspects of the Social Class Structure', *British Journal of Sociology*, 3, 2 (1952), pp. 148–72.
56. W. D. James, *Hamptonians at War: Some War Experiences of Old Boys of Hampton Grammar School* (1964).
57. Alan Wood quoted in Jeremy Crang, *The British Army and the People's War, 1939–1945* (Manchester, 2000), p. 29.
58. TNA LAB 19/319, Herts County Council Employment Service, Dacorum Division, Services Open Evening, 28 November 1952. The grammar school boys had attended en masse on an evening in May. None came on 28 November.
59. John Hills of Bradfield College, letter to *The Times*, 8 October 1949.
60. Max Poulter in Ken Drury (ed.), *Get Some In: Memories of National Service* (Great Dunmow, 2006), pp. 30–36, at p. 34.
61. Nottingham PRO, papers of Professor J. M. Lee, DD 393/1/3, typed note, 'The Henry Mellish Grammar School Bulwell Nottingham. The Sixth Form Leaver of 1949'.
62. *Daily Express*, 20 January 1949.
63. TNA LAB 19/298, London County Council, 'Unemployment of Boys Aged 17 – Effect of Impending National Service'. Report, signed John Brown, 11 September 1953.
64. King George's Jubilee Trust, *Citizens of Tomorrow*, p. 73.
65. Head of Daniel Stewart's College quoted in *The Scotsman*, 7 October 1954, cited in Ferguson and Cunnison, *In Their Early Twenties*, p. 5.
66. Crowther, II, p. 147.

67. Ferguson and Cunnison, *In Their Early Twenties*, p. 14.
68. Logan and Goldberg, 'Rising Eighteen'.
69. Lord Moran, 'VD and Conscription', *The Spectator*, 8 August 1947: 'Recently the Chairman of a Juvenile Employment Committee put it on record that . . . boys are restless; they will not settle to anything; they do not want to become apprentices, and they do not want to learn to become craftsmen or technicians.'
70. Gwylmor Prys Williams, *Teenagers' Problems: The Contemporary Social Background and Youth's Reaction to It* (1958), p. 3: 'Quite a number of youths go in for apprenticeships or the Merchant Navy because it affords a way of dodging National Service, and the status of apprenticeship has deteriorated to some extent.'
71. Ministry of Labour and National Service, *Report on the Enquiry into the Effects of National Service on the Education and Employment of Young Men* (1955), p. 10.
72. IWMSA 17819, Alan Sandland, reel 1.
73. M. E. M. Herford, letter to *The Times*, 19 December 1956.
74. IWMSA 26853, Thomas Hewitson, reel 2.
75. Ministry of Labour and National Service, *Effects of National Service*, p. 10.
76. Ibid.
77. TNA AIR 77/608, 'Morale of the National Service Airman on Entry and During Initial Training: Report I of an Investigation into the Morale of the National Service Man in the RAF', January 1949.
78. Ken Lynham, interviewed by Michael Cos, *Food: From Source to Salespoint*, 2005, British Library Sound & Moving Image Catalogue reference C821/165, track 3. © The British Library.
79. TNA WO 32/15604, point 9, 'Age of Call-up', attached to letter from H. A. Dilley, 26 June 1955: 'The Ministry of Labour point out that in the case of almost all apprenticeships the last year is already spent "working on the job".'
80. IWMSA 22606, Harry Sanson, reel 2.
81. Albert Balmer, *A Cyprus Journey: Memoirs of National Service* (2008), pp. 16–17.
82. IWMSA 18439, Albert Tyas, reel 1.
83. NAM 2003-08-61, Jack Gillett.
84. Brian Bushell in Eric Pegg (ed.), *The Royal Engineers and the National Service Years, 1939–1963: A Military and Social History* (2002), pp. 129–30, and Patrick Sumner in ibid., pp. 409–13.
85. IWMSA 14145, Richard Faint, reel 1.

86. IWMSA 26559, Leigh Parkes, reel 1.
87. Mannheim and Wilkins, *Prediction Methods in Relation to Borstal Training*, pp. 190–92.
88. IWMSA 29895, Paul Croxson, reel 1.
89. IWMSA 21582, David Davies, reel 1.
90. IWMSA 20802, Jack Coley, reel 1.
91. IWMSA 18825, Joseph Roberts, reel 1.
92. Leslie T. Wilkins, *Delinquent Generations* (1960).
93. TNA AIR 77/608, 'Morale of the National Service Airman on Entry and During Initial Training'.
94. Royston Salmon in Peter Chambers and Amy Landreth (eds.), *Called Up: The Personal Experiences of Sixteen National Servicemen, Told by Themselves* (1955), pp. 140–50, at p. 141.
95. Alan Sillitoe, *Life Without Armour* (1995), p. 40.
96. Ibid., p. 51.
97. IWM 6431, E. A. Dorking, 'Some Recollections of My Life During the Years 1930–1955'.
98. Geoffrey G. Field, *Blood, Sweat and Toil: Remaking the British Working Class, 1939–1945* (Oxford, 2011), p. 219.
99. IWMSA 10925, Bruce Kent, reel 1.
100. IWMSA 28361, Julian Thompson, reel 1.
101. IWMSA 22347, Edmund Bruford-Davies, reel 1.
102. A. E. Morgan, *Young Citizen* (1943), p. 51.
103. TNA AIR 77/608, 'Morale of the National Service Airman on Entry and During Initial Training'.
104. TNA AIR 20/12136, 'Morale of the National Service Airman (an Account of an Investigation Covering the Period October 1947–September 1950)', by A. S. Anthony, 24 July 1951. The same report can also be found in TNA AIR 77/270.
105. Logan and Goldberg, 'Rising Eighteen'. See also *The Times*, 7 December 1951. An enquiry among 200 boys and 198 girls who had left school in the summer of 1950 concluded that 70 per cent of boys and 74 per cent of girls had settled into employment.
106. *Ministry of Labour Gazette*, January 1957, p. 23.
107. E. R. Braithwaite, *To Sir, with Love* (1959), p. 179.
108. Leslie T. Wilkins, *The Adolescent in Britain* (1955), p. 31.
109. TNA LAB 19/222, Director of Education to Ministry of Labour and National Service, signed H. S. Magnay, 4 November (no year but seems to be 1950).

110. Ministry of Labour and National Service, *Effects of National Service*, p. 19.

111. Logan and Goldberg, 'Rising Eighteen'.

112. Letter from Ewen Montagu to *The Times*, 24 January 1949.

113. TNA LAB 19/298, minute sheet, from Parker to Taylor, 14 January 1949 at start of document but 5 April 1949 at its end.

114. James Maxwell, *Sixteen Years On: A Follow-up of the 1947 Scottish Survey* (1969), p. 67.

115. Riordan, *Comrade Jim*, p. 31.

116. TNA LAB 19/298, London County Council, 'Unemployment of Boys Aged 17 – Effects of Impending National Service'. Report, signed John Brown, 11 September 1953.

117. Ferguson and Cunnison, *In Their Early Twenties*, pp. 70 and 72.

118. Ibid., p. 71.

119. Arnold Wesker, *As Much as I Dare: An Autobiography (1932–1959)* (1994), p. 257.

120. Ferris, interview, 25 July 2012.

121. Fyvel, *The Insecure Offenders*, p. 40.

122. A. J. Leoni, letter to *The Times*, 8 May 1954.

123. TNA CAB 128/29/33, Cabinet, 22 September 1955.

124. Gwylmor Prys Williams, *Patterns of Juvenile Delinquency: England and Wales, 1946–1961* (1962), p. 22.

125. IWMSA 26097, Terrance Atkinson, reel 1.

126. Ken Lynham, interviewed by Michael Cos, *Food: From Source to Salespoint*, 2005, British Library Sound & Moving Image Catalogue reference C821/165, track 4. © The British Library.

127. IWM 1598, A. Cole, letter to family, 18 March 1959.

128. IWMSA 22261, Peter Whiteman. © Whistledown, 2000.

129. IWM 1779, I. W. G. Martin, extract from letter to Martin (dates from 1958 but not clear exactly when it was written or by whom): 'the Greeks, mostly Teddy boy types, are paying off a few old scores'. IWM 15316, P. J. Houghton-Brown, undated letter to mother, from Cyprus: 'It is the Teddy boy types that you have to watch.'

130. TNA INF 6/812, on the making of the film.

131. Basil Henriques, *The Home-menders: The Prevention of Unhappiness in Children* (1955).

132. TNA LAB 19/319, 'So You're Being Called Up', March 1954.

133. Ibid., Youth Employment Service – Southern Region, illegible signature, 9 August 1955, responding to a request for frank views of speakers.

134. Wilkins, *National Service and Enlistment*, p. 13.

NOTES TO PP. 105-11

135. Ibid., pp. 36 and 37.
136. NAMSA 2003-04-2, Field Marshal Sir John Chapple, reel 1.
137. IWMSA 9911, Samuel Osborne, reel 1.
138. TNA LAB 21/8, minutes of meeting of controllers, 10 June 1953.
139. King George's Jubilee Trust, *Citizens of Tomorrow*, p. 66.
140. TNA WO 32/16714, correspondence on this matter.
141. *The Times*, 2 March 1950, letter on 'young hooligans' from Elinor Birley, the wife of the headmaster of Eton.
142. King George's Jubilee Trust, *Citizens of Tomorrow*, p. 20.
143. Ibid., p. 18.

6. CALL-UP

1. Stuart Brisley, interviewed by Melanie Roberts, *NLSC: Artists' Lives*, 1996, British Library Sound & Moving Image Catalogue reference C466/43, track 2. © The British Library.
2. TNA LAB 19/319, National Joint Advisory Council, 26 October 1955, 'Minister's Quarterly Review of Certain Aspects of the Work of the Ministry'.
3. NAMSA 1995-05-93, Robin Ollington, reel 1.
4. TNA DEFE 10/332, Working Party on National Service Intakes, 18 May 1951. Roberts drew attention to the numbers, around 22 per cent, who might fail to register on the correct day.
5. TNA LAB 6/655, letter to Vivien, illegible signature, 2 April 1958. It was reckoned at this stage that around one man in seven was failing to register.
6. TNA LAB 6/692, this file contains statistical tables relating to failure to register or submit to medical examination.
7. TNA ADM 1/21985, head of Naval Law to Treasury Solicitor, 13 February 1951. By this date, the Home Office seems to have discouraged the payment of bounty.
8. TNA LAB 6/692, 'Analysis of Action by MR 1 on Reports of Failure to Register or to Submit to Medical Examination from 1st January 1949', undated.
9. TNA DEFE 10/332, Working Party on National Service Intakes, 16 January 1952, Appendix IV.
10. TNA RG 28/165, 'Notes on RX Operation Instituted to Assist the Ministry of Labour and National Service', 28 September 1948.
11. TNA WO 71/1261, court martial for mutiny at Shepton Mallet

detention centre, 28 April to 1 May 1959. Matters were made all the more complicated because some 'real' Irishmen had lied about their origins when they joined the British army. During a court martial in April 1959, a soldier from the Royal Army Service Corps disputed his own criminal record, which stated that he had been born in Lancashire. He claimed to have been born in County Donegal.

12. Hansard, 1 April 1953, statement by Sir David Maxwell Fyfe.

13. TNA HO 45/24214, 'Extract from Cabinet Working Party on Eire', undated.

14. TNA ADM 1/26594, 'Detention in the Royal Navy', the Commodore Royal Naval Barracks Portsmouth, 1 January 1956.

15. Charles Richardson, *My Manor* (1992), p. 87.

16. *The Times*, 26 January 1960.

17. Ibid., 20 October 1954.

18. Hansard, 9 November 1954, reply by Head.

19. Ibid., 21 March 1956, Anthony Marlowe.

20. TNA WO 32/15144, Brigadier Sandars to Reader of Civil Service Commission, 3 December 1953. Sandars suggested removing explicit reference to 'colour bar' from a document and substituting the stipulation that candidates for commissions for Sandhurst should 'fit into the corporate life of the Service'.

21. TNA DEFE 10/332, Working Party on National Service Intakes, 27 October 1954.

22. Robert Douglas, *Somewhere to Lay My Head* (2006), p. 254.

23. TNA BD 24/168, Sir Ifan ab Owen Edwards, 'The Welsh National Serviceman', report for the Council for Wales and Monmouthshire, June 1954.

24. TNA WO 32/15025, 'Report of the Welsh National Service Committee', signed Dalton, 13 November 1956. This is responding to a private report (presumably the one referred to above).

25. TNA BD 24/168, Sir Ifan ab Owen Edwards, 'The Welsh National Serviceman'.

26. TNA BD 24/167, minute, 19 February 1954, illegible signature.

27. IWM 1601, J. M. T. Grieve. See also TNA LAB 43/154.

28. TNA LAB 43/2, 'Treatment of Conscientious Objectors', unsigned and undated but seems from surrounding documents to be by Barnes and to date from 2 January 1947.

29. *The Times*, 13 December 1960.

30. Ibid., 7 October 1955.

31. Roger Bush, *FAU: The Third Generation – Friends Ambulance Unit, Post-war Service and International Service, 1946–1959* (York, 1998), p. 103.
32. TNA LAB 6/692, 'Failure to Attend Medical Examination under the National Service Act since January 1949', and 'Analysis of Action by MR1 on Reports of Failure to Register or to Submit to Medical Examination from 1st January 1949'. Both documents are undated but seem to have been produced in late 1960.
33. *The Times*, 8 July 1952. The Court of Appeal decided that Borstal was 'the least appropriate sentence for the offence in question' and substituted a four-month prison sentence.
34. Ibid., 16 June 1949.
35. TNA LAB 6/573, Lt Colonel Donovan to Under Secretary of State for War, 2 November 1951.
36. *The Times*, 22 October 1959.
37. Gabriel Newfield in Peter Chambers and Amy Landreth (eds.), *Called Up: The Personal Experiences of Sixteen National Servicemen, Told by Themselves* (1955), pp. 241–56, at p. 255.
38. *Daily Express*, 29 September 1960.
39. Hansard, 7 February 1956. Victor Yates claimed that Roger Hobbs, who had become a conscientious objector after completing his full-time service, had been paraded outdoors in his underpants. Hobbs was eventually excused further service.
40. TNA LAB 6/468, letter from housemaster, 2 June 1949; letter from headmaster, 27 July 1949.
41. TNA LAB 6/470, letter from the Labour Manager, Belliss and Morcom Limited, 9 September 1949.
42. Stephen Martin, 'Did Your Country Need You? An Oral History of the National Service Experience in Britain, 1945–1963' (PhD thesis, University of Wales, Lampeter, 1997), pp. 60 and 65.
43. Peter Duncumb, interview, 11 January 2013.
44. IWM 15595, David Batterham, 'National Service Recalled': 'I think that this thumbs down stemmed from having stood up to my interviewers' disparaging views. I think that I pointed out that one had to be quite brave to go against the grain of the system. After all I had failed that test myself!'
45. Interview with Lloyd by Alan Macfarlane, 7 June 2005, http://www.alanmacfarlane.com/DO/filmshow/lloyd1_fast.htm.
46. In 1952, a lawyer appealing against a sentence remarked that rejection

of his client's initial claim 'was almost inevitable as he did not belong to any religious organization of known pacifist views'. *The Times*, 8 July 1952.

47. *The Times*, 2 December 1952.

48. TNA LAB 6/496.

49. Hansard, 25 April 1950, question by Dr King.

50. Birkbeck College, papers of Bernard Crick, 1/3/3, typed statement to 'Ministry of Labour and National Service or the Tribunal for Conscientious Objectors as the Minister shall determine which body is relevant'. I am grateful to the literary executors of Sir Bernard Crick for permission to quote this document.

51. David Hockney in B. S. Johnson (ed.), *All Bull: The National Servicemen* (1973), pp. 243–7.

52. Newfield in Chambers and Landreth (eds.), *Called Up*, p. 255.

53. TNA LAB 6/499, case of Anthony Barrington Risley.

54. Methodist Youth Department, *Another Kind of National Service* (1957).

55. Bush, *The FAU*, p. 103.

56. TNA LAB 6/573, case of William Moulton, letter from Harold Cole, Sunday School teacher, 2 December 1951.

57. Bush, *The FAU*, p. 104.

58. IWMSA 10116, David Morrish, reels 1 and 2.

59. IWM 15595, David Batterham, 'National Service Recalled'.

60. TNA LAB 21/167.

61. *The Times*, 30 August 1957.

62. TNA LAB 6/696, Bryan Reed to Chair of Appellate Tribunal for Conscientious Objectors, 20 March 1962.

63. *The Times*, 13 December 1960.

64. TNA LAB 6/349, note, 21 January 1957.

65. TNA LAB 6/684, 'Outline of the History of National Service', 1960.

66. John Palmer, Obituary of Ken Coates, *Guardian*, 29 June 2010.

67. Leslie T. Wilkins, *The Social Survey: National Service and Enlistment in the Armed Forces. A Report on an Enquiry Made for Several Government Departments into the Attitudes of Young Men Prior to, and on Joining the Armed Forces* (1951), p. 12.

68. TNA DEFE 10/332, Working Party on National Service Intakes, 24 October 1951.

69. Ibid., 18 December 1951.

70. IWMSA 28670, David Wilson, reel 2.

71. IWMSA 19993, Ernest Dobson, reel 1.

72. Letter from Myra Hess, Ralph Vaughan Williams and others, *The Times*, 22 May 1947.
73. TNA PREM 11/477, Prime Minister's minute to Monckton, 3 May 1953.
74. See the correspondence on this matter in TNA PREM 8/611.
75. For Cherwell's position see, for example, *Daily Express*, 7 July 1955.
76. See, for example, TNA LAB 8/2476, documents relating to the case of Anthony Kelly. Kelly would have become liable for service in 1946 but deferred to study. He took a fellowship in Illinois and returned, two days after his twenty-sixth birthday. He was technically liable for conscription but the authorities seem to have decided not to call him up.
77. TNA LAB 6/691, 'History of the Deferment Arrangements for Science and Engineering Graduates', 9 October 1960.
78. J. W. Parr, letter to *The Times*, 11 January 1949.
79. *The Times*, 21 October 1959.
80. C. R. Hildyard, letter to *The Times*, 14 October 1959.
81. TNA LAB 19/319, 'Minister's Quarterly Review of Certain Aspects of the Work of the Ministry', National Joint Advisory Council, 26 October 1955.
82. TNA WO 32/17243, 'Report on the Training and Employment of National Servicemen, 1956'. The War Office recognized that it would have been better for recruits to be interviewed by serving officers but could not spare enough men for the task.
83. TNA WO 291/1215, AORG, 'The Testing of National Servicemen at Ministry of Labour Recruiting Centres', March 1952.
84. NAM 2002-08-61, Colin Metcalfe, 'Recollections of National Service'.
85. TNA WO 291/1215, 'The Testing of National Servicemen'.
86. TNA LAB 6/370, letter from Ministry of Labour to George Turner of War Office, 23 May 1955.
87. NAM 2002-08-61, Metcalfe, 'Recollections'.
88. Newfield in Chambers and Landreth (eds.), *Called Up*, p. 245.
89. NAM 2002-08-61, Metcalfe, 'Recollections'.
90. Newfield in Chambers and Landreth (eds.), *Called Up*, p. 255. Newfield and Metcalfe must have served in the same office at the same time. They do not mention each other but Metcalfe's papers contain a photograph of 'John Newfield'. Metcalfe says that the centre processed 25,000 recruits – presumably this means that 25,000 passed through in total but that only 4,000 of them were tested.
91. NAM 2002-08-61, Metcalfe, 'Recollections'.

92. TNA LAB 29/555, 'Instructions for the Guidance of Medical Boards under the National Service Act', pp. 33-5.

93. TNA LAB 19/319, Butler to Pillinger, 4 December 1952.

94. Roger G. Hall, *One-Two-Three-One! (A Nutter's Account of National Service)* (Twickenham, 2007), p. 13.

95. Hansard, 28 February 1956. Marcus Lipton complained that medical boards were passing 'crocks' as fit.

96. At an inquest in Birmingham on a conscript who died on weekend leave from the army, his father said that the boy had been classified A1 and called up in spite of the fact that his mother and grandfather had both died from a rare condition. *The Times*, 24 June 1953.

97. TNA DEFE 7/509, 'Alleged Treatment by the Army of Men Who Have Been Placed by the Ministry of Labour and National Service Medical Boards in Grade III as Only Fit for Certain Duties, but Whose Disabilities Are Ignored in the Initial Period of Training', in briefs for minister, attached to unsigned letter from Ministry of Defence to Sellar of Ministry of Labour, October 1953 (no more precise date).

98. TNA WO 32/17243, 'Report on the Training and Employment of National Servicemen', 1956.

99. *The Times*, 29 June 1953.

100. Dick Langstaff in Ken Drury (ed.), *Get Some In: Memories of National Service* (Great Dunmow, 2006), pp. 39-43, at p. 40.

101. Sidney Rosenbaum, 'Experience of Pulheems in the 1952 Army Intake', *British Journal of Industrial Medicine*, 14 (1957), pp. 281-6.

102. TNA WO 32/17243, 'Report on the Training and Employment of National Servicemen', 1956.

103. Some doctors believed that service would do unfit men good. See Dr M. E. M. Herford, letter to *The Times*, 4 August 1953. Herford believed that only 0.7 per cent of men classed as fit by Ministry of Labour medical boards were subsequently discharged by the army.

104. TNA WO 216/305, 'Report on Quality of National Service Intake', enclosed with note from AG to S of S and GIGS, 22 February 1949.

105. TNA DEFE 10/332, Working Party on National Service Intakes, 24 October 1951. It was anticipated that the introduction of mass mini radiography might raise rejection rates from 17 per cent to 18 per cent.

106. Ibid., 26 April 1951.

107. TNA LAB 6/694, table, undated but obviously from 1960.

108. Ministry of Labour and National Service, *Report on the Enquiry into the Effects of National Service on the Education and Employment of Young Men* (1955).

109. TNA AIR 2/10934, 'Brief for DGM on Allocation of National Servicemen to Trades', signed Lumgair, 6 February 1956. See also TNA AIR 77/271, 'Qualifications of National Service Personnel: Seasonal Variations in Mental Abilities of National Service Men on Entry', signed Anthony, October 1951.

110. TNA WO 32/10994, 'Observations on the Supply of Technical Manpower', P. E. Vernon, May 1952, quoting a recent Air Ministry study. Though Vernon's report was prepared for the Admiralty, it refers to all three services.

111. Sidney Rosenbaum, 'Home Localities of National Servicemen with Respiratory Disease', *British Journal of Preventative and Social Medicine*, 15 (1961), pp. 61–7.

112. T. Ferguson and J. Cunnison, *In Their Early Twenties: A Study of Glasgow Youth* (Oxford, 1956), p. 10.

113. TNA WO 32/10994, 'Observations on the Supply of Technical Manpower', P. E. Vernon, May 1952.

114. Michael Parkinson, *Parky: My Autobiography* (2008), p. 54.

115. Paul Bailey, *An Immaculate Mistake: Scenes from Childhood and Beyond* (1990), p. 128.

116. TNA AIR 2/12407, 'Homosexuality Within the Royal Air Force', note by DPS (PM), no date but prepared as part of submission to Wolfenden Committee.

117. TNA LAB 6/734, letter to a doctor concerning a patient of his, 4 December 1970.

118. TNA LAB 6/680, letter to Sellar, illegible signature, 11 April 1956.

119. TNA LAB 6/734. The letter relating to insurance was written on 11 January 1967 and concerned a medical of 1959; the letter relating to employment was sent on 25 March 1969 and concerned a medical in 1957; the letter relating to South Africa was written on 21 April 1967 and concerned a medical in 1958.

120. TNA DEFE 10/332, Working Party on National Service Intakes, 24 July 1951.

121. Wilkins, *National Service and Enlistment in the Armed Forces*, pp. 9 and 10. See also TNA AIR 77/281, 'Educational Qualifications of National Servicemen (RAF Entrants, 1951–1952)', 7 November 1952. The second of these surveys is more comprehensive with regard to airmen though lacks any comparative figures for the army. The most striking difference between the two sets of figures was that the air force survey suggested that over 14 per cent of national service airmen had

attended technical schools, while Wilkins felt that the figure was just 7 per cent for the air force and 5 per cent for the army.

122. TNA AIR 20/8671, cutting from *Sunday Express*, illegible date.

123. Ministry of Education, *15 to 18* (1959) (Crowther Report), II, pp. 155, 118 and 119.

124. TNA DEFE 10/332, Working Party on National Service Intakes, 26 April 1951.

125. TNA AIR 2/10933, letter, 22 October 1954, signed by a wing commander (name illegible).

126. Ibid., undated table dealing with the period 24 September to 12 October. It was reported that men at Brighton and Blackheath had not been processed by the RAF recruiters before the buildings closed for the day.

127. IWMSA 26563, John Robinson, reel 1.

128. NAM 2000-08-55, D. F. Barrett. Barrett worked for an electrical contractor and, unusually, the interviewing officer sought to persuade him to go into the Royal Electrical and Mechanical Engineers. He insisted, however, on the Middlesex Regiment. Barrett diary (this section is in fact autobiography rather than diary), vol. 1, p. 35.

129. Major General C. Lloyd, 'The Integration of National Service with the Country's Economic Future', *Journal of the Royal United Services Institution*, May 1955, pp. 187–201.

130. David Hall, *Fred: The Definitive Biography of Fred Dibnah* (2006), p. 43. Once he had been attached to a cavalry regiment, Dibnah seems to have escaped from the cookhouse and worked mainly on maintaining the stables.

131. IWM 7778, K. S. J. Hill.

132. NAM 2003-12-7, Charlie Reading.

133. TNA WO 71/1198, court martial, 16 and 17 May 1951, plea in mitigation by Captain Mulligan.

134. IWMSA 17333, John Noble.

135. Leslie Ives, *A Musket for the King: The Trials and Tribulations of a National Serviceman 1949–1951* (Tavistock, 1999), p. 1.

136. Ken Lynham, interviewed by Michael, Cos, *Food: From Source to Salespoint*, 2005, British Library Sound & Moving Image Catalogue reference C821/165, track 4. © The British Library.

137. Jack Spall, interviewed by Cathy Courtney, *NLSC: City Lives*, 1991, British Library Sound & Moving Image Catalogue reference C409/061, track 1. © The British Library.

138. IWM 161, A. E. Fisher.

7. BASIC TRAINING

1. TNA AIR 77/608, 'Morale of the National Service Airman on Entry and During Initial Training: Report I of an Investigation into the Morale of the National Service Man in the RAF', January 1949.

2. *Daily Express*, 23 July 1955. A sapper, prosecuted for not having a ticket, was released after he told the magistrate that he had never travelled on a train before.

3. IWMSA 19634, John Waller, reel 1.

4. Pat Barker in Adrian Walker (ed.), *Six Campaigns: National Servicemen at War, 1948-1960* (1993), pp. 8-14, at p. 8.

5. Wes Magee in B. S. Johnson (ed.), *All Bull: The National Servicemen* (1973), pp. 26-35, at p. 27.

6. John Barkshire interviewed by Kathy Burk, NLSC: *City Lives*, 1990, British Library Sound & Moving Image Catalogue reference C409/057, track 1. © The British Library.

7. NAM 2003-08-67, John Lyon-Maris.

8. IWMSA 18212, Derek Burke, reel 1.

9. Bruce Kent, *Undiscovered Ends: An Autobiography* (1992), p. 33.

10. IWMSA 24570, Piers Plowright, reel 2. Plowright recalled 'slippers chucked at me'.

11. NAMSA 2000-04-56, Michael Perry. Perry who served in the Medical Corps in 1951 and 1952 said his prayers every night and had no trouble. George Carey recalled that his nightly prayers in the RAF were greeted with 'courteous silence': George Carey, *Know the Truth: A Memoir* (2004), p. 28.

12. NAMSA 2000-04-55, John Hodgson, reel 1.

13. NAMSA 2000-04-56, Michael Perry, reel 1.

14. Nottingham PRO, papers of Professor J. M. Lee, DD 393/1/1, letter from Graham Mottershaw to Lee, 20 April 1949.

15. NAM 2003-08-63, Philip Firth.

16. Jeremy Morse, interviewed by William Reader, NLSC: *City Lives*, 1988, British Library Sound & Moving Image Catalogue reference C409/007, track 1. © The British Library.

17. William Rees-Mogg, *Memoirs* (2011), p. 80.

18. NAM 2006-12-77-82, Malcolm Edward Barker, letter to mother, 5 May 1952.

19. IWMSA 21672, Derek Johns. © Whistledown, 2000.

20. John Blair, *The Conscript Doctors: Memories of National Service* (Edinburgh, 2001), p. 24.

21. Letter from 'A mother' to *Observer*, 13 March 1955.

22. Tony Betts, *The Key of the Door: Rhythm and Romance in a Post-war London Adolescence* (Wimborne, 2006), p. 248.

23. Michael Heseltine, *Life in the Jungle: My Autobiography* (2000), p. 52.

24. Anthony Hampshire, interview, 15 May 2013.

25. Tom Baker, *Who on Earth is Tom Baker?* (1997), p. 54.

26. IWM 15608, G. J. W. Rosbrook, Rosbrook to parents, 2 April 1954.

27. Reg Martin, interviewed by Wendy Rickard, *HIV/AIDS Testimonies*, 1995, British Library Sound & Moving Image Catalogue reference C743/02, transcript p. 28. © The British Library.

28. NAM 2006-12-77-83, Malcolm Barker, 'Transcript of the Sporadic Diary Entries of a National Serviceman with the Queen's Royal Regiment (1st Battalion) in BAOR 1952–1953'. Barker described the day he passed out (11 June 1952) as the happiest of his life – though he added, when typing up his diary, that he was amused by his own naivety.

29. Frederick Hudson, *Loyal to the End: A Personal and Factual Account of National Service in Malaya* (Blackburn, 2006), pp. 41, 42, 35. IWM 9870, James Jacobs, p. 4. 'Korea: One Conscript's Work', Jacobs, who went to Korea, said: 'only those awful first few weeks of basic training are best forgotten'.

30. LHCMA, I. W. G. Martin, 'In the Service of Queen and Country', *Plebs*, 2, 2 (July 1978).

31. H. D. Chaplin, *The Queen's Own Royal West Kent Regiment, 1951–1961* (Maidstone, 1964), p. 10.

32. TNA AIR 77/608, 'Morale of the National Service Airman on Entry and During Initial Training': 'In other services this identification is by tradition attached to groups smaller than the Service as a whole – the regiment, the ship etc. In the RAF, it certainly exists, among NS recruits, for the Force as a whole.'

33. IWMSA 26546, Martyn Highfield, reel 14.

34. Ken Perkins, *A Fortunate Soldier* (1988), p. 26.

35. Cecil Blacker, *Monkey Business: The Memoirs of General Sir Cecil Blacker* (1993), pp. 119 and 121.

36. NAM 2003-08-63, Philip Firth.

37. IWMSA 11138, Ron Cassidy interviewed by Charles Allen, reel 1.

38. IWM, Trevor Royle, 66/211/1(1/36), Arthur Franks, 1951.

39. IWM 15595, David Batterham, 'National Service Recalled': 'I was interviewed by my Troop Officer, a conscript my own age, who was sur-

prised to find that I had a place at Cambridge in the same college as himself.'

40. IWM 12733, Cyril MacG Williams, letter to 'all', January 1952.
41. IWM 614, W. H. Butler, 'Derby to Derna (an Account of National Service Experiences)', p. 8: 'When the second lieutenant left the room the sergeant said "you can forget that lot".'
42. NAMSA 2003-04-2, Field Marshal Sir John Chapple, reel 1.
43. Leslie Ives, *A Musket for the King: The Trials and Tribulations of a National Serviceman 1949–1951* (Tavistock, 1999), p. 8.
44. NAMSA 2000-04-52, John Arnold, reel 1: 'I seem to remember a sort of general impression that they [the sergeants] had all been at Arnhem.'
45. NAM 2006-12-77-82, Malcolm Barker, letter to mother, 5 May 1952.
46. N. G. R. Sanders, letter to *Observer*, 20 March 1955.
47. TNA AIR 77/608, 'Morale of the National Service Airman on Entry and During Initial Training'.
48. *Manchester Guardian*, 8 January 1955.
49. *The Times*, 20 March 1953.
50. Ives, *A Musket for the King*, p. 16.
51. T. C. Sparrow, *Tales of a Schoolie: A Story of National Service* (Badsey, 2006), p. 27.
52. *Daily Express*, 6 March 1954.
53. IWMSA 24570, Piers Plowright, reel 2.
54. War Office, *Infantry Training: The National Serviceman's Handbook* (1955), lesson nine.
55. Alan Burns, 'Buster' in *New Writers* (1961), p. 84.
56. Arnold Wesker, *As Much as I Dare: An Autobiography (1932–1959)* (1994), p. 299.
57. Betts, *The Key of the Door*, p. 253.
58. IWM 675, A. R. Ashton, 'National Service: Royal Marine Commando Memoirs' (1990), p. 25.
59. IWMSA 11105, Michael McBain, reel 1.
60. IWMSA 26098, Benjamin Whitchurch, reel 3.
61. IWM 1598, A. Cole, letter home, 12 April 1959.
62. Tom Stacey in Peter Chambers and Amy Landreth (eds.), *Called Up: The Personal Experiences of Sixteen National Servicemen, Told by Themselves* (1955), pp. 47–65, at p. 60.
63. IWMSA 15433, Peter McAleese, reel 1.
64. NAMSA 2000-04-52, Arnold, reel 1.

65. Roger G. Hall, *One-Two-Three-One! (A Nutter's Account of National Service)* (Twickenham, 2007), p. 15.

66. IWM 11915, N. A. Martin, 'The Day the Sun Stopped Shining', p. 9.

67. P. J. Kavanagh, *The Perfect Stranger* (1966), p. 51.

68. Baker, *Who on Earth is Tom Baker?*, p. 82.

69. IWMSA 26098, Whitchurch, reel 3.

70. NAM 2003-08-29, Ronald Dominy, 'Memoirs, 1951–1953'.

71. IWMSA 21696, Brian Sewell. © Whistledown, 2000.

72. Brian Goodliffe, *Recollections of Gunner Goodliffe: Life of a National Serviceman in 1952 and 1953 from His Own Diaries* (Harrow, 2009), pp. 35, 55 and 91.

73. David Lodge, *Ginger, You're Barmy* (1962, this edn 1984), p. 19.

74. IWMSA 27811, Richard Wilson, reel 2.

75. TNA WO 32/15746, 'Accepted Candidates for National Service Commissions who do not Come with the Conditions of the War Office Scheme', appendix to letter from Stopford to Director of Infantry, 8 March 1954.

76. Christopher Hurst, *The View from King Street: An Essay in Autobiography* (1997), p. 115.

77. Stanley Price, 'The Fucking Army', unpublished chapter of autobiography.

78. Robin Chapman, *A Waste of Public Money, or The Education of Charlie Williams* (1962), p. 101.

79. Derek Seaton, *Memoirs of a Conscript: National Service 1950–1952* (Alton, 2002), p. 5.

80. IWMSA 23213, Gordon Lawrence Potts, reel 1; IWM 15595, David Batterham, letter to parents, 12 January 1952.

81. IWMSA 18338, David Wray Fisher, reel 1.

82. IWMSA 11138, Ron Cassidy, reel 1.

83. Nottingham PRO, papers of Professor J. M. Lee DD 393/1/1, Mottershaw to Lee, 2 April 1949.

84. R. A. C. Radcliffe, *The Times*, 17 January 1953.

85. Kent, *Undiscovered Ends*, p. 31.

86. IWM 15058, R. D. Cramond, memoir of national service.

87. NAMSA 2003-04-3, 'Mac' McCullogh, reel 1.

88. Joe Studholme, interviewed by Cathy Courtney, *NLSC: Artists' Lives*, 1996, British Library Sound & Moving Image Catalogue reference C466/74/02, transcript p. 6. © The British Library.

89. TNA WO 32/15746, 'Accepted Candidates for National Service Commissions'.

90. IWMSA 21688, Richard Ingrams. © Whistledown, 2000. Ingrams was

not commissioned but he was removed from the RASC and sent to the more civilized atmosphere of the Education Corps.

91. Stacey in Chambers and Landreth (eds.), *Called Up*, pp. 47–65.
92. *Manchester Guardian*, 12 September 1953. A gunner who was about to attend the War Office Selection Board was attacked in his barracks.
93. IWMSA 20471, William Purves reel 1.
94. Len Woodrup, *Training for War Games: One Man's National Service* (Lewes, 1993), p. 15.
95. Goodliffe, *Recollections of Gunner Goodliffe*, p. 16.
96. IWMSA 21690, Paul Foot. © Whistledown, 2000.
97. IWMSA 29895, Paul Croxson, reel 1.
98. Alan Sillitoe, *Life Without Armour* (1995), p. 96.
99. IWMSA 10669, Brian Vyner, reel 1.
100. IWMSA 21672, Derek Johns. © Whistledown, 2000.
101. Seaton, *Memoirs of a Conscript*, p. 7.
102. IWMSA 17335, L. H. Scribbins, reel 1.
103. IWM 11915, N. A. Martin, 'The Day the Sun Stopped Shining', p. 13. Martin recalls, of a recruit with whom he went through basic training: 'we even had to bathe him'.
104. Robert Robinson, *Skip All That* (1996), p. 52.
105. IWMSA 11138, Ron Cassidy, reel 1.
106. *Manchester Guardian*, 19 December 1951.
107. IWMSA 19993, Ernest Dobson, reel 2.
108. IWMSA 20307, Norman Woods. See also IWMSA 23217, Ingram Murray, reel 1. Murray alludes to one of his comrades in the Royal Artillery being taken to the showers (apparently by his fellow recruits) and scrubbed with stiff brushes.
109. IWMSA 8943, Derek Blake, reel 1.
110. IWMSA 24569, John Harlow, reel 1.
111. TNA WO 291/1408, AORG, 'Follow-up Study of Psychiatric Gradings Given at Arms Basic Training Units', February 1954, prepared by Basil Clarke and Dr J. Penton.
112. *The Times*, 10 January 1957.
113. *Daily Mail*, 29 June 1959 and 3 July 1959.
114. LHCMA, Martin, 'In the Service of Queen and Country'.
115. NAM 2004-02-106, Simon Bendall, 'Memoirs of a National Serviceman'.
116. NAM 2002-08-61, Colin Metcalfe, 'Recollections of National Service'.
117. IWMSA 26098, Benjamin Whitchurch, reel 1.
118. IWMSA 20268, Edwin Haywood, reel 1.
119. Betts, *The Key of the Door*, pp. 237, 248, 259.

120. IWMSA 21681, Ray Self. © Whistledown, 2000.

121. *Manchester Guardian*, 16 January 1957.

122. *The Times*, 25 January 1947.

123. *The Times*, 3 August 1954.

124. David Barron in Ken Drury (ed.), *Get Some In: Memories of National Service* (Great Dunmow, 2006), pp. 181–91, at p. 189.

125. IWM 16584, Michael Longley, letter home, 16 June 1949.

126. *Manchester Guardian*, 3 March 1951.

127. Ibid., 29 December 1954.

128. Ibid., 18 and 22 February 1956.

129. *The Times*, 1 February 1956.

130. *Manchester Guardian*, 27 March 1956.

8. MAKING MEN

1. Peter Burns (actually written by his brother Alan) in B. S Johnson (ed.), *All Bull: The National Servicemen* (1973), pp. 81–9, at p. 88.

2. TNA LAB 29/555, 'Instructions for the Guidance of Medical Boards under the National Service Acts', 1956.

3. David Morgan, *'It Will Make a Man of You': Notes on National Service, Masculinity and Autobiography* (Manchester, 1987), p. 65.

4. Derek Seaton, *Memoirs of a Conscript: National Service 1950–1952* (Alton, 2002), p. 5: 'officers hardly figured in our lives and when they did they appeared almost effete. Against a background of the macho NCO they seemed so ineffectual.'

5. Richard Davenport-Hines (ed.), *Letters from Oxford: Hugh Trevor-Roper to Bernard Berenson* (2006), p. 132, letter of 8 November 1953.

6. Patrick Higgins, *Heterosexual Dictatorship: Male Homosexuality in Post-war Britain* (1996).

7. NAM 2003-06-9, Nigel Hensman, documents relating to training at Mons. The Kinsey Report was suggested as a topic for discussion – along with Germany as an ally, race segregation in South Africa and church parades in the army.

8. TNA WO 291/1408, AORG, 'Follow-up Study of Psychiatric Gradings Given at Arms Basic Training Units', February 1954, prepared by Basil Clarke and Dr J. Penton.

9. IWMSA 20471, William Purves, reel 1.

10. IWMSA 10211, Peter Beadle, reel 2.

11. Neal Ascherson in Adrian Walker (ed.), *Six Campaigns: National Servicemen at War, 1948–1960* (1993), pp. 1–7, at p. 2.

12. P. J. Kavanagh implies that he lost his virginity in Japan shortly after his first experience of battle (*The Perfect Stranger* (1966), p. 99). John Hollands's autobiographical novel of the Korean War also recounts a loss of virginity during post-combat leave in Japan (*The Dead, the Dying and the Damned* (1956), p. 275).

13. NAM 2000–1-08-55, D. F. Barrett, diary entry, 24 September 1950.

14. TNA AIR 77/608, 'Morale of the National Service Airman on Entry and During Initial Training: Report 1 of an Investigation into the Morale of the National Service Man in the RAF', January 1949.

15. TNA WO 291/1510, AORG, 'The Different Officer Potentials of Various Regions of Great Britain', 1956, by L. J. Holman. Appendix D, 'Shortage of Officers from the North', CEO [Chief Education Officer], Northern Command.

16. TNA AIR 77/608, 'Morale of the National Service Airman on Entry and During Initial Training'.

17. TNA AIR 20/12136, 'Morale of the National Service Airman (an Account of an Investigation Covering the Period October 1947–September 1950)', by A. S. Anthony, 24 July 1951.

18. TNA ADM 1/23999, officer commanding Scotland and Northern Ireland to Secretary of the Admiralty, illegible signature, 20 December 1949.

19. *Daily Mirror*, 2 May 1956.

20. TNA DEFE 7/61, letter from Barrow-in-Furness, 14 July 1958.

21. TNA WO 32/15025, note on case of Private W. in the RAPC, unsigned and undated; note written on it by another officer is dated 28 February 1958.

22. NAM 2001-07-1187-46, Andrew Man, 'The National Service Soldier in Korea and his Background', May 1951.

23. Simon Raven, *The English Gentleman: An Essay in Attitudes* (1961), pp. 141–3.

24. NAMSA 2001-02-397, Barry Reed, reel 2.

25. *Daily Mirror*, 7 August 1953. The King George's Jubilee Trust claimed to have consulted 1,000 'women with sons serving in the forces'. *The Times*, 21 October 1955.

26. Michael Gannon, 'Your Son and the Call-up', *Evening News*, 29 March 1954; see also the preceding articles on 22, 23 and 24 March.

27. John Hall, 'Mother Isn't the Best Friend of the Army', *Daily Mail*, 29 July 1953. This article can be found in TNA DEFE 7/508.

28. Barbara Castle, for example, intervened in the case of an orphaned National Service reservist who wanted to be excused his annual camp so that he could look after his thirteen-year-old sister. *Daily Mirror*,

20 August 1955. Bessie Braddock intervened in the case of David Larder, who was disciplined in Kenya after complaining about army brutality.

29. Frederick Hudson, *Loyal to the End: A Personal and Factual Account of National Service in Malaya* (Blackburn, 2006), p. 35.

30. 'A National Serviceman', 'Band Night', *New Statesman*, 13 April 1957.

31. T. Ferguson and J. Cunnison, *The Young Wage-earner: A Study of Glasgow Boys* (Oxford, 1951), p. 7.

32. TNA WO 291/1074, AORG, 'Mental Attitudes of National Service Army Recruits Immediately Before Call-up', based on interviews conducted from July to November 1948.

33. IWM 1597, J. R. Christie, letter from Lt Colonel F. J. Swainson to Mrs Christie, 16 April 1956: 'I do not think you need have any worries about his welfare or physical well-being, but if you have, please write to me.'

34. NAM 2003-06-9-16, Nigel Hensman, 'The Problem of Increasing the Regular Content of the Regiment', by commanding officer 12th Lancers, November 1952.

35. TNA AIR 77/608, 'Morale of the National Service Airman on Entry and During Initial Training'.

36. Ibid. Views of a student, a glazier from Middlesbrough and a shop assistant from Newton Abbot.

37. TNA HO 345/13, Departmental Committee on Homosexual Offences and Prostitution, Wolfenden Committee, 25 May 2013. Lt Colonel Barron, 'Nearly all of them [young soldiers] make allotments to their mothers and so on.' On sending money home to mothers see, for example, Frank Dickinson, *Them Days 'ave Gone* (Ely, 2008), p. 71.

38. TNA AIR 77/608, 'Morale of the National Service Airman on Entry and During Initial Training'.

39. TNA AIR 20/12136, 'Morale of the National Service Airman'.

40. Stephen Martin, 'Did Your Country Need You? An Oral History of the National Service Experience in Britain, 1945–1963' (PhD thesis, University of Wales, Lampeter, 1997), p. 49.

41. IWM 12723, John Whybrow, letter to father, 9 February 1951.

42. NAM 1995-01-164, Robert Gomme, 'Korea: A Short Memoir, Forty Years On'.

43. Ascherson in Walker (ed.), *Six Campaigns*, p. 7.

44. IWM 2118, Peter Mayo, diary entry, 9 December 1956.

45. IWMSA 21688, Richard Ingrams. © Whistledown, 2000.

46. Lord Moran, 'VD and Conscription', *The Spectator*, 8 August 1947.

47. TNA WO 32/12436, minute signed 'DAE', 30 March 1948.
48. Ibid., Army Education Advisory Board, amended report by subcommittee, 26 May 1949.
49. NAM 2001-07-1187-63, papers of Andrew Man, 'Guide to Regimental Officers on the Problems of Venereal Disease', 7 March 1947.
50. IWMSA 10925, Bruce Kent.
51. Jeremy Crang, 'The Abolition of Compulsory Church Parades in the British Army', *The Journal of Ecclesiastical History*, 56 (2005), pp. 92–106.
52. Donald Manley, for example, was confirmed with several of his comrades during his service in the late 1940s. NAM 2004-06-64, 'Change Here for Aldershot. Memoirs of a National Serviceman'.
53. NAMSA 2000-04-55, John Hodgson; NAMSA 2000-04-56, Michael Perry; NAMSA 2003-04-4, Mike Gilman.
54. Letter to *Manchester Guardian*, 24 October 1955.
55. IWM 12733, Cyril MacG Williams, letter to parents, 23 November 1952.
56. TNA WO 216/238, Chief of Imperial General Staff, conference of army commanders, War Office, 11 November 1947.
57. TNA WO 384/1–44, the 'Abstract of Army Statistics' gives figures for infection rates.
58. John Blair, *The Conscript Doctors: Memories of National Service* (Edinburgh, 2001), p. 47.
59. John Cowell, *Elephant Grass* (Blackburn, 2007), p. 55.
60. IWM 7178, C. B. L. Barr, diary entry, 17 May 1954.
61. IWMSA 20494, Peter Featherby, reel 1.
62. TNA AIR 20/6457, 'Attitudes of Serving Airmen: Report of a Working Party, Oct.–Dec. 1948'.
63. Morgan, '*It Will Make a Man of You*', p. 51.
64. Blair, *Conscript Doctors*, p. 94.
65. NAM 2000-08-55, Barrett, diary entry, 17 December 1950.
66. Hansard, 11 March 1954, George Thomas.
67. NAM 2001-07-1187-63, papers of Andrew Man, F. M. Richardson, Brigadier, Deputy Director of Medical Services 1 (BR) Corps, pamphlet 'Advice on Sex', October 1955: 'The act is generally a misuse of an important bodily function.'
68. George Carey, *Know the Truth: A Memoir* (2004), p. 30.
69. Nottingham PRO, papers of Professor J. M. Lee, DD 393/1, letter from Graham Mottershaw to Lee, 2 April 1949.
70. IWM 2118, Mayo, diary entry, 6 January 1956.

71. Michael Lewis, *Killroy Was Here* (1961), p. 26.
72. IWM 161, A. E. Fisher.
73. Morgan, *'It Will Make a Man of You'*, p. 27.
74. TNA WO 32/12436, Army Education Advisory Board, report, 26 March 1949.
75. Douglas Findlay, *White Knees Brown Knees: Suez Canal Zone 1951–1954, the Forgotten Years* (Edinburgh, 2003), p. 74.
76. R. F. L. Logan and E. M. Goldberg, 'Rising Eighteen in a London Suburb: A Study of Some Aspects of the Life and Health of Young Men', *British Journal of Sociology*, 4, 4 (1953), pp. 323–45.
77. TNA WO 384/1, 'Abstract of Army Statistics'. The precise figures were 2 per cent for privates, 2.7 per cent for lance corporals, 2.8 per cent for corporals and 1.7 per cent for sergeants. Lance corporals and corporals would have been older than most privates. Many sergeants would have been members of the Royal Army Education Corps, and thus drawn from a class of men unlikely to marry young. Among officers under the age of twenty-five, 153 were married and 2,021 were unmarried; among those over the age of twenty-five, 386 were married and 633 were unmarried.
78. TNA WO 384/26, figures for 31 August 1957.
79. TNA WO 384/34, figures for 31 October 1959.
80. Nottingham PRO, papers of Professer J. M. Lee, DD 393/1/1, letter from Mottershaw to Lee, 2 April 1949.
81. Logan and Goldberg, 'Rising Eighteen': 'Finally 4 boys had become engaged and were saving up for marriage. Their histories, however, suggested that they had not progressed through the stage of "trying out" their attitudes towards girls, but had clung to one girl from early adolescence, who seemed to satisfy immature needs for a mother substitute.'
82. TNA WO 384/12, 'Abstract of Army Statistics', figures for 28 February 1954.
83. NAM 2001-07-1187-63, 'Advice on Sex', October 1955, quoting 'an experienced CO's view', p. 1.
84. TNA WO 291/1074, AORG, 'Mental Attitudes'.
85. Albert Balmer, *A Cyprus Journey: Memoirs of National Service* (2008), p. 107.
86. *The Times*, 17 August 1956.
87. David Baxter, *Two Years to Do* (1959), p. 57.
88. *Daily Mirror*, 24 December 1957. IWMSA 21672, Derek Johns. © Whistledown, 2000. Derek Johns, who undertook his training with

Wands, describes Wands and says that he committed suicide but apparently does not know the circumstances of the death.

89. NAM 2003-08-61, Jack Gillett.

90. TNA HO 345/13, Wolfenden Committee, 25 May 2013.

91. IWMSA 21675, Anne Collins. © Whistledown, 2000.

92. Richard Vaughan, interview, 23 January 2013.

93. Workers' Educational Association and East Lothian Council Library Service, *West Lothian and the Forgotten War: Experience of World War II, National Service and the Korean War* (Edinburgh, 2000), p. 16.

94. IWMSA 10211, Beadle, reel 2.

95. NAM 1995-01-164, Gomme, 'Korea: A Short Memoir'.

96. Joan Bakewell, *The Centre of the Bed* (2003). Bakewell mentions briefly the fact that most of her male contemporaries at Cambridge had been through national service and remarks that her first husband, Michael Bakewell, had failed to obtain a commission after expressing support for Red China to his commanding officer. Michael Bakewell's essay was published in Johnson (ed.), *All Bull*, pp. 188–200.

97. Logan and Goldberg, 'Rising Eighteen': 'In actual fact almost all the youths said they approved of pre-marital intercourse with a "steady" girl friend . . . A common inconsistency was that most said they wanted their wives to be virgins, and were also uncertain whether the sexual code to which they subscribed should apply also to their sisters.'

98. Stanley Price, 'The Fucking Army', unpublished chapter.

99. Sussex University, Mass Observation Archive MO 334, Borstal chaplain, diary entry, 4 March 1947.

100. Adrian Laing, *R. D. Laing: A Biography* (1994), p. 55.

101. NAMSA 1995-05-93, Robin Ollington, reel 1.

102. TNA WO 291/1408, AORG, 'Psychiatric Gradings'. It was reported that a private in the RASC – a 'small, puny man' who wrote to his wife every day – was the biggest user of the district brothels.

103. The Wolfenden Committee was set up to investigate prostitution as well as homosexuality, but the evidence that the armed forces provided to it was exclusively concerned with the latter. The War Office told the committee that 'Female prostitution has raised no problem in relation to members of the Forces in the United Kingdom.' TNA DEFE 70/96, memorandum by the War Office, n.d.

104. NAM 2001-07-1187-63, papers of Andrew Man, 'Guide to Regimental Officers on the Problems of Venereal Disease', 7 March 1947.

105. TNA WO 291/1408, 'Psychiatric Gradings'.

106. Peter Gaston in Peter Chambers and Amy Landreth (eds.), *Called Up: The Personal Experiences of Sixteen National Servicemen, Told by Themselves* (1955), pp. 35–46, at p. 42.
107. Leslie Ives, *A Musket for the King: The Trials and Tribulations of a National Serviceman 1949–1951* (Tavistock, 1999), pp. 101–2.
108. Roger Alford, *Life and LSE* (Sussex, 2009), p. 163.
109. Cowell, *Elephant Grass*.
110. IWMSA 24570, Piers Plowright, reel 4.
111. IWMSA 21582, David Davies, reel 1.
112. Hugh Chesters in Ken Drury (ed.), *Get Some In: Memories of National Service* (Great Dunmow, 2006), pp. 101–4, at p. 103.
113. Stuart Crampin in Johnson (ed.), *All Bull*, pp. 126–35, at p. 127.
114. John Scurr, *Jungle Campaign: A Memoir of National Service in Malaya, 1949–51* (Lewes, 1998), p. 47.
115. NAM 2000-08-55, Barrett, diary entry, 2 November 1950.
116. David Lodge discusses the difficulty of using real army language in the introduction to the second edition of *Ginger, You're Barmy*. David Baxter's national service memoir *Two Years to Do* (1959) used the word 'fucking' without causing trouble.
117. N. Dennis, F. M. Henriques and C. Slaughter, *Coal is Our Life: An Analysis of a Yorkshire Mining Community* (1956), p. 218.
118. Tom Baker, *Who on Earth is Tom Baker?* (1997), p. 85.
119. Baxter, *Two Years to Do*, p. 15.
120. Frederic Raphael, *Cracks in the Ice: Views and Reviews* (1979), p. 22.
121. Peter Nichols, *Feeling You're Behind: An Autobiography* (1984), p. 122.
122. *Sunday Times*, 5 October 1986, quoted in Morgan, 'It Will Make a Man of You', p. 76.
123. Logan and Goldberg's study of young men registering for the call-up found little relation between sexual experience and occupation except that 'none of the students reported "adult outlets"': Logan and Goldberg, 'Rising Eighteen'.
124. See 'Pokers and Stilettos' in *Times Educational Supplement*, 31 August 1956. The author, who had been a national service sergeant instructor, described teaching illiterate soldiers – many of whom were criminal and some of whom were homosexual.
125. IWMSA 14822, Rodney Giesler, reel 7. Giesler, however, recalling his own experience at Catterick, insisted that the working classes did not go into sexual detail in their letters.
126. John Boorman, *Adventures of a Suburban Boy* (2003), p. 66.
127. TNA WO 291/2193, AORG, 'Likes and Interests Test: A Report of the

Experimental Testing of Recruits Eligible for Consideration as Potential Officers', prepared by Joan Harris (1958).

128. Terence Blacker, *You Cannot Live as I Have Lived and Not End Up Like This: The Thoroughly Disgraceful Life and Times of Willie Donaldson* (2007), p. 32.

129. NAM 2001-07-1187-63, Andrew Man, draft speech to passing-out parade of signals officers, undated.

130. IWM 2775, J. C. A. Green, letter to parents, 11 October 1952, just after he has been put in a hut for Other Ranks I (i.e. potential officers): 'It is still feeling very nice to be among chaps who are not always moaning [and] talking about girls.'

131. Ronald Hyam, *My Life in the Past* (privately published, 2012), p. 92.

132. Tony Betts, *The Key of the Door: Rhythm and Romance in a Post-war London Adolescence* (Wimborne, 2006), p. 281.

133. Gordon M. Williams, *The Camp* (1966), p. 53.

134. Robin Chapman, *A Waste of Public Money, or The Education of Charlie Williams* (1962), p. 101.

135. John Goldthorpe, David Lockwood, Frank Bechhofer and Jennifer Platt, *The Affluent Worker: Industrial Attitudes and Behaviour* (Cambridge, 1968). An even more revealing remark about 'mateship' was scribbled on an interview form by one of the researchers in this project: 'I bet his mates hate him.'

136. Hansard, 2 February 1954, Arthur Lewis.

137. Basil Henriques, *So You're Being Called Up*, various editions 1947–52.

138. NAM 2001-07-1187-63, 'Advice on Sex, October 1955'.

139. Higgins, *Heterosexual Dictatorship*, p. 74.

140. Ibid.

141. TNA HO 345/13, Wolfenden Committee, 25 May 1955.

142. TNA ADM 1/26594, minute by Medical Director General, 23 April 1956: 'one sees more cases nowadays of pseudo homosexuality which before the war might have masqueraded as pathological enuresis'.

143. TNA AIR 2/12407, Wolfenden Committee, memorandum by the Air Ministry.

144. Cited in Higgins, *Heterosexual Dictatorship*, p. 76.

145. TNA AIR 2/12407, Departmental Committee on Homosexual Offences and Prostitution, memorandum by the War Office, Appendix A, 'Homosexuality in London. Summary of Statement by GOC London District on Aspects of the Problem Affecting the Army', attached to note signed Curtis, 15 April 1955.

146. Hansard, 14 July 1955, speech by Alport.

147. TNA AIR 2/12407, 'Homosexuality Within the Royal Air Force', note by DPS: 'Homosexuality is like an iceberg: the greater part remains unseen and undetected.'

148. Cited in Higgins, *Heterosexual Dictatorship*, p. 61.

149. TNA AIR 2/12407, 'Homosexuality Within the Royal Air Force', note by DPS.

150. Ibid.

151. Higgins, *Heterosexual Dictatorship*, p. 73.

152. IWM 614, W. H. Butler, 'Derby to Derna (an Account of National Service Experiences)', p. 68: 'what does seem somewhat surprising in retrospect is that there was not much evidence of homosexuality amongst that large male community'. Butler said that he came across 'three or four' who were 'suspect' and that there was no problem 'once things were made clear'. Ernest Dobson mentions 'puffs' on the boat returning from Korea and expresses hostile views of them. IWMSA 19993, Ernest Dobson, reel 25.

153. TNA AIR 2/12407, 'Homosexuality Within the Royal Air Force', note by DPS.

154. IWM 15608, G. J. W. Rosbrook, letter, 28 August 1954.

155. IWMSA 14786, Godfrey Raper, reel 3.

156. Cowell, *Elephant Grass*, p. 66.

157. Reg Martin, interviewed by Wendy Rickard, *HIV/AIDS Testimonies*, 1995, British Library Sound & Moving Image Catalogue reference C743/02, transcript p. 29. © The British Library.

158. Ibid., p. 28.

159. Ibid., p. 29.

160. Ibid., p. 30.

161. Ibid., p. 31.

162. Ibid.

163. Roy Strong, *Self-portrait as a Young Man* (Oxford, 2013).

164. NAMSA 2000-04-56, Perry, reel 2.

165. Sussex University, National Gay and Lesbian Survey, case 183.

166. Ibid., case 417.

167. Christopher Hurst, *The View from King Street: An Essay in Autobiography* (1997), p. 114.

168. Ibid., p. 140.

169. Ibid., p. 142.

170. Ibid., p. 135.

171. TNA AIR 77/608, 'Morale of the National Service Airman on Entry and During Initial Training'.

172. IWM 2118, Mayo, diary entry, 22 December 1956.
173. Ibid., 6 November 1956.
174. Ibid., 4 December 1956.
175. Ibid., 9 December 1956.

9. OFFICERS

1. IWMSA 14786, Godfrey Raper, reel 3.
2. The two near exceptions to this rule were graduates who, having been recognized as officer material before they joined the air force, went straight from kitting-out camp to officer training, and doctors, who were almost automatically commissioned.
3. TNA ADM 1/23211, report signed Admiral Commanding Reserve, 10 December 1951: 'there is a strong feeling in schools that the Army offers far better chances of obtaining a commission during National Service than does the Navy.' On the views of public school housemasters about naval commissions, see the letters that Harold Walker (of Winchester) wrote to his protégé Peter Jay while the latter was serving in the navy. Churchill College, Cambridge, Papers of Peter Jay 4/1/1.
4. TNA AIR 32/416, 'Outline of Suggested Procedure for the Selection of Candidates for National Service Commissions at RAF Station Hednesford', signed Mary Allan (Senior Psychologist) and Sqn Ldr Carmichael, 28 January 1952.
5. Ibid.
6. TNA AIR 32/466, 'Investigations into Potential Officer Material', 1957.
7. The Times, 24 February 1950.
8. TNA AIR 10/7398, 'Annual Digest of Air Force Statistics', 1953.
9. Ibid.
10. Ibid. By 1957, the national service component of the air force comprised 1,807 officers and 63,128 other ranks.
11. TNA AIR 2/13938, various documents on what national service officers in ground branches did.
12. TNA AIR 32/414, 'National Service Commissioning in Ground Branches', 1951.
13. TNA AIR 32/466, 'Potential Officer Material'.
14. TNA AIR 2/11603, note to D of M, illegible signature, 4 March 1953.
15. TNA AIR 32/466, 'Potential Officer Material'.
16. David Sharman, interviewed by Anthony Isaacs, Millennium Memory Bank, 1998, British Library Sound & Moving Image Catalogue reference

C900/18039. © BBC. David Cainey, interviewed by Andrew Vincent, *Millennium Memory Bank*, 1998, British Library Sound & Moving Image Catalogue reference C900/00543. © BBC.

17. TNA WO 384/15, 'Abstract of Army Statistics', 1954.

18. So far as the army is concerned, this would also fit in with statistics for the number of officer cadets. We know that there were around 3,000 officer cadets per year in the early 1950s (at a time when the army took a little over 100,000 national servicemen per year). It seems likely that the number of officer cadets increased later in the decade – partly because the number of men with the minimum educational level required to be officers increased and partly because the War Office sought to increase the number of commissions granted as a matter of policy.

19. TNA WO 291/1510, AORG, 'The Different Officer Potentials of Various Regions of Great Britain', L. J. Holman, 1956.

20. IWMSA 24570, Piers Plowright, reel 2. Plowright recalled the irritation that he felt towards Smart, an Oxford graduate, who was, as the sergeant always put it, 'smart by name and smart by appearance'. This is presumably the same Smart who eventually passed out top at Eaton Hall and was commissioned into the Intelligence Corps. A few of his papers can be found in IWM 2519.

21. IWMSA 20656, Michael Foulds, reel 2.

22. IWMSA 27184, John Akehurst, reel 2.

23. IWM, Trevor Royle, 66/211/2/(2/16), Neal Ascherson. Perhaps the question was harder than it sounded. In the army, as opposed to the marines, officers were sometimes discouraged from playing sport with other ranks. In an infantry regiment, the correct answer would probably have been 'Rugger's my game, sir.'

24. TNA WO 291/1510, AORG, 'Officer Potentials'. Men from northern England performed less well than those from the south at all stages of officer selection; the gap narrowed over the years (partly because of pressure from the War Office) but it narrowed less quickly with regard to USB than with regard to the centralized War Office Selection Board.

25. IWMSA 20656, Foulds, reel 1.

26. IWMSA 24569, John Harlow, reel 2.

27. Brian Thompson, *Clever Girl: Growing Up in the 1950s* (2007, this edn 2008), p. 72.

28. Bernard Fergusson, *The Trumpet in the Hall, 1930–1958* (1970), p. 246.

29. NAM 2003-08-59, W. J. R. Morrison.
30. John Scurr, *Jungle Campaign: A Memoir of National Service in Malaya, 1949–51* (Lewes, 1998), p. 23.
31. IWMSA 24570, Plowright, reel 1. Scurr and Plowright did eventually fail WOSB.
32. W. K. B. Crawford, 'Training the National Service Army Officer at Eaton Hall', *Journal of the Royal United Services Institution*, February 1951, pp. 134–8.
33. TNA WO 32/15146, 'The Future of the Officer Cadet Schools', paper prepared for a meeting of 24 November 1953.
34. Robert Douglas, *Somewhere to Lay My Head* (2006), p. 236.
35. So far as I am aware, there is only one account by a sergeant major who trained national service men. It is Eric Howard, *My Trinity* (Edinburgh, 1999).
36. Kevin O'Sullivan, http://wabbrown.co.uk.
37. IWMSA 27184, Akehurst, reel 3.
38. *Manchester Guardian*, 17 September 1955.
39. NAMSA 2000-04-52, John Arnold, reel 2.
40. TNA WO 305/204, 'School of Signals (OTW), Jan. 1949–Nov. 1958', by Lt Colonel Howarth, enclosed note dated 16 November 1958.
41. Crawford, 'Training the National Service Army Officer'. In the year to September 1953, just twenty-two cadets were returned to unit from Eaton Hall, *Manchester Guardian*, 16 January 1954.
42. TNA WO 32/13957, Memorandum from War Office to commandants at Mons and Eaton Hall, signed Director of Personnel Administration, 25 October 1956.
43. IWMSA 21564, John Cormack, reel 12.
44. TNA WO 291/1510, AORG, 'Officer Potentials'.
45. TNA WO 32/15743, 'Provision of NS Officers for the Reserve Army', Appendix B.
46. TNA WO 291/1510, AORG, 'Officer Potentials', Appendix D, 'Shortage of Officers from the North', by CEO [Chief Education Officer] Northern Command.
47. TNA WO 291/1510, AORG, 'Officer Potentials'.
48. Scurr, *Jungle Campaign*, p. 30.
49. TNA WO 291/1510, AORG, 'Officer Potentials': 'Scottish accents seem more acceptable than English ones to PSOs'.
50. Keith Taylor and Brian Stewart, *Call to Arms: Officer Cadet Training at Eaton Hall* (2006), p. 94.

51. Churchill College, Cambridge, papers of Peter Jay, 4/1/1, letters from Harold Walker to Peter Jay.

52. Taylor and Stewart, *Call to Arms*, p. 65.

53. Cecil Blacker, *Monkey Business: The Memoirs of General Sir Cecil Blacker* (1993), p. 120. The personnel selection officer in the training regiment commanded by Blacker said that the son of a minister was unsuitable for a commission. Blacker insisted that he was sent to WOSB and he passed.

54. IWMSA 20656, Foulds, reel 2.

55. C. M. Maclachlan, 'Officer Selection', *Journal of the Royal United Services Institution*, November 1949, pp. 615–22.

56. TNA WO 291/1510, AORG, 'Officer Potentials'.

57. Ibid.

58. TNA WO 32/15743, 'NS Officers – Geographical Distribution', report attached to note, signed Houghton-Beckford, 18 September 1953.

59. Tales from the University of Aberdeen Forestry Graduates of 1956. This can be found at homepages.abdn.ac.uk/forestry/ or at http://homepages.abdn.ac.uk/forestry/associated%20links/Tales%20from%20Aberdeen%20Foresters%20of%201956%20vs2.pdf.

60. TNA WO 32/15604, Appendix A to CRNC, 13 July 1954 interview with Dr McKay, Personnel Director, Imperial Chemical Industries: 'We find that chemists will do all they can to avoid National Service on the grounds that such service is a complete waste of time as few of them obtain commissions, and there is no opportunity of carrying out technical work. This attitude is not particularly noticeable in engineers who are usually able to find a job in the forces which will give them useful experience.'

61. TNA WO 32/15743, 'Note on Shortage of Officers in the North', brigadier commanding War Office Selection Board, 27 March 1953.

62. REME took four graduates in arts subjects and the Royal Engineers took twelve.

63. TNA WO 384/5, figures for June–December 1951. In the Armoured Corps, 193 who left school at eighteen had studied arts, 64 had studied science. In the artillery, 405 had studied arts and 147 had studied science.

64. *The Times*, 13 July 1956.

65. Alexander Thynn, The Marquess of Bath, *Strictly Private to Public Exposure (Series 1: A Plateful of Privilege, Book III: Two Bites of the Apple)* (2003), p. 11.

66. IWM, Royle, 66/211/1/(1/15), A. B. Carter.

67. David Baxter, *Two Years to Do* (1959), p. 17.

68. TNA WO 291/2193, AORG, 'Likes and Interests Test: A Report of the

Experimental Testing of Recruits Eligible for Commissions as Potential Officers', prepared by Joan Harris (1958). Of 135 in one sample who were rated as potential officers, forty-two did not attend USB.

69. IWMSA 29062, John 'Jack' Burn, reel 1.

70. John Kelly, *National Service, 1950s: Lancs, Bucks, Libya* (Cambridge, 2003), p. 30.

71. T. C. Sparrow, *Tales of a Schoolie: A Story of National Service* (Badsey, 2006).

72. TNA WO 32/15743, Advisory Committee on the Territorial Army, 'TA Officer Problem, Examination by West Lancs: T & AF Association, Paper by the Chairman, West Lancashire T and AF Associations for consideration by the Committee at their meeting to be held on 11th June 1953'.

73. TNA WO 291/1510, AORG, 'Officer Potentials'.

74. NAMSA 1995-05-93, Robin Ollington, reel 2.

75. IWM 15595, David Batterham, 'National Service Recalled'.

76. Tony Dipple in Ken Drury (ed.), *Get Some In: Memories of National Service* (Great Dunmow, 2006), pp. 125–7.

77. IWMSA 14053, David Henderson, reel 1.

78. IWM 1834, A. R. Eaton, letter to parents, 9 July 1953.

79. Ibid., 22 March 1954.

80. Ibid., 26 July 1953.

81. Ibid., 13 September 1953.

82. IWMSA 20668, Alan Bexon, reel 1.

83. IWM 2118, Peter Mayo, diary entry, 8 May 1955.

84. IWM 2775, J. C. A. Green, 86/47/1, letters to parents, 3, 10 and 22 October 1952.

85. Ibid., 11 October 1952.

86. Ibid., 30 September 1953.

87. IWM 15595, Batterham, 'National Service Recalled'.

88. IWM 3126, R. J. Miller, memoir.

89. TNA WO 32/13957, memorandum from commanding officer 14/20 Hussars to War Office, signed Lt Colonel Stephen, 10 July 1951.

90. Ibid., 'Internal Recruiting Intelligence Corps', 28 November 1960, illegible signature, reporting speech by Brigadier Crosthwaite Emerson.

91. IWMSA 24570, Plowright, reel 3.

92. Ibid., reel 6.

93. Ibid., reel 7.

94. Andreas Whittam Smith, interviewed by Louise Brodie, *An Oral History of the British Press*, 2007, British Library Sound & Moving Image Catalogue reference C638/08, track 1. © The British Library.

95. P. J. Kavanagh, *The Perfect Stranger* (1966), p. 61.

96. *News Chronicle*, 13 May 1955.

97. TNA WO 32/13957, 'Memorandum to all Commands', 29 April 1960.

98. *The Times*, 31 May 1958.

99. IWMSA 14822, Rodney Giesler, 8 reels.

100. IWMSA 20494, Peter Featherby, reel 2: 'they wanted you to be reasonably intelligent unless you were going into the cavalry'.

101. Eton College Archive, letter to Hugh Marsden from J. Smith, 28 April 1948.

102. NAM 2003-08-63, Philip Firth.

103. IWMSA 20668, Bexon, reel 2.

104. IWM 16584, Michael Longley, letter of 12 October 1947. Longley described the RASC as 'the easiest commission'.

105. Christopher Hurst, *The View from King Street: An Essay in Autobiography* (1997), p. 130.

106. Simon Raven, *The English Gentleman: An Essay in Attitudes* (1961), p. 141.

107. NAMSA 2003-04-2, Field Marshal Sir John Chapple, reel 1. Chapple does not seem to have minded serving with the artillery – though he did contrive to be commissioned into the Gurkhas (associated with the Rifle Brigade) when he returned to the army as a regular.

108. IWMSA 12663, Denys Whatmore, reel 1.

109. TNA WO 305/204, 'School of Signals (OTW)'.

110. IWMSA 22307, Anthony Howard. © Whistledown, 2000.

111. Michael Holroyd in B. S. Johnson (ed.), *All Bull: The National Servicemen*, pp. 136–48, at p. 141.

112. Terence Breden in Drury (ed.), *Get Some In*, pp. 77–97, at p. 79; Thompson, *Clever Girl*, p. 74.

113. John Nott, *Here Today, Gone Tomorrow: Recollections of an Errant Politician* (2002), p. 35.

114. John Barkshire, interviewed by Kathy Burk, *NLSC: City Lives*, 1990, British Library Sound & Moving Image Catalogue reference C409/057, track 1. © The British Library.

115. NAM 2001-07-1187-47, papers of Andrew Man, Lt Colonel A. E. Green DSO OBE to 'Andrew' (i.e. Man), 31 January 1951.

116. John Chynoweth, *Hunting Terrorists in the Jungle* (Stroud, 2007), p. 18.

117. Hansard, 26 February 1952. Statement by Secretary of State for War: 'The Brigade of Guards have stated emphatically that there is absolutely

nothing to prevent an officer joining the Brigade of Guards who has no private income whatever.'

118. IWMSA 10669, Brian Vyner, reel 1. Vyner was unusual in that he was commissioned into the 4th Hussars, after lunch at the Cavalry Club, without having previous associations with the regiment, just before it went to Malaya. He later obtained a regular commission, but after his regiment returned to Britain he decided that life in it would be too expensive and left the army.

119. NAM 2003-06-9-40, Nigel Hensman, 'List of Essential Clothing Required by an Officer on Joining the XII Lancers', undated.

120. John Sutherland, who went through Mons with a group of guards officers claimed: 'the Brigade wouldn't look at you unless you had £300 a year'. John Sutherland, *The Boy Who Loved Books* (2007, this edn 2008), p. 190. This is probably an overstatement. Auberon Waugh recalls that his father paid him £25 per month in the army, but stopped his allowance when he was seriously wounded and confined to hospital. Auberon Waugh, *Will This Do? An Autobiography* (1991, this edn 1992), p. 109.

121. Robin Chapman, *A Waste of Public Money, or The Education of Charlie Williams* (1962), p. 102.

122. TNA WO 32/15746, letter, Stopford to Director of Infantry, 6 March 1954 and attached list. Of the eight men who had left school, two were undergoing basic training and six were at Eaton Hall.

123. Oliver Lindsay, *Once a Grenadier . . . : The Grenadier Guards, 1945–95* (1996), p. 113.

124. TNA WO 32/16277, note to Under Secretary of State, illegible signature, 25 September 1951.

125. Lindsay, *Once a Grenadier . . .* , p. 117.

126. Churchill College, Cambridge, British Diplomatic Oral History Project, Martin Morland, interviewed by Malcolm McBain, 24 January 2006. Available online at https://www.chu.cam.ac.uk/media/uploads/files/Morland.pdf.

127. Eton College Archive, letter to Hugh Marsden, signed illegibly, 30 August 1948.

128. So far as I can discern from the *Eton College Chronicle*, seven of the sixteen men who went though Brigade Squad with W. G. Runciman (himself an Etonian) in 1953 were Etonians. The thirty-eight Grenadiers were those described as second lieutenants in the Army Emergency Reserve in the *Army List* for 1956. I've compared this list with names given in the *Eton College Chronicle* for 1948.

129. Hurst, *The View from King Street*, p. 121. Hurst went through Eaton Hall with a number of guards officers from Brigade Squad but also with an ordinary guardsman who was to be commissioned after a year in the ranks. He was not to be commissioned in the guards: 'his plebeian accent and demeanour explained why'.

130. John Milne, interviewed by Sue Bradley, *NLSC: Book Trade Lives*, 1999, British Library Sound & Moving Image Catalogue reference C872/17, reel 1. © The British Library.

131. TNA WO 291/1510, AORG, 'Officer Potentials'.

132. IWMSA 19061, Hugh Currie, reel 1.

133. Tom Stacey in Peter Chambers and Amy Landreth (eds.), *Called Up: The Personal Experiences of Sixteen National Servicemen, Told by Themselves* (1955), pp. 47–66.

134. W. G. Runciman, interview, 17 April 2013.

135. Bruno Schroder, interviewed by Cathy Courtney, *NLSC: City Lives*, 1992, British Library Sound & Moving Image Catalogue reference C409/076, track 2. © The British Library.

136. Thynn, *Two Bites*, p. 10.

137. At least, I can find no reference to a guards officer among the military records described in *The Monmouthian*.

138. TNA AIR 2/15389, minutes of meeting at Ministry of Defence on 'Call-Up of Graduates', 3 December 1959.

139. Waugh, *Will This Do?*, p. 95.

140. Hansard, 8 May 1963, question from George Thomas to Profumo (Secretary of State for War).

141. *Manchester Guardian*, 16 December 1953.

142. Ibid. The cadet giving evidence was Alistair Black.

143. Andrew Sinclair, *The Breaking of Bumbo* (1959, this edn 1961), p. 42.

144. *The Times*, 14 January 1954.

145. Elizabeth Basset, *Love is my Meaning: An Anthology of Assurance* (1973).

146. W. G. Runciman, interview, 17 April 2013.

147. *The Times*, 8 January 1954.

148. *Manchester Guardian*, 8 January 1954.

149. Ibid., 16 January 1954.

150. Hansard, 19 January 1954, answer by J. R. H. Hutchison.

151. Taylor and Stewart, *Call to Arms*, pp. 67, 94, 115, 128. An earlier suicide at Eaton Hall had attracted less attention. *Manchester Guardian*, 27 July 1948.

152. John Bingham in Chambers and Landreth (eds.), *Called Up*, pp. 83–98, at pp. 86–7.

153. *The Times*, 6 June 1951. Douglas Hurd, *Memoirs* (2003), pp. 81–2.

154. TNA DEFE 13/53, Hurd to Macmillan, 13 February 1955.

155. TNA WO 32/13775, 'The Continuing Need for National Service in the Army', undated and unsigned.

156. TNA WO 32/15604, 'Retrospect: A Survey of the Effects of National Service', 1954.

157. *The Times*, 13 July 1956.

158. Sutherland, *The Boy Who Loved Books*, p. 194.

159. Brian Jackson and Dennis Marsden, *Education and the Working Class: Some General Themes Raised by a Study of 88 Working-class Children in a Northern Industrial City* (1962, this edn 1966), p. 55.

160. Waugh, *Will This Do?*, p. 102.

161. IWM 15316, P. J. Houghton-Brown, undated letter to mother.

162. Bruce Kent, *Undiscovered Ends: An Autobiography* (1992), p. 41.

163. IWMSA 9395, Colin Bower, reel 2.

164. IWM, Royle, 66/211/1(1/17), Simon Coke.

165. IWM, Royle, 66/211/1(1/77), J. M. H. Radford, letter dated 28 April 1985.

166. NAM 2000-08-55, D. F. Barrett, diary entry, 19 February 1951.

167. NAMSA 2000-04-55, John Hodgson, reel 1.

168. Hurst, *The View from King Street*, p. 116.

169. TNA WO 291/1494, AORG, 'Field Follow-up of Young Regular and National Service Officers' by L. J. Holman, 1955.

170. Kent, *Undiscovered Ends*, p. 40.

171. John Peel, *Margrave of the Marshes: His Autobiography* (2005, this edn 2006), p. 145.

172. Hurst, *The View from King Street*, p. 144.

173. Peter Nichols, *Feeling You're Behind: An Autobiography* (1984), p. 93.

174. IWM 12733, Cyril MacG Williams, letter of 25 January 1953.

175. IWM, Royle, 66/211/1(1/17), Simon Coke.

176. IWM 3225, W. S. B. Loosmore, diary entry, 15 July 1958.

177. Ibid., 15 November 1957.

178. Ibid., 26 October 1957.

179. Ibid., 28 February 1958.

180. Ibid., 5 September 1958.

10. OTHER RANKS

1. IWMSA 22307, Anthony Howard. © Whistledown, 2000.

2. Dr John Lester cited in John Blair, *The Conscript Doctors: Memories of National Service* (Edinburgh, 2001), p. 22.

3. TNA AIR 2/10934, 'Brief for DGM on Allocation of National Servicemen to Trades', signed Lumgair, 6 February 1956.

4. Leslie Ives, *A Musket for the King: The Trials and Tribulations of a National Serviceman 1949-1951* (Tavistock, 1999), p. 26.

5. Karl Miller in B. S. Johnson (ed.), *All Bull: The National Servicemen* (1973), pp. 256-66, at p. 258.

6. IWMSA 20668, Alan Bexon, reel 1.

7. TNA AIR 20/6457, 'Attitudes of Serving Airmen: Report of a Working Party, Oct.-Dec. 1948'.

8. IWM, Trevor Royle, 66/211/1(1/27), J. Dinning.

9. Alan Sillitoe, *Life Without Armour* (1995), p. 91.

10. Don Wallace, 'The POM Has Landed', *Aviation News*, 8-21 August 1986.

11. Harold Evans, *My Paper Chase: True Stories of Vanished Times, an Autobiography* (2009, this edn 2010), p. 88.

12. Jimmy Reid, *Reflections of a Clyde-built Man* (1976), p. 29.

13. Wallace, 'The POM Has Landed'.

14. TNA WO 32/17657, 'The Effect of the Abolition of National Service and the Reduction in Size of the Army on Promotion Prospects of Regular Other Ranks', draft, attached to note Forster to Legh, 1 January 1959.

15. TNA WO 291/1080, AORG, 'The Promotion of National Servicemen to Non-commissioned Rank', July 1949.

16. NAM 2001-07-1187-46, Andrew Man, 'The National Service Soldier in Korea', May 1951.

17. NAM 2000-08-55, D. F. Barrett, diary entry, 29 December 1950.

18. TNA WO 384/20, 'Abstract of Army Statistics', March 1956.

19. TNA WO 32/14970, 'Substantive Promotion – Drivers', signed by Colonel Wilson, 26 September 1955.

20. TNA WO 291/1408, AORG, 'Follow-up Study of Psychiatric Gradings Given at Arms Basic Training Units', February 1954, prepared by Basil Clarke and Dr J. Penton.

21. TNA AIR 10/5478, 'Annual Digest of Royal Air Force Statistics', no. 2, 1953. TNA WO 384/12, 'Abstract of Army Statistics', March 1954.

22. TNA WO 32/17657, 'The Effect of the Abolition of National Service'.

23. TNA WO 384/22, 'Abstract of Army Statistics', September 1956.
24. IWMSA 21582, David Davies, reel 3.
25. T. C. Sparrow, *Tales of a Schoolie: A Story of National Service* (Badsey, 2006), p. 42.
26. NAM 2003-05-23, Patrick J. Wye, 'Royal Army Service Corps, March 15th 1951–March 1953'.
27. Frank Stokes in Ken Drury (ed.), *Get Some In: Memories of National Service* (Great Dunmow, 2006), pp. 63–8.
28. *Daily Mirror*, 26 August 1950.
29. IWM 3126, R. J. Miller, memoir.
30. Leslie T. Wilkins, *The Social Survey: National Service and Enlistment in the Armed Forces. A Report on an Enquiry Made for Several Government Departments into the Attitudes of Young Men Prior to, and on Joining the Armed Forces* (1951), p. 19.
31. Derek Seaton, *Memoirs of a Conscript: National Service 1950–1952* (Alton, 2002), pp. 9 and 10.
32. Ibid., p. 13.
33. Alan Watson in Drury (ed.), *Get Some In*, pp. 113–17.
34. IWMSA 26097, Terrance Atkinson, reel 1.
35. David Baxter, *Two Years to Do* (1959), p. 60.
36. IWM 3135, J. R. Beverland, memoir.
37. NAMSA 1995-05-93, Robin Ollington, reel 2.
38. Eric Pegg (ed.), *The Royal Engineers and the National Service Years, 1939–1963: A Military and Social History* (2002), p. 22.
39. *Daily Mirror*, 11 March 1955.
40. IWM 7178, C. B. L. Barr, diary entry, 4 February 1955.
41. Seaton, *Memoirs of a Conscript*, p. 16.
42. TNA WO 291/1510, AORG, 'The Different Officer Potentials of Various Regions of Great Britain', L. J. Holman, 1956.
43. IWMSA 29895, Paul Croxson, reel 2.
44. Ibid.; IWMSA 17223, Adrian Walker.
45. John Ockenden, 'Memoirs of a Computing Man' (unpublished manuscript).
46. NAMSA 2000-04-52, John Arnold, reel 1.
47. TNA AIR 32/414, 'National Service Commissioning in Ground Branches', 1951.
48. Geoffrey Elliott and Harold Shukman, *Secret Classrooms: An Untold Story of the Cold War* (2003), p. 50.
49. Brian Jackson and Dennis Marsden, *Education and the Working Class:*

Some General Themes Raised by a Study of 88 Working-class Children in a Northern Industrial City (1962, this edn 1966), p. 184.

50. IWMSA 26569, John Waine.
51. NAMSA 2000-04-52, Arnold.
52. NAM 2003-08-61, Jack Gillett.
53. TNA AIR 20/6457, 'Attitudes of Serving Airmen'.
54. TNA ADM 1/21623, 'Reduced NS Intake', signed head of Naval Branch, 11 November 1949.
55. Ministry of Education, *15 to 18* (1959) (Crowther Report), II, pp. 144 and 148.
56. TNA AIR 20/6457, 'Attitudes of Serving Airmen'.
57. TNA AIR 2/10933, 'Intakes from the NS Fields', signed Marchant, 22 October 1953.
58. *The Times*, 11 October 1960.
59. Ken Lynham, interviewed by Michael Cos, *Food: From Source to Salespoint*, 2005, British Library Sound & Moving Image Catalogue reference C821/165, track 4. © The British Library.
60. NAM 2001-07-1187-54, papers of Andrew Man, 'The Requirement for NS from the Army's Point of View', 27 May 1954. The document was designed to prepare speakers to justify national service at a conference of industrialists.
61. Wilkins, *National Service and Enlistment*, p. 19.
62. Ibid., p. 15.
63. TNA WO 32/15604, Appendix C to CRNC 185006, 13 July 1954, 'Discussion with Employers at Conference at Headquarters of North Midland District'.
64. IWMSA 27184, John Akehurst, reel 4. Akehurst remarked that a regular sergeant in his battalion was capable of 'coming the old soldier'.
65. Peter de la Billière, *Looking for Trouble: SAS to Gulf Command* (1994, this edn 1995), p. 56.
66. NAM 2001-07-1187-46, Andrew Man, 'The National Service Soldier in Korea'.
67. IWMSA 11139, David Storrie. National service officers were more sympathetic to regular other ranks in the marines. IWMSA 22268 Neal Ascherson. © Whistledown, 2000.
68. IWM 675, A. R. Ashton, 'National Service: Royal Marine Commando Memoirs' (1990).
69. Keith Jessop, *Goldfinder: The True Story of One Man's Discovery of the Ocean's Richest Secrets* (1998).

70. Robin Welch, interviewed by Hawksmoor Hughes, *NLSC: Craft Lives,* British Library Sound & Moving Image Catalogue reference C960/85, track 3. © The British Library.

71. Alun Pask in Adrian Walker (ed.), *Six Campaigns: National Servicemen at War, 1948–1960* (1993), pp. 115–21, at p. 117.

72. IWMSA 13645, General Forrester, Brigadier Flood, Brigadier Dawney, reel 1.

73. IWM 4102, Peter Burke, diary entry, 10 May 1956.

74. Ibid., 26 April 1956.

75. Adrian Walker, *A Country Regiment: 1st Battalion The Queen's Own Royal West Kent Regiment, Malaya, 1951–1954* (2001).

76. Frank Dickinson, *Them Days 'ave Gone* (Ely, 2008), p. 126.

77. Ibid., p. 200.

78. Ives, *A Musket for the King*, p. 20.

79. Peter Nichols, *Feeling You're Behind: An Autobiography* (1984, this edn 1985), p. 76.

80. NAMSA 1995-05-93, Robin Ollington, reel 1.

81. IWM, Trevor Royle, 66/211/1(1/37), Frank Gaff.

82. IWM, Royle, 66/211/1(1/38), Dennis Gane.

83. IWM, Royle, 66/211/1(1/35), W. Findlay.

84. IWM 15719, G. T. Kell, 'The Diary of 2266489 Kell', in fact more a memoir than a diary, p. 23.

85. TNA AIR 20/12136, 'Morale of the National Service Airman (an Account of an Investigation Covering the Period October 1947–September 1950)', by A. S. Anthony, 24 July 1951.

86. IWMSA 21681, Ray Self. © Whistledown, 2000.

87. IWM 15103, Bernard Parke.

88. TNA AIR 20/12136, 'Morale of the National Service Airman'.

89. Ibid.

90. Gordon M. Williams, *The Camp* (1966), p. 29.

91. IWMSA 14983, Albert Shippen, reel 14.

92. TNA WO 32/17243, 'Report of Committee on Employment of National Servicemen in the United Kingdom', 1956/57.

93. The War Office statistics in the WO 384 series are curiously unrevealing about the total number of men on three years' engagements. In a sample of people born in Scotland in 1936, 253 men had performed national service and 100 had served for three years – sixteen of the later group became regulars. James Maxwell, *Sixteen Years On: A Follow-up of the 1947 Scottish Survey* (1969), p. 167. Figures for various kinds of

engagements are given for 1957/1958 in TNA DEFE 7/1453, 'Recruiting and Prolongation: Statistics and Returns'. In this year, there were 26,065 regular recruits to the army, of whom 12,536 were three-year men; in the air force there were 15,755, of whom 5,991 signed up for three years. One assumes that the number of three-year engagements dropped as national service was coming to an end and most men could hope to avoid serving altogether.

94. TNA DEFE 13/53, Minister of Defence Service Ministers Committee, 'Full-time National Service. Report of Working-party on the Effect of Straight Reduction in the Period of Full-time from 2 Years to 21 Months', 20 January 1955.
95. TNA AIR 20/12136, 'Morale of the National Service Airman'.
96. Maxwell, *Sixteen Years On*, p. 167: thirty-seven out of 253 national servicemen had done something related to their civilian occupation; sixteen out of 100 three-year men had done so.
97. IWM 614, W. H. Butler, 'Derby to Derna (an Account of National Service Experiences)', p. 11.
98. Peter Hems in Drury (ed.), *Get Some In*, pp. 141–5.
99. TNA WO 32/15604, Appendix A to CRNC, dated 13 July 1954, reporting opinion of Clarke, Chapman and Co. Marine Engineers, Gateshead.
100. TNA DEFE 13/53, letter from head of BOAC to Sir Miles Thomas, 10 June 1955.
101. Ibid., BOAC pamphlet.
102. TNA AIR 2/10934, 'Selection of National Service Recruits and their Allocation to Ground Trades', signed Group Captain Lumgair, 19 June 1957.
103. IWM 2279, Brigadier P. J. Jeffreys, 'Account of 1st Btn Durham Light Infantry in Korea, September 1952 to September 1953'.

11. THE QUEEN'S HARD BARGAINS

1. TNA DEFE 13/53, note to minister, illegible signature, 22 July 1955. It was said that George Craddock MP planned to raise national service in the forthcoming adjournment debate and that he would argue that it was a 'contributory cause to delinquency'.
2. TNA WO 291/1408, AORG, 'Follow-up Study of Psychiatric Gradings Given at Arms Basic Training Units', February 1954, prepared by Basil Clarke and Dr J. Penton.
3. TNA ADM 1/26594, RN Detention Quarters: Statistical Report, 5 January 1956.

4. *Manchester Guardian*, 2 June 1955.
5. Ibid., 7 April 1958.
6. TNA WO 291/1408, AORG, 'Psychiatric Gradings'.
7. Hermann Mannheim and Leslie T. Wilkins, *Prediction Methods in Relation to Borstal Training* (1955), p. 187. The man in question was, in fact, turned away by the army on account of his poor scores on education tests.
8. T. C. N. Gibbens, 'Borstal Boys after 25 Years', *British Journal of Criminology*, 24, 1 (1984), pp. 49–61.
9. TNA WO 291/1455, AORG, 'Quality of Intake to RASC and Relationship Between General Ability and Driver Training Results', 1956.
10. Gibbens, 'Borstal Boys after 25 Years'.
11. TNA WO 32/13364, minute sheet, signed QMG, 3 October 1949.
12. TNA LAB 6/370, 'Draft Paper by DMP for Consideration at a Future Triangular Meeting', attached to letter from Waters to Hooper, 29 September 1954. See also table of men downgraded from January to June 1954. In all, 259 came from the infantry, 58 from the RASC, 36 from the Ordnance Corps, 34 from the Catering Corps, 79 from the artillery, 26 from the Armoured Corps, 10 from the Royal Engineers, 39 from the Signals, 28 from the Medical Corps and 6 from REME.
13. TNA WO 32/13849, Executive Committee of the Army Council, 11 October 1954, 'Provision of Military Labour for Administrative Installations in the United Kingdom'; TNA WO 32/16806, 'Recruiting for the Royal Pioneer Corps', 5 September 1958.
14. Mannheim and Wilkins, *Prediction Methods*, p. 189.
15. Royston Salmon in Peter Chambers and Amy Landreth (eds.), *Called-Up: The Personal Experiences of Sixteen National Servicemen, Told by Themselves* (1955), pp. 144–50.
16. NAM 2003-08-59, W. J. R. Morrison.
17. George Gardiner, *A Bastard's Tale: The Political Memoirs of George Gardiner* (1999), p. 72.
18. Jeff Nuttall in B. S. Johnson (ed.), *All Bull: The National Servicemen* (1973), pp. 17–25, at p. 21.
19. IWM 9870, James Jacobs, 'Korea: One Conscript's War'.
20. Leslie Ives, *A Musket for the King: The Trials and Tribulations of a National Serviceman 1949–1951* (Tavistock, 1999), p. 30.
21. TNA WO 291/1408, 'Psychiatric Gradings'.
22. TNA WO 32/10994, Director of Army Education, 'Review of Illiteracy and Sub-literacy among National Service Men', 3 March 1953. There are numerous discussions of this matter in WO 32/10994, WO 163/305 and LAB 6/370.

23. TNA WO 32/10994, note by DAE (Director of Army Education), 13 February 1948.

24. Ibid., minutes of meeting, 14 March 1947, contribution by Colonel Ungerson.

25. Hansard, 15 October 1952, Antony Head.

26. TNA WO 32/10994, Director of Army Education, 'Background Information', 14 January 1955. Apparently prepared in anticipation of a question in parliament. These figures differ slightly from those given in the 'Abstract of Army Statistics' – see Appendix VIII.

27. TNA WO 384/22, 'Abstract of Army Statistics', September 1956.

28. TNA WO 32/10994, Director of Army Education, 'Background Information'. Once again, the figures differ slightly from those given in the 'Abstract of Army Statistics'.

29. TNA WO 32/10994, loose minute, 'Education of Sub-literate NSM, Reference your Note 20 Jan.', 4 February 1954.

30. TNA WO 163/305, 'Activities and Responsibilities of the RAEC', attached to note from F. W. Armstrong and B. L. Rigby, 12 July 1951.

31. The Times, 13 February 1953.

32. TNA ED 34/185. The House of Commons statement was made on 15 October 1952. A civil servant minuted, of questions asked about literacy rates in the army, 'I have no doubt that this question arises out of some recent obiter dicta of a lieutenant colonel which were, I believe, promptly disavowed by the War Office.' Note by Bennet, 12 September 1952.

33. Ross Cranston, 'A Biographical Sketch: The Early Years' in Mads Andenas and Duncan Fairgrieve (eds.), Tom Bingham and the Transformation of the Law: A Liber Amicorum (Oxford, 2009), pp. li–lxxii, at p. lviii.

34. TNA WO 32/10994, 'For the Information of the Minister', 18 July 1953.

35. Ibid., 'The Battle Against Illiteracy', attached to note by John McCulloch, 12 March 1953.

36. IWMSA 18338, David Fisher, reel 2.

37. IWM 2775, J. C. A. Green, letter dated 'Monday 23rd'; it seems to have been written in 1952.

38. Daily Mirror, 18 April 1953.

39. TNA WO 291/1408, AORG, 'Psychiatric Gradings'.

40. IWMSA 26559, Leigh Parkes.

41. IWM 1779, I. W. G. Martin, letter of 4 May 1958.

42. The Times, 3 July 1953.

43. TNA WO 32/15021, psychiatric report on Gunner W., 26 April 1951, signed G. W. Hill.

44. TNA WO 32/15024, 'NSM considered unsuitable for service in the

TA', appendix to letter to Under Secretary of State for War from GOC-in-C, Anti-Aircraft Command, 28 November 1952.

45. *The Times*, 2 May 1959.
46. TNA WO 291/1408, AORG, 'Psychiatric Gradings'.
47. TNA WO 291/1152, AORG, 'The Military Value of the ex-Borstal Boy', report by J. Penton, November 1951.
48. Winifred Elkin and D. B. Kittermaster's *Borstal: A Critical Survey* (1950) suggests that in 1947 1,766 boys and 136 girls were committed to Borstal. A newspaper article of 1951 talked of '2,000 lads' being committed annually, *Manchester Guardian*, 17 August 1951.
49. TNA WO 32/15021, Butterfield to Hooper, 27 April 1955, Ministry of Labour to Brigadier Dewar, signed Hooper, 22 April 1955.
50. TNA HO 291/116, 23 February 1956, 'Case of G.'.
51. TNA WO 32/16185, 'Borstal Boys in the Army', unsigned and undated note.
52. TNA PCOM 9/1390, AORG, 'The Military Value of the ex Juvenile Delinquent', I. R. Haldane. The research on which the report was based seem to date from 1947–8, though it is attached to a letter from Snell to Colonel Penton, 17 May 1952.
53. David Baxter, *Two Years to Do* (1959), p. 11. Baxter recalled training with a man called Dartmoor because he had apparently been released from a long stretch in prison.
54. Roger Hood, *Homeless Borstal Boys: A Study of their After-care and After-conduct* (1966), pp. 41–2. The study took place from 1953 to 1957.
55. Mannheim and Wilkins, *Prediction Methods*, p. 181.
56. Ewen Montagu, letter to *The Times*, 24 January 1949.
57. TNA WO 32/16185, AG to S of S, 3 March 1958: 'I have had to guess at the proportion of NS with past criminal records, because the figures are withheld from us. I assume the figure to be about 5 per cent.'
58. TNA DEFE 7/141, Antony Head to Lloyd George [i.e. Gwilym Lloyd George, the Home Secretary], 16 November 1954.
59. Ibid., memorandum by Secretary of State for War, 21 January 1955.
60. *The Times*, 3 August 1960.
61. Ibid., 5 March 1955.
62. *Daily Mail*, 10 June 1960.
63. *Daily Mirror*, 15 and 23 November 1955.
64. James Maxwell, *Sixteen Years On: A Follow-up of the 1947 Scottish Survey* (1969), p. 71.
65. IWM 7178, C. B. L. Barr, diary entry, 17 January 1955.

66. *The Times*, 21 January 1960.
67. Hansard, 14 July 1955, Alport.
68. *Daily Express*, 12 January 1954. Halladay returned after three and a half years, was court-martialled and sentenced to nine months.
69. Mannheim and Wilkins, *Prediction Methods*, p. 191.
70. Ibid., pp. 200–202.
71. TNA WO 71/1200, court martial of Signalman Charles Connor, 19 June 1951, letter read out by defence.
72. Baxter, *Two Years to Do*.
73. *Daily Mirror*, 5 July 1957.
74. *Manchester Guardian*, 23 December 1952.
75. TNA MEPO 2/7822, note to M. R. Carter from chief inspector (name illegible), 23 June 1949.
76. Ibid., R. L. Jackson to Philip Allen at the Home Office, 17 July 1952.
77. Ibid., note to M. R. Carter from chief inspector (name illegible), 23 June 1949.
78. Hansard, 4 April 1950.
79. TNA DEFE 7/61, preparation for reply by Minister of Defence to parliamentary question, 23 July 1958.
80. TNA WO 384/1, 'Abstract of Army Statistics', Outflow by Arms, 1 April 1950–March 1951.
81. Hansard, 1 August 1952. Shillingford's career was described by James Simmons and George Wigg. The Under Secretary of State for War said that Shillingworth's last sentence had been quashed and that he had now been released from the army.
82. TNA WO 32/16185, AG to S of S, through PUS, 25 November 1957.
83. TNA PCOM 9/1390, memorandum by Secretary of State for War, 21 January 1955.
84. Hansard, 14 July 1955, Alport.
85. TNA WO 32/16185, VAG to S of S, 4 August 1961.
86. TNA WO 32/16806, 'Recruiting for the Royal Pioneer Corps', 5 September 1958.
87. *The Times*, 13 March 1961.
88. Hansard, 14 July 1955, Alport.
89. TNA WO 71/1198, court martial of Bates, RPC, and others, 16 and 17 May 1951. Plea in mitigation.

12. KOREA

1. IWM 12515, Sir Peter Holmes, 'Korean War Diary' (it is in fact mainly a memoir), p. 12.
2. Ibid., pp. 9 and 10.
3. Ibid., p. 14.
4. Ibid., p. 15 refers to 7 to 22 November 1951.
5. Ibid., p. 17, quoting diary entry for 1 December, describing events of 17 November 1951.
6. IWM 1324, A. L. Saunders, letter to 'mum and uncle', 13 September 1951.
7. Ibid., telegram from War Office, 13 November 1951; letter to Mrs Hilda Cole, signed Scotland, 3 March 1952.
8. TNA CAB 128/17/39, Cabinet meeting, 27 June 1950.
9. NAM 2000-08-55, D. F. Barrett, diary entry, 14 August 1950.
10. IWMSA 17987, Roy Vincent, reel 2.
11. NAM 2001-07-1187-64, papers of Andrew Man, notes for a lecture on Korea given at Catterick District Officers' Club, 10 September 1951.
12. TNA WO 384/1, 'Abstract of Army Statistics', 1951.
13. TNA DEFE 7/509, 'The Present Need for Sending Very Young National Servicemen to Action Theatres Abroad', first of briefs attached to letter from Ministry of Defence, no signature, to Sellar of Ministry of Labour, October 1953. The brief did not break down numbers in any more detail.
14. Hansard, 31 January 1956, answer by Antony Head.
15. By October 1952, 150 national servicemen had been killed or died of wounds in Korea and a further six had died as prisoners of war. All of these were soldiers. Hansard, written answer by Nigel Birch, 20 October 1952.
16. NAM 1995-01-164, Robert Gomme, 'Korea: A Short Memoir, Forty Years On'.
17. NAMSA 1995-05-93, Robin Ollington, reel 1.
18. IWMSA 18825, Joseph Roberts, reel 3. Roberts remembered his contemporaries being told that they could stay with the Argylls in Germany if they signed on for three years but 'no one bit that'. They were transferred to the Black Watch and sent to Korea. Emrys Hughes alluded to 'dictatorial methods' used to make men sign on for regular service, with the threat that they would be drafted 'to serve in the Far East'. He said that he had received letters from three different parts of the country describing such methods. The Secretary of State for War admitted that

members of the Queen's Regiment had been offered regular engagements in terms that made it clear that acceptance would get them out of drafts for Korea. Hansard, 10 March 1952.

19. John Hollands, *The Dead, the Dying and the Damned* (1956, this edn 1976), p. 11.

20. *Daily Telegraph*, obituary, 25 March 2004.

21. Tom King in Adrian Walker (ed.), *Six Campaigns: National Servicemen at War, 1948–1960* (1993), pp. 101–7, at p. 106.

22. IWM 15595, David Batterham 'National Service Recalled'.

23. IWMSA 21696, Brian Sewell. © Whistledown, 2000.

24. John Boorman, *Adventures of a Suburban Boy* (2003), p. 66.

25. IWMSA 22268, Neal Ascherson. © Whistledown, 2000.

26. TNA WO 71/1024, court martial of R. Bone and ten others for mutiny, 1951.

27. IWMSA 18338, David Wray Fisher, reel 3.

28. IWM 9870, James Jacobs, 'Korea: One Conscript's War', pp. 4 and 9.

29. IWM 12515, Holmes, 'Korean War', p. 15.

30. IWMSA 8850, Peter Farrar, reel 4.

31. Ibid.

32. NAM 1995-01-164, Gomme, 'Korea: A Short Memoir', citing letter from the front.

33. P. J. Kavanagh, *The Perfect Stranger* (1966), p. 97.

34. IWMSA 12663, Denys Whatmore, reel 1.

35. Max Hastings, *The Korean War* (1987), p. 253.

36. Stephen Martin, 'Did Your Country Need You? An Oral History of the National Service Experience in Britain, 1945–1963' (PhD thesis, University of Wales, Lampeter, 1997), p. 41.

37. Major Harry Legge-Bourke, quoted in Hastings, *The Korean War*, p. 329.

38. NAM 2000-08-55, Barrett, diary entry, 4 October 1950.

39. IWMSA 18439, Albert Tyas, reel 2.

40. George Brown in Walker (ed.), *Six Campaigns*, pp. 21–7, at p. 23.

41. IWMSA 17740, Desmond Barnard, reel 2.

42. NAMSA 2001-02-397, Barry Reed, reel 3.

43. Nottingham PRO, papers of Professor J. M. Lee, DD 393/1/1, Patrick Preston to J. M. Lee, 2 May 1951.

44. IWM 9870, Jacobs, 'Korea: One Conscript's War', p. 25.

45. IWMSA 10708, Jack Harrison, reel 1.

46. NAM 1995-01-164, Gomme, 'Korea: A Short Memoir'.

47. IWM 9870, Jacobs, 'Korea: One Conscript's War', p. 26.

48. Hastings, *The Korean War*, p. 103.
49. NAMSA 2001-02-398, Dr Stanley Boydell, reel 2.
50. IWM 9870, Jacobs, 'Korea: One Conscript's War', p. 60.
51. IWMSA 20471, William Purves, reel 1.
52. NAM 2001-07-1187-64, notes for a lecture on Korea given by Colonel Andrew Man at Catterick District Officers' Club, 10 September 1951.
53. IWMSA 26098, Benjamin Whitchurch, reel 2.
54. Cited in Hastings, *The Korean War*, p. 366.
55. IWMSA 20669, John Keays, reel 5.
56. NAM 2000-08-55, Barrett, diary entry, 5 September 1950.
57. IWM 9968, D. Oates, 'Memoirs of the British Commonwealth General Hospital, Kure, Japan during the Korean War, 1950–53'.
58. IWMSA 10302, Peter Bangs, reel 2.
59. IWMSA 12729, Dennis Matthews, reel 2.
60. IWMSA 26098, Whitchurch, reel 2.
61. IWMSA 12663, Whatmore, reel 1.
62. Ibid., reels 2 and 3.
63. S. P. MacKenzie, *British Prisoners of the Korean War* (Oxford, 2012); C. N. Barclay, *The First Commonwealth Division: The Story of British Commonwealth Land Forces in Korea, 1950–1953* (1954), p. 189.
64. On the experience of national service prisoners see IWMSA 26098, Whitchurch, and IWMSA 18439, Tyas.
65. Hansard, 20 October 1952, written answer by Nigel Birch.
66. IWM 12515, Holmes, 'Korean War', epilogue, p. 43.
67. Ibid., quoting diary entry, 1 December 1951, p. 18.
68. Kavanagh, *A Perfect Stranger*, pp. 104 and 105.
69. NAM 2000-08-55, Barrett, diary entry, 1 December 1950.
70. Ibid., diary entry, 17 February 1951: 'Another strong rumour going the rounds at this time is that the MO has let it be known he will always do his very best for us if we suffer a grievous wound and will not allow undue suffering.'
71. NAMSA 2001-02-398, Boydell, reel 1. Boydell was Medical Officer with the Middlesex. He carried a gun to protect men in his care but makes no reference to killing badly wounded patients.
72. IWM 26098, Whitchurch, reel 3.
73. NAM 1995-01-164, Gomme, 'Korea: A Short Memoir'.
74. IWMSA 20364, Francis Cheesman, reel 3.
75. IWMSA 21064, Thomas Nowell, reel 3.
76. IWMSA 20471, Purves, reel 2.

77. IWMSA 22138, Thomas Henson, reel 3.
78. NAMSA 2001-02-397, Reed, reel 5.
79. IWM 12515, Sir Peter Holmes, 'Korean War Diary', p. 2.
80. Ibid., p. 14.
81. Ibid., epilogue, p. 42.
82. An account of Whybrow's action can be found in his medal citation in TNA WO 373/116/65.
83. IWM 12723, John Whybrow, 'Korea, 1951–1952: Some Personal Impressions': 'To my shame and regret: one sadly neglected group are the men who saved my life on the night of 29 January 1952.' Whybrow tried to track down members of his platoon but Talbot, the man who had rallied the soldiers, was dead by the time Whybrow found his address.
84. Kavanagh, *The Perfect Stranger*, p. 93.
85. IWM 9870, Jacobs, 'Korea: One Conscript's War', p. 56.
86. Hollands, *The Dead, the Dying and the Damned*, p. 253.
87. IWM 12515, Holmes, 'Korean War', introduction.
88. On feelings towards the Gloucesters, see IWMSA 18439, Tyas, reel 4. Tyas was himself captured with the Ulster Rifles and resented the attention given to the Glosters when prisoners were returned. Holmes too drew attention to the fact that the Royal Ulster Rifles had fought their way out from circumstances similar to those in which the Glosters had found themselves caught, IWM 12515, Holmes, 'Korean War', introduction, p. 4.
89. IWM 2279, Brigadier P. J. Jeffreys, 'Account of 1st Btn Durham Light Infantry in Korea, September 1952 to September 1953'.
90. *Manchester Guardian*, 30 March 1954, 'Young Soldiers in Korea 1. Casualties at Night', by a 'Young National Service Officer who was in Korea before the armistice'. See also the articles by the same author on 31 March and 1 April.
91. IWM 12515, Holmes, 'Korean War', p. 3, quoting diary entry for October 1951.
92. Ibid., epilogue, p. 44.
93. IWMSA 20471, Purves, reel 2.
94. NAMSA 2001-02-397, Reed, reel 1.
95. IWM 12515, Holmes, 'Korean War', epilogue, p. 43.
96. IWM 12723, Whybrow, 'Korea, 1951–1952', letter to father, 9 February 1952: 'having weighed up the pros and cons, I think that life will still be almost as enjoyable when I finally recover'.
97. NAMSA 2001-02-397, Reed, reel 5.
98. IWMSA 20471, Purves, reels 3 and 4.

99. IWM 12723, Whybrow, 'Korea, 1951–1952'.

100. Berwick Coates, *Sam Browne's Schooldays: Experiences of a Typical Squad of Postwar National Service Recruits* (Bognor Regis, 2009), p. 2: 'I was at college with someone who had lost a leg in Korea and I did not detect a trace of bitterness in his make up or his speech.'

101. For information on John Whybrow's later life, I am grateful to his son Nicolas.

102. IWMSA 12663, Whatmore, reel 4.

103. IWMSA 12729, Matthews, reel 2.

104. IWMSA 20268, Edwin Haywood, reel 4.

105. IWMSA 18825, Roberts, reel 5.

106. IWMSA 26098, Whitchurch, reel 6.

107. Martin, 'Did Your Country Need You?', p. 246.

108. IWMSA 21593, Maynard Leslie Winspear, reel 5.

13. IMPERIAL EMERGENCIES

1. Crispin Worthington preface to Robert Bonner, *Jungle Bashers: A British Infantry Battalion in the Malayan Emergency, 1951–1954* (Knutsford, 2002).

2. *New Statesman*, 'London Diary', 31 December 1955. The French did not use conscripts in colonial wars. They sent them to Algeria precisely because they did not consider it a colony, but even there few of them resisted.

3. IWMSA 8736, John Harding, reel 38.

4. TNA WO 384/15, 'Abstract of Army Statistics'. In December 1954, 51 per cent of all soldiers served in the UK and 19 per cent served in BAOR. These figures refer only to soldiers and do not distinguish between regulars and conscripts.

5. TNA WO 384/22, 'Abstract of Army Statistics', figures for 30 September 1956.

6. Hansard, 20 March 1956, answer by Fitzroy Maclean.

7. Monmouth School, *The Monmouthian*, July 1954.

8. Ibid. It was reported that R. L. Patterson was undertaking a course in London 'to be a better bearer of the white man's burden. He bears this burden in Tanganyika.'

9. Antony Copley, 'Midshipman's Workbook', entry for 12 March to 11 April 1955. Copley was to become a historian of decolonization with a particular focus on Gandhi and the independence movement.

10. Antony Copley, private diary, extracts lent by author.

11. Leslie Thomas, *This Time Next Week* (1964, this edition 1991), p. 154.

12. John Catton, *Prickly Heat: A Cheerful Happy Gallop through Experiences in Africa with the King's African Rifles* (Brighton, 2011).

13. IWMSA 22307, Anthony Howard. © Whistledown, 2000. Michael Holroyd, *Basil Street Blues: A Family Story* (1999, this edn 2000); David Cesarani, *Major Farran's Hat: Murder, Scandal and Britain's War against Jewish Terrorism, 1945–1948* (2009).

14. IWM 7178, C. B. L. Barr, diary entry, 24 May 1954.

15. IWM 2775, J. C. A. Green, letter home, 'Monday 23rd', apparently March 1953.

16. IWMSA 29062, John 'Jack' Burn, reel 4.

17. Mark Girouard, interviewed by Paul Thompson, *NLSC: Architects' Lives*, 2009, British Library Sound & Moving Image Catalogue reference C467/92, track 1. © The British Library. Girouard was initially recruited into the Brigade of Guards, in which his father had served, but was posted to the Nigeria Regiment after officer training.

18. John Cowell, *Elephant Grass* (Blackburn, 2007). The book describes the author's national service in Cameroon and those locals whom he got to know with great affection.

19. IWM 3135, J. R. Beverland, memoir.

20. IWM 6431, E. A. Dorking.

21. Hansard, 27 January 1953.

22. Ibid., 11 March 1954.

23. According to the Ministry of Defence, 55 British soldiers died in 'Egypt/ Suez' between 1 January 1948 and 31 December 1960. Of these, 43 were killed by terrorist action, 10 were killed by enemy action and 2 died of wounds. It may be that all men killed in the Suez expedition of 1956 were recorded as the victims of enemy action and all those who died in the Canal Zone before 1955 were designated victims of terrorism (see Appendix III).

24. NAMSA 2002-07-358, anonymous.

25. Ibid.

26. IWM 12733, Cyril MacG Williams, letter to 'All', September 1952, otherwise undated.

27. Ibid., 23 November 1952.

28. Ibid., 16 February 1953.

29. Ibid., 22 March 1953.

30. Ibid., 25 July 1953.

31. J. B. P. R., 'The Emergency in Malaya: Some Reflections on the First Six Years', *The World Today*, 10, 11 (1954), pp. 477–87.

32. See Karl Hack, '"Iron Claws on Malaya": The Historiography of the Malayan Emergency', *Journal of Southeast Asian Studies*, 30, 1 (March 1999), pp. 99–125.

33. IWMSA 10316, Frederick Dobbs, reel 3.

34. IWMSA 24570, Piers Plowright, reel 4: 'I began to worry and have an almost hero worship of these guys who live in the jungle ... Fighting a desperate battle.'

35. John Chynoweth, *Hunting Terrorists in the Jungle* (Stroud, 2007), p. 150. Bonner, *Jungle Bashers*, p. xvii.

36. J. B. P. R., 'The Emergency in Malaya'.

37. IWM 11915, N. A. Martin, 'The Day the Sun Stopped Shining', p. 66.

38. Huw Bennett, '"A Very Salutary Effect": The Counter-terror Strategy in the Early Malayan Emergency, June 1948 to December 1949', *Journal of Strategic Studies*, 32, 3 (2009), pp. 415–44.

39. David French, *The British Way in Counter-insurgency, 1945–1967* (Oxford, 2011), pp. 122–4.

40. Hansard, 1 November 1949 gives the figures of killed from 1 May 1948; Hansard, 31 January 1956 gives the figures of killed and wounded from November 1949 to January 1956. At least 184 national servicemen were wounded in Malaya during this period.

41. TNA DEFE 13/843, transcript of interview with Sir Stafford Foster-Sutton on *World at One*, 2 February 1970.

42. Christopher Hale, 'Batang Kali: Britain's My Lai?', *History Today*, 62, 7 (2012).

43. Cited in the *People*, 1 February 1970, copy in TNA DEFE 70/101.

44. Both NCOs were 'lance sergeants' – a rank in the Foot Guards that is equivalent to corporal in regiments of the line.

45. TNA WO 296/41, sworn testimony of Cootes, 8 January 1970.

46. Ibid.

47. Ibid.

48. Statements of Tuppen, Remedios, Brownrigg and Cootes cited in the *People*, 1 February 1970, copy in TNA DEFE 70/101. The original sworn statements can be found in TNA WO 296/41.

49. Cited in the *People*, 1 February 1970.

50. TNA WO 296/41, sworn testimony of Cootes, 8 January 1970.

51. TNA DEFE 70/101, Director of Public Prosecutions to Sir James

Dunnett, 29 June 1970. The Director of Public Prosecutions does not mention the Batang Kali case in his memoirs: *Public Prosecutor: The Memoirs of Sir Norman Skelhorn, Director of Public Prosecutions 1964–1977* (1981).

52. TNA DEFE 70/101, 'Alleged Massacre at Batang Kali: Position of RSM Douglas SG', 13 August 1970, signed Tugwell.

53. Ibid., Lt Colonel Commanding Scots Guards, reference to MOD letter, 10 February 1970, 17 February 1970.

54. IWMSA 9936, Edward Russell, reel 2.

55. David Erskine, *The Scots Guards, 1919–1955* (1956), p. 478.

56. Tom Stacey in Peter Chambers and Amy Landreth (eds.), *Called Up: The Personal Experiences of Sixteen National Servicemen, Told by Themselves* (1955), pp. 47–65.

57. Chynoweth, *Hunting Terrorists*, p. 58.

58. Hansard, 4 February 1970.

59. Leslie Ives, *A Musket for the King: The Trials and Tribulations of a National Serviceman 1949–1951* (Tavistock, 1999), p. 109. IWMSA 17333, John Noble, reel 2.

60. David Loewe, interview, 19 July 2012.

61. IWMSA 14053, David Henderson, reel 2. Henderson compares Malaya with 'Aden' – though he seems to be referring to Cyprus.

62. IWM 4102, Peter Burke, diary entry, 29 February 1956.

63. Nottingham PRO, papers of Professor J. M. Lee, DD 393/1/1, Preston to Lee, 2 May 1951.

64. IWMSA 17333, Noble, reel 2.

65. Geoffrey Barnes, *With the Dirty Half-hundred in Malaya: Memories of National Service, 1951–52* (Royston, 2001), p. 137.

66. Bernard Wickstead, *Daily Express*, cited in Adrian Walker, *A Country Regiment: 1st Battalion The Queen's Own Royal West Kent Regiment, Malaya, 1951–1954* (2001), p. 24.

67. IWMSA 14053, Henderson, reel 2.

68. Ibid., reel 1.

69. IWMSA 10211, Peter Beadle, reel 2.

70. French, *The British Way*, p. 290, n. 108. Precise figures are available only for the period after 1953.

71. IWMSA 10211, Beadle, reel 2.

72. Barnes, *With the Dirty Half–hundred*, p. 70.

73. IWMSA 10742, Kenneth Bartley, reel 1.

74. Neal Ascherson in Walker (ed.), *Six Campaigns*, pp. 1–7.

75. IWMSA 24570, Plowright, reel 5.

76. Barnes, *With the Dirty Half-hundred*, p. 20.
77. Ibid., p. 108.
78. Ibid., p. 147.
79. Ibid., p. 140.
80. Ibid., p. 125.
81. Ibid., p. 161.
82. Ibid., p. 147.
83. Ibid., p. 60.
84. Cited in ibid., p. 99.
85. IWMSA 21876, Geoffrey Barnes, reel 3.
86. Barnes, *With the Dirty Half-hundred*, p. 97. 'H.' was a regular corporal – later awarded the Military Medal and promoted to sergeant.
87. Cited in ibid., p. 147.
88. Ibid., p. 101.
89. IWMSA 17333, Noble, reel 2. Noble, who worked in the officers' mess, recalled that Hands had been upset by the accidental drowning of one of his men.
90. IWMSA 28424, Leslie Hands, reel 4.
91. *Daily Telegraph*, obituary for Leslie Raymond Hands, 13 February 2012.
92. French, *The British Way*, p. 120.
93. Huw Bennett, *Fighting the Mau Mau: The British Army and Counter-insurgency in the Kenya Emergency* (Cambridge, 2012).
94. TNA WO 384/15, 'Abstract of Army Statistics', figures for December 1954.
95. TNA WO 384/1, 'Abstract of Army Statistics'.
96. Hansard, 9 December 1952, reply by Antony Head.
97. Hansard, 13 July 1954, written answer by James Hutchison.
98. Hansard, 24 March 1953, Antony Head.
99. IWMSA 11159, Thomas Hewitson, reel 2.
100. Brian Thompson, *Clever Girl: Growing Up in the 1950s* (2007, this edn 2008), p. 91.
101. French, *The British Way*, p. 290. Between October 1952 and April 1953, 8,400 alleged Mau Mau fighters were killed and 1,193 firearms were recovered.
102. From Simon Raven's *Bird of Ill Omen* (1989), cited in Howard Watson (ed.), *The World of Simon Raven* (2002), p. 196.
103. French, *The British Way*, p. 297.
104. IWMSA 18825, Joseph Roberts, reel 6.
105. Cited in Bennett, *Fighting the Mau Mau*, p. 217.

106. TNA WO 32/21720, Proceedings of McLean Court of Enquiry, evidence of 2nd Lt Ellis, 16 December 1953.

107. TNA WO 32/16103, interrogation of Innes Walker, answer 93.

108. TNA WO 71/1221, Proceedings of Second Court Martial of Captain G. S. L. Griffiths, evidence of Innes Walker, 9 March 1954.

109. Ibid., 8 March 1954.

110. TNA WO 32/21722, suggested answer, signed T. L. Binney, 4 December 1953.

111. Chynoweth, *Hunting Terrorists*, p. 102. Tom King also alludes to the case – though without naming Griffiths. See Tom King in Walker (ed.), *Six Campaigns*, pp. 101–7, at p. 104.

112. French, *The British Way*, p. 313.

113. TNA WO 32/21720, McLean Enquiry, 17 December 1953, evidence of Major Holmes.

114. David Larder, letter to *Guardian*, 10 June 2013.

115. TNA WO 93/56, list of court martials in Kenya, attached to loose minute, illegible signature, 13 January 1954. Larder was court-martialled at Sagana on 10 August 1953.

116. TNA WO 32/21720, McLean Enquiry, 29 December 1953, evidence of Lt Colonel Windeatt, commanding officer of the Devonshire Regiment.

117. Bennett, *Fighting the Mau Mau*, p. 119.

118. TNA WO 32/21720, McLean Enquiry, 29 December 1953, evidence of Reverend Squire.

119. Roy Fuller, *The Father's Comedy* (1961), p. 91.

120. TNA WO 32/21721, *Journal Devonshire Regiment*, November 1953.

121. Michael Barber, *The Captain: The Life and Times of Simon Raven* (1996), p. 123.

122. IWMSA 19064, William Fitt, reel 1.

123. Ibid., reels 1 and 2.

124. Thompson, *Clever Girl*, pp. 76–123.

125. Ibid., p. 110.

126. IWMSA 10010, Simon Maclachlan, reels 2 and 3.

127. IWM Trevor Royle, 66/211/1(1/37), Frank Gaff.

128. IWMSA 10145, Michael Harbottle, reel 1.

129. F. A. Godfrey, *The History of the Suffolk Regiment, 1946–1959* (1988), pp. 140–41.

130. French, *The British Way*, p. 169.

131. Ibid., p. 170.

132. David Lance, interviewed by Michelle Winslow, *Oral History of Oral*

History, 2005, British Library Sound & Moving Image Catalogue reference C1149/01, track 1. © The British Library.

133. Antony Copley, diary entry, 11 August 1956.

134. IWMSA 17223, Adrian Walker, reel 2.

135. Albert Balmer, *A Cyprus Journey: Memoirs of National Service* (2008), p. 192.

136. LHCMA, I. W. G. Martin, letter cited without date in Ian Martin, 'The "Cyprus Troubles", 1955–1960' in *Kampos: Cambridge Occasional Papers in Modern Greek* (1993). The originals of Martin's letters can be found in IWM 1779.

137. Letter cited without date in ibid.

138. Pat Baker in Walker (ed.), *Six Campaigns*, pp. 8–14, at p. 13.

139. Interview with Simon Coningham, 20 May 2013.

140. IWM 15316, P. J. Houghton-Brown, undated letter in part 2, and ibid., part 4, brief memoir between letters in part 4.

141. IWM 675, A. R. Ashton, 'National Service: Royal Marine Commando Memoirs' (1990), p. 183.

142. David Baxter, *Two Years to Do* (1959), p. 50.

143. Stephen Hugh-Jones, *Guardian*, 19 February 1960.

144. Owen Parfitt in Walker (ed.), *Six Campaigns*, pp. 108–14, at p. 111.

145. Balmer, *A Cyprus Journey*, p. 128.

146. IWMSA 21684, Tom Davis. © Whistledown, 2000.

147. TNA WO 32/16103, interrogation of Innes-Walker, answer 403.

148. TNA WO 32/21720, McLean Enquiry, 29 December 1953, evidence of Lt Colonel Windeatt, commanding officer of the Devonshire Regiment.

14. SUEZ

1. David Morgan, *'It Will Make a Man of You': Notes on National Service, Masculinity and Autobiography* (Manchester, 1987), p. 9.

2. TNA DEFE 7/808, letter to Richard Powell, illegible signature, 30 November 1956.

3. IWMSA 22307, Anthony Howard. © Whistledown, 2000.

4. John Ferris, interview, 25 July 2012.

5. A. J. P. Taylor, *A Personal History* (1983, this edn 1984), p. 273.

6. IWM 15316, P. J. Houghton-Brown, letter to mother, 5 November 1956.

7. Alan Watson in Ken Drury (ed.), *Get Some In: Memories of National Service* (Great Dunmow, 2006), pp. 113–17, at p. 116.

8. Francis Holford, interviewed by Cathy Courtney, *NLSC: City Lives*, 1992, British Library Sound & Moving Image Catalogue reference C409/067, track 1. © The British Library.

9. IWMSA 10145, Michael Harbottle, reel 1.

10. IWMSA 21690, Paul Foot. © Whistledown, 2000.

11. Antony Copley, diary entry, 1 November 1956.

12. IWMSA 10925, Bruce Kent.

13. John Barnes, *Diary of a National Serviceman in the Royal Navy* (Edinburgh, 1994), p. 43, letter to parents, 2 November 1956.

14. Alan Watkins, *The Spectator*, 7 April 1979.

15. Peter Jay, *The Spectator*, 18 August 2012.

16. Peter Jay, entry in 'Midshipman's Workbook', 14 September 1956, comment by superior officer.

17. Peter Jay, entry in Ibid., 9 December 1956.

18. Douglas Jay, *Change and Fortune: A Political Record* (1980), p. 268.

19. IWMSA 22307, Anthony Howard. © Whistledown, 2000.

20. John Ferris, interview, 25 July 2012.

21. IWM 2118, Peter Mayo, diary entry, 6 November 1956.

22. IWMSA 11146, General Sir Michael Gray, reel 4.

23. Alun Pask in Adrian Walker (ed.), *Six Campaigns: National Servicemen at War, 1948–1960* (1993), pp. 115–21, at p. 120.

24. IWM 675, A. R. Ashton, 'National Service: Royal Marine Commando Memoirs' (1990), p. 83.

25. Ibid., p. 92.

26. IWMSA 11142, Nicholas Vaux.

27. IWM 675, Ashton, 'National Service', p. 114.

28. Ibid., pp. 121–3.

29. IWM 2118, Mayo, diary entries, 22 September, 31 October, 2 November, 4 December 1956.

30. Copley, diary entry, 7 November 1956.

31. Ibid., 10/11 November 1956. Copley wishes to distance himself from these remarks, which he now regards as 'infantile'.

32. IWMSA 21674, Nick Harden. © Whistledown, 2000.

33. *The Times*, 23 November 1956.

34. TNA WO 71/1235, 'Report of Mutiny at Platres on 1 October 1956 and Events Leading to it', by Lt Colonel Baverstock, 2 December 1956.

35. TNA WO 71/1235, words reported in letter from Deputy Judge Advocate General to General Commanding Officer, Cyprus District, 24 November 1956.

36. Ibid., court martial proceedings, 7–12 November 1956.

37. TNA WO 32/16713, 'The Case of Mrs Margaret B', signed DP, 16 October 1956.
38. TNA WO 71/1234, letter to Driver Newall, signed Rosie, dated 'Monday'.
39. TNA WO 32/16713, 'Statement by Brigadier A. W. Brown, CBE, DSO, MC, Duty Commander, 10th Armoured Division, on Alleged Incident at Derna, Cyrenaica, Involving Men of the 1st Battalion KRRC on or about the Week-end 29th/30th September 1956'.
40. Ibid.
41. Ibid.
42. Ibid., telegram from commandant Malta, 'Incident Involving Other Ranks of 3 Grenadiers GDS Which Occurred Friday 5 October'.
43. NAMSA 2002-07-358, anonymous.
44. Ibid.
45. Ibid.
46. Ibid.
47. Ibid.
48. Ibid.

15. ENDING NATIONAL SERVICE

1. John Sutherland, *The Boy Who Loved Books* (2007, this edn 2008), p. 175.
2. Peter Cobbold, *The National Service Sailor* (Wivenhoe, 1993).
3. NAMSA 2003-04-4, Mike Gilman, reel 1.
4. TNA DEFE 7/1048, Maston to Mottershead, 15 August 1958, and attached memorandum.
5. Nigel Nicolson, *Alex* (1973), p. 302.
6. Shinwell apparently made this suggestion in an article for the *Sunday Pictorial*. See TNA PREM 11/201, note to Prime Minister by Jacobs, 4 September 1952.
7. Conservative Manifesto, cited in D. E. Butler, *The British General Election of 1955* (1955), pp. 18–19.
8. TNA PREM 11/201, Montgomery to Churchill, 6 September 1952.
9. Ibid., Head to Churchill, 24 July 1952, and Churchill to Head, 25 July 1952. Churchill was angry when Head initially sent him a brief factual account of how much money might be saved by shortening national service.
10. Ibid., Churchill to Jacob, 15 August 1952: 'considering that he [Shinwell] was the Ministerial author of two years Service and has on several

occasions shown patriotic inclinations I should like to know whether he has any foundation for his views'.

11. TNA PREM 11/494, Churchill to Head, 11 September 1953: 'The cogent arguments which you use would not I fear make two years popular and would only lend publicity and weight to Shinwell's inconsistent and unpatriotic activities. There is no doubt a plebiscite would negative two years, and eighteen months after that. The House of Commons is the best place for arguing this.'

12. Brigadier A. H. Head, MP, 'The Army We Need', *The Spectator*, 17 December 1948.

13. TNA WO 216/411, note by Antony Head (Secretary of State for War) to DCIGS and VAG, 21 February 1952.

14. TNA AIR 8/1656, Head to Eden, 23 November 1955.

15. TNA DEFE 7/808, letter from Naval Manpower Branch, 21 August 1956, illegible signature but apparently written on behalf of Admiral Bryant.

16. TNA CAB 139/505, Playfair of War Office to Campion of Central Statistical Office, 25 July 1956.

17. TNA WO 32/17657, AAG to DPA, 'The Effect of the Abolition of National Service and the Reduction in Size of the Army on Promotion Prospects of Regular Other Ranks', 12 January 1959. It was estimated that a man in an all-regular army would take four, rather than two, years to reach the rank of corporal.

18. TNA WO 32/16430, Major Freyburg (War Office) to Major Johnson (Grenadier Guards), 12 July 1960.

19. TNA CAB 139/505, Central Statistical Office, working group on regular recruiting possibilities after the termination of national service, 'Draft Review of the Estimates of Regular Recruiting, the Likely Period of Regular Service and the Strength of the Forces Which Would be Thereby Maintained after the Cessation of National Service', circulated by Ridley, 11 December 1956.

20. TNA PREM 11/1935, Home to Sandys, 22 February 1957.

21. TNA DEFE 7/808, Hailsham to meeting on future of national service, 4 October 1956.

22. TNA DEFE 7/808, note by N. S. Forward to Sir Richard Powell, summarizing meeting of Minister of Labour and service ministers, 6 June 1956. The meeting concluded: 'We must have national service . . . We cannot go on with the present policy of raising the age of intake . . . We must not cut down the period . . . Therefore, we must have some kind of selective draft.'

23. Ibid., meeting on future of national service, 4 October 1956.

24. TNA DEFE 13/53, Norman Dodds, MP for Dartford, to Eden, 1 September 1955.

25. TNA PREM 11/935, notes to Pitblado, illegible signature, 6 December 1955: 'I did not record this statement as I assumed that the Prime Minister would not specially wish to have a general prognostication of this kind included in the minutes.' Eden's words on this subject do not appear in the official minutes of the Cabinet meeting of 6 December 1955. See TNA CAB/128/29/45.

26. TNA PREM 11/1935, Eden to Minister of Defence, 1 July 1956.

27. Ministry of Labour and National Service, *National Service* (1955), cmd 9608.

28. Nigel Fisher, *Iain Macleod* (1973), p. 114.

29. TNA CAB 130/120, Cabinet committee on national service, 23 July 1956.

30. TNA PREM 11/1935, 'National Service', note by Lord President of the Council, initialled by Salisbury, 10 January 1957.

31. TNA DEFE 7/808, minute to Chilver, illegible signature, 16 November 1956.

32. IWM 12505, T. J. Hunt, Midshipman's Workbook, 20 January 1957.

33. Martin S. Navias, 'Terminating Conscription? The British National Service Controversy 1955-56', *Journal of Contemporary History*, 24 (1989), pp. 195-208.

34. TNA CAB 129/86/19, draft circulated by Sandys, 15 March 1957. The language of the final published paper was more measured.

35. Churchill College, Cambridge, papers of Duncan Sandys, 6/52, 'How the Total of 375,000 for the Forces Was Reached', apparently an aide memoire drafted for Sandys.

36. TNA CAB 129/86/41, 'Future of National Service', memorandum by the Minister of Labour and National Service, 5 April 1957.

37. Ministry of Labour and National Service, *Call Up of Men to the Forces, 1957/60* (1957), cmd 175.

38. TNA LAB 6/694, 'Run-down of National Service', 31 July 1959, attached to note, Bond to Maston, 5 August 1959.

39. TNA PREM 11/2088, 'National Service and Regular Recruiting', Faviell, 26 June 1957, sent to Bishop on 8 July 1957 by Michael Fraser of the Conservative Research Department and apparently seen by the Prime Minister before being forwarded to officials in the Ministry of Defence.

40. TNA CAB 128/31/32, 9 April 1957.

41. Churchill College, Cambridge, papers of Duncan Sandys, 8/10, Sandys to Wigg, 27 November 1961.

42. Hansard, 7 June 1956. Macleod said that the deferment of scientists had been announced in 1954 and that the number involved had risen sharply, and was expected to reach 1,400 in 1956. See also Hansard, 29 October 1957. The indefinite deferment of teachers with first- and second-class degrees had been announced in July of that year.

43. TNA LAB 6/624, 'National Service Acts: Programme of Medical Examinations', circular signed S. Price, 20 March 1959.

44. TNA LAB 6/694, 'Run-down of National Service', 31 July 1959.

45. Ibid., minutes meeting, 28 April 1960, chaired by Martyn: 'the judgement of doctors were affected by the standards applied by Service medical officers for retention in the services'.

46. Ibid., 'Run-down of National Service', 31 July 1959.

47. *The Times*, 13 August 1955.

48. TNA UGC 7/407, Master of Corpus Christi College, Cambridge to Murray of the UGC, 2 March 1956.

49. TNA LAB 6/694, letter from Neil Scott, Secretary to Nottingham University Careers and Appointments Board, to Whittington, Secretary to University Joint Recruitment Board, 22 October 1959.

50. TNA LAB 6/691, 'History of the Deferment Arrangements for Science and Engineering Graduates', 9 October 1960.

51. TNA LAB 6/694, 'Problem of Call Up in 1960', brief for minister, attached to note to Bond, illegible signature, 6 November 1959.

52. John Sainsbury, interview, 15 December 2011.

53. Churchill College, Cambridge, papers of Peter Jay, 4/1/1, Harold Walker to Jay, 2 May 1957.

54. IWM 2118, Peter Mayo, diary entry, 9 October 1956.

55. David Lodge, *How Far Can You Go?* (1980, this edn 1981), p. 50.

56. Antony Copley, diary entry, 4 November 1956.

57. TNA AIR 2/14647, various documents on this matter, particularly 'Extract from Minutes of Principal Personnel Officers' Committee', 12 October 1960.

58. Trevor Royle, *The Best Years of Their Lives* (1986), p. 222.

59. TNA LAB 6/694, Maston to Drew of Ministry of Defence, proposed draft of joint statement by their ministers, 1 June 1960.

60. TNA PREM 11/3037, note for Prime Minister, 'National Service Call Up', illegible signature, 9 August 1960.

61. TNA LAB 6/694, working party on national service intakes, minutes of meeting, 10 August 1960.

62. The outline script for this programme (written by Michael Nelson) and various correspondence relating to it are to be found in TNA DEFE 7/1037.

63. TNA DEFE 7/1037, Ministry of Labour to Minister of Defence, signed J. H., 16 November 1960.

64. The figure of '9,000 to 10,000' was given by Lord Shepherd in the House of Lords, Hansard (HOL), 27 February 1962. There were eighty-nine national service officers and 5,139 national service other ranks still serving in the army on 1 January 1963, by which point even the very last intake of national servicemen would have served for more than two years. Hansard, 31 January 1963, answer by Profumo.

65. Richard Vaughan, interview, 23 January 2013.

66. *The Times*, 13 May 1963.

67. Ibid., 12 August 1960.

68. NAMSA 2003-03-626, Peter Duffell, reel 1.

69. TNA LAB 6/741, Billing to Macdonald, 20 May 1976.

70. TNA LAB 6/694, 'Run-down of National Service', 31 July 1959.

71. IWMSA 26559, Leigh Parkes, reel 1.

72. Philip Naylor in Eric Pegg (ed.), *The Royal Engineers and the National Service Years, 1939–1963: A Military and Social History* (2002), pp. 413–19, at p. 415.

73. Letter to *The Times* from Peter Duffell, 8 October 1959.

74. TNA LAB 6/637, copy of statement made by Flynn.

75. *Daily Express*, 1 April 1960.

76. John Hoskyns, *Just in Time: Inside the Thatcher Revolution* (2000), p. 3.

77. Ministry of Defence, *Report of the Advisory Committee on Recruiting* (1958), cmd 545 (Grigg Report).

78. Stanley Price, 'The Fucking Army', unpublished chapter of autobiography and also his unperformed play, 'A Sergeant's Tale', partly about Wavell. Stanley Price, interview, 17 May 2013.

79. Denis Healey, *The Time of My Life* (1989, this edn 1990), p. 256.

80. TNA WO 32/19447, draft letter from Stockwell, undated, and 'Redundancy – AG's Personal Letter', note signed Hingston, 23 June 1960.

81. Resettlement Advisory Board, *Progress Report, 1957–1959* (1959), cmd 789, pp. 6–8.

82. Hansard, 17 April 1957.

83. Discussion of 19 November 1947 on the 'Supply and Training of Officers', *Journal of the Royal United Service Institution*, February 1948, pp. 45–68, comments by John Wolfenden, p. 62.

84. TNA PREM 11/2088, note by Faviell, 26 June 1957.

85. TNA WO 384/40, 'Abstract of Army Statistics', March 1961.
86. IWM 3300, Brigadier T. Hart Dyke.
87. C. B. Otley, 'Militarism and Militarization in the Public Schools, 1900–1972', *British Journal of Sociology*, 29, 3 (1978), pp. 321–39. The proportion of public school bursars with military backgrounds seems to have peaked at 38 per cent in 1972.
88. Resettlement Advisory Board, *Progress Report*, p. 11.
89. John Drummond, *Tainted by Experience: A Life in the Arts* (2000, this edn 2001), p. 86.
90. Michael Holroyd in B. S. Johnson (ed.), *All Bull: The National Servicemen* (1973), pp. 136–48, at p. 146.
91. 'A National Serviceman', 'The New Unemployables', *New Statesman*, 15 June 1957.
92. Ibid., 'Band Night', 13 April 1957.

16. A COLD-BLOODED VIEW

1. TNA PREM 11/201, Churchill to Jacob, 15 August 1952.
2. Oliver Franks, *Britain and the Tide of World Affairs: The BBC Reith Lectures, 1954* (1955), p. 2.
3. Stephen Martin, 'Did Your Country Need You? An Oral History of the National Service Experience in Britain, 1945–1963' (PhD thesis, University of Wales, Lampeter, 1997), p. 57.
4. Ibid., p. 59.
5. A few young seamen on unofficial strike were called up in 1955. Revealingly *The Times* suggested that continued deferment should be granted only to men on *official* strikes. *The Times*, 28 June 1955.
6. TNA LAB 6/19, Smieton to Sutherland, 23 September 1957.
7. IWSMA 26731, Leonard Knowles, reel 2. Knowles returned from the air force to find that his employer would re-employ him only as an apprentice. He resigned and was helped only because an official of the Communist Electricians' Union bent the rules to get him a union card, and hence the right to work.
8. Frank Myers, 'British Trade Unions and the End of Conscription: The Tripartite Committee of 1950–56', *Journal of Contemporary History*, 31, 3 (1996), pp. 509–20.
9. Quaker Meeting House, London, Friends Peace Committee Conscription Group, minutes, 30 November 1955, report by Eden Peacock: '70 per cent of the local Labour Parties voted against conscription and the

vote in relation to its continuance was only carried by the large number of votes registered by the Trade Union blocs.'

10. John Drummond belonged to the small group of men who managed to join the navy, the small group who became officers, the small group who learned Russian and the small group, even within this small group, who became interpreters rather than merely translators. Not surprisingly, he had fond memories of national service and he also wrote of his politics: 'I am a typical Butskellite of the post-war generation, and deeply resented the way in which the consensus politics of the middle years of the century fell victim to the Thatcherite need for confrontation.' John Drummond, *Tainted by Experience: A Life in the Arts* (2000, this edn 2001), p. 81.

11. In discussion after a sermon by the Bishop of Croydon about 'Christianity as opposed to Communism', Lt General Sir Giffard Le Quesne Martel said: 'Some of us have been trying to get rid of Communism in certain ways, such as among school teachers and so forth. We have studied this matter. In the olden days we should have cleared them out in five minutes and some of them would have been burnt at the stake, but in these days the Country is in a very timid state.' *Journal of the Royal United Services Institution*, November 1953, p. 522.

12. TNA WO 32/16246, 'Military Assistance in the Event of Civil Emergency', undated and unsigned but apparently attached to note to the Secretary of State from a lieutenant colonel, with illegible signature, 28 January 1958 about a forthcoming bus strike: 'Although the character of the Services has changed to some extent since 1926, mainly through the advent of National Service, there is no doubt that the reliability of the forces is beyond question. All emergencies dealt with in recent years have shown this quite clearly. Full employment and high wages have removed entirely the elements of sympathy that existed between troops and strikers in 1926, and apart from feelings of class or in some cases family loyalty, there will be few points of concord.'

13. TNA WO 32/15857, letter from W. H. Cuties, 9 September 1953, enclosing a cheque for £3,000 to be distributed to service charities from oil companies as a token of appreciation for help during a tanker drivers' strike.

14. TNA WO 32/10994, Army Educational Advisory Board, 11 October 1951.

15. TNA DPP 6/31, Hill to Mathew, 25 March 1953, and Mathew's reply, 27 March 1953.

16. Leslie Ives, *A Musket for the King: The Trials and Tribulations of a National Serviceman 1949–1951* (Tavistock, 1999), p. 100.

17. Arnold Wesker, *As Much as I Dare: An Autobiography (1932–1959)* (1994), p. 295. See also Jimmy Reid, *Reflections of a Clyde-built Man* (1976), p. 21.

18. David French, *Army, Empire, and Cold War: The British Army and Military Policy, 1945–1971* (Oxford, 2012), p. 156

19. Albert Balmer, *A Cyprus Journey: Memoirs of National Service* (2008), p. 80. NAM 2004-02-106, Simon Bendall, 'Memoirs of a National Serviceman'. Bendall, a gunner in Germany, was issued with 'what passed for anti-radiation clothing' and trained in how to use a Geiger counter – supposedly so that he could tell his comrades whether it was safe to emerge from their shelters after a nuclear attack.

20. IWM, Trevor Royle, 66/211/1(1/92), Richard Storey.

21. Bernard Palmer in B. S. Johnson (ed.), *All Bull: The National Servicemen* (1973), pp. 149–58.

22. Anthony Hampshire, interview, 15 May 2013.

23. French, *Army, Empire, and Cold War*, p. 104.

24. NAMSA 2000-04-56, Canon Michael Perry, reel 2.

25. TNA WO 32/17243, 'Interview of National Servicemen by Personnel Selection Officers', signed Director of Manpower Planning, 21 December 1956.

26. TNA WO 32/15021, AORG, 'Psychiatric Assessment of Borstal Entrants', 11 August 1952.

27. Geoffrey Barnes, *With the Dirty Half-hundred in Malaya: Memories of National Service, 1951–52* (Royston, 2001), p. 77.

28. IWMSA 11146, General Sir Michael Gray, reel 1.

29. Bruno Schroder, interviewed by Cathy Courtney, *NLSC: City Lives*, 1992, British Library Sound & Moving Image Catalogue reference C409/076, reel 1. © The British Library.

30. IWM, Royle, 66/211/1(1/51), Jim Laird. See also *Scottish Paraplegic Association Journal*, spring 1985.

31. Wesker, *As Much as I Dare*, p. 306.

32. TNA HO 344/28, Defence Committee, 8 December 1960.

33. Richard Pole, interviewed by Louise Brodie, *Down to Earth: An Oral History of British Horticulture*, 2006, British Library Sound & Moving Image Catalogue reference C1029/38, track 2. © The British Library.

34. TNA DEFE 7/808, meeting on future of national service, 4 October 1956.

35. Ministry of Defence, *Report of the Advisory Committee on Recruiting* (1958), cmd 545 (Grigg Report), paras 164 and 257.

36. David Lodge, *Ginger, You're Barmy* (1962, this edn 1984), p. 216.

37. Karl Miller in Johnson (ed.), *All Bull*, pp. 256–66, at p. 257.

38. IWMSA 8423, Peter Burke.

39. Jim Riordan, *Comrade Jim: The Spy Who Played for Spartak* (2008), p. 28. Ronald Hyam, *My Life in the Past* (privately published, 2012).

40. David Morgan, *'It Will Make a Man of You': Notes on National Service, Masculinity and Autobiography* (Manchester, 1987). Morgan does mention the relatively large number of grammar school boys in his intake and does say, though not in his published memoir, that he 'vaguely' understood Hednesford to be a camp for potential officers.

41. Jeremy Crang, *The British Army and the People's War, 1939–1945* (Manchester, 2000), p. 36.

42. Alan Sillitoe, *Life Without Armour* (1995), p. 38.

43. Michael Young, *The Rise of the Meritocracy* (1958, this edn 1963), p. 112.

44. TNA WO 163/107, Executive Committee of the Army Council, 'Future of the Royal Pioneer Corps (Memorandum by AG for Consideration by the Executive Committee of the Army Council at a Future Meeting)', 24 September 1948.

45. Peter Nichols, *Feeling You're Behind: An Autobiography* (1984), p. 120.

46. TNA AIR 77/608, 'Morale of the National Service Airman on Entry and During Initial Training', January 1949. TNA WO 32/15604, 'Retrospect: A Survey of Effects of National Service', 1955. The first concerned only airmen, the second only soldiers. 'Retrospect' dealt with men who had actually changed jobs whereas the survey of airmen looked at their expectations for the future.

47. Martin, 'Did Your Country Need You?', p. 54.

48. Cited in Adrian Walker, *A Country Regiment: 1st Battalion The Queen's Own Royal West Kent Regiment, Malaya, 1951–1954* (2001), p. 24.

49. Ministry of Education, *15 to 18* (1959) (Crowther Report), II, pp. 158–65.

50. Two papers by economists try to assess the impact of national service on long-term earnings. In his 'Long-term Effects of Conscription: Lessons from the UK', http://www.sole-jole.org/820.pdf, Paolo Buonanno argues that conscription had a markedly negative effect. Professor Buonnano uses 'a regression discontinuity approach to compare individuals born just after 1943 (affected) with those born just before 1943 (not affected)'. But no one born later than September 1939 and

relatively few men born in the year before that were called up, so Buon-nano is just comparing two different cohorts of post-conscription men.

In 'Above and Beyond the Call: Long-term Real Earnings Effects of British Male Military Conscription in the Post-war Years', IZA Discussion Paper No. 5563, March 2011, Julien Grenet, Robert A. Hart and J. Elizabeth Roberts argue that national service did not have a demonstrable effect on earnings – though they are sympathetic to the idea that it might have provided men with economically useful experience. After complicated discussions of statistics, Hart et al. resort to qualitative assertions about the value of 'teamwork' and 'leadership'.

51. IWM 15103, Bernard Parke. Parke was discharged from the RAF in 1958.
52. Anthony Heath and Clive Payne, 'Twentieth Century Trend in Social Mobility in Britain', Centre for Research into Elections and Social Trends, Working Paper 70 (1999), http://www.crest.ox.ac.uk.
53. TNA WO 32/15604, 'Retrospect: A Survey of Effects of National Service', 1955.
54. TNA AIR 20/12136, 'Morale of the National Service Airman (an Account of an Investigation Covering the Period October 1947–September 1950)', by A. S. Anthony, 24 July 1951.
55. TNA AIR 20/6457, 'Attitudes of Serving Airmen: Report of a Working Party, Oct.–Dec. 1948'.
56. Essex University, Affluent Worker Survey, 204.
57. IWMSA 21582, David Davies, reel 4. Having left grammar school relatively early, Davies trained as a teacher after national service. The sociologist John Ferris, who had left a secondary modern school at fifteen, and the historian Patrick O'Brien both returned to education after their service.
58. IWM 15595, David Batterham, letter to parents, 2 March 1953.
59. Philip Bell, interview, 21 May 2013.
60. NAM 1995-01-164, Robert Gomme, 'Korea: A Short Memoir'.
61. Abigail Wills, 'Delinquency, Masculinity and Citizenship in England, 1950–1970', Past and Present, 187 (2005), pp. 157–85.
62. Peter Duncumb, interview, 11 January 2013.
63. TNA AIR 20/6457, 'Report of a Working Party on the Attitudes of Serving Airmen, Oct.–Dec. 1948'.
64. IWM 16584, Michael Longley, letter, 9 April 1949.
65. Nottingham, PRO, papers of Professor J. M. Lee, DD 393/1/1, letter from Graham Mottershaw to Lee, 12 November 1950.
66. NAM 2005-09-145, John Joseph Wellington.

67. It may be that national service had helped underwrite the networks that linked the upper reaches of business to the Conservative party in the 1970s. Brian Wyldbore-Smith, *March Past: The Memoirs of a Major-General* (Spenneymoor, 2001), p. 130. Wyldbore-Smith believed that raising money for the Conservative party was relatively easy in this decade because so many businessmen had done national service. The Conservative minister George Younger sometimes said that William Purves, the banker, had saved his life in Korea – though, in fact, the two men were not on the front line at the same time. David Torrance, *George Younger: A Life Well Lived* (Edinburgh, 2008), p. 31.
68. Cecil Parkinson, *Right at the Centre: An Autobiography* (1992), p. 63.
69. Douglas Hurd, *Memoirs* (2003), p. 64.
70. Peter Sharp in Peter Chambers and Amy Landreth (eds.), *Called Up: The Personal Experiences of Sixteen National Servicemen, Told by Themselves* (1955), pp. 68–81, at p. 81.
71. Tom Stacey in ibid., pp. 47–65.
72. IWMSA 21690, Paul Foot. © Whistledown, 2000.

Bibliography

PUBLISHED SOURCES

Place of publication is London unless otherwise stated.

Individual articles in newspapers and periodicals have been cited only if they are particularly significant.

'A National Serviceman', 'Band Night', *New Statesman* 13 April 1957

—, 'The New Unemployables', *New Statesman*, 15 June 1957

'Young National Service Officer who was in Korea before the armistice', *Manchester Guardian*, 30 March, 31 March and 1 April 1954

Abrams, Mark, *The Teenage Consumer* (1959)

Adams, R. J. Q., 'The National Service League and Military Service in Edwardian Britain', *Armed Forces and Society*, 12 (1985), pp. 53–74

— and Poirier, Philip, *The Conscription Controversy in Great Britain, 1900–1918* (Columbus OH, 1987)

Alford, Roger, *Life and LSE* (Sussex, 2009)

Allport, Alan, *Demobbed: Coming Home after the Second World War* (2009)

Amery, Julian, 'How to Strengthen the British Army', *East and West*, 1957

Anderson, David, *Histories of the Hanged: The Dirty War in Kenya and the End of Empire* (New York, 2005)

Annan, Noel, *Our Age: The Generation that Made Post-war Britain* (1990)

Bailey, Paul, *An Immaculate Mistake: Scenes from Childhood and Beyond* (1990)

Baker, Mike, *The Last Intake: The Story of a Serviceman in Singapore and RAF Changi* (1995)

Baker, Tom, *Who on Earth is Tom Baker?* (1997)

Bakewell, Joan, *The Centre of the Bed* (2003)

Balmer, Albert, *A Cyprus Journey: Memoirs of National Service* (2008)

Barber, Michael, *The Captain: The Life and Times of Simon Raven* (1996)

Barclay, C. N., *The First Commonwealth Division: The Story of British Commonwealth Land Forces in Korea, 1950–1953* (1954)

Barnes, Geoffrey, *With the Dirty Half-hundred in Malaya: Memories of National Service, 1951–52* (Royston, 2001)

Barnes, John, *Diary of a National Serviceman in the Royal Navy* (Edinburgh, 1994)

Basset, Elizabeth, *Love is my Meaning: An Anthology of Assurance* (1973)

Baxter, David, *Two Years to Do* (1959)

Bayly, Christopher and Harper, Tim, *Forgotten Wars: The End of Britain's Asian Empire* (2007)

Bennett, Huw, ' "A Very Salutary Effect": The Counter-terror Strategy in the Early Malayan Emergency, June 1948 to December 1949', *Journal of Strategic Studies*, 32, 3 (2009), pp. 415–44

—, *Fighting the Mau Mau: The British Army and Counter-insurgency in the Kenya Emergency* (Cambridge, 2012)

Betts, Tony, *The Key of the Door: Rhythm and Romance in a Post-war London Adolescence* (Wimborne, 2006)

Billington, Michael, *Harold Pinter* (1996)

Blacker, Cecil, *Monkey Business: The Memoirs of General Sir Cecil Blacker* (1993)

Blacker, Terence, *You Cannot Live as I Have Lived and Not End Up Like This: The Thoroughly Disgraceful Life and Times of Willie Donaldson* (2007)

Blair, John, *The Conscript Doctors: Memories of National Service* (Edinburgh, 2001)

Blake, Robert, *The Unknown Prime Minister: The Life and Times of Andrew Bonar Law, 1858–1923* (1955)

Bonnaud, Robert, *Itinéraire* (Paris, 1962)

Bonner, Robert, *Jungle Bashers: A British Infantry Battalion in the Malayan Emergency, 1951–1954* (Knutsford, 2002)

Boorman, John, *Adventures of a Suburban Boy* (2003)

Bourke, Joanna, *An Intimate History of Killing: Face to Face Killing in Twentieth-century Warfare* (2000)

Braine, John, *Room at the Top* (1957)

Braithwaite, E. R., *To Sir, with Love* (1959)

Branche, Raphaëlle, *La Torture et l'armée pendant la guerre d'Algérie* (Paris, 2001)

Broad, Roger, *Conscription in Britain, 1939–1964: The Militarization of a Generation (Politics and Society)* (2005)

Burke, Peter, Harrison, Brian and Slack, Paul, 'Keith Thomas' in eid. (eds.), *Civil Histories: Essays Presented to Sir Keith Thomas* (Oxford, 2000), pp. 1–30

Burns, Alan, 'Buster' in *New Writers* (1961), p. 84

Bush, Roger, *FAU: The Third Generation – Friends Ambulance Unit, Post-war Service and International Service, 1946–1959* (York, 1998)

Butler, D. E., *The British General Election of 1955* (1955)

Carey, George, *Know the Truth: A Memoir* (2004)

Carr-Saunders, A. M., Caradog Jones, D. and Moser, C. A., *A Survey of Social Conditions in England and Wales* (Oxford, 1958)

Catton, John, *Prickly Heat: A Cheerful Happy Gallop through Experiences in Africa with the King's African Rifles* (Brighton, 2011)

Cesarani, David, *Major Farran's Hat: Murder, Scandal and Britain's War against Jewish Terrorism, 1945–1948* (2009)

Chambers, Peter and Landreth, Amy (eds.), *Called Up: The Personal Experiences of Sixteen National Servicemen, Told by Themselves* (1955)

Chaplin, H. D., *The Queen's Own Royal West Kent Regiment, 1951–1961* (Maidstone, 1964)

Chapman, Robin, *A Waste of Public Money, or The Education of Charlie Williams* (1962)

Chynoweth, John, *Hunting Terrorists in the Jungle* (Stroud, 2007)

Coates, Berwick, *Sam Browne's Schooldays: Experiences of a Typical Squad of Postwar National Service Recruits* (Bognor Regis, 2009)

Cobbold, Peter, *The National Service Sailor* (Wivenhoe, 1993)

Colville, John, *The Fringes of Power: 10 Downing Street Diaries, 1939–1955* (New York, 1985)

Conekin, Becky, Mort, Frank and Waters, Chris (eds.), *Moments of Modernity: Reconstructing Britain, 1945–1964* (1999)

Corbin, Alain, *Historien du sensible: Entretiens avec Gilles Heuré* (Paris, 2000)

Cowell, John, *Elephant Grass* (Blackburn, 2007)

Crang, Jeremy, *The British Army and the People's War, 1939–1945* (Manchester, 2000)

—, 'The Abolition of Compulsory Church Parades in the British Army', *The Journal of Ecclesiastical History*, 56 (2005), pp. 92–106

Cranston, Ross, 'A Biographical Sketch: The Early Years' in Mads Andenas and Duncan Fairgrieve (eds), *Tom Bingham and the Transformation of the Law: A Liber Amicorum* (Oxford, 2009), pp. li–lxxii

Crawford, W. K. B., 'Training the National Service Army Officer at Eaton Hall', *Journal of the Royal United Services Institution*, February 1951, pp. 134–8

Critchley, Julian, *A Bag of Boiled Sweets* (1994)

Crook, John, *Hilltops of the Hong Kong Moon* (1997)

Crossman, Richard, 'The Great Conscription Muddle', *Sunday Pictorial*, 14 August 1949

Danchev, Alex, 'The Army and the Home Front' in David Chandler and Ian Beckett (eds.), *The Oxford History of the British Army* (Oxford, 1994), pp. 298–315

Davenport-Hines, Richard (ed.), *Letters from Oxford: Hugh Trevor-Roper to Bernard Berenson* (2006)

de la Billière, Peter, *Looking for Trouble: SAS to Gulf Command* (1994)

Dennis, N., Henriques, F. M., and Slaughter, C., *Coal is Our Life: An Analysis of a Yorkshire Mining Community* (1956)

Dickinson, Frank, *Them Days 'ave Gone* (Ely, 2008)

Douglas, Robert, *Somewhere to Lay My Head* (2006)

Drummond, John, *Tainted by Experience: A Life in the Arts* (2000)

Drury, Ken (ed.), *Get Some In: Memories of National Service* (Great Dunmow, 2006)

Elkin, Winifred and Kittermaster, D. B., *Borstal: A Critical Survey* (1950)

Elkins, Caroline, *Imperial Reckoning: The Untold Story of Britain's Gulag in Kenya* (New York, 2005)

—, 'Alchemy of Evidence: Mau Mau, the British Empire, and the High Court of Justice', *The Journal of Imperial and Commonwealth History*, 39, 5 (2011), pp. 731–48

Elliott, Geoffrey and Shukman, Harold, *Secret Classrooms: An Untold Story of the Cold War* (2003)

Emsley, Clive, *Soldier, Sailor, Beggarman, Thief: Crime and the British Armed Services since 1914* (Oxford, 2014)

Erskine, David, *The Scots Guards, 1919–1955* (1956)

Evans, Harold, *My Paper Chase: True Stories of Vanished Times, an Autobiography* (2009)

Fancy, Harry, *'Remembered with Advantage': The National Service Memoirs of Lance Corporal (Unpaid) Harry Fancy* (Marple, 2009)

Ferguson, T. and Cunnison, J., *The Young Wage-earner: A Study of Glasgow Boys* (Oxford, 1951)

—, *In Their Early Twenties: A Study of Glasgow Youth* (Oxford, 1956)

—, 'The Impact of National Service', *British Journal of Sociology*, 10, 4 (1959), pp. 283–90

Fergusson, Bernard, *The Trumpet in the Hall, 1930–1958* (1970)

Field, Geoffrey G., *Blood, Sweat and Toil: Remaking the British Working Class, 1939–1945* (Oxford, 2011)

Findlay, Douglas, *White Knees Brown Knees: Suez Canal Zone 1951–1954, the Forgotten Years* (Edinburgh, 2003)

Fisher, Nigel, *Iain Macleod* (1973)

Franks, Oliver, *Britain and the Tide of World Affairs: The BBC Reith Lectures, 1954* (1955)

French, David, *The British Way in Counter-insurgency, 1945–1967* (Oxford, 2011)

—, *Army, Empire, and Cold War: The British Army and Military Policy, 1945–1971* (Oxford, 2012)

Fuller, Roy, *The Father's Comedy* (1961)

Fyvel, T. R., *The Insecure Offenders: Rebellious Youth in the Welfare State* (1961)

Gannon, Michael, 'Your Son and the Call-up', *Evening News*, 29 March 1954

Gardiner, George, *A Bastard's Tale: The Political Memoirs of George Gardiner* (1999)

Gibbens, T. C. N., 'Borstal Boys after 25 Years', *British Journal of Criminology*, 24, 1 (1984), pp. 49–61

Girardet, Raoul, *La Société militaire dans la France contemporaine (1815–1939)* (Paris, 1953)

—, *La Crise militaire française, 1945–1961* (Paris, 1964)

Glass, David (ed.), *Social Mobility in Britain* (1954)

Godfrey, F. A., *The History of the Suffolk Regiment, 1946–1959* (1988)

Goldthorpe, John, Lockwood, David, Bechhofer, Frank and Platt, Jennifer, *The Affluent Worker: Industrial Attitudes and Behaviour* (Cambridge, 1968)

Goodliffe, Brian, *Recollections of Gunner Goodliffe: Life of a National Serviceman in 1952 and 1953, from His Own Diaries* (Harrow, 2009)

Grieves, Keith, *The Politics of Manpower, 1914–18* (Manchester, 1988)

Hack, Karl, '"Iron Claws on Malaya": The Historiography of the Malayan Emergency', *Journal of Southeast Asian Studies*, 30, 1 (March 1999), pp. 99–125

Hale, Christopher, 'Batang Kali: Britain's My Lai?', *History Today* (July 2012)

—, *Massacre in Malaya: Exposing Britain's My Lai* (2013)

Hall, David, *Fred: The Definitive Biography of Fred Dibnah* (2006)

Hall, Roger G., *One-Two-Three-One! (A Nutter's Account of National Service)* (Twickenham, 2007)

Hardwick, Kit, *Brian Jackson: Educational Innovator and Social Reformer* (Cambridge, 2003)

Hastings, Max, *The Korean War* (1987)

Hayman, Ronald, *Arnold Wesker* (1970)

— (ed.), *My Cambridge* (1977)

Head, Brigadier, A. H., 'The Army We Need', *The Spectator*, 17 December 1948

Healey, Denis, *The Time of My Life* (1989)

Hennessy, Peter, *Having It So Good: Britain in the Fifties* (2006)
—, *Distilling the Frenzy: Writing the History of One's Own Times* (2012)
Henriques, Basil, *So You're Being Called Up* (1947)
—, *The Home-menders: The Prevention of Unhappiness in Children* (1955)
Heseltine, Michael, *Life in the Jungle: My Autobiography* (2000)
Hickman, Tom, *The Call-up: A History of National Service* (2005)
Higgins, Patrick, *Heterosexual Dictatorship: Male Homosexuality in Post-war Britain* (1996)
Himmelweit, H. T., Halsey, A. H. and Oppenheim, A. N., 'The Views of Adolescents on Some Aspects of the Social Class Structure', *British Journal of Sociology*, 3, 2 (1952), pp. 148–72
Hollands, John, *The Dead, the Dying and the Damned* (1956)
—, *The Court Martial* (2009)
—, *Heroes of the Hook* (2013)
Holroyd, Michael, *Basil Street Blues: A Family Story* (1999)
Hood, Roger, *Homeless Borstal Boys: A Study of their After-care and After-conduct* (1966)
Horne, Alastair with Montgomery, David, *The Lonely Leader: Monty, 1944–1945* (1995)
Hoskyns, John, *Just in Time: Inside the Thatcher Revolution* (2000)
Howard, Anthony, 'A National Serviceman's Postscript', *New Statesman*, 1 February 1958
Howard, Eric, *My Trinity* (Edinburgh, 1999)
Hudson, Frederick, *Loyal to the End: A Personal and Factual Account of National Service in Malaya* (Blackburn, 2006)
—, *National Secret Service: Deception and Conspiracy in Malaya* (Blackburn, 2008)
Hurd, Douglas, 'Soldiers at Salisbury', *The Spectator*, 9 August 1951
—, *Memoirs* (2003)
Hurst, Christopher, *The View from King Street: An Essay in Autobiography* (1997)
Ives, Leslie, *A Musket for the King: The Trials and Tribulations of a National Serviceman 1949–1951* (Tavistock, 1999)
J. B. P. R., 'The Emergency in Malaya: Some Reflections on the First Six Years', *The World Today*, 10, 11 (1954), pp. 477–87
Jackson, Brian and Marsden, Dennis, *Education and the Working Class: Some General Themes Raised by a Study of 88 Working-class Children in a Northern Industrial City* (1962)
James, W. D., *Hamptonians at War: Some War Experiences of Old Boys of Hampton Grammar School* (1964)

Jay, Douglas, *Change and Fortune: A Political Record* (1980)

Jessop, Keith, *Goldfinder: The True Story of One Man's Discovery of the Ocean's Richest Secrets* (1998)

Johnson, B. S. (ed.), *All Bull: The National Servicemen* (1973)

Judt, Tony, *Postwar: A History of Europe Since 1945* (New York, 2005)

—, *The Memory Chalet* (2010)

Kavanagh, P. J., *The Perfect Stranger* (1966)

Kelly, John, *National Service, 1950s: Lancs, Bucks, Libya* (Cambridge, 2003)

Kennaway, James, *Tunes of Glory* (1956)

Kent, Bruce, *Undiscovered Ends: An Autobiography* (1992)

Kent, John, 'Bevin's Imperialism and the Idea of Euro-Africa, 1945–49' in Michael Dockrill and John Young (eds.), *British Foreign Policy, 1945–56* (1989), pp. 47–76

Kerr, Madeline, *The People of Ship Street* (1958)

King George's Jubilee Trust, *Citizens of Tomorrow: A Study of the Influences Affecting the Upbringing of Young People* (1955)

Laing, Adrian, *R. D. Laing: A Biography* (1994)

Lascelles, Alan, *King's Counsellor: Abdication and War – The Diaries of Sir Alan Lascelles* (edited by Duff Hart-Davis) (2006)

Le Roy Ladurie, Emmanuel and Zysberg, André, 'Anthropologie des conscrits français (1868–1887)', *Ethnologie française*, 9, 1 (1979), pp. 47–68

Lewis, Michael, *Killroy Was Here* (1961)

Lewis, Roy and Maude, Angus, *The English Middle Classes* (1949)

'Lictor', 'The Production of Army Officers', *Journal of the Royal United Services Institution*, November 1948, pp. 584–9

Lindsay, Oliver, *Once a Grenadier . . . : The Grenadier Guards, 1945–95* (1996)

Lloyd, C., 'The Integration of National Service with the Country's Economic Future', *Journal of the Royal United Services Institution*, May 1955, pp. 187–201

Lodge, David, *Ginger, You're Barmy* (1962)

—, *How Far Can You Go?* (1980)

Logan, R. F. L. and Goldberg, E. M., 'Rising Eighteen in a London Suburb: A Study of Some Aspects of the Life and Health of Young Men', *British Journal of Sociology*, 4, 4 (1953), pp. 323–45

Loukes, Harold, *Secondary Modern* (1957)

Lowe, Eric, *Forgotten Conscripts: Prelude to Palestine's Struggle for Survival* (Trafford, 2006)

Lucas Keene, F., letter to the *British Medical Journal*, 19 June 1948

MacKenzie, S. P., *British Prisoners of the Korean War* (Oxford, 2012)

Maclachlan, C. M., 'Officer Selection', *Journal of the Royal United Services Institution*, November 1949, pp. 615–22

Macpherson, J. S., *Eleven-year-olds Grow Up* (1958)

Mannheim, Hermann and Wilkins, Leslie T., *Prediction Methods in Relation to Borstal Training* (1955)

Mauss-Copeaux, Claire, *Appelés en Algérie: La parole confisquée* (Paris, 1999)

Maxwell, James, *Sixteen Years On: A Follow-up of the 1947 Scottish Survey* (1969)

Methodist Youth Department, *Another Kind of National Service* (1957)

Miller, Keith, *730 Days Until Demob! National Service and the Post-1945 British Army* (2003)

Ministry of Defence, *Report of the Advisory Committee on Recruiting* (1958), cmd 545 (Grigg Report)

Ministry of Education, *15 to 18* (1959) (Crowther Report)

Ministry of Labour and National Service, *National Service* (1955), cmd 9608

—, *Report on the Enquiry into the Effects of National Service on the Education and Employment of Young Men* (1955)

—, *Call Up of Men to the Forces, 1957/60* (1957), cmd 175

Morgan, A. E., *Young Citizen* (1943)

Morgan, David, *'It Will Make a Man of You': Notes on National Service, Masculinity and Autobiography* (Manchester, 1987)

Morgan, Kevin, 'Militarism and Anti-militarism: Socialists, Communists and Conscription in France and Britain, 1900–1940', *Past and Present*, 202 (2009), pp. 207–44

Morse, Mary, *The Unattached* (1965)

Musgrove, F., *Youth and the Social Order* (1964)

Newton, C. C. S., 'The Sterling Crisis of 1947 and the British Response to the Marshall Plan', *Economic History Review*, 37, 3 (1984), pp. 391–408

Nichols, Peter, *Feeling You're Behind: An Autobiography* (1984)

—, *Plays: One* (1987)

Nicholson, Nigel, *Alex* (1973)

Nott, John, *Here Today, Gone Tomorrow: Recollections of an Errant Politician* (2002)

Oppenheim, A. N., 'Social Status and Clique Formation among Grammar School Boys', *British Journal of Sociology*, 6, 3 (1955), pp. 228–45

Osborne, John, *A Better Class of Person* (1981)

Otley, C. B., 'Militarism and Militarization in the Public Schools, 1900–1972', *British Journal of Sociology*, 29, 3 (1978), pp. 321–39

Parkinson, Cecil, *Right at the Centre: An Autobiography* (1992)

Parkinson, Michael, *Parky: My Autobiography* (2008)

Partridge, John, *Life in a Secondary Modern School* (1966)

Peel, John, *Margrave of the Marshes: His Autobiography* (2005)

Pegg, Eric (ed.), *The Royal Engineers and the National Service Years, 1939–1963: A Military and Social History* (2002)

Percival, Alicia, *Youth Will Be Led: The Story of the Voluntary Youth Organizations* (1951)

Perkin, Harold, *The Making of a Social Historian* (2002)

Perkins, Ken, *A Fortunate Soldier* (1988)

Pratt, F. W. H., Comments in discussion on 'The Supply and Training of Officers', *Journal of the Royal United Services Institution*, February 1948, pp. 45–68

Price, Stanley, *Somewhere to Hang My Hat: An Irish-Jewish Journey* (Dublin, 2002)

Prior, James, *A Balance of Power* (1986)

Prost, Antoine, *Carnets d'Algérie* (Paris, 2005)

Prys Williams, Gwylmor, *Teenagers' Problems: The Contemporary Social Background and Youth's Reaction to It* (1958)

—, *Patterns of Juvenile Delinquency: England and Wales, 1946–1961* (1962)

Ramsay, Roy, *Green on 'Go': National Service and the TA* (Harrow, 1989)

Raphael, Frederic, *Cracks in the Ice: Views and Reviews* (1979)

Raven, Simon, *The English Gentleman: An Essay in Attitudes* (1961)

Rees-Mogg, William, *Memoirs* (2011)

Reid, Jimmy, *Reflections of a Clyde-built Man* (1976)

Resettlement Advisory Board, *Progress Report, 1957–1959* (1959), cmd 789

Richardson, Charles, *My Manor* (1992)

Riordan, Jim, *Comrade Jim: The Spy Who Played for Spartak* (2008)

Rodgers, Bill, *Fourth Among Equals* (2000)

Rosenbaum, Sidney, 'Heights and Weights of the Army Intake, 1951', *Journal of the Royal Statistical Society*, 117, 3 (1954), pp. 331–47

—, 'Experience of Pulheems in the 1952 Army Intake', *British Journal of Industrial Medicine*, 14 (1957), pp. 281–6

—, 'Home Localities of National Servicemen with Respiratory Disease', *British Journal of Preventative and Social Medicine*, 15 (1961), pp. 61–7

Royle, Trevor, *The Best Years of Their Lives: The National Service Experience, 1945–63* (1986)

Roynette, Odile, *'Bon pour le service': L'expérience de la caserne en France à la fin du XIXe siècle* (Paris, 2000)

Runciman, W. G., *Relative Deprivation and Social Justice: A Study of Attitudes to Social Inequality in Twentieth-century England* (1966)

Saville, John, *Memoirs from the Left* (2003)

Scott, Len, *Conscription and the Attlee Governments: The Politics and Policy of National Service, 1945–1951* (Oxford, 1993)

Scurr, John, *Jungle Campaign: A Memoir of National Service in Malaya, 1949–51* (Lewes, 1998)

Seaton, Derek, *Memoirs of a Conscript: National Service 1950–1952* (Alton, 2002)

Shindler, Colin, *National Service: From Aldershot to Aden – Tales from the Conscripts* (2012)

Sillitoe, Alan, *The Key to the Door* (1961)

—, *Life Without Armour* (1995)

Sinclair, Andrew, *The Breaking of Bumbo* (1959)

Skelhorn, Norman, *Public Prosecutor: The Memoirs of Sir Norman Skelhorn, Director of Public Prosecutions 1964–1977* (1981)

Sparrow, T. C., *Tales of a Schoolie: A Story of National Service* (Badsey, 2006)

Stacey, Margaret, *Tradition and Change: A Study of Banbury* (1960)

Stouffer, Samuel et al., *The American Soldier: Adjustment During Army Life* (Princeton, NJ, 1949)

Strickland, Geoffrey, 'The Torture Lesson', *The Spectator*, 17 March 1984

Strong, Roy, *Self-portrait as a Young Man* (Oxford, 2013)

Supple, Barry, *Doors Open* (Cambridge, 2009)

Sutherland, John, *The Boy Who Loved Books* (2007)

Taylor, A. J. P., *A Personal History* (1983)

Taylor, Keith and Stewart, Brian, *Call to Arms: Officer Cadet Training at Eaton Hall* (2006)

Thomas, Leslie, *This Time Next Week* (1964)

—, *The Virgin Soldiers* (1966)

Thompson, Brian, *Clever Girl: Growing Up in the 1950s* (2007)

Thynn, Alexander, The Marquess of Bath, *Strictly Private to Public Exposure (Series 1: A Plateful of Privilege, Book III: Two Bites of the Apple)* (2003)

Tisdall, Laura, '"That Was What Life in Bridgeburn had Made Her": Reading the Autobiographies of Children in Institutional Care in England, 1918–1946', *20th Century British History*, 24, 3 (2013)

Torrance, David, *George Younger: A Life Well Lived* (Edinburgh, 2008)

Trewin, Ion, *Alan Clark: The Biography* (2009)

Wain, John, *The Contenders* (1958)

Walker, Adrian (ed.), *Six Campaigns: National Servicemen at War, 1948–1960* (1993)

— (ed.), *A Barren Place: National Servicemen in Korea, 1950–1954* (1994)

—, *A Country Regiment: 1st Battalion The Queen's Own Royal West Kent Regiment, Malaya, 1951–1954* (2001)

Walker, S. G., Trench Gascoigne Essay Competition 1947, *Journal of the Royal United Services Institution*, May 1948, pp. 177–86

Wallace, Don, 'The POM Has Landed', *Aviation News*, 8–21 August 1986

War Office, *Infantry Training: The National Serviceman's Handbook* (1955)

Ware, Michael, *Gap Year: A Saga of National Service* (2000)

Watson, Howard (ed.), *The World of Simon Raven* (2002)

Waugh, Auberon, *Will This Do? An Autobiography* (1991)

Webb, George, *Epitaph for an Army of Peacekeepers: British Forces in Palestine, 1945–1948* (Fleet Hargate, 2005)

Weber, Eugen, *Peasants into Frenchmen: The Modernization of Rural France, 1870–1914* (1976)

Wesker, Arnold, *As Much as I Dare: An Autobiography (1932–1959)* (1994)

Weston, Peter, *A Stranger to Khaki: Memoirs of a National Service Officer* (Penzance, 1997)

Wilkins, Leslie T., *The Social Survey: National Service and Enlistment in the Armed Forces. A Report on an Enquiry Made for Several Government Departments into the Attitudes of Young Men Prior to, and on Joining the Armed Forces* (1951)

—, *The Adolescent in Britain* (1955)

—, *Delinquent Generations* (1960)

Williams, Gordon M., *The Camp* (1966)

Williams, W. M., *The Sociology of an English Village: Gosforth* (1956)

Wills, Abigail, 'Delinquency, Masculinity and Citizenship in England 1950–1970', *Past and Present*, 187 (2005), pp. 157–85

Wood, Christopher, *'Terrible Hard', Says Alice* (1970)

Woodrup, Len, *Training for War Games: One Man's National Service* (Lewes, 1993)

Workers' Educational Association and East Lothian Council Library Service, *West Lothian and the Forgotten War: Experience of World War II, National Service and the Korean War* (Edinburgh, 2000)

Wright, 'Shiner', *Jack Strop, VD and Scar* (Edinburgh, 2002)

Wyldbore-Smith, Brian, *March Past: The Memoirs of a Major-General* (Spenneymoor, 2001)

Young, Michael, *The Rise of the Meritocracy* (1958)

Young, Michael and Willmott, Peter, *Family and Kinship in East London* (1957)

—, *Family and Class in a London Suburb* (1960)

SERIAL PUBLICATIONS AND NEWSPAPERS

Army List
Daily Express
Daily Mail
Daily Mirror
Eton College Chronicle
Guardian
Isis
Manchester Guardian (*Guardian* from 24 August 1959)
Ministry of Labour Gazette
The Monmouthian (Monmouth School)
The NAAFI Review
New Statesman
News Chronicle
Observer
Portcullis (Emanuel School)
The Spectator
Sunday Pictorial
The Times
The Times Educational Supplement

UNPUBLISHED PHD THESES

Jason Fensome, 'The Administrative History of National Service in Britain, 1950–1963' (University of Cambridge, 2001)

Stephen Martin, 'Did Your Country Need You? An Oral History of the National Service Experience in Britain, 1945–1963' (University of Wales, Lampeter, 1997)

David Mitchell, 'The Army League, Conscription and the 1956 Defence Review' (University of East Anglia, 2012)

Sidney Rosenbaum, 'Statistical Studies of the Health and Physique of Young Soldiers During the Period of National Service' (University of London, School of Hygiene and Tropical Medicine, 1960)

THE NATIONAL ARCHIVES, KEW (TNA)

ADMIRALTY
ADM 1/21623

ADM 1/21985
ADM 1/23211
ADM 1/23999
ADM 1/26594

AIR MINISTRY
AIR 2/10933
AIR 2/10934
AIR 2/11394
AIR 2/11603
AIR 2/12407
AIR 2/13938
AIR 2/14647
AIR 2/15389
AIR 8/1656
AIR 10/5478
AIR 10/7398
AIR 20/6457
AIR 20/8993
AIR 20/12136
AIR 20/8671
AIR 23/2899
AIR 32/414
AIR 32/416
AIR 32/466
AIR 77/270
AIR 77/271
AIR 77/281
AIR 77/608

CABINET OFFICE
CAB 128/17/39
CAB 128/29/33
CAB 128/29/45
CAB 128/31/32
CAB 129/86/19
CAB 129/86/41
CAB 130/120
CAB 139/505

MINISTRY OF DEFENCE
DEFE 7/61
DEFE 7/141
DEFE 7/145
DEFE 7/146
DEFE 7/508
DEFE 7/509
DEFE 7/808
DEFE 7/1037
DEFE 7/1048
DEFE 7/1453
DEFE 10/332
DEFE 13/53
DEFE 13/843
DEFE 70/96
DEFE 70/101

DIRECTOR OF PUBLIC PROSECUTIONS
DPP 6/31

MINISTRY OF EDUCATION
ED 34/185

HOME OFFICE
HO 45/24214
HO 291/116
HO 344/28
HO 345/13

MINISTRY OF INFORMATION
INF 6/812

MINISTRY OF LABOUR AND NATIONAL SERVICE
LAB 6/19
LAB 6/349
LAB 6/370
LAB 6/468
LAB 6/470
LAB 6/496
LAB 6/499
LAB 6/573

LAB 6/624
LAB 6/637
LAB 6/655
LAB 6/659
LAB 6/680
LAB 6/682
LAB 6/684
LAB 6/691
LAB 6/692
LAB 6/694
LAB 6/696
LAB 6/734
LAB 6/741
LAB 8/2476
LAB 19/222
LAB 19/298
LAB 19/319
LAB 21/8
LAB 21/167
LAB 29/555
LAB 43/2
LAB 43/154

METROPOLITAN POLICE
MEPO 2/7822

OFFICE OF THE PRIME MINISTER
PREM 8/598
PREM 8/611
PREM 8/1021
PREM 11/201
PREM 11/477
PREM 11/494
PREM 11/935
PREM 11/1935
PREM 11/2086
PREM 11/2088
PREM 11/3037

PRISON SERVICE
PCOM 9/1390

GENERAL REGISTER OFFICE
RG 28/165

UNIVERSITY GRANTS COMMITTEE
UGC 7/407

WAR OFFICE
WO 32/10994
WO 32/11578
WO 32/11848
WO 32/12436
WO 32/13364
WO 32/13775
WO 32/13849
WO 32/13957
WO 32/14970
WO 32/15021
WO 32/15024
WO 32/15025
WO 32/15144
WO 32/15146
WO 32/15604
WO 32/15743
WO 32/15746
WO 32/15857
WO 32/16103
WO 32/16185
WO 32/16246
WO 32/16277
WO 32/16430
WO 32/16713
WO 32/16714
WO 32/16806
WO 32/17243
WO 32/17657
WO 32/18704
WO 32/21720
WO 32/21721
WO 32/21722
WO 71/1024
WO 71/1198

WO 71/1200
WO 71/1221
WO 71/1234
WO 71/1235
WO 71/1261
WO 73/183
WO 93/56
WO 163/107
WO 163/305
WO 216/238
WO 216/305
WO 216/411
WO 291/1074
WO 291/1080
WO 291/1152
WO 291/1215
WO 291/1408
WO 291/1455
WO 291/1494
WO 291/1510
WO 291/2193
WO 296/41
WO 305/204
WO 373/116/65
WO 384/1–44. This archive reference encompasses successive editions of the 'Abstract of Army Statistics' for the years from 1950 to 1962.

WELSH OFFICE
BD 24/167
BD 24/168

NOTTINGHAM PUBLIC RECORD OFFICE,
NOTTINGHAM

Papers of Professor J. M. Lee, DD 393/1

BIRKBECK COLLEGE, LONDON

Papers of Sir Bernard Crick – 1/3/3

CHURCHILL ARCHIVE CENTRE, CHURCHILL COLLEGE, CAMBRIDGE

Papers of Duncan Sandys
6/52
8/10
Papers of Peter Jay
4/1/1

ESSEX UNIVERSITY

Affluent Worker Archives

ETON COLLEGE

Eton College Archive, Letters to Hugh Marsden

KING'S COLLEGE, LONDON

Liddell Hart Centre for Military Archives
LH 13/32
LH 15/5/114
LH 15/5/163

SUSSEX UNIVERSITY

Mass Observation Archive MO 334
National Gay and Lesbian Survey

QUAKER MEETING HOUSE, LONDON

Friends Peace Committee Conscription Group, minutes
Temp mss, 914, ECM/9, Central Board for Conscientious Objectors Executive Committee, minutes

IMPERIAL WAR MUSEUM. PRIVATE PAPERS (IWM)

A. R. Ashton, 675
H. Atkins, 1941
C. B. L. Barr, 7178
David Batterham, 15595
J. R. Beverland, 3135
Peter Burke, 4102
W. H. Butler, 614
J. R. Christie, 1597
A. Cole, 1598
R. D. Cramond, 15058
E. A. Dorking, 6431
A. R. Eaton, 1834
A. E. Fisher, 161
J. C. A. Green, 2775
J. M. T. Grieve, 1601
Brigadier T. Hart Dyke, 3300
K. S. J. Hill, 7778
Sir Peter Holmes, 12515
P. J. Houghton-Brown, 15316
T. J. Hunt, 12505
James Jacobs, 9870
Brigadier P. J. Jeffreys, 2279
G. T. Kell, 15719
Michael Longley, 16584
W. S. B. Loosmore, 3225
D. Lord, 714
I. W. G. Martin, 1779
N. A. Martin, 11915
A. S. Mason, 13121
Peter Mayo, 2118
R. J. Miller, 3126
J. T. Nye, 3438
David Oates, 9968
Bernard Parke, 15103
Colonel Pickard, 2856
G. J. W. Rosbrook, 15608
A. L. Saunders, 1324
I. M. H. Smart, 2519

L. G. G. Smith, 3368
B. E. Turberville, 1594
John Watson, 2717
John Whybrow, 12723
Cyril MacG. Williams, 12733

One particularly important set of papers was deposited by Trevor Royle and consists of the completed questionnaires, interviews and letters relating to his own book on national service. It was in the process of being catalogued as I sent this book to press and each individual serviceman studied by Royle was assigned his own reference number, which I have tried so far as possible to cite in the notes.

IMPERIAL WAR MUSEUM SOUND ARCHIVE (IWMSA)

John Akehurst, 27184, interviewed by Nigel de Lee, 2004
Neal Ascherson, 22268 © Whistledown, 2000
Terrance Atkinson, 26097, interviewed by Lindsay Baker, 2003
Peter Bangs, 10302, interviewed by Conrad Wood, 1988
Desmond Barnard, 17740, interviewed by Conrad Wood, 1998
Geoffrey Barnes, 21876, interviewed by Conrad Wood, 2001
Kenneth Bartley, 10742, interviewed by Conrad Wood, 1989
Peter Beadle, 10211, interviewed by Conrad Wood, 1988
Alan Bexon, 20668, interviewed by Peter Hart, 2009
Derek Blake, 8943, interviewed by Conrad Wood, 1985
Colin Bower, 9395, interviewed by Nigel de Lee, 1986
Edmund Bruford-Davies, 22347, interviewed by Nigel de Lee, 2001
Derek Burke, 18212, interviewed by Conrad Wood, 1998
Peter Burke, 8423, interviewed by Charles Allen, 1983
John 'Jack' Burn, 29062, interviewed by Peter Hart, 2006
Lt Colonel Mike Calvert, 9989, interviewed by Conrad Wood, 1987
Ron Cassidy, 11138, interviewed by Charles Allen, 1990
Francis Cheesman, 20364, interviewed by Conrad Wood, 2000
Jack Coley, 20802, interviewed by Harry Moses, 2000
Anne Collins, 21675 © Whistledown, 2000
John Cormack, 21564, interviewed by Nigel de Lee, 2001
Paul Croxson, 29895, interviewed by Lyn Smith, 2007
Hugh Currie, 19061, interviewed by Conrad Wood, 1999
David Davies, 21582, interviewed by Conrad Wood, 2001
Tom Davis, 21684 © Whistledown, 2000

Frederick Dobbs, 10316, interviewed by Conrad Wood, 1988
Ernest Dobson, 19993, interviewed by Michael Moses, 2000
Noel Dobson, 17571, interviewed by Conrad Wood 1997
Richard Faint, 14145, interviewed by Conrad Wood, 1994
Peter Farrar, 8850, interviewed by Conrad Wood, 1985
Peter Featherby, 20494, interviewed by Peter Hart, 2000
Anthony Firth, 19853, interviewed by Conrad Wood, 1999
David Fisher, 18338, interviewed by Conrad Wood, 1998
William Fitt, 19064, interviewed by Conrad Wood, 1999
Paul Foot, 21690 © Whistledown, 2000
General Forrester, Brigadier Flood, Brigadier Dawney, 13645, interviewed by
    Nigel de Lee, 1993
Michael Foulds, 20656, interviewed by Peter Hart, 2001
Rodney Giesler, 14822, interviewed by Lyn Smith, 1994
General Sir Michael Gray, 11146, interviewed by Charles Allen, 1992
Edward Grey, 16719, interviewed by Harry Moses, 1995
Leslie (Raymond) Hands, 28424, interviewed by Richard McDonough, 2005
Michael Harbottle, 10145, interviewed by Lyn Smith, 1988
Nick Harden, 21674 © Whistledown, 2000
Field Marshal Lord Harding, 8736, interviewed by Lyn Smith, 1984
John Harlow, 24569, interviewed by Peter Hart, 2002
Jack Harrison, 10708, interviewed by Conrad Wood, 1989
Edwin Haywood, 20268, interviewed by Conrad Wood, 2000
David Henderson, 14053, interviewed by Conrad Wood, 1994
Thomas Henson, 22138, interviewed by Conrad Wood, 2001
Thomas Hewitson, 26853, interviewed by Peter Hart, 2004
Martyn Highfield, 26546, interviewed by Peter Hart, 2003
Anthony Howard, 22307 © Whistledown, 2000
Richard Ingrams, 21688 © Whistledown, 2000
Derek Johns, 21672 © Whistledown, 2000
John Keays, 20669, interviewed by Peter Hart, 2001
Bruce Kent, 10925, interviewed by Lyn Smith, 1989
Leonard Knowles, 26731, interviewed by Jo White, 2004
Kenneth Lee, 9485, interviewed by Conrad Wood, 1986
George Lightley, 19632, interviewed by Harry Moses, 1999
Peter McAleese, 15433, interviewed by Bruce Jones, 1995
Michael McBain, 11105, interviewed by Harry Moses, 1992
Simon Maclachlan, 10010, interviewed by Conrad Wood, 1987
D'Arcy John Desmond Mander, 12401, interviewed by Conrad Wood, 1992
Dennis Matthews, 12729, interviewed by Conrad Wood, 1992

David Morrish, 10116, interviewed by Lyn Smith, 1988

Ingram Murray, 23217, interviewed by Nigel de Lee, n.d.

John Noble, 17333, interviewed by Conrad Wood, 1997

James Notley, 18565, interviewed by Nigel de Lee, 1998

Thomas Nowell, 21064, interviewed by Conrad Wood, 2001

Samuel Osborne, 9911, interviewed by Conrad Wood, 1987

Leigh Parkes, 26559, interviewed by Peter Hart, 2003

Piers Plowright, 24570, interviewed by Peter Hart, 2002

Gordon Lawrence Potts, 23213, interviewed by Nigel de Lee, 2002

William Purves, 20471, interviewed by Conrad Wood, 2000

Michael Randle, 12919, interviewed by Lyn Smith, 1992

Godfrey Raper, 14786, interviewed by Lyn Smith, 1994

Joseph Roberts, 18825, interviewed by Conrad Wood, 1999

John Robinson, 26563, interviewed by Peter Hart, 2004

Edward Russell, 9936, interviewed by Conrad Wood, 1987

Alan Sandland, 17819, interviewed by Conrad Wood, 1998

Harry Sanson, 22606, interviewed by Michael Moses, 2002

L. H. Scribbins, 17335, interviewed by Conrad Wood, 1997

Ray Self, 21681 © Whistledown, 2000

Brian Sewell, 21696 © Whistledown, 2000

Albert Shippen, 14983, interviewed by Harry Moses, n.d.

Alan Sillitoe, 21676 © Whistledown, 2000

Alberic Stacpoole, 12498, interviewed by Conrad Wood, 1992

David Storrie, 11139, interviewed by Charles Allen, 1992

Julian Thompson, 28361, interviewed by Nigel de Lee, 2005

Albert Tyas, 18439, interviewed by Conrad Wood, 1998

Nicholas Vaux, 11142, interviewed by Charles Allen, 1992

Roy Vincent, 17987, interviewed by Conrad Wood, 1998

Brian Vyner, 10669, interviewed by Conrad Wood, 1989

John Waine, 26569, interviewed by Vincent Dowd, 1986

Adrian Walker, 17223, interviewed by Conrad Wood, 1997

John Waller, 19634, interviewed by Harry Moses, 1999

Derek Watkins, 18217, interviewed by Conrad Wood, 1998

Denys Whatmore, 12663, interviewed by Conrad Wood, 1992

Benjamin Whitchurch, 26098, interviewed by Lindsay Baker, 2003

Peter Whiteman, 22261 © Whistledown, 2000

David Wilson, 28670, interviewed by Peter Hart, 2006

Richard Wilson, 27811, interviewed by Peter Hart, 2006

Maynard Winspear, 21593, interviewed by Conrad Wood, 2001

Norman Woods, 20307, interviewed by Conrad Wood, 2000

NATIONAL ARMY MUSEUM. PRIVATE PAPERS (NAM)

Malcolm Edward Barker, 2006-12-77
D. F. Barrett, 2000-08-55
Simon Bendall, 2004-02-106
Ronald Dominy, 2003-08-29
Philip Firth, 2003-08-63
Jack Gillett, 2003-08-61
Robert Gomme, 1995-01-164
Nigel Hensman, 2003-06-9
Herbert Bartley Hiscock, 2006-07-58
John Lyon-Maris, 2003-08-67
Andrew Man, 2001-07-1187 46-93
Donald Manley, 2004-06-64
Colin Metcalfe, 2002-08-61
W. J. R. Morrison, 2003-08-59
Charlie Reading, 2003-12-7
John Wellington, 2004-06-49
Patrick J. Wye, 2004-05-23

NATIONAL ARMY MUSEUM SOUND ARCHIVE (NAMSA)

Anonymous, 2002-07-358
The Very Reverend John Arnold, 2000-04-52
Dr Stanley Boydell, 2001-02-398
Field Marshal Sir John Chapple, 2003-04-2
General Sir George Cooper, 1989-05-258
Lt General Peter Duffell, 2003-03-626
Mike Gilman, 2003-04-4
Venerable John Hodgson, 2000-04-55
'Mac'McCullogh, 2003-04-3
Robin Ollington, 1995-05-93
Canon Michael Perry, 2000-04-56
Barry Reed, 2001-02-397
Col. P. J. Wilkinson, 1991-09-1

BRITISH LIBRARY SOUND ARCHIVE

Henry Askew, interviewed by Cathy Courtney, *NLSC: City Lives*, 1992, British Library Sound & Moving Image Catalogue reference C409/082. © The British Library

John Barkshire, interviewed by Kathy Burk, *NLSC: City Lives*, 1990, British Library Sound & Moving Image Catalogue reference C409/057. © The British Library

Stuart Brisley, interviewed by Melanie Roberts, *NLSC: Artists' Lives*, 1996, British Library Sound & Moving Image Catalogue reference C466/43. © The British Library

John Brooks, interviewed by Bernard Attard, *The Jobbing System of the London Stock Exchange: An Oral History*, 1990, British Library Sound & Moving Image Catalogue reference C463/25. © The British Library

David Cainey, interviewed by Andrew Vincent, *Millennium Memory Bank*, 1998, British Library Sound & Moving Image Catalogue reference C900/00543. © BBC

Mark Girouard, interviewed by Paul Thompson, *NLSC: Architects' Lives*, 2009, British Library Sound & Moving Image Catalogue reference C467/92. © The British Library

Francis Holford, interviewed by Cathy Courtney, *NLSC: City Lives*, 1992, British Library Sound & Moving Image Catalogue reference C409/067. © The British Library

David Lance, interviewed by Michelle Winslow, *An Oral History of Oral History*, 2003, British Library Sound & Moving Image Catalogue reference C1149/01. © The British Library

Ken Lynham, interviewed by Cos Michael, *Food: From Source to Salespoint*, 2005, British Library Sound & Moving Image Catalogue reference C821/165. © The British Library

Gordon Martin, interviewed by Louise Brodie, *NLSC: City Lives*, 1996, British Library Sound & Moving Image Catalogue reference C409/134. © The British Library

Reg Martin, interviewed by Wendy Rickard, *HIV/AIDS Testimonies*, 1995, British Library Sound & Moving Image Catalogue reference C743/02. © The British Library

Kenneth Matthews, interviewed by Rachel Cutler, *Oral History of British Athletics*, 2006, British Library Sound & Moving Image Catalogue reference C790/43. © The British Library

John Milne, interviewed by Sue Bradley, *NLSC: Book Trade Lives*, 1999,

British Library Sound & Moving Image Catalogue reference C872/17. © The British Library

Jeremy Morse, interviewed by William Reader, *NLSC: City Lives*, 1988, British Library Sound & Moving Image Catalogue reference C409/007. © The British Library

Richard Carew Pole, interviewed by Louise Brodie, *Down to Earth: An Oral History of British Horticulture*, 2006, British Library Sound & Moving Image Catalogue reference C1029/38. © The British Library

John Quinton, interviewed by Paul Thompson, *NLSC: City Lives*, 1988, British Library Sound & Moving Image Catalogue reference C409/001. © The British Library

David Scholey, interviewed by Kathy Burk, *NLSC: City Lives*, 1992, British Library Sound & Moving Image Catalogue reference C409/085. © The British Library

Bruno Schroder, interviewed by Cathy Courtney, *NLSC: City Lives*, 1992, British Library Sound & Moving Image Catalogue reference C409/076. © The British Library

David Sharman, interviewed by Anthony Isaacs, *Millennium Memory Bank*, 1998, British Library Sound & Moving Image Catalogue reference C900/18039. © BBC

Jack Spall, interviewed by Cathy Courtney, *NLSC: City Lives*, 1991, British Library Sound & Moving Image Catalogue reference C409/061. © The British Library

Joe Studholme, interviewed by Cathy Courtney, *NLSC: Artists' Lives*, 1996, British Library Sound & Moving Image Catalogue reference C466/74/02. © The British Library

Robin Welch, interviewed by Hawksmoor Hughes, *NLSC: Craft Lives*, British Library Sound & Moving Image Catalogue reference C960/85, track 3. © The British Library

Andreas Whittam Smith, interviewed by Louise Brodie, *An Oral History of the British Press*, 2007, British Library Sound & Moving Image Catalogue reference C638/08. © The British Library

DOCUMENTS IN PRIVATE HANDS

Antony Copley, private diary
Antony Copley, Midshipman's Workbook
Robert Hardy, unpublished autobiography
Anthony Hampshire, 'Autobiographical Notes'
Ronald Hyam, *My Life in the Past* (privately published, 2012)

Peter Jay, Midshipman's Workbook
John Ockenden, 'Memoirs of a Computing Man'
Stanley Price, 'The Fucking Army', unpublished chapter from autobiography
Stanley Price, 'The Sergeant's Tale', unperformed television play

THE WORLD WIDE WEB

Anthony Heath and Clive Payne, 'Twentieth Century Trend in Social Mobility in Britain', Centre for Research into Elections and Social Trends, Working Paper 70 (1999)

Julien Grenet, Robert A. Hart and J. Elizabeth Roberts, 'Above and Beyond the Call: Long-Term Real Earnings Effects of British Male Military Conscription in the Post-war Years', IZA, Discussion Paper No. 5563, March 2011

There are also many personal testimories on the web. A number of national service memoirs can be consulted online and many men run websites devoted to their own experiences or those of their comrades. Many of the interviews in the Imperial War Museum Sound Archive can be heard online.

Alan Macfarlane's interviews with leading thinkers (http://wwwalanmacfarlanecom) contain many references to national service, though only Peter Burke discusses the matter at any length and often the most revealing aspect of interviews is the brief and flippant way in which most successful men pass over their experience of peacetime conscription. I have referred briefly to Macfarlane's interview with Geoffrey Lloyd.

Barry Brown runs an interesting website (wabbrown.co.uk), which contains a whole section of national service memoirs. I have cited the memoir of Kevin O'Sullivan on officer training at Eaton Hall.

A transcript of the interview with Martin Morland, including his account of national service in the Grenadier Guards can be consulted at http://www.chu.cam.ac.uk/archives/collections/BDOHP/Morland.pdf.

The website of the Forestry Department of the University of Aberdeen has an interesting collection of memoirs – relating, in part, to national service: http://homepages.abdn.ac.uk/forestry/associated%20links/Tales%20from%20Aberdeen%20Foresters%200f%201956%20vs2.pdf.

INTERVIEWS CONDUCTED BY THE AUTHOR

David Baxter, 15 March 2012
Philip Bell, 21 May 2013

Simon Coningham, 20 May 2013
Antony Copley, 27 February 2013
Peter Duncumb, 11 January 2013
John Ferris, 25 July 2012
Anthony Hampshire, 15 May 2013
David Loewe, 19 July 2012
Martin Morton, 24 January 2013
Bernard Palmer, 29 May 2013
Stanley Price, 17 May 2013
W. G. Runciman, 17 April 2012
John Sainsbury, 15 December 2011
Robert Tollemache, 17 January 2013
Richard Vaughan, 23 January 2013

FREEDOM OF INFORMATION

In the course of my researches I made a number of requests for documents to be opened. Generally, these requests were granted – I was even shown a file on the liability of 'young murderers' for national service – and most refusals were rooted in a very understandable desire to respect the privacy of individuals. On two occasions, the results of my enquiries were so unexpected that I think it worth recording them here. First, the Ministry of Defence wrote that they had no information on suicide by servicemen between 1945 and 1963, in spite of the fact that the matter had sometimes been the subject of parliamentary questions. Secondly, one file in the National Archives at Kew (FCO 24/851) relates to allegations that British soldiers killed civilians in Malaya in 1948. This is an open document but has been removed from the National Archives by the Foreign and Commonwealth Office. When I made a Freedom of Information request, I was told that the document could 'not be located'.

Acknowledgements

I am grateful to Andrew Wylie and James Pullen, who encouraged me to start this book, and to Simon Winder, Marina Kemp and Richard Duguid at Penguin, without whom I could not have finished it. Bela Cunha overcame her anti-militarist feelings and agreed to deploy her skills as a copy-editor on a difficult text. Stephen Ryan and Michael Page read the proofs with remarkably sharp eyes. The Leverhulme Trust supported this project with the award of a major research fellowship, which allowed me to devote time to research and writing. I have been much impressed by the efficiency of the Trust as well as by its generosity. I owe a great deal to my students and colleagues at King's College London – especially Arthur Burns, Paul Readman and Adam Sutcliffe.

The archival research for this book was mainly done in the National Archives at Kew, the National Army Museum and the Imperial War Museum – it seemed oddly appropriate that my work on this topic should have begun in the beautiful but sinister domed reading room at what used to be Bedlam hospital. The staff of all these institutions were welcoming and helpful. Nigel Cochrane guided me through the archives of the Affluent Worker Survey at Essex University.

I have talked to a number of former national servicemen during my research. Formal interviews – conducted in line with the Research Ethics rules of King's College – are listed in the Bibliography. I should, however, stress that many people have provided helpful advice outside the framework of formal interviews and that even formal interviews were often useful for the questions my interviewees asked of me, or for the things they said when the recording had stopped, as much as for the remarks they made on the record. Particularly helpful have been David Baxter, Philip Bell, Peter Burke, Simon Coningham, Peter Duncumb, John Ferris, Anthony Hampshire, David Loewe, David Morgan, Martin Morton, Sir John Mummery, Bernard Palmer, Stanley Price, Lord Ramsbotham, Lord Runciman, Claude Scott, Robert Tollemache, Richard Vaughan, Don Wallace and John Waters. I owe particular debts to the late John Sainsbury, who gave me very useful advice in the early stages of my research, and to Antony Copley, who has taken a friendly interest in my work throughout the writing of this book.

Three distinguished national service veterans – Lord Hurd of Westwell, Peter Jay and the late Anthony Howard – were kind enough to give talks to my students in recent years. They were not speaking about their national service experience, but meeting them has helped me to understand their writing on the subject – which is not to say that they would agree with the interpretation I have put on it.

I have conducted relatively few formal interviews with former national servicemen, but I have listened to many recorded interviews at the Imperial War Museum, the National Army Museum and the British Library. I have come to feel great admiration for those who conducted these interviews with such skill and patience. I also owe a particular debt to Emily Hewitt of the British Library for her advice about using the sound archives there.

For permission to quote material of which they hold the copyright, and often for other practical help as well, I am grateful to Bernard Barr, David Batterham, Simon Bendall, W. H. Butler, Sue Coombe, John Green, Ken Hill, P. J. Houghton-Brown, Ronald Hyam, Ian Kell, Jane Kilsby, Michael Longley, Brian Loosmore, J. T. Nye, Giles and Julian Ockenden, Bernard Parke, Kevin O'Sullivan and Felicitas Whybrow. Birkbeck College and the Literary Executors of Sir Bernard Crick allowed me to quote from the papers of Bernard Crick. The Trustees of the Liddell Hart Centre for Military Archives allowed me to quote from those of Basil Liddell Hart. Kerry Sutton-Spence was very helpful in granting access to the National Gay and Lesbian Survey. Brian Bouchard, Mike Humphries and David Metters went to great lengths in helping me to locate photographs. I have made every effort to locate holders of copyright (Simon Offord of the Imperial War Museum and Alastair Massie of the National Army Museum helped in my search). If I have failed to acknowledge anyone's copyright, I will, of course, be happy to remedy this in subsequent editions.

I am grateful for the help that many school headmasters and archivists gave with what must have seemed a rather strange project to some of them. I owe particular debts to James Harrison at Monmouth, Patrick Mileham at Wellington, Penny Hatfield at Eton, Tony Jones at Emanuel and Anthony Wallersteiner at Stowe.

Three historians of national service – Keith Miller, Trevor Royle and Adrian Walker – not only tolerated my incursion into their field but also gave me a good deal of help and encouragement. David Prest and Charles Allen were also very generous in allowing me to quote from interviews they had conducted while making radio programmes that touched on national service. Dennis Mills and Simon Robbins allowed me to read their important unpublished work on, respectively naval linguists and the Cyprus Emergency.

Stephen Baxter, Huw Bennett, Jim Bjork, Peter Brooke, Charlotte Clements, Stephen Lovell, Jinty Nelson, Richard Overy, Munro Price, Miles Taylor, Pat Thane and Nicolas Whybrow provided useful advice. Rosie Germain was the first person to read parts of this book and helped to frame many of its arguments. Simon Ball, Lawrence Black and Helen Parr read the whole text and commented on it with a nicely balanced mixture of rigour and tact. David French has been enormously helpful at every stage of this project – advising about my research, reading the whole text and answering a stream of naive questions with good humour.

My greatest debts, as always, are personal. Alison Henwood's practical support made it possible to write this book. Her love reminded me that these is more to life than writing books. Our children – Emma and Alexander – were encouraging and tolerant, as was my sister Katie and my parents-in-law, David and Janice. Most of all my father – always my most demanding critic and my most enthusiastic supporter – has inspired this book.

Index